FOUNDATIONS OF LAW:
CASES, COMMENTARY,
AND ETHICS

The West Legal Studies Series

Your options keep growing with West Legal Studies

Each year our list continues to offer you more options for every area of the law to meet your course or on-the-job reference requirements. We now have over 140 titles from which to choose in the following areas:

Administrative Law

Alternative Dispute Resolution

Bankruptcy

Business Organizations/Corporations

Civil Litigation and Procedure

CLA Exam Preparation

Client Accounting

Computer in the Law Office

Constitutional Law

Contract Law

Criminal Law and Procedure

Document Preparation

Environmental Law

Ethics

Family Law

Federal Taxation

Intellectual Property

Introduction to Law

Introduction to Paralegalism

Law Office Management

Law Office Procedures

Legal Research, Writing, and Analysis

Legal Terminology

Paralegal Employment

Real Estate Law

Reference Materials

Torts and Personal Injury Law

Will, Trusts, and Estate Administration

You will find unparalleled, practical support

Each book is augmented by instructor and student supplements to ensure the best learning experience possible. We also offer custom publishing and other benefits such as West's Student Achievement Award. In addition, our sales representatives are ready to provide you with dependable service.

We want to hear from you

Our best contributions for improving the quality of our books and instructional materials is feedback from the people who use them. If you have a question, concern, or observation about any of our materials, or you have a product proposal or manuscript, we want to hear from you. Please contact your local representative or write us at the following address:

West Legal Studies, 3 Columbia Circle, P.O. Box 15015, Albany, NY 12212-5015

For additional information point your browser at

www.westlegalstudies.com

WEST

™

THOMSON LEARNING

FOUNDATIONS OF LAW: CASES, COMMENTARY, AND ETHICS

THIRD EDITION

Ransford C. Pyle
University of Central Florida

WEST

THOMSON LEARNING Australia Canada Mexico Singapore Spain United Kingdom United States

WEST
THOMSON LEARNING

WEST LEGAL STUDIES

Foundations of Law: Cases, Commentary, and Ethics, Third Edition
by Ransford C. Pyle

Business Unit Director:
Susan L. Simpfenderfer

Executive Editor:
Marlene McHugh Pratt

Senior Acquisitions Editor:
Joan M. Gill

Developmental Editor:
Rhonda Dearborn

Editorial Assistant:
Lisa Flatley

Executive Production Manager:
Wendy A. Troeger

Production Manager:
Carolyn Miller

Production Coordinator:
Matthew J. Williams

Executive Marketing Manager:
Donna J. Lewis

Channel Manager:
Nigar Hale

Cover Image:
Artville

Cover Design:
Dutton and Sherman Design

For permission to use material from this text or product, contact us by
Tel   (800) 730-2214
Fax   (800) 730-2215
www.thomsonrights.com

Library of Congress Cataloging-in-Publication Data

Pyle, Ransford Comstock, 1936–
   Foundations of law : cases, commentary, and ethics / Ransford C. Pyle.—3rd ed.
      p. cm.
   Includes index.
   ISBN 0-7668-3582-0
   1. Legal assistants—United States—Handbooks, manuals, etc. 2. Law—United States. I. Title.
KF320.L4 P95 2001
349.73—dc21   2001046791

NOTICE TO THE READER

CONTENTS

CHAPTER 8   The Law of Criminal Procedure   174

PREFACE

Foundations of Law is intended for introductory law courses at the post-secondary, undergraduate level of instruction, particularly pre-law, legal studies, paralegal programs, and business law programs that aim at a broader base than the "legal environment of business" text. At the time of writing, I was completing my twenty-fifth year of teaching in a Legal Studies Program, which was originally designed as a paralegal program but which changed gradually over the years as our students changed their goals to pre-law and business. While the curriculum changed, the introductory courses changed very little since it was my goal to provide what I thought to be the essential background in the law that any undergraduate ought to have, whether they intended to become lawyers or paralegals or simply wanted to fill that gap in knowledge of the law and legal system that our colleges and universities have inexplicably left unfilled in their standard instruction. *Foundations* approaches the law from a lawyer's viewpoint, covering basic fields of the law such as property, contracts, torts, and criminal law, as well as procedure in both civil and criminal cases. I have included historical and societal commentary where I think it helpful in understanding the law; I would have liked to include much more, but I have found that covering most of the basic fields and legal concepts is quite enough for a one-semester course.

Why I Wrote This Text

My original motivation for writing this text in 1990 was to find a compromise between those texts that were so vocationally oriented as to neglect, in my opinion, the conceptual framework of the law and those texts that were dryly expository, even encyclopedic. I used as a conceptual guide my first encounter with legal education; I included in the text all those terms and concepts I wish I had understood when I arrived at law school, along with an exposure to legal writing sufficient to be comfortable in reading cases and appreciating the common law tradition. In writing the text, my primary stylistic goal was *clarity* without oversimplification. I am happy to say that students and colleagues who have used the text have commented favorably on this feature.

Organization

The second edition and this third edition have developed empirically; changes have been based on the lessons I have learned in the classroom and, more recently, in distance education. The basic outline has not changed greatly, but the cases and questions have changed considerably. Inevitably, some cases prove to be too difficult, obscure, or stale to inspire the students. I have found that I must resist the temptation to include cases that I find intellectually intriguing because most of my students are not equipped to operate at higher levels of legal abstraction.

The basic topics of the course reflect our legal tradition, the basic fields found in the law and in legal education. The organization is simple and, I think, logical. I ease the students into the study of law with a narrative chapter on the legal profession, formerly two chapters, one on lawyers and one on paralegals. The second chapter covers legal ethics. I have experimented with saving this chapter for last in my course with the thought that legal ethics are better understood after a fuller acquaintance with the law; but, since the first chapter on the legal profession necessarily addresses what lawyers do and what others may *not* do, legal ethics, and especially unauthorized practice of law, follows some of the issues raised in the first chapter. Chapters 3 and 4 introduce the sources of the law in terms of cases and legislation. (The Constitution, another primary source of law, is introduced where appropriate to different chapters rather than squeezed into one or two awkward chapters.) Chapters 5 and 6 introduce the American court system under what I see to be major themes of our system, namely, trial and appeal, the federational aspect of the United States Constitution, and law and equity. Chapters 7 and 8 deal with procedure, civil and criminal respectively. Chapters 9 through 13 discuss major fields of substantive law, for example, property law, criminal law and contracts. Chapter 14 deals with administrative law and procedure, focusing on the latter. Although an important field, students find administrative law uninspiring in comparison with criminal law, personal injury, and divorce, which they can more easily conceptualize. Chapter 15 on law and computers is entirely rewritten from the second edition, reflecting the revolution in computer use since 1996 when the second edition first hit the street. I have retained Appendix A, How to Read a Case, which I encourage students to read as soon as possible. Appendix B contains the complete text of the United States Constitution, which should be pointed out to students who may not peruse the text on their own.

The chapters follow a general format in which subjects are explained in a running comment, interspersed with excerpts from state and federal appellate courts. Each case is introduced in the comment section, linking to the subject under discussion. Each case contains case questions at the end of the excerpted text designed to direct the attention of the students to features of the case worthy of inquiry or to relate the case to the subject matter of the commentary with which it is connected. Each chapter concludes with a summary followed by a provocative case scenario asking students to apply some of what they have learned in the chapter to a novel and difficult legal problem.

New to This Edition

Changes in the third edition have been driven by experience in the classroom as well as through on-line teaching. Three goals have driven the changes in the third edition:

1. **Facilitation of the acquisition of terminology and concepts**

   - The glossary has been expanded to include *all* legal terms mentioned in the text and cases.

   - Same-page definitions of textual terms have tripled and have been moved from footnote position to page margins. This reflects a change in approach. In the first two editions, terms explained in the text, for example, "stare decisis," were not defined in the margins, while undefined terms of less importance, for example, "dower," were boldfaced and defined in the margins. I found my students often spent more time learning these terms to the neglect of the important terms defined in the text.

   - Most terms are defined by the author, tailored to their use in the text. The practice of the second edition, borrowing exclusively from a legal dictionary, often resulted in awkward differences in nuance between the text and the definitions. While these nuances are important variations in meaning, they are often confusing to beginning students, who rely heavily on literal definitions. Many definitions were taken verbatim or modified minimally from *Oran's Dictionary of Law*, which I found quite suitable for my students. Instructors familiar with the second edition should be pleased with the harmony between the definition and the text, as well as with the improvement in the end-of-book glossary and index.

2. **The encouragement of critical/analytical thinking**

   - Case scenarios have been added at the end of each chapter. These replace the review questions, which have been put on the website for this book. The scenarios are a variation of *problem-based learning* methods, requiring students to apply what they have just learned to real-life problems. The particular approach used here is that of the "messy," cutting-edge legal problem, which as yet has no settled answer. The author has found that students learn more by becoming involved in active problem solving once they have acquired the basic concepts that apply to the field in which the problem resides.

3. **Currency**

   - Each new edition must reflect notable changes. For a general text on the law, changes tend to take place gradually except in areas that may reflect changes caused by forces outside the law. Twenty-four cases have been added and eighteen deleted. These were not motivated by any major change in law or society but by the need to remove some cases that were not especially helpful and replace them with cases that are more interesting, more insightful, or simply more current. I am happy with the new cases, and I think students will find them more interesting. I was more systematic in collecting cases than I had been in the past, and I believe instructors familiar with the second edition will see a marked improvement in "teachability." The one chapter that required massive revision was the last chapter, "Law in the Age of Computers."

It is not a long chapter, but it informs the students of some major areas of computer application to the law. It is natural to fear that such a chapter will become outdated quickly. I am less concerned than I was when I began to revise *Foundations* because I have seen a stabilization of the major legal databases along with standardization and slowdown in computer applications, software, and hardware. The solution to obsolescence can be found in the new computer environment. *Foundations* will now be accompanied by a website, which can be updated to reflect changes in the name, location, and ownership of the links that are listed in the text. It is quite possible that Chapter 15 will in the future be found on the Internet, a replacement for the printed version.

Supplemental Materials

- **Instructor's Manual with Test Bank**   Written by the author of the text, the Instructor's Manual contains briefs of all the excerpted cases in the book, answers to case questions, suggested approaches, and a test bank. The Instructor's Manual can also be found on-line at www.westlegalstudies.com. Please click on Resources, then go into the Instructor's Lounge.

- **Computerized Test Bank**   The Test Bank found in the Instructor's Manual is also available in a computerized format on CD-ROM. The platforms supported include Windows™ 3.1 and 95, Windows™ NT, and Macintosh. Features include:

  - Multiple methods of question selection

  - Multiple outputs—that is, print, ASCII, and RTF

  - Graphic support (black and white)

  - Random questioning output

  - Special character support

- **On-Line Resource**   Come visit our website at www.westlegalstudies.com where you will find valuable information specific to this book such as hot links and sample materials to download, as well as other West Legal Studies products.

- **Survival Manual for Paralegal Students**   Written by Bradene Moore and Kathleen Mercer Reed of the University of Toledo, it covers practical and basic information to help students make the most of their paralegal courses. Topics covered include choosing courses of study and note-taking skills.   ISBN 0-314-22111-5

- **Strategies and Tips for Paralegal Educators**   Written by Anita Tebbe of Johnson County Community College, it provides teaching strategies specifically designed for paralegal educators. A copy of this pamphlet is available to each adopter. Quantities for distribution to adjunct instructors are available for purchase at a minimal price. A coupon in the pamphlet provides ordering information.   ISBN 0-314-04971-1

- **WESTLAW®** West's on-line computerized legal research system offers students hands-on experience with a system commonly used in law offices. Qualified adopters can receive ten free hours of WESTLAW®. WEST-LAW® can be accessed with Macintosh and IBM PC and compatibles. A modem is required.

- **Court TV Videos** West Legal Studies is pleased to offer the following videos from Court TV, available for a minimal fee:
  - *"Flynn v. Goldman Sachs*—Fired on Wall Street: A Case of Sex Discrimination?"
    ISBN 0-7668-1096-8
  - *"Dodd v. Dodd*—Religion and Child Custody in Conflict"
    ISBN 0-7668-1094-1
  - *"Fentress v. Eli Lilly & Co., et al.*—Prozac on Trial"
    ISBN 0-7668-1095-X
  - *"In Re Custody of Baby Girl Clausen*—Child of Mine: The Fight for Baby Jessica"* ISBN 0-7668-1097-6
  - *"Northside Partners v. Page and New Kids on the Block*—Intellectual Property"* ISBN 0-7668-0426-7
  - *"Maglica v. Maglica*—Contract Law"* ISBN 0-7668-0867-X
  - *"Hall v. Hall*—Family Law"* ISBN 0-7668-0196-9

- **West's Paralegal Video Library** includes:
  - "The Drama of the Law II: Paralegal Issues Video"
    ISBN 0-314-07088-5
  - "I Never Said I Was a Lawyer: Paralegal Issues Video"
    ISBN 0-314-08049-X
  - "The Making of a Case Video" ISBN 0-314-07300-0
  - "Mock Trial Video—Anatomy of a Trial: A Contracts Case—Business Litigation"
    ISBN 0-314-07343-4
  - "Mock Trial Video—Trial Techniques: A Products Liability Case"
    ISBN 0-314-07342-6
  - "Arguments to the United States Supreme Court"
    ISBN 0-314-07070-2

These videos are available at no charge to qualified adopters.

Acknowledgments

I want to thank Daniel Oran for allowing me to use a number of his entries in *Oran's Dictionary of the Law* (West Legal Studies, 2000). Thanks go to my colleague Carol Bast for numerous helpful critical comments on the text. Carol Bast and Margie Hawkins furnished me advanced copies of the sections on computer-assisted legal research from their recent book *Foundations of Legal Research and Writing* (West Legal Studies, 2001), which filled in important gaps in my knowledge of this area. I borrowed a large number of glossary definitions from my book, *Bush v. Gore: Understanding American Law,* with the kind permission of Pearson Publications Company.

List of Reviewers

Joe Cagle
Gaston College, N.C.

Wendy Edson
Hilbert College, N.Y.

Deborah Howard
University of Evansville, Ind.

Pamela Sackerman
New York Career Institute, N.Y.

Melody Schroer
Maryville University, Mo.

Kathy Smith
Community College of Philadelphia, Pa.

Please note the Internet resources are of a time-sensitive nature and URL addresses may often change or be deleted.

Contact us a westlegalstudies@delmar.com

TABLE OF CASES

LAW AND THE PROFESSION OF LAW

Introduction

Not only is it quite difficult to provide a definition of *law* that will satisfy lawyers, legal scholars, and the general public, defining the *practice* of law is daunting as well. The people we call lawyers or, alternatively, attorneys, may be identified by the custom of licensing. One definition of a lawyer, then, is one who is licensed to practice law. As we shall soon see, what exactly a lawyer is licensed to do is problematic. Bar associations and state supreme courts have often despaired of finding a definition; in the latter part of this chapter we examine an area called "the unauthorized practice of law" in an attempt to find out what the practice of law is by looking at what those without licenses may *not* do. Some of this inquiry accompanies our discussion of legal assistants, or paralegals, who have become essential adjuncts to lawyers and law firms. The unauthorized practice of law is both a professional ethics and a criminal law problem.

An important theme of this chapter is the broad range of advice and services that lawyers provide the public. "Lawyering" is not simply a matter of giving legal advice, drafting legal documents, and appearing in court. Contemporary American life is complex in large part because of the regulation of all spheres of human endeavor. In many ways, law defines and regulates life, love, and death, not to mention property, business, crime, and injury. The author, having taught in higher education for nearly three decades, would today give advice that did not occur to him thirty years ago to anyone embarking on a teaching career: "Don't sign that teaching contract until you have shown it to an attorney; and make sure you have an attorney who specializes in academic contracts." It would be wise, in fact, to consult an attorney before making any important decision—buying a house, getting married, making a will, starting or investing in a business. Lawyers have a wealth of knowledge by virtue first of their legal training and second because they spend their days anticipating and solving a myriad of problems. As a result they can provide a great deal of advice about the law and about life.

Let us, then, inquire into who lawyers are and how they become lawyers. Then we discuss what they do, what they should not do, and what others may not do. All of this is important information about the legal profession, but it is also an important beginning step in understanding law and the legal system. Lawyers in general maintain and direct the law and its system. Those special lawyers we call *judges* enforce and define the law. Formal lawmaking is the province of legislators, who need not be lawyers but often are and who almost never make final decisions without legal consultation.

The Law and the Lawyer

Lawyers are named after the subject matter of the profession, the law. Unfortunately, the field of law is not as easily described as, say, electrical engineering. The problem of precisely defining law may be left to legal philosophers and scholars of **jurisprudence.** The primary concern of this study is with law in operation or "in practice." Lawyers are called professionals, but are also referred to as *practitioners*, referring to the professional application of learned skills. The practice of law includes a great variety of services furnished by lawyers to their clients.

For practical purposes, law may be defined as a process, a system, or a set of rules governing society. As a process, law can be viewed as the means by which rights and duties are created and exercised. As a system, law interconnects rules governing society with a hierarchy of courts served by the legal profession and the police. As a set of rules, law is a complex code of conduct and values formally established and published, backed by the threat of enforcement. This last view of law as rules is what law students regularly study and what the public generally views as the law.

Failure to understand law as system and process, however, leads to a distorted view of law and lawyers. For example, nonlawyers often regard **plea bargaining** as an unethical device used by criminal defense lawyers to circumvent justice. Plea bargaining only makes sense in the context of the pressures and problems inherent in the administration of criminal justice. It has become an indispensable aid, some might say a necessary evil, in resolving criminal cases in the context of overcrowded jails, overburdened court **dockets,** and overworked **prosecutors.**

One must never forget that law continually undergoes change. Not only do the rules change, but the legal system also changes. As society changes, so must law. Law has a particularly important place in American society, which is extremely diverse and complex in comparison with other societies. The various parts of American society express differing and often conflicting values, so a major task of law is to convert values into functioning rules. In the last thirty years, America has encountered major value confrontations over racial integration, civil

jurisprudence
Commonly defined as the science or philosophy of law; it is generally concerned with the nature of law and legal systems.

plea bargaining One accused of a crime can "bargain" through her attorney with the prosecutor; the bargain usually involves an agreement by the accused to plead guilty in return for favorable treatment, such as a lenient sentence, reduction to a lesser charge, or probation in lieu of incarceration.

docket The court calendar of proceedings.

prosecutor The attorney charged with prosecuting criminal cases on behalf of a state or the United States; a public employee commonly titled state attorney, district attorney, or United States attorney.

disobedience in the Vietnam era, gays in the military, and abortion. Although these are social, political, and even spiritual issues, Americans have looked to law and the legal system for their resolution.

The law we discuss in the following chapters is American law, the law of the American legal system as practiced by the legal profession. It might be more properly labeled "Anglo-American law," since we have more than nine hundred years of unbroken legal tradition from England. The severing of political bonds with England in 1776 did not bring a corresponding break with the English legal tradition. In fact, it has been argued convincingly that the American colonials were fighting for the rights normally accorded Englishmen in England but denied to Americans by colonial governments.

Law is concerned with rights, duties, obligations, and privileges and their enforcement. Under the U.S. constitutional model, political authority is divided among the executive, legislative, and judicial branches of government. The study of law generally focuses on the judiciary, because the courts in our system are entrusted with interpreting the law, and it is in the courts that disputes between opposing sides are resolved.

Disputes form the heart of our legal system, which has evolved as an **adversarial system** in which legal battle is waged by conflicting parties employing legal counsel to take their sides before an impartial judge and, if necessary, an impartial jury. The practice of law commonly involves advancing and protecting the interests of a client in a dispute, but equally important is preventing disputes. No ethical lawyer would write a **will** or **contract** or close a real estate transaction hoping that **litigation** would result. The test of a well-written will is whether its provisions are carried out uncontested; the test of a good contract is whether it has resolved all reasonably foreseeable conflicts in advance and allows the contracting parties to perform their obligations to their mutual satisfaction. Perhaps it is in this area of preventive law, in which lawyers foresee and avoid future problems, that they do their best work and provide their most valuable services. The public rarely recognizes that lawyers routinely perform this function. The uncontested will, the contract that is not **breached,** and the transaction that runs smoothly do not make headlines. For most lawyers, however, an appreciative and satisfied client is one of the frequent personal rewards of the practice of law.

Becoming a Lawyer

In order to represent a client before a court, a person must become a member of the bar. In a general sense of the term, the **bar** refers to licensed members of the legal profession, the community of American lawyers, just as the **bench** refers to all judges collectively. Requirements for membership, however, differ from state to state, and membership in one state bar does not confer membership in another state. In most states, licensing is regulated by a state bar association to which members pay annual dues. The state bar associations are responsible for maintaining standards of conduct within the profession and for

adversarial system
The U.S. legal system in which litigants, typically represented by attorneys, argue their respective sides in a dispute before an impartial judge and jury.

will A document through which a person directs how his or her property will be distributed at death.

contract An agreement that creates a legal relationship between two or more parties.

litigation A dispute brought to court; derived from the Latin *lis*, which means lawsuit.

breach of contract
When a party fails to render the performance required by a contract.

bar The term used to refer collectively to licensed members of the legal profession.

bench Drawn from the term referring to the seat occupied by judges in court, "the bench" refers to all judges collectively.

disbarment   The most severe professional disciplinary sanction, canceling an attorney's license to practice law.

bar examination   A written test required of applicants for license to practice law.

J.D.   The basic law degree; it stands for "juris doctor" and is equivalent to the more traditional **LL.B.**

LL.B.   The basic law degree, a "bachelor of laws," replaced in most law schools today by **J.D.** (juris doctor).

LSAT   "Law School Admissions Test," a written, largely multiple-choice test required at most law schools for admission.

associate   The title usually given to a full-time member of a law firm who has not yet been elevated to *partner.*

law review   Most accredited law schools publish a "law review" on a quarterly basis with scholarly articles and comments on legal issues.

law clerks   Law school students who work summers or part time for private attorneys; also, top law students who obtain clerkships with judges after graduating from law school.

justice   The title given to the judges of the Supreme Court of the United States and to the judges of the appellate courts of many of the states.

determining misconduct or assisting the court in disciplining members for misconduct with a variety of sanctions, the most severe of which is **disbarment.** Bar disciplinary boards are particularly concerned with misconduct in relations with clients, such as misuse of client funds or the failure to provide promised services. Bar associations also engage in review and reform of laws and provide a sounding board and even lobbying activities for the legal profession. If a state attempts to place new restrictions or taxes on lawyers, they will be quick to respond through their respective bar associations. The authority and activities of the different associations vary considerably from state to state.

Admission to the bar requires passing a **bar examination** and submission to scrutiny by the bar association. Traditionally, bar membership has required that each candidate be approved on the basis of moral character, as determined by the licensing association. In earlier times, the character and competence of an applicant for admission to the bar was vouched for by members of the bar; today some states conduct extensive inquiry into each applicant's background.

Approval of an application to take the bar examination generally requires completion of law school and the receipt of a law degree, usually called a **J.D.** (Juris Doctor) or **LL.B.** (Bachelor of Laws), although some states allow senior law students to take the examination prior to graduation. Admission to law school normally requires completion of a four-year undergraduate degree.

Law School

To understand how lawyers think, some appreciation of the law school experience is helpful. Law school provides a rigorous training that formally and informally molds a certain sort of thinking. Strict emphasis on critical and analytical reasoning sets a high standard for legal debate and discussion, but some have argued that the focus is too narrow.

Admission to law school is highly competitive. Prestige and reputation are important in the legal profession and equally so to the law student, because placement and salary upon graduation from law school depend upon the prestige of the law school and performance in law school. Entry to law school is based principally on undergraduate grade point average and scores obtained on the Law School Admissions Test (**LSAT**). The more prestigious the law school, the higher grades and scores must be to obtain admission. Intense competition is characteristic of law students and happily encouraged by their professors, most of whom were once law school achievers.

Among law schools, the most elite are considered "national law schools" because their orientations as well as their reputations are national. Yale Law School in New Haven, Connecticut, for example, is not a training ground for Connecticut lawyers but an entree to large New York law firms, the so-called "Wall Street firms," which represent national business interests. The archetype of the perfect new **associate** just hired by a law firm went to Harvard Law School, became editor of the *Harvard Law Review,* and served a year or two as a **law clerk** for a United States Supreme Court **Justice.** Such credentials would guarantee a handsome salary at a top law firm.

case method Since its introduction by Dean Langdell at Harvard Law School, the method of reading judicial opinions (cases) and analyzing them under the law professor's questioning has been the standard approach to law school instruction in America.

bailiff An officer of the court charged with keeping order in the courtroom, having custody over prisoners and the jury.

court reporter
A person who makes verbatim recordings of court proceedings and other sworn statements, such as depositions, which can be reduced to printed transcripts.

clinical programs
Programs found in most law schools in which students provide legal services to the public under the supervision of law professors and sanctioned by the courts and the bar; some schools require enrollment, but in most law schools "clinic" is a voluntary course for credit.

Law school training continues to follow a model established in the 1890s by Dean Christopher Columbus Langdell of the Harvard Law School. He invented the **case method** in which students read judicial opinions, or cases, rather than treatises about law, formerly the dominant method of studying law. Langdell reasoned that the practice of law in the United States was based on discovering the law through judicial decisions, because it was in the courts that law was interpreted and explained. A natural corollary to the case method is the *Socratic dialogue* between professor and student. Instead of lecturing, the law professor asks questions of the students about cases they have been assigned to read in order to determine the issues and reasoning in the opinions. For the freshman law student, this is a grueling and often humiliating experience and has been called a "game that only one (the professor) can play." It is a rite of passage in which students are forced to shed their former ways of thinking and reacting to issues and problems and begin to "think like lawyers." This method of teaching has been seriously criticized as promoting tunnel vision, but it succeeds in its goal of fostering analytical thinking and objective argument. Because of this criticism, however, many law schools have in recent years shown a greater sensitivity to the needs of students, offering counseling and tutoring by staff and peers.

The product of an American law school has read hundreds of judicial opinions and spent countless hours finding the way through an extensive law library, but may never have been in a courtroom and may not know the difference between a **bailiff** and a **court reporter.** In recent years law schools have initiated or expanded the number of **clinical programs** in which students practice law under the supervision of an instructor. In addition, many law students gain experience by serving as law clerks for law firms during the summers between academic years. Despite this occasional practical education, law schools focus on developing an attitude of mind that seeks the relevant legal issue in each human transaction and applies a technical analytical approach to solving problems.

Obtaining a License to Practice Law

To represent a client in legal matters, an attorney must be licensed in the jurisdiction in which he or she practices. Each state has its own requirements for admission to practice, and the federal courts have their own requirements. Many states relax their requirements for long-term members of the bar of other states, but the process by which the newly graduated law student becomes an attorney follows a similar pattern in most states.

Application for licensing generally requires graduation from a law school approved by the American Bar Association (in some states nonapproved law schools are allowed). The applicant must also show good moral character, but the extent to which this is scrutinized depends on the state. Moral fitness is difficult to define and must be determined on a case-by-case basis; but bar examiners are especially concerned about defects in character that suggest a potential for betraying a client's trust or deceiving a court. For example, an individual

perjury Committed by knowingly making a false statement under oath in a judicial proceeding; the false statement must concern a material issue or fact in the proceeding.

previously convicted of **perjury** would be a poor candidate for the practice of law, having demonstrated a disregard for the integrity of the justice system. Finally, admission is usually predicated on a passing score on the bar examination.

Bar Examination

Upon completion of law school or just before graduation, aspiring candidates face the dreaded ordeal of the bar examination. This generally consists of two or three days of a written examination, which in most states consists of two parts. One part is the **Multistate Bar Examination,** a standardized national test that contains two hundred multiple-choice questions based on general legal topics such as property, contracts, and constitutional law. Each question is based on a hypothetical fact situation, and the examination requires a thorough knowledge of **black letter law.** This mentally exhausting part of the examination lasts six hours.

Multistate Bar Examination
A standardized national test of general legal subjects, such as property, contracts, and constitutional law.

The Multistate is based on general principles of law, but most states require a second part that addresses law specific to the state administering the examination. This part of the examination often requires written essay questions based on hypothetical legal disputes and resembles the sorts of examinations typically given as final examinations in law school. Applicants must then wait several weeks, even months, to receive the final results. Each state licensing board is free to establish its own standards, so a passing grade on the Multistate in one state may be a failing grade in another. In most states between 65 and 90 percent of examinees pass. A failing candidate can usually retake the examination, though some states limit the number of times the examination can be taken.

black letter law
Lawyers' slang for the basic, well-established rules of law.

The bar examination not only establishes a minimum standard of competence for lawyers, but it also represents a psychological ordeal shared by attorneys; most recall vividly the examination. The Multistate in particular calls for an approach for which law students have not been prepared, namely, to command a broad knowledge of the law and apply it all at once to a series of multiple-choice questions. For this reason, most applicants take a bar review course lasting several weeks prior to the examination itself. Whereas law students have been accustomed to limiting their study to a particular subject over the course of an academic term, the bar examination requires the applicant to recall the sum of three years of legal study.

integrated bar
A state bar association in which membership is required in order to practice law.

In most states, a license to practice law is predicated on membership in the state bar association. This signifies an **integrated bar.** Because the bar also acts as a lobbying organization, some members may object when their dues are spent on political efforts with which they disagree.

Attorney Employment

house counsel Full-time attorneys employed by many corporations and other businesses as part of the administrative staff; distinguish from "outside counsel."

The vast majority of new bar members join private law firms, but significant numbers obtain employment as government attorneys or as **house counsel** for private corporations. A few brave souls decide to "hang out their shingles" and

bankruptcy Generally, the situation in which a person, business, or government cannot or will not pay its debts, so its property is entrusted to a "trustee in bankruptcy" who distributes the property to creditors.

zoning variance It is customary in the United States for local governments to create *zones* within city and county boundaries with restrictions primarily on the form of use, for example, agricultural, residential.

real estate closing Real estate transactions are completed by a closing, at which numerous documents are signed and exchanged, payment is made, and property deeds are transferred.

begin practicing law as sole practitioners or jointly with one or more law school colleagues. Despite three years of intensive training, few law school graduates are prepared for the demands of practice. They are unfamiliar with law office routine and management, the peculiarities of court systems, interviewing clients, negotiating settlements, and collecting for services. Successful practice requires interpersonal skills that are sorely neglected in law school. In addition, law school focuses on major legal issues presented in casebooks with national distribution. A law school graduate, before preparing for the bar exam, is likely to be totally ignorant of many areas of state law. A new lawyer is unlikely to know how to process a **bankruptcy,** do a tenant eviction, get a **zoning variance** from a city, or even conduct a **real estate closing.** Because of unfamiliarity with so many features of day-to-day practice, the new lawyer is most comfortable in the company of more experienced practitioners and their legal staff.

The competitive spirit of law school also directs many new lawyers to large firms. Already oriented toward achievement and success, graduating law students often measure themselves by starting salaries and the prestige of the law firms they join. Big city law firms compete with each other for top law school graduates, and the largest Wall Street firms offer starting salaries more than twice the average.

Fortunately for our society, not all law graduates are driven to enrich themselves. It is very common for a graduate to return to his or her home town to assume a respected position among friends and associates. Lawyers who choose this path inevitably find that the rewards of service to the community outweigh monetary compensation. The practice of law, like most other professions, offers an opportunity for personal satisfaction difficult to find in other kinds of employment.

Some law school graduates have specific goals for their training, such as preserving the environment, providing legal services to the poor, prosecuting criminals, or serving as elected legislators. The legal profession provides a unique foundation for contributing to change or improvement of one's society.

Obtaining prestigious employment, however, does not guarantee a successful career. New attorneys in a firm are called *associates*, a position from which they may never graduate. The traditional course of a legal career in a private firm entails working for a few years as an associate until invited to become a partner in the firm, which means moving from a salary to sharing in the profits of the firm. In the largest firms, only a small number of associates are ever asked to become partners. Associates who do not make partner commonly move to other firms or set up their own practices. This brutally competitive system has been improved somewhat by many firms by establishing intermediate positions like senior associate or junior partner. This allows firms to reward attorneys without forcing a partnership decision.

The pressures on attorneys to perform do not consist simply of providing good services to clients. A law firm is also a business, and attorneys who do not add significant profits to the business by way of new clients and many hours of work billable to clients are unlikely to become partners in a firm. For some, the advantage of employment with government or a private corporation is that an attorney is more often measured by the quality of work rather than the quantity of business generated.

Paralegals must understand the stresses involved in the work of attorneys in order to work better with their employers. One of the advantages of paralegal work over that of an attorney is that paralegals do not bear ultimate responsibility for the outcome of clients' problems. The difference in stress can be great. Paralegals occupy a position similar to corporate lawyers in that performance is measured by the quality of their work.

What Lawyers Do

The United States has more than a half a million lawyers. They are assisted by two hundred thousand paralegals. Obviously, a great deal of legal work exists to support this workforce. What exactly do lawyers do?

Acquisition of knowledge in law school is merely the first step in becoming a competent attorney; this knowledge must be put into practice. Just as the LSAT is an imprecise predictor of performance in law school, law school grades are an imperfect predictor of success in the practice of law. Even the bar examination fails to measure many qualities essential to future success. An attorney is not simply a repository of legal knowledge and technical skills. An attorney is a problem solver who must rely on imagination, creativity, common sense, and psychology as well as the analytical skills learned in school. The rules that make up the body of the law are abstractions that only take on meaning in the course of human events. Attorneys are frequently addressed as "counselor," and this perhaps comes closer than any other word to the nature of their work. Attorneys act as providers of legal services, advisors, counselors, negotiators, and agents for their clients.

Many states have attempted to define what lawyers do in order to clarify what is meant by *unauthorized practice of law (UPL)* since each state prohibits the unauthorized practice of law with fines and injunctions and on rare occasions with jail. In our legal system, we insist that crimes be clearly expressed by **statute.** Nevertheless, expressing what is prohibited under UPL has been difficult because it is difficult to articulate precisely what only lawyers may do. The South Carolina Bar attempted the "Herculean" task of defining the practice of law, which it submitted to the Supreme Court of South Carolina for approval. The court's response is reproduced in part in the accompanying case, in which it despairs of defining the practice of law and UPL and can only clarify what is *not* UPL!

statute A law enacted by the legislative branch of government declaring, commanding, or prohibiting something.

The Lawyer as Provider of Legal Services

The public most commonly pictures the lawyer as a furnisher of services in legal problem solving. Although this may be the primary function of an attorney, the following sections reveal that attorneys also play many other roles.

The dramatic popular image of the lawyer focuses on the trial lawyer, when in actuality very few attorneys spend a significant portion of their time in court.

In re unauthorized practice of law rules proposed by the SOUTH CAROLINA BAR
Supreme Court of South Carolina
309 S.C. 304, 422 S.E.2d 123 (1992)

In June 1991 the South Carolina Bar through a special subcommittee of the Unauthorized Practice of Law Committee (Committee) submitted to the Supreme Court a set of proposed rules governing the unauthorized practice of law (Proposed Rules). This comprehensive set of Proposed Rules represents the Committee's collective wisdom accumulated during its thirteen years of existence, as well as the efforts of the special subcommittee which spent over a year drafting these rules. The Proposed Rules attempt to define and delineate the practice of law, and to establish clear guidelines so that professionals other than attorneys can ensure they do not inadvertently engage in the practice of law.

It is impossible for anyone not familiar with the scope of the issues embraced by the Proposed Rules to truly appreciate the enormity of the task undertaken by the special subcommittee. After careful review of the Proposed Rules, the documentation in support of these rules, and the tremendous amount of memoranda in opposition to their adoption, we conclude that the Proposed Rules should not be adopted. We commend the subcommittee for its Herculean efforts to define the practice of law. We are convinced, however, that it is neither practicable nor wise to attempt a comprehensive definition by way of a set of rules. Instead, we are convinced that the better course is to decide what is and what is not the unauthorized practice of law in the context of an actual case or controversy.

The Constitution commits to this Court the duty to regulate the practice of law in South Carolina. . . . We take this opportunity to clarify certain practices which we hold do not constitute the unauthorized practice of law.

First, we recognize the validity of the principle found in S.C.Code Ann. § 40-5-80 (1986):

any individual may represent another individual before any tribunal, if (1) the tribunal approves of the representation and (2) the representative is not compensated for his services. We have refused, however, to allow an individual to represent a business entity under the statute. See State ex rel. *Daniel v. Wells*, 191 S.C. 468, 5 S.E.2d 181 (1939). We modify Wells today to allow a business to be represented by a non-lawyer officer, agent or employee, including attorneys licensed in other jurisdictions and those possessing Limited Certificates of Admission pursuant to Rule 405, SCACR, in civil magistrate's court proceedings. . . . [The court then recognizes an exception for "Certified Public Accountants (CPAs), attorneys licensed in other jurisdictions and persons possessing Limited Certificates of Admission to practice before state agencies which allow such representation," and goes on to recognize the special status of CPAs when working within their area of expertise.]

We also take this opportunity to reaffirm the rule that police officers may prosecute traffic offenses in magistrate's court and in municipal court. Only the arresting officer may prosecute the case, although if the officer is new or inexperienced, he may be assisted at trial by one of his supervisors. . . .

Finally, we recognize that other situations will arise which will require this Court to determine whether the conduct at issue involves the unauthorized practice of law. We urge any interested individual who becomes aware of such conduct to bring a declaratory judgment action in this Court's original jurisdiction to determine the validity of the conduct. We hope by this provision to strike a proper balance between the legal profession and other professionals which will ensure the public's protection from the harms caused by the unauthorized practice of law.

Let this order be published with the Administrative Orders of this Court.

IT IS SO ORDERED.

Case Questions

1. Why should the state Supreme Court have the final say on unauthorized practice of law rather than the state bar association?
2. Should the practice of law be defined case by case or by rule?

Many lawyers never try cases, and most trial lawyers spend most of their time preparing for trial. Lawyers are basically problem solvers. Sometimes the problems are actual disputes that may lead to lawsuits and eventually to trial. Most disputes never reach the trial stage, but are settled with the lawyer acting principally as negotiator or conciliator.

Much of the work that lawyers do has nothing to do with disputes. Many client problems do not involve an adversary, but range from matters as simple as changing one's legal name to something as complicated as obtaining approval for a major airport. Potential adversaries may be lurking on the sidelines, but most problems require legal help largely because they have legal consequences. Incorporating a business must be accomplished in accordance with state law; writing a will must be done with formalities dictated by state law. Although these may be done without an attorney, it is wiser and safer to employ professional services.

Most lawyers are specialists, whether they realize it or not. Some, for instance, handle only tax matters; others, who may call themselves general practitioners, may refuse to handle criminal or divorce cases. The body of the law is immense and constantly growing. No lawyer can adequately keep up with the changes in all areas of the law. If a lawyer accepts a case in an area in which she is not expert, it is her duty to educate herself before proceeding.

Because of specialization, the distribution of legal work for any particular lawyer varies considerably, but we may make some generalizations about how lawyers spend their time. They talk with clients, first to understand the problem, then to explain its legal ramifications to the client. They write many letters—to clients, to other attorneys, to a variety of sources to request information. They are constantly reading. They read contracts furnished by their clients; they read wills and deeds and many other legal documents to assess their clients' duties, rights, and risks. They read a lot of "law," which may be focused on research for a problem or a dispute or may be designed to keep them current on areas of law of particular concern. Lawyers must be well informed about matters affecting their clients. It has been said that some lawyers specializing in **medical malpractice** cases know more about many fields of medicine than the average physician. In short, the attorney must know enough to provide competent legal representation to a client, an ethical duty imposed by the ABA Canons of Ethics and every state bar association. (See Chapter 2 on current ethical codes.)

In short, lawyers must rely on their communication skills; they talk, they write, and they read. Those who view lawyers as merely clever manipulators of words fail to recognize that a primary function of law in our society is to reduce rules of conduct to precise language that can be applied to real situations. Lawyers exercise their verbal skills with a knowledge of the law and supported by analytical training. In a legal context, words simply may not be used in the manner of casual speech. The attorney must use not only legal terms in a precise way but ordinary words as well. When dealing with the written word, attorneys read with a verbal microscope, analyzing each word and phrase for its legal implications. They are adept at what we might call "legal semantics." Anyone

medical malpractice
A form of professional *misconduct* restricted to negligence in the medical field; an important field of legal specialization.

can memorize rules or fill out forms, but training, experience, and intelligence are required to use the special language of the law.

Lawyers are also organizers. Many transactions require detail and coordination. The merger of two corporations, for example, is a complex transaction that should be performed without leaving loose ends. Lawyers serve in such transactions to ensure that no legal problems will arise that could have been foreseen and avoided during the negotiations. They establish an orderly process to facilitate a smooth transition. Similarly, preparation for trial requires a step-by-step process in which all necessary information is collected and organized in a way that builds a logical and convincing presentation of the client's side of the lawsuit. As the case is built, it must be constantly reevaluated; lack of proper organization will produce poor results.

The State of Oregon has a typical prohibition against nonlawyers providing legal services in Oregon Revised Statutes 9.160:

> Except for the right reserved to litigants by ORS 9.320 to prosecute or defend a cause in person, no person shall practice law or represent that person as qualified to practice law unless that person is an active member of the Oregon State Bar.

***pro se* (Latin)** "For oneself," "in one's own behalf." American law recognizes not only the right to be represented by an attorney but also the right to represent oneself in court.

enjoin To prohibit (or require) a person from certain acts; an order typically emanating from an *injunction*.

While recognizing the right to sue ***pro se***, the statute prohibits nonlawyer representation of others. Oregon Revised Statutes 9.166 provides that the court may **enjoin** a person violating the preceding provision (ORS 9.160). While even the Oregon Court of Appeals is reluctant to define the practice of law ("We cannot, and will not, purport to derive an omnibus definition of 'practice of law' from [the cases]"), it was willing to approve a list of activities nonlawyers should not engage in. *Oregon State Bar v. Smith* details such a list.

The Lawyer as Advisor

Clients consult lawyers when they feel they need legal advice. Many transactions and events take place in our society that have legal significance, and common sense dictates that they be entrusted at least in part to someone knowledgeable in their legal ramifications. Probably most of these involve property transactions in some way, but those who are accused of a crime or are seeking compensation for injury can best protect their interests by employing an attorney.

A person making a will or buying a residence is involved in important property planning. For most, purchasing a home constitutes the largest investment of a lifetime, and the consequences of such a transaction should not be left to chance and ignorance. This transaction involves two principal areas of law—the law of real property and the law of contracts. Property law has evolved over many centuries and contains many relics of the past that present hidden traps for the unwary. The buyer may be presented with a standard contract for sale that provides reasonable protections for buyer and seller, or may be confronted with a contract that was designed primarily for the benefit of the seller. In either case, it is unlikely that the buyer understands the full import of the many

Oregon State Bar
v.
Robin Smith, and People's Paralegal Service, Inc., an Oregon corporation
Court of Appeals of Oregon
149 Or.App. 171, 942 P.2d 793 (1997)

HASELTON, Judge.

Defendants, People's Paralegal Service, Inc., and its president, Robin Smith, appeal from a judgment declaring them to have engaged in activities that constitute the unauthorized practice of law, ORS 9.160, and enjoining them from those activities. . . .

From 1987 until 1995, when the injunction issued, defendants operated a business providing "legal technician" services for a fee. The services included providing consumers with various legal forms available to the public through such sources as Stevens Ness Publishing Company, NOLO PRESS, bankruptcy courts, and the Oregon State Bar, and advising them with respect to their individual legal concerns. Defendants never attempted to represent consumers in court, nor did they sign any documents as attorneys. Moreover, People's Paralegal posted signs at its place of business advising consumers that its employees were not attorneys, and its intake sheets, which were signed by the consumers, included the following statement:

> "WE ARE NOT ATTORNEYS . . . IF YOU REQUIRE LEGAL ADVICE PLEASE SEE AN ATTORNEY."

"Plaintiff Oregon State Bar brought this action in April 1995, alleging that defendants were engaged in the unlawful practice of law under ORS 9.160 and seeking injunctive relief under ORS 9.166. . . . The trial court disagreed and granted the injunction, which provided, in part:

[Defendants] * * * are * * * enjoined from practicing law including:

(1) Enjoined from any personal contact with any persons in the nature of consultation, explanation, recommendation, or advice regarding their legal matters.

(2) Enjoined from meeting with any persons to discuss their individual facts and circumstances relating to their need or desire for legal forms, legal services or legal assistance.

(3) Enjoined from obtaining information orally, in writing, or in any other manner relating to individual facts and circumstances so as to assist any persons with their legal matters.

(4) Enjoined from advising any persons regarding their eligibility for or advisability of legal remedies to address any person's particular legal matters.

(5) Enjoined from advising any persons regarding procedural functions of the court system as it relates to any person's particular legal matters including advice regarding jurisdiction or venue.

(6) Enjoined from assisting in selecting particular forms, documents or pleadings for any persons to address their legal matters.

(7) Enjoined from assisting in any way with the preparation or filling out of legal forms, or any parts of such forms, documents or pleadings for any persons.

(8) Enjoined from assisting, suggesting or advising any persons how forms, documents or pleadings should be used to address or to solve particular legal problems.

(9) Nothing included in this Judgment and Decree precludes Defendant Smith from working for someone authorized to practice law so long as she is acting within the course of her duties and under the direction and supervision of an individual authorized to practice law."

On appeal, defendants renew and reiterate their constitutional challenges to ORS 9.160, both on its face and as applied.

[I]n *State Bar v. Security Escrows, Inc.,* . . . the court identified the essence of the "practice of law," as being the informed application of legal principles to address a particular person's individual circumstances and needs:

* * *

"For the purposes of this case, we hold that the practice of law includes the drafting or selection of documents and the giving of advice in regard thereto any time an informed or trained discretion must be exercised in the selection or drafting of a document to meet the needs of the persons being served. The knowledge of the customer's needs obviously cannot be had by one who has no knowledge of the relevant law. One must know what questions to ask. Accordingly, any exercise of an intelligent choice, or an informed discretion in advising another of his legal rights and duties, will bring the activity within the practice of the profession." . . .

[The] most recent, pertinent "unauthorized practice" decision is *Oregon State Bar v. Gilchrist,* 272 Or. 552, 538 P.2d 913 (1975). There, the court held that the advertising and sale of generic, noncustomized do-it-yourself divorce kits did not, without more, constitute the practice of law[.]

[T]he mere general dissemination of legal information by nonlawyers does not constitute the unauthorized practice of law. The court proceeded, however, to conclude that other, more personalized contact and advice was properly enjoined:

"[A]ll personal contact between defendants and their customers in the nature of consultation, explanation, recommendation or advice or other assistance in selecting particular forms, in filling out any part of the forms, or suggesting or advising how the forms should be used in solving the particular customer's marital problems does constitute the practice of law and must be and is strictly enjoined." . . .

We cannot, and will not, purport to derive an omnibus definition of "practice of law" from Johnston, Security Escrows, Miller, and Gilchrist. Indeed, Security Escrows cautions that a determination of unauthorized practice may depend on case-specific circumstances. . . .

Nevertheless, regardless of any uncertainty at the margins, certain core criteria are well settled. Most significantly, for present purposes, the "practice of law" means the exercise of professional judgment in applying legal principles to address another person's individualized needs through analysis, advice, or other assistance. . . .

Case Questions

1. How do the activities that are enjoined in the order conform to the definition of law at the end of the case?
2. Why does not the list of prohibited activities serve as a definition of what constitutes the practice of law.

clauses contained in the document. An attorney well-versed in property law can explain the contract and advise the client about its possible dangers and how to deal with them.

As an advisor in these circumstances, the attorney does not give only legal advice. The attorney is likely to have a wealth of practical knowledge that has nothing to do with law, strictly speaking, such as the current state of local real estate prices, the most favorable mortgage rates, and planned or proposed development in the area. The attorney may know that the airport is about to change its flight paths in such a way that flights will pass directly over the home in question. Such information may be more valuable to a client than the explanation of rights and duties or the legal consequences of the contract itself.

Attorneys may be successful for many reasons, including politics and even luck, but most attorneys succeed because they provide valuable services. They are in a position to acquire a great deal of practical knowledge because they deal

trust A device whereby title to property is transferred to one person, the trustee, for the benefit of another, the beneficiary.

estate "Estate" has several legal meanings, but when used in reference to a decedent it means the property rights to be distributed following death.

attorney-client privilege Confidential statements made by a client to an attorney may not be disclosed to others by the attorney without the client's permission.

on a daily basis with countless problems that arise in the course of practice. An attorney who specializes in wills and **trusts,** for example, has seen countless examples of what can happen when someone dies if relatives and in-laws fight over the deceased's **estate.** Writing a will for a client may appear to be a technical legal matter, yet an attorney's knowledge of human nature will influence the legal advice given.

This role of the lawyer as personal, practical advisor is also important with business clients. Many businesses frequently require legal help. Not only are they concerned with making contracts and buying and selling, but they must also be concerned with employee relations, government regulation, and taxation, not to mention the type of business organization that is appropriate to the enterprise. It is common for a close relationship to develop between an attorney and a business client. The attorney comes to understand the business and its needs, and the client often turns to the attorney for advice of a business and personal nature. The client also enjoys the **attorney-client privilege,** which allows the client to treat the attorney as a confidante who may be told matters that could not be disclosed to anyone else.

The Lawyer as Counselor

The role of counselor includes the role of advisor and more. The term is commonly used to refer to legal counsel, but in fact attorneys are often called upon to do much more. Certain areas of the practice of law entail personal counseling skills beyond legal skills, most notably divorce law. Lawyers must be prepared for the fact that clients deliver problems to them that the clients are not competent to handle themselves. When dealing with a client seeking divorce or one accused of a crime, the lawyer must be aware that the client is dealing with intensely emotional personal problems as well as immediate legal problems. Law school training rarely prepares the new attorney for this kind of conflict.

Although the function of the lawyer is to resolve a client's legal difficulties, the close personal and confidential relationship that often develops between lawyer and client can put the attorney in a role similar to that of a mental health counselor. Some lawyers avoid this role by taking a distant, strictly professional attitude toward their clients, but others feel that this can seem callous and insensitive to a client who may be very much in need of caring and understanding. To persons who may be full of guilt and pain and have low self-esteem, personal rejection by the person they are looking to for solutions can make them feel very alone.

On the surface, the lawyer's responsibility would seem to end with the furnishing of legal services, but the nature of the relationship between attorney and client affects the quality of the services rendered. A divorcing spouse or an incarcerated person may well be in an emotional state that weakens his or her ability to achieve a reasonable legal solution. Persons suing for compensation for personal injury often face loss of work, medical expenses, and other financial difficulties that render them vulnerable to unfair negotiations with an insurance company or corporation that views the dispute as merely a business transaction. An attorney insensitive to these personal problems may do a client a disservice.

Attorneys must also learn that a fine line must be drawn between caring and understanding and emotional involvement with a client's problems. It is one thing to have a personal relationship with a client and quite another to have a social or even romantic relationship. Taking a cue from mental health counselors, the lawyer should maintain a professional attitude without losing sight of the fact that clients are human beings deserving respect and understanding.

The Lawyer as Negotiator

The attorney must give a client the best representation possible. In the adversarial legal system, a lawyer often appears to be the "hired gun," using all the tricks of the trade to destroy the opposing party. This picture misrepresents the role of the lawyer, who is more often a negotiator, mediator, and conciliator. In a personal injury case, for example, the attorney must weigh a number of factors besides winning. If a person injured in an auto accident is suing an insurance company, both sides will have made an estimate of reasonable compensation. Their estimates are based on past experience, both in negotiations and with awards made by juries and judges. If the initial estimates, which are kept secret, are close, it is likely that the two sides can come to an early agreement. If this happens, a number of advantages accrue to the client. First, the client will not experience the considerable unpleasantness of a trial. Second, the client will not endure prolonged negotiations. Third, the expenses, including attorneys' fees, will be minimized.

The client in this case is best served by an attorney who is a persuasive negotiator and can convince the other parties that it is in their best interests to present reasonable offers of compensation. The attorney not only negotiates with the insurance company's attorney but must also apprise the client of the risks and strategies on both sides, so that the client has reasonable expectations. Although the client must make the final decision to accept or reject an offer of settlement, the attorney commonly acts as a mediator between the two sides, ultimately persuading the client that an offer should be accepted. It should be noted, however, that some insurance companies adopt a strategy of nonnegotiation, in which case the plaintiff's attorney must assume an aggressive and threatening posture.

The adversarial role is especially problematic in divorce cases. The legal process of divorce tends to aggravate an already painful and frequently hostile relationship between husband and wife. The best interests of clients go beyond maximizing economic benefits and parental rights. If minor children are involved, the divorcing parents need to establish at least a minimal basis of cooperation for the children's sake. A court battle is likely to leave everyone severely scarred emotionally. Nowhere are ethical and professional duties more perplexing than in divorce law. Divorce does not make unhappy people happy. Perhaps no other area of the practice of law produces so many dissatisfied clients. Interpersonal skills in negotiation, mediation, and conciliation are just as essential as legal skills in this field.

Negotiating skills are essential in commercial law as well. In business and real estate transactions, in contracts, and in structuring business organizations, the objective is usually to establish agreement among all concerned within the requirements of the law. Though different parties have different self-interests, business transactions are normally entered into because everyone benefits. The attorney acts as a facilitator and negotiator, at the same time protecting the client's interests. In some long-standing business relationships based on personal trust, legal counsel may actually be intrusive. If agreements have been customarily cemented with a handshake, the sudden appearance of a contract written by an attorney may be insulting and could damage the relationship. Again, the lawyer's legal skills must be tempered with sensitivity.

Paralegals/Legal Assistants

Origins

paralegal Refers generally to a worker in a law office who performs legal tasks under attorney supervision but who is not licensed to practice law. Some states allow paralegals to provide limited legal services without supervision. "Paralegal" as a title and a job is usually interchangeable with **legal assistant.**

The terms **paralegal** and **legal assistant** are today used interchangeably, though there has been some debate over which term was more descriptive. In some cities and even in individual law firms, the terms may be used to differentiate two jobs different in prestige, though there is no clear indication of which is higher. Thus, some lawyers and some legal staffers insist on two different meanings—it is simply a matter of custom. As with other areas of employment, the more skill and judgment required in a job, the more prestige it is likely to carry.

In general, paralegals do not perform any tasks that were not performed in law offices prior to the rise in importance of their field. In fact, paralegals do not perform any tasks that lawyers did not perform in the past. Paralegals assist lawyers in providing legal services to clients, but there are a number of things paralegals cannot do because they are not licensed to practice law, a matter discussed later in this chapter. Because paralegals are employees of lawyers and law firms, the nature of their work depends largely on how their work is defined by their employers, but the types of tasks they perform have become increasingly standardized, in part because of the uniformity of the formal training they are receiving in educational institutions.

Inns of Court For centuries, English lawyers were trained in the Inns of Court, where students learned the law in association with legal scholars, lawyers, and judges.

Although the paralegal profession is relatively recent in origin, lawyers have been using legal assistants in some form since the founding of our republic. Before bar associations, bar examinations, and law schools, it was the custom in the legal profession to learn law by apprenticeship in a law office, often called "reading the law." Except for those affluent enough to study law at the **Inns of Court** in London, early nineteenth-century lawyers learned law by assisting lawyers for a period of time, taking what opportunities they could to read cases and treatises about the law. This often took on an aspect of exploitation at low wages, but eventually the novice was sponsored by his employer to be accepted into practice by the courts of his jurisdiction. This form of legal education qualified bar applicants in most states well into the twentieth century, and contemporary law school students continue to serve much the same function when they work as law clerks in law offices during summer vacations from law school. It would be appropriate to refer to these students as paralegals, though the customary label is *clerk*. In communities with large law schools, law students and paralegals often compete for employment.

Before the rise of paralegalism, many lawyers trained their legal secretaries to perform legal tasks beyond the usual scope of secretarial work, and some attorneys still prefer this approach to hiring formally trained assistants. Many present-day paralegals were trained in this way. As the attorney's practice increased, the secretary was gradually converted into a full-time paralegal, and a new secretary was hired to do the secretarial work. The advantage of such an arrangement was that the lawyer was able to take an employee with whom a good working relationship had been established and train that person to do the specific auxiliary tasks the lawyer needed. The disadvantage was that both the lawyer and the secretary took time away from their work for the training.

The paralegal position would never have been invented if it had not proven economically advantageous to law firms. The prime movers in paralegalism have been the largest law firms in the largest American cities. In large law firms, attorneys tend to be highly specialized, which tends to produce attorneys very knowledgeable and competent within their field of practice. They charge premium fees because they can provide quick delivery of high-quality legal services to large corporate and affluent private clients. But this can be accomplished effectively only if the firm is a well-managed business. The lawyers are freed to concentrate on important tasks by the assistance of a competent staff, consisting primarily of law office managers, paralegals, and secretaries. The more support staff a lawyer has, the more time the lawyer can devote to delivering legal services and the more money can be brought into the firm. In many instances this benefits the clients, who can be billed for paralegal research, for example, at a significantly lower rate than the attorney's hourly rate. In short, paralegals came to occupy defined positions in large law firms simply because they were part of a rational allocation of work that improved the quality of legal services at the same time that it increased profit for the firm.

Paralegal Training

Because paralegals are as yet unlicensed, no formal training is required. As mentioned, many paralegals have been trained at work by their supervising attorney; some have even trained themselves. While we may call some persons paralegals by virtue of the completion of formal training, others are best defined by the nature of the work they do. In addition, many individuals working in law firms perform secretarial work as well as legal work that goes beyond what would normally be expected of a legal secretary. Whether we call such individuals legal secretaries or paralegals is presently a matter of choice.

Paralegal training is not currently monopolized by any one type of institution. This is unusual because training in most fields is clearly either vocational or academic. Paralegals should be viewed as professionals who must possess not only technical skills but also a firm grounding in the subject matter of their field, which is law. A *professional* is a person who applies a body of knowledge to aid people in solving their problems.

Perhaps an analogy with the English legal profession will be helpful. In England, the legal profession is divided into barristers and solicitors. **Solicitors** perform the day-to-day tasks of handling commercial transactions and advising clients with legal problems. **Barristers** are similar to what we in America call *trial lawyers*; they take from solicitors cases that cannot be resolved by negotiation and must be decided by trial in court. Although English solicitors have broader authority than American paralegals, the two are similar in the sense that their authority stops short of representation in court. Nevertheless, paralegals, like solicitors, are often present during trials to advise and assist the trial attorney. Solicitors are not merely technicians but must have an intimate knowledge of the law in order to adequately represent the interests of their clients.

Parallels with the English system are obvious, and recognition of paralegalism as a profession in its own right is imminent. To take their place beside the time-honored professions, paralegals must possess more than technical skills. They must also acquire a broad body of knowledge to help them exercise wise and effective judgments. With this in view, paralegal training takes on a serious mission.

Academic institutions conform to the traditions of academic training and the requirements of regional accrediting agencies, which monitor the activities of the institutions that seek continuing approval. The American Bar Association (ABA) has added its own approval process, which entails a detailed initial approval application and periodic review to maintain approval. Any program that has obtained ABA approval has received careful attention to ensure that it meets stringent requirements. Because the approval process is voluntary as well as costly and time-consuming, many fine programs have declined to seek ABA approval. The American Association for Paralegal Education (AAfPE) plays a significant role in discussing and setting standards for paralegal programs.

Regional accreditation subjects an educational institution as a whole to intense scrutiny, but does not necessarily subject its paralegal program to the same scrutiny, which is largely up to the institution itself. An institution like a community college or university that has both regional accreditation and ABA approval has undergone scrutiny through two processes. Though neither of these guarantees high quality, they demonstrate that a program has met important minimal standards. A less formal, but nonetheless important, measure of any program is its reputation among local attorneys. Like law schools and the legal profession in general, reputation and prestige are very important. Good programs that graduate good paralegals will ultimately be recognized through the legal grapevine, because attorneys have a serious interest in hiring competent paralegals.

Paralegal training programs can also be divided into degree programs and certificate programs. Degree programs are more typical of traditional academic programs, like those found in community college, college, and university settings, where a degree such as Associate of Science, Associate of Arts, or Bache-

solicitor A lawyer in England who handles all legal matters except trial work.

barrister An English lawyer who specializes in trial work.

lor of Arts is awarded. In these programs, the institution usually requires that the academic training meet a general standard that may require courses in addition to paralegal courses. In certificate programs, a certificate of satisfactory completion is conferred, and the programs usually limit themselves to the particular field of study. *Certificate programs* should not be confused with *certification* by the National Association of Legal Assistants (NALA), which conducts an optional examination of qualified paralegals leading to the designation *Certified Legal Assistant*. Although this designation has no official legal status, NALA was an early entry into the paralegal field, assigning itself the mission of establishing standards for practicing paralegals; certification, like passing a bar exam, is evidence of professional knowledge and competence.

Curriculum

substantive law That part of law that creates, defines, and regulates rights; compare to **procedural law** which deals with the method of enforcing rights.

pleadings Written formal documents framing the issues of a lawsuit, consisting primarily of what is alleged on the one side, for example, the plaintiff's *complaint*, or denied on the other, for example, the defendant's *answer*.

evidence The information presented at trial; the *rules of evidence* are part of the procedural law.

motions Requests that a judge make a ruling or take some other action.

jurisdiction The authority, capacity, power, or right of a court to render a binding decision in a case.

Paralegal courses echo those taught in law school. Both train legal practitioners, and the subjects are necessarily similar. Because of the variety of paralegal programs, the curriculum and pedagogy vary far more than they do in law school. Nevertheless, the basic subjects have changed little in name over the years. Both the law and legal curricula divide law into two major areas: **substantive law** and **procedural law.** [The distinction is extremely important in the law and perhaps should not be introduced here in what is largely descriptive content; but, like so many important legal themes and concepts, no obvious learning sequence presents itself.] Procedural law is aptly named since it deals with procedure, such things as **pleading, evidence, motions,** and **jurisdiction.** Substantive law in one sense covers all that is not procedural or, more specifically, the basic law of legal rights and duties. Procedural law is the means by which rights and duties may be enforced. *Substantive* is derived from *substance*, which is often contrasted to *form*. We are inclined to elevate substance over form in our personal values; but, in law, form—that is, procedure—is the structure that creates system rather than chaos and anarchy.

The word *right* conjures up fundamental rights, such as freedom of speech and equality before the law, but legal process is far more often involved in more mundane rights and duties. For example, the law recognizes that each of us has a right to be free of physical attack by others, to enjoy a reputation unsullied by malicious lies about our character, to enjoy our privacy, and to use our property in most ways that do not intrude on the rights of others. And each of us has a duty to not deprive others of those same rights. The substantive law delineates those rights. Later chapters of this book that discuss contracts, torts, and property law, among other issues, contain basic treatment of substantive rights and duties. The chapters on civil procedure and criminal procedure deal with basic procedural law. These subjects and others form a basic curriculum for both law schools and paralegal programs.

The difference between curricula of law schools and paralegal programs lies not so much in subject matter as in method. The case method discussed earlier in the chapter is a staple of law schools while used sparingly in undergraduate education. This book, by the way, uses a modified case method—case excerpts are found in each chapter but the bulk of the book consists of descriptive comments about the law. Paralegal programs typically include more courses based on practice, while law schools relegate this field to on-the-job training or the so-called "clinical courses," which are usually voluntary programs. Law schools are often the battlegrounds for theoretical disputes about law, such as feminist legal theory and the radical critique that, in the late twentieth century challenged the traditional business—some might call "patriarchal"—focus of law school training. Paralegal training tends to avoid theoretical issues, except to the extent that they are encountered in a four-year curriculum that emphasizes a liberal arts focus over vocational training. The emphasis, of course, depends not merely on the formal curriculum but also on the orientation of the faculty.

Paralegals regularly receive training in law office skills that are absent in law school training. These may include computer programs, law office management, and specific legal clerical tasks. Paralegal training tends to be far more task-oriented than law school training, which emphasizes analytical and verbal training. Paralegals frequently serve as interns, doing many of the tasks law students perform as summer law clerks. Many paralegals ultimately decide to go on to law school to be transformed into attorneys.

What Paralegals May Not Do

Before we discuss what paralegals actually do, it may be helpful to clarify what they may *not* do. This summary does not include all the areas in which paralegals may run into difficulties, such as fee-splitting with attorneys, soliciting business for attorneys, and other ethical problems covered in Chapter 2; for now we confine the discussion to work tasks.

Problem areas are found under what is called *unauthorized practice of law.* Some things may be done legally only by licensed attorneys, and most states have a statute that restricts the practice of law to attorneys. Limited exceptions may be made for realtors and accountants, for example, within their respective fields, and paralegals may enjoy limited privileges if the state has specifically authorized them. Those few states that have addressed this issue by statute have been largely concerned with what paralegals cannot do rather than with what they can do. It is incumbent upon paralegals to become familiar with restrictions and privileges in effect in their state. Because many states are currently investigating the need for and desirability of regulating and licensing paralegals, we can anticipate that the range of permissible activities for paralegals will vary widely among the states and gradually settle into basic principles recognized nationally. Several national paralegal associations and the American Bar Association encourage uniformity among the states. In the meantime, individual paralegals must stay informed of the requirements of their states.

Despite variations among the states, it is possible to arrive at general principles, because there is a consensus on what an attorney's license permits. Lawyers are privileged to provide legal advice and legal representation to clients. Legal advice means advising a client about legal rights and duties and especially about the proper course of action as it relates to the law. For instance, a paralegal may properly advise someone, "I think you ought to see a lawyer," but it would not be proper to say, "I think you ought to file a motion to dismiss." This extends even to matters of law clearly within the paralegal's knowledge and competence. *The temptation to advise must be resisted.* This proscription extends beyond actual clients—whenever a paralegal gives legal advice, she may be engaged in the unauthorized practice of law. The line is not always easy to draw. Consider the example of a friend laboring under the misconception that the **statute of limitations** is four years when the paralegal knows it to be only two. Should she quietly sit by and let her friend lose a suit? Without advising the friend on a course of legal action, the paralegal can certainly question the friend's knowledge and suggest a visit to an attorney or provide a copy of pertinent state statutes, without interpretation that might constitute legal advice.

Legal representation includes a number of important activities, including representation before a court, which is the privileged domain of attorneys. This monopoly of the bar is necessary to exercise control over attorneys who act improperly and to enable clients who are improperly represented to sue their attorneys for malpractice. Nonlawyers may not represent others in court, may not sign documents submitted to the court in any proceeding, nor sign any documents that call for attorneys' signatures. The paralegal is not an agent of a client and must avoid any appearance of being one. There may be limited exceptions to this rule, but paralegals act at their peril in such matters and must be very clear on state law when interviewing clients or engaging in negotiations.

Observing two cardinal rules can avoid the dangers of legal representation by the paralegal. First, the client must always be aware that the paralegal is not an attorney. In any consultations with a client in which the paralegal may participate, especially in initial contacts, the status of paralegal should be clear to the client. Letters written on law firm stationery (some states do not allow paralegals' names on the letterhead) should make clear that the letter is not from an attorney, for example, "As Mr. Clinton's paralegal, I have been asked to write concerning . . . [signed] Erin Summer, Paralegal." Even this might not be sufficient if legal advice is offered. Many clients do not know that paralegals are not lawyers.

The second rule concerns attorney supervision. As long as the paralegal is under the control and supervision of an attorney and the attorney exercises supervision properly, nearly all potential problems are avoided. Many legal documents, including pleadings are prepared by paralegals and signed by lawyers. The attorney is responsible for ascertaining the paralegal's competence to prepare the documents and must review and amend the documents before signing them. Responsibility rests with the supervising attorney, who may be disciplined by the court or the bar association for problems created by a failure to supervise properly, but the paralegal must be aware of the dangers of such situations. Other activities that could constitute unauthorized practice of law include:

1. Negotiating fees or legal representation on behalf of the attorney

2. Discussing the merits of a case with attorneys for the other side

3. Assisting others in the unauthorized practice of law

statute of limitations   A federal or state law that specifies time limits within which suits must be filed for civil and criminal actions; they vary from state to state and from action to action.

Legal Technicians

legal technicians
Persons who provide legal services for compensation without attorney supervision.

The terms *paralegal* and *legal assistant* both imply attorney supervision. There are also a number of persons now calling themselves **legal technicians,** who provide legal services without attorney supervision. A movement toward licensing appears to have started in California, where a significant number of independent paralegals risked legal sanctions for providing services to the public. Although the California Bar Association disapproved the proposed licensing of paralegals in November 1990, the issue survives. Several states have formalized licensing bills in the state legislatures, including Illinois, Minnesota, Washington, and Oregon. In 1994, Arizona followed other states in postponing comprehensive regulation and licensing. Until a consensus is built in the bar of at least one state, or until someone frames a case for the courts, the problem of regulation is likely to be tabled for the time being, but it will not go away as long as the number of nonlawyers offering legal services continues to increase. The issue of the 1990s is likely to shift from *whether* to license paralegals to who will be responsible for regulating them.

The courts and the bar association are most likely to take action for unauthorized practice of law where someone impersonates an attorney or gives every appearance of being an attorney although technically disclaiming any attorney status. While it might appear that attorneys are merely protecting their own turf, the justification for bar membership and discipline is the protection of the public. A person who innocently, perhaps naively, believes another to be an attorney and acts to her misfortune on that advice does not have the remedies available that she would have with a licensed professional. Her remedy might be fraud and misrepresentation rather than malpractice, for which attorneys usually insure themselves. Nor could she count on an attorney's fear of losing the license to practice law. The *Telford* case gives the appearance of someone who borrowed the indicia of a lawyer without actually assuming that label. The New Mexico Bar dislikes this sort of conduct.

What Paralegals Do

appellate brief A formal statement submitted to the appellate court. When a case is appealed, the appellant submits a written statement to the appellate court raising legal issues to be decided. The appellee then has a period within which the appellee's brief must be filed, challenging the appellant's arguments on the issues.

Once impermissible tasks are eliminated, paralegals may do anything from typing and filing to preparing **appellate briefs.** An efficiently run law office will clarify the boundaries between paralegal work and the work of the rest of the office staff. Routine typing and filing should be assigned to the secretarial staff simply because such tasks do not effectively utilize the knowledge and skills of the paralegal. Appellate briefs probably should be written by attorneys, though paralegals can provide valuable assistance.

Rather than catalog the myriad tasks that a paralegal can do, it is more instructive to consider what a paralegal might do in a case. In a complex case that may result in litigation, a paralegal may be assigned extensive duties of management and coordination. A supervising attorney can delegate tasks to a trusted and experienced paralegal to free the attorney from time-consuming, routine activities. In our hypothetical case, the attorney is working on a

CINCINNATI BAR ASSOCIATION
v.
TELFORD
Supreme Court of Ohio
85 Ohio St.3d 111, 707 N.E.2d 462 (1999)

In December 1997, relator, Cincinnati Bar Association, filed a complaint with the Board of Commissioners on the Unauthorized Practice of Law of the Supreme Court ("board"), charging that respondent, Stephen Mark Telford, had engaged in the unauthorized practice of law. The board heard the matter in May 1998.

. . . [T]he board found that respondent is not an attorney and is not licensed to practice law in Ohio. In 1996, respondent began operating a business known as Kennedy, Katz & Rose. Despite its name, respondent was the sole operator of Kennedy, Katz & Rose.

In his business, respondent searched a Hamilton County court index for recent filings of foreclosure proceedings and debt collection lawsuits. Respondent then mailed letters to the defendants in these debt-related lawsuits requesting that they hire him to settle the cases. The letters contained a statement that Kennedy, Katz & Rose did not include attorneys and that the business could not represent the debtors or advise them in legal proceedings. When a defendant expressed interest in becoming a client, respondent had the defendant sign a power of attorney and a work agreement authorizing the respondent's business to negotiate a settlement in exchange for compensation. Respondent then would send a letter to the attorney representing the plaintiff in the debt-related litigation in an effort to settle the dispute.

The board found that respondent was retained by John F. Gallant in connection with a collection matter filed by A.F.Y. Security Distributors, Inc. ("A.F.Y.") in Hamilton County Municipal Court against Gallant and Linda J. Kniepp. In January 1997, respondent wrote to the plaintiff's attorney, requesting some time to develop a payment plan to settle the debt

issue and to have Kniepp's name removed from the lawsuit because "[s]he had no involvement or liability for Mr. Gallant's business." A.F.Y. refused to dismiss Kniepp from the case.

James Kersting retained respondent in connection with a collection matter filed in Hamilton County Municipal Court by Quality Supply Co. In November 1996, respondent wrote a letter to the plaintiff's counsel, stating that Kersting did not believe he owed the alleged debt and that respondent "would like to review the facts and decide the merit of this claim" himself. In December 1996, respondent advised Kersting that if he did not have a certified check in the amount of $3,426.43 made out to the plaintiff by a certain time, "we run the risk of triple damages in the amount of $17,706.37." The plaintiff, however, requested only a sum of $5,900.79 in its complaint, which already included treble damages. . . . [Several other incidents are briefly mentioned in which respondent was retained to handle collection matters.]

The board concluded that respondent's actions, including giving legal advice and counsel to defendants in collection and foreclosure proceedings, constituted the unauthorized practice of law in Ohio. The board recommended that respondent be prohibited from engaging in such practices in the future.

PER CURIAM.

We adopt the findings, conclusions, and recommendation of the board. Under Gov.Bar R. VII(2)(A), the "unauthorized practice of law is the rendering of legal services for another by any person not admitted to practice in Ohio * * *." The practice of law is not restricted to appearances in court; it also encompasses giving legal advice and counsel. . . .

Respondent gave legal advice to defendants in pending lawsuits in an attempt to settle those cases. In fact, in the Kersting matter, respondent gave erroneous legal advice to Kersting by specifying a potential damage liability far exceeding the actual sum requested by the plaintiff in that case. In the Gallant matter,

(continued)

(continued)

respondent informed the plaintiff's attorney that he should remove a third party from the lawsuit, and in the Brownstone case, respondent sent a proposed settlement of the suit to the plaintiff's counsel.

As we recently held, the practice of law includes "making representations to creditors on behalf of third parties, and advising persons of their rights, and the terms and conditions of settlement." . . . Neither respondent's state-ments in his solicitation letters that he was not an attorney and was not giving legal advice nor the powers of attorney executed by his clients insulated respondent, a non-attorney, from the unauthorized practice of law. . . .

Based on the foregoing, we find that respondent engaged in the unauthorized prac-tice of law. Respondent is hereby enjoined from the further practice of law in Ohio. Costs taxed to respondent.

Judgment accordingly.

Case Questions

1. Which of the basic acts of unauthorized practice of law was Telford found to be practicing?
2. Why was Telford's advice concerning triple damages particularly damaging to his case?

contingency fee contracts Agreements between an attorney and a client in which the attorney will receive compensation in the form of a percentage of money recovered in a lawsuit; used predominantly in personal injury cases.

contingency fee basis, so the final fee will be the same regardless of who per-forms the work. In such a situation, the use of paralegals, who presumably earn considerably less than the supervising attorney, is very cost-efficient. Keep in mind that consultations with the attorney should be frequent, and the attorney should directly supervise the paralegal's work. Depending on the complexity of the case, a paralegal may actually supervise other paralegals.

Hypothetical case: The parents of a five-year-old boy who has a rare form of cancer consult a personal injury firm concerning a possible lawsuit against a business adjacent to their residence that has been investigated for and charged with dumping toxic waste in back of the business premises. It has been deter-mined by a public investigating agency that some of the effluent has caused contamination of the well water serving the surrounding neighborhood. The parents have received information that the particular chemicals disposed of have been linked elsewhere with their son's form of cancer. After a preliminary investigation, the law firm decides that the business wrongfully dumped toxic waste that caused contamination of the water supply, that a strong case can be made for a causal connection between the contamination and the child's can-cer, and that the injuries sustained were sufficient to pursue the case on a con-tingency fee basis. What are some of the tasks that might be assigned to the para-legal working on the case?

Numerous tasks could be performed by a paralegal assigned as case man-ager. A paralegal may be put in charge of many tasks and report directly to a supervising attorney. Some tasks may be delegated to a secretary or another assisting paralegal. Without a paralegal, some tasks, such as telephone calls to collect information and arrange meetings, would be performed by a legal sec-retary, while others would be performed by an attorney.

An attorney may prefer to have the paralegal present from the outset in any consultations with a client. In fact, the client may see the paralegal first in an interview to determine the nature of the case. All this depends on the practices of the firm and the relationship between attorney and paralegal. An advantage of having a paralegal present is that the client can be introduced in a setting in which the client perceives the paralegal as a trusted assistant to the attorney. In addition, the paralegal can take notes, thus freeing the attorney from talking and taking notes at the same time. If the paralegal is not present, the attorney must later take time to explain the case to the paralegal.

The paralegal will engage in some investigative activities. The facts as represented by a client are necessarily incomplete. Facts must thus be collected from other sources to get a complete picture and also to minimize any distortions the client may have conveyed. A report of the agency investigating the dumping of wastes will be sought. Any action taken against the business will be researched and its status followed through any final decision. The paralegal may make a visit to the site to take pictures of the client's property and its relation to the property on which the chemicals were dumped. The paralegal may question neighbors named by the client who have suffered illness they believe to be caused by the dumping of waste. In short, a full picture of the background in which these events took place should be established, both through informal investigation and questioning and through public and private records.

discovery A pretrial procedure in which parties to a lawsuit ask for and receive information such as testimony, records, or other evidence from each other.

Pretrial preparation also involves formal devices for collecting information from the opposing party, called **discovery.** The paralegal can be instrumental in the pretrial process. He can arrange for depositions to be taken of the employees of the business and any other witnesses for the opposition. During the case, the attorney will develop what is often loosely called the "theory" of the case, that is, the most probable legal basis for winning the case, tying it into the facts of the case. It is called *theory* for two reasons: First, no one can be certain that the judge or jury will agree until the final decision. Second, the approach and even the basis for the lawsuit may change as the factual basis becomes clearer. Like a scientific theory, the theory of the case is a tentative explanation or working hypothesis that remains to be proved and may be adjusted if it is not working.

interrogatories A *discovery* device, pretrial written questions sent from one party to the other party.

In a good working relationship, attorney and paralegal share the story of a case and develop a strategy to deal with it. If a paralegal enjoys the confidence of the attorney, the paralegal can formulate questions for depositions, draft **interrogatories** to opposing counsel to obtain basic information, and participate in and sometimes direct other discovery processes such as requesting documents from the other side. The fact that the attorney is responsible for reviewing and approving or signing appropriate documents does not prevent the paralegal from doing most of the work. Oral depositions must be arranged at times convenient to attorneys for both sides as well as the person to be deposed. It is more economical for a paralegal or secretary to make such arrangements than an attorney. The case manager can track the process on the attorney's calendar to see that these tasks are completed. Obviously secretaries can perform such tasks, but it is more efficient to have someone in charge of the loose ends of a particular case to ensure that everything has been done.

Whether or not the paralegal is directly involved in the deposition itself, in a complicated case it is essential that the deposition be summarized and indexed. The court reporter typically reduces the deposition to a verbatim written **transcript,** which can often run to several hundred pages. Long transcripts are unmanageable without summaries and references to the pages of important topics discussed. Summarizing and indexing should be done by someone familiar with the case and its theory. This is a time-consuming job that can be accomplished by a paralegal, allowing better time management by the attorney.

Extensive legal research will be necessary in the case. As much as possible, the client's legal position must be bolstered by persuasive legal authority. This is not only important to persuade the trial judge but is also instrumental in negotiations with opposing counsel. If a defendant's attorney is convinced that, under the law, his client has a losing case, focus will change from fighting the case to saving the client money by a favorable negotiation. A strong case built on solid research is an essential part of the negotiation process. Although some attorneys insist on doing most or all of the legal research, many paralegals are accomplished researchers. The most important ingredients in good research are thoroughness and perseverance.

Management of a complex case requires an orderly filing system. The many documents that accumulate in the course of the case must be readily available for review and preparation for trial. In our computer age, file management has been made much easier. Many software packages are available for litigation files, and a program can be tailored for specific styles of organization. Material can be stored by computers in ways that make retrieval fast and efficient. Nevertheless, a human being is still necessary to record and file the material on the computer, and paralegal case managers often perform or delegate these responsibilities.

Writing can also be an important activity for the paralegal. In complex litigation, a paralegal case manager may at many points in the case have a greater mastery of the legal and factual details of the case than the attorney, who as the decision-maker has an overview of the case. The attorney may ask the paralegal to write memoranda about the case, and especially the legal issues of the case, so that the major issues are summarized in an analytical form that makes a quick review of the case and its status possible. Although analysis and writing require more skill than does research, experience is a great teacher. The fortunate paralegal works for an attorney who will take time to help build these skills.

Paralegals can also be instrumental in maintaining good client relations. One of the most frequent client complaints is difficulty in reaching attorneys by phone and in receiving return calls. Paralegals often have direct contact with clients and may have a better feel for clients' concerns. Clients may be reluctant to discuss all their concerns with the attorney, especially if they think of that two-dollar-a-minute clock ticking. The paralegal is often a more sympathetic and patient listener and can reassure the client that the case is proceeding in a timely fashion, as well as relay the client's concerns to the attorney. Clients often feel that nothing is happening in their case if their attorney has not corre-

transcript A written verbatim version of an oral statement. In law, transcripts are used most frequently in reference to depositions and trials.

sponded with them for some time. It is helpful for a client to know that more than one person is concerned about the case. The paralegal can call, receive calls, make sure that copies of letters and legal documents are sent to the client, and in other ways make the client appreciate that the case is receiving attention. The paralegal can also alert the attorney to angry clients and help head off unpleasant confrontations.

The tasks performed by paralegals are too numerous to catalog completely, but the following lists give some indication of paralegal duties in two specialized areas of the law. They borrow heavily from lists prepared by the Subcommittee on Legal Assistance of the New York State Bar Association:

Real Estate Transactions

1. Review the contract for sale of real property.
2. Request and obtain title searches.
3. Request and obtain survey of the property.
4. Prepare deeds.
5. Review title opinion and/or title insurance documents.
6. Prepare and review closing statements.
7. Forward, receive, and track documents for closing.
8. Monitor closing file for completeness and accuracy.
9. Track deadlines.

Wills and Trusts

1. Maintain files and indexes.
2. Conduct initial interview with fiduciary.
3. Prepare and file probate documents.
4. Arrange for publication and service of citation.
5. Prepare application for tax identification number.
6. Value assets.
7. Transfer property to trust.
8. Prepare decedent's final income tax return.
9. Prepare estate tax return.
10. Prepare applications for life insurance benefits.
11. Inventory investments, bank accounts, etc.
12. Pay decedent's debts and costs of administration.
13. Cancel credit cards.
14. Prepare final accounting.
15. Prepare final probate petition.

Similar lists could be compiled for corporate paralegals, tax paralegals, bank-ruptcy paralegals, or virtually any other specialty using paralegals. The lists indi-cate the variety of formal document preparation and management required for activities involving property transfers. A great deal of work is required to ensure that these events are handled accurately, completely, and in a timely fashion.

The *Winder* case draws a fine line between what is the practice of law and what is not. In drawing its conclusions, it cites a case involving a well-known book titled *How to Avoid Probate!*, which caused considerable consternation among state bar associations. **Probate** is the court procedure whereby the estate of a deceased person is administered and distributed. When poorly planned by the decedent, the estate may be subject to significant costs during the probate process, which in some jurisdictions has been abused by lawyers and judges. In writing his book, Dacey appealed to the fears of those who had heard horror stories of pro-bate. There are a number of legal devices for passing on property without going through probate. Members of the legal profession, nevertheless, were properly concerned that a general book about probate failed to take into account the pecu-liarities of various state laws and the individualized needs of those who sought a proper division of their property.

probate   The process of handling the will and the estate of a deceased person.

Summary

Law school training and admission to the bar are the first steps in becoming a competent attorney. Although law school imparts a basic knowledge of impor-tant fields of the law, it emphasizes the development of analytical skills and does not provide either training for the daily tasks of the practice of law or the com-munication skills necessary for rendering valuable legal services. Law students often clerk in law offices during summer terms to gain experience in the prac-tical side of the profession.

Lawyers are problem-solvers; they help remove the legal hurdles from a client's path. Sometimes this means fighting a legal battle in the courtroom, but more often it involves resolving a dispute without going to trial. Perhaps attor-neys spend an even greater portion of their time preventing disputes and aiding in personal and business transactions by anticipating potential conflicts.

The practice of law entails many skills that are not taught in law school and are often absent from the popular image of the lawyer. These are primarily interpersonal communication skills that cast the attorney in the role of advisor, counselor, and negotiator.

The last years of the twentieth century witnessed a boom in large law firms and a trend toward specialization even in small ones. This accompanied an increase in personnel and technology. This same period saw the establishment of paralegal employment as an essential adjunct to the law office, part of a more businesslike emphasis in the legal profession. Paralegals, or legal assistants, per-form a variety of tasks in law offices that depend largely on the needs of the firm. Paralegals today do many things only lawyers did in the past, but there are cer-tain things only lawyers may do, and anyone else who attempts to engage in

The STATE of New York, Respondent,
v.
James A. WINDER, Individually and dba
Divorce Yourself,
Do It Yourself Divorce Kits
and Divorce Aid
Service Enterprises, Appellant
Supreme Court, Appellate Division,
Fourth Dept.
348 N.Y.S.2d 270 (1973)

The Divorce Yourself Kit offered for sale by defendant, a layman, purports to offer forms and instructions in law and procedure in certain areas of matrimonial law and the judicial process. In *Matter of New York Co. Lawyers' Ass'n v. Dacey,* 28 A.D.2d 161 . . . , the court dealt with the publishing of a book "How to Avoid Probate!" consisting of 55 pages of text and 310 pages of forms. In the dissenting opinion adopted by the Court of Appeals, Justice Stevens, analyzing the pertinent rules of law, stated . . . : "It cannot be claimed that the publication of a legal text which purports to say what the law is amounts to legal practice. And the mere fact that the principles or rules stated in the text may be accepted by a particular reader as a solution to his problem does not affect this. . . . Apparently it is urged that the conjoining of these two, that is, the text and the forms, with advice as to how the forms should be filled out, constitutes the unlawful practice of law. But that is the situation with many approved and accepted texts. Dacey's book is sold to the public at large. There is no personal contact or relationship with a particular individual. Nor does there exist that relation of confidence and trust so necessary to the status of attorney and client. This is the essential of legal practice—the representation and the advising of a particular person in a particular situation. . . . At most the book assumes to offer general advice on common problems, and does not purport to give personal advice on a specific problem peculiar to a designated or readily identified person." Similarly the defendant's publication does not purport "to give personal advice on a specific problem peculiar to a designated or readily identified person," and because of the absence of the essential element of "legal practice—the representation and the advising of a particular person in a particular situation" in the publication and sale of the kits, such publication and sale did not constitute the unlawful practice of law in violation of Sec. 478 of the Judiciary Law and was improperly enjoined by paragraph I of the judgment appealed from. There being no legal impediment under the statute to the sale of the kit, there was no proper basis for the injunction in paragraph G against defendant maintaining an office for the purpose of selling to persons seeking a divorce, separation, annulment or separation agreement any printed material or writings relating to matrimonial law or the prohibition in the memorandum of modification of the judgment against defendant having an interest in any publishing house publishing his manuscript on divorce and against his having any personal contact with any prospective purchaser. The record does fully support, however, the finding of the court that for the charge of $75 or $100 for the kit, the defendant gave legal advice in the course of personal contacts concerning particular problems which might arise in the reparation and presentation of the purchaser's asserted matrimonial cause of action or pursuit of other legal remedies and assistance in the preparation of necessary documents. The ordering paragraphs of the injunction A through F, H and J all enjoin conduct constituting the practice of law, particularly with reference to the giving of advice and counsel by the defendant relating to specific problems of particular individuals in connection with a divorce, separation, annulment of [sic] sought and should be affirmed.

Judgment unanimously modified on the law and facts in accordance with Memorandum and as modified affirmed without costs.

Case Questions

1. What does the court describe as the essential ingredient of legal practice?
2. Why may a nonlawyer give advice in a book but not in person?

these activities risks being charged with unauthorized practice of law. Representing clients in court and giving final legal advice top the list of activities that require membership in the bar. Independent paralegals, often called "legal technicians," must therefore walk a fine line. Licensure for paralegals has been considered for several years but has yet to come to pass.

Scenario

marital settlement agreement A contract drawn up for a divorcing couple to distribute marital property and set the terms for child custody, child support payments, and alimony.

You have been working as a paralegal for five years for an attorney specializing in divorce and family law. A close friend comes to you for help. He says that his wife has filed for divorce and has presented him with a **marital settlement agreement** drawn up by her attorney, and he wants you to read it and tell him what you think of it. You have prepared many of these agreements yourself and know that in your jurisdiction the judges routinely approve such agreements when signed by both parties unless they appear grossly unfair to one party. Your friend says that the agreement appears to him to reflect his oral agreements with his wife before she consulted an attorney. He has consulted several attorneys, and all want at least $1,500 to represent him. He says he cannot afford this additional expense and will not hire an attorney unless absolutely necessary. If you do not read the agreement, he says, he will simply take his chances by signing it. He knows you are a paralegal and not licensed to practice law.

What are the ethical considerations?

1. Does it matter whether your friend pays you for this service?

2. Must you advise your friend to consult an attorney?

3. Must you refuse to read the agreement?

4. If you read the agreement and are convinced that it is fair and legally sound, can you so inform your friend?

5. If you read the agreement and have doubts about some of its clauses, what can you tell your friend?

6. Can you advise your friend with a disclaimer to the effect that you are not an attorney, that your advice may be incorrect, and that he should consult an attorney?

ETHICS

CHAPTER OUTLINE

Introduction

ethics Concerns right or proper conduct and often refers to the fairness and honesty of a person's character. In philosophy, it covers the area of inquiry into right conduct.

legal ethics Synonymous with "professional responsibility"; the legal profession promulgates specific rules to cover important areas of professional misconduct and disciplines transgressors.

The study of ethics is a branch of philosophy. The **ethics** discussed in this chapter is more appropriately labeled **legal ethics,** which has developed over the last century from an intuitive sense of duty and responsibility to an explicit set of rules governing the professional conduct of attorneys. Violation of the rules subjects attorneys to disciplinary action.

It must be cautioned at the outset that a strong sense of right and wrong will not guarantee avoidance of the violation of professional ethics, though it certainly minimizes the danger. The practice of law involves duties to clients, to the public, to the courts, and to colleagues. Lawyers have access to sensitive, confidential information about their clients, information that must often necessarily be shared with law office staff. In the representation of clients, attorneys are frequently faced with ethical dilemmas that are not easily solved. Ethical codes are designed to provide answers to most of these dilemmas, but they cannot precisely address every possible situation. Clients can be unpredictable and even unscrupulous, consciously or unconsciously putting attorneys in positions that lead to unfavorable outcomes. It is only by strictly following the ethical codes and acting in utmost good faith that attorneys can avoid the many traps that the practice of law entails.

In the last two decades, the legal profession has expended great effort to define and refine the principles governing the ethical conduct of attorneys. More than any other profession, the legal profession has embarked on a campaign to identify and police unethical conduct and fulfill its primary duty of serving the public and the legal system.

31

History of Ethical Rules

Formulating ethical principles has been an ongoing task of the American Bar Association, which established Canons of Ethics as early as 1908. The ABA has no disciplinary authority, but it is the appropriate forum for discussing ethical principles because it represents the bar nationwide. The Canons are general statements of principle urging proper conduct. They have been elaborated over the years through the addition and amendment of *Disciplinary Rules* and *Ethical Considerations*, which describe more specifically conduct that is subject to discipline (*Disciplinary Rules*) and conduct that, though improper, is not subject to discipline (*Ethical Considerations*).

In 1970, these principles crystallized in the ABA's *Model Code of Professional Responsibility* and were quickly adopted by nearly all states. Once these principles were adopted, the Multistate Bar Examination devised a separate ethics test, which most states then made a part of their state bar examination. The ABA additionally provided advisory opinions on specific applications of the *Model Code*, and many state bar associations have similarly answered ethical questions posed by their members in formal opinions.

In 1983, after several years of intense study and dialogue, the ABA reformulated legal ethics in the *Model Rules of Professional Conduct*. The *Model Rules* (as distinguished from the earlier *Model Code*) attempted to reflect changes in the legal profession; for instance, the former prohibition against advertising legal services was found by the U.S. Supreme Court to be an unconstitutional invasion of freedom of speech. The *Model Rules* also addressed conduct more specifically, narrowing the principles to increase clarity and enforceability. The *Model Rules* did away with *Disciplinary Rules* and *Ethical Considerations*, substituting "shall" and "shall not" ("a lawyer shall not seek to influence a judge, juror . . . except as permitted by law or the rules of court") as language warranting disciplinary action and "may" ("a lawyer may refuse to offer evidence that the lawyer reasonably believes is false") as language expressing conduct that is discretionary and not subject to disciplinary action.

The *Model Code* must be discussed along with the more recent *Model Rules* for three reasons:

1. The basic principles are quite similar.

2. Because the *Model Code* was the initial set of rules adopted in the states, a host of opinions and judicial decisions serve as precedents for interpretations of the *Rules*.

3. The *Model Rules* have not received the same degree of acceptance from state bar associations as the *Model Code* enjoyed previously.

The *Model Code* and the *Model Rules*

The Canons of Professional Responsibility of the *Model Code* are listed here with corresponding sections of the *Model Rules*. Although the same issues are addressed, a comparison reveals a distinct difference. The Canons somewhat resemble the Ten Commandments, a moral code to live by, whereas the *Model Rules* reflect a more sophisticated legislative approach, organized into related subject areas with specific proscriptions that provide better guidance to disciplinary boards and tribunals. The *Model Rules* are eminently more practical, both in terms of enforcement and in terms of the clarity provided to attorneys.

Keep in mind that the Canons were extensively supplemented by *Disciplinary Rules* and *Ethical Considerations* that spelled out specific problems. Nor does displaying the *Model Rules* in this way show their higher degree of organization. The *Model Rules* were published with supplementary comments that address problems routinely confronted by attorneys and are a practical improvement over the *Model Code* as guidelines for attorneys. Nevertheless, because the *Model Rules* are more specific and more clearly enforceable, not all sectors of the bar have been satisfied with them, and the states have not received the *Model Rules* with the same wholehearted approval that the *Model Code* received.

Codes for Legal Assistants

Legal assistant organizations have also formulated ethical codes designed specifically for paralegals. Since paralegals are not licensed, infractions of the rules do not invoke any legal sanctions. This fact should not obscure the need for paralegals—and other office staff, for that matter—to be aware of legal ethics. When a paralegal in a law firm breaches ethical standards, he very likely subjects his attorney supervisor to disciplinary action. For example, if a paralegal discloses a client's confidential statements to someone outside the firm, an ethical breach has occurred and the supervising attorney may be held responsible. The ABA has promulgated *Model Guidelines for the Utilization of Legal Assistant Services*, which hold the attorney responsible for paralegal conduct under the attorney's direction or delegation and effectively assign attorneys the duty of ensuring that paralegals are aware of professional ethics. Legal ethics prohibit attorneys from assisting in the unauthorized practice of law, a violation of legal ethics more likely to be committed by a paralegal than a lawyer because the paralegal is unlicensed. There is, of course, a sanction that can be imposed on a paralegal: employment termination.

One of the most common ethical dilemmas for a paralegal occurs when an attorney delegates tasks that should only be performed by an attorney. Experienced paralegals are knowledgeable and competent and could, for example, often provide clients with sound legal advice but are ethically prohibited from doing so. Paralegals commonly draft legal documents for attorneys. When an attorney submits or files such documents without reading them, an ethical breach has occurred even if the document is without a blemish. A paralegal is put in a delicate position when she becomes aware that this is happening; it is difficult to chastise the boss.

The National Association of Legal Assistants drafted a *Code of Ethics and Professional Responsibility* in 1975, the most recent revision of which was published in 1995. It is composed of nine canons, in the ABA tradition, but, in contrast to the old ABA *Model Code*, concentrates on the unauthorized practice of law. The National Association of Legal Assistants produced its *Model Code of Ethics and Professional Responsibility* in 1993 and in 1997 published the *Model Disciplinary Rules*, which follow the ABA *Model Code* tradition as well, with disciplinary rules and ethical considerations. Both of these codes express general duties in a somewhat moralistic manner characteristic of the original ABA Canons. When and if paralegals are licensed, we can anticipate more specific prohibitions like the ABA's *Model Rules*.

MODEL CODE AND *MODEL RULES* COMPARED	
Model Code *of Professional Responsibility*	Model Rules *of Professional Conduct*
Canons:	**Rules:**
1. A lawyer should assist in maintaining the integrity and competence of the legal profession.	*8 Maintaining the integrity of the profession.*
	8.3 Reporting professional misconduct. (a) A lawyer having knowledge that another lawyer has committed a violation of the *Rules of Professional Conduct* . . . shall inform the appropriate professional authority.
2. A lawyer should assist the legal profession in fulfilling its duty to make legal counsel available.	*6 Public service.*
	6.1 Pro bono publico service. A lawyer should render public interest legal service . . .
	6.2 Accepting appointments. A lawyer shall not seek to avoid appointment by a tribunal to represent a person except for good cause . . .
3. A lawyer should assist in preventing the unauthorized practice of law.	*5.5 Unlicensed (or unauthorized?) practice of law.* A lawyer shall not: (a) practice in a jurisdiction where doing so violates the regulation of the legal profession in that jurisdiction; or (b) assist a person who is not a member of the bar in the performance of activity that constitutes the unauthorized practice of law.

Model Code of Professional Responsibility	Model Rules of Professional Conduct
Canons:	**Rules:**
4. A lawyer should preserve the confidences and secrets of a client.	*1.6 Confidentiality of information.* (a) A lawyer shall not reveal information relating to representation of a client . . . unless the client consents after disclosure to the client.
5. A lawyer should exercise independent professional judgment on behalf of a client.	*5.4 Professional independence of a lawyer.* (a) A lawyer or law firm shall not share legal fees with a nonlawyer, except . . . (b) A lawyer shall not form a partnership with a nonlawyer if any of the activities of the partnership consist of the practice of law. (c) A lawyer shall not permit a person who recommends, employs, or pays the lawyer to render legal services for another to direct or regulate the lawyer's professional judgment in rendering such legal services.
6. A lawyer should represent a client competently.	*1.1 Competence.* A lawyer shall provide competent representation to a client. Competent representation requires the legal knowledge, skill, thoroughness, and preparation reasonably necessary for the representation.
7. A lawyer should represent a client zealously within the bounds of the law.	[Canon 7 is arguably spread among the many subsections of Rules 1 (Client-Lawyer Relationship), 2 (Counselor), and 3 (Advocate).]
8. A lawyer should assist in improving the legal system.	[Canon 8 is primarily exhortatory rather than disciplinary and is implied in many of the Rules and the Preamble.]
9. A lawyer should avoid even the appearance of professional impropriety.	[The vagueness of Canon 9 has been resolved by addressing specific improprieties within the Rules.]

Ethical standards have always required attorneys to provide "zealous representation" to their clients. Canon 7: "A lawyer should represent a client zealously within the bounds of the law." Attorneys are, however, officers of the court and thereby charged with a duty to uphold the judicial system, as well as maintain the dignity of the courts and the legal profession. A problem often arises when an attorney's *zeal* for a client's case or cause exceeds the boundaries of proper practice. In the *Tweedy* case, attorney Craig Tweedy seemed to have become so zealous in his involvement in some cases that he acted improperly. Among the allegations not included in the case excerpts were "communication with a person who is represented by counsel" and "false and reckless statements about a judge." The primary issue, however, dealt with "his continued filing of frivolous and vexatious motions and pleadings after being directed by two levels of federal courts not to do so." He was suspended from practice before the federal courts in Oklahoma, and this resulted in the Oklahoma Bar Association bringing complaints.

Tweedy demonstrates the limits of ethical considerations. When attorneys act improperly, judges are usually quick to admonish them and the improprieties usually end. When the conduct occurs in the courtroom, a judge may threaten contempt of court, which ordinarily frightens the attorney into an apology and the exercise of restraint. Tweedy's conduct was interesting in that he went too far in certain cases but was otherwise cooperative and appropriate. An important feature of the case is the issue of disbarment. The Oklahoma Supreme Court indicates its reluctance to invoke this most serious of professional disciplinary action.

Disclosure

Many ethical problems can be resolved or mitigated by full disclosure to clients. Many conflict-of-interest situations may be eliminated by disclosure of the conflict to the client and opposing party and consent by both to continued representation. Even if an attorney represents a client in the mistaken belief that the ethical problem has been resolved, evidence of full disclosure indicates a good faith attempt by the attorney to resolve the ethical problem and may mitigate any resulting disciplinary action.

In addition to disclosure to the parties, ethical questions over which some uncertainty exists may be addressed to an appropriate state bar ethics committee for an opinion on the ethical issues, if such a procedure is available.

Defining the Practice of Law

The practice of law may be defined in two ways as it relates to professional ethics. The first definition addresses the question of whether an attorney is rendering legal services. For example, a lawyer may engage in **mediation** activities, which does not entail providing legal services and therefore is not covered by legal ethics

mediation   A form of conflict resolution often used in conjunction with litigation or as an alternative to it. Mediation deals with adversarial parties, as in divorce mediation, but is not an adversarial process. The mediator's task is to facilitate agreement and resolution, bringing the parties together without taking sides.

State of Oklahoma ex rel. Oklahoma Bar Association
v.
Craig R. Tweedy
Supreme Court of Oklahoma
2000 OK 37
May 9, 2000

As Corrected May 18, 2000.

The Complainant Oklahoma Bar Association (OBA) brought disciplinary proceedings against Respondent Attorney, Craig R. Tweedy (Respondent)[.] . . .

The allegations against Respondent in Complaint I had their genesis in his handling of three separate matters in the United States District Court for the Northern District of Oklahoma (Northern District) and the United States Court of Appeals for the Tenth Circuit (Tenth Circuit), between 1986 and 1993. Both courts sanctioned Respondent for pursuing baseless legal claims and remedies in the three cases. The Tenth Circuit eventually disbarred Respondent and the Northern District suspended him from practice for three years. The Northern District refused to subsequently reinstate Respondent upon the expiration of his three-year suspension. . . .

After a hearing, the PRT [Professional Responsibility Tribunal] found there was clear and convincing evidence that Respondent violated the ORPC [Oklahoma Rules of Professional Conduct], Rule 3.2 by making frivolous claims and contentions, Rule 8.2 by making false or reckless statements concerning the qualifications or integrity of a judge, Rule 8.4(d) by conduct prejudicial to the administration of justice, and Rule 1.1 by incompetent representation of clients. The PRT also found that Respondent violated the RGDP Rule 1.3 by conduct that discredits the legal profession. . . .

Upon these findings, the PRT recommended Respondent be disbarred for "his continued filing of frivolous and vexatious motions and pleadings after being directed by two levels of federal courts not to do so," for his refusal to acknowledge the unprofessional nature of his conduct, and for being suspended and denied reinstatement by the Northern District and disbarred by the Tenth Circuit. . . .

In considering the PRT's recommendations, we review the entire record de novo[.] . . .

III. Complaint I, Count I, Graham Litigation

In 1987, Respondent entered his appearance for the plaintiff, Graham, in her suit alleging wrongful termination, discrimination and harassment against American Airlines (Graham 1). The case was tried in the Northern District over a period of days. After the trial, in August of 1989, the court entered judgment for the defendant, American Airlines. After judgment in Graham 1, Respondent filed two cases in the state district court in Tulsa County regarding the same claim (Graham 2 and Graham 3). . . . American Airlines removed both cases to the [federal courts.] . . .

During the course of the Graham litigation, Respondent filed a myriad of post-trial motions. . . . In addition, he commenced two appeals to the Tenth Circuit both of which he later sought to dismiss. He also sought two writs of mandamus in the Tenth Circuit. Ultimately the Tenth Circuit sanctioned Respondent indicating that "[t]he record in this case is replete with multiple and vexatious filings by Plaintiff . . . so numerous and multiplicative we . . . have determined that sanctions are appropriate in this case."

. . . Regardless of his convictions to Graham's cause, Respondent was required to heed the law regarding the method of attacking judgments and the mandates of the Oklahoma Rules of Professional Conduct. Respondent failed in this regard. We find that the evidence establishes, by a clear and convincing standard, that Respondent's actions, as alleged in Count I, Complaint I, were prejudicial to the administration of justice . . . .

(continued)

(continued)

[The court goes on to the *Mullen* and *Burggraf* cases, which involved conduct strikingly similar to the *Graham* case. Other misconduct is discussed and the court notes throughout that Tweedy denied all wrongdoing and "either blamed the federal judicial system, his opposing parties, or a favored relationship between the two."]

An attorney must be zealous in his advocacy on behalf of his clients, but the rule is not without limits and the attorney must remain within the bounds of the law and ethical considerations. Respondent's conduct in the Graham, Mullen and Burggraf litigation exceeded these bounds.

In imposing discipline, our purpose is not to punish the involved attorney, but to inquire into his continued fitness to practice law with a view to safeguarding the public, the courts and the legal profession. . . .

. . . Respondent has consistently cooperated with the OBA throughout this proceeding. Also, Respondent has apparently practiced law throughout the pendency of this matter without any further grievances. Both these factors tend to mitigate the severity of the punishment.

The PRT has recommended that Respondent be disbarred. We reject that recommendation for two primary reasons. . . . [First . . .] A review of cases in which this Court imposed disbarment as a discipline reveals the existence of conduct of a more serious degree of culpability.

Second, we are persuaded that the discipline imposed by the Northern District and Tenth Circuit (the jurisdictions in which the misconduct occurred) has effectively served to deter Respondent from subsequent acts of professional misconduct. Respondent has apparently practiced law in the intervening seven years without any reported grievances. In view of this recent record, we are convinced that we can fulfill our purpose to protect the public and the courts generally by crafting a discipline short of disbarment.

For the reasons stated herein, Respondent is suspended from the practice of law for a period of six (6) months from the effective day date of the filing of this pronouncement opinion. Respondent is ordered to pay costs in the amount of $1,340.25 relating to the investigation and disciplinary proceedings against him not later than ninety (90) days after this opinion becomes final.

Case Questions

1. What seems to be the line between *zealous* representation of a client and over-zealous representation?
2. Why did the court hand out a less severe penalty than what had been recommended?

Note: The case citation, 2000 OK 37, differs from other citations in this book because Oklahoma has adopted the universal citation format designed by the Association of Legal Writing Directors (ALWD). This format is called the "public domain citation form" by the *Bluebook,* the longtime standard for citation, officially titled, *A Uniform System of Citation.* It remains to be seen how many other states may adopt this system as the official state citation system.

per se, but any linkage of mediation services and the practice of law raises ethical problems. For example, an attorney might mediate a divorce between husband and wife and then represent one of them in the divorce or refer them to the attorney's firm for representation. Such action would invoke ethical problems of conflict of interest and confidentiality constituting a serious breach of ethics. Thus, an attorney may engage in activities other than the practice of law, but such activities must be consistent with the attorney's professional responsibilities.

The practice of law is defined differently when addressing the question of the unauthorized practice of law. In this instance, it is not so much what lawyers do as what may be done *only* by lawyers that defines the practice of law. For ethical purposes, the practice of law is best defined in the context of unauthorized practice of law, which is subject to criminal and civil sanctions by the court. In applying these sanctions, the courts have been forced to address the definition of the practice of law.

Unauthorized Practice of Law

The following discussion should be supplemented with a review of the comments already made on this subject in Chapter 1.

Each state restricts the practice of law to licensed attorneys and provides for a penalty, commonly criminal, to enforce these prohibitions. The problem lies in defining what constitutes the practice of law, which varies widely among the states. From an ethical standpoint, the restrictions on providing legal services can be justified only by an interest in protecting the public and not in preserving a professional monopoly. There are two issues in protecting the public: (1) the public should be protected against incompetence, and (2) some agency, usually a court, must have the power to protect the public. Licensing protects the public by requiring a level of competence necessary to obtain the license and by establishing authority to revoke the license for misconduct. Those without licenses can be punished for practicing law.

Lawyers are agents of their clients; they can represent clients before the court, sign certain documents on behalf of their clients, and act as direct contacts in matters in which they represent their clients. Because of this agency relationship, the lawyer is held to ethical standards in representing clients and can be disciplined for misconduct, even sued by the client for breach of the limits of the relationship. Abuse of the representation can have serious consequences to the client and so justifies this control over attorney misconduct. Unlicensed persons providing legal services are much less subject to the scrutiny of the court and the profession.

The practice of law is much less narrow than the practice of other professions, such as medicine and dentistry. For example, lawyers give advice on the conduct of personal and business affairs, but so do many others, such as accountants, real estate brokers, stock brokers, insurance agents, bankers, etc. These persons commonly give advice concerning the legal consequences of their clients' personal and business decisions. In fact, advice that could be considered legal is furnished by just about everyone. Anyone arrested for speeding, anyone buying land, or anyone getting a divorce can find many people offering advice on the legal aspects of each of these. When are such people practicing law?

The answer to this question is by no means easy, as a review of court cases on unauthorized practice of law attests. It is not sufficient to define the practice of law, as some early cases did, as what lawyers traditionally do. Lawyers do a great many things that do not require legal expertise. For the purposes of unauthorized practice of law, the issue has come down to identifying what it is that only lawyers may do. Although the states vary considerably on the specific activities restricted to lawyers, three activities are universally identified:

1. Legal representation before a court
2. Preparation of legal documents
3. Giving legal advice

Note that the first two categories relate to the attorney-client agency relationship under control of the court, whereas the third category is concerned with legal competence.

For instance, Louisiana regulates the practice of law with the following statutes:

> It is a crime for a non-lawyer to practice law, hold himself out as an attorney, or advertise that he alone or jointly has an office for the practice of law.

La. Rev. Stat. Ann. § 37:213.

> The practice of law is defined as appearing as an advocate, drawing papers, pleadings or documents, performing any act in connection with pending or prospective court proceedings or, if done for consideration, the advising on the "secular" law and doing any act on behalf of another tending to obtain or secure the prevention or redress of a wrong or the enforcement or establishment of a right.

La. Rev. Stat. Ann. § 37:212.

Legal Representation before a Court

Because of the technical requirement of procedural law, as well as the intricacies of specific kinds of lawsuits, a litigant without a lawyer is severely disadvantaged, especially if the opposing party has legal representation. In our legal system, it is not required that a person have an attorney to bring or defend a suit, but a person may not be represented by someone other than a licensed attorney. The court relies on the competence and accountability of attorneys.

A successful outcome to a trial generally requires legal skills, experience, and knowledge of a high order; the adversarial system does not work fairly when one of the parties lacks legal representation. However, many nontrial court appearances involve routine matters that do not involve legal argument or expertise and could easily be managed by legal staff acting on behalf of an attorney at a great savings to clients without risk.

The appearance of the attorney in court is certainly necessary when a legal argument may ensue or rights and duties of clients are decided, otherwise the court need only be reassured that an attorney is ultimately responsible for the action taken. The legal system and the practice of law would be more efficient and less costly if paralegals were authorized to perform a number of routine tasks. Nevertheless, no nonlawyer should ever appear in court to represent a client unless absolutely certain that this is permissible.

Many administrative agencies, like the Social Security Administration, permit representation by any person of the claimant's choosing. Before undertaking such representation, a nonlawyer should ascertain the extent and scope of such representation under the agency's rules and regulations and make certain the person represented consents (in writing) to such representation with full knowledge that the representative is not a member of the bar.

Although the *Alexander* case is more than thirty years old, the court struggles with a continuing problem: What is, and what is not, the practice of law? The law student clerk charged with unauthorized practice of law might today be described as a paralegal. The trial court took a broad view of the practice of law, a protectionist attitude toward the bar, and was perhaps affronted by the appearance of a nonlawyer in the courtroom. The appellate court, however, showed a progressive attitude toward the allocation of legal services benefiting the bench, the bar, and the public.

Note that the individual in question was not prosecuted for anauthorized practice of law but was disciplined by the court for contempt of court, a sanction available to a judge for punishing misconduct in court.

PEOPLE of the State of Illinois, Plaintiff-Appellee
v.
Walton ALEXANDER, Defendant-Appellant
Appellate Court of Illinois, First District, Fourth Division
53 Ill. App. 2d 299, 202 N.E.2d 841 (1964)

This is an appeal from a judgment order adjudging defendant guilty of contempt of court for the unauthorized practice of law. The Supreme Court transferred this case to our court and it is to be considered here as a direct contempt.

Defendant is a clerk employed by a firm of attorneys and is not licensed as a lawyer, although he is studying to be an attorney. On October 19, 1962, defendant was present in court when the case of *Ryan v. Monson* was called. Thereafter, he prepared an order spreading of record the fact that after a trial of the case of *Ryan v. Monson* the jury had disagreed and continuing the case until October 22. The trial judge added to that order "a mistrial declared."

Before entering the contempt order, the court issued a rule to **show cause** and a hearing was held at which only defendant testified. He was examined by his attorney, cross-examined and also interrogated by the judge. . . .

In his testimony defendant stated that after the case was called on October 19, he and plaintiff's attorney in the *Ryan v. Monson* case stepped up; that the judge inquired whether they knew of the disagreement by the jury; that the court requested that an order be prepared spreading the mistrial of record; that both defendant and plaintiff's lawyer sat down at a counsel's table and defendant wrote the order which they then presented to the judge in **chambers**.

An order of court reciting the verdict of a jury or setting out its failure to agree on a verdict is the responsibility of the court and the court clerk is usually ordered by the court to enter an order showing the result of a jury's deliberations. This is reflected in *Freeport Motor Casualty Co. v. Tharp*, 406 Ill. 295, at 299, 94 N.E.2d 139, at 141. . . .

(continued)

(continued)

The preparation of an order, in the instant case, with the collaboration of opposing counsel was a ministerial act for the benefit of the court and a mere recordation of what had transpired. We cannot hold that this conduct of defendant constituted the unauthorized practice of law.

The opinion of the trial court also states as a basis for contempt that on October 22 the judge inquired of defendant whether the case of *Ryan v. Monson* was settled and that defendant answered in the negative. It appears that on that date the court held the case for trial. Defendant testified that he advised the court that the trial attorney was actually engaged in a trial in the Federal Court. The court held that the appearance of defendant constituted the unauthorized practice of law.

Plaintiff contends that any appearance by a non-lawyer before a court for the purpose of apprising the court of an engagement of counsel or transmitting to the court information supplied by the attorney in the case regarding the availability of counsel or the status of the case is the unauthorized practice of law.

In the case of *People ex rel. Illinois State Bar Ass'n v. People's Stock Yards State Bank,* 344 Ill. 462, at page 476, 176 N.E. 901, at page 907, wherein a bank was prosecuted for the unauthorized practice of law, the following quotation is relied upon:

> "According to the generally understood definition of the practice of law in this country, it embraces the preparation of pleadings, and other papers incident to actions and special proceedings, and the management of such actions and proceedings on behalf of clients before judges and courts * * *."

Since this statement relates to the appearance and management of proceedings in court on behalf of a client, we do not believe it can be applied to a situation where a clerk hired by a law firm presents information to the court on behalf of his employer.

We agree with the trial judge that clerks should not be permitted to make **motions** or participate in other proceedings which can be considered as "managing" the litigation. However, if apprising the court of an employer's engagement or inability to be present constitutes the making of a motion, we must hold that clerks may make such motions for continuances without being guilty of the unauthorized practice of law. Certainly with the large volume of cases appearing on the trial calls these days, it is imperative that this practice be followed.

Case Questions

1. The court distinguishes between appearance in court "in behalf of a client" and appearance "in behalf of the attorney-employer." Is this a relevant distinction?
2. Is there an implied distinction between "management of proceedings" and routine clerical activities? What is meant by "ministerial act"?

Case Glossary

show cause   A court may issue a rule to show cause when it wants a hearing on the question why it should not take certain action. A party shows cause by providing a compelling reason to prevent the action.

chambers   The private office of a judge where matters not required to be heard in open court can be discussed and appropriate orders issued.

motion   Generally, a formal request by a party for a ruling by the court in favor of that party. There are many types of motions; dismissal motions are discussed in Chapter 7.

Preparation of Legal Documents

This category refers to "preparation of legal instruments and contracts by which legal rights are secured." A major function of paralegals is the preparation of such documents; real estate agents ordinarily prepare contracts for sale that allocate legal rights and duties in great detail; and accountants prepare tax forms. So the word "preparation" may be a poor choice, as it is not the preparation per se that is at issue but the final product at the time it takes legal effect. The person who takes ultimate responsibility for the document must be licensed to practice law.

In many instances, paralegals prepare documents that are signed by attorneys. There is no ethical problem with this as long as the supervising attorney reads and approves the document prior to signing. Many documents require little skill in draftsmanship, sometimes only requiring that names, dates, and the like be inserted into a standard form. Nevertheless, the attorney is responsible for the legal sufficiency of documents prepared for clients. There is a danger that an attorney with a large workload assisted by a seasoned, competent paralegal may place too much reliance on the paralegal and begin signing documents without reading them, even when the documents are not standard forms. The concern here is not the competence of the paralegal but a proper allocation of responsibility.

In reality, a paralegal may be more knowledgeable about a particular legal matter than an attorney, but in theory the paralegal is a trained technician while the attorney is a legal analyst. This is an excellent combination of skills to serve clients; paralegal and attorney working as a team provide legal services of high quality. If the attorney, however, relies on the paralegal entirely, the equation fails; the client has not received the services contracted.

Giving Legal Advice

Paralegals must be careful not only to refrain from giving legal advice but also to avoid even giving that impression. It is important that each client clearly understand that the paralegal is not a lawyer and is not licensed to practice law. Clients will often seek advice from paralegals, especially when the attorney is temporarily unavailable. Paralegals possess a competence and knowledge of the law that tends to encourage clients and friends to ask for legal advice.

Defining *legal advice* is not an easy task because there is a fine line between providing information and giving advice. For example, it is neither unethical nor an unauthorized practice of law to sell standard legal forms (office supply stores regularly sell legal forms). Nor is furnishing typing services improper. A logical conclusion might be that assisting a person in typing in the blanks on a standard legal form is not improper or illegal. In the course of filling out a form, however, a client may ask a question concerning the legal consequences of an item in the form.

As a practical matter, the paralegal should be alert to making statements to a client. Statements that may induce the client to do or refrain from doing something that may have legal consequences may be construed as legal advice. There is a big difference between saying "Don't do that" and "You ought to talk to an attorney before doing that." When pressed for advice, the paralegal must always refer the questions to the attorney. Although often a conduit or messenger between attorney and client, the paralegal must exercise care in conveying information or advice. Even when instructions are unambiguous, such as "Tell the client to go ahead and sign the contract," a paralegal should ascertain the exact instructions to be conveyed and indicate to the client that the instructions are those of the attorney. Of course, it is far better for the attorney to communicate directly with the client.

Ironically, a paralegal is more constrained in giving legal advice than is the man-in-the-street. The justification for this is that the paralegal is knowledgeable in the law, so paralegal advice is likely to be construed as correct and thus be acted upon. Presumably, individuals understand that legal advice from the man-in-the-street has no authority behind it. Paralegals must be aware of their special vulnerability in this regard. In coming years the boundaries of paralegal responsibilities will undoubtedly undergo significant clarification. It should be noted that at present the states differ significantly in where they draw these boundaries.

Confidentiality

Perhaps the most important topic in legal ethics is confidentiality. In the course of legal consultation, a client typically reveals information that is personal, private, and often secret. Legal services are predicated on the assurance that none of these private facts will be disclosed to third parties beyond the attorney and the attorney's staff. To deal effectively with client affairs, the attorney must be fully informed about all matters relating to the client's need for legal service and advice. For this reason, statements made in confidence to an attorney by a client are privileged and may be disclosed only with the consent of the client or when special circumstances provide clear exceptions to the rule.

The privilege extends to law firm employees who necessarily have access to confidential material in order to provide legal services, including especially legal secretaries, clerks, and paralegals. Although paralegals are not subject to disciplinary actions for improper disclosures, a supervising attorney can be held responsible both by attorney disciplinary rules and by a possible suit by the client.

The paralegal must be scrupulous in protecting clients' confidences. It is a great temptation for attorneys and paralegals alike to relate the facts of an interesting case to friends and associates outside the law firm, but any disclosure incurs the risk that the listener may identify a client and thereby learn facts that are privileged. If third parties not covered by the privilege learn confidential communications, the disclosures may lose their confidential status. Extreme caution must be exercised in discussing specific matters involving specific clients. Attorneys and law firms routinely warn staff about confidentiality, but paralegals must also constantly remind themselves of their responsibilities toward the clients.

Confidentiality can lead to bizarre predicaments, as illustrated by the following real-life situation. A woman was working as an intake paralegal for a Legal Aid office that provided legal services in civil cases for indigents. As such, she interviewed prospective clients for the office. A woman seeking divorce came to the office and was accepted as a client. The attorney in charge of the case was encountering difficulties finding the woman's husband to serve notice of the pending divorce action. It so happened that the husband later came to the office for legal representation. In the course of collecting intake information, the paralegal recognized that the man was the husband of a client of the office. Although the office could not represent both husband and wife, it was now in possession of the husband's address and telephone number—but that information was now considered privileged information because the husband had furnished it in confidence in attempting to establish a lawyer-client relationship.

Although the attorney for the wife was informed that the husband had furnished this information, she and the paralegal concluded that it might be improper to give it to the wife's attorney, so the husband's file was locked away where the attorney did not have access to it. (Fortunately, the husband's whereabouts were discovered through another source.) The lesson, however, is that the paralegal and the attorney were appropriately sensitive to the confidentiality question.

A client's actions may render disclosures nonconfidential. Statements made before third parties who are not covered by confidentiality are disclosable (see *People v. Mitchell*). If, for instance, the client brings a friend along to a meeting with the attorney and the friend has no relation to the case, statements made are not confidential. Attorneys and paralegals are careful to exclude third parties from discussions, especially when confidential statements are expected. The problem with nonconfidential statements is that their content is subject to discovery by the opposing side, and in criminal cases, the third parties may be required to disclose the statements on the witness stand.

Whether or not the confidential attorney-client relationship applies depends on the circumstances. Even though an attorney may have represented a client in the past, statements made with regard to an unrelated current problem may not be confidential if the client has not expressed an intention to retain the attorney in the current matter.

In contrast, the attorney-client relationship may be understood to be ongoing. A client who employs an attorney on all business matters may

general retainer The
first payment made in
hiring an attorney. A
general retainer occurs
when a client furnishes a
sum of money to an
attorney to ensure that
the attorney will
represent the client in
whatever legal matters
may arise.

implicitly intend all business statements to be confidential. A client may also
pay an attorney a **general retainer** with the understanding that the attorney
and client have a continuing relationship. Once confidentiality is established,
the confidentiality does not end with the termination of client representation,
though it may not extend to subsequent nonconfidential information.

The duty to preserve the confidentiality of a client differs somewhat from
the lawyer/client privilege. This is an evidentiary rule designed to protect a
client by preventing the disclosure of confidential communications. The
Restatement of Law (Third) Law, Governing Lawyers, provides four elements
necessary for invoking the lawyer/client privilege: (1) a communication (2)
made between privileged persons (3) in confidence (4) for the purpose of
obtaining or providing legal assistance for the client.

The rationale for the privilege is based on the need for the client to make
disclosures to the attorney so that the attorney may effectively represent the
client's interests. Presumably, the attorney is far better at assessing the relevance
of facts and developing a legal theory to aid the client than the client could
without an attorney. A frank discussion between attorney and client is protected
by the privilege. Perhaps many clients would be unwilling to disclose pertinent
facts if unprotected by the privilege.

The effect of the privilege is to foreclose the attorney from disclosing the
confidential communications in legal proceedings. The attorney may not be
required to disclose these communications; and the privilege is absolute in that
the relevance of the communications to a legal proceeding or to the truth has
no bearing. Only the specific exceptions made by the law can intrude on this
privilege that belongs to the client.

**The PEOPLE of the State of New York,
Respondent
v.
John C. MITCHELL, Appellant
Court of Appeals of New York
58 N.Y.2d 368, 448 N.E.2d 121 (1983)**

Defendant was a resident of Waterloo, New
York, and, at the time these events occurred,
he was under **indictment** for causing the stab-
bing death of his girlfriend, Audrey Miller, in
February, 1976. He was represented on that
charge by Rochester attorney Felix Lapine. In
January, 1977, defendant went to Rochester to
take care of some personal matters and registered at the Cadillac Hotel. On the evening of

January 5 while sitting at the hotel bar, he met
O'Hare McMillon. They had two or three high-
balls and then were seen to leave the bar
about 11:00 p.m. and take the elevator to the
floor on which Mitchell's room was located.
No one saw either of them leave defendant's
room that night or the next morning, but in
the afternoon of January 6, on a tip from
attorney Lapine, the police went to defendant's hotel room and found the partially clad
dead body of O'Hare McMillon on the bed. She
had been stabbed 11–12 times in the face,
chest and back. At least four of the wounds
were sufficient to cause her death by
exsanguination.

After leaving the hotel room that morning,
defendant went to attorney Lapine's office.

Lapine was not in but defendant met and spoke to a legal secretary, Molly Altman, in the reception area. She testified that he seemed nervous and as if he was looking for someone. Apparently he could not find whomever it was he was looking for so he left only to return a minute later and start telling her about what happened the night before. She testified that he said: "he wanted to go out and have a last fling * * * he had been out drinking and met a girl and then he woke up in the morning and she was dead. He had stayed there all night and then he walked out again."

While he was talking to Ms. Altman, Judith Peacock, another legal secretary, entered the reception area. She testified that defendant was kind of rambling on but he said that: "he had laid next to someone all night and they didn't move, and he [was] in a bar and * * * in a hotel * * * this person who he had laid next to was black and he was worried because when the black people find out about it, they protect their own and he would be in danger." She also testified that he muttered something about a knife.

Ms. Pope-Johnson entered the room. She asked defendant what was wrong and he told her: "that there was a dead body and he felt that he had done it and that the person was dead, that she was dead because of being stabbed."

Shortly thereafter, Lapine entered the office and talked privately with defendant. After defendant left Lapine called the police and had them check defendant's hotel room. The body was discovered, defendant's identification learned from the hotel registration and defendant found and arrested at a bar near the courthouse.

* * *

On this state of the record, we conclude that defendant has not met his burden of establishing that when he spoke to these unknown women in a common reception area, his statements were intended to be confidential and made to an employee of his attorney for the purpose of obtaining legal advice. The only evidence identifying the women came from Lapine who responded to a question whether he had "any female employees" by saying "Yes, Robin Pope-Johnson." She, it turns out, was the last woman in the office to hear defendant's inculpatory statements and even if statements made to her at the time could have been privileged, the privilege was lost because of the prior **publication** to nonemployees and the utterance of the statements to Pope-Johnson in front of the nonemployees [Cc.] Taking this view we need not consider whether the statements could be privileged because of an ongoing retainer between defendant and Lapine or if they could be privileged if made to the attorney's employee before a formal retainer was agreed upon.

Case Questions

1. What circumstances argued most strongly for defeating the attorney-client privilege?
2. What argument can be made in Mitchell's behalf?

Case Glossary

indictment   A written accusation by a *grand jury* charging the accused with a crime. Also called a "true bill." When the grand jury does not indict, it is called a "no bill."

publication   Making a statement publicly, orally, or in writing, i.e., to a third person.

Exceptions to Confidentiality

Rule 1.6 Confidentiality of information.*

(a) A lawyer shall not reveal information relating to representation of a client except as stated in paragraphs (b), (c), and (d) unless the client consents after disclosure to the client.

(b) A lawyer shall reveal such information to the extent the lawyer believes necessary:

(1) To prevent a client from committing a crime; or

(2) To prevent a death or substantial bodily harm to another.

(c) A lawyer may reveal such information to the extent the lawyer believes necessary:

(1) To serve the client's interest unless it is information the client specifically requires not to be disclosed;

(2) To establish a claim or defense on behalf of the lawyer in a controversy between the lawyer and client;

(3) To establish a defense to a criminal charge or civil claim against the lawyer based upon conduct in which the client was involved;

(4) To respond to allegations in any proceeding concerning the lawyer's representation of the client; or

(5) To comply with the *Rules of Professional Conduct*.

(d) When required by a tribunal to reveal such information, a lawyer may first exhaust all appellate remedies.

The exceptions to confidentiality privilege are primarily aimed at protecting the public [(b)(1) and (b)(2)] and protecting the attorney in a conflict with the client [(c)]. Although confidential statements about past crimes and misconduct are privileged, a client's intention to commit a crime in the future is not. An attorney has an ethical duty to attempt to dissuade a client from committing a crime and a duty to inform appropriate authorities if unable to dissuade the client. The most difficult case arises when a client plans to commit perjury at trial and, despite the attorney's admonitions, proceeds to lie on the witness stand. Attempted withdrawal by the attorney at that stage of the process will ordinarily be refused by the court, but the attorney also is not free to disclose the confidences that would reveal the perjury.

Conflicts of Interest

A common conflict-of-interest problem arises when an attorney leaves one firm for another and the second firm represents a party suing or being sued by a

---

*Source: ABA Model Rule of Professional Conduct.

client of the former firm. The risk of disclosure of attorney-client confidences by the attorney to the new employers raises serious ethical concerns. Extreme cases are not difficult to decide. If the attorney worked on the client's case at his first employment, it would be clearly unethical to work for the opposing party. However, if an attorney moves from one large law firm to another and had no exposure to the case at either firm, the risk of disclosure is minimal. The risk can be further minimized by erecting a "Chinese wall" between the attorney and those dealing with the case, that is, preventing access to the case file and warning all concerned not to discuss the case with the firm-switching attorney. If no exception is made, an attorney working for a large firm becomes a "typhoid Mary," virtually unemployable at other large firms for fear the firm may have or may take on a client who may be involved in a dispute against a client of the other firm.

Because paralegals regularly deal with confidential material, an identical problem arises; the entire firm may be disqualified from representing a client if the court concludes that the risk of improper disclosure cannot be purged. In fact, some paralegals will have contact with a greater number of files than any single attorney.

This particular form of conflict of interest poses a practical as well as an ethical problem, because the firm representing a client can request that the court disqualify an opposing firm's representation. This action has resulted in numerous reported decisions of the courts that not only clarify the ethical principles but also give them the force of law. In *Silver Chrysler Plymouth, Inc. v. Chrysler Motors Corp.*, 518 F.2d 751 (2d Cir. 1975), the court articulated the "substantially related" test subsequently adopted by the courts of many jurisdictions. *Silver Chrysler* distinguished between the activities of a lawyer or law clerk at a former law firm that were substantially related to representation in a current case at a second law firm employing the attorney. The court thereby attempted to distinguish situations in which a distinct risk of confidential disclosures exists from those in which the risk is insignificant.

The ABA *Model Rules* adopted the "substantially related" test in 1980:

> **Rule 1.9** A lawyer who has formerly represented a client in a matter shall not thereafter:
>
> (a) represent another person in the same or a substantially related matter to which that person's interests are materially adverse to the interests of the former client unless the former client consents after consultation; or
> (b) use information relating to the representation to the disadvantage of the former client except as Rule 1.6 would permit with respect to a client or when the information has become generally known.

The Canons of Ethics, formerly the primary standard in all states, expressed general ethical principles. These gave rise to philosophical discussions in some cases, like the *Horan* case. The conflict of interest appears obvious, yet the attorney involved probably acted decently and in good faith in the matter. The court, however, held him to a higher standard.

STATE v. HORAN
Supreme Court of Wisconsin
21 Wis. 2d 66, 123 N.W.2d 488 (1963)

Mr. Horan, a bachelor 46 years old, has practiced law in Friendship, Wisconsin, for over 20 years. He enjoys a good reputation in his community and was a close friend and advisor of Wellington B. Barnes, a widower, who died on October 11, 1959, at the age of 87 leaving an estate of approximately $265,000. Upon Barnes' death the only **heir** at law was Myrtle Marks, a first cousin of the half-blood. He also left a relative Elizabeth Hover, a first cousin once removed. After Mrs. Barnes' death and between April 28, 1955, and November 29, 1958, Horan drew six wills for Barnes and a **codicil** on February 14, 1959. The general scheme of the wills provided specific **bequests** and a proportion of the residuary estate to various friends and to Myrtle Marks, Elizabeth Hover and Horan. The first will contained a bequest to Mr. Horan of $12,633 and a proportional share of the residuary estate. In each succeeding will, as other beneficiaries were eliminated or their share cut down, the specific bequest or the share of the residuary estate to Horan was increased . . . . No claim is made the testator was incompetent or the defendant used **undue influence** in procuring the financial benefit to himself under the will.

[The will was entered into probate after an agreement among the various parties which left Horan with a share worth $38,817.22.]

Posed for consideration is the specific question of whether Mr. Horan's conduct subjects him to any disciplinary action and a broader question of whether an attorney under any circumstances may draft and supervise the execution of a will for his client wherein he is named a substantial beneficiary without violating the rules of professional conduct. No claim is made [that] Horan exercised any undue influence in drafting the wills in which he became a substantial beneficiary. If he did, his conduct would involve moral turpitude and would demand that this court impose more severe discipline than it does in this case. . . . The practice of the law is not a business but a profession—a form of public trust, the performance of which is entrusted only to those who can qualify by fitness, not the least of which is good moral character. While within his power, an attorney has no right to jeopardize the performance of his duties or the confidence, approval and esteem of the public which the legal profession has traditionally enjoyed. An attorney has a duty not to harm but to maintain the integrity of the legal profession even though this may call for a personal sacrifice of the omission of acts which are not intrinsically bad. "The profession of the law, in its nature the noblest and most beneficial to mankind, is in its abuse and abasement the most sordid and pernicious." [Lord Bolingbroke]. . . .

Many lawyers in their practice have been confronted with the situation of drawing a will for a friend or a relative who wishes to make a bequest to him or to a member of his family. Perhaps sufficient consideration of the problem involved has not been given by lawyers or by the bar. The recurrence of the problem in the practice does not dull its serious dangers. The conflict of interests, the incompetency of an attorney-beneficiary to testify because of a transaction with the deceased, the possible jeopardy of the will if its admission to probate is contested, the possible harm done to other beneficiaries and the undermining of the public trust and confidence in the integrity of the legal profession, are only some of the dangers which a lawyer must consider.

The Canons of Professional Ethics, which may be considered as broad but not all-inclusive standards, do not expressly mention the drafting of wills. Canon 6 makes it unprofessional conduct "to represent conflicting interests, except by the express consent of all concerned given after a full disclosure of the facts." Canon 11 requires "The lawyer should refrain from any action whereby for his personal benefit or gain he abuses or takes advantage of the confidence reposed in him by his client." [The Court then discusses meager authorities suggesting that an attorney in this situation advise the client to seek advice of other counsel or have another attorney draw up a codicil to include the attorney's bequest.] . . .

[O]rdinary prudence requires that such a will be drawn by some other lawyer of the testator's own choosing so that any suspicion of undue influence is thereby avoided. . . .

An attorney's duty of fidelity to his client involves more than refraining from exercising undue influence. A client has a right to full and disinterested advice. The "right to make a will is a sacred and a constitutional right and that right includes a right of equal dignity to have it carried out." When Mr. Horan was drafting the wills for Barnes he failed to recognize the conflict of interests which existed between him as an attorney for his client and his position as a beneficiary of a substantial sum of money. It was his duty to fully advise his client that the will was vulnerable to attack because of the inference of undue influence which arose and his incapacity to give testimony to support it. Nor should he have placed himself in a position of drafting the will where his self-interest might have prevented his giving disinterested advice . . . . Because the law on this subject has not been clearly defined or well understood by the members of the legal profession and no undue influence is involved, we deem a reprimand and the payment of costs to be sufficient.

Case Questions

1. Why might Myrtle Marks, the heir, be interested in contesting the will or the attorney's share in the will?
2. How could Horan have handled this matter in such a way as to ethically participate in the distribution of his client's estate?

Case Glossary

heirs The persons who take the property of a deceased when no valid will is present. Heirs are determined by intestate succession according to state law. A living person does not have heirs.

codicil A supplement to a will that modifies or adds to the will without revoking it.

bequest A gift in a will. Traditionally this referred to personal property but it is today often used for testamentary gifts of real property (real estate) as well.

undue influence Excessive pressure placed on a person by another person, usually in a position of influence, such that the will of the other overcomes the will of the first person. Used primarily to challenge the voluntariness of a person making a contract.

Common sense would tell us that an attorney cannot represent both sides in an adversarial proceeding. Law firms are often put in the difficult position of representing clients who inadvertently become legal adversaries. Disclosure of the conflict and even waiver of objection by the parties may not be sufficient. Attorneys owe undivided loyalty to their clients. A fairly common exception to the rule is the uncontested divorce. In general, parties to an uncontested dispute may be represented by a single lawyer or a single law firm, provided disclosure and consent by the parties is evident. It may be that businesses that are in an amicable ongoing relationship may dispute the terms of a contract but not wish to undermine their relationship. Still there are dangers and these occur with some frequency in divorce. What begins as an amicable divorce often ends as battle royale. The *Ishmael* case shows that an attorney may ultimately be responsible for the tricks played by the client. Roberta Ishmael trusted her husband mistakenly, but the attorney who represented her and her husband should have been looking out for both of them. It should be noted as well that no attorney likes being sued by a client.

Roberta M. ISHMAEL
v.
Robert MILLINGTON
District Court of Appeal, Third District, California
241 Cal.App.2d 520, 50 Cal.Rptr.592 (1966)

This is a legal malpractice action in which the plaintiff-client appeals from a summary judgment granted the defendant-attorney. The factual narrative will possess heightened significance against a backdrop of general doctrine:

Quite without reference to the four basic elements of the traditional negligence analysis, a 1931 California appellate decision announced the following statement of essentials in the pleading and proof of legal malpractice: " 'First, that there existed the relationship of attorney and client; second, that in connection with such relationship advice was given; third, that he [the client] relied upon such advice and as a result thereof did things that he would not otherwise have done; fourth, that as a direct and proximate result of such advice and the doing of such acts, he suffered loss and was damaged thereby.' " (*McGregor v. Wright,* 117 Cal.App. 186, 193.)

In this case the defense is that the client sought no advice from the attorney and was given none; by the client's express admission, she did not rely on the attorney, thus, that her alleged damage was not proximately caused by the attorney's cause of action.

Roberta Ishmael, the plaintiff, was formerly married to Earl F. Anders. The couple had three children. They lived in Gridley, where Mr. Anders was a partner in a family trucking business. Domestic difficulties resulted in a separation, and Mrs. Anders moved to Sacramento where she secured employment. She and her husband agreed upon a divorce and property settlement. She knew that she was entitled to one-half the marital property.

Mr. Anders called upon defendant Robert Millington, a Gridley attorney who had for some time represented him and his trucking firm. . . . For one reason or another there was a decision that the wife rather than the husband would apply for divorce. At Anders' request Mr. Millington agreed to act as the wife's attorney, to prepare the necessary papers and to file a divorce action for her. He drew up a complaint and a property settlement agreement and handed these documents to Mr. Anders, who took them to Sacramento and had his wife sign them. She knew that Mr. Millington had represented her husband in the past. Faulty recall prevents ascertainment whether Mrs. Anders ever met personally with the attorney before the papers were drawn. She did not discuss the property settlement agreement with the attorney before she signed it. Mr. Millington believed the divorce and property settlement arrangements were "cut and dried" between the husband and wife; he "assumed that she knew what she was doing"; he believed that she was actually getting half the property but made no effort to confirm that belief.

In her deposition the former Mrs. Anders testified that in signing the complaint and property settlement agreement she relied solely on her husband and did not rely on the attorney. Later, when so instructed, she traveled to the courthouse at Oroville, where she and her corroborating witness met Mr. Millington. He escorted her through a routine ex parte hearing which resulted in an interlocutory divorce decree and judicial approval of the property settlement.

According to her complaint, the former Mrs. Anders discovered that in return for a settlement of $8,807 she had surrendered her right to community assets totaling $82,500. Ascribing her loss to the attorney's negligent failure to make inquiries as to the true worth of the community property, she seeks damages equivalent to the difference between what she received and one-half the asserted value of the community.

By the very act of undertaking to represent Mrs. Anders in an uncontested divorce suit,

Mr. Millington assumed a duty of care toward her, whatever its degree.

A lawyer owes undivided loyalty to his client. Minimum standards of professional ethics usually permit him to represent dual interests where full consent and full disclosure occur. The loyalty he owes one client cannot consume that owed to the other.

> The Rules of Professional Conduct of the State Bar, approved by the Supreme Court provide:
>
>> "Rule 6. A member of the State Bar shall not accept professional employment without first disclosing his relation, if any, with the adverse party, and his interest, if any, in the subject matter of the employment."
>>
>> "Rule 7. A member of the State Bar shall not represent conflicting interests, except with the consent of all parties concerned."

Divorces are frequently uncontested; the parties may make their financial arrangements peaceably and honestly; vestigial chivalry may impel them to display the wife as the injured plaintiff; the husband may then seek out and pay an attorney to escort the wife through the formalities of adjudication. We describe these facts of life without necessarily approving them. Even in that situation the attorney's professional obligations do not permit his descent to the level of a scrivener. The edge of danger gleams if the attorney has previously represented the husband. A husband and wife at the brink of division of their marital assets have an obvious divergence of interests. Representing the wife in an arm's length divorce, an attorney of ordinary professional skill would demand some verification of the husband's financial statement; or, at the minimum, inform the wife that the husband's statement was unconfirmed, that wives may be cheated, that prudence called for investigation and verification. Deprived of such disclosure, the wife cannot make a free and intelligent choice. Representing both spouses in an uncontested divorce situation (whatever the ethical implications), the attorney's professional obligations demand no less. He may not set a shallow limit on the depth to which he will represent the wife.

Judgment reversed

Case Questions

1. Why was not the wife responsible for her own lack of care in trusting her husband?
2. What does the court mean when it states "the attorney's professional obligations do not permit his descent to the level of a scrivener"?

Solicitation

solicitation In legal ethics, using improper means to drum up business. For example, the practice of "ambulance chasing," such as approaching hospital patients to solicit business, is unethical.

For many years, the legal profession banned advertising legal services, and many disciplinary cases considered such issues as listings in the yellow pages, the sending of Christmas cards, the size of law office signs, and so on. In 1977, the U.S. Supreme Court, in *Bates v. State Bar of Arizona*, 433 U.S. 350, held that the ban on advertising violated First Amendment freedom of speech. Since that time, ethical concerns have aimed at distinguishing advertising from **solicitation.** The bar continues to attempt to thwart "ambulance chasing," the practice of hunting down injured parties and twisting their arms to hire the attorney. Although *Bates* made it clear that attorneys were free to announce their services to the public in general, the aggressive solicitation of individual clients is still condemned.

Model Rules of Professional Conduct:
Rule 7.3 Direct contact with prospective clients.
A lawyer may not solicit professional employment from a prospective client with whom the lawyer has no family or prior professional relationship, in person or otherwise, when a significant motive for the lawyer's doing so is the lawyer's pecuniary gain. The term "solicit" includes contact in person, by telephone or telegraph, by letter or other writing, or by other communication directed to a specific recipient. . . .

An attorney is also prohibited from soliciting through another person, including a paralegal. Paralegals must be careful in generating business for the attorneys for whom they work. It is very tempting, when hearing a story of a personal injury or some other promising legal case, to encourage a visit to the law office, but paralegals must be cautious in their treatment of such situations. Certainly it is unethical to loiter at the hospital handing out business cards to accident victims, but it is not necessary to keep one's employment a secret or, when asked, to recommend an attorney. Suggesting that a person seek legal help is ethical if the paralegal has not sought out clients. The paralegal should not disparage other attorneys nor encourage a person to switch from one attorney to another nor criticize an attorney's handling of a client. When learning of possible misconduct by an attorney, the paralegal should discuss the matter with an attorney associate, who has an ethical duty to address attorney misconduct.

Fees

The *Model Rules* treat fee arrangements with much more specificity than did the *Model Code*. Fees are based on contracts between the attorney and the client and should be specifically discussed by the attorney with the client. Whenever fees have not been adequately explained to a client, a potential conflict emerges. If at all possible, a contract signed by the client should clearly explain the basis on which the fees are established. When the *Model Rules* were debated, the framers wanted to require that all fee arrangements be in writing, but sole practitioners and rural lawyers argued that this would hurt their relationships with many of their clients, so the writing was not made mandatory.

A recurring issue regarding fees concerns contingency fees, whereby the attorney is paid a percentage of the award or recovery received by the client. There is a strong national movement favoring limitations on contingency fees. Personal injury cases are typically based on contingency fees, which are unethical in criminal cases and divorce proceedings. It is essential that the client understand that the percentage does not include costs other than the attorney's services. In cases using expert witnesses, the costs can be quite large; the client must be aware of this and the fact that the client must pay the costs regardless of who wins the case.

Work performed by a paralegal is commonly billed to a client. Ordinarily the paralegal's work is charged at a rate significantly less than that for an attorney, though not necessarily proportional to the compensation paid the paralegal. Clients should not be charged for attorney's work if paralegals actually did the work, nor should they be billed for more time than was actually spent. The latter is not only unethical but illegal as well. Even though paralegals may not be responsible for the billing, they should not participate, actively or passively, in a fraud on the client.

Reporting Misconduct

Model Rules of Professional Conduct:
Rule 8.3 Reporting professional misconduct.
(a) A lawyer having knowledge that another lawyer has committed a violation of the *Rules of Professional Conduct* . . . shall inform the appropriate professional authority.

Although lawyers are understandably reluctant to inform on each other, this rule is clear, and failure to report misconduct is an ethical violation. The object is not simply to punish the wrongdoer but to protect the public and the legal system. Choice of the authority to which the misconduct should be reported depends on whether the misconduct is a professional matter or matter before the court.

The duty of paralegals to report misconduct is more problematic. If the misconduct is also criminal, a legal duty to report a crime falls upon the paralegal. If the misconduct is of a professional, noncriminal nature, the duty is less clear. There is an ethical duty in an abstract sense, but not one that subjects the paralegal to discipline, as the paralegal is not a member of the bar. If misconduct results in an injury to a client, the paralegal who overlooks the misconduct may be viewed as contributing to the injury. In any event, such matters must be treated with great delicacy. Accusations of misconduct can have serious ramifications for an attorney. The paralegal is quite vulnerable as well, having a subordinate position in the legal hierarchy. In such a situation, it is to be hoped that the paralegal will know a lawyer who can give counsel. If the misconduct can be corrected, approaching the wrongdoer rather than informing may be the best policy. In any event, diplomacy and caution should be exercised.

Trust Accounts

trust account In the practice of law, a special bank account in which fees paid by clients are kept until an attorney may properly claim the funds for fees or expenses.

One of the most common reasons for attorney discipline involves the misuse of client funds. This is considered by disciplinary committees to be one of the most serious transgressions. Clients deposit funds with attorneys for a number of reasons besides paying fees. Money held for a client must never be commingled (mixed) with an attorney's personal accounts, nor should separate **trust accounts** be commingled in any way. Accurate recordkeeping is essential to properly account for monies received and disbursed.

Malpractice

Disciplinary action is not the only risk facing an attorney. When a client has been injured by the negligence of an attorney, he or she may bring a civil action for **malpractice**, seeking compensation from the attorney for the injury. Malpractice refers to professional negligence, and negligence in turn refers to a cause of action falling in the class of private suits called torts, explained in greater detail in Chapter 10. Ordinary negligence occurs when a person fails to exercise reasonable care and because of carelessness causes injury to another person or to property. Persons (usually licensed) holding themselves out as professionals are held to a professional rather than an ordinary standard of care. After all, lawyers are hired because of their presumed competence and skill in legal representation. The lawyer who fails to meet the standards of the profession should compensate those injured by this failure. Much of a lawyer's work involves judgments that may prove mistaken but are nevertheless defensible even in retrospect. It may not be difficult in such situations for an attorney to get other attorneys to testify that the judgment was within the standards of the profession. The most provable instance of attorney malpractice occurs when an attorney negligently allows a statute of limitations to run, barring further action on a client's lawsuit. There may be other consequences from such conduct as well.

malpractice Professional negligence; those who are licensed professionals are held to a higher standard of care for their services than is required in ordinary negligence.

Paula Corbin JONES
v.
William Jefferson CLINTON
36 F.Supp.2d 1118, E.D.Ark. (1999)

Memorandum Opinion and Order

SUSAN WEBBER WRIGHT, Chief Judge.

What began as a civil lawsuit against the President of the United States for alleged sexual harassment eventually resulted in an impeachment trial of the President in the United States Senate on two Articles of Impeachment for his actions during the course of this lawsuit and a related criminal investigation being conducted by the Office of the Independent Counsel ("OIC"). The civil lawsuit was settled while on appeal from this Court's decision granting summary judgment to defendants and the Senate acquitted the President of both Articles of Impeachment. Those proceedings having concluded, the Court now addresses the issue of contempt on the part of the President. . . . For the reasons that follow, the Court hereby adjudges the President to be in contempt of court for his willful failure to obey this Court's discovery Orders.

I.

Plaintiff Paula Corbin Jones filed this lawsuit seeking civil damages from William Jefferson Clinton, President of the United States, and Danny Ferguson, a former Arkansas State Police Officer, for alleged actions beginning with an incident in a hotel suite in Little Rock, Arkansas on May 8, 1991, when President Clinton was Governor of the State of Arkansas.

. . . It was at a hearing on January 12, 1998, to address issues surrounding the President's deposition and at the deposition itself that the Court first learned of Monica Lewinsky, a former White House intern and employee, and her alleged involvement in this case.

At his deposition, the President was questioned extensively about his relationship with Ms. Lewinsky. . . . [T]he President testified in response to questioning from plaintiff's counsel and his own attorney that he had no recollection of having ever been alone with Ms. Lewinsky and he denied that he had engaged in an "extramarital sexual affair," in "sexual relations," or in a "sexual relationship" with Ms. Lewinsky. Id. at 52–53, 56–59, 78, 204.

. . . On August 17, 1998, the President appeared before a grand jury in Washington, D.C., as part of OIC's criminal investigation and testified about his relationship with Ms. Lewinsky and his actions during this civil lawsuit. That evening, the President discussed the matter in a televised address to the Nation. In his address, the President stated that although his answers at his January 17th deposition were "legally accurate," he did not volunteer information and that he did indeed have a relationship with Ms. Lewinsky that was inappropriate and wrong. . . . It was during the President's televised address that the Court first learned the President may be in contempt. . . .

. . . [I]t is now time to address the issue of the President's contempt as all other proceedings that heretofore have precluded this Court from addressing the issue have concluded. Id. Accordingly, it is that issue to which the Court now turns.

II.

* * *

A.

. . . Two requirements must be met before a party may be held in civil contempt: the court must have fashioned an Order that is clear and reasonably specific, and the party must have violated that Order. . . .

1.

. . . [T]he record demonstrates by clear and convincing evidence that the President responded to plaintiff's questions by giving false, misleading and evasive answers that were designed to obstruct the judicial process. . . . Although there are a number of aspects of the President's conduct in this case that might be characterized as contemptuous, the Court addresses at this time only those matters which no reasonable person would seriously dispute were in violation of this Court's discovery Orders and which do not require a hearing, namely the President's sworn statements concerning whether he and Ms. Lewinsky had ever been alone together and whether he had ever engaged in sexual relations with Ms. Lewinsky.

[Excerpts from Clinton's deposition and his grand jury testimony included to show contradictory statements.]

b.

. . . Simply put, the President's deposition testimony regarding whether he had ever been alone with Ms. Lewinsky was intentionally false, and his statements regarding whether he had ever engaged in sexual relations with Ms. Lewinsky likewise were intentionally false, notwithstanding tortured definitions and interpretations of the term "sexual relations." . . .

. . . The Court therefore adjudges the President to be in civil contempt of court pursuant to Fed.R.Civ.P. 37(b)(2).

2.

. . . Accordingly, the Court imposes the following sanctions:

First, the President shall pay plaintiff any reasonable expenses, including attorney's fees, caused by his willful failure to obey this Court's discovery Orders. . . .

Second, the President shall reimburse this Court its expenses in traveling to Washington, D.C., at his request to preside over his tainted deposition. The Court therefore will direct that the President deposit into the registry of this Court the sum of $1,202.00, the total expenses incurred by this Court in traveling to Washington, D.C. In addition, the Court will refer this matter to the Arkansas Supreme Court's Committee on Professional Conduct for review and any disciplinary action it deems appropriate for the President's possible violation of the Model Rules of Professional Conduct. Relevant to this case, Rule 8.4 of the Model Rules provides that it is professional misconduct for a lawyer to, among other things, "engage in conduct involving dishonesty, fraud, deceit or misrepre-

(continued)

(continued)

sentation," or to "engage in conduct that is prejudicial to the administration of justice." The President's conduct as discussed previously arguably falls within the rubric of Rule 8.4 and involves matters that the Committee on Professional Conduct may deem appropriate for disciplinary action.

[The Aftermath

Following the contempt order, charges were brought against President Clinton with regard to possible disbarment from the Arkansas Bar Association. The inquiry into his affairs by the Office of Independent Counsel continued under the leadership of Robert Ray, who replaced Kenneth Starr, the longtime investigator of President Clinton's conduct, which started with questionable real estate transactions that came to be known as "Whitewater." Mr. Ray and President Clinton reached an agreement settling the issues relating to this affair. President

Clinton faced the prospect of formal criminal charges for his false testimony in the Paula Jones cases that might be brought by the OIC. He received immunity from those charges by making a a statement admitting he "testified falsely," surrendered his license to practice law in Arkansas for five years, paid a $25,000 fine, and agreed not to receive reimbursement for his legal fees from the United States Treasury.

While President Clinton's enemies thought he was treated too leniently and his friends thought the penalties harsh, the important feature of this case is that lawyers may be disciplined by the bar for acts having nothing to do with the practice of law. State bar associations take very seriously any conduct by attorneys that perpetrates a fraud on the court, obstructs justice, or interferes with the justice system. It is fair to say that the bar and the courts are reluctant to take away a professional license, *except* when an attorney fails the primary duty to preserve the integrity of the judicial system.]

Case Questions

1. What is required for establishing civil contempt?
2. Was President Clinton punished for his sexual misconduct?

Misconduct outside the Practice of Law

Attorneys are subject to disciplinary action for conduct unrelated to the practice of law. Violations of the law by attorneys, such as driving while intoxicated, may be scrutinized by the bar in addition to criminal charges. Criminal or improper conduct that reflects on an attorney's fitness to practice law may result in sanctions. An attorney may act to undermine the integrity of the legal system even when not acting in the role of an attorney, as President Clinton discovered to his dismay. He had testified falsely, albeit with a semantic deftness that seemed at first to be technically truthful. He was understandably reluctant to reveal his sexual improprieties with Monica Lewinsky, but the false testimony that he gave presented the court and the bar with a transgression that begged for inquiry. As Judge Wright concluded in *Jones v. Clinton*, the president in such matters must be treated like other citizens, like other attorneys.

Summary

The legal profession is governed by a code of professional ethics that is enforced by the courts and the profession. Each state has an ethical code for lawyers. The ABA has been the leader in developing ethical codes, adopting the *Model Code of Professional Responsibility* in 1970 and the *Model Rules of Professional Conduct* in 1983. Most states have adopted these codes nearly verbatim, so there is considerable uniformity in principle, at least.

The interpretation of the codes in the courts shows some disparities, especially in defining the unauthorized practice of law, which is of special concern to paralegals because they risk unauthorized practice of law if they engage in activities permitted only to licensed attorneys, namely:

1. Legal representation before a court

2. Preparation of legal documents

3. Giving legal advice

The unauthorized practice of law may be prosecuted under criminal statutes or by the court as contempt of court.

Confidentiality of client statements is protected by the attorney-client privilege, which extends to law office personnel. Paralegals must take great pains not to disclose confidential information on clients to persons not covered by the privilege. The attorney-client privilege belongs to the client and not the attorney. Major exceptions to the privilege occur when a client proposes to commit a crime or when the client sues the attorney.

Confidentiality gives rise to problems of conflict of interest when an attorney or a paralegal changes employment from one firm to another. If the new firm represents a party adverse to a party represented by the firm from which the new employee came, the risk that confidential information may be disclosed to the disadvantage of a former client is great. The entire firm may be disqualified. However, in this age of large law firms, lawyers and paralegals frequently have no contact with a client of the firm in which they work. As a result, the courts and the *Model Rules* have adopted the "substantially related" test: The adverse representation must be substantially related to matters with which the attorney dealt in prior employment. Law firms must additionally take pains to isolate the attorney from the case, the so-called "Chinese wall" approach.

Scenario

Part I

You are defending a man accused of murder; we will call him Sammy. He has a history of crime and violence. The incident giving rise to the murder charge involved an altercation he had with another man on the street. Both Sammy and his victim, Joey, have been involved in the drug trade. Sammy shot Joey in front of witnesses that made it virtually impossible to defeat the accusation that Sammy shot Joey. Since the two men had a long history of hostility, you feel your only defense is self-defense. Sammy has told you that he believed Joey had a knife and was reaching for it when Sammy fired his pistol. It becomes clear that the self-defense argument is weak since Sammy and Joey were sufficiently far apart that Sammy was not in immediate danger from Joey's knife, especially considering Sammy was armed with a pistol. Sammy asks if his case would be a lot better if he had thought that Joey had a gun. Of course you acknowledge that would be a better scenario for self-defense but you and Sammy both know that Joey did not have a gun and Sammy did not believe he had a gun. Nevertheless, Sammy offers to testify that he saw the glint of something in Joey's hand he thought was a gun.

You tell Sammy that such testimony would be perjury and attempt to dissuade him from making such statements. When he insists, you tell him that you will withdraw from the case and tell the judge of the proposed perjury (it is one thing to keep a client's statements of past crimes confidential and quite another to refuse to disclose proposed criminal acts). Sammy reluctantly agrees. When put on the witness stand, however, Sammy tells the gun, rather than the knife, story. As he begins to tell this story, what should you do?

Before answering the question, consider the following proposed standard:

ABA Project on Standards for Criminal Justice; Proposed Defense Function Standard 4-7.7 (2d Ed. 1980).

(a) If the defendant has admitted to defense counsel facts which establish guilt and counsel's independent investigation established that the admissions are true but the defendant insists on the right to trial, counsel must strongly discourage the defendant against taking the witness stand to testify perjuriously.

(b) If, in advance of trial, the defendant insists that he or she will take the stand to testify perjuriously, the lawyer may withdraw from the case, if that is feasible, seeking leave of the court if necessary, but the court should not be advised of the lawyer's reason for seeking to do so.

(c) If withdrawal from the case is not feasible or is not permitted by the court, or if the situation arises immediately preceding trial or during the trial and the defendant insists upon testifying perjuriously in his or her own behalf, it is unprofessional conduct for the lawyer to lend aid to the perjury or use the perjured testimony. Before the defendant takes the stand in these circumstances, the lawyer should make a record of the fact that the defendant is taking the stand against the advice of counsel in some appropriate manner without revealing to the court the client's intent to perjure himself. The lawyer may identify the witness as the defendant and may ask appropriate questions of the defendant when it is believed that the defendant's answers will not be perjurious. As to matters for which it is believed the defendant will offer perjurious testimony, the lawyer should seek to avoid direct examination of the defendant in the conventional manner; instead, the lawyer should ask the defendant if he or she wishes to make any additional statement concerning the case to the trier or triers of the facts. A lawyer may not later argue the defendant's known false version of facts to the jury as worthy of belief, and may not recite or rely upon the false testimony in his or her closing argument.

The difficulty of adhering to these standards might best be examined by a mock examination in which someone plays the witness and someone the witness's attorney in an unscripted and spontaneous exchange.

Does it matter that the judge will very likely know exactly what is going on and the jury will be very curious?

Part II

Sammy is convicted of murder, and he files a habeas corpus petition on the grounds that he was denied "effective assistance of counsel" as guaranteed by the United States Constitution's right to counsel. He argues that you turned against him and were no longer zealously defending him. He claims this on the basis of your attitude following his proposal to use the gun defense and later at the trial when you suddenly stopped fighting in his behalf.

Have you violated ethical principles?

Is there substance to his argument that he was not properly represented?

Note that these two questions are independent.

SOURCES OF
THE LAW: CASES

Law and the Courts

The law in practice revolves around disputes and problems. The primary forum for dispute resolution is the court. Even though most disputes brought to lawyers do not result in trials, the courts, through their spokespersons, the judges, are the final arbiters of what the law is. Because courts are the last legitimate resort of disputants, judges must decide. No matter how difficult or complex a case, the judge may not plead ignorance, frustration, or indecision. In deciding a case, the judge must provide reasons and rules, the final product of the process of adjudication. Without reasons and rules, decision making is purely political. This is particularly true in our constitutional system in which the lines between the judicial function and the administrative and legislative functions are relatively distinct.

Where does a judge find the rules? The judicial imagination is not sufficient authority, even though some judicial decisions seem to suggest otherwise. There are several sources for the law, the primary ones being the Constitution, legislation, and prior judicial decisions. This last is the subject matter of this chapter.

Judicial Restraint

In the American judiciary, a principle has evolved called **judicial restraint.** The United States Constitution set the stage by separating executive, legislative, and judicial functions into the three basic branches of government. Taking their cues from European Enlightenment thinkers of the eighteenth century, the framers of the Constitution established a political charter designed to break completely

judicial restraint
An accepted, customary policy of courts to restrict themselves to consideration of the questions presented to them and to restrain from legislating or interfering unduly with the executive or legislative branches. The principle also refers to the customary restraint federal courts exercise to leave questions of state law to state courts.

from the archaic remnants of feudalism, in which power and status were based on the accident of birth and society was ruled by an aristocracy with ultimate power residing in the monarch. The Constitution, by contrast, attempted to create a "government of laws and not of men" and allocated authority to the three branches of government in such a way that each could serve as a check on the other.

From the beginning, the president and the members of Congress were elected officials and ipso facto involved in politics and the political process. The political nature of the courts was not clearly defined in the Constitution, and it can fairly be said that Chief Justice John Marshall, who dominated the United States Supreme Court during the early nineteenth century, singlehandedly defined the role of the federal judiciary. Among the important doctrines Marshall established, two stand out as fundamental principles that have guided American law ever since:

1. Marshall argued that the U.S. Constitution was the "law of the land," meaning that no law or official act that violated the Constitution was lawful; the Constitution stood as the guiding light superior to every other law. Because the U.S. Supreme Court is the final interpreter of the meaning of the Constitution, this doctrine of constitutional supremacy provided the Supreme Court with great political power. This phrase in the Constitution is referred to as the **supremacy clause.** The power of the court to examine legislative and executive acts is called **judicial review.**

2. This power was severely limited by another principle established by Marshall, which was dubbed *judicial restraint.* Because ultimate authority resides in the Court, which is made up of judges who are appointed for life subject only to removal by impeachment, it is necessary that judges restrain themselves from actively entering the political arena. This can be effectively accomplished by judges devoting themselves to deciding cases according to existing law. In simple terms, this means that judges interpret the law rather than make it, the latter function being reserved to the legislature. Ideally, judicial decisions are based on the authority of legal principles already in existence and not on the moral, political, or social preferences of the judges.

In *Bush v. Gore*, the U.S. Supreme Court was asked to overturn the order of the Florida Supreme Court to the Florida counties to examine ballots that had been rejected to see whether the intent of the voter could be determined and then tabulated, effectively recounting the Florida vote for purposes of certifying electors for the electoral college in the 2000 presidential and vice-presidential races. The Court was faced with fundamental questions concerning Article II of the U.S. Constitution, which gives state legislatures full authority over the selection of electors. As most of us will remember for a long time, the U.S. Supreme Court in a 5 to 4 decision stopped the counting, reversed the Florida Supreme Court, and concluded that there was not enough time remaining to recount the vote, effectively ensuring the election of George W. Bush.

supremacy clause
Article VI of the U.S. Constitution, which provides: "This Constitution and the laws of the United States which shall be made in pursuance thereof; and all treaties made, or which shall be made, under the authority of the United States, shall be supreme law of the land, and the Judges in every State shall be bound thereby, any thing in the Constitution or laws of any State to the contrary notwithstanding."

judicial review
Review by an appellate court of a determination by a lower court; also, the power of the federal courts to declare acts contrary to the Constitution null and void.

The correctness of that decision will be debated for some time, but what is interesting for our pupposes is the way in which precedents were argued by both sides. Attorneys engage in disputes over the application of precedent, one side arguing that a precedent favorable to her client should rule in the case, while the other side argues the prior case is *inapposite*, not similar to the situation in the case at hand, and perhaps citing another case, friendly to his client, as the rule that should be applied. We often find the same sort of argument in appellate decisions when a dissenting opinion is written. In *Bush v. Gore*, one of the issues that troubled the Court was judicial restraint. This arose not in the context discussed earlier in the chapter of restraining the court from entering the political arena but as restraint toward state courts. Under our system of federalism, discussed more fully in Chapter 6, state courts have final authority over the interpretation of state law. One notable exception arises when state law conflicts with federal law, but even here, the U.S. Supreme Court has followed a tradition of reluctance to interfere in the exercise of state authority absent a clear challenge to the U.S. Constitution or the U.S. Code. Chief Justice Rehnquist argued in a concurring opinion (the case was decided by a **per curiam** opinion) that this electoral issue was just such a case, for which he cited precedential authority. Justice Ginsburg strongly disagreed. In the portion of her dissenting opinion reproduced in *Bush v. Gore*, she attacks the chief justice's precedents as inapposite, urging judicial restraint. Of course, siding with the minority, Justice Ginsburg's view did not prevail; it is offered here as an example of the sort of legal argumentation to which lawyers aspire. Her argument is quite persuasive, but, then, she, like the chief justice, is a brilliant judicial author. We should keep in mind that dissents do not make precedents, so that dissenters have greater liberty to take off the gloves and assume an adversarial role. Dissenting opinions are often more persuasive than majority opinions. While we might feel in some instances that the majority is *wrong*, the majority is always *right* by virtue of being the majority. Justice Ginsburg's statements should not be interpreted to mean that the author of this book endorses either side.

The Common Law

The American legal system is said to follow the **common law** tradition inherited from England. We are perhaps unique, along with England, Canada, Australia, and New Zealand, in enjoying nine hundred years of virtually uninterrupted legal evolution since the Norman Conquest of England in 1066. Since that time, England has not been invaded by foreign powers imposing their own legal institutions, nor have political or legal revolutions seriously disrupted the steady development of English law. When the British came to America, they brought their law with them. The American Revolution made a political break with the mother country and established a more democratic political organization, but it did not change the fundamental process of the law. When our judges sought legal authority for their decisions, they logically turned to the basic principles of English law, which they knew and trusted even if they did not trust George III.

per curiam (Latin) "By the court." Per curiam opinions are anonymous opinions, departing from the custom of naming the author of the majority opinion. These are often used in unanimous opinions lacking extensive argumentation. [*Bush v. Gore* was unusual in having a per curiam opinion followed by a concurring opinion and four dissenting opinions.]

common law In the first century after the Norman Conquest, the Normans established a legal regime for the entire kingdom of England, with laws common to all inhabitants of the realm. Under the system three common law courts were established (Kings bench, common pleas, exchequer). The decisions of these courts and especially the decisions of the appeals of these courts became binding precedents on lower courts under a doctrine called *stare decisis*.

BUSH
v.
GORE
United States Supreme Court
121 S.Ct. 525 (2000)

Justice GINSBURG, with whom Justice STEVENS joins, and with whom Justice SOUTER and Justice BREYER join as to Part I, dissenting.

I

THE CHIEF JUSTICE acknowledges that provisions of Florida's Election Code "may well admit of more than one interpretation." Ante, at 534. But instead of respecting the state high court's province to say what the State's Election Code means, THE CHIEF JUSTICE maintains that Florida's Supreme Court has veered so far from the ordinary practice of judicial review that what it did cannot properly be called judging. . . . I might join THE CHIEF JUSTICE were it my commission to interpret Florida law. But disagreement with the Florida court's interpretation of its own State's law does not warrant the conclusion that the justices of that court have legislated. . . .

This Court more than occasionally affirms statutory, and even constitutional, interpretations with which it disagrees. . . . Not uncommonly, we let stand state-court interpretations of federal law with which we might disagree. Notably, in the **habeas** context, the Court adheres to the view that "there is 'no intrinsic reason why the fact that a man is a federal judge should make him more competent, or conscientious, or learned with respect to [federal law] than his neighbor in the state courthouse.' " *Stone v. Powell*, 428 U.S. 465, 494, n. 35, 96 S.Ct. 3037, 49 L.Ed.2d 1067 (1976) . . .

* * *

In deferring to state courts on matters of state law, we appropriately recognize that this Court acts as an " 'outside[r]' lacking the common exposure to local law which comes from sitting in the jurisdiction." *Lehman Brothers v.*

Schein, 416 U.S. 386, 391, 94 S.Ct. 1741, 40 L.Ed.2d 215 (1974). That recognition has sometimes prompted us to resolve doubts about the meaning of state law by certifying issues to a State's highest court, even when federal rights are at stake. [C.] . . . Notwithstanding our authority to decide issues of state law underlying federal claims, we have used the certification device to afford state high courts an opportunity to inform us on matters of their own State's law because such restraint "helps build a cooperative judicial federalism." *Lehman Brothers,* 416 U.S., at 391, 94 S.Ct. . . .

Rarely has this Court rejected outright an interpretation of state law by a state high court. *Fairfax's Devisee v. Hunter's Lessee,* 7 Cranch 603, 3 L.Ed. 453 (1813), NAACP v. Alabama ex rel. Patterson, 357 U.S. 449, 78 S.Ct. 1163, 2 L.Ed.2d 1488 (1958), and Bouie v. City of Columbia, 378 U.S. 347, 84 S.Ct. 1697, 12 L.Ed.2d 894 (1964), cited by THE CHIEF JUSTICE, are three such rare instances. See ante, at 535, 536, and n. 2. But those cases are embedded in historical contexts hardly comparable to the situation here. *Fairfax's Devisee,* which held that the Virginia Court of Appeals had misconstrued its own forfeiture laws to deprive a British subject of lands secured to him by federal treaties, occurred amidst vociferous States' rights attacks on the Marshall Court. G. Gunther & K. Sullivan, Constitutional Law 61–62 (13th ed.1997). The Virginia court refused to obey this Court's Fairfax's Devisee mandate to enter judgment for the British subject's successor in interest. That refusal led to the Court's pathmarking decision in *Martin v. Hunter's Lessee,* 1 Wheat. 304, 4 L.Ed. 97 (1816). Patterson, a case decided three months after *Cooper v. Aaron,* 358 U.S. 1, 78 S.Ct. 1401, 3 L.Ed.2d 5 (1958), in the face of Southern resistance to the civil rights movement, held that the Alabama Supreme Court had irregularly applied its own procedural rules to deny review of a contempt order against the NAACP arising from its refusal to disclose membership lists. We said

(continued)

(continued)

that "our jurisdiction is not defeated if the nonfederal ground relied on by the state court is without any fair or substantial support." 357 U.S., at 455, 78 S.Ct. 1163. Bouie stemming from a lunch counter "sit-in" at the height of the civil rights movement, held that the South Carolina Supreme Court's construction of its trespass laws—criminalizing conduct not covered by the text of an otherwise clear statute— was "unforeseeable" and thus violated due process when applied retroactively to the petitioners. 378 U.S., at 350, 354, 84 S.Ct. 1697.

THE CHIEF JUSTICE'S casual citation of these cases might lead one to believe they are part of a larger collection of cases in which we said that the Constitution impelled us to train a skeptical eye on a state court's portrayal of state law. But one would be hard pressed, I think, to find additional cases that fit the mold. As Justice BREYER convincingly explains, see post, at 552–555 (dissenting opinion), this case involves nothing close to the kind of recalcitrance by a state high court that warrants extraordinary action by this Court. The Florida Supreme Court concluded that counting every legal vote was the overriding concern of the Florida Legislature when it enacted the State's Election Code. The court surely should not be bracketed with state high courts of the **Jim Crow** South.

THE CHIEF JUSTICE says that Article II, by providing that state legislatures shall direct the manner of appointing electors, authorizes federal superintendence over the relationship between state courts and state legislatures, and licenses a departure from the usual deference we give to state court interpretations of state law. Ante, at 535 ("To attach definitive weight to the pronouncement of a state court, when the very question at issue is whether the court has actually departed from the statutory meaning, would be to abdicate our responsibility to enforce the explicit requirements of Article II."). The Framers of our Constitution, however, understood that in a republican government, the judiciary would construe the legislature's

enactments. See U.S. Const., Art. III; The Federalist No. 78 (A. Hamilton). In light of the constitutional guarantee to States of a "Republican Form of Government," U.S. Const., Art. IV, § 4, Article II can hardly be read to invite this Court to disrupt a State's republican regime. Yet THE CHIEF JUSTICE today would reach out to do just that. By holding that Article II requires our revision of a state court's construction of state laws in order to protect one organ of the State from another, THE CHIEF JUSTICE contradicts the basic principle that a State may organize itself as it sees fit. See, e.g., *Gregory v. Ashcroft*, 501 U.S. 452, 460, 111 S.Ct. 2395, 115 L.Ed.2d 410 (1991) ("Through the structure of its government, and the character of those who exercise government authority, a State defines itself as a sovereign."); *Highland Farms Dairy v. Agnew*, 300 U.S. 608, 612, 57 S.Ct. 549, 81 L.Ed. 835 (1937) ("How power shall be distributed by a state among its governmental organs is commonly, if not always, a question for the state itself."). Article II does not call for the scrutiny undertaken by this Court.

The extraordinary setting of this case has obscured the ordinary principle that dictates its proper resolution: Federal courts defer to state high courts' interpretations of their state's own law. This principle reflects the core of federalism, on which all agree. "The Framers split the atom of sovereignty. It was the genius of their idea that our citizens would have two political capacities, one state and one federal, each protected from incursion by the other." *Saenz v. Roe*, 526 U.S. 489, 504, n. 17, 119 S.Ct. 1518, 143 L.Ed.2d 689 (1999) (citing *U.S. Term Limits, Inc. v. Thornton*, 514 U.S. 779, 838, 115 S.Ct. 1842, 131 L.Ed.2d 881 (1995) (KENNEDY, J., concurring)). THE CHIEF JUSTICE'S solicitude for the Florida Legislature comes at the expense of the more fundamental solicitude we owe to the legislature's sovereign. U.S. Const., Art. II, § 1, cl. 2 ("Each State shall appoint, in such Manner as the Legislature thereof may direct," the electors for President and Vice President) (emphasis added); ante, at 539–540 (STEVENS, J., dissenting). Were the other members of this Court as mindful as they generally are of our system of dual sovereignty, they would affirm the judgment of the Florida Supreme Court.

* * *

In sum, the Court's conclusion that a constitutionally adequate recount is impractical is a prophecy the Court's own judgment will not allow to be tested. Such an untested prophecy should not decide the Presidency of the United States.

I dissent.

Case Glossary

habeas corpus   An ancient remedy used to challenge the lawfulness of a detention by a government.

Jim Crow laws   Enacted by Southern states following the Civil War and Reconstruction to enforce segregation of African Americans primarily in lodging and public transportation. In retrospect, these laws are viewed as an outrageous denial of civil rights under color of law.

Case Questions

1. What does Justice Ginsburg find at fault in Justice Rehnquist's argument?
2. Who determines whether there is time to conduct a recount or not?
3. Who was right, Ginsburg or Rehnquist?

When the Normans organized England into a unified kingdom, they eliminated the pockets of local authority and jurisdiction characteristic of continental European countries at the height of the Middle Ages. Although local legal process continued for a time for purely local matters, England gradually became a nation in the true sense of the word and gave birth to the "common law of England," under which developed a body of law common to all citizens of the nation. This undoubtedly led eventually to the reverence for the rule of law in the minds of the British people.

The common law has come to mean something more than simply English law. In American jurisprudence, the common law refers to judge-made law, distinguishing it from continental European legal systems, which are civil law systems. From the seventeenth century onward, with the rise of European nationhood, centralized governments were formed that required corresponding national legal institutions. Rather than building on existing custom and institutions, these governments compiled sets of laws into codes, borrowing heavily from the *Corpus Juris* of the Roman Emperor Justinian, the first European to attempt to collect and organize legal principles into comprehensive written form. This movement had significantly less impact on England, which had long enjoyed a central government and a national court system.

Although the sources of English law included edicts of the monarch and acts of Parliament, the daily life of the law was conducted in the courts, where pronouncements of the law were made on matters great and small. Today we are accustomed to view the legislature as the source of new law and expect judges to exercise judicial restraint by merely interpreting and enforcing the laws, but this was not always so. Until well into the nineteenth century, the English Parliament, the U.S. Congress, and the various state legislatures were by modern standards virtually inactive. The law was declared by judges in the process of resolving disputes, relying on traditional principles. In modern times society and polity have grown more complex at an accelerating rate, and it is no longer possible to deal with modern problems by relying on slowly evolving legal principles. As a result, modern legislatures have assumed the major burdens of lawmaking, and the courts have assumed a sharply reduced role.

Judges Make Law

It is currently part of the American democratic folklore that judges merely interpret but do not "make" law. The fallacy of this notion lies in the fact that the power to interpret the law inevitably leads to making the law. Every time a judge is called upon to interpret the law, lawmaking occurs. Because judges ordinarily rely on the authority of existing law, judicial interpretation of the law invokes changes that are nearly imperceptible, but when faced with novel or difficult cases, judges occasionally formulate statements of the law that form important new principles.

It may be helpful to give an example of judicial lawmaking. In the landmark case of *MacPherson v. Buick Motor Co.*, 217 N.Y. 382, 111 N.E. 1050 (1916), Justice Cardozo of the New York Court of Appeals wrote an opinion that ushered in a new era in liability of manufacturers for injuries caused by their products, leading many years later to the field of **product liability.** Mr. MacPherson sued for injuries caused by the collapse of a defective wooden spoke wheel on the Buick he had purchased. The company defended against the suit on the grounds that it had sold the car to a dealer, which in turn sold the car to MacPherson. Because Buick did not have a contractual relation with MacPherson, it was not liable, stated attorneys for the company. In a carefully reasoned opinion, Cardozo explained why the company could not be protected by the traditional principle of **privity of contract** and held the company liable. The appearance of the automobile on the American scene put in the hands of the American public a potentially dangerous machine. Cardozo held that the manufacturer was responsible for inspection of the vehicles it sold and refused to allow the manufacturer to pass liability on to the dealer under the guise of privity of contract. In handing down his decision, Cardozo charted a course for compensation law in the United States.

Stare Decisis

Today the importance of the common law tradition lies largely in the principle of **precedent,** or stare decisis, by which judicial lawmaking is rendered orderly, predictable, and legitimate. The principle of **stare decisis** dictates that in making decisions judges should follow prior precedents. In practice, this means that

product liability A branch of tort law that assigns liability to a manufacturer when injury occurs due to a "dangerously defective product." It dispenses with traditional requirements of proving fault, as in *intentional torts* and *negligence*.

privity of contract The relationship between two parties to a contract. Originally, this was a bar to a suit brought by a consumer against a manufacturer when the consumer bought through a dealer and directly from the manufacturer. Modern product liability law does away with this impediment.

precedent Prior decisions of the same court, or a higher court, which a judge must follow in deciding a subsequent case presenting similar facts and the same legal problem. Precedent consists of the rule applied in a case and encompasses the reasoning that requires it. In a given decision, the precedent may be distinguished from *dictum*, which includes extraneous or conjectural statements not necessary to the decision and which are not binding on future decisions.

stare decisis The doctrine that judicial decisions stand as precedents for cases arising in the future. It is a fundamental policy of our law that, except in unusual circumstances, a court's determination on a point of law will be followed by courts of the same or lower rank in later cases presenting the same legal issue. It means to stand by a decision. The conventional translation is "Let the decision stand," probably not very helpful.

case of first impression A case that presents a fact situation that has never been decided before by that court.

disputes involving similar fact situations should be decided by similar rules. Former decisions are thus called precedents and are examined for guidance in making present decisions. When the court is faced with a novel fact situation (**case of first impression**) and formulates a rule to decide the case, the court "sets a precedent" that should be followed should a similar case arise.

As an example, let us suppose that a state court is faced with the following situation: a man and woman who have been living together for several years without benefit of marriage separate; the woman sues the man for breach of contract, claiming that when they entered into a cohabitation arrangement, the man promised to share his earnings equally with her if she refrained from employment and provided him with homemaking services and companionship, to which she agreed. The man defends on the basis of an established principle of contract law that a contract to perform illegal acts is unenforceable. Because sexual cohabitation is illegal in the state and that was the purpose of any promises that might have been exchanged, claims the man, the contract cannot be enforced.

Assuming the court has never been faced with this precise situation before, it must apply the rules of contract law and set a precedent for cohabitation agreements. Judging from similar cases already decided in several states, the court will probably rule that a cohabitation agreement is enforceable like any other contract unless its purpose is compensation for sexual services. Once this precedent has been set, the next dispute over a cohabitation agreement should be decided by application of the same rule. In this way, the first case is precedent for the second. If the rule is applied in many similar cases over a period of time, the court is likely to refer to it as a "well-established principle of law."

The force of a precedent depends upon the court that hands it down. A precedent is considered binding on the court that sets it and all lower courts within its jurisdiction. In a typical state court system, decisions can be rendered at three levels: trial court (lowest), court of appeals (intermediate appellate), and state supreme court (highest). Decisions of the highest state court are binding on all state courts. Decisions of courts of appeals are binding on that court and on lower courts within its jurisdiction. There is frequently more than one court of appeals, each with specific regional jurisdiction within the state. The hierarchy of federal courts also follows this pattern.

It sometimes happens that different courts of appeals within the same system (i.e., a state or the federal system) will formulate different rules for the same fact situation, creating considerable confusion. Trial courts in the First Circuit may feel bound by a different rule than those in the Fifth Circuit, and courts in the Third Circuit, whose court of appeals may not have decided an equivalent case, may be in a quandary about whether to follow the First Circuit rule or the Fifth Circuit rule. The logical solution is to obtain a ruling from the highest court, which is at liberty to adopt either rule or even a different rule, which would then be binding on all the courts within its jurisdiction.

The quagmire of American jurisdiction can be clarified by certain important principles. First, not only are federal and state court systems separate, but state and federal laws are separate as well. Where federal law is concerned, federal courts set the precedents, and the U.S. Supreme Court has final authority in declaring what the law is. In matters of state law, state courts have authority, and the highest court of a state has final authority to declare what the law is. Many Americans labor under the misconception that the U.S. Supreme Court is the final authority for interpreting state law. On the contrary, the highest court of each state is the ultimate authority for the law of that state. One of the reasons for the confusion arises from the supremacy clause of the U.S. Constitution, under which the U.S. Supreme Court may declare state law, whether judicial precedent or state statute, invalid if it is deemed to be in violation of the U.S. Constitution. This power of the U.S. Supreme Court is not derived from any authority to define state law but from authority to interpret the meaning of the U.S. Constitution, which is the "supreme law of the land."

The *Li* case is an example of a court overruling a well-established precedent and thus substituting a new rule. The issue facing the Supreme Court of California was whether to abolish the doctrine of contributory negligence and replace it with the doctrine of comparative negligence. Negligence is discussed in some detail in the chapter on torts, but in layman's terms, negligence occurs when one person injures another by failing to exercise care (for example, if someone carelessly causes an auto accident). Because negligence is grounded in fault, the courts in the nineteenth century developed the doctrine of *contributory negligence*, which held that a negligent defendant would not be liable if it could be shown that the plaintiff's negligence also contributed to the

---

LI

v.

YELLOW CAB COMPANY OF CALIFORNIA et al., Defendants and Respondents

13 Cal. 3d 804, 532 P.2d 1226,

119 Cal. Rptr. 858 (1975)

In this case we address the grave and recurrent question [of] whether we should judicially declare no longer applicable in California courts the doctrine of **contributory negligence,** which bars all recovery when the plaintiff's negligent conduct has contributed as a legal cause in any degree to the harm suffered by him, and hold that it must give way to a system of **comparative negligence,** which assesses liability in direct proportion to fault. . . .

It is unnecessary for us to catalogue the enormous amount of critical comment that has been directed over the years against the "all-or-nothing" approach of the doctrine of contributory negligence. The essence of that criticism has been constant and clear: the doctrine is inequitable in its operation because it fails to distribute responsibility in proportion to fault.

* * *

It is in view of these theoretical and practical considerations that to this date 25 states have abrogated the "all or nothing" rule of contributory negligence and have enacted in its place general apportionment statutes calculated in one manner or another to assess liability in proportion to fault. In 1973 these states were joined by Florida, which effected the same result by judicial decision. (*Hoffman v. Jones* (Fla. 1973) 280 So.2d 431.) We are likewise persuaded that logic, practical experience, and fundamental justice counsel against the retention of the doctrine rendering contributory negligence a complete bar to recovery—

and that it should be replaced in this state by a system under which liability for damage will be borne by those whose negligence caused it in direct proportion to their respective fault. . . .

It is urged that any change in the law of contributory negligence must be made by the Legislature, not by this court. Although the doctrine of contributory negligence is of judicial origin . . . subsequent cases of this court, it is pointed out, have unanimously affirmed that . . . the "all-or-nothing" rule is the law of this state and shall remain so until the Legislature directs otherwise. . . .

[There follows a discussion of why the court may nevertheless abolish the doctrine of contributory negligence followed by a discussion of the different forms of comparative negligence adopted in the other states.]

For all of the foregoing reasons we conclude that the "all-or-nothing" rule of contributory negligence as it presently exists in this state should be and is herewith superseded by a system of "pure" comparative negligence, the fundamental purpose of which shall be to assign responsibility and liability for damage in direct proportion to the amount of negligence of each of the parties.

* * *

The judgment is reversed.

* * *

CLARK, J., dissenting. . . . [T]he Legislature is the branch best able to effect transition from contributory to comparative or some other doctrine of negligence. Numerous and differing negligence systems have been urged over the years, yet there remains widespread disagreement among both the commentators and the states as to which one is best. . . . This court is not an investigatory body, and we lack the means of fairly appraising the merits of these competing systems. Constrained by settled rules of judicial review, we must consider only matters within the record or susceptible to judicial notice. That this court is inadequate to the task of carefully selecting the best replacement system is reflected in the majority's summary manner of eliminating from consideration all but two of the many competing proposals—including models adopted by some of our sister states.

By abolishing this century old doctrine today, the majority seriously erodes our constitutional function. We are again guilty of judicial chauvinism.

Case Questions

1. Is abolishing contributory negligence a question more properly addressed by the legislature than the court? (Consider this question when reading the section comparing adjudication and legislation.)
2. If the court sets a "bad" precedent, must it wait for the legislature to rectify the mistake?
3. What if the California legislature, after the decision in *Li*, passed a law unequivocally declaring that contributory negligence and not comparative negligence was the law of California? Does a legislature have authority to do this? Must the court follow the statute?

Case Glossary

negligence   A cause of action based on a failure to meet a reasonable standard of conduct that results in an injury.

contributory negligence   A principle by which a recovery will be denied a plaintiff for defendant's negligence if plaintiff is also found to have been at fault. It is an affirmative defense that has been replaced by *comparative negligence* in most states.

comparative negligence   A principle whereby damages are apportioned between plaintiff and defendant according to their relative fault in a negligence case where both are found to have been at fault.

injury. It soon became apparent that the doctrine was inequitable in cases in which the defendant's negligence was great and the plaintiff's negligence was minimal. For example, railroad workers commonly worked under dangerously unsafe conditions and sometimes contributed to their own injuries through momentary inattention. Gradually the states began to replace contributory negligence with the doctrine of *comparative negligence,* which apportioned fault between plaintiff and defendant so that the plaintiff, even if also negligent, could recover a diminished amount if the jury found the plaintiff less responsible for the cause of the injury (e.g., plaintiff 20 percent at fault and defendant 80 percent at fault).

In *Li,* the plaintiff made an improper turn through an intersection and was struck by the defendant, who was racing to pass through the intersection while the stoplight was yellow. The case was heard without a jury. The judge found both plaintiff and defendant negligent and entered a judgment in favor of the defendant based on California law. The plaintiff then appealed in the hope that she could persuade the Supreme Court of California to overrule prior precedent, in which effort she was successful.

A careful reading of the case reveals that four of the six justices ruling on the case wanted to change the law. Their decision was complicated by the fact that although contributory negligence originally arose through judicial decision, the California legislature had enacted a statute in 1872 establishing the doctrine of contributory negligence. In a lengthy discussion of the statute and its history (omitted here), the court concluded that the statute had not been intended to permanently establish contributory negligence as the law of the state.

Adjudication versus Legislation

legislation The act of giving or enacting laws; preparation and enactment of laws; lawmaking, ordinarily the prerogative of legislatures or legislative bodies.

Although judges may be said to "make law," they do so in a way quite unlike that of legislators. **Legislation** is a very different process with a different orientation. Whereas adjudication can be said to be particularized in the sense that cases focus on particular events and particular parties, legislation is generalized in that it is designed to make rules that apply to everyone.

Adjudication: Narrow Focus on Past Events

adjudication The formal act of deciding disputes by a court or tribunal.

Judges resolve disputes between parties; **adjudication** refers to the process of making these decisions. In the American system, a person (which can also be a business, a corporation, or a city) files a lawsuit against another to redress an injury or to establish rights and duties. When a case reaches trial, the judge is faced with past events that have been framed by attorneys for both sides for submission to the judge for resolution. Ordinarily only the facts of the events relating to the dispute are relevant to its resolution. Evidence presented at trial will reveal those facts in great detail in order to determine which rule of law is applicable. The judge will decide which laws are relevant to the facts as determined by the evidence presented in court. Thus, the process of adjudication focuses on past events specific to one dispute, and only the law the judge deems appropriate to that case will be applied.

In short, the judge looks through a magnifying glass at one case and declares what law is applicable. If law is made in the process, it is a byproduct of the case. The function of the judge is to settle the dispute, not to determine how the law applies to other cases in the future. The judge will look to the authority of the past to make the decision.

Legislation: Universal Application and Future Effect

The characteristics of legislation are universal application and future effect. Legislators do not resolve individual cases, though they are often motivated by dissatisfaction with the outcomes of cases decided in the courts. For example, the *Baby M* case in New Jersey (*In re Baby M*, 109 N.J. 396, 537 A.2d 1227 [1988]), in which a surrogate mother fought unsuccessfully to gain custody from the couple who had arranged for the baby's adoption, resulted in many legislatures, including New Jersey, enacting laws regulating surrogate mother contracts. But the New Jersey legislature did not decide the *Baby M* case nor change the ruling of the court; its enactment governed contracts between surrogate mothers and adoptive parents in future cases.

The legislative process typically operates by first recognizing a problem and then, through investigation and deliberation, attempting to solve the problem by enacting a law. When the legislative process is complete, the law is a matter of public record, and everyone must comply or risk legal consequences. Only rarely can legislation apply retroactively. The surrogate mother case brought to public attention the moral issues in the commercialization of pregnancy and adoption. Some people felt that such contracts should be illegal or unenforceable, some felt that the natural mother should have the option to revoke the contract, and others felt that ordinary contract law provided sufficient protection. State legislatures deliberated these questions and arrived at laws designed to deal with the question. These laws, however, did not change adoptions that had already taken place, but instead served as the legal standards that would govern surrogate mother contracts subsequent to enactment of law.

The *Colby* and *Higgins* cases illustrate the difference between legislation and adjudication and illuminate the judicial attitude exemplified in the doctrine of stare decisis.

American courts in the nineteenth century created or expanded immunity to suit for several categories of parties, including charitable institutions, the subject of *Colby* and *Higgins*. Immunity from suit leaves an injured party without a remedy, and in the twentieth century the courts and legislatures of our country began to question the wisdom and legality of immunity to suit. The rise of the insurance industry made such immunities obsolete. Individuals and institutions can protect themselves from catastrophic losses by purchasing insurance. The Supreme Judicial Court of Massachusetts was presented with an archaic

Edwin A. COLBY, Administrator
v.
CARNEY HOSPITAL
356 Mass. 527, 254 N.E.2d 407 (1969)

The plaintiff **administrator** brings this action of tort and contract for the death and conscious suffering of his **intestate**. The defendant hospital set up, among other things, the defence of charitable immunity. The plaintiff **demurred** to this part of the answer, stating that it "does not set forth a valid or legal defense, in that said defense as alleged violates and abrogates certain rights, privileges and immunities granted to, and preserved for the citizens of the Commonwealth" under arts. 1, 10, 11, 12, 20, and 30 of our Declaration of Rights and also under the Fifth and Fourteenth Amendments to the Constitution of the United States. A judge in the Superior Court overruled the demurrer, and the plaintiff appealed.

The demurrer was rightly overruled. Nothing has been brought to our attention suggesting that the doctrine of charitable immunity is repugnant to any provision of the Constitutions of the United States and the Commonwealth.

In the past on many occasions we have declined to renounce the defence of charitable immunity set forth in *McDonald v. Massachusetts Gen. Hosp.*, 120 Mass. 432, and *Roosen v. Peter Bent Brigham Hosp.*, 235 Mass. 66, 126 N.E. 392, 14 A.L.R. 563. We took this position because we were of opinion that any renunciation preferably should be accomplished prospectively and that this should be best done by legislative action. Now it appears that only three or four States still adhere to the doctrine. . . . It seems likely that no legislative action in this Commonwealth is probable in the near future. Accordingly, we take this occasion to give adequate warning that the next time we are squarely confronted by a legal question respecting the charitable immunity doctrine it is our intention to abolish it.

Order overruling demurrer affirmed.

John HIGGINS
v.
EMERSON HOSPITAL
328 N.E.2d 488 (1975)

This appeal brings before us the issue whether, by reason of the language in *Colby v. Carney Hosp.*, 356 Mass. 527, 528, 254 N.E.2d 407 (1969), we should hold that the defense of charitable immunity is not available to the defendant hospital. . . .

The plaintiff brought an action in tort and contract for injuries allegedly sustained by him on June 17, 1970, while he was an inpatient at the defendant hospital. The case was tried on June 20, 1974, before a Superior Court judge and a jury. The plaintiff's attorney made an opening statement that asserted the facts of the plaintiff's accident and injury, including a stipulation that the defendant hospital . . . was operated exclusively for charitable purposes. The judge thereupon **directed verdicts** for the defendant as to both counts of the plaintiff's declaration.

. . . The parties and the judge have clearly considered that the single issue is whether, by reason of the *Colby* case, or any other consideration, we should hold that charitable immunity is not applicable in this case. We hold that the doctrine is applicable and the judge properly directed verdicts for the defendant as to both counts.

The injury here occurred after the date of the decision of the *Colby* case (December 23, 1969), but before the effective date, September 16, 1971, of [the statute] which abolished the doctrine of charitable immunity. We have since held that the statute is not retrospective in effect . . . , and it is thus clear that the plaintiff here takes no benefit from the statute.

The plaintiff contends that, because of the intimation in the *Colby* case as to the possible future abolishment of charitable immunity, that doctrine is not applicable in this case. He argues that from the date of the decision the various charitable institutions, as well as the insurance industry and members of the public, were clearly given notice of and could conform their conduct in reliance on the fact that claims of charitable immunity raised with respect to incidents occurring after the date of the decision, December 23, 1969, would be rejected.

He further contends that had the Legislature not acted on the subject matter in 1971 there would be no question that this court would rule the charitable immunity doctrine abolished as to the instant case.

We reject the arguments. In *Colby v. Carney Hosp.*, 356 Mass. 527, 528, 254 N.E.2d 407, 408 (1969), we said that any renunciation of the doctrine of charitable immunity "should be accomplished *prospectively* and that this should be best done by legislative action"

(emphasis supplied). At no time has this court abolished the doctrine. In *Ricker v. Northeastern Univ., supra*, _____ at _____, 279 N.E.2d at 672, we said, speaking of the *Colby* case, "This language does not by itself abolish the doctrine of charitable immunity as of December 23, 1969 . . . [the language] makes it clear that no change of the doctrine was then being made." The Legislature chose to act subsequent to the *Colby* decision. We recognize the factual distinction between the instant case and the *Ricker* case, to wit, that the injury to Ricker occurred prior to December 23, 1969, the date of our decision in the *Colby* case, while the injury underlying this action occurred subsequent to that decision. Nevertheless, we see no persuasive reason now to rule, as in practical effect the plaintiff urges here, that the doctrine of charitable immunity does not apply to an injury which occurred after December 23, 1969, but before the effective date of [the statute].

* * *

Judgment affirmed.

Case Questions

1. If the court was so clearly opposed to charitable immunity, why did it not simply abolish it in *Colby*?
2. Since the doctrine of charitable immunity was a judicial creation in the first place, why did the court look to the legislature to abolish it?
3. How do these cases express the judicial attitude toward precedent in Massachusetts?
4. If you had been Higgins's attorney in *Higgins v. Emerson Hospital*, would you have predicted a win or a loss in the Supreme Judicial Court?

Case Glossary

administrator A person appointed by a court to manage the distribution of the estate of a deceased person.

intestate A person who dies without a will. Also used as an adjective to refer to the state of dying without a will.

demurrer A motion to dismiss a case, alleging that the complaint is insufficient to state a legal cause of action.

directed verdict The judge may order a verdict against the plaintiffs when they have failed to meet their burden of proof. Formerly the judge ordered the jury to enter a verdict against the plaintiff. Today the judge grants a motion for a directed verdict and enters a judgment.

principle of charitable immunity that it had created a century before. By the time these cases were decided, nearly every other state had abolished charitable immunity by statute or by the highest state court overruling its own prior decisions.

Even though the court was inclined to abolish charitable immunity, it found itself in a dilemma. Because the precedents were clear (i.e., charitable institutions were immune from suit according to a well-established line of precedents), the Supreme Judicial Court was reluctant to change the rule suddenly, but at the same time the doctrine of charitable immunity had just as clearly been discredited as a principle of American law. Charitable institutions should be able to rely on the law as stated by the courts. Why should a nonprofit hospital buy insurance if it cannot be sued?

Obiter Dictum

dictum, dicta, obiter dictum *Dictum* is a Latin word meaning "said" or "stated." *Obiter* means "by the way" or "incidentally." *Obiter dictum*, then, means something stated incidentally and not necessary to the discussion, usually shortened to *dictum* or its plural *dicta*. In law, it refers to a part of a judicial decision that goes beyond the scope of the issues and is considered mere opinion and not binding precedent.

Not everything that is expressed in an opinion is precedent. The author of an opinion is free to make comments that go beyond the immediate issues to be decided. The remarks, opinions, and comments in a decision that exceed the scope of the issues and the rules that decide them are called **dictum**, plural **dicta**, from the older Latin phrase **obiter dictum**, and are not binding on future cases. As we have already seen, the process of adjudication commonly results in the making of new rules or the interpretation of existing rules. This is an unavoidable result of the necessity of resolving disputes. However, when a judge attempts to expand an argument to issues or facts not before the court in the dispute, adjudication ends and legislation begins. Although these statements are worthy of consideration in subsequent cases, they are not considered binding precedent and need not be followed; they are *dicta* rather than rule.

Analytically, the way to distinguish *dictum* from the rule of law is to determine the legal and factual issues presented by a dispute and analyze the reasoning that leads to their resolution. Anything outside this reasoning and the rule behind it is *dictum*.

This can be applied to the *Colby* and *Higgins* cases. In *Colby*, the court faced the issue of whether charitable immunity was still the rule in Massachusetts. Although the court expressed its disapproval of the rule, it nevertheless followed prior precedent and held that charitable immunity was still in effect, suggesting that it would be better for the legislature to abolish the doctrine. The court added that it intended to abolish the doctrine the next time it was faced with the same issue. This assertion of the court's future intentions was *dictum*. When the trial court in *Higgins* was faced with the same issue five years later, it upheld charitable immunity and directed verdicts in favor of the defendant. The trial court was legally correct, because the Supreme Judicial Court in *Colby* had not abolished the doctrine but merely expressed its intention to do so. The Supreme Judicial Court agreed with the lower court that the doctrine had not been abolished by the court and indicated that its expression of future intentions had no legally binding force on Massachusetts courts. As a practical matter, the fact that the legislature had subsequently abolished charitable immunity meant that the Supreme Judicial Court need not take it upon itself to abolish the doctrine, which only affected those unfortunate few who were injured prior to the legislative act.

A more obvious example of *dictum* can be found in *State v. Butler*, which demonstrates that precedent is law and *dictum* is not.

The STATE of Ohio
v.
BUTLER
Supreme Court of Ohio
19 Ohio St.2d 55, 249 N.E.2d 818 (1969)

SCHNEIDER, Judge

Appellant's contention is that the prosecution violated his Fifth Amendment right against self-incrimination by using statements of his which were made to police during in-custody interrogation with no warning of his right to silence or to counsel. The questioning occurred after arrest, on November 20, 1965, which was prior to the United States Supreme Court decision in *Miranda v. Arizona* (1966). 384 U.S. 436 . . . It was held there that the prosecution's use of statements of an accused, made to police without prior warnings of his rights to remain silent, to counsel and appointed counsel if indigent, was a violation of the accused's Fourteenth and Fifth Amendment right against self-incrimination. In *Johnson v. New Jersey* (1966), 384 U.S. 719 . . . the court held that the rule of Miranda applied to all trials commenced after its date of announcement, June 13, 1966. The delayed trial in the instant case occurred on May 15, 1968, making Miranda applicable.

The appellant took the stand and, on cross-examination by the prosecution, he made assertions as to the facts surrounding the crime. A recorded statement appellant made to a detective after arrest was then read to him to show a prior inconsistent statement. Counsel objected, but the court allowed the statement to be used as evidence to impeach the witness' credibility. Appellant contends that this use of the statements, made without cautionary warnings, violated his Fifth Amendment rights as defined by *Miranda v. Arizona*. . . .

We cannot agree. First, the statements used by the prosecution were not offered by the state as part of its direct case against appellant, but were offered on the issue of his credibility after he had been sworn and testified in his own defense. Second, the statements used by the prosecution were voluntary, no claim to the contrary having been made. . . .

. . . In the case of the Fifth Amendment, . . . reason exists to distinguish between statements of an accused used in the prosecution's direct case and used for impeachment in cross-examining the accused when he takes the stand. We must not lose sight of the words of the Fifth Amendment: '* * * nor shall be compelled * * * to be a witness against himself * * *.' This is a privilege accorded an accused not to be compelled to testify, nor to have any prior statements used by the prosecution to prove his guilt. . . .

We do not believe that the case of *Miranda v. Arizona*, . . . dictates a conclusion contrary to ours. In Miranda, the court indicated that statements of a defendant used to impeach his testimony at trial may not be used unless they were taken with full warnings and effective waiver. . . . However, we note that in all four of the convictions reversed by that decision statements of the accused, taken without cautionary warnings, were used by the prosecution as direct evidence of guilt in the case in chief.

We believe that the words of Chief Justice Marshall regarding the difference between holding and dictum are applicable here.

'It is a maxim not to be disregarded, that general expressions, in every opinion, are to be

(continued)

(continued)

taken in connection with the case in which those expressions are used. If they go beyond the case, they may be respected, but ought not to control the judgment in a subsequent suit when the very point is presented for decision. The reason of this maxim is obvious. The question actually before the court is investigated with care, and considered in its full extent. Other principles which may serve to illustrate it, are considered in their relation to the case decided, but their possible bearing on all other cases is seldom completely investigated.' . . .

The court, in *Miranda,* was not faced with the facts of this case. Thus, we do not consider ourselves bound by the dictum of *Miranda.*

The 'linch pin' (as Mr. Justice Harlan put it, 384 U.S. at 513, 86 S.Ct. 1602) of *Miranda* is that police interrogation is destructive of human dignity and disrespectful to the inviolability of the human personality. In the instant case, the use of the interrogation to impeach the voluntary testimony of the accused is neither an assault on his dignity nor disrespectful of his personality. He elected to testify, and cannot complain that the state seeks to demonstrate the lack of truth in his testimony.

Finally, we emphasize that the statements used by the prosecution were voluntarily made. The decision in *Miranda* did not discard the distinction between voluntary and involuntary statements made by an accused and used by the prosecution. . . . Lack of cautionary warnings is one of the factors to consider in determining whether statements are voluntary or not. However, appellant here has never claimed that the statements used to impeach were involuntary. . . .

Judgment affirmed.

DUNCAN Judge (dissenting in part).

* * *

In *Miranda,* Chief Justice Warren stated, at page 476, 86 S.Ct., at p. 1629:

'The warnings required and the waiver necessary in accordance with our opinion today are, in the absence of a fully effective equivalent, prerequisites to the admissibility of any statement made by a defendant. No distinction can be drawn between statements which are direct confessions and statements which amount to 'admissions' of part or all of an offence. The privilege against selfincrimination protects the individual from being compelled to incriminate himself in any manner; it does not distinguish degrees of incrimination. Similarly, for precisely the same reason, no distinction may be drawn between inculpatory statements and statements alleged to be merely 'exculpatory.' If a statement made were in fact truly exculpatory it would, of course, never be used by the prosecution. In fact, statements merely intended to be exculpatory by the defendant are often used to impeach his testimony at trial or to demonstrate untruths in the statement given under interrogation and thus to prove guilt by implication. These statements are incriminating in any meaningful sense of the word and may not be used without the full warnings and effective waiver required for any other statement. . . .'

This specific reference to impeachment, I believe, forecloses the use of defendant's in-custody statement in the instant case.

I would reverse.

Case Questions

1. What is the difference between statements used for the direct case and the same statements used for impeachment?
2. What practical policy justifies disregarding Chief Justice Warren's *dicta* in *Miranda?*

Nonbinding Authority

In practical terms, the law consists of state and federal constitutions, statutes, and judicial opinions. If a trial court in Rhode Island is faced with a difficult legal issue, it will attempt to determine the applicable law by resorting to Rhode Island statutes and case law that conforms to mandates of the Rhode Island and federal constitutions. It is bound by these authorities alone. Nevertheless, the court may confront an issue that clearly demands judicial resolution and for which the usual binding sources of the law provide little or no guidance. Typically this arises in a case of first impression in which the factual situation giving rise to the dispute has never been decided by a court of the state nor been addressed by the state legislature.

Reasoning from Authority   To arrive at a reasonable solution, the court will use the best authority it can find. It may reason from existing state law using logic and analogy to infer a rule. For instance, until recently state courts universally rejected the notion that a professional license was property that could be used to establish property settlements upon divorce. This was particularly problematic in cases in which spouses, usually wives, had worked to support their husbands through professional school, only to be divorced soon afterward, when their professional husbands had not yet practiced long enough to acquire much property to be divided between husband and wife. In attempting to classify professional licenses, the courts, though admitting the license clearly had value for its holders, noted that the licenses did not have the usual attributes of property (namely, they could not be transferred, sold, leased, or given away) and noted that they could be revoked by the licensing authority. Although many courts obviously felt that this traditional definition of property resulted in an injustice to many wives, they felt compelled to follow the law. Finally, in *O'Brien v. O'Brien*, 489 N.E.2d 712 (N.Y. 1985), the New York court defined professional licenses as "marital property," justifying its departure from prior law on the basis of recent divorce legislation that provided a broad definition of marital property in divorce.

Law from Sister States   When binding authority is absent, the court often looks to nonbinding authority from other states. An issue unique in one state may very well have been decided in another. It seems reasonable to examine such decisions to see whether the rules handed down and the reasoning behind them are applicable to the law of the state faced with a case of first impression. Often the pioneering state will give its name to the principle; for example, one of the comparative negligence rules mentioned in *Li* as the "50 percent" rule might also be referred to as the "Wisconsin rule," as opposed to the "Florida rule," which is normally referred to as "pure" comparative negligence.

Decisions of other state courts are commonly referred to as **persuasive authority;** they command respect because they represent the law of another American jurisdiction even though they are not binding outside that jurisdiction. The persuasiveness of such authority is greatest in areas of common law,

persuasive authority   Authority that carries great weight even though not qualifying as precedent, for example, decisions of other state courts.

community property
A regime in which the earning of husband and wife curing marriage are owned equally by both; eight states borrowing from French (Louisiana) or Spanish (Texas west to California) law incorporated the concept of community property into marital law.

equitable distribution   Designed to equalize the marital shares of husband and wife for purposes of divorce.

Uniform Commercial Code   Commonly referred to simply as the UCC, a set of comprehensive statutes governing most commercial transactions that has been adopted in every state except Louisiana.

secondary authority
Authoritative statements of law other than statutes and cases, such as law review articles, treatises, and the Restatements.

treatises   In the legal context, scholarly books about the law, usually covering one of the basic fields of law, such as torts or contracts, or a significant subfield of the law, such as worker's compensation.

Restatements of the Law   The compilation of general interpretations of major fields of common law, sponsored and published by the American Law Institute, founded in 1923.

especially torts, and weakest in decisions based on statutory interpretation. For example, in the area of family law, there is considerable variation among the states concerning divorce law, so the reasoning of the court of one state may be considered inappropriate in another by virtue of differences between their respective statutes. For example, California is a **community property** state, whereas New York is an **equitable distribution** state, making California decisions regarding the distribution of property upon divorce often inapplicable to New York cases. In contrast, because the **Uniform Commercial Code** (UCC) has been adopted in every state except Louisiana, decisions interpreting the UCC are often used as persuasive authority.

Secondary Sources   In addition to cases from other states, a vast array of legal materials used in arguments by lawyers and opinions by judges that are not officially the law anywhere are called **secondary authority**. Principal among these are law review articles, **treatises,** and the **Restatements.** Law review articles written by legal scholars commonly address contemporary problems in the law and suggest carefully reasoned solutions. For example, the surrogate motherhood question that arose in New Jersey in the *Baby M* case gave rise to numerous articles critiquing the court's decision and discussing appropriate solutions to the issues raised. Treatises by eminent scholars are often cited in cases, and the Restatements are especially respected because they attempt to provide a general statement of American law rather than focus on any particular state.

In addition to cases of first impression, courts, usually the highest state courts, are sometimes presented with cases that reveal serious weakness in prior precedents and urge their overruling. In rationalizing the departure from what otherwise appears to be binding precedent, the court will muster all the available persuasive authority and secondary authority it can.

Because cases raise serious legal issues and judges are entrusted with the administration of justice, decisions are not mechanical products of legal scholarship. Much attention is given in written opinions to fairness to the parties and the consequences to society of the rules that are constructed or enforced. The search for authority on which to base a rule helps to ensure that judges do not act merely on their own personal value systems but instead reflect a consensus of the wisdom of their peers. This is the legacy of the common law, a system of judicial decision making that has endured many centuries of political and social change and has perhaps greatly assisted in making those changes.

Summary

The Anglo-American legal tradition has a rich history of judge-made law known as the common law. It is governed by the principle of stare decisis, which urges that the courts abide by past precedents unless there is a compelling reason to depart from them. The process of adjudication focuses on disputes, in contrast to the legislative process, which enacts general laws for future application.

In determining and interpreting the law, courts base decisions on authority, principally statutes and prior case law. When these do not provide a clear answer to the case at hand, secondary authority may be the source of reasoning and rules.

The statements of the law made in higher courts must be followed by the lower courts, but the force of precedent applies only to that part of the decision pertinent to the facts of the dispute before the court and not to incidental statements of the author of a judicial opinion.

Scenario

Precedent and Unpublished Cases

In the 1960s and 1970s, appellate courts found their caseloads increasing significantly. This tendency has continued since that time without a corresponding increase in appellate judges and their budgets. Faced with numerous cases that could be decided on well-established precedents and offering little of interest to those other than the parties, judges in the last few decades have increasingly decided some decisions were not worthy of inclusion in the reporters. These cases are deemed "unpublished" because they do not appear in the official printed reports. This practice allowed judges to skimp on writing, focusing their attention simply on the facts and issues necessary to explain the decision to the parties without extensive discussion needed for opinions serving as stare decisis. Of course, the decisions were "official" in the sense that they decided the winners and losers, adjudicating the rights of the parties; but they were not published in the usual sources that attorneys would research. In recent times, these unpublished opinions have been made available on Westlaw and Lexis, the two primary databases, as well as other sources so that they are readily searchable on the Internet.

These unpublished decisions were deemed by many jurisdictions not to have precedential force. An apparently logical conclusion followed that attorneys should not cite them. The U.S. Court of Appeal for the 8th Circuit formulated its own rule in this regard:

> **Rule 28 A (i) Citation of unpublished opinion.** Unpublished opinions are not precedent and parties generally should not cite them. . . . Parties may also cite an unpublished opinion of this court if the opinion has persuasive value on a material issue and no published opinion of this or another court would serve as well. A party who cites an unpublished opinion in a document must attach a copy of the unpublished opinion to the document. A party who cites an unpublished opinion for the first time at oral argument must attach a copy of the unpublished opinion to the supplemental authority letter required by FRAP 28(j). When citing an unpublished opinion, a party must indicate the opinion's unpublished status.

The 8th Circuit rule has been challenged as unconstitutional. The U.S. Constitution divides governmental powers into three branches, judicial, legislative, and executive, which is the basis for the longstanding policy of judicial restraint. Given the history and importance of precedent, the separation of powers, and judicial restraint, how does Rule 28A (i) conflict with this system?

Here is the scenario. This is a tax case. The appellant taxpayer filed suit for a refund of $10,000. The IRS argued that the taxpayer's claim for a refund had not been filed within the requisite time limits. The Federal District Court agreed, and the 8th Circuit Court of Appeals affirmed. As is usual, the district court heard this as a three-judge panel.

In making its case, the IRS cited an unpublished opinion, *Arthur v. United States.* The panel considered itself bound by this decision, arguing that Rule 28A (i), which specified that unpublished opinions have no precedential effect, was unconstitutional, as purporting to confer upon the courts a power that went beyond the "judicial," within the meaning of Article III of the Constitution.

While the case was under advisement by the panel, the Second Circuit decided *Fernandez v. United States,* which was in direct conflict with *Arthur.* While noting *Fernandez,* the panel considered itself bound by in-circuit precedent that could only be changed by the Court en banc, that is, by the entire circuit court sitting together on the case. In the meantime, the IRS changed its mind and gave the taxpayer her refund. Not content, she appealed to get her attorney's fees as well.

Has the case become moot by reason of these events subsequent to the filing of the panel opinion? The taxpayer says no. In her view, the case is not moot for two main reasons. First, the issue of the status of unpublished opinions is of great importance to the bar and bench. Second, the taxpayer claims that she is entitled to an award of attorneys' fees under 26 U.S.C. § 7430, a claim that has not yet been decided, and that the existence of this claim, which presumably the government will dispute, prevents the case from becoming moot.

Query The issue of whether unpublished opinions are precedent, persuasive authority, without value, or even disallowed is very controversial. It may well be that the taxpayer here should take her money and run; the issues raised are not trivial. They go to the essence of stare decisis and the proper role of bench and bar. Try to state the reasons for both sides in this case in the context of the significance of decision and precedent in our legal system.

SOURCES OF THE LAW: LEGISLATION

Introduction

Historically, judicial decisions have played the major role in the evolution of Anglo-American law, but the courts as the source of law have been eclipsed in modern times by the ascendancy of legislatures as primary lawmaking bodies.

Evolution of Legislation

During most of the development of Anglo-American law, the pronouncement of law was accomplished by courts deciding cases in which customs, practices, and informal principles of conduct were formalized in written decisions. Although Anglo-American law largely escaped the **codification** movements that revolutionized continental European law, the nineteenth century brought a new attitude in America with regard to legislation. The English Parliament enacted numerous statutes over the centuries that clarified or changed the common law, but its legislative output was minor in comparison to the courts as a source of law.

codification The term *codify* may refer to the simple process of turning a custom or common law rule into legislation, but usually it refers to making *codes*.

The American situation was different. The United States had approved a written federal constitution that allocated political authority among the three branches of government, providing specific important spheres of authority for *Congress*. (See Appendix B; U.S. Const. Art. I, §§ 1 and 8.) The legal profession and the courts were viewed by some with suspicion because of the elitist tradition of these institutions in England and colonial America. Congress, in contrast, was elected by the people and thus viewed as representative of the people. It was natural that antiaristocratic sentiment in the new republic would turn to Congress and the state legislatures for lawmaking, which is their constitutional and customary function.

The last half of the nineteenth century saw a major movement toward codification in the United States. In addition to the reasons previously given for favoring legislation, two others provided impetus. First, Americans had learned through revolution and the establishment of the Constitution that the people could guide their own destiny by making law through their representatives, a democratic and rational process. Second, the country was undergoing rapid change and development, and Americans were disinclined to preserve ancient customs simply because they were ancient. Americans were ambitious and ready for change. To wait for the evolution of legal principles through the cumbersome and conservative judicial process was probably never truly part of the American character.

momentum

The most renowned spokesman for codification was David Dudley Field, a New York lawyer who was appointed to a law revision commission that authored the *Code of Civil Procedure* enacted in 1848, often called simply the "Field Code." Although Field advocated and authored several other codes, their reception in New York and other eastern states was poor. Western states, on the contrary, wholeheartedly jumped at the chance for ready-made law, perhaps because their brief history and lack of tradition made them impatient for a system of laws from which they could set new horizons.

The complex problems of the twentieth century encouraged timely responses from legislative bodies, which have became politically very powerful, often seeming to eclipse the common law tradition. Although the states differ in the extent to which they have codified state law, every state has enacted a complex body of statutes that serves as a principal source of law. The rise of the power of legislatures is reflected in the courts, which now defer to the statutes. Nevertheless, because disputes over the law must ultimately be resolved in the courts, the meaning of legislation is decided by the courts and applied to specific cases.

The Nature of Legislation

In Chapter 3, legislation was distinguished from judge-made law by its characteristics of "universal application and future effect." The line drawn between the characteristics of legislation and adjudication has not always been clear. In the past, legislatures have often passed special bills to define narrow rights of individuals or local entities, but this practice has always been viewed with suspicion (see the 1851 case of *Ponder v. Graham*). When a legislative body narrows its focus to resolve a particularized dispute, it may be challenged in court as violating the principle of separation of judicial and legislative powers embodied in federal and state constitutions.

Legislation strives to reduce principles of law to a coherent written form in which the intent of the law can be determined from the words alone—statutes are pure rules, often without policy statements or statements of intent. In this respect they differ in nature from the common law, which, while relying on past precedent when available, may be characterized as customary law because it is based on unwritten principles of justice and proper conduct rooted in the values of society and is elaborated in often lengthy critical comments in the decisions. The rules in judicial decisions are formulated to apply to the case before the court and are tailored to that dispute. They express an underlying principle rather than an exact rule, as is the case with legislation. The reasoning is as much a part of the rule as the precise statement of the rule in the decision.

The common law treats law as an evolving process. Ultimately it is what a case comes to stand for rather than what it actually states. For example, the landmark school case *Goss v. Lopez*, 419 U.S. 565 (1975), which defined the rights of public school students in certain disciplinary actions, is frequently cited as establishing a constitutional right to a public education. In fact, *Goss v. Lopez* did not hold that there was such a right in the U.S. Constitution, but rather that once a state (Ohio) established such a right, it could not take that right away without due process of law. Nonetheless, if the U.S. Supreme Court or state courts dealing with state law declare that *Goss v. Lopez* holds that there is a constitutional right to a public education, then that principle becomes the law, regardless of the actual language of the prior case. Because all states provide public education, the distinction is largely academic, but the point here is that judicial statements of law are not always taken literally in the way that statutes are. Because judicial decisions are narrowly framed by reference to particularized disputes, the rules they express frequently require further refinement and explanation when used as precedent for subsequent cases.

This distinction may be shown more simply by the difference in attitude of a court in dealing with legislation as opposed to judicial precedent. The court "interprets" statutes, that is, attempts to determine the meaning of the words and phrases in the statute, whereas the specific rules laid down in cases are examined to determine the underlying principles on which they are based. For example, in *Goss v. Lopez*, the majority concluded with the statement:

> We should also make it clear that we have addressed ourselves solely to the short suspension, not exceeding 10 days. Longer suspensions or expulsions for the remainder of the school term, or permanently, may require more formal procedures.

In so stating, the court made its ruling quite limited, leaving clarification for future cases. Such an imprecise approach would be unacceptable for legislation. The end result of legislation is the enactment of written laws with an effective date and publication in the statute books. From the lawyer's point of view, the quality of legislation is measured by its clarity and lack of ambiguity. Because lawyers must be able to predict the outcomes of their clients' disputes, carefully framed statutes are an important aid. But legislators are not clairvoyant; they cannot predict every future scenario and provide for every possibility. Numerous cases arise in which the applicability of a statute to a particular case is unclear. A court may ultimately be asked to define the statute with regard to its application to a real-life dispute. Keep in mind, however, that when statutes are later found to be faulty or unclear, the legislature is free to amend or change the statute to reflect its intent.

The *Ponder* case reflects a fundamental difference between legislative and adjudicative functions in our political system, but it also reveals an interesting facet of the history of family law. In England, prior to American independence, family law matters were handled by ecclesiastical courts. There was no divorce in the modern sense, although a cumbersome procedure involving common law courts and an act of Parliament could result in a legal divorce. It was rare and, practically speaking, available only to men of influence and power. Because the United States did not incorporate ecclesiastical courts into the legal system, family law eventually fell within the courts of equity (see Chapter 6 for a discussion of courts of law and equity) rather than the common law courts. In the meantime, several state legislatures borrowed from the English practice of legislative divorce and passed special acts divorcing married couples. In the twentieth century, state legislatures have regulated marriage and divorce through statute, and the courts have assumed the task of granting divorces and determining the rights of divorcing parties. When *Ponder v. Graham* was decided, this separation of function was still evolving.

The Legislative Process

Although individual states are free to regulate and order the process of lawmaking, we find a common pattern by which principles are enacted into law. The following discussion describes a formal political process. It does not take into account the influence on legislation of informal political activities, the conflicts inherent in the two-party system, lobbying, interest groups, constituencies, and the like, because their interaction varies from issue to issue and locality to locality.

The hallmark of the legislative process is discussion and debate. (Note that their absence was criticized implicitly in the legislative divorce that the Supreme Court of Florida invalidated in *Ponder v. Graham*.) Passage of a bill into law ultimately requires open debate within the legislative body, which may be quite extensive with complex or controversial legislation, or quite brief with laws on which there is a general consensus or lack of interest.

Among the many problems that arise in our society, some come to the attention of lawmakers as problems that may be helped by the enactment of laws. Typically, legislators serve on legislative committees that deal with a defined area of interest. These committees are assigned to conduct an examination of proposed legislation and frame the law. In studying the problem, the committee collects a wide range of data and information and often conducts hearings on the subject. The purpose is to frame the legislation in the best way to solve the underlying problem, and this is best accomplished if legislators are fully informed about the problem so they can estimate the effectiveness of the solution. Each legislature has rules by which the proposed legislation reaches the floor of the legislature for open debate and vote. All states except Nebraska have a **bicameral** legislature modeled on the U.S. Senate and House of Representatives; the different views of these two bodies often require compromise for passage of a law.

bicameral   Referring to a legislature with two bodies, such as a House of Representatives and a Senate; only Nebraska has a single, or *unicameral*, legislature.

William G. PONDER, Executor of Archibald Graham, Appellant

v.

Mary GRAHAM, Appellee
4 Fla. 23 (1851)

[Mary Graham was not satisfied with the provisions made for her by her husband, Archibald Graham, in his will, and petitioned to take her **dower** right to one-third interest in his estate in lieu of the will. Ponder was appointed under the will to distribute Archibald's estate and challenged Mary's right on the grounds that she was not lawfully married to Archibald. The jury found for Mary and the court awarded her a one-third interest in Archibald's real estate.]

The facts of the case are succinctly these: The respondent, then Mary Buccles, about the year 1820, in South Carolina, intermarried with one Solomon Canady. Some time afterwards, they removed to, and resided in Georgia, but soon, in consequence of domestic dissensions, separated. Mary went to reside with Graham, a bachelor, and continued to live with him, under circumstances from which an adulterous **cohabitation** might be inferred.

In 1832, and while the said cohabitation continued, a bill was passed by the Legislative Council of the then Territory of Florida, entitled "An act for the relief of Mary Canady."

By this act, the Legislative Council, for the cause expressed in the preamble, assumed to judge and declare that the said Mary Graham was thereby divorced from her said husband, Solomon, and that the bonds of matrimony subsisting between them, were thereby to be entirely and absolutely dissolved, as if the same had never been solemnized. . . . There does not appear to have been any petition, **affidavit**, or proofs—a reference to a committee to ascertain the facts, or any notice to the absent husband. In 1834, the cohabitation between Mary and the testator still subsisting, the ceremony of marriage is celebrated between them, and from the time up to the period of the testator's death, which occurred in 1848, he lived with her, and acknowledged her as his wife, and in his will he provides for her by that name, and in that relation.

* * *

The main question raised in this case, as to the power of a Legislative body, *as such*, to grant divorces, is not altogether a new one. It has been investigated by some of the American Courts, and grave constitutional questions have been necessarily involved in the discussion; and yet the question still remains an open one—opinions clashing—nothing settled. . . .

No one doubts the right of the people by their constitution, to invest the power in the Legislature, or any where else; but the question is, when the constitution is silent on the subject, in what department of government does this authority rest? [M]uch, if not the whole difficulty, has arisen from overlooking some of the great principles which enter into the constitutional government of the States, and from not preserving the obvious distinction between legislative and judicial functions—by confounding the *right* which a legislative body has to pass *general laws* on the subject of divorce, with the *power* of dissolving the marriage *contract*.

* * *

[The court goes on to dispute the notion that the English Parliament granted divorces, noting that both ecclesiastical courts and common law courts were required to rule on a divorce before it went for approval by the House of Lords, which served as the English supreme court as well as a legislative body.]

In every respect in which I have been able to see this case, I can find no reason to sustain the act of the legislature. It appears by the record, that the parties were domiciled in the State of Georgia, where, it is alleged, the desertion and ill treatment occurred. The wife, living with the testator, Graham, removed to Florida—while the husband returned to Carolina, his former residence. The bill was introduced into the legislature one day, and passed the next. It is very clear that this divorce would not be recognized

(continued)

(continued)

by the courts of Georgia or Carolina, were any rights asserted under it in those States. . . .

I am, therefore, of opinion that the act of the Legislative Council of February 11th, 1832,

was in conflict with the organic law of Florida and the Constitution of the United States, and is, therefore, void.

Per Curiam—Let the judgment of the court below be reversed.

Case Questions

1. What does Mary Graham get as a result of this decision?
2. What are the relative powers of legislature and court with regard to divorce?

Case Glossary

dower   Property interests acquired in a husband's estate upon marriage. At old common law, a wife was entitled to one-third of her husband's real property upon his death. Today husband and wife have equal rights as surviving spouses, but these vary from state to state.

cohabitation   Living together in a marital-like relationship. Sometimes simply refers to a sexual relationship.

affidavit   A statement in writing sworn to before a person authorized to administer an oath.

The process is quite different from adjudication, in that the legislators must view the law in its general effect for the future, taking into consideration the effects on all who may be subject to the law. Enactment into law makes a public record and serves as notice to the public of the requirements of the law.

Judicial Invalidation of Legislation

Although the courts are bound to uphold legislation, there are two grounds on which courts have struck down legislation:

1. *Defective procedure.* The passage of the law may have been procedurally defective as measured by state law. Because our legislatures have been operating for many decades, the legal requisites of statutory enactment are well known and generally orderly, so procedural challenges are uncommon.

2. *Unconstitutionality.* The law itself may violate principles of state or federal constitutions. Statutes may also be declared unconstitutional in substance rather than procedure. A statute may be unconstitutional "on its face," meaning that a careful reading of the statute reveals that it violates some constitutional prohibition; or a statute may be unconstitutional in its effects or applications, which is more difficult to establish.

Judicial Deference to Legislation

Our constitutional system allocates legislative powers to Congress and authority to decide cases and "controversies" to the federal judiciary. This constitutional mandate has been followed by state constitutions so that the principle of separation of legislative and judicial functions is a fundamental part of our legal system. Inherent in this scheme is the notion that legislatures make law and courts interpret and enforce them.

The *Papachristou* case held a Jacksonville, Florida, vagrancy ordinance unconstitutional both on its face and in its potential for abuse by the police, an abuse made apparent from the facts of the various parties to the case. Note that local legislative bodies, such as a county commission or a city council, enact legislation, commonly called **ordinances,** which have the force of law and are subject to the same constitutional requirements as state and federal statutes. The principal challenge to the ordinance was based on the principle of **void for vagueness,** which applies to a statute that "fails to give a person of ordinary intelligence fair notice that his contemplated conduct is forbidden by the statute." This principle is based on the notion that statutes serve as public notice of the conduct required by law. If a law cannot be understood as written, it does not furnish notice. The void-for-vagueness doctrine is derived from the constitutional requirement in the Fourteenth Amendment that no state shall "deprive any person of life, liberty, or property, without due process of law."

The Jacksonville ordinance included peculiar language that came from much earlier English poor laws used to control the working class:

ordinance Legislation at the local level, typically, city councils, county commissions.

void for vagueness A constitutional principle of substantive due process that is used to invalidate legislation that fails to give a person of ordinary intelligence fair notice that his contemplated conduct is forbidden by the statute.

> Rogues and vagbonds, or dissolute persons who go about begging, common gamblers, persons who use juggling or unlawful games or plays, common drunkards, common night thieves, pilferers or pickpockets, traders in stolen property, lewd, wanton and lascivious persons, keepers of gambling places, common railers and brawlers, persons wandering or strolling around from place to place without any lawful purpose or object, habitual loafers, disorderly persons, persons neglecting all lawful business and habitually spending their time by frequenting houses of ill fame, gaming houses, or places where alcoholic beverages are sold or served, persons able to work but habitually living upon the earnings of their wives or minor children shall be deemed vagrants and, upon conviction in the Municipal court shall be punished as provided for Class D offenses. (Jacksonville Ordinance Code § 26–57.)

This does not abolish the common law system, which is still held in high esteem. Nevertheless, legislatures have surpassed the courts as the major source of new law. The evolution of a complex society and legal system in America brought these two legal institutions into direct and frequent confrontation. The separation of powers and the self-imposed custom of judicial restraint ultimately resulted in judicial subservience to statutes. If a statute is procedurally correct and constitutional in substance, American courts are bound to enforce it. Individual judges and courts have expressed dislike for particular statutes at the same time that they have upheld them. If the legislature passes a "bad" law, it is the job of the legislature, not the courts, to revise the law. Courts often send

Margaret PAPACHRISTOU et al.,
Petitioners,

v.

CITY OF JACKSONVILLE
405 U.S. 156 (1972)

The facts are stipulated. Papachristou and Calloway are white females. Melton and Johnson are black males. Papachristou was enrolled in a job-training program sponsored by the State Employment Service at Florida Junior College in Jacksonville. Calloway was a typing and shorthand teacher at a state mental institution located near Jacksonville. She was the owner of the automobile in which the four defendants were arrested. Melton was a Vietnam war veteran who had been released from the Navy after nine months in a veterans' hospital. On the date of his arrest he was a part-time computer helper while attending college as a full-time student in Jacksonville. Johnson was a tow-motor operator in a grocery chain warehouse and was a lifelong resident of Jacksonville.

At the time of their arrest the four of them were riding in Calloway's car on the main thoroughfare in Jacksonville. They had left a restaurant owned by Johnson's uncle where they had eaten and were on their way to a night club. The arresting officers denied that the racial mixture in the car played any part in the decision to make the arrest. The arrest, they said, was made because the defendants had stopped near a used-car lot which had been broken into several times. There was, however, no evidence of any breaking and entering on the night in question.

Of these four charged with "prowling by auto" none had been previously arrested except Papachristou who had once been convicted of a municipal offense.

* * *

[The court goes on to describe each of the arrests of the several petitioners—including those in companion cases, which were consolidated upon appeal—none of whom were engaged in conduct that would be criminal except for the ordinance.] . . . [Heath and his companion] and the automobile were searched. Although no contraband or incriminating evidence was found, they were both arrested, Heath being charged with being a "common thief" because he was reputed to be a thief. The codefendant was charged with "loitering" because he was standing in the driveway, an act which the officers admitted was done only at their command.

* * *

This ordinance is void-for-vagueness, both in the sense that it "fails to give a person of ordinary intelligence fair notice that his contemplated conduct is forbidden by the statute," *United States v. Harriss,* 347 U.S. 612, 617, and because it encourages arbitrary and erratic arrests and convictions.

Living under a rule of law entails various suppositions, one of which is that "[all persons] are entitled to be informed as to what the State commands or forbids."

* * *

The Jacksonville ordinance makes criminal activities which by modern standards are normally innocent. "Nightwalking" is one. . . .

"[P]ersons able to work but habitually living upon the earnings of their wives and minor children"—like habitually living "without visible means of support"—might implicate unemployed pillars of the community who have married rich wives.

"[P]ersons able to work but habitually living upon the earnings of their wives or minor children" may also embrace unemployed people out of the labor market, by reason of a recession or disemployed by reason of technological or so-called structural displacements.

* * *

Another aspect of the ordinance's vagueness appears when we focus, not on the lack of notice given a potential offender, but on the effect of the unfettered discretion it places in the hands of the Jacksonville police. . . .

A direction by a legislature to the police to arrest all "suspicious" persons would not pass constitutional muster. A vagrancy prosecution may be merely the cloak for a conviction which could not be obtained on the real but undisclosed grounds for the arrest. . . .

The Jacksonville ordinance cannot be squared with our constitutional standards and is plainly unconstitutional.

Reversed.

Case Questions

1. What was the purpose of the Jacksonville ordinance?
2. Why did this decision invalidate vagrancy statutes throughout the United States?
3. What constitutional provision supports the void-for-vagueness doctrine?

strong messages to the legislature by way of their written decisions, but the legislature may or may not heed these messages.

In the evolutionary process of defining legislative and judicial functions, legislative bodies have also been subject to certain constraints. Although legislatures enact laws and even provide for the means of enforcement by establishing and funding regulatory, judicial, and law enforcement agencies, the task of enforcement is not a legislative function. The courts are the final arbiters of disputes that arise under the laws, whether common law or legislation. The power of the legislature to make the rules is counterbalanced by the power of the judiciary to interpret and apply them. It is not uncommon for a court to give lip service to the language of a statute at the same time that its interpretation of the statute makes serious inroads into its intended purpose. Lawmaking and interpretation take place in a political, social, and economic environment that is often more influential than legal technicalities or even the Constitution.

Statutory Interpretation

rules of construction
A tradition of customs for statutory interpretation; **construe** is the verb from which the noun *construction* is derived and is very close in meaning to *interpret*.

For the legal practitioner, the most important problem with legislation is interpretation. Over the course of many years, a number of principles have been developed to guide the courts in resolving disputes over the meaning of statutes. The principles governing statutory interpretation are commonly called **rules of construction,** referring to the manner in which courts are to **construe** the meaning of statutes. The overriding principle governing statutory interpretation is to determine the intent of the legislature and give force to that intent. The rest of this section discusses some of the rules and priorities employed to further this goal.

Legislative Intent

legislative intent
That which the legislature wanted or intended to achieve when it enacted a statute; the determination of which is the goal of the court when the language of a statute is in doubt.

The underlying purpose behind statutory construction is the search to determine **legislative intent.**

The Plain Meaning Rule

plain meaning rule

A rule of statutory construction that states that if the language of a statute is unambiguous, the terms of the statute should be construed according to their ordinary meaning.

This rule can actually be used to ~~evade~~ *avoid* legislative intent. The **plain meaning rule** states simply that if the language of a statute is unambiguous and its meaning clear, the terms of the statute should be construed and applied according to their ordinary meaning. Behind this rule is the assumption that the legislature understood the meaning of the words it used and expressed its intent thereby. This rule operates to restrain the court from substituting its notion of what the legislature *really* meant if the meaning is already clear.

The application of the plain meaning rule may in fact undermine legislative intent. Although legislation is usually carefully drafted, language is by its nature susceptible to ambiguity, distortion, or simple lack of clarity. Because legislation is designed to control disputes that have not yet arisen, the "perfect" statute requires a degree of clairvoyance absent in the ordinary human being, including legislators, so that a statute may apply to a situation not foreseen by the legislators, who might have stated otherwise had they imagined such a situation.

The plain meaning rule obviates the need to pursue a lengthy inquiry into intent. Consider the nature of the legislative process. First, legislative intent is difficult to determine. The final product of the legislative process, the statute, would thus seem to be the best evidence of legislative intent. Legislatures are composed of numerous members who intend different things. In many instances, legislators do not even read the laws for which they vote. To believe there is a single legislative intent is to ignore reality. Many statutes are the result of compromise, the politics of which are not a matter of public record and cannot be accurately determined by a court. The precise language of the statute, then, is the best guide to intent. If, in the eyes of the legislature, the court errs in its application of the statute, the legislature may revise the statute for future application.

Limitations on the Plain Meaning Rule

Adherence to the plain meaning rule is neither blind nor simple-minded. A statute that is unambiguous in its language may be found to conflict with other statutes. Statutes are typically enacted in "packages," as part of a legislative effort to regulate a broad area of concern. Thus, alimony is ordinarily defined in several statutes embraced within a package of statutes covering divorce, which in turn may be part of a statutory chapter on domestic relations. The more comprehensive the package, the more likely some of its provisions may prove to be inconsistent. A sentence that seems unambiguous may be ambiguous in relation to a paragraph, a section, or a chapter.

Language must thus be interpreted in its context. In fact, this principle often operates to dispel ambiguity. Comprehensive statutes commonly begin with a preamble or introductory section stating the general purpose of the statutes collected under its heading. This statement of purpose is intended to avoid an overly technical interpretation of the statutes that could achieve results contrary to the general purpose.

uncertainty

The preamble is frequently followed by a section defining terms used in the statutes. This, too, limits the application of the plain meaning rule, but in a different way: The definitions pinpoint terms that have technical or legal significance to avoid what might otherwise be a nontechnical, ordinary interpretation.

On occasion, a provision in a statute may turn out to defeat the purpose of the statute in a particular set of circumstances; the court is then faced with the problem of giving meaning to the purpose of the statute or the language of the clause within the statute. In *Texas & Pacific Railway v. Abilene Cotton Oil Co.*, 204 U.S. 426 (1907), the U.S. Supreme Court was called upon to interpret the Interstate Commerce Act, which set up the Interstate Commerce Commission (ICC) and made it responsible for setting rates and routes for the railroads. A disgruntled shipper sued the railroad under an old common law action for "unreasonable rates." The Act had a provision, commonly included in legislation, stating that the Act did not abolish other existing remedies. However, the court reasoned that if persons were able to bring such actions any time they were unhappy with the rates, the rate structures established by the ICC would have little meaning, depending instead upon what a particular jury or judge considered reasonable. The court limited the effect of the clause and argued that Congress could not have intended for the clause to be used to completely undermine the purpose of the Act; "in other words, the act cannot be held to destroy itself."

The court will not ordinarily disregard the plain meaning of a statute, especially in a criminal case.

Aids to Statutory Interpretation

Single statutes do not exist in a legal vacuum. They are part of a section, chapter, and the state or federal code as a whole. Historically, statutes developed as an adjunct to the traditional common law system that established law from custom.

Like case law, statutory construction relies heavily on *authority*. Interpretation is a formal reasoning process in the law, which in our legal tradition depends less on the creative imagination than on sources of the law. In the reasoning process, an overriding judicial policy insists that the body of laws be as consistent and harmonious as possible. It was for this reason that the court held in *Abilene Oil*, that the statute "cannot be held to destroy itself."

If a clause seems to conflict with its immediate statutory context, it will be interpreted so as to further the general legislative intent, if such can be ascertained. In a sense, this is simply intelligent reading; words and phrases take their meaning from their contexts. The principle can be extended further, however. Statutes taken from different parts of a state or federal code may be found to conflict. The court will interpret the language to harmonize the inconsistency whenever possible. Legislative intent may become quite obscure in such situations because the presumption that the legislature meant what it said is confronted by the problem that it said something different elsewhere. In reconciling the conflict, the court may use its sense of overall legislative policy and even the general history of the law, including the common law. The obvious solution to these conflicts is action by the legislature to rewrite the statutes to resolve the inconsistencies and provide future courts with a clear statement of intent.

Strict Construction

Words by their nature have different meanings and nuances. Shades of meaning change in the context of other words and phrases. Tradition has determined that certain situations call for broad or liberal constructions, whereas others call for narrow or **strict construction,** meaning that the statute in question will not be expanded beyond a very literal reading of its meaning.

strict construction
Narrowly interpreted by a very literal reading of the statutes; criminal statutes, in particular, are *strictly construed.*

"Criminal statutes are strictly construed." This rule of construction has its source in the evolution of our criminal law, in particular, in the many rights we afford those accused of crime. Out of fear of abuse of the criminal justice system, we have provided protection for the accused against kangaroo courts, overzealous prosecutors, and corrupt police. It is an accepted value of our legal system that the innocent must be protected even if it means that the guilty will sometimes go free.

Although many basic crimes, such as murder, burglary, and assault, were formulated by the common law in the distant past, today most states do not recognize common law crimes but insist that crimes be specified by statute. We consider it unjust for someone to be charged with a crime if the conduct constituting the crime has not been clearly prohibited by statute. Conversely, if a statute defines certain conduct as criminal, "ignorance of the law excuses no one" (*ignorantia legis neminem excusat*). If public notice of prohibited conduct is an essential ingredient of criminal law, strict construction is its logical conclusion. If conduct is not clearly within the prohibitions of a statute, the court will decline to expand its coverage.

A second category of statutes that are strictly construed is expressed by the principle that "statutes in derogation of the common law are strictly construed." State legislatures frequently pass laws that alter, modify, or abolish traditional common law rules. The principle that such changes are narrowly construed not only shows respect for the common law, but also reflects the difference between legislative and judicial decision making. Whereas judicial decisions explain the reasons for the application of a particular rule, allowing for later interpretations and modifications, statutes are presumed to mean what they say. The intent of the legislature is embodied in the language of the statute itself, which if well drafted can be seen to apply to the situations for which it was intended.

A statute should stand alone, its meaning clear. Unfortunately, this is not always possible. If there is some question of meaning, a statute that appears to conflict with prior principles of the common law can be measured against that body of law. In other words, the court has recourse to a wealth of time-tested principles and need not strain to guess legislative intent. This is particularly helpful when the statute neglects to cover a situation that was decided in the past. If the statute is incomplete or ambiguous, the Court will resolve the dispute by following the common law.

Legislative History

legislative history
Recorded events that provide a basis for determining the legislative intent underlying a statute enacted by a legislature; the sources for legislative history include legislative committee hearings and debates on the floor of the legislature.

If the application of a statute remains unclear in its language and in its written context, the intent of the legislature may be ascertained by researching the statute's **legislative history**. This includes the records and documents concerning the process whereby the statute became law. The purpose and application of the statute may sometimes become clear with these additional materials. Several committees may have held hearings or discussions on the law during its enactment that have become part of the public record and demonstrate the concerns of legislators and the reasons for enactment. Inferences may be made based on different drafts of the statute and the reasons expressed for the changes. If two houses of the legislature began with different language, the final compromise language may also suggest conclusions. Legislative debates may similarly clarify legislative intent.

Research into legislative history can be a lengthy process involving extensive analytical skills; but an examination of the entire process for a particular enactment will tend to dispel plausible, but incorrect, interpretations of legislative intent. The informal politics of negotiation and compromise, however, are not always reflected in the record, so the reasons for the final decisions on the language of the statute may remain obscure.

A Caveat on Statutory Interpretation

We have touched here on only a few of a multitude of rules of interpretation employed by the courts in resolving issues of statutory meaning. In fact, there are so many rules and exceptions to them that the courts enjoy considerable freedom to select the rules that support the interpretation that a given court or judge favors. For example, any specific rule may be avoided by declaring that it conflicts with the primary intent of the legislature. There is a subjective element to this analysis that provides a court great discretion.

Courts ordinarily attempt to give force to legislative intent. They are assisted by a great variety of technical rules of construction that have been developed in the precedents of prior judges faced with the problem of statutory meaning. But judges differ in their thinking from legislators. They not only deal with abstract rules, but on a daily basis must also resolve difficult problems with justice and fairness. Very few judges will blindly follow a technical rule if the result would be manifestly unfair. They can justly reason that the legislature never intended an unjust result. When arguing the interpretation of a statute, a lawyer or paralegal must keep in mind the importance of persuading the court that the proposed interpretation is not only correct but also fair and just.

Statute and Precedent

It would be a mistake to think that the existence of a statute suspends the common law principle of precedent. Although a statute may supersede a common law rule, the court's interpretation of the statute is law. When researching a case covered by statute, it is not enough to look merely to the statute. One must look at the cases that have interpreted the statute. In many instances, the application of a statute to a client's case is clear; if any doubt exists, judicial decisions must be examined.

The *Cox* case involves two distinct but common problems in interpreting statutes. Cox was convicted of selling crack cocaine within 1,000 feet of a school. In order to prove the elements of the crime, the prosecution must prove the existence of a school; since criminal statutes are strictly construed, there is no getting around this requirement. Normally, this fact would be easy to prove, but the prosecution was careless. In criminal cases especially, the court compares the facts to the statute and if it does not fit, the law cannot be applied. Cox was not home free, however, since he was still convicted of selling cocaine.

peremptory challenge
Each side in a trial is allowed a specific number of exclusions of individual jurors without the necessity of giving reasons for the exclusions.

The second problem involved the number of **peremptory challenges** Cox was entitled to use because he came under Florida's habitual offender law, which meant that his conviction could mean life imprisonment. It is clear that he would have ten challenges under Florida law if he were tried for a capital crime, like murder, but only six for noncapital felonies, such as selling crack cocaine. Since his conviction could mean life imprisonment, is he entitled to six challenges or ten? The Florida Statutes do not contemplate this detail; the court looks to prior interpretations of the statutes for guidance.

Anthony COX
v.
STATE of Florida
District Court of Appeal of Florida, First District
764 So.2d 711 (2000)

On January 12, 1999, appellant was charged in a two-count information with: Count I—sale, manufacture or delivery of a controlled substance within 1,000 feet of a school, contrary to section 893.13(1)c)l, Florida Statutes; and Count II—actual or constructive possession of cocaine contrary to the provisions of section 893.13(6)(a), Florida Statutes. . . .

During the jury selection process, appellant's counsel advised the trial court that he believed both the state and the defense were entitled to ten peremptory challenges, because appellant was subject to a sentence of life imprisonment by virtue of the habitual felony offender statute. The trial court indicated each side would have six challenges, unless either defense counsel or the prosecutor could produce legal authority to the contrary. . . . Counsel urged that pursuant to the plain meaning of rule 3.350(a)(1), of the Florida Rules of Criminal Procedure, a defendant charged with an offense punishable by death or imprisonment for life is entitled to ten peremptory challenges during the jury selection process. The trial court adhered to its original ruling. In doing so, the court reasoned that appellant had been charged with a plain first-degree felony, and was subject to a life sentence only because of the habitual offender statute.

At trial, the state adduced evidence that appellant sold crack cocaine to undercover narcotics detectives. The state also adduced evidence that a structure known as the Academy of Excellence was located across the street at a distance of 137 feet from the area where the drug transaction took place. However, the state failed to adduce evidence which established that the Academy of Excellence was a school at the time of the subject offense. . . .

The statute applicable, section 893.13(1)(c), Florida Statutes, provides in pertinent part:

(c) Except as authorized by this chapter, it is unlawful for any person to sell, manufacture, or deliver, or possess with intent to sell, manufacture, or deliver, a controlled substance in, on, or within 1,000 feet of the real property comprising a child care facility as defined in s. 402.302 or a public or private elementary, middle, or secondary school between the hours of 6 a.m. and 12 a.m. . . . .

It is incumbent upon the state to introduce competent evidence of each element of the offense charged. If the evidence of an element of the offense charged does not conform to the date of the offense alleged in the information, the defendant's motion for judgment of acquittal should be granted. . . .

In *McKinney v. State,* 640 So.2d 1183 (Fla. 2d DCA 1994), the court approved the trial court's **judicial notice** that Lakeland Christian School is a school for purposes of section 893.13(1)(c), Florida Statutes, finding such notice authorized by section 90.202(11) and (12). The court noted that it had published at least one opinion in which Lakeland Christian School had been the school relied upon for a conviction under section 893.13(1)(c). . . . The court recognized that the status of the school had been established previously in another case and was well known within the jurors' community. . . .

Appellant in this case concedes the state presented evidence which established that two years before the offense charged, the Academy of Excellence was a school within the meaning of section 893.13(1(c). Nevertheless, the only competent evidence that the academy was a school in December 1998, when the offense occurred, consisted of an officer's testimony that he observed children playing outside the building with adults present. Unlike the situation in *McKinney,* here the state has not directed our attention to, nor has our independent research revealed, a prior case from this court which recognized the Academy of Excellence as a school. Further, we infer from the appellate record that the school status of the Academy of Excellence is not common knowledge within the territorial jurisdiction of Duval County Circuit Court.

Therefore, we conclude the state failed to prove an essential element of the charged offense, i.e., that the offense was committed within 1,000 feet of a school. Since the state proved appellant committed the offense of sale of cocaine, the conviction for sale of cocaine within 1,000 feet of a school must be vacated and remanded with directions to enter a judgment of conviction and sentence for sale of cocaine, in accordance with the provisions of section 924.34, Florida Statutes.

As to the second issue, we affirm the trial court's ruling limiting appellant and the state to six peremptory challenges each. The statute applicable, section 913.08, provides in pertinent part:

(1) The state and the defendant shall each be allowed the following number of peremptory challenges:

(a) Ten, if the offense charged is punishable by death or imprisonment for life;

(b) Six, if the offense charged is punishable by imprisonment for more than 12 months but is not punishable by death or imprisonment for life;

(c) Three for all other offenses. . . .

The argument raised by appellant on this point has been considered and rejected by the second, third, and fourth district courts of appeal. [Cites cases from each district] In each of the cited cases, the defendant maintained that because he was charged with a first degree felony which became punishable by life imprisonment by virtue of the state's decision to seek habitual offender sentencing, he was entitled to ten peremptory challenges. In [the *Inmon* case], the court focused on the penalty attributable to the charged offense, rather than the possible penalties attributable to habitual offender enhancement. See *Inmon,* 383 So.2d at 1104.

(continued)

(continued)

The third and fourth districts agreed with the rationale expressed in *Inmon*. . . . Among other things, the courts were persuaded that the respective defendants' interpretation would lead to inconsistent treatment, because a defendant whose notice to habitualize was filed before jury selection would receive ten peremptory challenges, while a defendant who received notice later in the proceedings would be limited to six peremptory challenges . . .

[A]ppellant urges this court to reject the prior rulings of those courts, and find that a defendant subject to a life sentence by virtue of the habitual offender statute should be entitled to ten peremptory challenges.

In our view, appellant has failed to show a flaw in the reasoning and the interpretation adopted by the [cases].

. . . Therefore, appellant cannot prevail on this issue.

Accordingly, we reverse the conviction and sentence for sale of cocaine within 1,000 feet of a school, and remand this cause with directions to enter a conviction for sale of cocaine and to impose sentence accordingly. In all other respects, the trial court's rulings are affirmed.

Case Questions

1. Why was Cox not convicted of sale of a controlled substance within 1000 feet of a school?
2. By virtue of his prior criminal record, Cox could be sentenced to life imprisonment as an habitual offender and the statute says that a defendant is allowed ten peremptory challenges "if the offense charged is punishable by death or imprisonment for life." Why was Cox only allowed six peremptory challenges?

Case Glossary

judicial notice   The act of a judge in recognizing the existence or truth of certain facts without bothering to make one side in a lawsuit prove them.

Summary

In modern times, legislation has replaced the common law as the major source of changes in the law. Legislative bodies enact laws to be applied generally to future situations rather than deciding existing disputes, which is the task of the courts. Unless they are procedurally defective or unconstitutional, statutes must be enforced by the court without changing or distorting their language. For cases in which the application of a statute is unclear, the courts have developed a multitude of rules of construction with the purpose of ascertaining the intent of the legislature. Once a higher court has interpreted the meaning of a statute, that decision becomes precedent for it and lower court. The legislature always has the option of rewriting the statute for clarification or revision, or if it objects to the interpretation the court has given it.

Scenario

As president of the faculty senate for Denizen College, a small liberal arts college in Ohio, you are charged with writing new rules for disciplining students for plagiarism, which has been a growing problem at the college, apparently a nationwide tendency. You will chair a committee that will draw up new rules on the subject of plagiarism that will be submitted to the full senate for discussion and debate and the final product will be sent to the college president for her approval. To prevent becoming mired in endless debate, you have decided to propose rules for the committee to consider. Legislatively, you have two issues: (1) Define plagiarism in a way that makes it clearly identifiable and gives notice to students and faculty alike as to what constitutes plagiarism—the substantive aspect; and (2) Outline a procedure to follow when plagiarism is suspected, so that a faculty member discovering plagiarism can follow to confront the student and present the case to the college, including appropriate remedies and penalties—the procedural aspect.

In charging you with these tasks, the president has told you of problems other colleges and universities have encountered with this problem. In particular, she noted the experience with one school that allowed students to hire attorneys to represent them in plagiarism hearings with the result that students who could afford attorneys inevitably won their cases because either the rules or the procedures were sufficiently vague to make enforcement a clear violation of due process of law. While due process limitations in these situations do not require attorneys or full-blown trial-type hearings, the inclusion of attorneys tends to convert the process into a legal one. Since yours is a private college, the issue of due process is much weaker than for a state school acting as an agent of the state; it lurks in the background because of a state charter of incorporation and state and federal funds.

In a private college, the issue normally becomes contractual. The old rule states simply that a student found to have plagiarized was subject to receiving a failing grade for the course in which it occurred or suspension from the college, at the discretion of a faculty committee convened to inquire into the accusations. The college attorney has advised the president that this rule is too vague to satisfy due process and fails as well as a contractual term if challenged by a competent attorney. At the very least, the president wants rules and procedures that demonstrate fair procedure for a student accused of plagiarism and can be included in the student conduct code to be read by all incoming students before enrolling in Denizen College so that they will receive notice of its requirements and also be construed as a contractual obligation for students, faculty, and the college.

In the proceedings, an attorney will represent neither the student nor the college. This does not mean that attorneys may not be consulted. Both the student and the college are entitled to consult attorneys about the rights involved, but all inquiries and hearings will be conducted without attorneys present. Naturally, recourse to the courts may be had by right; your rules will not preclude, but it is hoped that through a clear definition of plagiarism and fair procedure, the likelihood of a contest in court will be minimized.

You may utilize a student court or faculty board of inquiry or both. You must provide for a reasonable appeal process within the college.

Draw up the rules and procedures you will propose to your committee.

TRIAL AND APPELLATE COURTS

The Adversary Process

The American legal system is based on certain assumptions that are responsible for its organization and structure, its strengths and its weaknesses. The system is a competitive one that reflects the political process and the competitive market economy. In the legal arena, this competitive form is referred to as the **adversarial system.** Every legal system must assert justice as its primary goal in order to claim legitimacy. Our system maintains that justice can best be achieved on the basis of rules that provide a fair procedure for those engaged in a dispute. The procedure embodies a search for truth by allowing disputing parties to present their cases through partisan, legally competent agents before an impartial tribunal. The agents are duly licensed attorneys, and the impartial tribunal is composed of a disinterested judge and a disinterested jury.

The adversarial process has been likened to a game and a fight, but as a game it has serious consequences and as a fight it is controlled by numerous rules that attempt to make the fight fair and civilized. Whichever metaphor is used, the judge may be viewed as an "umpire," ensuring that the rules are followed and each party is treated with fairness.

Although there may be several parties to a lawsuit, there are only two sides. Each side is provided with equal opportunity to present its evidence and arguments and to challenge the evidence and arguments from the other side. It is to be expected that each side will present a very different picture of the dispute, but the underlying assumption is that objective observers will be able to come close to the truth of the events behind the dispute and that the judge, trained and

adversarial system
The U.S. legal system in which litigants, typically represented by attorneys, argue their respective sides in a dispute before an impartial judge and jury; often contrasted with an inquisitorial system in which an accused is questioned by officials without rights of defense in a relentless search for the truth.

100

experienced in the law, will be able to weigh the legal arguments of both sides and come to a correct application of the law in each case.

Critics of the adversarial system point to certain inherent weaknesses: the partisanship of the attorneys often operates to cloud the truth rather than reveal it; judges and juries are neither objective nor totally disinterested; the competitive market model reflects a patriarchal, elitist, capitalist bias that prevents litigants from obtaining equality before the law; the system is old-fashioned, awkward, and inefficient. There is some truth to all of these criticisms, yet the Anglo-American legal system has made remarkable achievements that have been out of reach for legal systems based on a different model.

Like any human institution, the legal system has its faults, but it has within it the means to diminish or eliminate its own weaknesses. A major means of correcting mistakes in the system lies in the appellate process, which provides the opportunity to litigants to challenge the propriety of the results of trial. Ambrose Bierce in his *Devil's Dictionary* defines *appeal* as "in law, to put the dice into the box for another throw." This is not quite true; the appellate process aims at rectifying serious mistakes made in the course of trial. The appellate courts are there to ensure that the rules of the game are enforced.

Fact and Law

To understand the difference between trial and appellate courts, an appreciation of the fact/law distinction is necessary. As the modern court system has developed, the functions of judge and jury have become distinct. The word **trial** refers to *trial of fact*; the factfinder at trial is also called the **trier of fact.** In jury cases, the jury is the trier of fact; if there is no jury (for example, if the parties have waived a jury trial), the judge, sometimes simply referred to as the *court*, is the trier of fact. The trier of fact determines, from the evidence presented, the facts of the case in dispute. Once the facts are determined, appropriate law is applied. Decision, declaration, and determination of the law are the sole province of the judge. The jury's factfinding is called the **verdict,** and upon the verdict the judge makes a **judgment,** which determines the respective rights and obligations of the parties.

Facts in a legal case must be distinguished from what is considered fact in the layperson's sense of the word and from what might be considered scientific fact. Although the purpose of trial is to get at facts and truth, neither of these is clear at the outset or there would be no need for a trial; if both parties agree to all the facts relevant to a case, there is nothing left to do but apply the law—no jury is necessary. In a trial, each side presents a different version of the facts. The jury, or the judge in a nonjury trial, must decide what actually happened based on inferences and conclusions drawn from the evidence. The jury (or judge) may believe one side and disbelieve the other, or it may conclude that the truth lies somewhere in between. In many cases, the truth is not readily apparent.

---

trial   A judicial examination, in accordance with the law, of a criminal or civil action. It is an "on-the-record hearing," which means the determination is to be made on the basis of what is presented in court. It is a trial of fact with judgment entered on the law.

trier of fact   Also called *factfinder*, the entity that determines fact in a trial. In a jury trial, the jury is entrusted with factfinding; in a bench trial, the judge necessarily must find the facts as well as make conclusions of law.

verdict   The factfinding by a jury; for example, in a civil case, the jury might find the defendant liable in a dollar amount; in a criminal case, the verdict is usually *guilty* or *not guilty* of each criminal charge.

judgment   The official decision of a court about the rights and claims of each side in a lawsuit; usually a final decision after trial based on findings of fact and making conclusions of law.

question of law
A question for the judge, i.e., a question as to the appropriate law to be applied, or the correct interpretation of the law.

question of fact
A question for the jury in a jury trial or for the judge in a bench trial. Fact questions are evidentiary questions of who, when, where, and what.

substitution of judgment The standard of review of conclusions of law made by a lower court.

prejudicial error
Mistakes made at trial that are sufficiently serious to prejudice the result. Also called **reversible error.**

clearly erroneous
The test or standard used at the appellate level to determine if *judicial* factfinding at trial constitutes prejudicial error. Highly deferential toward the trial court.

substantial evidence
The test or standard used at the appellate level to determine if *jury* factfinding at trial constitutes prejudicial error. Often used interchangeably with **clearly erroneous.**

Sometimes fact determinations are supported by very persuasive evidence, but sometimes they are not. Suppose, for example, two litigants were involved in a head-on collision, and each asserts that the other crossed the median line and caused the collision. Assuming one is telling the truth, how is the jury to determine the facts months after the accident? The jury would be very much aided by disinterested eyewitnesses who confirmed one version rather than the other. Expert witnesses may be called upon to reconstruct the accident by skidmarks, the position of the cars after the accident, and the nature of the injuries. But eyewitnesses and expert witnesses can be as equivocal as the participants. Jurors may rely on other inferences—the experience of the drivers, the evidence that one driver had been drinking, and the demeanor of the parties as witnesses (one may seem honest and sincere, the other furtive and evasive). The absolute truth may never be known, but the jury is obliged to draw conclusions about the facts. If standards of scientific proof of fact were required, cases could not be resolved.

Under the adversary system, then, the facts are assumed to be as concluded by the trier of fact. Even though inferences drawn by the trier of fact may differ from the absolute truth, the assumption of the legal system is that when impartial, reasonable persons deliberate about the facts, their conclusions are as close to the truth as possible and that the process of arriving at the facts is fair to both parties.

Distinguishing fact from law is not a simple matter. Generally facts are concerned with what happened—answers to questions of who, when, what, and how. These are questions or issues of fact. A question of law involves the application or meaning of law. As a rule of thumb, questions of law and fact are distinguished by whether a particular question requires legal training or knowledge. For example, whether or not the defendant in an auto accident/negligence case was drinking prior to the accident is a question requiring no special legal training. A judge is no better qualified to answer that question from the evidence presented than a layperson, thus identifying this as a question of fact. In contrast, the issue of whether particular evidence of the defendant's drinking is admissible in court is a question of law; the judge is trained and experienced in the rules of evidence and must decide which evidence may properly be presented and which is inadmissible.

The fact/law distinction is not important only for the assignment of labor between judge and jury; it can be critical on appeal. Once a trial has reached final judgment, a disappointed party may seek reversal on appeal. The appellate courts treat **questions of law** and **questions of fact** quite differently. Questions of law decided by the trial court judge are not treated deferentially by an appellate court that disagrees. For example, if the trial judge gave the jury an instruction that the appellate court concludes was an incorrect statement of the law, the appellate court would **substitute its judgment** for that of the trial court and order a new trial if the improper instructions were **prejudicial,** or **reversible, error.** Factfinding by judge or jury, however, is treated by the appellate court with great deference and will be overturned only if it is **clearly erroneous** or without **substantial evidence** to support it. This standard makes it extremely difficult to challenge factfinding on appeal.

Questions of law and questions of fact are not always distinct. For example, the meaning of words may be either a law or a fact question. The common

Label of the Standard	Issue	Deference Paid Trial Court or Jury
Substitution of judgement	Law	None—appellate court "substitutes its judgment" for that of trial court.
Clearly erroneous	Fact	Great deference—This is commonly applied to the trial judge's factfinding.
Substantial evidence	Fact	Great deference—When referring to jury factfinding, appellate courts rarely overturn findings of fact.

meaning of a word is a question of fact; the interpretation of a legal term is a question of law. Although judges may not be more competent than laypersons to define *tree*, *employee* may be used in either a legal sense or an everyday sense. So if *employee* is used in a statute, its meaning would seem to be a question of law. However, it may not have been used with any particular legal reference and may have been used simply as an ordinary term. Whether a person is an employee for the purposes of inclusion in a collective bargaining unit under the National Labor Relations Act could be treated as either a question of law or a question of fact. Who decides which it is? The judge, of course, or, as put by Isaacs: "Whether a particular question is to be treated as a question of law or a question of fact is not in itself a question of fact, but a highly artificial question of law" [22 *Col. L. Rev.* 1, 11–12 (1922)].

The *Kindle* case is an example of an appellate court reversing a trial court's factfinding. Note the short statute of limitations for bringing actions against local government. Note also the standard for mental incapacity, one resembling contractual capacity but different from criminal intent or insanity, as we shall see in later chapters.

Trials and Trial Courts

A trial is an "on-the-record" evidentiary hearing. *On the record* refers to the requirement that the facts be determined exclusively on the basis of evidence presented at trial. Evidence of disputed facts is presented by both sides. The plaintiff attempts to establish facts substantiating claims against the defendant, and the defendant attempts to counter the plaintiff's case by questioning and objecting to the plaintiff's evidence as well as presenting additional evidence. Evidence takes several forms, including witness testimony, **physical evidence,** and documents. The evidence forms the **record.** Naturally the jury will make factual inferences based on common sense and experience gained outside the trial, but it is improper for jurors to use knowledge of events that gave rise to the dispute acquired outside of the record. It would be improper, for instance, for a juror to visit the scene of the crime or ask questions of witnesses or bystanders.

physical evidence
Physical objects introduced as evidence, such as a gun, a lock, drugs, and so on.

record   All the evidence presented at trial, whether or not recorded.

What should the appellate court do when the record from the court below is insufficient? In the *Kingman* case, the trial court did not provide findings of fact on which the appellate court could determine the adequacy of factfinding. The trial court treated this case quite casually, apparently because it seemed a relatively routine exercise of the state's power to take private property for a public use (**eminent domain**). The only requirement placed on the state to obtain judicial approval was to show that the property was being taken for a "public use and necessity." It is usually a fairly easy task to get this rubber-stamped by the court. Apparently the trial judge gave his reasons for denial orally but did not make them part of the record.

eminent domain The power of the government to take private property for a public use, for which just compensation is required by the Constitution.

In re Martha KINDLE Claims Against City and County Employees, Agents and Officers for Damages Arising From Assault by Joseph Kindle
Supreme Court of South Dakota
509 N.W.2d 278 (1993)

Hand County, the City of Miller and agents and officers thereof appeal a trial court's order granting Martha Kindle's motion to extend the time for filing notice of a claim against a public entity or its employees. We reverse.

FACTS

On May 24, 1991, Martha Kindle (hereinafter Kindle) was abducted from her job at a Miller, South Dakota, day-care center by her estranged husband, Joseph Kindle. [Joseph Kindle beat Martha, stabbed her with a knife and threatened to kill her. He was arrested, charged with various crimes, and eventually pled guilty to kidnapping.]

Kindle sought to file an action against Hand County, the City of Miller and their agents and officers (hereinafter Defendants). Kindle asserted that city and county law enforcement officials had earlier promised her protection after she reported she had been raped, subjected to physical violence and threatened by her estranged husband. She claimed said officials still took no action to safeguard her before she was kidnapped and assaulted.

Under [state statute], in order to maintain a lawsuit against a public entity for an injury caused by that entity or its employee, a party is required to serve notice upon the entity within 180 days of the injury. Defendants did not receive notice by the time the statute of limitations . . . . Kindle moved the circuit court for an extension of time to serve notice. She claimed she had been mentally incapacitated by extreme fear, anxiety and post-traumatic stress syndrome during the time the statute of limitations was running.

The trial court held a hearing where both sides presented expert testimony as to mental incapacity. The court concluded that: "Mental incapacity . . . should be defined more narrowly than a condition where a person cannot generally make sound decisions concerning the general aspects of their life." It found Kindle was mentally incapacitated under the statute "to make any decisions concerning any claims she may have had against law enforcement officers connected with the assaults upon her" and ordered she be permitted to file notice on Defendants. This appeal followed.

DECISION

I. THE TRIAL COURT ERRED AS A MATTER OF LAW IN DEFINING MENTAL INCAPACITY . . . . The legal definition of "mental incapacity" is a question of law. . . .

Under South Dakota law, no action for damages may be maintained against a public entity or official unless written notice of the injury is given to that entity within 180 days of the injury.

[T]he 180-day notice requirement may be extended for up to two years if the injured party is a minor or mentally incapacitated. . . . There is no statutory definition of mental incapacity contained in [state statute chapter on liability for public officials]. Therefore, we must look to other statutory and case law to determine what the legislature intended when it used the term "mentally incapacitated."

This court has never decided a case dealing specifically with the definition of mental incapacity . . . . However, there is one recurrent and prevailing theme to cases dealing with mental incapacity, mental illness, mental infirmity, unsound mind, or mental impairment as justification to toll statutes of limitation—did the person understand the nature and consequences of his or her action? The analysis of whether a person meets this definition involves an examination of the person's conduct of his or her everyday affairs.

* * *

In determining whether a person comprehends the nature and effect of his or her actions, a trial court should examine all relevant facts and circumstances of a person's overall ability to function in society and comprehend and protect his or her legal rights.

* * *

Defendants attack the sufficiency of the evidence to support the trial court's findings on the question of Kindle's mental incapacity. We review a trial court's findings of fact under the clearly erroneous standard. We will not disturb the court's findings unless they are clearly erroneous; the question is whether, after a review of all the evidence, we are left with a definite and firm conviction that a mistake has been made. However, the findings of fact must support the conclusions of law.

* * *

The trial court found that Kindle was able to make decisions concerning the everyday functions of her life but had a tendency to avoid situations involving her abduction. These findings are not clearly erroneous based on the evidence presented. However, the evidence and findings are insufficient to support the trial court's legal conclusion that Kindle was "mentally incapacitated" under the test we have adopted.

Mental incapacity . . . means the failure to understand the nature and effect of one's actions. The trial court found Kindle possessed the overall ability to function in society. Kindle exercised her legal rights to the degree she consulted with her attorney, obtained a divorce, and cooperated in the criminal prosecution of Joseph Kindle. Additionally, she was represented by her divorce attorney during at least part of the time the statute of limitations was running. These findings are insufficient to support the legal conclusion that she was "mentally incapacitated". . . .

The order of the trial court is reversed.

Case Questions

1. What is the plaintiff claiming she was too mentally incapacitated to do?
2. Has the court enunciated a test for mental incapacity that would make it virtually impossible for someone in the plaintiff's circumstances to bring suit?
3. The 180-day limitation period for suits against a public entity is relatively short. Should this fact influence the interpretation of mental incapacity in this case?

The STATE of Washington, Petitioner,
v.
W. Kenneth KINGMAN
and Julia E. Kingman, his wife,
et al., Respondents
Supreme Court of Washington
Department 1 463 P.2d 638 (1970)

By writ of certiorari, the state seeks review of an order denying its petition for an order of public use and necessity.

* * *

It appears from briefs of counsel (a) that the land to be acquired is a 300 foot strip of waterfront approximately 150 feet wide between the public highway and Lake Chelan; . . . specifically, it is to preserve a beautiful view of Lake Chelan and the foothills beyond. Photographs illustrate the state's position.

Except for the phrase "good cause appearing," the trial court, in its order after trial, gives no reasons for denying the certificate of public use and necessity.

* * *

Here we run into a void. For some reason, which does not appear in the record, the trial court did not make and enter findings of fact and conclusions of law.

* * *

A judgment entered in a case tried to the court where findings are required, without findings of fact having been made, is subject to a motion to vacate within the time for the taking of an appeal. After vacation, the judgment shall not be re-entered. . . .

The order denying the petition for public use and necessity is set aside; the case is remanded for further proceedings not inconsistent with this opinion.

It is so ordered.

Case Questions

1. Why was the case remanded?
2. When should a court make and enter findings of fact and conclusions of law?

Jury Instructions

The jury is given detailed instructions by the judge about its functions in the lawsuit. Judges vary in their explanations of the proceedings before and during the trial, but the most important instructions are given to the jury at the close of the evidence as the jury prepares to deliberate its verdict. These instructions provide only as much explanation of the law as is needed for the jury to dispose of factual questions. For example, in a lawsuit for slander, the judge would instruct the jury about the facts it would need to find to hold the defendant liable for slander; namely: (1) the utterance alleged to be slanderous was communicated to a third party and (2) injured the reputation of the plaintiff. In addition, the judge would instruct the jury that if it found the statement to be true, the defendant would not be liable. The jury would also be instructed on what would constitute compensation for injuries sustained. The specifics of these instructions could vary considerably from case to case.

In short, the court delineates the facts the jury must decide in making its verdict according to the nature of the case, confining the jury to its factfinding function. When the jury reaches a consensus on the facts and presents the judge with its results, the judge makes conclusions of law and enters a judgment.

Before and during trial, the judge makes a series of decisions on the law, of which the most important concern motions to dismiss the lawsuit in favor of one of the parties, admission of evidence and the propriety of its presentation, and instructions to the jury. In each decision, the judge applies legal principles, which the judge could interpret or apply incorrectly. The correctness of the judge's rulings forms the basis for appeal.

Appellate Courts

appellate courts As distinguished from *trial courts*, appellate courts function primarily to correct errors of the lower, trial courts and do not ordinarily serve as factfinders. The two common forms of appellate courts are intermediate appellate courts, usually called courts of appeal(s), and the highest courts, usually called supreme courts.

The courts above the trial court level to which appeals may be taken are called **appellate courts.** The most common arrangement in the state hierarchy echoes that of the federal court system, with an intermediate appellate court and a court of last resort (e.g., Colorado Court of Appeals, Colorado Supreme Court). Some states have a two-tiered trial court system in which one court handles cases of lesser import, often limited by a dollar amount, and misdemeanor cases, whereas the other court has jurisdiction over felonies and civil cases above the specified dollar amount. In this arrangement the "higher" court may serve as an appellate court for cases decided in the lower court.

Although the drama of the courtroom receives greatest attention from the media and the public, legal professionals are primarily concerned with appellate court decisions because of stare decisis. Trial courts interpret and apply the law, but appellate courts state the law with greater authority. Because they establish precedent for future cases, appellate courts not only settle disputes but also have an impact beyond the case at hand.

The appellate process is quite different from trial. The appellate court does not retry facts, does not call witnesses. It receives a record from the trial court, which includes a written transcript of the testimony at trial, exhibits introduced during trial, copies of the pleadings and motions filed with the court before and during trial, and written briefs submitted by the attorneys for **appellant** and **appellee** arguing the issues raised on appeal.

appellant The party bringing an appeal against the other party, the **appellee.**

Attorneys for the parties are given a limited time to make oral arguments before the appellate court, during which the appellate judges may ask questions concerning the case. Deliberation of the case following oral argument is governed by the customs of the particular court, but at some point a vote is taken and usually a single judge will be assigned to write the opinion for the court in consultation with the other judges. Judges disagreeing with the result may write dissenting opinions; judges agreeing with the result may wish to add comments in a concurring opinion. There can be a considerable lapse of time between the oral argument and the issuance of a written opinion, depending largely on the complexities of the legal issues raised and the extent of disagreement among the judges.

Although the appellate court is limited to the record before it with regard to the dispute, its research of the law and its legal arguments may go beyond the cases and arguments made by attorneys for appellant and appellee in their briefs and oral arguments. Because decisions of the appellate courts may establish precedent for future cases, appellate judges are not concerned simply with resolving the dispute at hand but also with the impact of their interpretation of the law on future cases. At trial, the judge is constrained to proceed in a timely fashion, making rulings that will not delay the process and issuing a decision as soon as possible to define the rights of the parties. By contrast, the appellate process may be described as deliberative. The attorneys representing the parties have the opportunity to reflect on their arguments and craft carefully reasoned briefs, and the appellate court will take the time necessary to examine the law to write a reasoned decision. Steadily rising case loads in appellate courts have put pressure on the courts, but it is fair to say that cases of great import receive corresponding attention by appellate courts.

Appellate courts have two primary functions in deciding appeals: (1) resolve the dispute and (2) state the law. Many cases raise minor issues, dispute well-established rules, or have no particular merit (e.g., many criminal appeals are at government expense, so the convicted party has nothing to lose by appealing). When no significant issue of law is decided, or if prior law is followed, many jurisdictions do not require that the opinion be published. In some instances the court will write a cursory **memorandum** or **per curiam opinion** that disposes of the case without elaborate reasoning. Lengthy reasoning is reserved for cases that raise new or controversial legal issues.

Prejudicial Error

The appellate court examines the record and arguments to determine whether prejudicial, also called reversible, error occurred at the lower court level. The court does not impose an impossibly perfect standard on the trial court, but must determine whether mistaken actions constitute grounds for reversal. For example, the court may conclude that one of the instructions to the jury was not an exact statement of the law but, given the facts and circumstances of the case, a precise statement of the law would not have changed the jury's verdict. This would be considered harmless error that did not prejudice the case and would not be grounds for reversal. In some instances the appellate court may agree with the trial court's result but disagree with its reasoning, in which case the court may substitute its reasoning in an affirming opinion or remand the case for the lower court to rewrite the decision in accord with the appellate court's instructions. A remand for a new decision would also be appropriate when no error was committed in factfinding, but there was prejudicial error in application of law. For instance, the appellate court might hold that the trial court had no authority to award **punitive damages**, so that portion of the decision would be deleted, leaving the award of **compensatory damages** intact.

Reversible error may or may not call for a new trial. The appellate court might find, for example, that the trial court was incorrect in ruling that the statute of limitations had not run, thereby barring further suit. The appellate

memorandum decision
A court's decision that gives the ruling (what it decides and orders done), but no opinion (reasons for the decision). A **memorandum opinion** is the same as a **per curiam opinion,** which is an opinion without a named author, usually a brief and unanimous decision.

punitive damages
Sometimes awarded beyond mere compensation (see **compensatory damages**) to punish a defendant for outrageous conduct in tort.

compensatory damages   Awarded to an injured party to make her whole, that is, in tort, to compensate for all injuries, and, in contract, to put the nonbreaching party in the position he would have been in if the contract had been performed.

STATE of Kansas, Appellee,
v.
Clifton Lorrin STAFFORD, Appellant
Supreme Court of Kansas
223 Kan. 62, 573 P.2d 970 (1977)

The testimony comprising the state's case came from twelve witnesses. Defendant was the only person to testify on his behalf. Thirty pages of defendant's testimony were transcribed, but another fifty pages were lost. On order of the district court an attempt was made to reconstruct the missing transcript through testimony of defendant's trial attorney. The lost transcript formulates defendant's first point on appeal.

* * *

The inability of the state to provide a full transcript of the trial proceedings does not entitle a defendant to a new trial per se. Before defendant can claim he is entitled to a new trial he must demonstrate that despite a good faith effort it is impossible to reconstruct the missing portion of the record and this precludes effective appellate review of the issues.

* * *

The rest of defendant's claims of error relate to instructions given by the trial court. The trial court instructed on first and second degree murder and voluntary and involuntary manslaughter . . . . The court did not define "heat of passion". . . . There was an instruction on the effect of voluntary intoxication. The jury was instructed on defendant's presumption of innocence, weight of the testimony of the witnesses, and the duty to reach a verdict in light of all the evidence.

It is to be noted that none of the objections to instructions now raised were presented to the trial court; therefore, our scope of review is limited to a determination of whether the instructions are "clearly erroneous." An instruction is clearly erroneous when the reviewing court reaches a firm conviction that if the trial error had not occurred there was a real possibility the jury would have returned a different verdict.

* * *

We find no reversible error and the judgment is affirmed.

Case Questions
1. Because the correctness of jury instructions is a question of law rather than a question of fact, why did the reviewing court apply the clearly erroneous test rather than substitution of judgment?
2. Was the loss of the transcript prejudicial to the defendant?

court may conclude that the trial court was wrong in granting plaintiff's motion for judgment notwithstanding the verdict, the effect of which was to reject the verdict in favor of defendant and enter a judgment in favor of plaintiff; the result of the appellate reversal would be to reinstate the jury's verdict and enter a judgment in favor of defendant. In contrast, the appellate court might find that instructions to the jury or a ruling on admissibility of evidence so prejudiced the factfinding process that the error can only be corrected by a new trial.

In short, reversible error refers to the reversal of the *judgment* of the lower court. Because the judgment is based on findings of fact and conclusions of law, either or both could constitute harmful error, and the order of the appellate court is designed to correct the error in the most expeditious manner.

In *Stafford*, the defendant-appellant was convicted of second-degree murder, but a significant portion of the stenographic record of the trial was lost. Errors in serious felony cases are scrutinized much more critically than in lesser crimes and civil cases. The defendant wanted a new trial because of the incomplete record. The defendant also challenged the jury instructions.

Impact of the Appellate System

Appellate courts serve as a brake on the arbitrariness of trial judges as well as a forum for establishing uniformity in the interpretation of the law. The right to appeal is a fundamental custom of our legal system. Trial court judges naturally dislike being reversed, so the threat of appeal that lurks behind every case encourages them to conform to the law as stated by higher authority. In states having both intermediate courts and courts of last resort, a disappointed litigant has two opportunities for appellate review of the case. Courts of last resort have great discretion in choosing cases for review and decline to hear most cases. Intermediate appellate courts also have significant discretion in the cases they hear and the time they wish to devote to a case.

These factors limit the numbers of appeals, as does the prohibitive cost. Not only are substantial attorney's fees involved in preparing for appeal, but the cost of reproducing the trial transcript in a lengthy trial is an economic burden as well. Appeals therefore tend to involve cases in which the cost of appeal is borne by the government, as in criminal cases, or which involve significant amounts of money. Some appeals are subsidized by outside groups that have an interest in setting a precedent or in representing appellants, such as in a civil rights action. Because of these factors, appeals are not a representative sample of the cases that go to trial.

Appellate decisions also affect lawyers, who must evaluate their client's chances by predicting the outcome of trial and appeal. Most cases are settled without going to trial or appeal; settlement is encouraged by well-established principles of law that allow attorneys to assess whether a case is a winner or a loser. Indirectly, the costs of trial and appeal encourage litigants to make realistic decisions about whether to proceed.

In the murder trial, *Carruthers v. State*, the evidence was conclusive that Carruthers slit Jannette Williams' throat and stabbed her eleven times in the chest. On appeal, there was no credible argument against the guilty verdict. In murder cases in Georgia, however, once guilt has been determined, the jury must then choose between life imprisonment and death in the sentencing phase of the trial. Prosecutor and defense attorney are likely to make impassioned arguments before the jury to persuade the jurors of either of these sentences. On occasion, the prosecutor may go too far and make improper remarks that an appellate court may find to be prejudicial. The appeal in this situation presents a special feature—since murder trials have two phases, error in the sentencing phase may be separable from the trial of fact phase. The jury has been dismissed, however; what is the court to do?

Anthony CARRUTHERS
v.
STATE
Supreme Court of Georgia
528 S.E.2d 217 (2000)

Anthony Carruthers was convicted of the malice murder of Jannette Williams and sentenced to death. Carruthers contends that the assistant district attorney made several improper arguments that warrant reversal of the death sentence. Finding no reversible error in the guilt/innocence phase of Carruthers' trial, we affirm the jury's verdict of guilt on all charges. However, because we conclude that the trial court erred in allowing the state to urge the jury to follow the religious mandates of the Bible rather than Georgia law, we reverse the sentence of death and remand the case for another jury to consider the proper sentence for the murder. . . .

The United States Constitution and the Georgia Constitution guarantee criminal defendants the right to due process at trial. In addition, OCGA § 17-10-35 requires this Court to review the death sentence to determine whether it "was imposed under the influence of passion, prejudice, or any other arbitrary factor."

Carruthers filed a motion in limine to exclude during closing argument any Bible passages that appealed to the passion of the jury and would encourage it to impose a death sentence based on religion. During a pre-argument hearing, the prosecutor said that he intended to cite passages from the Books of Romans, Genesis, and Matthew. The defendant objected to the biblical references, but the trial court overruled the objection and allowed the three passages.

During closing argument, the state urged the jury to impose a death sentence because the Bible states that society must deter criminals by taking the life of persons who kill other people. The state argued as follows:

Now, ladies and gentlemen, let me talk to you a moment about some biblical references that help us in this case. Deterrence is very important and the Bible suggests to us why deter-

rence is appropriate. Romans tells us that every person is subject to the governing authority, every person is subject. And in Matthew it tells us, who sheddeth man's blood by man shall his blood be shed for in the image of God made [he] man. For all they who take the sword shall die by the sword, and this is a message that is very clear, that society must deter criminals.

This Court has noted its concern about the use of biblical authority during closing arguments in death penalty trials. . . . By quoting these texts during closing arguments, prosecutors may "diminish the jury's sense of responsibility and imply that another, higher law should be applied in capital cases, displacing the law in the court's instructions."

Although we have long declined to disapprove of passing, oratorical references to religious texts in arguments by counsel, we have distinguished those fleeting references from more direct references that urge that the teachings of a particular religion command the imposition of a death penalty. In contrast to biblical law, Georgia law gives the jury the discretion to recommend life imprisonment or death, provides stringent procedures and safeguards that must be followed during the trial, and permits the jury to impose the death penalty only in limited circumstances.

In addition, we have specifically disapproved of a prosecutor quoting verses from the Bible to support the death penalty. In *Hammond v. State*, we concluded that it was improper for the assistant district attorney to argue that the defendant had violated the law of God that "whoever sheds the blood of man by man shall his blood be shed." Despite this disapproval and repeated admonitions, prosecutors have continued to quote the Bible and urge its teachings, and trial courts have continued to permit the arguments.

Unlike previous cases, however, where the defendant failed to object to the state's religious arguments at trial, the defense in this case anticipated the argument and tried to prevent it by filing a motion in limine, but the trial court denied the motion. Because the defendant received an adverse ruling on his objection, the standard of

(continued)

(continued)

review in this case is not whether the improper argument in reasonable probability changed the result of the trial, but simply whether the argument was objectionable and prejudicial.

It is difficult to draw a precise line between religious arguments that are acceptable and those that are objectionable, but we conclude that the assistant district attorney in this case overstepped the line in directly quoting religious authority as mandating a death sentence. In citing specific passages, he invoked a higher moral authority and diverted the jury from the discretion provided to them under state law. . . .

Therefore, we find that Carruthers' right to due process as secured by OCGA § 17-10-35, the Georgia Constitution, and the Constitution of the United States was abridged when the trial court allowed the inappropriate arguments from the Bible over objection. Because we cannot conclude beyond a reasonable doubt that the violation of Carruthers' state and federal constitutional rights was harmless, we reverse the jury's death sentence and remand the case for resentencing. . . .

Judgment affirmed in part and reversed in part. All the Justices concur, except Carley, J., who concurs in part and dissents in part.

CARLEY, Justice, concurring in part and dissenting in part.

. . . A reversal of the death sentence on this basis runs counter to the long-standing principle that "the range of discussion (during closing argument) is wide—very wide. . . . [The prose-

cutor's] illustrations may be as various as are the resources of his genius; his argumentation as full and profound as his learning can make it; and he may, if he will, give play to his wit, or wing to his imagination." "Counsel may bring to his use in the discussion of the case well-established historical facts and may allude to such principles of divine law relating to transactions of men as may be appropriate to the case." Counsel for the State may forcibly or even extravagantly attempt to impress upon the jury "the enormity of the offense and the solemnity of their duty in relation thereto." *Conner v. State,* . . . . Here, the prosecutor used Biblical references only to illustrate the historical and moral underpinnings of deterrence as a justifying factor for imposing the death penalty. He did not improperly argue that Carruthers deserved to die for any reason other than that authorized under the secular law of this state. Instead, he made only an emotional exhortation that our contemporary reliance upon the deterrent effect of capital punishment has its roots in religious teachings. In the State's argument, the Bible did not supplant applicable statutes, but rather explicated those enactments. . . .

In *Conner v. State,* supra at 122 (5), this Court noted that it had never "invalidated a death penalty simply because the prosecutor made an impassioned argument to the jury during the sentencing phase of the trial." With today's opinion, that is no longer true. Henceforth, death sentences are subject to reversal if an emotional argument by the State does not satisfy the sensibilities of a majority of the Justices on this Court. . . .

Case Questions

1. What was improper about the prosecutor's remarks with regard to sentencing?
2. What was the basis of the dissent's disagreement concerning the propriety of the prosecutor's remarks?

Miscellaneous Judicial Duties

In attempting to learn the law, one tends to concentrate study on appellate decisions, which provide authoritative statements of the law. Most of these are appeals from final judgments from trials, but judges engage in many other duties that consume much time and energy.

Trial Courts

no-fault divorce
Contemporary divorce that does away with the need to prove fault, that is, state grounds, against the other spouse.

Lower court judges must act on a number of problems that are not truly adversarial in nature but that require orders from a court. The advent of **no-fault divorce,** for example, has converted a formerly adversarial proceeding into one that frequently involves a judge simply approving a marital settlement agreement negotiated by the divorcing parties through their attorneys. A five- or ten-minute hearing disposes of the matter. The major purpose of no-fault divorce laws has been to diminish the adversarial aspect of divorce and give the parties rather than the court control over their destinies. Of course, if the parties cannot agree on the distribution of marital assets, alimony, and child support, the proceedings take on the former adversarial character, forcing the judge to decide these issues.

garnishment An action by which one who is owed a debt may collect payments through a third party, often an employer.

Some actions, like a legal name change, in which no defendant is involved, are rather perfunctory actions requiring a court order. Others, like **garnishment** of wages, can be adversarial but usually are not. In addition, the court must take action on issues prior to trial and enforce judgments after trial. And, depending on the jurisdiction, judges may spend a good deal of time on purely administrative duties.

Appellate Courts

In general, appellate courts are responsible for overseeing the orderly process of the court system. This includes not only hearing appeals, but also ruling on requests for delays in the appellate process, staying decisions of lower courts, applications for bail, and so on. Appellate courts may also be involved in matters relating to admission to the bar and disciplinary actions.

Appellate courts also have responsibility for administrative duties, managing their own activities, as well as some supervisory functions over the lower courts. Onerous administrative duties are often bestowed on the chief judge of a district or circuit, or the chief justice of a supreme court. The time spent in administrative duties may be directly related to the staff available to a judge.

Unlike trials, which are conducted by a single judge, appellate proceedings involve three or more judges, usually an odd number to prevent evenly divided decisions. Assignment of duties also becomes an administrative matter, as someone must make the assignments. Many appellate courts have panels of judges, from which a subset is selected, to hear certain cases. The U.S. Court of Appeals is the most familiar example.

writ of prohibition
An order by a higher court directing a lower court not to do something.

The *Lee* case is an example of the regulatory feature of appellate courts. The newspaper in the case was charged with contempt of court for violating a "gag" order of the court in a juvenile case by publishing letters from the parents. The newspaper petitioned for a **writ of prohibition,** which is a common law remedy asking an appellate court to restrain a lower court from doing something it has no authority to do.

**MINNEAPOLIS STAR
AND TRIBUNE COMPANY,
La Crosse Tribune Company,
and Northwest Publications, Inc.,
Petitioners,
v.
Honorable Robert E. LEE,
Judge of Country Court
for Houston County,
Respondent
Court of Appeals of Minnesota
353 N.W.2d 213 (1984)**

FACTS

The petitioners request a writ of prohibition. In June 1984, the trial court issued an order that all parties in what was presumably a juvenile dependency case cease and desist from publishing letters or statements having to do with the proceeding. Subsequently, the minor's parents wrote two letters to the editor of a newspaper in the area. On July 27, 1984, the trial court, believing the letters to be a violation of its order, ordered a contempt hearing. . . .

ISSUE

May a court issue an order forbidding publication of information about a juvenile case obtained from involved parties and at the contempt hearing which was open to the public?

ANALYSIS

* * *

Prior restraints of speech have long been deemed unconstitutional except in the most drastic of situations.

* * *

Such a restraint must be "necessitated by a compelling governmental interest, and * * * narrowly tailored to serve that interest."

* * *

In this case, the governmental interest is not constitutional but statutory: privacy in a juvenile proceeding. It is an important and substantial government interest, but also with limits.

* * *

In this case, there has been no showing of any illegality; the trial court simply wanted to stop people from reading about the case. [The trial court judge] said he wanted to protect the child and have a better relationship between Houston County Social Services and the parties. Such an interest does not rise to the level required to justify a prior restraint. The order violated a fundamental constitutional right. Although the court's motives were honorable, nonetheless it was a violation of a fundamental right. There is no adequate remedy at law to redress such a violation and, therefore, the writ must issue.

DECISION

The trial court's order was an unconstitutional prior restraint of speech. It is hereby vacated.

The writ of prohibition is granted.

Case Questions

1. Why does the court note that there is no adequate remedy at law?
2. Could a court ever use a gag order prior to trial?
3. Under what provision of the Constitution is this case decided?

Case Glossary

prior restraint   An action by the government to impose limits on the exercise of free speech, especially publication, prior to its exercise, as distinguished from punishing a person after publication.

Summary

In the United States, the judicial system has a hierarchy that is divided into trial and appellate courts. The function of the trial court is to resolve disputes between parties in an adversarial process in which an impartial and disinterested judge presides over the presentation of evidence of fact by attorneys for the two sides. When a jury is present at trial, it determines issues of fact, whereas the judge applies the law in the conduct of the trial and renders a judgment on the verdict. In a non-jury trial, the judge serves as the trier of fact and then applies the law.

The distinction between law and fact is important on appeal. The appellate court does not try facts, although it is sometimes called upon to determine whether the trial record indicates that factfinding at the trial was clearly erroneous, warranting reversal. This is a much higher standard than the appellate court exercises in reversing an application of law by the trial judge. On questions of law, the appellate court is free to substitute its judgment for that of the lower court and need not show any deference to the lower court. As a result, most reversals are based on legal rather than factual arguments.

For an appellant to win a reversal on appeal, the appellate court must be convinced that there was reversible error at the trial level. Reversible error is a mistake in the law or the facts that was so prejudicial to appellant that a different result might have resulted if the mistake had not occurred. Minor mistakes may be deemed to be nonprejudicial or harmless error. In some cases reversible error requires a new trial; in others the error can be corrected by the appellate court or remanded to the lower court to write a new decision and order.

The appellate process provides a means to make the actions of trial courts consistent with the law, decide new issues of law, and protect litigants from misapplication of the law.

Scenario

Return to Chapter 3 and the *Colby* and *Higgins* cases. *Higgins* declared that the single issue on appeal is "whether, by reason of the *Colby* case, or any other consideration, we should hold that charitable immunity is not applicable in this case."

Treat the *Higgins* decision as if it were the trial court decision—*Higgins* affirms the trial court, so this should not be difficult—and write a new appellate decision to explain why the trial court decision is weakly reasoned and unfair to the plaintiff/appellant. In other words, you are writing a new appellate decision that reverses the trial court instead of affirming it. Give the reasons why the court now abolishes charitable immunity and explain what its effects and limits will be in light of legislation on the matter. Although an appellate decision commonly cites a wealth of authorities, you may treat this simply as a well-reasoned policy statement. You can cite *Colby* and, if appropriate, the *Ricker* case cited in *Higgins*.

This exercise should not only make you think about trial and appeal, but also make you look at both sides of the argument. The author often has his students write an appellate brief and then make them write the brief for the appellee without having told them in advance that this was the next writing assignment.

STATE AND FEDERAL COURTS

Introduction

The United States has a unique court system. Whereas most developed countries have a hierarchical court system in which all courts are subordinate to a central supreme court, the United States has two separate court systems, federal and state; also, each state is independent from every other and is free within constitutional limits to make its own laws and administer its own system of justice. This chapter discusses the interrelationships of this court system and its ramifications.

The United States Constitution

The U.S. Constitution allocates power between the federal and state governments. The aspects of the Constitution discussed here are far more important and complex than this summary treatment suggests, but acquaintance with certain constitutional provisions is essential for an understanding of state and federal court systems.

When the American colonies united into a federal republic, their representatives framed a charter, the United States Constitution, which allocated governmental authority between state and federal governments. The Constitution reflects a certain distrust of government based on the experience of abuses of traditional legal principles by the British colonial governors under a monarchy. Not only was there a distrust of government in general but also a degree of mutual distrust among the states due to differences in local economies (e.g.,

independent self governing

plantation economies of Virginia and the Carolinas versus commercial economies of New York, Massachusetts, and Pennsylvania) and differences in size and population (e.g., Rhode Island versus New York). As a result, the Constitution was framed to limit the power of the federal government while preserving governmental autonomy among the states.

The Constitution was viewed as a granting of power by the states to the federal government such that the federal government's powers were limited to those enumerated in the Constitution. All other governmental authority remained in the states, without need to specify that authority in the Constitution itself. This principle is embodied in the Ninth and Tenth Amendments: *list*

> AMENDMENT IX. The enumeration in the Constitution of certain rights shall not be construed to deny or disparage others retained by the people.
> AMENDMENT X. The powers not delegated to the United States by the Constitution, nor prohibited by it to the States, are reserved to the States respectively, or to the people.

This language reflects that the federal government exercises its authority "by grant," whereas the states exercise authority "by reservation." Note that this language is the language of property law, such as when a property owner transfers or "grants" property rights to another, "reserving" those rights not granted. Like a property transaction, the grant of power is a contract between the people and the government. This is not merely a philosophical point; constitutional cases may best be conceptualized as enforcing property rights in a contractual relationship in which the federal government is bound by the original bargain.

The scope of federal control over the states can be expanded or restricted by constitutional interpretation. In the twentieth century, it was greatly expanded by a broad interpretation of the *commerce clause*, Article I, Section 8, cl. 3, which gives Congress power to regulate interstate commerce. Because most business is in some way involved in interstate commerce, Congress has allowed pervasive regulation of American business. In contrast, in recent decades the U.S. Supreme Court has recognized inherent privacy rights into which neither the states nor the federal government may intrude (e.g., abortion rights).

Supreme Law of the Land

preemption The principle or doctrine that federal statutes that overlap or are in conflict with state statutes will take preference and prevail, even to the point of invalidating state statutes entirely.

Article VI, Section 2, of the Constitution provides that the Constitution "shall be the supreme law of the land." It was early established by the U.S. Supreme Court that this clause meant that neither state nor federal legislatures could enact laws in conflict with the Constitution, nor could any official or agency of government act in violation of the Constitution (refer to *judicial review* in Chapter 3). Because the U.S. Supreme Court is the ultimate authority with regard to the interpretation of the Constitution, it can exercise significant authority over state action.

The doctrine of **preemption** governs the conflict between federal and state statutes. Although the Constitution allocates authority between the federal government and the states, that authority is often overlapping. In particular, the authority over regulation of interstate commerce is given to the federal government and, in the twentieth century, the U.S. Supreme Court interpreted the interstate commerce clause of the Constitution to give the federal government broad powers. Since states have the authority to regulate state businesses, it happens from time to time that state and federal law conflict. The question then arises as to whether the federal law *preempts* state law, which it usually does. The *Shaw* case demonstrates, however, that the preemption question is not always a simple one. In their relative spheres of regulation, state and federal government may step on each others' toes without meaning to be in conflict. In *Shaw*, the defendant tobacco company raised an ingenious argument about cigarette warning labels preempting a state claim based on damages incurred from secondhand smoke. This case examines the limits and extent of the preemption doctrine.

Robert T. SHAW and Beatrice Shaw,
v.
BROWN & WILLIAMSON TOBACCO CORP.
United States District Court, D. Maryland
973 F. Supp. 539 (1997)

I.

Plaintiffs allege the following facts. Robert T. Shaw was employed as a long distance truck driver with the Kelly-Springfield Tire Company from 1968 to 1991. From May 1, 1973 to November 14, 1984, Shaw routinely traveled in an enclosed truck with a co-worker who smoked Raleigh cigarettes, which are manufactured, produced, and distributed by Brown & Williamson. Shaw did not smoke cigarettes at any time during his employment with Kelly-Springfield. Nevertheless, Shaw was diagnosed with lung cancer in 1992. Shaw and his wife allege that he developed lung cancer as a result of his exposure to second-hand or environmental tobacco smoke (hereinafter "ETS") emitted from the Raleigh cigarettes. . . .

III. Preemption

The Court will first consider defendant's contention that plaintiffs' claims for negligent misrepresentation, negligent failure to warn, and intentional misrepresentation are preempted by the 1969 Act.

The Supremacy Clause provides that the laws of the United States "shall be the supreme Law of the Land; . . . any Thing in the Constitution or Laws of any State to the Contrary notwithstanding. . . . A preemption analysis "start[s] with the assumption that the historic police powers of the States [are] not to be superseded by [a] Federal Act unless that [is] the clear and manifest purpose of Congress." . . . Accordingly, " 'the purpose of Congress is the ultimate touchstone' " of a preemption analysis. . . .

The Supreme Court has explained that congressional intent "may be 'explicitly stated in the statute's language or implicitly contained in its structure and purpose.' " . . . "In the absence of an express congressional command, state law is pre-empted if that law actually conflicts with federal law, or if federal law so thoroughly occupies a legislative field as to make reasonable the inference that Congress left no room for the States to supplement it." . . .

On the other hand, when Congress enacts a provision defining the preemptive reach of a statute, " 'there is no need to infer congressional intent to pre-empt state laws from the substantive provisions' of the legislation, . . . so long as the "provision provides a 'reliable indicium of congressional intent with respect to state authority.' " . . . Matters beyond the preemptive reach of such a provision are not preempted. . . . Thus, when an act contains a section that explicitly addresses pre-emption, the Court's task is to "identify the domain expressly preempted by" the section. Id.

. . . In accordance with its first purpose, the 1965 Act [Federal Cigarette Labeling and Advertising Act] required that each cigarette package be labeled with the warning statement "Caution: Cigarette Smoking May Be Hazardous to Your Health." Id. at § 4. The 1965 Act recognized its second purpose by including a preemption clause: "No statement relating to smoking and health, other than the statement required by section 4 of this Act, shall be required on any cigarette package." Id. at § 5.

The 1969 Act strengthened the warning by changing the required label to "Warning: The Surgeon General Has Determined That Cigarette Smoking Is Dangerous to Your Health." In addition, Congress changed the statute's pre-emption clause to its present form: "No requirement or prohibition based on smoking and health shall be imposed under State law with respect to the advertising or promotion of any cigarettes the packages of which are labeled in conformity with the provisions of this Act." 15 U.S.C. § 1334(b).

* * *

Plaintiffs argue that § 5 is addressed only to consumers of cigarettes, and that it therefore does not preempt the claims of persons affected by second-hand smoke . . . In an effort to ascertain congressional intent as to the meaning of this provision, the Court will now turn to other sources, such as additional language from the Labeling Acts and the legislative history of the Acts.

. . . While [Surgeon General's list regarding the adverse health effects of cigarette smoking] is replete with references to "smoking" and to "cigarette smoking," and also includes a reference to "women who smoke," it does not include any language broad enough to warn of the dangers associated with the inhalation of ETS. . . . Thus, this list of risks clearly does not indicate an intent to dissuade the public from breathing second-hand smoke. Indeed, it becomes apparent upon reading the list that the references to "smoking" allude only to one's own smoking, not to the smoking of others.

. . . None of these [required] warnings refer in any way to the risks associated with ETS. . . . The House Report for the 1965 Act states that "[t]he principal purpose of the bill is to provide adequate warning to the public of the potential hazards of cigarette smoking." . . . In these references to the legislative history of the Labeling Acts, it is again plain that the word "smoking" is intended to refer only to one's own smoking.

The Court should not affix to the term "smoking" a broader meaning in the preemption provision of § 5 than it has in the remaining provisions of the labeling Acts or in the legislative history of the Acts. . . . Restraint in this regard is particularly important where, as here, the Court is obligated to give the term a fair but narrow interpretation. The Court is persuaded, therefore, that the "based on smoking and health" language in § 5 encompasses only claims that concern one's own smoking. Accordingly, the claims of a nonsmoker such as Shaw do not constitute claims "based on smoking and health" under § 5(b), and are impliedly not preempted.

For all of the aforementioned reasons, the Court holds that plaintiffs' negligent misrepresentation, negligent failure to warn, and intentional misrepresentation claims are not preempted by § 5. . . .

Case Questions

1. Does this decision require tobacco companies to warn against second-hand smoke?
2. On the basis of this case, does the court take a broad or narrow view toward the interpretation of federal statutes that may pre-empt state statutes?

Due Process

federal statutes

due process of law
A guarantee of the Fifth Amendment and the Fourteenth Amendment to the U.S. Constitution. It provides that law administered through courts of justice is equally applied to all under established rules that do not violate fundamental principles of fairness. The process that is due before government may deprive a person of life, liberty, or property.

procedural due process That due process that is concerned with the fairness of *notice* and *hearing* provided by government in the adjudication of rights and duties.

substantive due process A theory of due process that emphasizes judging the content of a law by a subjective standard of fundamental fairness; the government may not act arbitrarily or capriciously in making, interpreting, or enforcing the law.

notice In law, represents the time requirement of notification of the opposing party. Under *procedural due process*, the fairness of legal procedure requires that a party must have sufficient notice to prepare a response to legal action.

hearing The presentation of evidence and argument before a tribunal. Under *procedural due process*, the hearing, usually the trial, must be fair and evenhanded. Most of the elements of a fair hearing have been established by custom and precedent.

The most important phrase in the Constitution for operation of the legal system is the **due process clause** of the Fifth and Fourteenth Amendments. The Fifth Amendment provides that no person "shall be deprived of life, liberty or property, without due process of law." Because this applied only to the federal government, the Fourteenth Amendment was ratified in 1868, including the language: "nor shall any State deprive any person of life, liberty, or property, without due process of law." In this way actions by state officials, legislatures, and courts become federal constitutional issues if denial of due process is alleged.

Due process is an elusive concept at best. It has been defined as requiring "fundamental fairness" in judicial process and prohibiting legislation that is "unreasonable, arbitrary, or capricious." These are subjective concepts—fairness and reasonableness are in the eyes of the beholder. As long as the court has the last word, what the court says is fair *is* fair, and what the court says is reasonable *is* reasonable. Unbridled power of the judiciary is mitigated, however, because the principles of *stare decisis* and judicial restraint constrain judges from arbitrarily imposing their views on society, and the appellate process encourages trial court judges to stay within the bounds of established law.

Due process has been divided into **procedural** and **substantive due process**. *Procedural due process* treats the issues of **notice** and **hearing.** *Notice* requires that a person threatened with legal action or whose legal rights are being affected be notified in such a way as to be able to prepare to protect those rights. *Hearing* requires that the form and nature of legal proceedings be fundamentally fair (e.g., an impartial tribunal, right to counsel, right of cross-examination, etc.). *Substantive due process* requires that legislation be reasonable, that it have a legitimate purpose, that it use reasonable means to effect a reasonable end, and so on. The void-for-vagueness doctrine is an example of a reasonableness test.

Because the fairness and reasonableness standards of due process are developed on a case-by-case basis, to understand due process one must become acquainted with the principal cases that have interpreted it. But judges tend to perceive as unfair what most citizens perceive as unfair, so the anger and frustration that a person may feel toward treatment at the hands of the law or the courts will often strike a resonant chord in the minds of judges. Whenever the government acts to the detriment of an individual, a due process argument lurks in the background.

It is not possible to catalog all the possibilities for denial of due process, but consider the following in terms of potential lawsuits against government:

1. A state university has a policy not to release course transcripts if a student has a debt outstanding to the university. George Shylock fails to be admitted to law school because his transcripts were not sent due to a $2.00 library fine he failed to pay. George had not been notified of the fine and now must wait an additional year to enter law school.

2. The Town of Uppercrust, Connecticut, passes a new zoning plan that requires residential building lots to be at least half an acre in area.

Mohammed Hussein owns a lot that is four tenths of an acre, sufficient under the old ordinance for a building site, but his application for a variance (an exception to the ordinance) is denied, so he cannot build on his lot.

3. Under state law a person can be convicted of manslaughter if involved in a fatal auto accident while driving intoxicated, even if the intoxication did not contribute to the accident.

4. In a rulemaking hearing held by the Interstate Commerce Commission, representatives of the railroad and trucking industries are permitted to offer oral testimony of expert witnesses concerning the impact of proposed transportation regulations but are not permitted to cross-examine witnesses.

These hypothetical situations raise additional constitutional issues. The zoning case would be challenged as taking private property without just compensation under the Fifth Amendment; the manslaughter case would undoubtedly raise the Eighth Amendment issue of cruel and unusual punishment. Due process questions are commonly raised along with other issues.

Equal Protection

equal protection of the laws
A Constitutional guaranty that specifies that every state must give equal treatment to every person who is similarly situated or to persons who are members of the same class; this protection is a requirement of the Fourteenth Amendment enacted originally to protect former slaves.

The Fourteenth Amendment also prohibits states from denying "any person within its jurisdiction the **equal protection of the laws.**" This language was designed originally to protect former slaves from discriminatory treatment after the Civil War. Its coverage, however, has been expanded to invalidate all laws and procedures that unreasonably discriminate. It has been invoked when classes of persons have been treated unequally by the law; for instance, alimony statutes in many states provided alimony only for women, thus discriminating against men, or public schools budgeted more for male athletics than female athletic programs, discriminating against women. The discriminatory aspect of the law may be more subtle, such as when cable TV companies objected to regulation of their broadcasting that was not also applied to noncable broadcasting. All laws by their nature discriminate—drunken-driving statutes discriminate against drinkers—but such forms of discrimination are benign, protecting society and its members. Equal protection of the laws is designed to protect a stigmatized group from discrimination rather than to control or punish offensive conduct.

Cases and Controversies

standing   "Standing to sue" is a person's right to bring a lawsuit because he or she is directly affected by the issues presented, having a stake in the outcome of the suit.

Article III of the Constitution vests judicial power in the "Supreme Court, and in such inferior courts as the Congress may from time to time ordain and establish." Article III, Section 2, refers to judicial power over "cases" and "controversies." These words have been interpreted by the U.S. Supreme Court to restrict access to the federal courts in several ways, the most important of which concerns the question of **standing.** In our legal system, not every person may seek redress for every deprivation of a legal right. Standing is a limitation on who may bring an action. In general, only a person who has a "personal stake in the outcome" of a case may bring suit. This gloss on the Constitution encourages litigants to frame their suits in terms of property rights, but even in the violation of abstract rights, such as freedom of speech, suits are limited to those persons directly affected—a person may not sue the government for the abuse of power if that abuse is unrelated to the person desiring to sue.

Case and controversy have also been interpreted as referring to actual disputes between real parties. Not every slight, rebuke, or annoyance is a legal matter. And the courts have refused to hear cases concerning remote or hypothetical questions. This does not mean that some injury or wrong must necessarily have already occurred, but there must at least be an immediate threat of invasion of a right. In the *Waddell* case, a high school referee's call was taken all the way to the Georgia Supreme Court.

Full Faith and Credit

Article IV of the Constitution begins: "**Full faith and credit** shall be given in each State to the public acts, records, and judicial proceedings of every other State." As a practical matter, this means that the courts of each state must recognize the validity of the laws and judicial orders of other states. Divorce provides a useful example. Frequently after divorce, an ex-husband ordered to pay child support or alimony moves to another state and stops making payments. The ex-wife may bring an action in the state to which the former husband has moved to collect arrears in payments. In the action, the court must recognize the validity of the divorce and the order to make payments.

Full faith and credit has some limitations. A court may find that the law or court order of another state is repugnant to public policy, a rare occurrence. This statement will undoubtedly be tested in the light of New Hampshire's statutory approval of certification of same-sex partnerships. Many have pondered the question that will inevitably arise when the first state allows same-sex marriage: What happens when a homosexual married couple moves to a state that does not allow such marriages? Another basis for denying recognition is

case and controversy
Terms used in Article III, Section 2, of the U.S. Constitution regarding the judicial power; the terms have been interpreted to mean that the courts have authority over real disputes between real parties, as opposed to hypothetical disputes or nonadversarial parties. The courts do not answer questions about the law but decide actual disputes.

full faith and credit
The Constitution requires that each state respect the legal pronouncements of sister states: "Full faith and credit shall be given in each State to the public acts, records, and judicial proceedings of every other State" (Article IV).

GEORGIA HIGH SCHOOL ASSOCIATION
v.
WADDELL et al.
Supreme Court of Georgia
248 Ga. 542, 285 S.E.2d 7 (1981)

On October 23, 1981, a football game was played between R.L. Osborne and Lithia Springs High Schools, members of region 5 AAAA established by the Georgia High School Association. The winner of this game would be in the play-offs, beginning with Campbell High School.

The score was 7 to 6 in favor of Osborne. With 7 minutes, 1 second, remaining in the game, Osborne had the ball on its 47 yard line, 4th down and 21 yards to go for a first down. Osborne punted but "roughing the kicker" was called on Lithia Springs. The referee officiating the game with the approval and sanction of the Georgia High School Association assessed the 15 yard penalty, placed the ball on the Lithia Springs 38 yard line, and declared it was 4th down and 6 yards to go.

The rules of the National Federation of State High School Associations provide that the penalty for roughing the kicker shall be 15 yards *and* 1st down. There is a dispute as to whether the Osborne coaches properly protested to the referee, before the ball was put in play, the error in the referee's failing to declare a 1st down.

From Lithia Springs' 38, Osborne punted again. Lithia Springs received the punt and drove down the field to score a field goal. Now 2 points behind, Osborne passed. Lithia Springs intercepted and scored again. The final score was Lithia Springs over Osborne, 16 to 7.

* * *

On November 12, suit was filed in the Superior Court of Cobb County by parents of Osborne players against the GHSA. Hearing was held on November 13. The court found that it had jurisdiction, found that the referee erred in failing to declare an automatic first down, and found that a protest was lodged with the proper officials of GHSA. The court found that the plaintiffs have a property right in the game of football being played according to the rules and that the referee denied plaintiffs and their sons this property right and equal protection of the laws by failing to correctly apply the rules.

The court then entered its order on November 13 canceling the play-off game between Lithia Springs and Campbell High School scheduled for 8 p.m. that evening and ordered " . . . that Lithia Springs High School and R.L. Osborne High School meet on the football field on November 14, 1981 at an agreed upon time between the parties and resume play at the Lithia Springs thirty eight yard line with the ball being in the possession of R.L. Osborne High School and it be first down and ten yards to go for a first down and that the clock be set at seven minutes one second to play and that the quarter be designated as the fourth quarter."

Asserting that the trial court's order was erroneous under *Smith v. Crim,* 240 Ga. 390, 240 S.E.2d 884 (1977), and would disrupt the play-off games not only between Lithia Springs and Campbell but succeeding play-offs, the GHSA filed a motion for **supersedeas** in this court on November 13, 1981, and the court entered its order suspending the trial court's order, pending further order of this court.

In *Smith v. Crim, supra,* we held that a high school football player has no right to participate in interscholastic sports and has no protectable property interest which would give rise to a due process claim. Pretermitting the question of "state action" which is the threshold of the 14th Amendment, we held that Smith was not denied equal protection by the rule of GHSA there involved. Similarly we find no denial of equal protection by the referee's error here. Were our decision to be otherwise, every error in the trial courts would constitute a denial of equal protection. We now go further and hold that courts of equity in this state are without authority to review decisions of football referees because those decisions do not present judicial controversies. The stay granted by this court on November 13, 1981, is hereby reaffirmed.

All the Justices concur.

Case Questions

1. Why is "state action" the threshold question for an inquiry into a denial of equal protection of the law under the Fourteenth Amendment?
2. Why did the football players have no right and no property interest to qualify for due process protection?
3. Did the players receive fair procedure?

Case Glossary

supersedeas   An order staying the execution of judgment by a trial court. Suspension of the trial court's power, as where an appeal halts the court's power to execute judgment.

subject matter jurisdiction   The jurisdiction of a court to hear and determine the type of case before it. For example, in Florida, election contests are heard in the circuit court but not in county court. The reference to Leon County in "the Circuit Court for Leon County" refers to the location of the court—it is a circuit court, not a county court.

bankruptcy   Generally, the situation in which a person, business, or government cannot or will not pay its debts, so its property is entrusted to a "trustee in bankruptcy" who distributes the property to creditors.

patent   An exclusive right granted by the government to use one's invention.

trademark A distinctive mark in symbols or words used to distinguish products of manufacturers or merchants.

copyright   A right in literary property giving an author exclusive rights over her works for a limited period of time.

admiralty   That branch of law pertaining to maritime commerce and navigation.

general subject matter jurisdiction A court's authority to hear and decide a broad range of cases.

jurisdiction. One state may conclude that the court of another state did not have jurisdiction over the matter in the first place. A court without jurisdiction has no authority and its orders no validity. For example, husband and wife separate and live in different states. One brings a divorce action in one state and the other in another state. Only one state should have jurisdiction—two conflicting divorce decrees make no legal or practical sense. A court may conclude that the court of another state did not have jurisdiction and refuse to enforce its orders.

This may have unanticipated results; consider the following case. A man from North Carolina obtained a "quickie" divorce in Nevada, immediately remarried in Nevada, and returned to North Carolina with his new wife. North Carolina charged and convicted him of bigamy, and the case went to the U.S. Supreme Court twice. This created the anomalous situation in which a man was a "bigamist for living in one state with the only one with whom the other state would permit him lawfully to live" [Justice Douglas, *Williams v. North Carolina*, 317 U.S. 287 (1942)]. The Court required North Carolina to respect the Nevada decree (with vigorous dissenting opinions). The advent of no-fault divorce has mitigated the need for divorce havens like Nevada, but jurisdictional problems can still create a tangled web in divorce cases.

Subject Matter Jurisdiction

Although jurisdiction may properly be treated as part of civil and criminal procedure, the distinction between federal and state court systems is grounded on jurisdiction as well. The power and authority of a court in a particular dispute are based on jurisdiction. Without jurisdiction, a court has no authority; its orders are not valid. **Subject matter jurisdiction** refers to the kinds of disputes a court has the authority to decide. For example, the Constitution provides that the federal government has exclusive control over **bankruptcy, patent, trademark, copyright,** and **admiralty.** A state court has no power to decide a bankruptcy case; if it should do so, its orders would have no validity.

General and Limited Jurisdiction

Courts are classified as having **general** or **limited subject matter jurisdiction.** Courts of general jurisdiction have authority to decide a wide variety of cases and apply the full range of judicial remedy and relief. Major trial courts in each jurisdiction fit into this category. However, most states have also established courts of limited jurisdiction to handle only a restricted class of cases. A probate court, for example, handles matters concerning decedents' estates (many probate courts also have jurisdiction over some areas of law relating to juveniles). Thus, a probate court does not hear cases of tenant evictions. Some states divide their courts into criminal and civil courts; Texas even divides appeals into civil and criminal appeals at the supreme court level.

There is a wide variety of lower courts handling minor matters with limited subject matter jurisdiction; one example is small claims court (limited to cases involving a low maximum monetary amount and having limited

limited subject matter jurisdiction A court's restricted authority to decide only certain kinds of cases; for example, a probate court only hears cases concerning decedents' estates.

remedial powers—it cannot grant divorces, issue injunctions, etc.). Municipal courts are common in the United States, typically handling violations of city ordinances and other minor civil and criminal matters. Many of these lesser courts are conducted with less formality than higher trial courts. Small claims courts are designed to provide litigants with an inexpensive means to resolve disputes. Lawyers do not usually participate, court reporters are usually not present (therefore no transcript is made), and court costs are minimal; the judge tends to take a more active role in the process because the litigants are unfamiliar with the technicalities of the law.

Federal Subject Matter Jurisdiction

Federal jurisdiction applies to two categories of cases: (1) federal question cases and (2) diversity of citizenship cases.

Federal Question Cases

federal question Federal courts have subject matter jurisdiction over cases arising under the Constitution, laws, and treaties of the United States; these raise "federal questions."

The Constitution provides that the federal courts have jurisdiction over cases arising under the Constitution, laws, and treaties of the United States. These are called **federal question** cases. A case may directly raise a constitutional issue, or it may arise under a federal statute enacted by Congress (e.g., federal civil rights violations, environmental protection issues).

Each state (and the District of Columbia) has at least one U.S. District Court, the federal trial court to which federal question cases are brought. Many cases involve both state law and federal questions and can be brought in state courts, which must then decide issues of both state and federal law. For instance, the drunken driving manslaughter case in our hypothetical situations considered earlier would begin as a state prosecution in which the defendant would raise defense arguments based on the due process and cruel and unusual punishment clauses of the U.S. Constitution, as well as their counterparts in the state constitution (and factual defenses, of course). If convicted, the defendant could appeal to the state court of appeals and the state supreme court, and then petition the U.S. Supreme Court for a **writ of certiorari** on the federal constitutional issues.

writ of certiorari A writ issued by a higher court to a lower court requiring the certification of the record in a particular case so that the higher court can review the record and correct any actions taken in the case that were not in accordance with the law.

A case originating in the federal district court will stay in the federal system even if an issue of state law must be decided. A case originating in the state courts will remain in the state court system until decided or denied consideration by the state's highest court, from which appeal is made (by way of **certiorari**) to the U.S. Supreme Court. A defendant may challenge federal question jurisdiction in a case in a U.S. District Court, which would force the case into state court if the challenge is successful. Similarly, a defendant may petition the U.S. District Court for removal from state court to the federal court and will succeed if the federal court concludes that the case could have been brought originally in the federal court.

certiorari To be informed of, to be made certain in regard to.

Keep in mind that state courts have the final authority to declare state law, and federal courts have final authority to declare federal law. State courts will thus use federal cases to determine federal law, while federal courts will rely on decisions of state courts where state law is concerned. The exceptions to this are: (1) if state and federal laws overlap and conflict (e.g., certain state and federal labor laws may give rise to an inconsistency between them), state law must yield to federal law; and (2) any state statute or court decision that is held to be in conflict with the U.S. Constitution is invalid and without authority as to the part that is unconstitutional.

Federal question cases commonly arise in those areas in which the federal government has a special stake by virtue of the authority it has through the Constitution for interstate commerce, copyright, patent, bankruptcy, the military, customs, and so on. In each of these areas, a body of federal law has been developed by Congress and defined by the federal courts.

The U.S. government registers trademarks that are used in interstate commerce through the U.S. Patent and Trademark Office. Since trademarks are used to identify products and the businesses that produces them, they can become quite valuable to a business and many businesses are continually on guard to prevent others from copying, using, or imitating their trademarks. Infringement of U.S. registered trademarks raises a federal question to be heard in the federal court. In recent years, trademark and copyright problems have multiplied due to the Internet, which inadvertently facilitates copying and shady entrepreneurship. *GoTo.com v. Disney* presents the sort of federal question that has become common. GoTo.com obtained a preliminary **injunction,** an appropriate remedy for one who is trying to prevent the loss of business due to the misuse of a trademark, in this case a "remarkably" similar trademark. To determine whether the District Court was correct in issuing an injunction, the Court of Appeals uses two tests, one to determine whether an injunction was appropriate:

> A plaintiff is entitled to a preliminary injunction in a trademark case when it demonstrates either (1) a combination of "probable success on the merits" and "the possibility of irreparable injury" or (2) the existence of "serious questions going to the merits" and that "the balance of hardships tips sharply in his favor." . . .

and the second to determine "irreparable injury in the context of federal trademark law" (The Lanham Act), applying eight factors established in the *Sleekcraft* case:

> . . . To prevail on a claim under the Lanham Act, GoTo must establish that Disney is using a mark confusingly similar its own, which [GoTo] began using a year earlier. . . .
>
> The likelihood of confusion is the central element of trademark infringement, and the issue can be recast as the determination of whether "the similarity of the marks is likely to confuse customers about the source of the products. . . . We have developed eight factors, the so-called Sleekcraft factors, to guide the determination of a likelihood of confusion. . . . Applied to this case, they are (1) the similarity of the marks; (2) the relatedness of the two companies' services; (3) the marketing channel used; (4) the strength of GoTo's mark; (5) Disney's intent in selecting its mark; (6) evidence of actual confusion; (7) the likelihood of expansion into other markets; and (8) the degree of care likely to be exercised by purchasers. . . .

injunction A court order that commands or prohibits some act or course of conduct; it is preventive in nature and designed to protect a plaintiff from irreparable injury to his or her property or property rights by prohibiting or commanding the doing of certain acts; a form of equitable relief.

GOTO.COM, INC.
v.
THE WALT DISNEY COMPANY
United States Court of Appeals
for the Ninth Circuit
202 F.3d 1199 (2000)

We must decide whether two remarkably similar logos used commercially on the World Wide Web are likely to confuse consumers under federal trademark law.

I

The Walt Disney Company ("Disney") appeals the district court's grant of a preliminary injunction against it that was sought by GoTo.com ("GoTo"). The injunction prohibits Disney from using a logo confusingly similar to GoTo's mark. GoTo operates a web site that contains a pay-for-placement search engine, which allows consumers to locate items on the Web using a search algorithm weighted in favor of those advertisers who have paid to have their products given a priority by the engine. In December 1997, GoTo began using on its web site one of the two logos at issue in this appeal. The GoTo logo consists of the words "GO" and "TO" in a white font stacked vertically within a green circle. Although this green circle has been displayed against backgrounds of various colors, it is very often rendered against a square yellow background. To the right of the word "TO" are the characters ".com" in black, spilling out of the green circle onto the background color.

In preparing to launch a web site of its own, Disney commissioned a design firm, U.S. Web/CKS ("CKS"), to devise a logo for its Web portal, the Go Network, in April 1998. The Go Network is an interconnected collection of web sites, all belonging to Disney properties, designed to provide an easy starting point for consumers who use the Web. . . . CKS designed a logo that resembles a traffic light: it contains a green circle within a yellow square,

with details and contouring that is suggestive of a traffic light with a single lens. Within the green circle, the word "GO" appears in a white font, and next to the traffic light, the word "Network" appears in a black font. . . .

We review the district court's grant of a preliminary injunction for an abuse of discretion. . . . The grant of a preliminary injunction will be reversed only when the district court has based its decision on an erroneous legal standard or on clearly erroneous findings of fact. . . . We review a legal and factual determination of likelihood of confusion under the trademark laws for clear error. . . .

. . . In the context of the Web in particular, the three most important Sleekcraft factors are (1) the similarity of the marks, (2) the relatedness of the goods or services, and (3) the "simultaneous use of the Web as a marketing channel." . . .

Because the similarity of the marks is such an important question, we must begin our analysis by comparing the allegedly infringing Disney logo to the GoTo mark. . . .

With a single glance at the two images, one is immediately struck by their similarity. Both logos consist of white capital letters in an almost identical sans serif font rendered on a green circle. The circle in turn is matted by a square yellow background.

Quibbles over trivial distinctions between these two logos are unimpressive. The logos are glaringly similar. . . .

We have no difficulty concluding that the two marks are overwhelmingly similar.

B

The first of the other two controlling Sleekcraft considerations is that "related goods are generally more likely than unrelated goods to confuse the public as to the producers of the goods." . . . With respect to Internet services, even services that are not identical are capable of confusing the public. . . .

(continued)

(continued)

In this case, the services offered by GoTo and Disney are very similar. Both entities operate search engines and are, therefore, direct competitors on this score. . . .

C

Both GoTo and Disney use the Web as a substantial marketing and advertising channel, and we have given special consideration to that forum. . . . [T]he Web, as a marketing channel, is particularly susceptible to a likelihood of confusion since, as it did in this case, it allows for competing marks to be encountered at the same time, on the same screen.

In determining whether there is a likelihood of confusion, we rely heavily on the fact that the marks are similar, that Disney and GoTo offer very similar services, and that they both use the Web as their marketing channel. This trinity constitutes the most crucial body of the Sleekcraft analysis, and, in this case, it suggests that confusion is indeed likely. . . .

We conclude that the district court correctly found that two remarkably similar marks displayed commercially on the Web were likely to cause consumer confusion. . . .

AFFIRMED; preliminary injunction REINSTATED.

Case Questions

1. What is the primary question when examining a trademark challenge?
2. What factor from the *Sleekcraft* decision is specifically aimed at the World Wide Web?

Diversity of Citizenship Cases

diversity of citizenship The subject matter jurisdiction of federal courts to hear cases between citizens of different states.

Article III of the Constitution placed suits between citizens of different states under federal jurisdiction. This jurisdiction is not exclusive, so a plaintiff of Maryland suing a defendant from Virginia may elect to sue in a state court (most likely Virginia) or in a U.S. District Court. The differences in state citizenship are referred to as **diversity of citizenship,** and jurisdiction is based on the status of the parties without regard to the subject matter of the case; that is, no federal law other than the diversity clause of the Constitution is required. Diversity cases additionally require that the amount in controversy exceed $75,000.

Diversity jurisdiction requires total diversity—if there are multiple plaintiffs or defendants and any plaintiff is a citizen of the same state as any defendant, diversity jurisdiction will be denied. Like federal question cases, a petition for removal is available to the defendant if the plaintiff elects to bring the suit in the state court. The petition, however, is not available if suit is brought in the defendant's state. The rationale for this exception is based on the original purpose of the diversity clause. Apparently when the Constitution was framed, it was feared that parties might face prejudice when suing or being sued in a state other than their own. Federal jurisdiction was made available on the belief that federal courts would be less inclined to partiality. Thus, when a defendant is sued at home, the rationale for federal jurisdiction no longer holds.

William M. FINE, et al., Plaintiffs,

v.

DELALANDE, INC., Defendant
United States District Court,
S.D. New York
545 F. Supp. 275 (1982)

This lawsuit began on April 1, 1982, in the New York Supreme Court, New York County, the same day on which the defendant Delalande, Inc. filed an action in this Court against the plaintiffs herein based upon claimed diversity of citizenship. Delalande removed this action from the state court on April 20, 1982, pursuant to 28 U.S.C. § 1441(c).

By motion docketed May 5, 1982, the *Fine* plaintiffs seek the remand of this action to the

state court as improvidently removed, because Delalande, Inc. is a citizen of New York by reason of its principal place of business of this state.

For purposes of 18 U.S.C. § 1441, a corporation is deemed to be a citizen of the state wherein it has its principal place of business, and of the state of its incorporation. 28 U.S.C. § 1332(c).

For reasons discussed more fully in this Court's Memorandum and Order of this date in the companion *Delalande* action, 545 F. Supp. 268, familiarity with which is assumed, this Court finds that Delalande has its principal place of business in New York. Accordingly, there is not complete diversity because at least eleven of the plaintiffs are also citizens of New York.

Plaintiff's motion to remand this action to the state court is granted.

Case Questions

1. If Delalande's principal place of business is New York, on what basis was it claiming diversity of citizenship?
2. Why would the plaintiff prefer state court or defendant federal court?

In the *Fine* case, both sides filed suit on the same day, one in state court and one in federal court. As the case indicates, a corporation may be a "citizen" of more than one state for the purposes of diversity jurisdiction. Although a defendant sued in state court may petition for removal to federal court, claiming diversity jurisdiction, a defendant sued in federal court in a diversity case may move to remand to the state court, claiming a lack of diversity jurisdiction. Note that a removal should be distinguished from a *remand*, which in a diversity case would seek a transfer from a federal court back to the state court. Both removal and remand may be distinguished from a motion to dismiss for lack of jurisdiction.

Many have argued that the diversity clause no longer makes sense and unnecessarily clogs federal courts, which ought to be deciding cases of federal rather than state law.

The *Erie* Doctrine

In 1938, the U.S. Supreme Court decided the case of *Erie Railroad v. Tompkins*, 304 U.S. 64, which altered the nature of diversity cases forever. Tompkins was injured by a train while walking along a path beside the railroad tracks, when an open door on a refrigerator car hit him. Tompkins was a citizen of Pennsylvania, and the incident occurred in Pennsylvania; but Erie was a New York corporation. Tompkins brought a diversity case in federal court in New York and was awarded $30,000 in damages. The Second Circuit Court of Appeals affirmed the award, but the railroad petitioned and received certiorari from the U.S. Supreme Court.

At issue was the substantive law to be followed in a diversity case. The trial judge instructed the jury that the railroad was liable under general law if the jury found simple negligence. The railroad argued from the beginning that the common law of Pennsylvania, the site of the injury, should apply. Under Pennsylvania law, Tompkins would be considered a trespasser, as he was walking on the railroad's right of way, so the railroad would not be liable to a trespasser on the basis of ordinary negligence but only if the jury found gross negligence (i.e., wanton and reckless misconduct). In Pennsylvania, a landowner such as the railroad owes a lower duty of care to a trespasser than to nontrespassers. For this reason, Tompkins's attorneys chose to bring the case in federal court rather than the Pennsylvania state court.

Section 34 of the Federal Judiciary Act of 1789 had provided for the recognition and application of state common law in appropriate cases, but in *Swift v. Tyson*, 41 U.S. 1 (1842), the court had held that the federal courts were free to disregard specific decisions of state common law in favor of general principles of common law.

The effect of *Swift v. Tyson* was to encourage the creation of a general federal common law that could differ significantly from the law of a particular state. This would encourage litigants for whom diversity jurisdiction was available to select the court, state or federal, in which they would have the greatest likelihood of success, precisely what Tompkins's lawyers did. In *Erie*, the Supreme Court overruled *Swift v. Tyson* and declared that, henceforth, the federal courts in diversity cases would follow the common law of the state.

Mr. Tompkins lost his case.

Erie has been applied to substantive law but not procedure—when suing in federal court, federal procedure is followed.

In the *Brown* case, like the *Fine* case, the principal issue is diversity jurisdiction. Once the court determines it has jurisdiction, the case is summarily dismissed by interpreting state law as *Erie* requires. The *Brown* plaintiff is suing for wrongful discharge, but she is an "at-will" employee, which means that she does not have an employment contract that guarantees a period of employment, so she can be discharged at any time.

Some states allow suits for wrongful discharge for at-will employees; Missouri does not. Why is the plaintiff trying desperately to get into a Missouri state court? The answer may lie in the *Erie* doctrine itself. Although the federal court in a diversity case will be extremely reluctant to upset established Missouri precedent, the plaintiff might be able to persuade a Missouri court to overrule precedent in light of a trend in other states to recognize an action for wrongful discharge of an at-will employee.

Deborah BROWN, Plaintiff,

v.

**SOUTHLAND CORPORATION,
et al., Defendants
United States District Court,
E.D. Missouri, E.D.
620 F. Supp. 1495 (1985)**

Plaintiff, a resident of Missouri, brought this action for damages in the Circuit Court of the City of St. Louis against Southland Corporation, a Texas corporation, and Clyde Tinsley, a resident of Missouri.

The action arises out of the circumstances surrounding plaintiff's discharge from defendant Southland Corporation's (Southland) employment. Plaintiff was employed as the store manager of a "7-Eleven" store owned by defendant Southland at the time of her discharge in May 1980. Plaintiff alleges that she was wrongfully discharged pursuant to a corporate policy implemented to cover-up top-level employees' negligence. . . .

28 U.S.C. § 1441(b) gives a defendant who meets certain requirements the right to remove a civil action from a state court to a federal district court on the basis of diversity of citizenship. The requirement of complete diversity between plaintiffs and defendants is fully applicable to § 1441(b). A federal court, however, will not allow removal to be defeated by the collusive or fraudulent joinder of a resident defendant. . . .

In the present action, plaintiff's complaint alleges that Tinsley was the zone manager with ultimate supervisory responsibility over the store where plaintiff worked. In support of his removal petition, defendant Tinsley submitted affidavits and plaintiff's own deposition statements to the effect that at the time of the occurrences alleged in plaintiff's complaint, he was not the zone manager of the district in which plaintiff's store was located and that he had no involvement in the said occurrences. Plaintiff states in her deposition that she never spoke with defendant Tinsley. Plaintiff has not disputed this evidence. The Court concludes that defendants have met their burden of proving that defendant Tinsley was improperly joined and dismisses him pursuant to Rule 21, Fed.R.Civ.P. Accordingly, plaintiff's motion to remand is denied.

The next matter for consideration is defendants' motion to dismiss for failure to state a claim. Plaintiff does not allege any contractual or statutory provision that would bar her termination. In Missouri, it is firmly established that an at-will employee cannot maintain an action for wrongful discharge. . . .

The above rulings dispose of all claims in plaintiff's complaint against each defendant. Judgment for defendants.

Case Questions

1. Why does the plaintiff want the case remanded to state court?
2. What reasons are given for denial of the petition to remand?
3. What result does *Erie* achieve in this case?

conflict of laws Also called *choice of law;* concerns the problem that arises when there is a question about which state law should apply in a particular case.

Conflict of Laws

Separate state jurisdictions within one nation have also presented a special problem called **conflict of laws** or *choice of law.* Suppose two Connecticut residents are involved in an auto accident in Massachusetts. With a Connecticut plaintiff and a Connecticut defendant, suit is logically brought in Connecticut, although it could be brought in Massachusetts where the accident occurred. Should Connecticut or Massachusetts law apply? This is a conflict of laws problem. Whatever state is chosen for the suit (the *forum* state), its procedural laws will be followed; but a question may arise as to which forum's substantive law should apply. In some respects this parallels the issue in *Erie*: the result of the lawsuit should not depend on the choice of the forum. Because of differences in state law, a defendant may be liable under the law of one state but not under the law of another, making the defendant's state of residence the determining factor in the result.

Conflict of laws rules resolve this problem to some extent. Each state has its own rules to decide the choice of law. If the Connecticut plaintiff sues in Connecticut, Connecticut choice of law must apply. Assuming that Connecticut is in no way involved with the accident (i.e., the accident and its causes occurred wholly within Massachusetts), the substantive law of Massachusetts would apply, just as it would if the case were brought in Massachusetts. Connecticut law would require that the substantive law of Massachusetts govern the outcome of the case.

There is logic to this result. Whether conduct is wrongful should be determined by the law of the place where it occurs. The Connecticut driver in Massachusetts must obey Massachusetts law. To illustrate, many states allow a driver to turn right at a red light after stopping and determining it is safe to turn. Suppose a resident of such a state follows this custom in a state that does not allow turning on red. It would certainly be no defense, either civil or criminal, that the driver's home state has a different rule. Suppose that the turn on red caused an accident and that an injured party sued the nonresident in his home state. Should the defendant's conduct be judged differently because it is legal in his home state, the state where the suit was brought? No, wrongful conduct should not be magically transformed into proper conduct by the choice of the forum.

Unfortunately, conflict of laws is not always this simple. Suppose, for example, that the two drivers were crossing the Connecticut-Massachusetts border as the accident occurred. The wrongful act of one driver may have occurred in Connecticut but the injuries inflicted in Massachusetts. Choice of law will depend on the conflict of laws principles of the forum state. In tort cases like an auto accident, two rules are generally applied. The ancient rule, **lex loci delicti,** or "the law of the place of the wrong," holds that choice of law will fall on the site of the last act necessary to make the actor liable, that is, where the tortious act is complete. In recent times another test, called the **significant relationship test** has been adopted in many states. Under this test, all the circumstances of the tort are considered in deciding which state has the greatest connection with the wrong.

Contract cases present far more problems for conflict of laws. As a somewhat absurd, but not impossible, example, consider the following:

> Two corporations with nationwide activities negotiate a complex contract. One corporation is incorporated in California, the other in New York. The contract is negotiated and signed in Illinois. The contract is to be performed primarily in Texas but is breached in Louisiana. The contract specifically provides, "in case of breach, this contract will be construed under the law of Michigan." The California corporation sues the New York corporation in New Jersey, its principal place of business.

---

lex loci delicti (Latin) "The law of the place of the wrong." In a *conflict of laws* question in a tort action, this ancient rule held that the court would apply the law of that place (state) where the last act necessary to complete the tort occurred or the last act necessary to make the actor liable occurred.

significant relationship test The modern rule followed in a *conflict of laws* setting; it is used in both tort and contract contexts and makes the court apply the law of the state that had the most "significant relationship" to the cause of action.

Theoretically, the law of one of several states might be chosen. If suit is brought in New Jersey and the New Jersey court agrees that it has jurisdiction, the choice of law would depend on New Jersey rules on conflict of laws. New Jersey conflict of laws may be very different from those of Texas or Illinois. Most states give great weight to the agreement of the parties to specify the law that governs, here that of Michigan. But many contracts are silent in this regard, and there may be policy reasons for not enforcing that part of the contract.

There are several conflict of laws principles with regard to contracts, and frequently different rules apply to different circumstances. Like torts, there has been a strong trend toward the significant relationship test, which aims at choosing the state having the greatest connection with the contract. Except for those rare experts on conflict of laws, anyone with a problem in this area can anticipate doing considerable research. To achieve the best results, one should consider which state's law might apply; which would be most favorable; and which of the possible forum states has conflict rules that would invoke the favorable state's law.

In the *Newman* case, a conflict of laws problem becomes a pivotal issue, because the plaintiff might well lose in New York and win in Illinois. Note that the case was filed in a federal court in New York, which under *Erie* followed New York law, specifically New York conflict of laws, to determine whether New York or Illinois law should apply. *Newman*, a suit for damages for the cost of recreating a lost manuscript, was decided in the days before photocopying and word processing. Today the court might hold the plaintiff contributorily negligent for not making a copy of the valuable lost manuscript.

Although the court does not discuss them in detail, it uses two of the traditional bases for choice of law in contract cases: (1) the place where the contract was made, and (2) the place where the contract was performed.

NEWMAN
v.
CLAYTON F. SUMMY CO.
Circuit Court of Appeals, Second Circuit
133 F.2d 465 (1943)

Appellee, a composer, sent a manuscript, insured for $500, by Railway Express from Florida to appellant, a music publisher, in Chicago. Appellant later procured appellee's permission to send the manuscript to appellant's New York office. But, unknown to appellee, appellant, in shipping the script to New York, also by Railway Express, described the package as containing merely "sheet music." The script was lost in transit. Appellee, having retained no copy, spent considerable time in reproducing the script and later contracted with another publisher who published it under a royalty agreement.

* * *

The manuscript had no market value and was unique, so that it was proper to measure its value by the reasonable worth of the time and effort spent by appellee in reproducing it. On the basis of evidence, the verdict was not excessive. And appellee's failure to keep a copy of her script did not bar recovery. . . .

(continued)

(continued)

Appellant asserts that the trial judge erred in instructing the jury as follows: "What is the duty which the bailee, the Summy Company, owed to the bailor, Miss Newman? Being a **bailment,** the Summy Company owed the plaintiff the duty of exercising reasonable care in handling her manuscripts and in dealing with her manuscripts. * * * Negligence is usually defined in these words: Negligence is the failure to exercise a care commensurate to the hazard. That is, the amount and kind of care that would be exercised by an ordinarily prudent person in the same or similar circumstances, or that degree of diligence which the manner and the nature of the employment make it reasonable to expect. The question, therefore, that you must decide is whether the defendant failed in its duty to observe that degree of care in looking after the manuscript which had been entrusted to it." Appellant maintains that the judge should have instructed the jury that it was not liable unless it was **grossly negligent** because, appellant claims under *Erie R.R. v. Tompkins,* 304 U.S. 64 . . . New York law governs. By the law of New York where the trial was held, appellant was a gratuitous bailee, and a gratuitous bailee is not liable except for gross negligence. There is, however, no need for us to consider what would be the law of New York applicable to such a transaction occurring in New York, for here we must apply the New York doctrine of conflict of laws and that doctrine is to the effect that the applicable legal rules are those of Illinois. There can be no doubt that the arrangements for the bailment were made in Illinois, and that "performance," i.e., the shipment of the manuscripts, occurred in that state. In such circumstances, the New York courts hold that the Illinois law as to bailments should be applied.

Turning then to the Illinois decisions, it appears that the rule is that, regardless of whether or not there was a **gratuitous bailment** or one for "mutual benefit," the bailee must use the same care as he would with respect to his own property; there is no discussion of "gross negligence." . . .

The instruction given by the trial court in the instant case was not literally in accord with the language used in those cases. Perhaps the differences are not substantial. But even if they are, that is of no import, since, in the trial court, appellant did not except to the instruction on the ground of any such differences but only because of the failure to give instructions as to gross negligence. Accordingly there was no reversible error.

The judgment of the trial court is affirmed.

Case Questions

1. Why is a different standard of care applied to gratuitous bailment and bailment for hire in New York?
2. To what law (and why) does the federal court look to determine what substantive law to apply?
3. What would be an example of a bailment for hire? A gratuitous bailment?

Case Glossary

bailment   When the owner of personal property delivers possession without intent to pass title, as when one leaves an automobile with an auto mechanic.

gross negligence   Negligence reflecting a reckless disregard for the rights of others, in contrast to *ordinary negligence,* which is commonly characterized by simple carelessness or inattention.

gratuitous bailment   A *bailment* for which no compensation is made.

Law and Equity

legal remedy
A remedy under the common law, as distinguished from an *equitable remedy*.

equitable remedy
A special remedy, such as an injunction, or specific performance, not available at common law.

equity   A system for ensuring justice in circumstances where the remedies customarily available under conventional law are not adequate to ensure a fair result. Also see **chancery**.

chancery   Equity, equitable jurisdiction, a court of equity; a court that administers justice and decides controversies in accordance with the rules, principles, and precedents of equity and that follows the forms and procedure of chancery; as distinguished from a court having the jurisdiction, rules, principles, and practice of the common law.

writ   A written order directing that a specific act be performed.

complaint   The initial pleading in a civil action in which the plaintiff alleges a cause of action and asks that the wrong done to the plaintiff be remedied by the court.

trespass   Originally covered a wide variety of wrongs, one species of which, **trespass** *quare clausum fregit* constituted "trespass to land," which is a wrongful intrusion on the land of another.

History has left the American legal system with an arbitrary division of remedies into *legal* and *equitable*. **Legal remedies** refer to relief granted by common law courts, and **equitable remedies** to those afforded by courts of **equity**, also called **chancery**. Although this subject is usually treated under the heading of remedies, it is related to jurisdiction, because many states restrict equitable jurisdiction to their highest trial courts.

The existence of legal and equitable remedies can be adequately understood only in historical context. Anglo-American law began with the administrative organization of England in the aftermath of the Norman Conquest. Although the Normans left local tribunals in operation, often applying principles of former English law, the organization of a centralized kingdom included the establishment of laws common to the entire kingdom; hence the name common law. Courts were established that had jurisdiction over the common law. In these courts, actions were initiated by **writs,** a word that does not have an exact counterpart in modern law. A writ stated a cause of action, so it is similar to the modern pleading we now call a **complaint.** But writs had specific names, such as the writ of **trespass** *quare clausum fregit*, which corresponds to our modern cause of action for trespass to land, or the writ *de ejectione firmæ*, corresponding to modern ejectment or eviction. The writs were essentially formulas applied to recognized legal wrongs, almost like a catalog of actions in which a party would fill in the blanks. Each action was required to fit precisely into a specific writ. In the first years of the common law courts, new writs were constantly created as different disputes arose that varied from already established actions. Gradually, however, the system crystallized, and the common law courts became formal and rigid, resisting the establishment of new writs so that novel cases that did not fall within established writs were rejected by the courts.

This development did not leave litigants without a remedy, however, because from the beginning subjects of the kingdom enjoyed the right of petitioning the king for justice. As more and more cases arose that were not recognized by the common law courts, parties sought relief from the king, who then presented these cases to the chancellor, originally an ecclesiastical office staffed by priests—not to be confused with ecclesiastical courts under the authority of the Church that applied the principles of canon law. Because of a gradually mounting case load, chancery developed its own courts independent of the common law courts and referred to as courts of equity. Courts of law and equity existed side by side until recent years, when the states merged law and equity into a single court having authority to order both legal and equitable remedies. Despite the merger, features of the historical differences between the two courts remain of importance in modern legal practice.

Courts of equity treated the cases before them somewhat differently than the common law courts. Because petitions in equity sought special justice and presented novel situations, equity courts required greater flexibility and discretion than common law courts. The aim of equity was to provide relief appropriate to merits of the case; thus, courts of equity were described as *courts of conscience,* governed by the moral issues of the case rather than *stare decisis*. Theoretically this is still true today: a judge sitting in equity is not bound by precedent. As a practical matter, modern judges rule in equity on the basis of authority, that is, prior equity cases, and expect attorneys to provide precedential authority in their arguments. Nonetheless, since judges sitting in equity sometimes exercise discretion, ignoring precedent, appeal from a case in equity is frequently premised on the basis of "abuse of discretion" by the lower court judge. If a judge departs from well-established principles of equity as revealed by prior cases, an appellant may use this effectively to persuade an appellate court that the lower court judge abused discretion. Thus, justices sitting in equity are urged to follow consistent principles in a manner similar to *stare decisis* in the common law.

Jury Trials

Because courts of equity exercised moral authority and originally were cloaked with the spiritual authority of the clergy and the secular authority of the king, juries were deemed unnecessary and inappropriate. This custom remains today; there is no right to a jury trial in a case seeking equitable relief alone. The merger of law and equity compounds the jury question, as both legal and equitable remedies may be sought in the same suit, and legal as well as equitable issues may be raised in a suit for equitable relief.

Adequacy of Remedy at Law

replevin A common law cause of action to recover personal property wrongfully possessed by another person.

ejectment A common law cause of action designed to return rightful possession of real property; commonly called *eviction* in modern landlord and tenant law.

writ of mandamus An order requiring a public officer to perform a duty.

specific performance An equitable remedy that asks the court to order a party to a contract to perform the terms of the contract.

Equitable jurisdiction was always discretionary. Because equity courts were originally established to provide remedies when the common law was unavailing, the equity courts refused to hear cases if there was an adequate remedy at law. This became the threshold question in every equity action. The usual common law remedy is *damages*, specifically, monetary compensation for an injury or wrong. There are a number of specific common law actions, such as **replevin** and **ejectment**; various extraordinary remedies titled *writs* (e.g., **writ of mandamus,** writ of prohibition) are common law remedies.

To invoke the equitable jurisdiction of the court, the claim must be based on some special feature that monetary compensation will not redress. A common request for equitable relief is for an injunction, usually a prohibitory injunction, which asks the court to order someone *not* to do something. Injunctions are based on an alleged threat of imminent irreparable injury, asking equity to prevent the injury rather than waiting for the injury to occur and then suing for damages. Affirmative injunctions requiring a party to act (e.g., requiring a school to desegregate) are viewed less favorably by the courts, because of enforcement problems.

Inadequacy of legal remedy is often asserted when the subject matter of a contract is unique or irreplaceable. For example, if someone has made a contract to purchase and the seller refuses to deliver the goods, the remedy of **specific performance** may be sought on the grounds that the goods have some unique quality, such as a family heirloom or a one-of-a-kind classic car. Real property (i.e., land and its improvements) has long been regarded as unique, making available the remedy of specific performance for contracts for the sale of real property. If the goods may be readily purchased elsewhere on the market, however, the remedy is to purchase them and sue the original seller for the difference between the cost of replacement and the cost under the contract. Money damages would then be an adequate remedy, because the final cost would correspond to the price promised under the contract.

output contract
A contract that binds the buyer to buy and the seller to sell the entire product produced by the seller.

Campbell Soup Company had a practice of making **output contracts** with farmers, providing seed and agreeing to purchase the entire crop at prices fixed in advance. The Wentz brothers were Pennsylvania farmers who grew Chantenay carrots for Campbell. During the 1947 season, because of the scarcity of these carrots, the price per ton rose to $90. Because the contract price was $30, the Wentz brothers were not eager to honor the contract and sold 62 of their 100 tons of carrots to Lojeski, who sold half of them to Campbell. Ordinarily, Campbell could pursue a legal remedy by purchasing the carrots elsewhere at the market price and suing for the difference between the market and contact price and so receive the benefit of its bargain. Unfortunately, the carrots were unavailable on the market. Campbell was also undoubtedly concerned about the possibility of other farmers under contract acting similarly in the future and so a brought suit for specific performance, an equitable remedy asking the court to order performance of the contract.

Clean Hands Principle

equitable maxim
A general rule or principle guiding decision making in courts of equity, often serving the function that *precedent* would serve in a common law court.

Although equity is not bound by *stare decisis*, a number of principles of equity have developed over the years expressed in the form of **equitable maxims.** A maxim is often stated in a form resembling a moral commandment. One has already been discussed: equity will not intervene if there is an adequate remedy at law. Other maxims reflect the moral basis for equitable relief, one of the important maxims being the **clean hands doctrine.** Because equity is a court of conscience based on moral principles and dispenses special justice, an equity court may refuse to give relief if the petitioner has not acted in good faith or is otherwise undeserving of special consideration.

clean hands doctrine
An *equitable maxim* according to which the court of equity will refuse to provide a remedy to a petitioner who has acted in bad faith (with "unclean hands").

Statutes of Limitation and Laches

laches An equitable principle, roughly equivalent to a statute of limitations at common law; it prevents a party from bringing a petition (suit) where there has been an unreasonable delay in doing so.

Another difference between legal and equitable remedies arises in the context of delay in bringing suit. Common law actions may be barred by statutes of limitation. Each state has legislated that suits must be brought within a certain period of time, usually measured in years. Some statutes creating causes of action fix the period within which suit can be brought. Unless the state legislature has otherwise specified a time period, equity follows the maxim expressed by the word **laches.** Rather than fixing precise periods of time, laches may be used as a defense to an action in equity if the action is unreasonably delayed to

CAMPBELL SOUP CO.
v.
WENTZ et al.

CAMPBELL SOUP CO.
v.
LOJESKI
United States Court of Appeals, Third Circuit
172 F.2d 80 (1948)

On January 9, 1948, Campbell, suspecting that defendant was selling its "contract carrots," refused to purchase any more, and instituted these suits against the Wentz brothers to enjoin further sale of the contract carrots to others, and to compel specific performance of the contract. . . .

We think that on the question of adequacy of the legal remedy, the case is one appropriate for specific performance. It was expressly found that at the time of the trial it was "virtually impossible to obtain Chantenay carrots in the open market." This Chantenay carrot is one which the plaintiff uses in large quantities, furnishing the seed to the growers with whom it makes contracts. It was not claimed that in nutritive value it is any better than other types of carrots. Its blunt shape makes it easier to handle in processing, and its color and texture differ from other varieties. The color is brighter than other carrots. It appears that the plaintiff uses carrots in 15 of its 21 soups. It also appeared that it uses these Chantenay carrots diced in some of them and that the appearance is uniform. . . .

The trial court concluded that the plaintiff had failed to establish that the carrots, "judged by objective standards," are unique goods. . . . [T]hat the test for specific performance is not necessarily "objective" is shown by the many cases in which equity has given it to enforce contracts for articles—family heirlooms and the like—the value of which was personal to the plaintiff.

. . . Here the goods of the special type contracted for were unavailable on the open market, the plaintiff had contracted for them long ahead in anticipation of his needs, and had built up general reputation for its products as part of which reputation uniform appearance was important. We think if this were all that was involved in the case, specific performance should have been granted.

The reason that we shall affirm instead of reversing with an order for specific performance is found in the contract itself. We think it is too hard a bargain and too one-sided an agreement to entitle the plaintiff to relief in a court of conscience. . . . This form has quite obviously been drawn by skillful draftsmen with the buyer's interests in mind.

[The Court then discusses the contract paragraph by paragraph, demonstrating that it gives Campbell numerous powers and protections while affording no protection to the farmers and concludes the contract is "unconscionable."]

. . . That equity does not enforce unconscionable bargains is too well established to require elaborate citation.

. . . As already said, we do not suggest that this contract is illegal. All we say is that the sum total of its provisions drives too hard a bargain for a court of conscience to assist.

The judgments will be affirmed.

Case Questions
1. How is it that the appellate court totally disagreed with the trial court yet affirmed the trial court's decision?
2. What is Campbell Soup's remedy in future cases like this?
3. What is meant by "unconscionable"?

the prejudice of a party who has changed position during the delay. Circumstances might dictate that a party bring an action very promptly or, conversely, that because no one was harmed by a long delay, no injustice would occur by allowing the action.

Domestic Relations

Prior to the establishment of the American republic, family law matters fell within the jurisdiction of ecclesiastical courts and were governed by canon law. With the American separation of church and state, the law of domestic relations, having no common law precedent, fell within equity jurisdiction. This has had a profound effect on the law, as equity entails great discretion. This is generally appropriate because, with divorce and custody questions, problems tend to be particularized and each case must be examined on its own merits. No-fault divorce, however, has discouraged divorce contests and encouraged parties to negotiate the conditions of custody and the division of property. State legislatures have been active in recent years in setting the standards for child support and providing the means to collect it.

Language

It is important to note that the historical separation of law and equity has given rise to different terms. Because equity actions are brought by petition, the parties to an action in equity are called *petitioner* and *respondent* rather than their common law equivalents, *plaintiff* and *defendant*. Judges sitting in equity are in some jurisdictions referred to as **chancellor** or **master in equity.**

chancellor   A judge of a court of chancery or court of equity; also called a **master in equity.**

Summary

The American legal system is complicated by the existence of separate state and federal jurisdictions. Not only do these have different spheres of authority, but the states themselves are also independent jurisdictions. The division of judicial power is expressed in the U.S. Constitution, which grants specific power to the federal government and reserves the remaining authority to the states. The Constitution is the supreme law of the land, and no official act, law, or judicial order may violate it. The federal judiciary exercises significant authority over state law under the due process and equal protection clauses of the Fourteenth Amendment. The Constitution also requires that the states honor the acts, laws, and judicial orders of other states under the full faith and credit clause.

The Constitution also dictates subject matter jurisdiction of the federal courts, which have jurisdiction over federal question cases, those arising under the Constitution, laws, and treaties of the federal government, and diversity of citizenship cases, those given federal jurisdiction because of the grant of authority over citizens of different states. In diversity cases, by virtue of the decision in

Erie Railroad v. Tompkins, the federal courts apply state law rather than developing a general federal common law.

In cases in which there is some question as to which state's substantive law should apply, each state has its own rules, called conflict of laws, to determine whether it should apply its own law or that of a state more closely involved with the facts giving rise to the lawsuit.

A further complication in the American legal system is the historical existence of common law courts and courts of equity. Equity court first arose several centuries ago in England to provide remedies for disputes the common law courts would not hear. Equity developed special remedies differing from the usual common law remedy of monetary compensation (damages) and developed its own principles based on moral principles. As a result, equitable remedies are more flexible and bound less by precedent than legal remedies. One important feature that distinguishes law from equity is the traditional absence of the right to a jury in equity.

Today law and equity have merged, so that American judges provide both equitable and legal relief, and legal and equitable remedies may be requested in the same suit. Nevertheless, many of the traditional differences have been maintained.

Scenario

The year is 2008. After many years debating the appropriateness of same-sex marriage, the state of Vermont, which pioneered legislation recognizing *civil unions,* is the first state in 2008 to pass a law allowing same-sex marriage:

> Vermont Revised Statutes (2008), § 28.101. Effective January 1, 2009, no person otherwise eligible to contract marriage may not be denied a marriage license on the grounds of sexual preference, including a person contracting marriage with another person of the same sex. Any person who obtains a marriage license in accordance with this statute shall enjoy all rights and be subject to all duties of married persons now recognized by statute or case law, any statute or case precedent to the contrary notwithstanding. Eligibility to marry shall be established by residence in the state of Vermont for three days (72 hours).

The residency requirement for voter registration in Vermont is six months' continuous residence in the state. Anyone living in Vermont for more than one month is required to obtain a state driver's license to drive legally in the state if that person is employed within the state, except for students whose legal residence is another state. These statutes have been upheld in Vermont and federal courts when challenged on due process and equal protection grounds.

Alice Murphy and Nancy Gibson, after cohabiting in a relationship of emotional, sexual, and economic unit for several years in the state of West Carolina, decide to contract marriage in Vermont and adopt a child. Fortuitously, they have a friend, Camille, living in Vermont who is dying of cancer and has a three-year-old daughter she wants Alice and Nancy to adopt. The requisite papers are drawn up, and Alice and Nancy go to Vermont to stay with Camille. After staying there for four days, they go before the clerk of court before whom they swear that they have resided in Vermont for 72 hours and intend to make Vermont their place of residence. The clerk of court asks them to raise their right hands and swear that the statements they have made are correct, after which the clerk asks them standard marital oaths that they answer in the affirmative and the clerk validates the marriage license, which is then recorded. One week later, the adoption is recorded with the court. They stay with Camille for another month, at which time she is about to be put on life support at the hospital. Camille takes leave of her daughter, and Alice and Nancy return to West Carolina

In 1996, Congress passed an act called the Defense of Marriage Act, which reads as follows:

> **28 U.S.C. §1738C. Certain acts, records, and proceedings and the effect thereof.**
> No State, territory, or possession of the United States, or Indian tribe, shall be required to give effect to any public act, record, or judicial proceeding of any other State, territory, possession, or tribe respecting a relationship between persons of the same sex that is treated as a marriage under the laws of such other State, territory, possession, or tribe, or a right or claim arising from such relationship.

Many legal scholars have attacked this act as unconstitutional, but it has not been tested because no state—until the Vermont law changed—had allowed same-sex marriage.

Alice and Nancy want to live in West Carolina. While they wish to have a legal marriage, they are more concerned that the adoption be recognized in West Carolina. Children and Family Services of West Carolina brings an action to take custody of the child; Alice and Nancy defend on the basis of the Vermont marriage and adoption. The trial judge denies the writ on the grounds that West Carolina has passed a Defense of Marriage Act (DOMA) clearly prohibiting same-sex marriage in accord with 28 U.S.C. 1738C. West Carolina law also prohibits adoption by homosexuals. The judge adds that Alice and Nancy were West Carolina residents at the time of the marriage, invalidating that marriage even under the law of Vermont.

You represent Alice and Nancy on appeal. Formulate the issues for appeal and make an argument for each based on policy grounds. Ordinarily the appellate brief would have numerous citations to pertinent cases, but we may treat this as a first draft, making the arguments that would then direct us to research supporting and challenging cases.

The issues might be stated something like this: "ISSUE I: Whether the defendants met the residency requirements for the state of Vermont, making the marriage valid in Vermont."

The arguments might start out like this: "ARGUMENT—ISSUE I: The prior and subsequent residence of the defendants in West Carolina did not invalidate the Vermont residency because . . . "

This scenario is designed to make you think through the nature of "full faith and credit" and the federal system in general.

PROCEDURE IN CIVIL CASES

Introduction

Procedural law is the oil that greases the legal machine. No area of law has more theoretical or practical importance. From a theoretical perspective, procedural law informs us about the basic premises of the legal system itself. The adversarial premise of the American legal system maintains that our system is based on competition and that individuals act in their own self-interest and cannot be trusted unless their power positions are equalized by a disinterested and perhaps indifferent tribunal. The fact that we preserve the jury system suggests that we do not even trust the impartiality of our judges. The rules that exclude evidence suggest that we do not trust the capacity of juries to sift good evidence from bad.

The theoretical premise at the heart of our procedure is: If the means by which conflict in society is resolved are fair and equal, justice will, on the whole, be achieved. Acceptance of this premise is a virtual catechism of lawyers. When criminal defense attorneys are asked, "Would you defend a guilty man? Would you help a guilty man be acquitted and go free?," the answer is usually the same: "Every person is entitled to competent legal representation; it is not for the attorney to judge; it is the job of the prosecution to prove guilt beyond a reasonable doubt." This response can only be understood in the context of a system that places procedure on a pedestal.

The practical importance of procedure is equal to its philosophical importance. Rights have no meaning without a means to enforce them. Without a procedure for enforcement, the statement of a right is merely symbolic.

Each state and the federal system have compiled their own set of rules of civil procedure, which henceforth are referred to as "the rules." These treat some procedural questions with great specificity, allowing little room for interpretation, but other questions may be adequately understood only by researching rules of court, judicial interpretations, or even local procedural customs. The competent practitioner must have a thorough understanding of the rules of the jurisdictions in which practice is to be conducted, but that is beyond the scope of the treatment of civil procedure here. What follows is merely a model and an overview.

Procedure is arbitrary and technical, yet it is always subject to attack for its fairness under the due process clause of the Fourteenth Amendment. Cases concerning procedural due process tend to be exceedingly complex and difficult. One of the reasons may be that the social values underlying the rules are obscure at best. In comparison, substantive areas of law, such as tort and contract, may rely on values supported by a general consensus. For example, in contract law, it is a premise of our society that a person should fulfill lawful promises; in tort law, it is a premise that a person who wrongfully injures another should compensate the injured party. In contrast, is there any fundamental reason that a jury may not be exposed to hearsay evidence, or that a hearing be adversarial rather than mediatory in nature, or that a complaint must state a cause of action?

Procedural Framework of Legal Disputes

A basic model of the legal processing of a dispute underlies American procedural law. In its minute details, it differs from jurisdiction to jurisdiction, but the basic idea is the same. This chapter delineates its outline, as follows:

1. One who proposes to seek relief through the legal system must formally state to a court the basis for a grievance, and the grounds asserted must amount to a grievance that the law recognizes as enforceable.

2. The opponent in a legal action must be notified of the suit and given the opportunity to prepare for a defense.

3. Parties to a lawsuit will have every reasonable means prior to a trial to become fully informed of the factual and legal arguments of the other side.

4. If a dispute proceeds to trial, it will be conducted as an adversarial proceeding in which each side has every opportunity to challenge the arguments of the other side.

5. In an adversarial trial, decisions of the court must be based on the evidence and arguments presented in court before an impartial tribunal.

service of process
Delivery of a summons, writ, complaint, or other process to the opposite party or other person entitled to receive it, in such manner as the law prescribes.

original service   The first presentation of legal documents to the defendant, after which service is usually made to the defendant's attorney.

process   In criminal law, the document commanding a party to do or not to do something; see **service of process.**

personal service
The presentation of the summons and complaint upon the defendant personally.

substituted service
Service of process to someone other than the defendant, such as a relative living at the defendant's abode; requirements usually defined by statute.

publication   In reference to *service of process*, a means of service by publishing notice in the legal section of a newspaper periodically as prescribed by statute.

long-arm statutes
Statutes that provide a state with jurisdiction over persons or entities ordinarily beyond its territory and usual jurisdiction.

6. Any departure from procedural rules will provide a basis for challenging the fairness of the process.

7. Procedural error takes precedence over substantive goals. The corollary to this is that if the procedure was fair, the results cannot be questioned except in extraordinary circumstances.

Determining the Proper Court for the Suit

In addition to the problems of subject matter jurisdiction discussed in Chapter 6, a number of obstacles may arise concerning the exercise of the court's authority in a particular case.

Service of Process

The notification of the defendant in a lawsuit is accomplished by **service of process.** This refers to the presentation to the defendant of a copy of the complaint, along with a summons, which informs the defendant that an answer to the complaint must be served on the plaintiff's attorney within a specified number of days, commonly twenty. It is an essential component of procedural due process, the other being a (fair) hearing. *Service* refers to presentation of the documents; service of the complaint and summons is **original service.** (After original service, documents may be served on the attorneys for the parties by mail.) **Process** refers to the document commanding a party to do or not do something. At common law, original process was formerly called an original writ or writ of process. In equity, it was called a subpoena. Today original process is usually simply called a summons.

Service of process is effected by filing the complaint and summons with the court, followed by presentation to the defendant of the complaint and summons by one authorized to do so, typically a sheriff or deputy or a U.S. Marshal for federal cases. Private process-servers may also be authorized by the law and are typically used if the defendant may be purposely avoiding service or may be difficult to locate. Deputies and marshalls have many duties and cannot be expected to go to great efforts in serving process in civil cases. Attorneys commonly offer assistance in locating defendants, such as informing the sheriff of the defendant's place of work or the hours the defendant is likely to be at home. The place, time, and manner of service of process must be in accord with the rules or other statutes of the jurisdiction in which process is served.

Presenting the summons and complaint personally to the defendant is called **personal service** and is the ideal form of service, especially in jurisdictions in which the defendant signs a paper, thus assuring the court that the defendant was properly notified of the suit and making it difficult for the defendant to later challenge the service. The rules or statutes also provide for **substituted service** whereby process can be served on someone other than the defendant, such as a relative living at the defendant's abode. Substituted service that does not

seduction Inducing (usually by deception or promise to marry) a person (usually a chaste, unmarried woman) to have sex.

heart balm suits Now largely discredited lawsuits for emotional injuries such as *seduction, breach of promise to marry, criminal conversation*, and *alienation of affections*.

breach of promise to marry A cause of action based on breaking off an engagement to marry.

criminal conversation Causing a married man or woman to commit adultery. Despite its name, this is a tort, not a crime, and it is generally abolished in most states as a cause of action.

alienation of affection Taking away the love, companionship, or help of another person's husband or wife; still recognized in a few states.

default judgment May be entered against a party failing to file a required document in a lawsuit, particularly failing to file an answer.

in personam, or personal jurisdiction The power a court has over the person of a defendant to subject that person to decisions and rulings made in a case.

strictly comply with the law is invalid. Service may also be made by publication in a newspaper of general circulation if a diligent search for the defendant fails to reveal the defendant's whereabouts. **Publication** refers to the publication of a legal notice in an authorized periodical, such as a newspaper of general circulation. Again, the manner of service by publication must strictly follow the law.

The rules provide for service in special situations. Business entities, for example, call for different service—a corporation may be served by service upon an authorized agent of the corporation; partnerships may be served by service upon a partner. Minors, prisoners, military personnel on active duty, legal incompetents, and the like may call for special treatment.

Service of nonresidents is accomplished under the authority of **long-arm statutes,** with the cooperation of the officers of the state of residence of the defendant. If the nonresident is present in the state in which the suit is filed, personal service is effective within the state.

Service other than personal service will be scrutinized carefully by the judge if the defendant does not answer and does not appear for a judicial proceeding. Judges are understandably reluctant to determine the rights of an absent defendant.

The *Wyman* case presents several interesting procedural features, some of which are difficult to reconstruct because of the age of the case. In 1937, personal service of process was preferred even more than today. At that time, the causes of action for seduction and breach of promise to marry were recognized in most states as in Florida, which later abolished them, but they were in disrepute, particularly in New York, which may explain why the complaint was filed in Florida rather than New York. (**Seduction** is one of the so-called **heart balm suits,** along with **breach of promise to marry, criminal conversation,** and **alienation of affections,** which were designed to compensate for loss of or interference with intimate relationships. Most states have abolished such causes of action through what have come to be known as *anti–heart balm statutes.*) Because the defendant did not answer the Florida complaint, the Florida court entered a **default judgment,** which the plaintiff then attempted to enforce in New York.

In Personam Jurisdiction

In personam or **personal jurisdiction** refers to the authority of the court to determine the rights of the defendant in a lawsuit. (Personal jurisdiction over the plaintiff results from filing the suit.) When service of process is deficient or not in accordance with law, the court does not have personal jurisdiction over the defendant. The defendant may simply be beyond the reach of the court. If a resident of Oregon is involved in an accident in Oregon with a resident of California, the Oregon resident can object to personal jurisdiction in California—California would have personal jurisdiction under its long-arm statute only if the accident occurred in California.

WYMAN
v.
NEWHOUSE
Circuit Court of Appeals, Second Circuit
93 F.2d 313 (2d Cir. 1937)

This appeal is from a judgment entered dismissing the complaint on motion before trial. The action is on a judgment entered by default in a Florida state court, a jury having assessed the damages. The recovery there was for money loaned, money advanced for appellee, and for seduction under promise of marriage.

* * *

Appellant and appellee were both married, but before this suit appellant's husband died. They had known each other for some years and had engaged in meretricious relations.

The affidavits submitted by the appellee deemed to be true for the purpose of testing the alleged error of dismissing the complaint established that he was a resident of New York and never lived in Florida. On October 25, 1935, while appellee was in Salt Lake City, Utah, he received a telegram from the appellant, which read: "Account illness home planning leaving. Please come on way back. Must see you." Upon appellee's return to New York he received a letter from appellant stating that her mother was dying in Ireland; that she was leaving the United States for good to go to her mother; that she could not go without seeing the appellee once more; and that she wanted to discuss her affairs with him before she left. Shortly after the receipt of this letter, they spoke to each other on the telephone, whereupon the appellant repeated, in a hysterical and distressed voice, the substance of her letter. Appellee promised to go to Florida in a week or ten days and agreed to notify her when he would arrive. This he did, but before leaving New York by plane he received a letter couched in endearing terms and expressing love and affection for him, as well as her delight at his coming. Before leaving New York, appellee telegraphed appellant, suggesting arrangements for their accommodations

together while in Miami. She telegraphed him at a hotel in Washington, D.C., where he was to stop en route, advising him that the arrangements requested had been made. Appellee arrived at 6 o'clock in the morning at the Miami Airport and saw the appellant standing with her sister some 75 feet distant. He was met by a deputy sheriff who, upon identifying appellee, served him with process in a suit for $500,000. A photographer was present who attempted to take his picture. Thereupon a stranger introduced himself and offered to take appellee to his home, stating that he knew a lawyer who was acquainted with the appellant's attorney. The attorney whom appellee was advised to consult came to the stranger's home and seemed to know about the case. The attorney invited appellee to his office, and upon his arrival he found one of the lawyers for the appellant there. Appellee did not retain the Florida attorney to represent him. He returned to New York by plane that evening and consulted his New York counsel, who advised him to ignore the summons served in Florida. He did so, and judgment was entered by default. Within a few days after the service of process, the appellant came to New York and sought an interview with the appellee. It resulted in their meeting at the home of the appellee's attorney. She was accompanied by her Florida counsel.

These facts and reasonable deductions therefrom convincingly establish that fraud perpetrated upon him by the appellant in falsely representing her mother's illness, her intention to leave the United States, and her love and affection for him, when her sole purpose and apparent thought was to induce him to come within the Florida jurisdiction so as to serve him in an action for damages. Appellant does not deny making these representations. All her statements of great and undying love were disproved entirely by her appearance at the airport and participation in the happening there. She never went to Ireland to see her mother, if indeed the latter was sick at all.

In asking for judgment based on these Florida proceedings, appellant relies upon arti-

cle 4, section 1, of the United States Constitution, providing that "Full Faith and Credit shall
be given in each State to the public Acts,
Records, and Judicial Proceedings of every
other State.". . .

This judgment is attacked for fraud perpetrated upon the appellee which goes to the

jurisdiction of the Florida court over his person.
A judgment procured fraudulently, as here,
lacks jurisdiction and is null and void. A fraud
affecting the jurisdiction is equivalent to a lack
of jurisdiction. The appellee was not required to
proceed against the judgment in Florida. . . .

Judgment affirmed.

Case Questions

1. Did the Florida trial court have any reason to believe that the service of process was accomplished
   by fraud?
2. Does the court's opinion suggest a union of a conniving plaintiff and an unscrupulous attorney?

---

special appearance
A defendant may make a
special appearance for the
purpose of challenging
personal jurisdiction
without the fact of the
appearance conferring
personal jurisdiction, as it
would otherwise do.

in rem jurisdiction
Describes a lawsuit
brought to enforce rights
in a thing against the
whole world as opposed
to one brought to enforce
rights against another
person; see **personal
jurisdiction** (p. 145).

attachment Formally
seizing property in order
to bring it under the
control of the court; this is
usually done by getting a
court order to have a law
enforcement officer take
control of the property.

quasi in rem Actions
that are really directed
against a person, but are
formally directed only
against property.

Appearance by the defendant in court confers personal jurisdiction despite
deficient service of process. In many jurisdictions, the defendant may enter a
special appearance solely for the purpose of contesting personal jurisdiction,
and the appearance will not be construed as conferring personal jurisdiction.
Challenges to personal jurisdiction must follow the rules to avoid a waiver of
defenses to personal jurisdiction. Of course, a nonresident may remain silent and
later challenge jurisdiction of the original court if the plaintiff attempts to
enforce a judgment under full faith and credit in the defendant's home state, but
a significant risk is involved because the defendant's state might reject the
defenses and enforce the judgment, leaving the defendant without an opportunity to defend the case on its merits.

In Rem Jurisdiction

Under certain circumstances, the purpose of a suit may be to determine the status of property rather than to determine personal rights, and an **in rem** action
may be brought. *Rem* is from the Latin word *res*, roughly translated as "thing."
Courts generally have jurisdiction over real and personal property located
within their jurisdictions. In rem proceedings are often brought to prevent the
removal of property from the jurisdiction, typically in **attachment** proceedings
to secure court control over property subject to a debt. Some actions involve
property but operate only between parties to the suit and are called **quasi in
rem**. Conceptually, it is difficult to distinguish quasi in rem from in personam
actions. In rem actions are fairly rare because the primary purpose of most lawsuits is to determine the respective rights of persons.

Certain real property actions in equity are in rem or quasi in rem actions,
such as suits to quiet title or to remove a cloud on title. These suits are usually
brought in connection with a real estate transaction when an attorney (or title
company) discovers some potential defect in the title that should be cleared up
prior to completing the transaction. For example, a person can acquire title by

adverse possession; that is, someone without rightful possession of real property who nevertheless enters on the land and occupies it for a certain number of years (twenty at common law, less under most state statutes) may acquire title. The presence at some past time of adverse possession may raise doubts about title that can be settled in the suit. Essentially, then, the suit is against the property rather than against specific persons. Whenever the parties are known, caution suggests that they should be included as defendants.

res   Thing. In Latin, nouns have different forms for subjective and objective positions in the sentence. Thus res is the same noun as rem in "in rem," except that the latter takes a different ending because it follows the preposition. Note that "in personam" also adds an "m" to "persona" because it follows the preposition.

Another example of an in rem action is suit for divorce. In theory, the **res** in a divorce action is the marriage—divorce has the effect of changing the status from married to unmarried. In practice, courts are extremely reluctant to treat divorce actions as in rem proceedings because ordinarily divorce actions involve the adjudication of personal rights. Alimony and child support, for example, are considered in personam questions.

These examples demonstrate that in rem proceedings must be restricted to special circumstances; frequently, as in attachment, they are ancillary to a larger in personam suit. Whenever a known person's rights are involved, personal jurisdiction should be established to prevent a later attack on the judicial order.

In Personam, in Rem, and Quasi in Rem Compared

In personam, in rem, and quasi in rem are difficult to distinguish in the abstract. The cases, the history, and the difference between jurisdictional definitions have left the distinctions quite confused. With this confusion in mind, the following is designed as a rule-of-thumb guide:

In personam jurisdiction has a party—a person—as a defendant.

> *Example:* Johnson sues Jackson for breach of contract.

In rem jurisdiction has property as a defendant.

> *Example:* State seizure of property for taxes.

Quasi in rem jurisdiction brings suit against property to satisfy a personal claim.

> *Example:* Plaintiff sues for attachment and sale of property to satisfy a debt owed by another party who has property located within the forum state but is beyond the reach of the personal jurisdiction of the court.

Quasi in rem is used when personal jurisdiction would have been obtained if the defendant could have been served personally. The court has in rem jurisdiction over property within the state but does not have in personam jurisdiction over out-of-state residents who have no contact with the state other than their ownership of property located within the state.

The distinctions are often obscure, and an inherent due process issue always lurks when rights may be affected without opportunity to be heard. This problem of definition underscores the difficult problems of civil procedure, namely, measuring very technical rules and concepts against the broad, flexible concept of due process.

Venue

venue The *place* where jurisdiction is exercised—many courts may have jurisdiction over a case, but it is filed in only one place.

Venue refers to the place where jurisdiction is exercised. Venue is easily confused with jurisdiction, but the two must be clearly distinguished. For example, the issue of whether a case should be heard in a state or federal court is a matter of subject matter jurisdiction, as discussed in Chapter 6. Venue concerns the question of which court within a system should be the *place* where jurisdiction is exercised. An example from divorce law in Florida may clarify this problem.

forum non conveniens
If two or more courts both have proper *venue* for a case, a judge may rule that a lawsuit must be brought in the other court for either the convenience of or fairness to the parties.

Florida circuit courts have jurisdiction over divorce cases (now called "dissolution of marriage"). The jurisdictional requirement for bringing a divorce action is that the petitioner must have resided in the state for six months prior to bringing the action. The action may be brought in any circuit in the state; in fact, some actions are brought in a venue far from the residences of either party to the action in order to avoid local public scrutiny. However, if the respondent objects to the place where the suit is filed, venue may be challenged, and the court will transfer the case to the circuit in which the respondent resides. It is not that the original court does not have jurisdiction but, rather, that another court with similar jurisdiction is determined to be the more appropriate site of the lawsuit.

complaint The initial pleading in a civil action in which the plaintiff alleges a cause of action and asks that the wrong done to the plaintiff be remedied by the court.

The divorce example is based on the allegation of *inconvenient venue*, commonly referred to by the Latin phrase **forum non conveniens.** Another venue challenge is based on the allegation that a party cannot obtain a fair trial where the action has been brought (e.g., the plaintiff may have unusual influence over the local population so that the defendant fears that a fair trial is difficult or impossible).

answer A pleading that responds to the complaint, admitting and denying specific allegations and presenting defenses.

Pleadings

petition Sometimes also known as a *complaint* or *pleading*, it alleges a cause of action. It is a formal, written request, addressed to a person or body in a position of authority.

Many technical problems may arise concerning proper and necessary parties to a lawsuit, that is, who may or must be included in the lawsuit. Problems of multiple plaintiffs or defendants, class action suits, and other special problems must be left to a more detailed study of litigation and procedure. Discussion here is limited to the basic documents that frame the issues for trial.

subpoena A court's order to a person that he or she appear in court to testify in a case.

Modern pleading borrows heavily from both law and equity. The basic documents of pleading, the **complaint** and the **answer,** echo the procedure of equity, which required the suitor to file a **petition** or bill in equity. The petition initiated the suit much like a complaint does today, except that the petition was a lengthy recitation of the facts of the case, much restricted today. After the bill was filed, a **subpoena** was issued requiring the respondent to appear, and the respondent provided an answer, which presented the respondent's defenses, thereby closing the pleadings and requiring the plaintiff to go forward to prove the allegations.

joinder The bringing in of a new person who joins together with the plaintiff as a plaintiff or the defendant as a defendant.

Equity also provided for **joinder,** which consolidated related claims and related parties, thus avoiding the necessity of hearing numerous cases. If a

counterclaim A cause of action brought by a defendant against the plaintiff in a single case, e.g., in an auto collision, both drivers often sue each other, one files a complaint and the other counterclaims.

cause of action In order to bring a lawsuit, one must state a *cause of action*. The court must recognize the action (suit) as one of the many kinds that a court can decide. In a sense, a cause of action is a label for a type of lawsuit. For example, slander, breach of contract, invasion of privacy, and trespass are causes of action.

elements The specific parts of a cause of action that must be alleged and proved to make out that cause of action.

ultimate facts The general statements of fact that support a cause of action, for example, the allegations of fact in the complaint. Compare to **evidentiary facts.**

evidentiary facts The specific facts presented at trial, as distinguished from the more general **ultimate facts.**

caption The heading of a court paper, usually including the names of the parties, the court, and the case number.

respondent had a claim against the petitioner, this could be brought through a *cross-bill,* analogous to the modern **counterclaim.**

Equity also provided for petitioner's (and later respondent's) discovery of information possessed by the adverse party in order to prepare for hearing.

All these features of equity procedure were incorporated with changes into modern pleading. Common law procedure, in contrast, was complex and formal. Common law pleading had two principal objects. First, it was necessary for the plaintiff to fit the case into a *form of action* that would support the court's issuing a corresponding writ or order to the sheriff to compel the defendant to satisfy the plaintiff's claim or appear in court to show cause why he or she need not do so. The form of action corresponds to the **cause of action,** still required in modern pleading; the specific facts required by the formula for each form of action correspond to the **elements** presently required to state a cause of action.

Second, common law pleading was designed to focus the lawsuit on a single issue, and it did this by a series of responsive pleadings back and forth between plaintiff and defendant until the issue was clearly framed. This was a highly technical process with numerous pitfalls. The parties were not allowed to present multiple actions or defenses, and attempt to do so would result in a holding for the other side.

The advantage of common law pleading was its precision; the disadvantages were its inflexibility and technicality. The advantages of equity procedure were its flexibility and attention to substance over technicality; its disadvantage was the time-consuming process of setting the case for hearing—the relative simplicity and flexibility of equity procedure failed to focus the case and restrain the parties.

Modern code pleading attempts to borrow the advantages of both processes while minimizing their disadvantages. Equity pleadings are restricted to the allegation of **ultimate** rather than the more detailed **evidentiary facts.** Rather than focusing on a single issue, the pleadings are designed to establish a cause of action and present defenses. Issues are narrowed largely by the pretrial process, including discovery, a concept borrowed from equity. Liberalized pleading allows complaints to be amended, shifting emphasis toward substantive rather than purely technical issues. It must be noted, however, that civil procedure is by its nature technical, and inattention to the rules can be costly.

The Complaint

The complaint is designed to inform the court and the defendant that a lawsuit has been filed, invoking the attendant legal process. The complaint itself—that is, the document filed with the court and served on the defendant—may be divided into several parts:

1. The **caption** is the heading of the complaint and names the court in which the complaint is filed, the names of the parties to the suit, and the case number of the suit (assigned by the clerk). The caption begins each document filed with the court. Below the case number (on the right underneath

the name of the court) or below the caption itself is the label of the document, e.g., "COMPLAINT," "ANSWER," "MOTION FOR SUMMARY JUDGMENT."

2. The first paragraph of the complaint contains the jurisdictional allegation, which states the grounds for subject matter jurisdiction of the court wherein the complaint has been filed.

3. The remaining numbered paragraphs of the complaint present a brief allegation of general facts designed to state a cause of action and provide notice to the defendant of the basis for the suit.

4. The complaint ends with a **prayer for relief,** sometimes called the **wherefore clause** because it traditionally begins with something like "WHEREFORE, the Plaintiff prays for judgment. . . ."

prayer for relief   Also known as *demand for relief,* it is that portion of a complaint or claim for relief that specifies the type of relief to which the plaintiffs feel they are entitled and they are requesting. See **wherefore clause.**

wherefore clause
Meaning "for this reason," this refers to the *prayer for relief,* the final clause in a complaint asking the court for some sort of remedy: "Wherefore, the plaintiff prays that. . . ."

The complaint example should be familiar to most readers. It is the case of *Gore v. Harris,* which started out in the Florida court and ultimately ended in the U.S. Supreme Court as *Bush v. Gore* (Governor Bush, later President Bush, was one of the original defendants, who petitioned successfully for a writ of certiorari from the U.S. Supreme Court, resulting in his name being listed first in the case.) The original complaint is twenty-five pages long. The answer, which follows, by Florida Secretary of State Katherine Harris, was originally thirty-one pages. A great many complaints and answers are much shorter because the plaintiff often needs only to assert enough allegations of fact to establish the elements of a traditional cause of action; for example, in an auto collision, the plaintiff alleges the defendant ran a stop sign and thereby caused plaintiff's injury; defendant denies he ran the stop sign. Complaints and answers are sometimes almost that simple. In *Gore v. Harris,* a complicated electoral process with different counties counting ballots differently and confusing Florida statutes combined to necessitate a detailed outline of pertinent facts.

The Answer

affirmative defense
A claim made by the defendant that, if it prevails, will negate the plaintiff's case.

To defend the suit, the defendant must file an answer, although other procedural devices to attack the complaint are available at this time. The answer is responsive to the complaint and admits allegations in the complaint that defendant does not wish to contest. It contains denials of allegations in the complaint that the defendant disputes, which allegations then become questions for proof and argument. The answer may also contain **affirmative defenses,** which contain matter not included in the complaint that defendant alleges will prevent the plaintiff from obtaining relief. For example, the defendant may contend that the statute of limitations has run, barring plaintiff's suit. If the plaintiff cannot overcome this defense, the suit must be dismissed. The answer may also present a counterclaim, which is a claim by the defendant against the plaintiff that must contain sufficient allegations to state a cause of action on its own.

Sample Complaint

IN THE CIRCUIT COURT OF THE SECOND JUDICIAL CIRCUIT,
IN AND FOR LEON COUNTY, FLORIDA CIVIL DIVISION

ALBERT GORE, Jr., Nominee of the Democratic Party)
of the United States for President of the United)
States, and)
JOSEPH I. LIEBERMAN, Nominee of the Democratic)
Party of the United States for Vice President of the)
United States,)
)
Plaintiffs,)
)
v.)   CASE NO. 00-2808
)
KATHERINE HARRIS, as SECRETARY OF STATE, STATE)
OF FLORIDA, and SECRETARY OF AGRICULTURE)
BOB CRAWFORD, SECRETARY OF STATE KATHERINE)
HARRIS And L. CLAYTON ROBERTS, DIRECTOR,)
DIVISION OF ELECTIONS, individually and as)
member of and as THE FLORIDA ELECTIONS)
CANVASSING COMMISSION,)
)
and)
)
THE MIAMI-DADE COUNTY CANVASSING BOARD,)
LAWRENCE D. KING, MYRIAM LEHR, and DAVID C.)
LEAHY as members of and as THE MIAMI-DADE)
COUNTY CANVASSING BOARD, and DAVID C.)
LEAHY, individually and as Supervisor of Elections,)
)
and)
)
THE NASSAU COUNTY CANVASSING BOARD,)
ROBERT E. WILLIAMS, [etc. . . .])
)
and)
)
THE PALM BEACH COUNTY CANVASSING BOARD,)
THERESA LEPORE. [etc. . . .])
)
and)
)
GEORGE W. BUSH, Nominee of The Republican)
Party of the United States for President of the)
United States, and RICHARD CHENEY, Nominee of)
the Republican Party of the United States for Vice)
President of the United States,)
)
Defendants.)

COMPLAINT TO CONTEST ELECTION

1. This is an action to contest the certification that George W. Bush and Richard Cheney received more votes in the Presidential election in the State of Florida than Al Gore and Joe Lieberman. The vote totals reported in the Election Canvassing Commission's certification of November 26, 2000 are wrong. They include illegal votes and do not include legal votes that were improperly rejected. The number of such votes is more than sufficient to place in doubt, indeed to change, the result of the election.

2. The Plaintiffs, Albert Gore, Jr., nominee of the Democratic Party of the United States for President of the United States in the 2000 General Election (Al Gore) and Joseph I. Lieberman nominee of the Democratic Party of the United States for Vice-President of the United States in the 2000 General Election (Joe Lieberman), contest the November 26, 2000 certification by the Elections Canvassing Commission of the results of the Presidential election and the determination of the winning Presidential election and the determination of the winning Presidential Electors in Florida. Al Gore and Joe Lieberman further contest the Secretary of State's certification of the electors for Defendants George W. Bush and Richard Cheney as elected.

3. The Election Canvassing Board certified 2,912,790 votes for George W. Bush and Richard Cheney and 2,912,253 votes for Al Gore and Joe Lieberman, a difference of 537 votes. The difference was <u>entirely</u> the result of:

    (a) rejecting the results of the complete manual count in Palm Beach County (which resulted in approximately 215 additional net votes for Gore/Lieberman) and the results of a manual count of approximately 20% of the precincts in Miami-Dade County (which resulted in approximately 160 additional net votes for Gore/Lieberman); and

    (b) including changes to the certified results of the Nassau County Canvassing Board which, over the Thanksgiving weekend, changed its previously certified results—not based on a manual count, but by adding votes in violation of Florida law from earlier tabulations that had previously been rejected by that Board as illegal (which resulted in a total of approximately 50 additional net votes for Bush/Cheney).

    (c) not counting approximately 4,000 ballots in Palm Beach County that were marked by the voter with an indentation but which were not (in most cases at least) punctured that the Palm Beach County Canvassing Board reviewed but did not count as a vote . . .

    (d) not counting approximately 9,000 ballots in Miami-Dade County that have not been recorded as a vote for any presidential candidate . . .

Common Allegations

4. This is an action to contest an election under section 102.168, Florida Statutes (2000).

5. Section 102.168(5), Florida Statutes (2000) establishes Leon County as the proper venue for this action.

(continued)

(continued)

6. Section 102.168(8), Florida Statutes (2000) empowers the judge in a contest action to:

> fashion such orders as he or she deems necessary to ensure that each allegation in the complaint is investigated, examined or checked to prevent or correct any alleged wrong, and to provide any relief appropriate under such circumstances.

[There follow factual allegations leading to:]

17. On November 26, 2000 the Elections Canvassing Board declared George W. Bush and Richard Cheney as winners of Florida's electoral votes.

Count I (Miami-Dade County Canvassing Board)

[Factual allegations specific to the Canvassing Board]

35. If the uncounted ballots in Miami-Dade County are counted, it will show that a person other than the person certified by the Elections Canvassing Commission as a winner of Florida's Presidential election was elected.

Count II (Miami-Dade County)

[Paragraphs 36–39 present factual allegations concerning Miami-Dade County.]

Count III (Nassau County)

[Paragraphs 40–56 concern Nassau County.]

[Paragraphs 57–88 provide additional allegations for Counts IV–VI, after which is the Prayer for Relief:]

Prayer for Relief

WHEREFORE, Plaintiffs pray the court:

As to Count I (Miami-Dade County Canvassing Board)

A. Order that the Miami-Dade County Canvassing Board and Supervisor of Elections immediately transmit the approximately 10,750 uncounted ballots cast in the year 2000 presidential election to the Clerk of this Court for safe keeping.
B. Cause the uncounted ballots cast in Miami-Dade County for President and Vice President of the United States to be manually counted by or under the direction of this Court, counting each ballot cast unless it is impossible to determine the intent of the voter, in order to determine the true and accurate returns of the general election for President and Vice President from Miami-Dade County.
C. Order that the Elections Canvassing Commission include in the certified results for Presidential electors all votes counted in the Miami-Dade County election including the results of this court's count.

[Plaintiffs request specific orders regarding the other counts and ask also for "universal relief" concluding with:]

H. Order that the Elections Canvassing Commission, Secretary of State, and the Division of Elections certify as elected the presidential electors of Al Gore and Joe Lieberman.

I. And grant such other relief as the court deems right and just.

Certificate of Service

I HEREBY CERTIFY that a true copy of the foregoing has been furnished by United States mail, hand delivery or facsimile transmission this [27th] day of November, 2000 to the following:

Barry Richard Cheney
Greenberg Traurig
101 East College Avenue
Tallahassee, FL 32301
for Governor Bush

Deborah Kearney, General Counsel
Florida Department of State
400 South Monroe Street, PL 02
Tallahassee, FL 32399
for Secretary Katherine Harris and
the Elections Canvassing Committee

[There follow the names and addresses of five additional attorneys. And the signature of the submitting attorney.]

Respectfully submitted this [27th] day of November, 2000

COUNSEL FOR ALBERT GORE, JR., AND JOSEPH I. LIEBERMAN

[Names, addresses and signatures of six attorneys]

Complaint Questions

1. Why is the case commonly referred to as *Gore v. Harris?*
2. What governs the choice of the allegations in the first paragraphs?
3. Why are they suing in Leon County (in Tallahassee, the state capital)?
4. Why is there a section called "Common Allegations"?
5. The "Wherefore" clause: The prayer for relief is complex because somewhat different relief is requested for the different countries. Note that the last paragraph contains the catch-all: "And grant such other relief as the court deems right and just."
6. Explain the Certificate of Service and the final signature section.

Answer and defenses by Harris, Secretary of State, and L. Clayton Roberts, Director, Division of Elections.

IN THE CIRCUIT COURT OF THE SECOND JUDICIAL CIRCUIT,
IN AND FOR LEON COUNTY, FLORIDA CIVIL DIVISION

ALBERT GORE, Jr., Nominee of the Democratic Party)
of the United States for President of the United)
States, and)
JOSEPH I. LIEBERMAN, Nominee of Democratic)
Party of the United States for Vice President of the)
United States,)
)
Plaintiffs,)
)
v.) CASE NO. 00-2808
)
KATHERINE HARRIS, as SECRETARY OF STATE, STATE)
OF FLORIDA, et al.)
)
Defendants.)

ANSWER AND DEFENSES OF KATHERINE HARRIS, AS
SECRETARY OF STATE, STATE OF FLORIDA,

and

SECRETARY OF AGRICULTURE BOB CRAWFORD,
SECRETARY OF STATE KATHERINE HARRIS AND L.
CLAYTON ROBERTS, DIRECTOR, DIVISION OF
ELECTIONS, Individually and as Members of

THE FLORIDA ELECTIONS CANVASSING COMMISSION

Katherine Harris, as Secretary of State, and Secretary of Agriculture Bob Crawford, Secretary of State Katherine Harris and L. Clayton Roberts, Director, Division of Elections, Individually and as Member Of and as the Florida Elections Canvassing Commission provide their Answer and Defenses to the Complaint to Contest Election as follows:

ANSWER AND FIRST DEFENSE

As their first defense, the responding defendants answer specifically each allegation of the complaint:

1. This is an action to contest the certification that George W. Bush and Richard Cheney received more votes in the Presidential election in the State of Florida than Al Gore and Joe Lieberman. The vote totals reported in the Election Canvassing Commission's certification of November 26, 2000 are wrong. They include illegal votes and do not include legal votes that were improperly rejected. The number of such votes is more than sufficient to place in doubt, indeed to change, the result of the election. **ANSWER:** Admitted that the plaintiffs have brought this action to contest and election, but deny that they are entitled to any relief. Otherwise denied.

2. The Plaintiffs, Albert Gore, Jr., nominee of the Democratic Party of the United States for President of the United States in the 2000 General Election (Al Gore) and Joseph I. Lieberman nominee of the Democratic Party of the United States for Vice President of the United States in the 2000 General Election (Joe Lieberman), contest the November 26, 2000 certification by the Elections Canvassing Commission of the results of the Presidential election and the determination of the winning Presidential election and the determination of the winning Presidential Electors in Florida. Al Gore and Joe Lieberman further contest the Secretary of State's certification of the electors for Defendants George W. Bush and Richard Cheney as elected.

   ANSWER: Admitted, but deny that they are entitled to any relief.

3. The Election Canvassing Board certified 2,912,790 votes for George W. Bush and Richard Cheney and 2,912,253 votes for Al Gore and Joe Lieberman, a difference of 537 votes. The difference was <u>entirely</u> the result of:

   (a) . . . [All allegations are identical to the complaint.]

   (d) not counting approximately 9,000 ballots in Miami-Dade County that have not been recorded as a vote for any presidential candidate . . .

   ANSWER: The first sentence is admitted, otherwise denied.

Common Allegations

4. This is an action to contest an election under section 102.168, Florida Statutes (2000).

   ANSWER: Admitted that the plaintiffs have brought this action under section 102.168, Florida Statutes to contest an election, but denied that the plaintiffs are entitled to any relief under this statute or otherwise.

5. Section 102.168(5), Florida Statutes (2000) establishes Leon County as the proper venue for this action.). [sic]

   ANSWER: Admitted.

6. Section 102.168(8), Florida Statutes (2000) empowers the judge in a contest action to:

   > fashion such orders as he or she deems necessary to ensure that each allegation in the complaint is investigated, examined or checked to prevent or correct any alleged wrong, and to provide any relief appropriate under such circumstances.

   ANSWER: Admitted.

[The Answer continues in this fashion to respond paragraph by paragraph until all are answered. Then the Defendants raise additional defenses:]

Second Defense

As their second defense, the responding defendants state that the complaint fails to state a cause of action.

(continued)

(continued)

Third Defense

As their third defense, the responding defendants state that manually recounting votes of Palm Beach County, Miami-Dade County, and Nassau County cannot change or place in doubt the result of the election.

Fourth Defense

As their fourth defense, the responding defendants state that any manual recount of votes in a statutory contest of a statewide election for a federal office under section 102.168, Florida Statutes, must to the extent applicable, as a matter of law, include a recount of all votes cast statewide to ensure compliance with the requirements of equal protection and due process.

* * *

Ninth Defense

As their ninth defense, the responding defendants state that the plaintiffs have alleged no claims against the members of the Elections Canvassing Commission in their individual capacities, and that they are immune from such claims in any event.

Respectfully submitted,
/s/ Al Lindsay
Joseph P. Klock, Jr.
Gerry S. Gibson
Thomas M. Karr
Alvin S. Lindsay, III
STEEL HECTOR & DAVIS LLP
215 South Monroe, Street, 6th Floor
Tallahassee, FL, 32301
Telephone: (850) 555-1234
Fax: (850) 555-5678

Certificate of Service

I HEREBY CERTIFY that a true copy of the foregoing has been furnished by United States mail and facsimile transmission this [30th] day of November, 2000 to the following:

[Eight attorneys representing both sides are listed in the following format:]

Barry Richard Cheney
Greenberg Traurig
101 East College Avenue
Tallahassee, FL 32301
for Governor Bush

Things to Note with Regard to the ANSWER AND DEFENSES

Although the pleading repeats each paragraph of the Complaint and responds (ANSWER:), admitting indisputable facts, such as that Gore is the nominee of the Democratic Party, while denying others or denying entitlement to relief, there are other formats for answers, e.g., "Plaintiff admits paragraphs 1–4 and denies paragraphs 5–8, 10–14, and has no knowledge of paragraph 9."

The Second Defense is a demurrer.

The Fourth Defense raises an Equal Protection argument: If some counties are to be recounted, but not others, the others have been denied Equal Protection of the law.

The Ninth Defense is designed to remove Harris and Roberts as individuals in the suit, leaving them only defendants in their official capacities (members of the Elections Canvassing Commission, as Secretary of State).

The Reply

reply A pleading made by a plaintiff when a defendant makes a counterclaim or affirmative defenses that require a response.

Although filing an answer usually ends the pleadings, the plaintiff must file a **reply** if the defendant has made a counterclaim, in order to present denials and defenses to the counterclaim. Affirmative defenses do not necessarily require the filing of a reply, but the cautious attorney may do so to avoid certain technical problems later on.

Discovery

Discovery refers to pretrial devices for obtaining information relevant to the suit. It is a modern adaptation of procedures in equity and has come to play a major role in civil cases. Long delays in bringing suit to trial are most often related to the discovery process, which has been severely criticized for its contribution to delays and the resulting costs that give a significant advantage to wealthy parties. Although it is unethical to delay as a strategy for wearing down an opponent or as leverage to induce settlement, and is subject to sanctions in some states, it is difficult to prove that attorneys have used procedural devices solely for the purpose of delay. Defense attorneys in personal injury suits have little incentive to effect prompt resolution of a case—their clients are not eager to pay sooner than necessary, and the attorneys continue to receive compensation as the process is prolonged. This is not purely self-serving on the attorneys' part. In the end, the client may save a great deal of money in the settlement, despite increased attorneys' fees. And any eagerness to settle tends to be regarded as weakness by the other side. This is one of the prices we pay for having an adversarial system that encourages both sides to engage in strategies, tricks, and traps to win.

The discovery process involves a great deal of work that is currently accomplished by paralegals. It requires knowledge of the law and the legal system, but does not require the pivotal decision making that is the responsibility of the attorney.

Depositions

deposition   Oral examination of a witness transcribed by a court reporter. Ordinarily, attorneys for both sides are present, one having requested the deposition. A deposition is part of the pretrial procedure called *discovery* and is usually conducted without any participation by the judge.

A primary tool of discovery is the **deposition.** It consists of an oral questioning of a witness or the parties themselves; present are attorneys for both sides and a court reporter recording verbatim the questions and answers for later transcription. The ostensible purpose of the deposition is to gather information, but it serves also to gauge the credibility of the witness and to make a record of statements under oath to preserve testimony for trial, usually effectively preventing a witness from later changing testimony. The merits of a case are usually reevaluated following the deposition of an important witness, based on the information gathered and the impact the witness is likely to make on judge and jury. Settlement offers are often raised or lowered following a deposition.

Attorneys often arrange for a deposition through their paralegals; scheduling can be difficult because the attorneys and the witness must all be available at the same time. Although several depositions may be taken in succession on the same day, attorneys frequently arrange one deposition at a time, prolonging the pretrial period for several months or even years.

Paralegals frequently draft questions for depositions and may even sit beside an attorney and pass notes concerning objections and follow-up questions to responses made by the deponent.

Interrogatories and Requests for Admissions

interrogatories
A discovery device, pretrial written questions sent from one party to the other party.

requests for admissions   One side in a lawsuit giving a list of facts to the other and requesting that they be admitted or denied; those admitted need not be proved at trial.

production of documents   Requests used in *discovery* to obtain documents from the other side of a case that are pertinent to issues in the case.

Attorneys submit written questions, called **interrogatories,** to the opposing party asking for specific information, usually information not easily denied, such as vital statistics, employment, and historical facts of the case. Time of reply is often protracted, although undue delay may be countered by motions to the court to compel compliance. **Requests for admissions** ask the opposing party to admit specific facts, which once admitted may no longer be put in dispute, thereby narrowing the issues for trial.

Requests for Documents and Mental and Physical Examinations

A party may demand the **production of documents** and records relevant to the case (e.g., business records, receipts), as well as mental and physical examinations of a party if it can be shown that an examination is relevant to the case (this is especially common in personal injury actions).

Scope of Discovery

Discovery inquiry is measured by very broad standards and is not limited by the more restrictive standards of admissibility applied to evidence at trial. Discovery is normally conducted through the attorneys without the intervention of the judge, who may have little knowledge of what is happening. The court becomes involved only when the process breaks down and a party seeks an order from the court requiring the other party to comply with the discovery process.

In theory, discovery is based on the rationale that justice is served by both sides being fully informed and prepared for trial. It is a counterpoise to the "gunslinger" approach to trial in which trial is a battle of wits between great performers, a view favored by popular dramatists. In practice, the trial is a performance that has been carefully rehearsed—both sides are aware of the facts and arguments of the other, the only uncertainty being the unpredictability of the jury.

On the surface, discovery appears to be a reasonable feature of the search for truth and the equalization of the positions of the parties. In fact, it is as much subject to subterfuge as any other part of a lawsuit. Deponents are prepared for depositions as are witnesses for trial and are warned by attorneys not to expand on their answers, to answer merely "Yes" or "No" to questions that can be answered simply by yes or no responses. Answers to interrogatories are drafted by attorneys, rather than the parties, to provide as little information as possible. In short, discovery has become a negotiating tool used as much for strategic purposes as for investigation. It is a part of a lengthy pretrial process devoid of judicial scrutiny, encouraging a continual reevaluation of a case for negotiating settlements. It is responsible for pretrial settlements more than any other feature of civil procedure. The question remains whether this mechanism is fairer, more efficient, or more just than procedure without it.

The discovery process typically proceeds without the involvement of the court. When one party is uncooperative, the other may ask for the court's intervention. If this fails to bring the uncooperative party into line, the court may impose sanctions, including dismissal of the case.

Pretrial Hearing

pretrial conference or **hearing**   A meeting of attorneys in a case with the judge to discuss the issues in the case and plan for the trial.

In a great many cases, a **pretrial conference** or **hearing** is held at an advanced stage of the pretrial process. It is frequently held in the judge's chambers rather than in open court and is attended by the judge and attorneys for the parties. A general discussion is held on the issues of the case and the merits of the claim. Matters such as discovery, logistics, and the like are discussed as well. Ostensibly the pretrial hearing helps the judge assess the progress of the pretrial process and plan for trial time. Depending on the judge and the jurisdiction, pretrial is often used to encourage settlement. The judge may urge the attorneys to focus on real issues and suggest areas for compromise. Attorneys may show a willingness to settle in the pretrial hearing that they were reluctant to show previously. The judge may express some impatience with frivolous claims and issues and ask the attorneys to submit written arguments on questions of law.

Depending on the judge, the attorneys may come away from the conference with a clear idea of where the judge stands on the law and even the judge's attitude toward the merits, weaknesses, and defenses with regard to the claim. It is not that the judge prejudges the lawsuit, but a frank discussion of the case takes place in which the judge can act as a mediator to resolve the dispute and obviate the necessity for going to trial. It is often in the interests of all present to forgo the time and expense of trial. At the pretrial conference, the adversaries finally come face to face with the one person whose job it is to resolve the dispute.

Procedure at Trial

Trial is conducted as an orderly sequence of steps. The model presented here is followed quite generally in federal and state courts.

Jury Selection

voir dire The examination of potential jurors to qualify them for the trial.

The means and manner of selecting a jury vary considerably among jurisdictions, and even different judges differ in the extent to which they wish to control the process. The jury pool is typically selected from the list of registered voters within the jurisdiction, a number of whom are called for jury duty when the court is in session. From a number larger than the number of jurors required in a case, the jury will be selected by an examination called *voir dire,* during which the attorneys and/or the judge will ask the prospective jurors questions with regard to their qualifications to serve in the case. In addition to statutory disqualifications, jurors who are prejudiced with regard to the parties or subject matter of the case or who cannot reasonably be expected to judge the facts impartially may be excluded from the jury. An attorney who wishes to exclude such a juror makes a **challenge for cause.** These are unlimited in number, on the theory that no party should be tried by a biased jury. Cases that receive widespread publicity prior to trial may involve lengthy voir dire in the attempt to find impartial jurors, though the problem is usually encountered in sensational criminal trials.

challenge for cause In qualifying jurors during *voir dire*, either party may challenge the seating of a juror for bias or other disqualification. Challenges for cause are unlimited.

In addition to challenges for cause, each party is allowed a specific number of **peremptory challenges,** which allow the parties to exclude jurors they suspect are unsympathetic to their side of the case but who are not otherwise disqualified. Attorneys do not give reasons for exercising peremptory challenges.

peremptory challenge Exclusion of a juror without requiring justification. Each side is allowed a limited number of peremptory challenges as dictated by statute.

Jury selection is extremely important. Cases commonly go to trial because there are two believable versions of the facts or simply because the facts could be viewed to favor either side. A case may be won or lost on the basis of the jury selection. After all, a decision on the value of "emotional distress" or an award of punitive damages is arbitrary and subjective.

opening statements The introductory statements made at the start of a trial by lawyers for each side. The lawyers typically explain the version of the facts best supporting their side of the case, how these facts will be proved, and how they think the law applies to the case.

Conduct of the Trial

With the jury selected, the trial begins with **opening statements** by each side, plaintiff first and then defendant, who may reserve opening remarks until later. Opening statements are designed to inform the jury of the nature of the case and the facts each side proposes to show or dispute. In a **bench trial** (a nonjury trial), opening statements are usually waived because the judge ordinarily does not need to be prepared in this way.

bench trial A trial before a judge without a jury; a nonjury trial.

case-in-chief The main evidence offered by one side in a lawsuit. This does not include evidence offered to oppose the other side's case.

burden of proof The duty of proving a fact that is in dispute. In a trial, the plaintiff has the burden of proving through the presentation of evidence the allegations on which the case is brought. If the plaintiff fails to present sufficient evidence to prevail if that evidence were believed, the burden of proof has not been met and the case should be dismissed in defendant's favor.

prima facie case A case that will win unless the other side comes forward with evidence to disprove it.

direct examination The first questioning of a witness in a trial by the side that called the witness.

cross-examination The questioning of an opposing witness during a trial or hearing.

redirect When the party calling a witness asks questions of the witness following *cross-examination.*

recross The questioning of a witness by the party that did not call the witness following *redirect.*

The plaintiff then presents the evidence that forms the **case-in-chief.** The plaintiff has the **burden of proof,** meaning that there must be sufficient proof of the allegations of the complaint to sustain a verdict in favor of the plaintiff if the evidence is believed. This is called making a **prima facie case.**

Questioning of witnesses proceeds with the party calling the witness conducting a **direct examination,** followed by **cross-examination** by the other side. Cross-examination aims at showing flaws in the witness's testimony or discrediting the witness. The initial party then has the opportunity to **redirect** questions concerning issues raised "on cross." This is followed by **recross.**

When the plaintiff finishes the case-in-chief, the defendant produces witnesses favorable to the defense, who are questioned in similar fashion, with the defense conducting the direct examination. The plaintiff then has the opportunity to present evidence rebutting the defendant's presentation, followed by rebuttal by the defendant.

Finally, each side makes a **summation,** or **closing argument,** before the jury, with the defendant usually first (in opposite order of opening statements). The function of the closing argument is to summarize the evidence and present an interpretation of the facts consistent with the evidence that favors the party making the argument. Considerable latitude is given the attorneys in their closing arguments, provided they stay within the scope of the evidence presented and conduct themselves properly.

Verdict and Judgment

Before the jury retires to deliberate the facts, the judge **charges** them, that is, gives them instructions. The jury returns when it reaches consensus and reads the verdict before the court. The judge then asks each juror if he or she concurs in the verdict. After dismissing the jury, the judge may enter judgment on the verdict immediately or wait for a period, during which the parties may make posttrial motions.

In a nonjury trial, the judge is the trier of fact, so no verdict is entered, though the judgment should include findings of fact beyond what would be appropriate in a jury trial. Final judgment is in written form, dated and signed by the judge and filed with the court records.

The Rules of Evidence

Evidentiary rules form an independent subject for study that cannot be treated in satisfactory fashion here. In general, the rules of evidence are designed to exclude evidence that is irrelevant, repetitious, or unreliable. They help to prevent filibustering (delaying tactic) by attorneys representing losing causes. But the rules also reveal a distrust of the jury. Much that is excluded could be helpful in learning the truth, but is not admissible because of questions of reliability, thus questioning the jury's ability to weigh the import of unreliable evidence. Because the jury may find facts based only on the evidence that it hears and sees, it often receives a limited picture of the circumstances of the case.

summation or **closing argument** Each lawyer's presentation of a review of the evidence at the close of trial.

charges to the jury Jury instruction, given to the jury prior to their deliberations.

expert witness When qualified as an expert, a witness may offer opinion testimony, which would be objectionable in a "lay" witness.

hearsay rule Excludes from testimony out-of-court statements made by a person not present in court; a complex rule with many exceptions.

movant The party making a motion.

nonmoving party The party against whom a motion is made.

The ancient forerunner of the modern jury was composed of members of the community who knew the defendant and could judge the veracity of the plaintiff's claim. Today the jurors are strangers to the parties as well as the facts and are limited by the rules of evidence in what they can know of the case.

Two examples of evidentiary rules may illustrate this problem. First, one rule of evidence holds that a nonexpert witness, or layperson, may not give opinion testimony. A person qualifying as an **expert,** let us say a psychiatrist, may express an opinion on the facts of the case as long as the opinion is within the expert's field of expertise. As a result, an eye-witness friend of the defendant may not declare that the defendant was "insane," whereas a psychiatrist who entered the case long after the events took place may talk at length about how Oedipal conflicts caused the defendant to act as he did.

Second, the **hearsay rule** excludes from testimony out-of-court statements made by a person not present in court ("My friend told me that Joe had been drinking"). There are more than a dozen major exceptions to the hearsay rule, but it excludes what might otherwise be extremely relevant evidence on the grounds of unreliability and the lack of opportunity to cross-examine the person who made the statement.

Motions

Parties to a case have at their disposal numerous motions that ask the court to take particular action by granting or denying the motion. Because the ruling on each motion requires the exercise of legal judgment, and therefore raises a question of law, denial of a motion may be the basis for appeal by the **movant** (person making the motion), and granting the motion may provide a basis for appeal by the **nonmoving party** on the grounds of prejudicial error. The discussion here is confined to a handful of motions that are designed to terminate the case favorably to the moving party if granted. They have several names but much in common; their differences depend largely on their timing, and so they are often classified as pretrial, trial, and posttrial motions.

Fact/Law Distinction

The purpose of trial must be kept in mind in order to understand the function of these motions. Trial refers to trying facts. Assuming a typical jury trial of a damage suit, the plaintiff must prove the elements of a cause of action and the amount of the damages. The jury must find facts supporting each element and fix the dollar amount of damages in order for the plaintiff to recover. The only issues before the jury are those of disputed fact. If no facts are in dispute, the jury has no function. The parties may stipulate the truth of certain facts, thus taking those fact questions out of dispute. For example, in a suit for damages, the defendant might acknowledge liability for compensation to the plaintiff, not disputing the amount claimed as compensation by the plaintiff, but arguing that punitive damages are not allowed under the circumstances of the case. Whether punitive damages are allowable is a legal question. If the judge agrees with the defendant's argument, there would be no task for the jury; if the judge disagrees, the jury must determine whether the facts of the case warrant punitive damages according to the instructions given the jury by the judge. If the jury finds punitive damages appropriate, the amount must be fixed by the jury.

The simple model of dispute resolution describes a two-step process in which (1) facts are determined from the evidence presented and (2) law is applied to the facts to establish the prevailing party and the form of relief, if any, to be awarded. This assumes, first, that facts will be found—this is almost always the case, but on rare occasions the jury finds it impossible to reach a consensus, resulting in a **mistrial.** The model also assumes that the law is there to be found and applied. This is somewhat problematic, because the judge will always make conclusions of law, but the peculiarities of a given case may present novel legal issues not easily answered on the basis of existing law.

mistrial   A trial that the judge ends and declares will have no legal effect because of a major defect in procedure or because of the death of a juror, a deadlocked jury, or other major problem.

If no material facts are in dispute, the only task before the court is to apply the law. Whether there are facts in dispute is a question of law for the judge. The judge may take the case out of the hands of the jury or take a fact question away from jury determination by converting it into a question of law. This sleight of hand is justified with language such as, "reasonable persons could not disagree. . . ." The rationale here is that the jury is needed only if some doubt exists with regard to the facts. If the judge concludes that no doubt exists, even though the parties dispute the facts, the question can be decided "as a matter of law" ("reasonable persons could not disagree"). Disputed facts should normally go to the jury; a judge who oversteps the authority to decide facts will be reversed on appeal.

In its simplest form, the conversion of a fact question into a question of law is seen in the taking of judicial notice. The court may relieve a party of the burden of proving a fact by taking judicial notice of that fact. Ordinarily notice is taken on the basis of common knowledge of a fact (it is dark in Omaha at midnight; Mario Cuomo was governor of New York in 1989). Of course, self-evident facts are rarely disputed, so the court does not need to bother with such questions, but sometimes facts that seem clear are nevertheless disputed, as when a party attempted to argue that wine is not intoxicating and the judge took judicial notice of the fact that wine is an intoxicating beverage.

In the 1940s, the great silent film actor Charlie Chaplin was sued by Joan Berry over paternity of her daughter, Carol Ann Berry. Chaplin agreed to pay support for the child if blood tests indicated he could be the father. To the contrary, the blood tests indicated he could *not* have been the father. Carol Ann had blood type B, while Joan had A and Charlie had O. Because Carol Ann must have inherited B from a parent who had a B or AB type blood, Charlie could not have been the father. Joan won a suit that was characterized by histrionics, including putting Charlie and Carol Ann side by side to show a family resemblance. The court refused to take judicial notice of the blood tests as conclusive and sent the case to the jury, which concluded that Charlie was the father. Although judicial notice is usually reserved for matters of common knowledge, the question arises as to whether the court should take fact-finding away from the jury when scientific certainty compels a factual conclusion. Compare *State v. Gray.*

STATE OF OHIO ex rel. HOPE A. STEIGER, COMPLAINANT, v. BRUCE GRAY, DEFENDANT.
Juvenile Court of Ohio, Cuyahoga County
145 N.E.2d 162 (1957)

Complainant, an unmarried woman, filed a complaint in bastardy alleging that the defendant is the father of her child born to her December 1, 1956.

Defendant himself did not testify on his own behalf. He called but one defense witness—Dr. Roger W. Marsters, a clinical pathologist, who had been appointed by the court to conduct the blood grouping tests of the child, the complainant and the defendant, as requested by the defendant. . . .

Dr. Marsters' qualifications as an expert serologist were not questioned by the complainant. He testified that he carefully tested the blood specimens of the complainant, the defendant and the child "for the International OAB, M and N, and C, D, E, and c blood factors by using known blood controls along with the unknowns". . . .

"The data on the International OAB blood group factors are inconclusive because the mating of a type A individual with a type O individual may produce offspring of either type A or type O.

"The data on the M–N factors are inconclusive. . . .

"The data on the Rh blood factor D are inconclusive. . . .

"The data on the Rh blood factor E are inconclusive. . . .

"The data on the [Rh] factor c are inconclusive. . . .

"The data on the Rh factor C however indicate that an exclusion of paternity is established on this basis. Both Hope Steiger and Bruce Gray are negative for the C factor and therefore lack this particular blood antigen. On the other hand Baby Norma June Steiger is C-positive and therefore possesses this particular blood antigen. Since these blood factors can only be inherited from the parents and since both of these adults lack the C, then some other man than Bruce Gray must be the father of this child.

"In conclusion, an exclusion of paternity is established by the demonstration of the C factor in this child, Norma Steiger, without the presence of this particular blood factor in the blood of either of these two adults, Hope Steiger or Bruce Gray."

Dr. Marsters stated that he and his associates made five separate blood tests and that all proper safeguards were taken to protect the integrity and accuracy of the blood grouping tests. The accuracy of his conclusion of the exclusion of defendant as the father of the child was not rebutted by any counter medical evidence submitted by complainant. . . .

This court further believes that the near unanimity of medical and legal authorities on the question of the reliability of blood grouping tests as an indicator of the truth in questioned paternity cases justifies the taking of judicial notice of the general recognition of the accuracy and value of the tests when properly performed by persons skilled in conducting them. The law does not hesitate to adopt scientific aids to the discovery of the truth which have achieved such recognition. . . .

I hold, further, that because this great weight must be accorded to the blood grouping test results as testified to by Dr. Marsters, complainant has failed to prove the guilt of the defendant by a preponderance of the evidence.

Accordingly, I find the defendant not guilty as charged in the complaint.

Case Questions

1. Why did the defendant not testify in his own behalf?
2. On what does the court base its justification for taking judicial notice?

Note that bastardy, usually called paternity, proceedings are "quasi-criminal" proceedings used to establish paternity for related civil suits. The court uses **preponderance of the evidence** rather than **guilt beyond a reasonable doubt** as the standard of proof.

**preponderance
of the evidence**
The standard of proof
required in most civil
actions. The party whose
evidence, when fairly
considered, is more
convincing as to its truth
has the *preponderance of
evidence* on its side.

**guilt beyond
a reasonable doubt**
The standard of proof the
prosecution must meet in
a criminal case.

Dismissal Motions

On motion, a judge may end a case because one side has no legal basis for its claims or because no material fact is in dispute and it is time to enter judgment. Because the granting of such motions cuts short further discussion and presentation of facts and denies a person's "day in court," the court uses a strict test. Although it is phrased somewhat differently according to the motions, generally it states that the court will test the motion by looking at the case "in the light most favorable to the nonmoving party." This test must be examined by considering the motions.

The Demurrer

The first dismissal motion that can arise in a case is one made by the defendant attacking the complaint by a "motion to dismiss for failure to state a claim upon which relief can be granted." This is quite a mouthful, so it is abbreviated to "motion to dismiss for failure to state a claim," "motion to dismiss for failure to state a cause of action," or, borrowing from equity, a "**demurrer.**" Granting this motion stops the action dead in its tracks. With a demurrer, the defendant argues that the complaint is legally insufficient, that it does not state a cause of action, or that the law has no remedy for the grievance asserted by the plaintiff.

demurrer   A motion to
dismiss for failure to state
a claim upon which
relief may be granted.
This asks the court to
dismiss a case because
the complaint is legally
insufficient; it fails to
state a cause of action.

The test used by the court for a demurrer is as follows: If all the allegations of the complaint were true, the complaint would still not allow the plaintiff any relief. In a sense, the demurrer says, "So what?" Some essential ingredient is missing. The *Georgia High School Association* case in Chapter 6 is a case that *should* have been dismissed if the trial court judge had taken the position the appellate court did; namely, that the plaintiffs had no property rights that were infringed by the referee's bad call. The law does not allow relief for such a case—no cause of action exists.

The assumption of the truth of a plaintiff's allegations is made only for the purpose of testing the demurrer. By making the demurrer, the defendant does not admit the allegations are true for any other purpose. If the demurrer is denied (the usual outcome), the defendant may proceed to dispute the facts alleged.

Summary Judgment

**summary judgment,
motion for**   A dismissal
motion that is a pretrial
motion and also a trial
motion in a *bench trial*.

A **motion for summary judgment** can be both a trial and a pretrial motion. As a pretrial motion, it is made at some point before trial, when it appears that one side must win. For example, although the complaint may appear to state a cause of action, after all pleadings have been filed and discovery has taken place, the plaintiff's case may reveal some fatal weakness, so the defendant moves for summary judgment. In such a case, the test to be applied is whether, viewing the case in the light most favorable to the plaintiff, the nonmoving party, the plaintiff could not win. Again, if material facts are in dispute, the motion will be denied.

Motion for a Directed Verdict

directed verdict, motion for a
A dismissal motion commonly made by the defendant at the close of plaintiff's *case-in-chief* and by both sides at the close of all the evidence.

At trial, after the plaintiff has presented its case-in-chief, the defendant may make a **motion for a directed verdict.** Construing all the evidence in the light most favorable to the plaintiff, the motion will be granted if it appears that the plaintiff has not provided sufficient proof to prevail. If granted, judgment is entered for the defendant and the case is over. Usually there are sufficient facts that a jury might find in the plaintiff's favor, so the case will continue. The motion for directed verdict is made routinely, and almost as routinely denied, so that the defendant preserves the right to appeal on the basis of its denial. Even if the plaintiff's case is weak, the judge may be reluctant to take the factfinding away from the jury.

At the close of all the evidence, both sides commonly make motions for a directed verdict. At first glance, it might seem that one would be granted, but because each is measured in terms most favorable to the nonmoving party, if there is a reasonable dispute over the facts, the evidence could be interpreted to support either side. Thus, both motions are denied and that task is left to the jury.

In a nonjury trial, the judge is the factfinder, so the appropriate motions are called motions for summary judgment, as the judge may immediately enter judgment. Formerly judges directed the juries to enter verdicts, which explains the "directed verdict" label of the motion, but this is no longer done. A motion for a directed verdict is also called a motion for nonsuit in some jurisdictions.

judgment n.o.v., motion for   The abbreviation **n.o.v.** stands for the Latin *non obstante veredicto*, meaning "notwithstanding the verdict." This is a motion made at the end of a trial asking the judge to enter a judgment contrary to the jury's verdict on the grounds that the verdict is against the manifest weight of the evidence. Also called a *motion for judgment notwithstanding the verdict.*

The *Hodge* case demonstrates the peculiarities of a motion for a directed verdict. Plaintiff appeals the granting of such a motion, which dismissed the case as against only one of the defendants, the insurance company. Plaintiff had a difficult battle, since he was attempting to blame the collision on a "phantom vehicle," one he was following when it swerved to avoid a van stopped in the left lane, with which plaintiff then collided. Understanding this case will be assisted by reviewing the fact/law distinction and recognizing how a judge may determine certain facts to be true or proved "as a matter of law." Also helpful would be a review of *Li v. Yellow Cab* and the accompanying discussion of negligence and comparative negligence.

Motion for Judgment Notwithstanding the Verdict

After the jury has returned a verdict, either party may make a motion for judgment notwithstanding the verdict, usually referred to as a **motion for judgment n.o.v.,** from the Latin *non obstante veredicto* ("notwithstanding the verdict").

Ray HODGE,

v.

LANZAR SOUND, INC., Robert L. Wempe, and Shelter Mutual Insurance Co., Inc.
Court of Appeals of Kansas
25 Kan.App. 2d 592, 966 P.2d 92 (1998)

Plaintiff Ray Hodge appeals from a directed verdict in a personal injury action. We affirm.

Plaintiff requests this court to decide if plaintiff submitted sufficient evidence to raise a jury question as to whether the negligence of a phantom motorist was a causal factor in this personal injury action.

The material facts are as follows:

Defendant Robert Wempe was driving in the left lane on Interstate 35 when a tire on his van blew out. The blowout happened in a construction zone. The highway had narrowed to two lanes in each direction, and there were no side lanes or medians. Traffic was heavy but moving fast. After unsuccessfully trying to merge into the right lane, Wempe stopped his van in the left lane, blocking traffic, and exited safely.

Plaintiff entered the construction zone following an unidentified passenger vehicle (phantom motorist) at about five car lengths. Suddenly, the phantom motorist swerved from the left lane into the right lane, and plaintiff was confronted with Wempe's stalled van. Plaintiff braked hard but collided with the rear of Wempe's van. Plaintiff suffered serious injuries.

Plaintiff filed suit against defendant Robert Wempe, the driver of the van; defendant Lanzar Sound, the owner of the van; and Wempe's insurance company, defendant Shelter Mutual Insurance Company (Shelter) under the **uninsured motorist coverage**. *Shelter stipulated that under its policy it is responsible for the liability of the phantom motorist which plaintiff was following.* [Emphasis added.]

At trial plaintiff alleged the phantom vehicle swerved at the last instant, without using a signal. As a result, plaintiff did not see the stalled van until it was too late for him to avoid a collision. The district court granted partial summary judgment for Shelter, holding the phantom motorist had no duty to warn plaintiff of plaintiff's approach to Wempe's vehicle.

At the close of defendants' cases, the district court entered a *directed verdict for defendant Shelter, holding the phantom motorist's actions were not causal factors as a matter of law.* [Emphasis added.] The court also dismissed Lanzar Sound on the plaintiff's motion. The jury assigned 50% fault to Wempe and 50% to plaintiff. Plaintiff appeals from the court's directed verdict dismissing defendant Shelter.

In ruling on a motion for a directed verdict, the district court is required to resolve all facts and inferences reasonably to be drawn from the evidence in favor of the party against whom the ruling is sought. Where reasonable minds could reach different conclusions based on the evidence, the motion must be denied. A similar analysis must be applied by an appellate court when reviewing the grant or denial of a motion for directed verdict. [C.]

To recover in a negligence action, the plaintiff must prove that the defendant owed a duty to the plaintiff, that defendant breached that duty, and that the breach of duty was the proximate cause of damages sustained by the plaintiff. The existence of a duty is a question of law, subject to unlimited review by an appellate court. [C.] Here, we must determine if any interpretation of the evidence would indicate the phantom motorist breached any duty owed to plaintiff.

Plaintiff alleges the last-second maneuvering of the phantom motorist placed plaintiff at a disadvantage because plaintiff did not see the stalled van in time to avoid a collision. According to plaintiff, by avoiding the van earlier, or by using a signal to warn of a lane change, the phantom motorist would have allowed plaintiff more time to prevent the collision. In order to prevail, plaintiff must show the phantom motorist had a duty to drive in a manner that allowed plaintiff sufficient opportunity to

(continued)

(continued)

see and avoid the road hazard. In addition, assuming the phantom motorist breached this duty, plaintiff must show that the phantom's actions were a proximate cause of the accident and plaintiff's injuries.

This is a matter of first impression in Kansas. Normally, the primary duty of a motorist is to look ahead. *Hallett v. Stone,* 216 Kan. 568, 572, 534 P.2d 232 (1975). One Kansas case seems to instruct that when a vehicle blocks the view of the road ahead, in certain circumstances the driver of that vehicle has the duty to warn of upcoming hazards. *Strimple v. O.K. Warehouse Co.,* 151 Kan. 98, 104, 98 P.2d 169 (1940). In *Strimple,* the lead vehicle, a large truck, blocked the view of a vehicle trailing behind. The truck slowed suddenly when it encountered a "slow" sign, and the following car collided with the truck. . . . Here, the lead vehicle was a passenger car. Plaintiff has not alleged the phantom motorist blocked plaintiff's vision more than would normally be expected. *Strimple* does not control here.

Similarly, we are convinced plaintiff cannot prove causation. The phantom motorist did not execute a maneuver that interfered with plaintiff. There is no indication the phantom motorist was even aware of plaintiff. Even if the phantom motorist failed to keep a lookout, such failure played no part in causing the collision. The negligence of the phantom motorist would be a factor if the phantom motorist struck or interfered with other motorists, but the concept of proximate cause would be stretched too far if a lead driver were saddled with the negligence of the trailing driver. Assuming a reasonable clear line of sight to the hazard, the trailing car is not put in a worse position than if the lead car slammed on the brakes and stopped successfully. The phantom motorist was entitled to assume that plaintiff would be exercising ordinary care, *Hallett,* 216 Kan. at 572, 534 P.2d 232, and keeping a sufficient interval to deal with any foreseeable emergency. Holding for plaintiff would place an unreasonable burden on drivers to keep a lookout to the rear at all times, which clearly is not the law. See *Hallett,* 216 Kan. at 572, 534 P.2d 232. If there was any negligence on the part of the phantom motorist, such could not have been a proximate cause of the collision.

We are convinced this court should follow the lead of other jurisdictions and hold that under normal circumstances, a lead car is under no general duty to evade a hazard in sufficient time to allow a following car to avoid the hazard as well.

Affirmed.

Case Glossary

stipulate   To arrange or settle definitely so that proof is not required.

uninsured motorist coverage   Supplemental coverage in auto insurance that covers the insured in the event that there is a collision with an uninsured motorist to cover the liability of the latter.

Case Questions

1. Why does the insurer of the van that broke down stipulate that it will insure the liability of the so-called "phantom motorist"?
2. Why is not the phantom motorist liable for the accident (although not to be found, the phantom motorist's liability extends to Shelter Mutual Insurance as indicated in the first question)?

This will be granted if the judge finds as a matter of law that the verdict is against the manifest weight of the evidence. On occasion a jury will return a verdict that appears absurd on the basis of the record, or the jury's factfinding may be legally inconsistent. For example, the jury may find that the plaintiff was negligent as well as the defendant, giving the defendant an absolute defense to the suit (in a state that recognizes contributory negligence), and yet award compensation to the plaintiff. In such a case, the judge would enter a judgment in favor of the defendant on a motion for judgment n.o.v.

The aforementioned motions terminate the proceedings if granted. Usually they are denied; in most instances a case should not proceed to trial if one side's case is fatally flawed—the case should have been settled short of trial. Nevertheless, the expense of trial is a threat that is used for bargaining, and sometimes both sides are so stubborn in the negotiating process that trial is held regardless of the merits of the case. When the dispute is based on novel or controversial interpretations of the law, the trial may be primarily a prelude to appeal. Negotiations may continue during trial and prior to appeal. In addition, there are posttrial motions designed to set aside the judgment or to ask for a new trial. These and other pretrial procedures will be left to further study. Specific devices of civil procedure vary considerably from one jurisdiction to another, and it is best to learn the peculiarities of the jurisdiction in which one intends to practice.

Res Judicata and Collateral Estoppel

res judicata Latin for "the thing has been judged." This is an affirmative defense that prevents a civil case from being brought a second time.

Although it is possible to obtain a new trial if an appellate court has determined that prejudicial error in the first trial justifies relitigating the case, the losing plaintiff does not have the right to a retrial simply by filing the cause of action again. This is the essence of the principle of *res judicata*, Latin for "the thing has been decided." A party may not bring a suit over and over again until a favorable result is achieved. *Res judicata* is an affirmative defense that bars further suit. It is also called *merger and bar,* referring to the principle that the claim of the winning plaintiff is "merged" in the judgment of the court and enforceable by the judgment, but the claim is "barred" from further suit when the plaintiff loses.

Although this seems straightforward, a number of problems complicate the principle. Overlapping state and federal jurisdictions allow a claim in either or both courts. State and federal law may cover similar subjects in different ways. The problem then becomes whether a suit brought in one court is really the same case as that later brought in another. And, because the law provides different causes of action that can arise from the same events (e.g., threatening someone with physical harm might be grounds for assault or intentional infliction of mental distress), the question can arise as to whether one suit bars the later suit.

There are important conflicting policies in claim preclusion (*res judicata*). On the one hand, fairness would prevent a defendant from being forced to defend the same case more than once. On the other hand, the plaintiff should have full access to the courts. The court will not invoke *res judicata* if there is a difference in the parties to the claim or if the case involves issues different from those brought in the first case. This discussion seriously oversimplifies *res judicata*, which can become very complex with multiple parties and multiple claims.

collateral estoppel
Bars the relitigation of issues that have been previously adjudicated.

Collateral estoppel is directly related to *res judicata*; it is a bar to the relitigation of specific issues that have been previously adjudicated, even though the suits may not satisfy the requirements of *res judicata* (if all the issues in a new suit are identical to those in the prior suit, collateral estoppel and *res judicata* may both be said to apply). Occasionally a new suit raises issues presented in a former case as well as additional issues not barred by the prior suit. Nevertheless, those issues raised in the former suit and decided in it may not again be raised, because of collateral estoppel.

Res judicata and collateral estoppel are simple in principle but often difficult in application.

Summary

Civil procedure has both theoretical and practical importance. Theoretically, examination of our system of civil procedure reveals an adversarial system in which the fairness of the procedural rules takes on special significance. Reliance is placed on procedure to achieve justice. Practically, the legal practitioner must understand the procedure of the jurisdiction, both to enforce the rights of clients and to protect them from the maneuvers of the opposing side.

Lawsuits are initiated by the filing of a complaint and service of process on the defendant. In order to determine the rights of the parties, the court must have personal jurisdiction over them. In restricted cases, a suit may be filed against a thing (*in rem* jurisdiction). When there is a choice of courts having jurisdiction over a case, proper venue is determined by the rules and the circumstances of the parties.

Most American jurisdictions follow code pleading, which is a statutory refinement of common law, and equity pleading, which requires that a complaint state a cause of action, to which the defendant files a responsive pleading called an answer. In some cases the plaintiff then files a pleading responding to the answer.

An important feature of pretrial procedure is the discovery process, in which the parties enjoy great latitude in learning about the case for the other side through deposition, interrogatories, requests for documents, and so on.

Key features of the jury trial are jury selection and presentation of evidence. Each side has ample opportunity to present evidence and challenge the evidence for the other side. The plaintiff carries the burden of proving the elements of the cause of action.

Each side has at its disposal several motions at the pretrial, trial, and post-trial stages. The most important of these are motions that test the validity of the case for the other side, such as a motion for summary judgment. When granted, these motions terminate the litigation at that point.

Scenario

You represent Fred Goodbody, sued by the Internal Revenue Service for unpaid taxes. The IRS challenges his claim of charitable nonprofit status. Fred is a computer consultant for retail businesses. He sets up retail systems with in-store networks that connect point-of-sale computers for collecting cash, checks, and credit card purchases with back office computers that are designed for tracking inventory, making wholesale purchases, and compiling data for accounting and tax purposes. In short, Fred can go into a store and design a computer system that will take care of all of the store's business needs.

Fred has all payments for his service made by check made out to the Church of Narcissism. Fred received a bachelor's degree in computer science and a master's degree in business administration, both from accredited schools. In addition, Fred has a Doctor of Theology from the East Texas Theological Seminary in Dallas, Texas, an unaccredited institution. In order to obtain his doctorate, Fred sent the seminary a check for $200 and received in return two books: (1) the Holy Bible, and (2) *How to Set Up a Tax Exempt Church.* He was required to submit a letter swearing before God that he had read both books, and in return he received his doctoral diploma. Fred had previously read the Bible while attending Sacred Heart Academy, and he read the other book very carefully. Fred established the Church of Narcissism, registering it with the secretary of state for his state and applying for nonprofit status with the IRS. For two years, Fred has collected his consulting payments in the name of the church and paid taxes only on the salary he pays himself as archbishop of the church. He set up a meditation room in his home, the physical location of the church, where he does yoga and meditation each morning, usually accompanied by his wife, the only other member of the church.

The IRS took no action on his application until recently, when, upon investigation, it claimed the Church was a sham, having no religious purpose.

Fred is about to go to trial, and you are preparing questions for voir dire. Your problem is that you are unsure who would be sympathetic to Fred's device to avoid paying taxes. What questions would you ask? Remember that you have both challenges for cause that are unlimited and a limited number of peremptory challenges. Fortunately, the judge is known to be tolerant of voir dire questioning, as well as generous in accepting challenges for cause.

List the questions you would ask and then think through the follow-up questions for different answers. Keep in mind that you do not want to offend the jurors if possible, and you want them to like you and be predisposed toward your client.

THE LAW OF CRIMINAL PROCEDURE

> It is better that ten guilty persons escape than one innocent suffer.
>
> —William Blackstone

The Constitutional Basis of Criminal Procedure

Criminal procedure follows many of the patterns of civil procedure, but major differences are largely due to the special provisions of the U.S. Constitution, which are usually echoed in state constitutions. The Constitution, and especially the first ten amendments (the Bill of Rights), expresses a basic code of criminal procedure by enumerating rights of the citizens against government intrusion and rights of those accused of crimes. The provisions of the Constitution have been subject to intense scrutiny by state and federal courts, particularly since the 1950s. Criminal procedure cannot be understood without reference to these rights. The following excerpts from the Constitution highlight these rights, with brief annotations or explanations of the terms emphasized in *italics*.

Excerpts from the Constitution of the United States

Article I
Section 9:
(2) The privilege of the *Writ of Habeas Corpus* shall not be suspended, unless when in Cases of Rebellion or Invasion the public Safety may require it.

Article III
Section 2:

(3) The trial of all Crimes, except in Cases of Impeachment, shall be by *Jury*; and such Trial shall be held in the State where the said Crimes shall have been committed; but when not committed within any State, the Trial shall be at such Place or Places as the Congress may by Law have directed.

Amendment IV

The right of the people to be secure in their persons, houses, papers, and effects, against *unreasonable searches and seizures*; shall not be violated, and *no warrants shall issue, but upon probable cause, supported by oath or affirmation, and particularly describing the place to be searched, and the persons or things to be seized.*

Amendment V

No person shall be held to answer for a capital, or otherwise infamous crime, unless on a presentment or *indictment of a grand jury*, except in cases arising in the land or naval forces, or in the militia, when in actual service in time of war or public danger; nor shall any person be subject for the same offense to be *twice put in jeopardy* of life or limb; nor shall be compelled in any criminal case to be a *witness against himself, nor be deprived of life, liberty, or property, without due process of law*; nor shall private property be taken for public use, without just compensation.

Amendment VI

In all criminal prosecutions, the accused shall enjoy the *right to a speedy and public trial*, by an *impartial jury* of the State and district wherein the crime shall have been committed, which district shall have been previously ascertained by law, and to be informed of the *nature and cause of the accusation*, to be *confronted with the witnesses against him*; to have *compulsory process* for obtaining witnesses in his favor, and to have the *assistance of counsel for his defense.*

Amendment VIII

Excessive bail shall not be required, nor excessive fines imposed, nor *cruel and unusual punishments* inflicted.

Amendment XIV

. . . No State shall make or enforce any law which shall abridge the privileges or immunities of citizens of the United States; nor shall any State deprive any person of life, liberty, or property, without *due process of law*; nor deny to any person within its jurisdiction the *equal protection of the laws*. . . .

Annotations

writ of habeas corpus Brought by petition to challenge the lawfulness of a detention.

A **writ of habeas corpus** is brought by a petition, the purpose of which is to challenge the lawfulness of a detention by the government. This includes institutions other than prisons, although most habeas corpus petitions are brought by imprisoned criminals. It is often used as a form of federal review after state appeals have failed.

ex post facto law
A penal law that operates
retroactively.

jury   The right to a jury
in the Constitution refers
to a petit jury, which is
the trier of fact in a
criminal case. Also see
grand jury.

warrant   Written
permission given by a
judge to arrest a person
or conduct a search or
make a seizure.

grand jury   A body of
citizens who receive
complaints and
accusations of crime and
decide whether an
indictment should issue.

indictment   A written
accusation by a **grand
jury** charging the
accused with a crime.
Also called a "true bill."
When the grand jury
does not indict, it is
called a "no bill."

An **ex post facto law** is a penal law that operates retroactively. For example, under such a law a person could be charged with a crime for an action that was not a crime at the time it took place, or a person's sentence for a crime could be increased to a greater sentence than was permissible at the time the crime occurred.

The right to a **jury** trial applies to all criminal prosecutions. Disciplinary actions in prisons do not fall into this category.

The right to be free from unreasonable searches and seizures is designed primarily to protect citizens from excessive intrusions by government and police into their homes and persons, but interpretation of search and seizure has extended its application to places of business as well. The reasonableness of a search must necessarily remain a subjective judgment.

". . . [No] **warrants** shall issue, but upon probable cause, supported by oath or affirmation, and particularly describing the place to be searched, and the persons or things to be seized." Warrants are carefully scrutinized by criminal defense attorneys to determine whether they conform to this constitutional requirement. If the warrant or the search exceeds constitutional limits, the evidence seized may be excluded from trial, which is often fatal to the case for the prosecution. For example, drugs illegally seized may not be used as evidence at trial, so the prosecution then has no case.

A **grand jury indictment** requires a hearing before a special body of citizens gathered to review the prosecutor's evidence in support of taking the accused to trial. If the grand jury concludes that there is probable cause to believe the accused committed the crime, it issues an *indictment*, which is a written accusation by the grand jury charging the accused with a criminal act. It is also referred to as a *true bill*, but when the grand jury does not indict, it is called a *no bill*. The grand jury proceeding is controlled by the prosecutor to such an extent that a chief judge of the New York Court of Appeals remarked that a grand jury would indict a ham sandwich if the prosecutor recommended it.

A grand jury, although composed of citizens, is different from the petit jury which serves at trial. The grand jury has been used as an investigatory tool of the prosecutor's office on many occasions, as where the federal prosecutor investigated activities of the Black Panther Party, whose leaders had indicated an intent to kill President Nixon and had advocated sabotage by Black soldiers in Vietnam. Since witnesses before the grand jury are not represented in the hearings by their attorneys and since the grand jury cannot convict, the prosecutor enjoys a freedom from the usual limitations imposed at trial, [so] the grand jury can be used oppressively.

In 1734, William Cosby, the English governor of New York, sought to have the publisher of a radical newspaper with extremely limited circulation indicted for criminal libel. The grand jury twice refused to indict. Thereafter, the publisher, Peter Zenger, was charged with libel, and one of the most celebrated trials in American history followed. [After a dramatic trial characterized by hostility between an arrogant judge appointed specially by Governor Cosby and a brave and unrelenting defense attorney, Mr. Zenger was found by the jury to be *not guilty*, a historic victory for the people and the cause of freedom of speech and of the press.] It was with this and similar precedents fresh in their memories that our founding fathers incorporated into the Fifth Amendment the requirement that no person shall be held to answer for an infamous crime except upon the presentment or indictment of a grand jury.

Today, courts across this country are faced with an increasing flow of cases arising out of grand jury proceedings concerned with the possible punishment of political dissidents. It would be a cruel twist of history to allow the institution of the grand jury that was designed at least partially to protect political dissent to become an instrument of political suppression.

Bursey v. United States, 466 F.2d 1059 (9th Cir. 1972).

double jeopardy
Prevents a person from being tried twice for the same crime.

Double jeopardy prevents a person from being tried twice for the same crime. Jeopardy attaches once the accused has been put on trial before judge or jury; until that time, the case may be postponed without violating this provision. Double jeopardy applies to bringing the same charges in the same jurisdiction even if the courts are different (e.g., a lower criminal court versus a higher criminal court). This does not apply to state and federal jurisdictions. In the famous case of the three civil rights workers who were killed in Mississippi, an acquittal of homicide in the state court was followed by prosecution and conviction in federal court for depriving the victims of their civil rights.

privilege against self-incrimination
A person accused of a crime cannot be required to testify against himself.

A person cannot be held to be a "witness against himself." This is usually referred to as the **privilege against self-incrimination,** generally restricted to a testimonial privilege; that is, a person may not be required to testify to matters that would tend to incriminate him or her. Blood tests, fingerprints, and most documents that might incriminate are not considered "testimony" and are not covered by this privilege. This provision of the Fifth Amendment is the basis for the *Miranda* rights, particularly the right to remain silent during a police interrogation. The privilege against self-incrimination in the Fifth Amendment is zealously guarded by the U.S. Supreme Court, as the *Griffin* case demonstrates.

due process of law
A guarantee of the Fifth Amendment and the Fourteenth Amendment to the U.S. Constitution. It provides that law administered through courts of justice is equally applied to all under established rules that do not violate fundamental principles of fairness. The process that is due before government may deprive a person of life, liberty, or property.

"[No person may . . .] be deprived of life, liberty or property, without **due process of law**" is an important feature of criminal law because of the inclusion of the words *life* and *liberty*, as the primary means of punishing criminals are execution and incarceration. Any criminal procedure can be scrutinized for fairness on the basis of the due process clause. Although the Fifth Amendment applies to federal action, a similar clause in the Fourteenth Amendment applies to the states, subjecting state action to review by federal courts.

The defendant has a "right to a speedy and public trial." Most state and federal jurisdictions have by statute fixed a time period within which a criminal case must be brought. If the prosecutor exceeds the time limit, the accused may not be tried. The right to a public trial is designed to prevent abuse that might occur in a closed hearing. When appropriate, and with the court's approval, the defendant may waive this right and close the trial to the public.

The right to an "impartial jury" is fundamental to our criminal justice system, as police and prosecutor assume an accusatorial role. Great pains are often taken to guarantee that the jury is untainted by pretrial publicity or acquaintance with the facts of the case.

GRIFFIN

v.

CALIFORNIA
U.S. Supreme Court
380 U.S. 609 (1965)

Petitioner was convicted of murder in the first degree after a jury trial in a California court. He did not testify at the trial on the issue of guilt, though he did testify at the separate trial on the issue of penalty. The trial court instructed the jury on the issue of guilt, stating that a defendant has a constitutional right not to testify. But it told the jury:

> As to any evidence or facts against him which the defendant can reasonably be expected to deny or explain because of facts within his knowledge, if he does not testify or if, though he does testify, he fails to deny or explain such evidence, the jury may take that failure into consideration as tending to indicate the truth of such evidence and as indicating that among the inferences that may be reasonably drawn therefrom those unfavorable to the defendant are the more probable. . . .

Petitioner had been seen with the deceased the evening of her death, the evidence placing him with her in the alley where her body was found. The prosecutor made much of the failure of petitioner to testify:

> . . . He would know how she got down the alley. He would know how the blood got on the bottom of the concrete steps. He would know how long he was with her in that box. He would know how her wig got off. He would know whether he beat her or mistreated her. . . .
> These things he has not seen fit to take the stand and deny or explain.
> And in the whole world, if anybody would know, this defendant would know.
> Essie Mae is dead, she can't tell you her side of the story. The defendant won't.

The death penalty was imposed and the California Supreme Court affirmed. . . .

The question remains whether, statute or not, the comment [on defendant's refusal to testify] rule, approved by California, violates the Fifth Amendment.

We think it does. It is in substance a rule of evidence that allows the State the privilege of tendering to the jury for its consideration the failure of the accused to testify. No formal offer of proof is made as in other situations; but the prosecutor's comment and the court's acquiescence are the equivalent of an offer of evidence and its acceptance. The Court in the *Wilson* case stated: ". . . It is not every one who can safely venture on the witness stand though entirely innocent of the charge against him, . . . will often confuse and embarrass him to such a degree as to increase rather than remove prejudices against him. It is not every one, however honest, who would, therefore, willingly be placed on the witness stand. The statute, in tenderness to the weakness of those who from the causes mentioned might refuse to ask to be a witness, particularly when they may have been in some degree compromised by their association with others, declares that the failure of the defendant in a criminal action to request to be a witness shall not create any presumption against him."

. . . What the jury may infer, given no help from the court is one thing. What it may infer when the court solemnizes the silence of the accused into evidence against him is quite another. That the inference of guilt is not always so natural or irresistible is brought out in the *Modesto* opinion itself: "Defendant contends that the reason a defendant refuses to testify is that his prior convictions will be introduced in evidence to impeach him and not that he is unable to deny the accusations. It is true that the defendant might fear that his prior convictions will prejudice the jury, and therefore another possible inference can be drawn from his refusal to take the stand."

. . . We take that in its literal sense and hold that the Fifth Amendment, in its direct application to the Federal Government, and in its bearing on the States by reason of the Fourteenth Amendment, forbids either comment by the prosecution on the accused's silence or instructions by the court that such silence is evidence of guilt.

Reversed.

MR. JUSTICE STEWART, with whom MR. JUSTICE WHITE joins, dissenting. . . .

We must determine whether the petitioner has been "compelled . . . to be a witness against himself." Compulsion is the focus of the inquiry. Certainly, if any compulsion be detected in the California procedure, it is of a dramatically different and less palpable nature than that involved in the procedures which historically gave rise to the Fifth Amendment guarantee. When a suspect was brought before the Court of High Commission or the Star Chamber, he was commanded to answer whatever was asked of him, and subjected to a far-reaching and deeply probing inquiry in an effort to ferret out some unknown and frequently unsuspected crime. He declined to answer on pain of incarceration, banishment, or mutilation. And if he spoke falsely, he was subject to further punishment. Faced with this formidable array of alternatives, his decision to speak was unquestionably coerced.

Those were the lurid realities which lay behind enactment of the Fifth Amendment, a far cry from the subject matter of the case before us. I think that the court in this case stretches the concept of compulsion beyond all reasonable bounds, and that whatever compulsion may exist derives from the defendant's choice not to testify, not from any comment by court or counsel.

Case Questions

1. The case refers to a right not to testify; the Fifth Amendment is commonly described as stating a privilege. What is the difference between a right and a privilege in this context?
2. Why does the majority consider the remarks of the judge and prosecutor sufficiently prejudicial to require a new trial?
3. What reasons does the *Modesto* case give justifying an innocent defendant's refusal to testify? For what other reasons might an innocent person refuse to testify?
4. Why does the dissent dwell on the word *compulsion* in reference to self-incrimination?

Nota bene: The phrase "a jury of one's peers" is commonly thought to be a constitutional right, but it appears nowhere in the U.S. Constitution. The Sixth Amendment only guarantees the right to "a speedy and public trial, by an impartial jury. . . ." In recent decades, however, there have been successful challenges to the composition of the jury, especially where minorities appear to have been intentionally and systematically excluded, but these challenges have been based on the equal protection clause of the Fourteenth Amendment rather than the impartial jury phrase of the Sixth.

The Article III guarantee of a jury trial applies to federal cases. The right to an impartial jury of the Sixth Amendment, originally a federal right, applies to the states through the due process clause of the Fourteenth Amendment. Like most of the rights in the Bill of Rights, this right of the federal Constitution has been "incorporated" by the Fourteenth Amendment to apply to the states. Nonetheless, the right to a jury trial at the state level need not be total. The

Melvin R. BLANTON and Mark D. Fraley, Petitioners

v.

CITY OF NORTH LAS VEGAS, NEVADA
Supreme Court of the United States
489 U.S. 538 (1989)

Justice MARSHALL delivered the opinion of the Court.

The issue in this case is whether there is a constitutional right to a trial by jury for persons charged under Nevada law with driving under the influence of alcohol (DUI). . . .

DUI is punishable by a minimum term of two days' imprisonment and a maximum term of six months' imprisonment. . . . Alternatively, a trial court may order the defendant "to perform 48 hours of work for the community while dressed in distinctive garb which identifies him as [a DUI offender]." The defendant also must pay a fine ranging from $200 to $1,000. . . . In addition, the defendant automatically loses his driver's license for 90 days, . . . and he must attend, at his own expense, an alcohol abuse education course. . . . Repeat DUI offenders are subject to increased penalties.

Petitioners Melvin R. Blanton and Mark D. Fraley were charged with DUI in separate incidents. Neither petitioner had a prior DUI conviction. The North Las Vegas, Nevada, Municipal Court denied their respective pretrial demands for a jury trial. On appeal, the Eighth Judicial District Court denied Blanton's request for a jury trial but, a month later, granted Fraley's. Blanton then appealed to the Supreme Court of Nevada, as did respondent city of North Las Vegas with respect to Fraley. After consolidating the two cases along with several others raising the same issue, the Supreme Court concluded, inter alia, that the Federal Constitution does not guarantee a right to a jury trial for a DUI offense because the maximum term of incarceration is only six months and the maximum possible fine is $1,000. . . . We granted certiorari to consider

whether petitioners were entitled to a jury trial, . . . and now affirm.

It has long been settled that "there is a category of petty crimes or offenses which is not subject to the Sixth Amendment jury trial provision." . . . In determining whether a particular offense should be categorized as "petty," our early decisions focused on the nature of the offense and on whether it was triable by a jury at common law. . . . In recent years, however, we have sought more "objective indications of the seriousness with which society regards the offense." . . . "[W]e have found the most relevant such criteria in the severity of the maximum authorized penalty."

In using the word "penalty," we do not refer solely to the maximum prison term authorized for a particular offense. A legislature's view of the seriousness of an offense also is reflected in the other penalties that it attaches to the offense. . . . Primary emphasis, however, must be placed on the maximum authorized period of incarceration. . . . Indeed, because incarceration is an "intrinsically different" form of punishment, . . . it is the most powerful indication whether an offense is "serious."

. . . [A] defendant is entitled to a jury trial whenever the offense for which he is charged carries a maximum authorized prison term of greater than six months. . . . The possibility of a sentence exceeding six months, we determined, is "sufficiently severe by itself" to require the opportunity for a jury trial. . . . As for a prison term of six months or less, we recognized that it will seldom be viewed by the defendant as "trivial or 'petty.'" . . . But we found that the disadvantages of such a sentence, "onerous though they may be, may be outweighed by the benefits that result from speedy and inexpensive nonjury adjudications." . . .

. . . A defendant is entitled to a jury trial in such circumstances only if he can demonstrate that any additional statutory penalties, viewed in conjunction with the maximum authorized period of incarceration, are so severe that they clearly reflect a legislative determination that the offense in question is a "serious" one. This standard, albeit somewhat imprecise, should ensure the availability of a jury trial in the rare situation where a legislature packs an offense it deems "serious" with onerous penalties that nonetheless "do not puncture the 6-month incarceration line." . . .

Applying these principles here, it is apparent that petitioners are not entitled to a jury trial. The maximum authorized prison sentence for first-time DUI offenders does not exceed six months. A presumption therefore exists that the Nevada Legislature views DUI as a "petty" offense for purposes of the Sixth Amendment. Considering the additional statutory penalties as well, we do not believe that the Nevada Legislature has clearly indicated that DUI is a "serious" offense.

Viewed together, the statutory penalties are not so severe that DUI must be deemed a "serious" offense for purposes of the Sixth Amendment. It was not error, therefore, to deny petitioners jury trials. Accordingly, the judgment of the Supreme Court of Nevada is Affirmed.

Case Questions

1. Does it seem that drunken driving is serious enough for national campaigns to stamp it out and levy severe penalties against but not serious enough to guarantee a jury trial? Explain your answer.
2. If you read the Sixth Amendment, would you think that a jury trial would be guaranteed in a criminal proceeding that could result in a six-month incarceration? Explain your answer.
3. Is there something in the nature of a DUI charge that suggests that a jury is unnecessary? Explain your answer.
4. Consider that many states have reduced the blood alcohol level required for a presumption of drunken driving and are under pressure to reduce it further. Automatic sentences have also been introduced. Is this not conviction by machine? Explain your answer.
5. In many states, some lawyers specialize exclusively in DUI defenses and are apparently very successful (challenging the accuracy of the machine, the way the test was administered, etc.). Is this case an appropriate remedy? Explain your answer.

Blanton case, in fact, suggests that there may be quite a large category of criminal cases exempt from the Sixth Amendment right to jury.

The defendant must be informed of the *nature and cause of the accusation* in order to prepare a defense. This simply spells out the notice requirement that would otherwise be implied by the due process clause.

The right of the defendant to be *confronted with the witnesses against him* is a protection against anonymous accusers and ensures the right to cross-examine witnesses.

Compulsory process refers to the power of the defendant in a criminal case to force witnesses to attend trial under a subpoena issued by the court. If appearance were voluntary, the defendant would be at a severe disadvantage.

In England, at common law, defendants in felony cases were forbidden to have an attorney. The Sixth Amendment was intended to do away with this prohibition. The right to effective *assistance of counsel* for the defendant has become a cherished right only in the last few decades. For many years, the right to counsel was considered applicable only to federal cases and then only when the accused could afford to pay or was accused of a capital offense (*Powell v. Alabama*, 287 U.S. 45 [1932]) — until the famous exchange between Gideon and the Florida judge:

> *The Court:* Mr. Gideon, I am sorry, but I cannot appoint Counsel to represent you in this case. Under the laws of the State of Florida, the only time the Court can appoint Counsel to represent a Defendant is when that person is charged with a capital offense. I am sorry, but I will have to deny your request to appoint Counsel to defend you in this case.
>
> *The Defendant:* The U.S. Supreme Court says I am entitled to be represented by Counsel.

Gideon v. Wainwright, 372 U.S. 335 (1963).

Mr. Gideon was not exactly correct when he made this statement, but after he presented his own defense and was convicted, he took the case to the U.S. Supreme Court, which agreed with him. *Argersinger v. Hamlin*, 407 U.S. 25 (1972) extended the right to petty offenses involving possible imprisonment. A defendant who cannot afford an attorney must be furnished one by the government.

The right to be free from the imposition of *excessive bail* is self-explanatory; what is excessive may be judged relative to what is usual bail under similar circumstances. This is a limitation on the judge's discretion.

The right against the imposition of *cruel and unusual punishments* is also a relative concept. This particular principle has been viewed as an evolving standard — what was not considered "cruel and unusual" fifty years ago may be considered uncivilized and barbaric by today's standards.

The *due process* clause demands fair procedure and reasonable laws; it is a standard that the courts can invoke when injustice is apparent.

The *equal protection* clause imposes a test of equality before the law against discriminatory practices. There must be no difference in treatment in the statement of the law itself or in its application. In recent years the differential impact of the laws with regard to minorities has raised equal protection claims; for example, it has been shown statistically that blacks receive a disproportionate number of death sentences.

The Exclusionary Rule

The exclusionary rule is a special feature of criminal procedure that has developed from a series of U.S. Supreme Court interpretations of the Fourth, Fifth, and Fourteenth Amendments. It applies to excluding evidence illegally obtained by the government and enforces the adversarial principle in criminal proceedings. Because of the disparity between the power and resources of the government and the relative powerlessness of the criminal defendant, a number of protections, such as those enumerated in the Constitution, are afforded the defendant to equalize the respective positions in a criminal proceeding. The exclusionary rule operates to protect the defendant from abusive procedures by a more powerful opponent.

Basically, the exclusionary rule excludes from trial evidence obtained in violation of the defendant's constitutional rights. It first arose in *Weeks v. United States*, 232 U.S. 383 (1914), which held that evidence illegally obtained by federal officers could be excluded from evidence, but *Weeks* failed to apply the principle to the states. *Wolf v. Colorado*, 338 U.S. 25 (1949) held that search and seizure provisions of the Fourth Amendment were applicable to the states under the due process clause of the Fourteenth Amendment but did not exclude illegally obtained evidence from state prosecutions. *Wolf* was overruled in 1961 by *Mapp v. Ohio*, 367 U.S. 643, which held that the products of a search violating Fourth Amendment rights may not be used in state prosecutions.

Suppose the police exact a confession from a suspect through torture. Should the confession be presented to the jury and the defendant allowed to disavow the confession because it was involuntary? Should the jury be allowed to weigh the relevance of the confession in light of the circumstances under which it was obtained? Our law answers in the negative. Coerced confessions have no place in the trial. This principle needs little justification; it is a reasonable interpretation of the meaning and intent of the due process clause of the Fourteenth Amendment.

In *Miranda v. Arizona*, 384 U.S. 486 (1966), Chief Justice Warren wrote an opinion that linked the right to counsel of the Sixth Amendment with the privilege against self-incrimination of the Fifth Amendment, both applicable to the states under the Fourteenth Amendment due process clause. The four dissenters argued that the Fifth Amendment was historically unconnected to the exclusion of involuntary confessions, but Warren and his four brethren prevailed, and police have been reading *Miranda* rights ever since. (Warren pointed out that these rights had been FBI policy for some time.) The precise requirements were spelled out in Chief Justice Warren's majority opinion:

> Our holding will be spelled out with some specificity in the pages which follow but briefly stated it is this: the prosecution may not use statements, whether exculpatory or inculpatory, stemming from custodial interrogation of the defendant unless it demonstrates the use of procedural safeguards effective to secure the privilege against self-incrimination. By custodial interrogation, we mean questioning initiated by law enforcement officers after a person has been taken into custody or otherwise deprived of his freedom of action in any significant way. As for the procedural safeguards to be employed, unless other fully effective means are devised to inform accused persons of their right of silence and to assure a continuous opportunity to exercise it, the following measures are required. *Prior to any questioning, the person must be warned that he has a right to remain silent, that any statement he does make may be used as evidence against him, and that he has a right to the presence of an attorney, either retained or appointed.* The defendant may waive effectuation of these rights, provided the waiver is made voluntarily, knowingly and intelligently. If, however, he indicates in any manner and at any stage of the process that he wishes to consult with an attorney before speaking there can be no questioning. Likewise, if the individual is alone and indicates in any manner that he does not wish to be interrogated, the police may not question him. The mere fact that he may have answered some questions or volunteered some

statements on his own does not deprive him of the right to refrain from answering any further inquiries until he has consulted with an attorney and thereafter consents to be questioned [emphasis added].

In most jurisdictions, a *motion to suppress* (physical evidence or a confession) is a pretrial motion that tests the applicability of the exclusionary rule to the circumstances of the case. If the prosecution's case relies on such evidence, the granting of the motion will be followed by a dismissal of the charges or a motion by the defense for a judgment of acquittal. The motion to suppress is the defense's first line of attack in cases in which confessions or physical evidence are critical elements. A surprising majority of criminal defendants confess in spite of being advised of their right to remain silent and their right to an attorney. When first contacted, the criminal defense attorney's first words of advice are likely to be: "Do not say anything to the police until I get there."

The criminal courts have been inundated for many years by drug crimes. In most of these, the defense's best attack is to suppress the evidence, so search and seizure appeals abound. Search and seizure law has come to draw extremely fine lines between proper and improper searches.

In order to attack evidence seized by police under a search warrant, criminal defense attorneys look to the warrant itself and the affidavit underlying it to see if some fatal mistake was made that would make the search itself illegal and the fruits of the search excludable. Police have been protected for a few years by the *good faith* exception, which applies where the warrant proves invalid but the officer reasonably believed it to be valid. The *Sheppard* case describes this exception along with a discussion of the validity of search warrants.

MASSACHUSETTS, Petitioner
v.
Osborne SHEPPARD
Supreme Court of the United States
468 U.S. 981 (1984)

Justice WHITE delivered the opinion of the Court.

The badly burned body of Sandra Boulware was discovered in a vacant lot in the Roxbury section of Boston at approximately 5 a.m., Saturday, May 5, 1979. . . . After a brief investigation, the police decided to question one of the victim's boyfriends, Osborne Sheppard. Sheppard told the police that he had last seen the victim on Tuesday night and that he had been at a local gaming house (where card games were played) from 9 p.m. Friday until 5 a.m. Saturday. . . .

By interviewing the people Sheppard had said were at the gaming house on Friday night, the police learned that although Sheppard was at the gaming house that night, he had borrowed an automobile at about 3 o'clock Saturday morning in order to give two men a ride home. Even though the trip normally took only 15 minutes, Sheppard did not return with the car until nearly 5 a.m.

On Sunday morning, police officers visited the owner of the car Sheppard had borrowed. . . . Bloodstains and pieces of hair were found on the rear bumper and within the trunk compartment. In addition, the officers noticed strands of wire in the trunk similar to wire strands found on and near the body of the victim. . . .

On the basis of the evidence gathered thus far in the investigation, Detective Peter O'Malley drafted an affidavit designed to support an application for an arrest warrant and a search warrant authorizing a search of Sheppard's residence. The affidavit set forth the results of the investigation and stated that the police wished to search for[.] . . .

Detective O'Malley showed the affidavit to the District Attorney, the District Attorney's first assistant, and a sergeant, who all concluded that it set forth probable cause for the search and the arrest. . . .

Because it was Sunday, the local court was closed, and the police had a difficult time finding a warrant application form. Detective O'Malley finally found a warrant form previously in use in the Dorchester District. The form was entitled "Search Warrant—Controlled Substance G.L. c. 276 §§ 1 through 3A." Realizing that some changes had to be made before the form could be used to authorize the search requested in the affidavit, Detective O'Malley deleted the subtitle "controlled substance" with a typewriter. He also substituted "Roxbury" for the printed "Dorchester" and typed Sheppard's name and address into blank spaces provided for that information. However, the reference to "controlled substance" was not deleted in the portion of the form that constituted the warrant application and that, when signed, would constitute the warrant itself.

Detective O'Malley then took the affidavit and the warrant form to the residence of a judge who had consented to consider the warrant application. The judge examined the affidavit and stated that he would authorize the search as requested. Detective O'Malley offered the warrant form and stated that he knew the form as presented dealt with controlled substances. He showed the judge where he had crossed out the subtitles. After unsuccessfully searching for a more suitable form, the judge informed O'Malley that he would make the necessary changes so as to provide a proper search warrant. The judge then took the form, made some changes on it, and dated

and signed the warrant. However, he did not change the substantive portion of the warrant, which continued to authorize a search for controlled substances; nor did he alter the form so as to incorporate the affidavit. The judge returned the affidavit and the warrant to O'Malley, informing him that the warrant was sufficient authority in form and content to carry out the search as requested. O'Malley took the two documents and, accompanied by other officers, proceeded to Sheppard's residence. The scope of the ensuing search was limited to the items listed in the affidavit, and several incriminating pieces of evidence were discovered. Sheppard was then charged with first-degree murder.

At a pretrial suppression hearing, the trial judge concluded that the warrant failed to conform to the commands of the Fourth Amendment because it did not particularly describe the items to be seized. The judge ruled, however, that the evidence could be admitted notwithstanding the defect in the warrant because the police had acted in good faith in executing what they reasonably thought was a valid warrant. App. 35a. At the subsequent trial, Sheppard was convicted.

On appeal, Sheppard argued that the evidence obtained pursuant to the defective warrant should have been suppressed. The Supreme Judicial Court of Massachusetts agreed. A plurality of the justices concluded that although "the police conducted the search in a good faith belief, reasonably held, that the search was lawful and authorized by the warrant issued by the judge,". . . the evidence had to be excluded because this Court had not recognized a good-faith exception to the exclusionary rule. . . .

II

Having already decided that the exclusionary rule should not be applied when the officer conducting the search acted in objectively reasonable reliance on a warrant issued by a detached

(continued)

(continued)

and neutral magistrate that subsequently is determined to be invalid, . . . the sole issue before us in this case is whether the officers reasonably believed that the search they conducted was authorized by a valid warrant. There is no dispute that the officers believed that the warrant authorized the search that they conducted. Thus, the only question is whether there was an objectively reasonable basis for the officers' mistaken belief. Both the trial court, App. 35a, and a majority of the Supreme Judicial Court, concluded that there was. We agree.

The officers in this case took every step that could reasonably be expected of them. Detective O'Malley prepared an affidavit which was reviewed and approved by the District Attorney. He presented that affidavit to a neutral judge. The judge concluded that the affidavit established probable cause to search Sheppard's residence, . . . and informed O'Malley that he would authorize the search as requested. O'Malley then produced the warrant form and informed the judge that it might need to be changed. He was told by the judge that the necessary changes would be made. He then observed the judge make some changes and received the warrant and the affidavit. At

this point, a reasonable police officer would have concluded, as O'Malley did, that the warrant authorized a search for the materials outlined in the affidavit.

Sheppard contends that since O'Malley knew the warrant form was defective, he should have examined it to make sure that the necessary changes had been made. However, that argument is based on the premise that O'Malley had a duty to disregard the judge's assurances that the requested search would be authorized and the necessary changes would be made. . . .

In sum, the police conduct in this case clearly was objectively reasonable and largely error-free. An error of constitutional dimensions may have been committed with respect to the issuance of the warrant, but it was the judge, not the police officers, who made the critical mistake. "[T]he exclusionary rule was adopted to deter unlawful searches by police, not to punish the errors of magistrates and judges." . . . Accordingly, federal law does not require the exclusion of the disputed evidence in this case. The judgment of the Supreme Judicial Court is therefore reversed, and the case is remanded for further proceedings not inconsistent with this opinion.

It is so ordered.

Case Questions

1. Was the court influenced by the fact that a homicide was involved? Explain.
2. Why did the court support the police but not the magistrate? Explain.

Plea Bargaining

The criminal justice system cannot be appreciated without an understanding of the custom of plea bargaining. The prosecuting attorney and the defense attorney usually engage in a form of negotiation, which until recent years has been a largely unofficial part of criminal procedure. Nearly all convictions are the result of negotiation. The defendant agrees to plead guilty in return for beneficial treatment by the prosecution. The prosecution may agree to drop some of the charges, reduce the offense—say, from first-degree murder to second-degree murder or from burglary to criminal trespass—thereby lessening the penalty, or recommend a lenient sentence or probation, which recommendation is usually accepted by the judge.

The present system could not work without plea bargaining. If every defendant demanded a jury trial, there would not be enough courts and prosecutors to try all the cases. Less than 5 percent of criminal cases go to trial (the same is true of civil cases). The presumption is that in most cases a trial would result in a conviction, thus encouraging defendants to make the best deal they can. Nevertheless, the custom of plea bargaining has come under severe criticism because negotiation takes place outside of public and judicial scrutiny and suggests a degree of collusion between prosecutors and defense attorneys.

The Steps in Processing a Crime

The steps in criminal procedure tend to follow a more consistent routine than those of civil procedure because of legal limitations. The burden of proving guilt beyond a reasonable doubt, as opposed to "a preponderance of the evidence," forces police and prosecutor to monitor cases carefully. The exclusionary rule makes evidence or confessions unlawfully obtained inadmissible at trial and thus requires that great care be taken in investigation, arrest, interrogation, and search and seizure of evidence, lest the case fail for improper procedure. The constitutional right to a speedy trial forces police and prosecutor to organize investigation, charges, and trial within a limited timeframe. In addition, the constitutional protections afforded an accused require that cases be carefully prepared to avoid infringement of the accused's rights. (See Figure 1.)

The following is an outline of the steps involved in the criminal process, which are followed virtually universally in criminal cases, though the terminology may differ from one jurisdiction to another:

1. Detection of crime.
    a. Report of crime.
    b. Police investigation.
2. Identification of a suspected criminal.
3. Arrest.
    a. Arrest without a warrant before the filing of a complaint.
    b. Arrest with a warrant after the filing of a complaint.
4. Initial appearance before a magistrate.
    a. Inform the accused of the charges and legal rights.
    b. Set bail or the terms of release from custody.
5. Preliminary hearing.
    a. Determine probable cause that accused committed a crime.
    b. Release accused or bind over for grand jury.
6. Indictment.
    a. Grand jury decides whether accused should be tried, or
    b. Prosecutor indicts by "information."

7. Arraignment before the court.
   a. Accused informed of charges brought.
   b. Accused enters plea.
      i. If plea of guilty or nolo contendere, the defendant may be sentenced.
      ii. If plea of not guilty, accused requests or waives jury.
8. Pretrial preparation.
   a. Pretrial motions.
   b. Discovery.
   c. Plea bargaining.

FIGURE 1
Steps in Processing a Crime. A large number of crimes go unsolved or unreported. Of those where action is taken, only a small percentage will make it to trial.

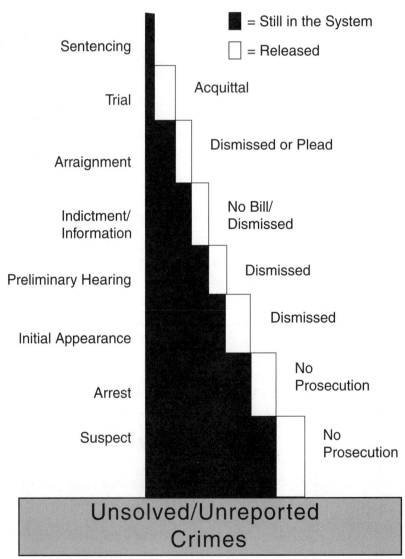

■ = Still in the System
□ = Released

Sentencing

Trial — Acquittal

Arraignment — Dismissed or Plead

Indictment/Information — No Bill/Dismissed

Preliminary Hearing — Dismissed

Initial Appearance — Dismissed

Arrest — No Prosecution

Suspect — No Prosecution

Unsolved/Unreported Crimes

9. Trial.
    a. Acquittal results in release of defendant.
    b. Conviction leads to sentencing.
10. Optional posttrial motions, appeals, and habeas corpus.

Detection of Crime

The initial intervention of law enforcement officers is prompted by the report of a suspected crime by victims or witnesses or the police themselves, who may witness a crime or discover one during a police investigation into suspected criminal activities. The criminal act may be apparent from the circumstances, as when police encounter bank robbers in the act of robbing a bank, or there may simply be suspicious activities that require investigation or surveillance.

Although it may be clear that a crime has been committed, the identity of the perpetrator may not be immediately apparent. The objective of police inquiry is to establish facts to support the conclusion that a crime has been committed and that a specific person or persons committed that crime. Detection of crime is simply the first step; the police must also furnish the prosecutor with sufficient evidence to form the basis for a probable conviction of the offender.

Statements made in the absence of Miranda warnings in the course of a custodial interrogation may be excluded from evidence at trial. What exactly is a *custodial interrogation* has been the subject of numerous cases, including the *Bruder* case.

Arrest and Complaint

arrest   Usually refers to detaining someone to answer for a crime.

Arrest is not an easy term to define in all circumstances and cases, but it generally refers to detaining someone for the purposes of having him or her answer to an allegation of a crime. The *complaint* is the formal allegation that the accused has committed a crime.

Legal process begins with a complaint. The complaint may be filed before or after arrest. When an arrest is made without a warrant during the commission of a crime, the complaint is filed at the defendant's initial appearance before the court or magistrate. When a crime has been completed and the police have information linking a person to the crime, the complaint is filed and an arrest warrant issued, which then serves as the basis for arresting the suspect.

In either case, an initial determination must be made as to whether there is *probable cause* to believe that a crime has been committed and that the defendant committed it. The complaint is accompanied by sworn statements, **affidavits,** which must present sufficient allegations to persuade the magistrate that a warrant should issue. If an arrest is made without a warrant, the arresting officer must have probable cause to believe that the suspect has committed a crime.

affidavit   A statement in writing sworn to before a person authorized to administer an oath.

The arrest powers of police are limited by constitutional and statutory requirements. When police exceed their authority in making an arrest, they

PENNSYLVANIA
v.
Thomas A. BRUDER, Jr.
U.S. Supreme Court
488 U.S. 9, 102 L. Ed. 2d 172,
109 S. Ct. 205 (1988)

In the early morning of January 19, 1985, Officer Steve Shallis of the Newton Township, Pennsylvania, Police Department observed Bruder driving very erratically along State Highway 252. Among other traffic violations, he ignored a red light. Shallis stopped Bruder's vehicle. Bruder left his vehicle, approached Shallis, and when asked for his registration card, returned to his car to obtain it. Smelling alcohol and observing Bruder's stumbling movements, Shallis administered field sobriety tests, including asking Bruder to recite the alphabet. Shallis also inquired about alcohol. Bruder answered that he had been drinking and was returning home. Bruder failed the sobriety tests, whereupon Shallis arrested him, placed him in the police car and gave him Miranda warnings. Bruder was later convicted of driving under the influence of alcohol. At his trial, his statements and conduct prior to his arrest were admitted into evidence. On appeal, the Pennsylvania Superior Court reversed, on the ground that the above statements Bruder had uttered during the roadside questioning were elicited through custodial interrogation and should have been suppressed for lack of Miranda warnings. The Pennsylvania Supreme Court denied the State's appeal application.

In *Berkemer v. McCarty,* which involved facts strikingly similar to those in this case, the court concluded that the "noncoercive aspect of ordinary traffic stops prompts us to hold that persons temporarily detained pursuant to such stops are not 'in custody' for the purposes of Miranda." . . .

The facts in this record, which Bruder does not contest, reveal the same noncoercive aspects as the *Berkemer* detention: "a single police officer ask[ing] respondent a modest number of questions and request[ing] him to perform a simple balancing test at a location visible to passing motorists." Accordingly, *Berkemer's* rule, that ordinary traffic stops do not involve custody for purposes of Miranda, governs this case. The judgment of the Pennsylvania Superior Court that evidence was inadmissible for lack of Miranda warnings is reversed.

Case Questions
1. Where does the court draw the line between a custodial and a noncustodial stop?
2. From the language of the case, can we infer that an interrogation did or did not take place?

may subject themselves to civil suit by the arrestee for the tort of false arrest or to a civil rights suit. An arrest made in the good faith belief that it is lawful and under the authority of a warrant and conducted with reasonable force is the ideal standard against which allegedly improper arrests are tested. There is a large body of constitutional cases on arrest, because arrest commonly involves incidental searches and the discovery of evidence later used in prosecution.

initial or **first appearance**   A person arrested for a crime must be brought before a magistrate promptly after arrest to be informed of the charges and the legal rights of the accused.

Initial Appearance

State and federal statutes require that an arrestee be brought before a magistrate without undue delay, commonly within twenty-four hours. This is called **initial** or **first appearance** and is designed to protect individuals from being jailed without charges or bonds in the absence of scrutiny by an impartial magistrate. The accused will be informed of the charges and legal rights, especially the right to an attorney, and that an attorney will be appointed at state expense if the accused does not have funds to pay an attorney.

Bail is set at the initial appearance. The purpose of bail is to assure the defendant's appearance at further hearings. The Eighth Amendment prohibits excessive bail, and the defendant may request a hearing to reduce the bail. Under federal law, the court must set the least restrictive conditions to assure appearance. Defendants are frequently released on their own recognizance if, for instance, the defendant has steady employment, has a stable residence, presents little threat to society, and the nature of the crime suggests little likelihood that the defendant will flee the jurisdiction. Extreme circumstances may justify a denial of bail. The court may impose certain conditions on release, such as restrictions on travel.

Preliminary Hearing

preliminary hearing
A criminal defendant is ordinarily afforded an opportunity to challenge the case before the judge in a hearing which determines the sufficiency of the charges without a determination of guilt.

A **preliminary hearing** is frequently called to examine the basis for the charges against the defendant, although this is frequently waived by the defendant. Because in the American system the prosecutor enjoys unrestricted authority over whether to prosecute, the preliminary hearing provides a defendant the opportunity to challenge the prosecution's case before the court. The preliminary hearing does not determine guilt but examines the legal basis for the charges against the defendant. The judge determines whether there is sufficient evidence to send the case to the grand jury or whether to release the defendant instead. Not all states require a grand jury indictment, so the preliminary hearing may be the only opportunity to challenge the charges prior to trial.

Indictment and Information

infamous crime
A major crime, for which a heavy penalty may be awarded. Used in the Constitution but now out of date and would probably mean *felony* today.

felony A serious crime, commonly defined by a penalty of a year or more in prison.

information A written accusation made by a public prosecutor.

Although the Constitution requires a grand jury for **infamous crimes** and many states require a grand jury indictment for **felonies,** many cases are brought on the basis of an **information,** which is a written accusation by a public prosecutor. The practice differs from jurisdiction to jurisdiction, but the defendant must be formally charged by an indictment or information.

Grand jury hearings are not truly adversarial; they are secret hearings in which the prosecutor is given wide latitude to present the case for the guilt of the defendant. The grand jury does not decide guilt but determines whether probable cause exists that the defendant committed the crime. If the grand jury finds no probable cause, the defendant is discharged; otherwise, the defendant is indicted and the case goes to trial.

Arraignment

arraignment Brings the defendant before the court to make a plea.

After indictment or upon an information, the defendant is brought before the court to answer the charge. At **arraignment,** the defendant makes a plea. In minor crimes (misdemeanors), the arraignment may be part of the preliminary hearing—the defendant is informed of the charges and asked to make a plea. Felonies requiring a grand jury and indictment separate the preliminary hearing and the arraignment, which follows the indictment.

The defendant has three pleas available:

1. *Not guilty.* A plea of not guilty results in a trial. The defendant may waive a jury, but the Constitution guarantees the right to a jury trial in criminal cases.

2. *Guilty.* The defendant admits commission of the crime and submits to the sentence of the court. Guilty pleas are usually the result of a plea negotiation between the prosecution and the defense attorney, with the acquiescence of the defendant.

3. *Nolo contendere* (not available in some jurisdictions; often not available in felony cases). Nolo contendere, literally "I do not wish to contest," is equivalent to a guilty plea except that it does not admit guilt. It is treated the same as a guilty plea for the purposes of sentencing, but it cannot be used in later civil or criminal cases as an admission of guilt.

The court has discretion to accept a guilty or nolo contendere plea. The court may require a defendant to plead guilty or not guilty rather than nolo contendere and may also in its discretion refuse to accept a guilty plea. If the defendant refuses to make a plea, the court will assume this refusal to be a plea of not guilty and set the case for trial.

A special plea of "**not guilty by reason of insanity**" is available in many jurisdictions; this subject is more fully covered in Chapter 9. This plea admits commission of the acts with which the defendant is charged but negates the critical element of criminal intent on the basis of the defendant's insanity.

nolo contendere (Latin) "I do not want to contest." Accepts responsibility without an admission of guilt.

not guilty by reason of insanity A plea in a criminal case that admits commission of the acts charged but denies intent on the basis of defendant's insanity.

Pretrial

In many respects the pretrial phase is reminiscent of civil procedure. Pretrial motions are available, such as the motion to suppress evidence. Discovery procedures are similar except for protections against self-incrimination. Plea bargaining bears some resemblance to the strategies for negotiating settlements in civil cases.

Ethical dilemmas in life and in law involve not only determining the right course of action, but also sometimes doing what appears to be morally wrong because it is ethically right, as illustrated by the *Belge* case. It concerns the issue of attorney-client confidentiality. With a few exceptions, lawyers may not reveal statements made to them by clients in confidence without the consent of the clients. This allows clients to truthfully disclose facts to the attorney without fear that these facts will be disclosed to others.

PEOPLE
v.
BELGE
390 N.Y.S.2d 867 (1976)

[In 1973 Robert Garrow, who was charged with child molestation, was represented by attorney Frank Armani. On July 28 of that year, Garrow encountered four young campers in the Adirondacks and held them at gunpoint. He then stabbed and killed one of them, Philip Domblewski. The three remaining campers later identified Garrow, who was captured several days later. Garrow requested that Armani represent him and Armani asked the help of Francis Belge in the defense. Both attorneys were appointed by the court as defense attorneys.

The attorneys persuaded Garrow to reveal the facts of his past, guaranteeing him that his disclosures were confidential and could not be revealed without his consent. Garrow admitted to three other killings, one involving a sixteen-year-old high school girl whom he had raped and killed and buried near a cemetery. He had also killed two university students who were camping, killing the young man first and then abducting his female companion for three days, raping her, and finally killing her and leaving her body in an abandoned mine shaft.

In an effort to check their client's story, Armani and Belge went to find the bodies of the two women and found them where Garrow said he had left them. Armani was uncertain as to his duties under the circumstances (parents of the two women were then attempting to find them); he posed a hypothetical situation similar to his dilemma before an appellate judge. The judge concluded that such information was confidential and advised Armani that he might be disbarred for disclosing it.

The attorneys attempted to plea bargain in Garrow's behalf, offering to provide information on unsolved crimes if Garrow's charges were reduced from murder to second-degree manslaughter. The offer was refused and the attorneys ultimately decided that, given three eyewitnesses to the Domblewski killing, Garrow's best defense was insanity. Garrow's personality and background of extensive abuse as a child made the insanity plea plausible. At trial Garrow also admitted to the other killings, but was nevertheless convicted of Domblewski's murder.

Following Garrow's testimony, Armani and Belge held a press conference to disclose their knowledge of the prior crimes and discovery of the bodies, but insisted that they had no choice but to keep the information secret, despite the continuing agony suffered by the families of the victims. The public was outraged by the attorneys' behavior and both were summoned before a grand jury on charges that they had violated New York law requiring a decent burial and reporting of death without medical attendance. Belge was indicted by the grand jury, but the case was later dismissed by the trial judge on the grounds that Belge was protected by his duty of nondisclosure and "the interests of justice." This decision was affirmed on appeal.]

Case Questions

1. Could the defense attorneys have ethically disclosed the whereabouts of the bodies through another means? Explain.
2. What limits on confidentiality could be imposed that could have changed the attorneys' conduct in this case? Explain.

Trial

In most respects the criminal trial is conducted in the same way as a civil trial. The prosecutor has the burden of proving the case. Each side presents its witnesses and cross-examines witnesses for the other side. There are opening statements, closing arguments, and so on. The major difference in the nature of the proceedings comes from the much higher standard that the prosecutor must meet, that of proving guilt beyond a reasonable doubt. Another major difference is that the defendant may not be compelled to testify. In one respect this right is illusory. It is human nature to expect the defendant to take the witness stand and declare innocence. If a criminal defendant declines to testify, the judge will instruct the jury that they should not draw any conclusions from this since the defendant is exercising a constitutional right. Human nature, however, slants jurors toward a negative inference when the defendant refuses to take the opportunity to urge his or her innocence.

Sentencing

sentencing guidelines
Many states have adopted guidelines that establish specific sentences for specific crimes. Some states have also adopted minimum sentences for certain crimes.

probation An alternative to incarceration that sets a period of time during which the probationer must adhere to conditions set by the court and be supervised by a probation officer. Violation of the conditions may result in incarceration.

pretrial diversion
Postpones and usually obviates the need for trial if the accused meets certain conditions, typically the performance of community service.

Sentencing procedures differ widely among the states. Historically, judges had wide discretion in sentencing because the range of imprisonment was broad (e.g., "one to ten years"). But some states have adopted guidelines that establish customary sentences for crimes. The judge must justify imposing a sentence more severe than the guidelines or risk reversal on appeal. Some crimes in some states now call for mandatory minimum imprisonment, limiting the judge's discretion. Federal prosecutions follow **sentencing guidelines** as well.

There are a number of alternatives to incarceration. In recent years, judges have become reluctant to send convicted criminals to jail. This is partly because our jails are full and partly because numerous studies have shown that incarceration tends to breed career criminals rather than prepare them for a return to society. It is now rare for a person on first conviction of nonviolent lesser crimes to be sent to prison.

Among alternatives to incarceration, the oldest is probation. **Probation** is ordered for a fixed period of time, during which the probationer is subject to stringent conditions, the violation of which may result in incarceration. The probationer is monitored by a probation officer, who ideally not only checks for violations of probation but also serves as a personal counselor to aid the probationer in obtaining employment and making appropriate choices in conduct and career.

A convicted criminal may be sentenced to perform community service. The accused may also avoid conviction by having the judge withhold adjudication under specified conditions. Some jurisdictions allow **pretrial diversion** which postpones and usually obviates the need for trial if the accused meets certain conditions, typically the performance of community service. The criminal justice system recognizes that incarceration can be detrimental not only to the criminal but also to society. In addition, the effect of conviction may be a serious impediment to a person's career, so young first offenders are often treated leniently.

Prison alternatives are frequently the result of plea bargaining and offer the judge considerable discretion in the treatment of offenders. This feature of the criminal justice system distinguishes it from civil procedure. In criminal cases, the court is not concerned simply with the determination of guilt and the award of penalties, but also with the regulation of conduct and the protection of society.

Many states have addressed the problem of habitual offenders by passing laws such as California's "three strikes [and you're out]" law. Under such laws, a person convicted of three felonies is subject to a special sentence of very long duration or lifetime imprisonment. This is properly aimed at habitual *violent* offenders but occasionally applies to situations where the offense seems to pose little threat to society at large. In the *Taylor* case, the three strikes rule was applied to Taylor's conviction of possessing 0.04 grams of crack (rock cocaine), a minimal amount, perhaps sufficient to provide Taylor with one "high." Nevertheless, Taylor was sentenced to twenty-five years to life. His prior convictions had been for robbery and assault with a deadly weapon (a pair of scissors). He was on parole when arrested for possession of cocaine.

Taylor represented himself at trial, waived his jury right, and apparently proceeded to annoy the judge. His main concern here is not to argue his innocence but rather to escape the harshness of the three strikes law. Judges are often uncomfortable with the legislature's intrusions on judicial discretion. In reading this case, one sees that the court is often concerned with justice over the *letter* of the law.

The PEOPLE, Plaintiff and Respondent,
v.
Frederick R. TAYLOR, Defendant and Appellant
Court of Appeal, Second District, Division 7, California
95 Cal.Rptr.2d 357 (2000)

JOHNSON, Acting P. J.

Discussion

* * *

III. THE TRIAL COURT ABUSED ITS DISCRETION BY CONSIDERING INAPPROPRIATE FACTORS IN DENYING TAYLOR'S MOTION TO DISMISS THE PRIOR STRIKE ALLEGATIONS UNDER SECTION 1385.

Taylor had previously been convicted of two violent or serious felonies within the meaning of the "three strikes" law: a robbery in 1991 and assault with a deadly weapon (a pair of scissors) in 1992. He was on parole when he was arrested for possession of 0.04 grams of cocaine in 1998 which led to the current conviction and a sentence of 25 years to life under the "three strikes" law (§ 667, subd. (e)(2)(A).)

The trial court denied Taylor's motion to dismiss the allegations of one or both of his "strikes" in furtherance of justice under section 1385. (*People v. Superior Court* (Romero) (1996) 13 Cal.4th 497, 53 Cal.Rptr.2d 789, 917 P.2d 628.) On appeal, Taylor contends the trial court abused its discretion in denying his motion and sent him to prison for life for being a bad lawyer and a public nuisance.

A split of authority exists as to whether the denial of a request to dismiss a strike under section 1385 is appealable. The majority of courts have found such an order is appealable. [Cc.] We believe the majority view is correct. Furthermore, even under *People v. Benevides,* supra, if the trial court expresses "clearly

(continued)

(continued)

improper reasons" for refusing to dismiss a "strike" the appellate court "must correct the error." [C.]

Rulings on Romero motions are reviewed for abuse of discretion. [C.] Discretion is abused where the trial court's decision is "irrational or arbitrary[C.] Discretion is also abused when the trial court's decision to strike or not to strike a prior is based on improper reasons [Cc.] or the decision is not in conformity with the "spirit" of the law [Cc.]

As the trial court acknowledged, there were a number of factors supporting a dismissal of one or more of Taylor's "strikes." The present felony was "minor," involving a "miniscule amount" of drugs. The present felony did not involve violence. The present felony did not place any person or property in danger. Taylor was employed and productive for the majority of the year prior to his current arrest. He had "strong support from many friends and family members."

On the other hand, the trial court identified two factors it believed militated against granting Taylor's motion. His two prior strikes, a 1991 robbery conviction and a 1992 conviction for assault with a deadly weapon were not "remote in time" from his 1998 drug arrest and he was on probation at the time of his current drug arrest.

However, what tipped the balance against Taylor were two factors which had nothing to do with the nature and circumstances of his present crime, his prior felony convictions, or the particulars of his background, character, and prospects. [C.]

After reviewing the above-stated factors for and against striking the priors, the court launched into an attack on Taylor for the way he had conducted his pro per defense.

The court accused Taylor of misconduct in appealing to the jury for sympathy. The court stated Taylor had misled the jury in telling them he had been in custody for six months awaiting trial "when you well [knew] that that

was only because you continued the case. . . . [Y]ou're telling the jury your rights have been violated, you were in custody for six months, and that was outrageous." The court also noted Taylor told the jury he was defending himself because he could not afford an attorney when in fact he had a court-appointed standby counsel at his side throughout the trial and had been provided by the court with funds for telephone calls, postage and to hire an investigator. In addition, Taylor told the jury he was concerned about the amount of time he was facing if convicted and, while the jury was passing through the courtroom during a break in deliberations, Taylor "loudly said: Please don't take my life."

Taylor's other misconduct cited by the court included calling one of the police officer witnesses "a liar" and attempting to use his opening statement and closing argument as testimony in lieu of taking the stand himself.

After describing these instances of misbehavior, the trial court asked Taylor: "Now tell me why that deserves any kind of consideration on my part that you have corrected your [past criminal behavior]. . . . I don't see that you're deserving of any leniency." Taylor responded he was "desperate" and gave a long account of his past life and his efforts at rehabilitation. The court then reacted with more criticism of Taylor's courtroom behavior, telling Taylor he had not "adhere[d] to the rules": "You cheated throughout the trial. You cheated in your opening statements to the jury, you cheated during the presentation of the evidence, cheated during your argument to the jury at the end, and you cheated after they were selected and they were going out pleading with them not to take your life, telling them this was a life sentence and not to take your life. . . . Nothing that you've done has shown me that you can correct your conduct in the future. And that's what three strikes is all about."

The trial court's remarks during the hearing on the Romero motion also show the court denied the motion because it viewed Taylor as a public nuisance who should be removed from the streets. The court made this point not just once but five times in the course of the hearing. . . .

We fail to see how Taylor's amateurish mistakes in conducting his own defense have any bearing on the question whether he may be deemed outside the spirit of the "three strikes" law, in whole or in part. The trial court attempted to make Taylor's actions during the trial a "character" issue [C.] by accusing Taylor of failing to follow the "rules" of proper trial conduct and of "cheating" in his presentation to the jury. [C.] [In exercising discretion whether to treat crime as "wobbler" court may consider defendant's "traits of character as evidenced by his behavior and demeanor at the trial"].) We perceive no correlation, however, between the way Taylor conducted his defense and the interests of society in longer prison terms for repeat felons. (§ 667, subd. (b).)

Furthermore, although there is no requirement the third "strike" be a serious or violent felony, we do not believe that in enacting the "three strikes" law the Legislature or the people intended the law be turned into a nuisance statute used as a way of ridding society forever of persons who are a mere public annoyance or embarrassment. [C.]That the trial court was using the statute in this manner is apparent from the court's numerous references to Taylor smoking his small rock of cocaine in public rather than in his home. This is not what the Supreme Court had in mind when it instructed the trial courts to consider "the nature and circumstances" of the defendant's present felony.[C.] Indeed, the power to dismiss prior strikes is intended to protect the defendant's right not to suffer disproportionate punishment. [C.] A sentence of life in prison for possession of 0.04 grams of cocaine is no more proportional to the crime because the possession occurred in public than if it had occurred in private.

For the reasons set forth above, we conclude the trial court abused its discretion in denying Taylor's motion to dismiss one or both of his prior strike allegations because it considered factors extrinsic to the statutory scheme. [C.] Because this is a close case and it is reasonably probable the trial court might have reached a more favorable decision had it not considered improper factors, the error was prejudicial. However, other than limiting itself to the factors discussed in *Williams,* supra, we express no view on how the trial court should exercise its discretion on remand.

Disposition

The judgment of conviction is affirmed. The sentence is vacated and the cause remanded to the trial court to reconsider whether to dismiss one or both of the prior strike allegations.

WOODS, J., concurs.

NEAL, J., Concurring and Dissenting.

Case Questions

1. What does the court mean by "we express no view on how the trial court should exercise its discretion on remand"?
2. What should Taylor do at this point?

Appeal

In most respects criminal appeals are similar to those in civil procedure. Appellate courts, however, jealously guard against infringements of basic constitutional rights, such as involuntary confessions and illegal searches and seizures, in an effort to ensure fairness to the accused. The right to counsel is the subject

pro bono (publico)
(Latin) "For the
(public) good."
Traditionally, members of
the bar were under a
moral obligation to
render free services to the
public, typically to
provide services to people
who could not afford to
pay. States now make this
a requirement of
membership in the bar,
typically with specific
minimum contributions
of time.

of many appeals. Indigent defendants are appointed counsel from the public defender's office or private counsel. Public defenders typically have heavy case loads and may not always be able to devote as much attention to each case as it deserves. Private attorneys often serve on a ***pro bono*** basis and are under pressure to devote their time to paying clients. This may or may not result in neglect of criminal cases, but those who are convicted often use this argument to claim ineffective assistance of counsel, in an effort to obtain a new trial.

Although prejudicial error is the basis for reversal of rulings on the law, jury instructions, and so on, as in civil cases, the test of error in factfinding is necessarily different in a criminal trial because the test is guilt beyond a reasonable doubt. On appeal, a verdict of guilty is tested against a standard that asks whether "no trier of fact could have found proof beyond a reasonable doubt." Like "clearly erroneous" and "substantial evidence," this test shows great deference to factfinding at trial and makes it difficult to challenge on this basis.

In *Fulminante*, we come across *harmless error* once again, but this case demonstrates that the difference is application to different burdens of proof. In civil cases, the burden of proof is *preponderance of the evidence*; while in criminal cases, the prosecution must prove *guilt beyond a reasonable doubt*. A moment's reflection reveals that the standard for appeal would be more strict in criminal cases. *Fulminante* resulted in considerable disagreement among the justices, as the first paragraph in the case indicates. This might make any precedent here difficult to apply in future cases. Nevertheless, the issues are revealed even though how they were resolved is confusing. In trying to keep everything straight, it is important to remember that, no matter how confusing, every opinion attempts to make a sequence of statements that lead to a final logical conclusion. When nine eminent legal thinkers do not agree on the reasoning, the court's opinion may be a bit murky.

ARIZONA, Petitioner
v.
Oreste C. FULMINANTE
Supreme Court of the United States
Argued Oct. 10, 1990
499 U.S. 279 (1991)

WHITE, J., delivered an opinion, Parts I, II, and IV of which are for the Court, and filed a dissenting opinion in Part III. MARSHALL, BLACKMUN, and STEVENS, JJ., joined Parts I, II, III, and IV of that opinion; SCALIA, J., joined Parts I and II; and KENNEDY, J., joined Parts I and IV. REHNQUIST, C. J., delivered an opinion,

Part II of which is for the Court, and filed a dissenting opinion in Parts I and III, post, p. 1261. O'CONNOR, J., joined Parts I, II, and III of that opinion; KENNEDY and SOUTER, JJ., joined Parts I and II; and SCALIA, J., joined Parts II and III. KENNEDY, J., filed an opinion concurring in the judgment, post, p. 1266.

The Arizona Supreme Court ruled in this case that respondent Oreste Fulminante's confession, received in evidence at his trial for murder, had been coerced and that its use against him was barred by the Fifth and Fourteenth Amendments to the United States Constitution. The court also held that the harmless-error rule could not be used to save the conviction. We affirm the judgment of the Arizona court, although for different reasons than those upon which that court relied.

I

Early in the morning of September 14, 1982, Fulminante called the Mesa, Arizona, Police Department to report that his 11-year-old stepdaughter, Jeneane Michelle Hunt, was missing. He had been caring for Jeneane while his wife, Jeneane's mother, was in the hospital. Two days later, Jeneane's body was found in the desert east of Mesa. She had been shot twice in the head at close range with a large caliber weapon, and a ligature was around her neck. Because of the decomposed condition of the body, it was impossible to tell whether she had been sexually assaulted.

Fulminante's statements to police concerning Jeneane's disappearance and his relationship with her contained a number of inconsistencies, and he became a suspect in her killing. When no charges were filed against him, Fulminante left Arizona for New Jersey. Fulminante was later convicted in New Jersey on federal charges of possession of a firearm by a felon.

[H]e became friends with another inmate, Anthony Sarivola, then serving a 60-day sentence for extortion. The two men came to spend several hours a day together. Sarivola, a former police officer, had been involved in loansharking for organized crime but then became a paid informant for the Federal Bureau of Investigation. While at Ray Brook, he masqueraded as an organized crime figure. After becoming friends with Fulminante, Sarivola heard a rumor that Fulminante was suspected of killing a child in Arizona. Sarivola then raised the subject with Fulminante in several conversations, but Fulminante repeatedly denied any involvement in Jeneane's death. . . .

Sarivola said that he knew Fulminante was "starting to get some tough treatment and whatnot" from other inmates because of the rumor. App. 83. Sarivola offered to protect Fulminante from his fellow inmates, but told him,

" 'You have to tell me about it,' you know. I mean, in other words, 'For me to give you any help.' " Ibid. Fulminante then admitted to Sarivola that he had driven Jeneane to the desert on his motorcycle, where he choked her, sexually assaulted her, and made her beg for her life, before shooting her twice in the head. . . .

. . . On September 4, 1984, Fulminante was indicted in Arizona for the first-degree murder of Jeneane.

Prior to trial, Fulminante moved to suppress the statement he had given Sarivola in prison, as well as a second confession he had given to Donna Sarivola, then Anthony Sarivola's fiancee and later his wife, following his May 1984 release from prison. He asserted that the confession to Sarivola was coerced, and that the second confession was the "fruit" of the first. . . . Following the hearing, the trial court denied the motion to suppress, specifically finding that, based on the stipulated facts, the confessions were voluntary. Id., at 44, 63. The State introduced both confessions as evidence at trial, and on December 19, 1985, Fulminante was convicted of Jeneane's murder. He was subsequently sentenced to death.

Fulminante appealed, arguing, among other things, that his confession to Sarivola was the product of coercion and that its admission at trial violated his rights to due process under the Fifth and Fourteenth Amendments to the United States Constitution. After considering the evidence at trial as well as the stipulated facts before the trial court on the motion to suppress, the Arizona Supreme Court held that the confession was coerced, but initially determined that the admission of the confession at trial was harmless error, because of the overwhelming nature of the evidence against Fulminante. . . . Upon Fulminante's motion for reconsideration, however, the court ruled that this Court's precedent precluded the use of the harmless-error analysis in the case of a coerced confession. . . . The court therefore reversed

(continued)

(continued)

the conviction and ordered that Fulminante be retried without the use of the confession to Sarivola. Because of differing views in the state and federal courts over whether the admission at trial of a coerced confession is subject to a harmless-error analysis, we granted the State's petition for certiorari. . . . Although a majority of this Court finds that such a confession is subject to a harmless-error analysis, for the reasons set forth below, we affirm the judgment of the Arizona court.

II

[T]he Arizona Supreme Court stated that a "determination regarding the voluntariness of a confession . . . must be viewed in a totality of the circumstances," . . . and under that standard plainly found that Fulminante's statement to Sarivola had been coerced.

In applying the totality of the circumstances test to determine that the confession to Sarivola was coerced, the Arizona Supreme Court focused on a number of relevant facts. First, the court noted that "because [Fulminante] was an alleged child murderer, he was in danger of physical harm at the hands of other inmates." In addition, Sarivola was aware that Fulminante had been receiving " 'rough treatment from the guys.' " . . . Using his knowledge of these threats, Sarivola offered to protect Fulminante in exchange for a confession to Jeneane's murder, . . . and "[i]n response to Sarivola's offer of protection, [Fulminante] confessed." . . . Agreeing with Fulminante that "Sarivola's promise was 'extremely coercive,' " . . . the Arizona court declared: "[T]he confession was obtained as a direct result of extreme coercion and was tendered in the belief that the defendant's life was in jeopardy if he did not confess. This is a true coerced confession in every sense of the word." . . .

. . . Nevertheless, "the ultimate issue of 'voluntariness' is a legal question requiring independent federal determination." . . .

Although the question is a close one, we agree with the Arizona Supreme Court's con-

clusion that Fulminante's confession was coerced. The Arizona Supreme Court found a credible threat of physical violence unless Fulminante confessed. Our cases have made clear that a finding of coercion need not depend upon actual violence by a government agent; a credible threat is sufficient. As we have said, "coercion can be mental as well as physical, and . . . the blood of the accused is not the only hallmark of an unconstitutional inquisition." . . . [T]he Arizona Supreme Court found that it was fear of physical violence, absent protection from his friend (and Government agent) Sarivola, which motivated Fulminante to confess. Accepting the Arizona court's finding, permissible on this record, that there was a credible threat of physical violence, we agree with its conclusion that Fulminante's will was overborne in such a way as to render his confession the product of coercion.

[Part III, a dissenting opinion, has been omitted.]

IV

Since five Justices have determined that harmless-error analysis applies to coerced confessions, it becomes necessary to evaluate under that ruling the admissibility of Fulminante's confession to Sarivola. . . . In so doing, it must be determined whether the State has met its burden of demonstrating that the admission of the confession to Sarivola did not contribute to Fulminante's conviction. . . .

In the Arizona Supreme Court's initial opinion, in which it determined that harmless-error analysis could be applied to the confession, the court found that the admissible second confession to Donna Sarivola rendered the first confession to Anthony Sarivola cumulative. . . . The court also noted that circumstantial physical evidence concerning the wounds, the ligature around Jeneane's neck, the location of the body, and the presence of motorcycle tracks at the scene corroborated the second confession. Ibid. The court concluded that "due to the overwhelming evidence adduced from the second confession, if there had not been a first confession, the jury would still have had the same basic evidence to convict" Fulminante. . . .

We have a quite different evaluation of the evidence. Our review of the record leads us to conclude that the State has failed to meet its burden of establishing, beyond a reasonable doubt, that the admission of Fulminante's confession to Anthony Sarivola was harmless-error. Three considerations compel this result.

First, the transcript discloses that both the trial court and the State recognized that a successful prosecution depended on the jury believing the two confessions. Absent the confessions, it is unlikely that Fulminante would have been prosecuted at all, because the physical evidence from the scene and other circumstantial evidence would have been insufficient to convict.

Second, the jury's assessment of the confession to Donna Sarivola could easily have depended in large part on the presence of the confession to Anthony Sarivola. Absent the admission at trial of the first confession, the jurors might have found Donna Sarivola's story unbelievable. . . . [I]t is clear that the jury might have believed that the two confessions reinforced and corroborated each other. . . . While in some cases two confessions, delivered on different occasions to different listeners,

might be viewed as being independent of each other, . . . it strains credulity to think that the jury so viewed the two confessions in this case, especially given the close relationship between Donna and Anthony Sarivola. . . .

Third, the admission of the first confession led to the admission of other evidence prejudicial to Fulminante . . . , for it depicted him as someone who willingly sought out the company of criminals. . . .

Finally, although our concern here is with the effect of the erroneous admission of the confession on Fulminante's conviction, it is clear that the presence of the confession also influenced the sentencing phase of the trial. . . .

Because a majority of the Court has determined that Fulminante's confession to Anthony Sarivola was coerced and because a majority has determined that admitting this confession was not harmless beyond a reasonable doubt, we agree with the Arizona Supreme Court's conclusion that Fulminante is entitled to a new trial at which the confession is not admitted. Accordingly the judgment of the Arizona Supreme Court is

Affirmed.

[RENQUIST, C. J., delivered a dissenting opinion in parts I and III, and a part II which is for the courts, all of which has been omitted.]

Case Questions

1. Did Fulminante win because the justices were in such disagreement?
2. What precisely was the rule, or rules, laid down by the court?

Habeas Corpus

The writ of habeas corpus provides prisoners with a remedy not available in civil cases. Because it challenges the lawfulness of detention, habeas corpus is often used as a means to obtain review of a case in addition to appeal.

Summary

Criminal procedure is similar to civil procedure in the steps it follows from pretrial to trial, in the presentation of evidence, and in the adversarial nature of the proceedings. There are important differences, however, many of which are based on constitutional rights of the accused. The Bill of Rights forms a skeletal code of criminal procedure that has been elaborated through appellate decisions. Among the more important rights guaranteed an accused are the privilege against self-incrimination, the right to an attorney even for those who cannot afford one, the right to a speedy and public trial, the right to be free of cruel and unusual punishment, and the right against the imposition of excessive bail.

Criminal procedure involves initial steps to assure that the accusation of crime is well grounded: the requirement of probable cause for arrest and for warrants (arrest or search warrants); of initial appearance before a magistrate after arrest; of preliminary hearing; and of grand jury indictment and arraignment.

The major differences between criminal and civil trials are the right of the accused in a criminal trial not be compelled to testify, the exclusion of improperly obtained evidence, and the burden of proof on the prosecution to prove guilt beyond a reasonable doubt.

Scenario

(Note: The following scenario is loosely based on Florida law and Florida fact; it is fictional but not unrealistic.)

The State of Florida is the southernmost of the continental United States and, as such, is one of the favorite entry points for illegal drugs coming from the Caribbean and South America. Miami and its environs play a major part in the drug traffic. Dealers and distributors commonly drive Interstate I-95 through Florida to Miami, bringing money to Miami and drugs back north. I-95 passes through Ambrosia County, which has discovered a lucrative device to fund the county and especially the sheriff's department. The deputy sheriffs of Ambrosia County have "profiles" of likely drug dealers, described by race, type of car, driving habits, and so on, which allows the deputies to stop cars most likely to be driven by drug dealers. The deputies can either stop the cars for actual traffic or safety violations or manufacture them, for example, failure to signal when changing lanes. Once stopped, the deputies are adept at judging the likelihood that the detained persons are drug dealers, letting the apparently innocent go with a warning while wheedling a consent to search out of most of the apparently guilty.

Ambrosia County deputies concentrate on southbound vehicles because, as Willie Sutton put it, "That's where the money is." Florida law provides that law enforcement officers may confiscate money they have a reasonable suspicion is being used or is about to be used for illegal purposes. The Florida Supreme Court has held that anyone carrying more than $5,000 on his person without a clearly defined legitimate purpose, for example, bank courier, raises such a reasonable suspicion. On this basis, the deputies have successfully confiscated about $3 million per year for the last three years. Although the purpose of the law is the forfeiture of money destined for an illegal purpose, the sheriff's department often keeps the money even though criminal charges are dropped. The forfeiture is classified as civil in nature, but many attorneys have argued that the label is a sham since the money is forfeited in connection with alleged criminal activity. Owners of the seized money must sue to get it back if the sheriff's department does not voluntarily return it. Of course, if the owners are convicted of crimes such as drug possession or other drug crimes, they will not succeed in getting the return of the money.

John and Nanci Martinez are driving down I-95 to Miami where they will stay with relatives while they look for work and housing, intending to move from New York City to Miami. Because John does not trust banks, he keeps his money in cash. They sold most of their possessions in New York, and they have $12,000 in cash, $6,000 in John's wallet and $6,000 in Nanci's purse. While driving through Ambrosia County, they are stopped by Deputy Birddog for driving in the left lane when not passing. Deputy Birddog asks if he can search the car and the persons of John and Nanci. They agree, believing they have done nothing wrong and not knowing about cash forfeitures. Birddog discovers the money, confiscates it, and finds the remains of a marijuana cigarette underneath John's (the driver's) seat. Birddog arrests John and Nanci. Later, when the state attorney's office is presented with the case, it declines to prosecute because of a policy to dismiss cases involving less than .1 ounces of marijuana. When John and Nanci ask for the return of their money, the sheriff's department refuses, claiming the money was forfeited in connection with drug activity and was about to be used to purchase drugs to be sold out of state. They cite the fact that John was convicted five years previously in New York of purchasing an ounce of marijuana. (He was given three years probation, which he served without incident.) The sheriff's department offers to return half of the money that was in Nanci's possession if John and Nanci will sign a release promising not to sue for the rest of the money.

You are the attorney for John and Nanci. Although the letter of the law seems to support Ambrosia County, a new circuit court judge has been elected and is handling this case. This judge has been known to criticize the forfeiture law and will entertain wide-ranging arguments in behalf of your clients. Build an argument drawing from whatever principles you can find in criminal procedure and the Bill of Rights to obtain the return of their money.

CRIMINAL LAW

Introduction

With a basic knowledge of criminal procedure, we can now turn to the substantive law of crimes. Because substantive criminal law varies from state to state, a concise catalog of American crimes is not possible. Instead, this chapter concentrates on underlying issues related to criminal concepts of fault and culpability involved in the criminal act and in criminal intent, especially the latter.

Criminal Law in Practice

Many criminal defense attorneys work as sole practitioners or in small firms where a large staff is not cost-efficient. The government employs lawyers and paralegals in prosecutors' offices and in **public defenders' offices.** In addition, many government agencies have positions in which legal training and skills are useful. No understanding of American law is complete, however, without studying the basics of criminal law.

public defender's office A government agency that provides criminal defense services to indigents.

Definition

crime An act that violates the criminal law. If this seems redundant, compare *Orans:* "Any violation of the government's penal laws. An illegal act."

There is no adequate substantive definition of **crime.** The condemnation of heinous acts against persons, such as murder, is a common feature of human societies; but property crimes, crimes against the state, and regulatory crimes—and the penalties for their violation—reflect arbitrary decisions of rulemakers that vary considerably from nation to nation and even from one American state to another, depending on perceived needs to regulate behavior. The criminal law as presently constituted is a compilation of specific prohibited acts. In a sense, a *crime* may be defined simply as an act that violates the criminal law. In the American legal system, a line has been drawn between acts that are regulated by criminal law process and those for which redress is sought through the civil law process depending on whether punishment or compensation is sought. In many instances, a specific act may give rise to both civil and criminal legal actions.

criminal law   The list of crimes promulgated by the state, including the mental states required for particular crimes, for example, specific intent, premeditation.

Thus, **criminal law** may be defined as the list of crimes promulgated by the state. This list is essentially arbitrary in the sense that the state may penalize conduct that was formerly not criminal and may decriminalize conduct that was formerly criminal. Slavery was once legal in the United States; now it is not. Using cocaine was once legal; now it is not. It was once criminal to libel the president; now it is not.

Criminal law may be practically defined by concentrating on procedural distinctions. Crime is defined as a "wrong against society." This really means that the means to redress that wrong are monopolized by the state. Our system has evolved to put the redress of criminal conduct wholly in the hands of public officials, so we have created agencies of police, prosecutors, and judges to accomplish the task. A criminal case can be distinguished from a civil case by the fact that it is brought by the public prosecutor, enforcing a criminal statute.

In short, a crime is a crime because the legislature (or in some cases the court) says it is a crime.

Crime and Morality

There is a cliché that says, "You can't legislate morality." This is patently false, as that is exactly what law, especially criminal law, does. However, if the statement really means that immorality cannot be eliminated simply by passing criminal laws, then the statement is correct.

To say that a crime is a wrong against society is to assert that it is immoral; otherwise, it might merely be a wrong against a person and of little consequence to the public at large. There are certain offenses, like murder, which are virtually universally condemned in our society, and others, such as using marijuana, over which there is widespread disagreement. As social mores change, so too will the law. In part, the criminal law is a reflection of societal values, but it is also an effort by lawmakers to control and regulate conduct they consider politically undesirable. In the latter sense, the criminal law may impose morality rather than merely reflect it.

mala in se (Latin) "Wrong in and of itself"; crimes that are morally wrong.

mala prohibita (Latin) "Prohibited wrongs." Crimes that are not inherently evil, usually regulatory crimes.

Mala in Se and *Mala Prohibita*

Some crimes, such as murder, are considered inherently wrong—*mala in se.* Others, which are not wrong in themselves but are nonetheless penalized (usually as a regulatory measure, such as failure to file an income tax return), are called *mala prohibita.* The recent proliferation of the latter offenses is derived from the growth of a highly bureaucratized and regulated political organization in the form of the state.

Consider the difference in nature between driving while intoxicated and driving with an expired automobile registration. The former represents a danger to the public and is *mala in se*, whereas the latter is primarily designed for revenue collection and recordkeeping and is *mala prohibita*.

In simpler times, a person could rely, with good reason, on the shared values of society to avoid breaking the moral injunctions of the law. Today, the bewildering complexity of a regulated society requires its members to consult the requirements of the law at every turn. The moral basis of the penal law has become obscure.

The confusion is exacerbated by rules penalizing offenses that are not criminal, a development of recent decades. Parking violations may no longer be misdemeanors (smaller crimes), as they were in the past. That ne'er-do-well who lets his auto registration expire will most certainly pay an extra fee when he renews, but why is he penalized? He was not caught, not charged, not convicted; he incurred no extra administrative expense. No doubt the late fee is called a *civil penalty*, something of a contradiction in terms. It is not labeled criminal, but it looks like a wrong and certainly not a private wrong, which would be a tort and covered by compensation law (see Chapter 10).

In short, a crime is not a crime if the legislature says it is not a crime.

Note on the Model Penal Code

The American Law Institute, which publishes the *Restatement of Torts* and the *Restatement of Contracts*, is also responsible for the *Model Penal Code*, an additional attempt to encourage uniformity in state law. Some areas of criminal law present a bewildering assortment of treatments among the states, and the *Model Penal Code* is often a leader in these areas rather than merely a restatement of the law. Many state laws are a hodgepodge of custom, past practice, and reformulation of the common law of crimes. The *Model Penal Code* attempts a more consistent and coherent statement of criminal law, but it has no official standing in state law that departs from it. Nevertheless, it is perhaps the most modern statement of American criminal law and is occasionally referred to here. It is an important research resource for those examining the law and is often quoted in judicial opinions.

Fault

Fault is as much a part of public wrongs (crimes) as it is of private wrongs (torts). In criminal law, however, the element of intent to do wrong is far more important than in tort law or contract law, where the law's attention is drawn to the injured party. Criminal law is primarily concerned with **punishment,** or **retribution,** of the criminal and the **deterrence** of crime; Anglo-American law aims at punishing those who deserve it. Traditionally, two components have been required to hold a person responsible for a crime: criminal act and criminal intent.

punishment, or retribution Has as the primary goal of criminal law punishing a person for criminal conduct. The other theories of the treatment of criminals are **deterrence** of crime (defined elsewhere); *incapacitation*, that is, removing the criminal from society through incarceration; and *rehabilitation*, helping the criminal toward a productive role in society.

deterrence Theory in criminal law that holds that the purpose of the sanctions imposed by the law is to deter, rather than simply punish, criminal conduct.

Criminal Act and Criminal Intent

actus reus Criminal act; conduct that the law prohibits or absence of conduct that the law requires.

mens rea Literally, "criminal mind"; criminal intent.

To find a person guilty of a crime, there first must be a criminal act or *actus reus,* conduct that the law prohibits or absence of conduct that the law requires. With most crimes there must also be criminal intent or *mens rea* (literally, "criminal mind"). Before defining these requisites for a crime, consider the following cases:

1. A prostitute, knowing she has AIDS, continues to ply her trade and is charged with attempted murder. *depends – (intent needs to be found)*

2. Four seamen adrift in a lifeboat for twenty days decide that one of them must be sacrificed and eaten in order to save the rest. A young cabin boy in weakened condition is killed and eaten. The others are charged with murder.

3. A parent who belongs to a religious sect that believes that physical illness must be cured by prayer and faith refuses medical aid for a child suffering from leukemia. When the child dies, the parent is charged with manslaughter. *can charge for inaction only –*

4. A young woman is kidnapped by a revolutionary gang, put in a closet for several weeks, and occasionally raped by her kidnappers. For several months she is subjected to political indoctrination and finally agrees to participate in a bank robbery with her abductors to get funds to continue the revolutionary cause. When finally found, she is charged with bank robbery. *insanity - duress*

5. A man meets a young woman in a bar; when asked by the bartender for identification proving her age, she shows a driver's license and is served a beer. She states to the man that she is twenty, and he believes it. Later they go to his apartment and have sexual relations. He is later charged with the crime of statutory rape, "sexual relations with a person under the age of 18." *not strict liability –*

6. A woman believes her husband to be dead and remarries. When her first husband reappears, she is charged with bigamy. *honest mistake*

7. A man picks up the wrong suitcase at an airport, believing it to be his, but later finds out his mistake and returns the suitcase. He is charged with theft. *honest mistake*

8. A physician assists a terminally ill person to commit suicide by preparing and providing the means to end her life in a painless and comfortable way. He is charged with murder. *not guilty – [crime is accessory to suicide]*

9. A game warden makes an image of a deer and puts it in the woods. When hunters shoot at the deer, the game warden arrests them for hunting deer out of season. *not guilty wrong charge – attempted hunting out of season* *not a real deer*

10. A man shoots a person intending to kill. It later turns out that the victim was already dead, although the shooting would have killed him if he had still been alive. The shooter is charged with homicide. *already dead not guilty*

Criminal Act

Under early English law, most crimes were treated in the courts as common law crimes. Today, most crimes are statutory, though many of these are simply statutory refinements of the old common law crimes (e.g., murder, rape, burglary, embezzlement, etc.). In an earlier, settled, agricultural society, values relating to wrongs against persons and property were widely shared and understood, so that the courts could turn to customary values and religious principles to define criminal misconduct. Today, in our diverse and complex society, it is not always clear exactly what should be prohibited and what should not. The underlying policy of the criminal law is that a person should not be punished for conduct not expressly prohibited by the law. This requires the articulation of criminal law by the legislatures rather than the courts. All states have criminal statutes, and most do not allow conviction for common law crimes. Judges are not supposed to impose their perceptions of wrongful conduct; they must find that the conduct falls clearly within a criminal statute in order to hold a person guilty of a crime. Ultimately, a court must determine the meaning of the statute as it applies to a particular incident; but, as already noted, criminal statutes are strictly construed.

voluntary When used in reference to criminal law, *voluntary* means an act of free will, though this is different from its use in contract law, where coercion may negate voluntariness. In criminal law, acts are not voluntary when occurring during sleep, unconsciousness, or hypnosis or by reflex or convulsions.

Actus reus requires that the criminal act be **voluntary**. At first blush, this would seem to be a feature of the mental state of the accused, part of the criminal intent (*mens rea*). *Voluntariness*, however, refers to whether the act was a product of free will and does not address issues of motivation specific to *mens rea*. Examples of involuntary acts are those occurring during sleep, unconsciousness, or hypnosis and those caused by reflexes or convulsions.

Thoughts alone are not criminal; an act must occur. In general, speech is protected by the First Amendment, but speech is conduct and sometimes constitutes a crime, as with inciting to riot or promoting a conspiracy.

The failure to act, an omission, may also constitute *actus reus* in cases in which the law imposes a duty to act; for instance, when a parent fails to provide nourishment to a child or a person with knowledge of a felony fails to report such knowledge (misprision of a felony). Failure to meet a *moral* obligation to act is not a crime if there is no *legal* duty to act. Historically, American law has not recognized a duty to rescue; a person may stand by and watch another drown, even if saving the drowning person offers no risk to the potential rescuer. A duty arises only if the rescuer was in some way responsible for the peril or enjoys a status requiring rescue, such as a lifeguard.

Because criminal act is typically shown by physical evidence, it presents far fewer problems than criminal intent, in which a mental state must usually be inferred from the circumstances of the events of the crime.

Criminal Intent

An act may be voluntarily accomplished without entailing *mens rea*. The man who mistakenly took the wrong suitcase at the airport acted voluntarily but without criminal intent. The nature of the intent required for guilt varies significantly from one crime to another, and some strict liability crimes require no proof of criminal intent.

General Intent   The broadest form of intent is called **general intent,** to be distinguished from specific intent, discussed in the next section. General intent is the traditional form of *mens rea* derived from the common law. It requires that the actor intended a harmful act but not that the specific result was intended. This may extend to reckless and negligent acts in which the actor acted with a "conscious disregard of a substantial and unjustifiable risk of harm" (recklessness) or, though lacking conscious disregard, nevertheless acted when a "reasonable person would have recognized a substantial and unjustifiable risk" (negligence). A person throwing a firecracker into a crowd of people would be guilty of resulting harm covered by a crime requiring only general intent.

Criminal intent is more convincingly shown if malice can be proven. General intent is a somewhat cloudy area because of the variety of harmful acts and the mysteries of the human mind and human motivation. With a few exceptions requiring powerful deterrents, the law and judicial decisions reflect a desire not to punish involuntary, innocent, and accidental acts. The elements that make up a specific crime indicate the intention required.

Specific Intent   As a rule of thumb, statutes that use the words "knowingly," "willfully," or "maliciously" require **specific intent.** These statutes are most easily satisfied when the defendant intended the precise results of the wrongful act (e.g., shooting someone in the head at close range). Defendants will naturally assert a lack of intent or knowledge, but the courts and juries are disinclined to accept such assertions. It may be enough that a knowledge of a high risk was present, as measured by what a reasonable person would know. The problem is that this is a subjective measure, that is, what the defendant knew or intended. Because only the defendant knows for certain what his or her knowledge and intent were, the defendant theoretically is the most reliable witness as to that intent. However, in practice, the defendant's statements are highly unreliable because self-interest often distorts the truth. What was intended may be inferred from the defendant's conduct, and the defendant's self-serving statements may be treated with skepticism. The *Jewell* case demonstrates the court's reluctance to accept a defendant's self-serving assertions.

Mens rea is a confusing area of criminal law because it attempts to define subjective knowledge, volition, and intent. To paraphrase one justice's comments about the definition of contracts, perhaps the definition of *mens rea* consists of the totality of the cases that define it. As a practical matter, this means that applying criminal intent to a given case requires fitting that case into similar cases of the past. It then becomes clear that the method of the common law prevails even in an area that ostensibly has been preempted by statute.

Long ago, *mens rea* may have appeared to be a relatively simple concept, but as we come to know more about the complexity of the human psyche, the legal concept has become more and more difficult to state with certainty. In questionable cases, a great deal of research into precedents may be appropriate.

general intent   For criminal law, *general intent* requires merely that the actor intended a harmful act, not necessarily the specific result. Also see **specific intent.**

specific intent   In criminal law, *specific intent* requires that the actor intended the precise result of a harmful act. Also see **general intent.**

All the research in the world, however, means little to the jury. Through its deliberations, the jury mysteriously arrives at conclusions about the defendant's intent. The jury is likely to pay more attention to common sense and experience than the technicalities of the jury instructions. In the *Jewell* case, some jurors must have asked, "Why did he have a secret compartment in his trunk? Surely he must have known, or at least guessed, there was marijuana in the secret compartment." Preparation of a jury case must pay at least as much attention to the mentality of the jury as to the law.

Specific Problems of Criminal Intent   The nature and degree of criminal intent required varies from crime to crime. In some instances, intent refers simply to the knowledge the accused must have. For example, crimes involving theft commonly require that the defendant intended to deprive someone permanently of property, knowing that the property belonged to another. Such a requirement would save our airport suitcase mistake because there was neither an intent to permanently deprive nor a knowledge of true ownership at the time of the taking.

**UNITED STATES of America,
Plaintiff-Appellee
v.
Charles Demore JEWELL,
Defendant-Appellant
U.S. Court of Appeals, 9th Circuit
532 F.2d 697 (9th Cir. 1976)**

[This is an appeal from a conviction for violating the Comprehensive Drug Abuse Prevention and Control Act of 1970. Jewell was found to have knowingly transported marijuana in the trunk of his car from Mexico to the United States. The marijuana was concealed in a secret compartment behind the back seat of his car. Jewell insisted that he did not know the marijuana was in the secret compartment. Whether he knew or did not know was a fact question for the jury. If he knew, he was guilty of the crime; but the trial judge was concerned that even a lack of knowledge could have been the result of "deliberate ignorance" and gave the following instruction to the jury:

The Government can complete their burden of proof by proving, beyond a reasonable doubt, that if the defendant was not actually aware that there was marijuana in the vehicle he was driving when he entered the United States his ignorance in that regard was solely and entirely a result of his having made a conscious purpose to disregard the nature of that which was in the vehicle, with a conscious purpose to avoid learning the truth.

Jewell appealed on the grounds that this instruction was not an accurate statement of the law with regard to criminal intent and that the jury should have been instructed that to find guilt, they must find that he knew he was in possession of marijuana. The court of appeals upheld the trial court's jury instruction with the following reasoning:]

The substantive justification for the rule is that deliberate ignorance and positive knowledge are equally culpable. The textual justification is that in common understanding one "knows" facts of which he is less than absolutely certain. To act "knowingly," therefore, is not necessarily to act only with positive knowledge, but also to act with an awareness of the high probability of the existence of the fact in question. When such awareness is present, "positive" knowledge is not required.

* * *

[D]efining "knowingly" makes actual knowledge unnecessary. "[T]hose who traffic in heroin will inevitably become aware that the product they deal with is smuggled, *unless they practice a studied ignorance to which they are not entitled.*"

. . . Holding that this term [knowingly] introduces a requirement of positive knowledge would make deliberate ignorance a defense. It cannot be doubted that those who traffic in drugs would make the most of it. This is evident from the number of appellate decisions reflecting conscious avoidance of positive knowledge of the presence of contraband—in the car driven by the defendant or in which he is a passenger, in the suitcase or package he carries, in the parcel concealed in his clothing.

* * *

The conviction is affirmed.

Kennedy, J., dissenting: [T]he "conscious purpose" jury instruction is defective in three respects. First, it fails to mention the requirement that Jewell have been aware of a high probability that a controlled substance was in the car. It is not culpable to form "a conscious purpose to avoid learning the truth" unless one is aware of facts indicating a high probability of that truth. . . .

The second defect in the instruction as given is that it did not alert the jury that Jewell could not be convicted if he "actually believed" there was no controlled substance in the car. . . .

Third, the jury instruction clearly states that Jewell could have been convicted even if found ignorant or "not actually aware" that the car contained a controlled substance. This is unacceptable because true ignorance, no matter how unreasonable, cannot provide a basis for criminal liability when the statute requires knowledge.

Case Questions

1. Why did the majority not adopt the dissent's approach?
2. In a portion of the dissenting opinion omitted in this case, the dissenting judge declared his approval of the *Model Penal Code § 2.02(7)*, which reads:

   Requirement of Knowledge Satisfied by Knowledge of High Probability. When knowledge of the existence of a particular fact is an element of an offense, such knowledge is established if a person is aware of a high probability of its existence, unless he actually believes that it does not exist.

   Does this imply the dissent's conclusion that "true ignorance, no matter how unreasonable, cannot provide a basis for criminal liability when the statute requires knowledge . . ."?
3. Perhaps when Jewell spoke with his attorney, the attorney said, "The statute requires that you *knowingly* transported controlled substances. You didn't know that what was in the secret compartment was *actually* marijuana, *did* you?" And suppose Jewell responded, "I didn't actually *see* marijuana put in the car; I didn't actually *know* there was marijuana in there." Can attorney and client then in good conscience go to court and base their defense on lack of knowledge? Is it unethical for the attorney to lead the client in this way? Argue both sides.
4. Is not subjective knowledge always arguable? If Jewell actually knew there was marijuana placed in the secret compartment, but he left his car for an hour, would he *know* the marijuana was still there if he did not check to see? Does this deliberate ignorance principle furnish a reasonable alternative to the philosophical problem of knowledge?
5. Does the rule in *Jewell* accord with the principle of strict construction of criminal statutes? Explain.
6. Do you think the jury would have found differently if it had been instructed as the dissent suggested?

Crimes against property, such as burglary, embezzlement, and larceny, are usually economically motivated, so intent can readily be inferred. Unless these involve violence or large amounts of money, they receive only modest attention in the press, which tends to focus on bizarre and violent crime. As a result, the popular conception of crime is distorted.

Other crimes require special ingredients for criminal intent that make them quite distinct. Murder, rape, and conspiracy are examples.

murder The wrongful killing of another human being with malice aforethought (premeditation).

Murder **Murder** is the unlawful killing by one human being of another with malice aforethought. It is distinguished from manslaughter (also called murder in the second degree) by the requirement of "malice aforethought," often referred to as premeditation or malice prepense, depending on one's preference for Old English, new Latin, or French. The requirement of premeditation removes from this most heinous of crimes homicides that are accidental but blameworthy (i.e., caused by culpable negligence) and those occurring in a moment of passion or anger. At the very least, murder requires some reflection about what one is doing or sufficient time between the beginning of the act and its completion to provide an opportunity to desist from following through. Obviously, a planned killing satisfies premeditation. In other cases, proof of premeditation typically takes the form of showing that the accused thought about what he or she was doing and then did it.

Murder cases present a very distorted picture of the criminal law. One reason is the requirement of evil intent; another is the availability of the death penalty in most states. Because of our fear of sending an innocent person to the gallows, a mistake that can never be corrected, the propriety of conduct by the police and prosecution and the conduct of the trial are scrutinized to a degree unusual in other cases. Because of media attention to these cases, the public forms a strange picture of the criminal law and criminal procedure.

rape At common law, this was forcible sexual intercourse by a man on a woman against her will. Add to this modern *statutory rape*, which makes consent irrelevant because of the status or mental state of the victim. Modern law recognizes a variety of sexual assaults.

Rape Forcible **rape** is the most serious of sex crimes. At present, there is little uniformity either in terminology or definition among the states with regard to sex crimes. On the one hand, we have seen a strong movement toward decriminalizing consensual sexual relations, but different states have shown different approaches depending on whether the partners are married, heterosexual, or homosexual. On the other hand, there has been a movement to refine the definitions of sex crimes to protect specific categories of victims—the young, the elderly, the mentally and physically handicapped. Because this is presently a dynamic area of legislation, we encounter a lack of uniformity among the states.

With regard to the mental state required for forcible rape, the problem is compounded by its nonconsensual element. Not only the defendant's mental state is at issue but also the victim's. It is a defense to forcible, as opposed to statutory, rape that the alleged victim consented to the sexual act. Because sexual relations usually occur in private without witnesses, ascertaining the mental states of perpetrator and victim presents difficult problems of proof.

An essential element of rape is the use of force. What constitutes force is problematic, and the relationship between force and consent raises additional questions. If a man holds a knife to a woman's throat and asks her if she wants to have sexual relations, is her affirmative answer consent? Consent under duress is not consent at all.

Rape is a serious crime that occurs with significant frequency in our society and is likely to leave victims with permanent emotional damage, yet it is difficult to prove and usually goes unreported. The commands of the criminal law have failed to control primal urges toward violence and sex.

Recently, focus has changed toward victim-oriented services and enlightened treatment of victims in court. Because of the consent defense, victims have in the past been questioned regarding their prior sexual contacts and sexual conduct in general. Much of this has been curtailed by law because of its questionable relevance—the factual issue is always whether the victim actually consented in this instance. A great many jurisdictions have also turned to victim advocacy and fought antifemale stereotypes on the part of traditionally male-dominated law enforcement. Officers have been sensitized to the plight of the victim and her responses to the trauma of rape. Rape counselors are often called in to assist in the aftermath of rape.

conspiracy A crime involving two or more persons who agree to commit a crime or agree to plan a crime.

Conspiracy   **Conspiracy** presents problems for both *mens rea* and *actus reus*, in that it addresses the planning of crime rather than its actual commission:

(1) *Definition of Conspiracy.* A person is guilty of conspiracy with another person or persons to commit a crime if with the purpose of promoting or facilitating its commission he:

   (a) agrees with such other person or persons that they or one or more of them will engage in conduct which constitutes such crime or an attempt or solicitation to commit such crime; or

   (b) agrees to aid such other person or persons in the planning or commission of such crime or of an attempt or solicitation to commit such crime.

* * *

(5) *Overt Act.* No person may be convicted of conspiracy to commit a crime, other than a felony of the first or second degree, unless an overt act in pursuance of such conspiracy is alleged and proved to have been done by him or by a person with whom he conspired.

(6) *Renunciation of Criminal Purpose.* It is an affirmative defense that the actor, after conspiring to commit a crime, thwarted the success of the conspiracy, under circumstances manifesting a complete and voluntary renunciation of his criminal purpose.

Model Penal Code, § 5.03.

Under these rules, one may effectively be charged with conspiracy for participating in the planning of a bank robbery even if one did not plan to participate in the actual bank robbery, conduct that society may appropriately condemn as criminal; but the crime of conspiracy may cast a wide net to include many persons marginally associated with others engaged in criminal conduct.

The *Lauria* case involves call girls and the telephone answering service they used. One may wonder why the police and prosecutor were anxious to find the owner of the answering service guilty of conspiracy to commit prostitution. The answer may lie in an effort to find another crime against the call girls. When the conspiracy count against Lauria failed, it also failed against the call girls.

An interesting wrinkle on conspiracy has been the ever-expanding use of the Racketeer Influenced and Corrupt Organizations Act (RICO), which was originally designed against organized crime and corrupt labor unions. In recent years, RICO has been used generously in white collar crime where "racketeering" has been given a broad interpretation. In particular, a variety of financial and stock manipulations have been attacked under RICO.

attempt to commit a crime   An act that goes beyond mere preparation to commit a crime but that is not completed.

Attempt   The **attempt to commit a crime** is also a crime. In its simplest form, an attempt is a crime that failed. The deterrent aspect of the criminal law should apply with equal force to attempts as to successful crimes (for instance, it would seem useful to deter bank robbers whether or not they are successful). The punitive aspect of the criminal law, however, has traditionally been more lenient with attempted crimes, which are usually of lesser grade or carry a lesser sentence. *Model Penal Code*, § 5.05(1), treats attempts as equal to the crime attempted, and a few states have adopted this policy.

The PEOPLE of the State of California, Plaintiff and Appellant

v.

Louis LAURIA et al., Defendants and Respondents
California District Court of Appeal, Second District, Division 2
251 Cal. App. 2d 471, 59

Cal. Rptr. 628 (1967)

In an investigation of call-girl activity the police focused their attention on three prostitutes actively plying their trade on call, each of whom was using Lauria's telephone answering service, presumably for business purposes. . . .

On April 1 Lauria and the three prostitutes were arrested. Lauria complained to the police that this attention was undeserved, stating that Hollywood Call Board had 60 to 70 prostitutes on its board while his own service had only 9 or 10, that he kept separate records for known or suspected prostitutes for the convenience of himself and the police. On a subse-

quent voluntary appearance before the Grand Jury Lauria testified he had always cooperated with the police. But he admitted he knew some of his customers were prostitutes. . . .

Lauria and the three prostitutes were indicted for conspiracy to commit prostitution, and nine overt acts were specified. Subsequently the trial court set aside the indictment as having been brought without reasonable or probable cause. The People have appealed, claiming that a sufficient showing of an unlawful agreement to further prostitution was made. . . .

Under what circumstances does a supplier become a part of a conspiracy to further an illegal enterprise by furnishing goods or services which he knows are to be used by the buyer for criminal purposes? . . .

Both the element of *knowledge* of the illegal use of the goods or services and the element of *intent* to further that use must be present in order to make the supplier a participant in a criminal conspiracy.

Proof of *knowledge* is ordinarily a question of fact and requires no extended discussion in the present case. The knowledge of the supplier was sufficiently established when Lauria admitted he knew some of his customers were prostitutes and admitted he knew that Terry, an active subscriber to his service, was a prostitute. . . .

The more perplexing issue in the case is the sufficiency of proof of *intent* to further the criminal enterprise. The element of intent may be proved either by direct evidence, or by evidence of circumstances from which an intent to further a criminal enterprise by supplying lawful goods or services may be inferred. . . .

Essentially, the People argue that knowledge alone of the continuing use of his telephone facilities for criminal purposes provided a sufficient basis from which his intent to participate in those criminal activities could be inferred.

1. Intent may be inferred from knowledge, when the purveyor of legal goods for illegal use has acquired a stake in the venture. . . .

In the present case, no proof was offered of inflated charges for the telephone answering services furnished the codefendants.

2. Intent may be inferred from knowledge, when no legitimate use for the goods or services exists. . . .

However, there is nothing in the furnishing of telephone answering service which would necessarily imply assistance in the performance of illegal activities. Nor is any inference to be derived from the use of an answering service by women, either in any particular volume of calls, or outside normal working hours. . . .

3. Intent may be inferred from knowledge, when the volume of business with the buyer is grossly disproportionate to any legitimate demand, or when sales for illegal use amount to a high proportion of the seller's total business. . . .

No evidence of any unusual volume of business with prostitutes was presented by the prosecution against Lauria. . . .

With respect to misdemeanors, we conclude that positive knowledge of the supplier that his products or services are being used for criminal purposes does not, without more, establish an intent of the supplier to participate in the misdemeanors. With respect to felonies, we do not decide the converse, viz. that in all cases of felony knowledge of criminal use alone may justify an inference of the supplier's intent to participate in the crime. . . .

Under these circumstances, although proof of Lauria's knowledge of the criminal activities of his patrons was sufficient to charge him with that fact, there was insufficient evidence that he intended to further their criminal activities, and hence insufficient proof of his participation in a criminal conspiracy with his codefendants to further prostitution. Since the conspiracy centered around the activities of Lauria's telephone answering service, the charges against his codefendants likewise fail for want of proof.

In absolving Lauria of complicity in a criminal conspiracy we do not wish to imply that the public authorities are without remedies to combat modern manifestations of the world's oldest profession. Licensing of telephone answering services under the police power, together with the revocation of licenses for the toleration of prostitution, is a possible civil remedy. The furnishing of telephone answering service in aid of prostitution could be made a crime. Other solutions will doubtless occur to vigilant public authorities if the problem of call-girl activity needs further suppression.

The order is affirmed.

Case Questions

1. Why is knowledge of a criminal purpose not sufficient for conspiracy?
2. Did the state fail to establish Lauria's criminal intent? What were the issues with regard to intent?

strict criminal liability
A few crimes may be proven without proving intent; see **strict liability**.

felony-murder rule   Provides for conviction of murder where someone is killed during the commission of a felony; premeditation need not be proven.

Strict Liability   Underlying the *mens rea* requirement is the traditional legal principle in criminal law of a *presumption of innocence. Mens rea* imposes a burden on the prosecution to show that the defendant acted out of evil intent. In recent years, however, legislatures have sometimes imposed strict criminal liability, thereby either eliminating the burden of proving *mens rea* or shifting to the defendant the burden of proving innocent motive.

Some precedent for **strict criminal liability** can be found in the common law **felony-murder rule,** under which a person can be found guilty of murder without proof of premeditation if a person is killed during the perpetration of a felony. Some justification in the rule can be found in an attempt to deter the use of unreasonable force in the commission of a felony, but on rare occasions the rule has been applied with peculiar results, as when one of the felons is killed by police and the other co-felons are held accountable for felony-murder. The felony-murder rule has been subject to much criticism and is severely qualified in some jurisdictions.

Another example of traditional strict liability is covered in the crime of statutory rape, in which sexual relations with a person under a certain age eliminate the defense of consent and in many states denies the defendant the defense of a good faith belief that the victim was above the prescribed age. Again, a reasonable objective of protecting young and innocent or naive girls from predatory older males is used to justify strict liability.

The growth of strict liability, however, has occurred primarily in regulatory statutes. On the one hand, strict liability has been justified when a class of persons, such as the young, seem to warrant special protection, or when the danger to the public is particularly hazardous—as with alcohol, firearms, drugs, poisons.

While common law crimes have been done away with, criminal intent continues its common law tradition, except when the legislature passes a new regulatory law, *malum prohibitum* (the singular form of *mala prohibita*). Typically, such regulatory law is silent about intent and the courts have shown an inclination to interpret the legislative acts as strict liability crimes when they cannot be classified as civil penalties. The *Morissette* case presents us with a brief history of mens rea and its demise in the last century with regard to *mala prohibita*. If we believe Morissette's protestations of innocent intent, the case provides little comfort to those who confront the government, in light of the fact that he only succeeded by taking his case to the highest court in the land.

The Insanity Defense

No discussion of *mens rea* would be complete without mention of the insanity defense. A criminal defendant may plead "not guilty by reason of insanity." This plea acknowledges the commission of the criminal act but negates criminal intent because of the defendant's insanity. The policy basis for the defense is to hold accountable for crimes only those persons who freely chose to commit crimes. An additional reason for the defense is the inappropriateness of putting insane persons in with the general prison population. The insanity defense is

MORISSETTE

v.

UNITED STATES

Supreme Court of the United States
342 U.S. 246; 72 S. Ct. 240; (1952)

On a large tract of uninhabited and untilled land in a wooded and sparsely populated area of Michigan, the Government established a practice bombing range over which the Air Force dropped simulated bombs at ground targets. . . .

Spent bomb casings were cleared from the targets and thrown into piles "so that they will be out of the way." They were not stacked or piled in any order but were dumped in heaps, some of which had been accumulating for four years or upwards, were exposed to the weather and rusting away.

Morissette, in December of 1948, went hunting in this area but did not get a deer. He thought to meet expenses of the trip by salvaging some of these casings [for which he received] $84.

The loading, crushing, and transporting of these casings were all in broad daylight, in full view of passers-by, without the slightest effort at concealment. When an investigation was started, Morissette voluntarily, promptly, and candidly told the whole story to the authorities, saying that he had no intention of stealing but thought the property was abandoned, unwanted, and considered of no value to the Government. He was indicted, however, on the charge that he "did unlawfully, willfully and knowingly steal and convert" property of the United States of the value of $84, in violation of 18 U. S. C. § 641, which provides that "whoever embezzles, steals, purloins, or knowingly converts" government property is punishable by fine and imprisonment. Morissette was convicted and sentenced to imprisonment for two months or to pay a fine of $200. [The maximum sentence was one year, $1,000, or both.] The Court of Appeals affirmed, one judge dissenting.

Morissette believed the casings were cast-off and abandoned, that he did not intend to steal the property, and took it with no wrongful or criminal intent. . . . The court refused to submit or to allow counsel to argue to the jury whether Morissette acted with innocent intention.

The Court of Appeals ruled that this particular offense requires no element of criminal intent.

I.

The contention that an injury can amount to a crime only when inflicted by intention is no provincial or transient notion. It is as universal and persistent in mature systems of law as belief in freedom of the human will and a consequent ability and duty of the normal individual to choose between good and evil. A relation between some mental element and punishment for a harmful act is almost as instinctive as the child's familiar exculpatory "But I didn't mean to," and has afforded the rational basis for a tardy and unfinished substitution of deterrence and reformation in place of retaliation and vengeance as the motivation for public prosecution. Unqualified acceptance of this doctrine by English common law in the Eighteenth Century was indicated by Blackstone's sweeping statement that to constitute any crime there must first be a "vicious will." Common-law commentators of the Nineteenth Century early pronounced the same principle, although a few exceptions not relevant to our present problem came to be recognized. [e.g., statutory rape]

Crime, as a compound concept, generally constituted only from concurrence of an evil-meaning mind with an evil-doing hand, was congenial to an intense individualism and took deep and early root in American soil. As the states codified the common law of crimes, even if their enactments were silent on the subject, their courts assumed that the omission did not signify disapproval of the principle but merely recognized that intent was so inherent in the idea of the offense that it required no statutory affirmation. Courts, with little hesitation or division, found an implication of the

(continued)

(continued)

requirement as to offenses that were taken over from the common law. . . .

[There is] a century-old but accelerating tendency, discernible both here and in England, to call into existence new duties and crimes which disregard any ingredient of intent. [Some of the causes for increasing regulation have been workers' injuries since the industrial revolution, injuries from the automobile, health and welfare problems in congested cities, and the need for consumer protection for the wide distribution of food and goods.]

While many of these duties are sanctioned by a more strict civil liability, lawmakers, whether wisely or not, have sought to make such regulations more effective by invoking criminal sanctions to be applied by the familiar technique of criminal prosecutions and convictions. This has confronted the courts with a multitude of prosecutions, based on statutes or administrative regulations, for what have been aptly called "public welfare offenses." These cases do not fit neatly into any of such accepted classifications of common-law offenses, such as those against the state, the person, property, or public morals. . . . While such offenses do not threaten the security of the state in the manner of treason, they may be regarded as offenses against its authority, for their occurrence impairs the efficiency of controls deemed essential to the social order as presently constituted. In this respect, whatever the intent of the violator, the injury is the same, and the consequences are injurious or not according to fortuity. Hence, legislation applicable to such offenses, as a matter of policy, does not specify intent as a necessary element. . . . Also, penalties commonly are relatively small, and conviction does no grave damage to an offender's reputation. Under such considerations, courts have turned to construing statutes and regulations which make no mention of intent as dispensing with it and holding that the guilty act alone makes out the crime. This has not, however, been without expressions of misgiving. The pilot of the move-

ment in this country appears to be a holding that a tavernkeeper could be convicted for selling liquor to an habitual drunkard even if he did not know the buyer to be such. . . . Later came Massachusetts holdings that convictions for selling adulterated milk in violation of statutes forbidding such sales require no allegation or proof that defendant knew of the adulteration. . . .

After the turn of the Century, a new use for crimes without intent appeared when New York enacted numerous and novel regulations of tenement houses, sanctioned by money penalties. Landlords contended that a guilty intent was essential to establish a violation. Judge Cardozo wrote the answer:

". . . But in the prosecution of minor offenses, there is a wider range of practice and of power. Prosecutions for petty penalties have always constituted in our law a class by themselves. . . . That is true though the prosecution is criminal in form." . . .

Thus, for diverse but reconcilable reasons, state courts converged on the same result, discontinuing inquiry into intent in a limited class of offenses against such statutory regulations.

Before long, similar questions growing out of federal legislation reached this Court. Its judgments were in harmony with this consensus of state judicial opinion, the existence of which may have led the Court to overlook the need for full exposition of their rationale in the context of federal law.

It was not until recently that the Court took occasion more explicitly to relate abandonment of the ingredient of intent, not merely with considerations of expediency in obtaining convictions, nor with the *malum prohibitum* classification of the crime, but with the peculiar nature and quality of the offense. We referred to ". . . a now familiar type of legislation whereby penalties serve as effective means of regulation," and continued, "such legislation dispenses with the conventional requirement for criminal conduct—awareness of some wrongdoing. In the interest of the larger good it puts the burden of acting at hazard upon a person otherwise innocent but standing in responsible relation to a public danger."

. . . State courts of last resort, on whom fall the heaviest burden of interpreting criminal law in this country, have consistently retained the requirement of intent in larceny-type offenses. If any state has deviated, the exception has neither been called to our attention nor disclosed by our research. . . .

We hold that mere omission from § 641 of any mention of intent will not be construed as eliminating that element from the crimes denounced.

. . . The law under some circumstances recognizes good faith or blameless intent as a defense, partial defense, or as an element to be considered in mitigation of punishment.

Congress, by the language of this section, has been at pains to incriminate only "knowing" conversions. Had the statute applied to conversions without qualification, it would have made crimes of all unwitting, inadvertent and unintended conversions. . . .

. . . Probably every stealing is a conversion, but certainly not every knowing conversion is a stealing. "To steal means to *take away from*

one in lawful possession without right with the *intention to keep wrongfully.*" . . . Conversion, however, may be consummated without any intent to keep and without any wrongful taking, where the initial possession by the converter was entirely lawful.

We find no grounds for inferring any affirmative instruction from Congress to eliminate intent from any offense with which this defendant was charged.

III.

* * *

We think presumptive intent has no place in this case. . . . That the removal of [the casings] was a conscious and intentional act was admitted. But that isolated fact is not an adequate basis on which the jury should find the criminal intent to steal or knowingly convert, that is, *wrongfully* to deprive another of possession of property. Whether that intent existed, the jury must determine, not only from the act of taking, but from that together with defendant's testimony and all of the surrounding circumstances.

Reversed.

Case Questions

1. Why is the Court resisting the intrusion of strict liability into traditional categories of common law crimes?
2. This case was decided in 1952. Since then, a blurring of notions of fault and free will has occurred. How might this case be decided differently today?

very much like the defense of an involuntary act or the absence of criminal intent. The difference lies in acknowledging insanity, which typically results in commitment to a mental institution if insanity is proven.

The principal problem with insanity is defining it. Understanding the subjective states of the human mind is difficult even for psychologists and psychiatrists with extensive training and experience. Although some persons may be found to be insane by almost any measure, the line between sanity and insanity cannot be drawn with accuracy, yet the law requires that the line be drawn.

The English rule originating in the nineteenth-century *M'Naghten* case (10 Cl. & F. 200, 8 Eng. Rep. 718 [1843]) is still followed, with some modifications, in many American jurisdictions. Daniel M'Naghten suffered delusions that the prime minister was out to get him; M'Naghten shot and killed the prime minister's secretary, mistakenly believing the secretary to be the prime minister. Public outrage over M'Naghten's acquittal ultimately led to a consideration of the insanity defense by the House of Lords (England's "Supreme Court"). Consensus resulted in what is often called the "right-wrong test," namely, whether the accused suffered from a defect of mind such that he did not understand the nature of his act or did not know that it was wrong. This is a difficult test to meet because it requires a very serious mental imbalance.

The fields of psychology and psychiatry in recent decades have shown that we are much less in control of our minds and actions than was formerly believed, so other insanity tests have been adopted that lower the threshold of insanity for legal purposes. The issue of legal accountability for acts committed by someone with diminished mental capacity is very murky at present.

Insanity defenses frequently involve several highly paid expert witnesses. Prosecution witnesses testify that the defendant was sane at the time of the act, while defense witnesses argue precisely the opposite; the jury must attempt to arrive at the "truth" of the defendant's mental state as described by experts who reconstruct that mental state after the fact.

A satisfactory resolution of these and other problems related to the insanity defense does not appear to be forthcoming.

Summary

Although the practice of criminal law tends to focus on problems of proof and other procedural issues, the substantive law of crimes is largely the concern of legislative enactments. There is considerable variability in the definitions of specific crimes from state to state. A general definition of crime is difficult to state, but crime may be identified procedurally by recourse to statutes that define crimes and delegate authority to police and prosecutors for the resolution of misconduct so labeled.

The criminal law penalizes conduct that offends the moral sentiments of the people. However, in our diverse society, moral commands are not always a matter of consensus. In addition, lawmakers provide criminal and civil penalties to encourage people to conform to an increasingly regulated state.

Traditionally, a crime requires both a criminal act and criminal intent on the part of the actor. The criminal act is defined by the elements of specific crimes, and it is up to the courts to determine whether a particular act falls within the prohibitions of the law.

Criminal intent, or *mens rea*, requires that the defendant in a criminal case be shown to have had a specific state of mind at the time of commission of the criminal act. Because subjective states of mind are difficult to ascertain, the intent of the defendant is a frequent issue in trials. Specific crimes often require or infer a specific state of mind. Questions of motivation, willfulness, premeditation, accident, knowledge, and intent are fact questions for the jury that may be quite confusing to resolve. The insanity defense is particularly problematic because of the inconsistency of legal and psychiatric definitions of insanity.

Scenario 1

A woman and a man meet in a bar; the woman is scantily clad, with a hemline that reveals that she is wearing no underwear. She agrees to have sexual intercourse with the man for money, and they leave in his van. She later accuses him of rape. She has prior convictions for prostitution and, on a prior occasion, charged rape against another man under roughly similar circumstances. He is wanted in another state on a rape charge. He promised her money for sex but refused to pay her up-front, and she claims she refused to have sex with him.

Assume that in the trial for rape, the prior convictions are admitted into evidence as relevant to the issue of consent (but not necessarily proving consent).

1. Frame the argument for the prosecution, telling the story as she would have represented it.

2. Frame the argument for the defense, telling the story as he would have represented it.

Briefly give the discussion a jury of six men and six women would have made, coming up with a unanimous verdict of guilty or not guilty. In other words, how do you think a jury would evaluate the stories? Remember that the standard of proof is guilt beyond a reasonable doubt.

Scenario 2

A man and a woman meet in a singles bar. The woman is dressed provocatively and plays the temptress. After many drinks, they end up in her apartment. She puts on a nun's habit and declares she is a virgin and married to God. Then she takes her clothes off and has intercourse with the man; all the while, she is saying, "No. No. No. I'm a virgin," (which she is not). The man is of below-average intelligence. He acknowledges overcoming some slight efforts of physical resistance on her part.

The woman is diagnosed as psychotic by a prosecution psychiatrist, although a defense psychiatrist testifies from his interviews with the woman that she has emotional problems without delusionary tendencies and does not have multiple personalities. On the witness stand, she is emotional but otherwise appears normal.

1. Frame the argument for the prosecution.

2. Frame the argument for the defense.

Briefly give the discussion a jury of six men and six women would have made, coming up with a unanimous verdict of guilty or not guilty. In other words, how do you think a jury would evaluate the stories? Remember that the standard of proof is guilt beyond a reasonable doubt.

TORTS, PERSONAL INJURY, AND COMPENSATION

Introduction

torts A major area of substantive law including causes of action to redress injuries that arise out of noncontractual events. Tort includes three major divisions: *intentional torts*, *negligence*, and *strict liability*.

slander An injury to reputation ordinarily caused by the communication of lies to third parties. It is the spoken form of defamation, *libel* being written defamation.

The traditional term for the field of personal injury and compensation law is **torts.** Generally, torts have specific legal labels, each considered a different cause of action, such as trespass, **slander,** negligence, and product liability. They often seem to have little in common except that the law recognizes that private interests can be subject to injury, the remedy of which is typically compensation if responsibility for the injury can be attributed to another party. The difference in terminology reflects a difference in attitude. The term *torts* suggests a set of fixed, labeled causes of action; the term *compensation for injuries* reflects a more flexible category recognizing new interests as tort law evolves. For example, electronic eavesdropping has come to be recognized as an impermissible intrusion on privacy subsumed under the cause of action invasion of privacy. Despite the more descriptive and realistic "compensation for injuries," "torts" continues to be favored for saving seven syllables or twenty keystrokes.

Definition

In the word *tort* we have a rare example of legal custom providing a doctrinaire but reliable definition: "A tort is a private wrong not arising out of contract." Unfortunately, the definition states what a tort is *not* without stating exactly what it *is*. It is not a public wrong, that is, it is not a crime and it is not based on a contract.

Tort versus Crime

Legal scholars have argued whether in ancient times crime and tort were separable. In modern times, the distinction between the two is clear because the rise of the modern state resulted in the assumption of authority by the state over misconduct it deemed criminal. Public wrongs are often characterized as "wrongs against society." It is doubtful that the victim of a rape or robbery meditates on the social impact of the crime. Nevertheless, in our legal system the public has a legitimate interest in preventing such crimes.

Distinguishing tort from crime is clearest from a procedural standpoint. If the public prosecutor seeks a remedy (usually punishment) for misconduct, the wrong is public—it is a crime. If the victim sues in his or her own right for compensation, the wrong is private, a cause of action in tort. If conduct constituting a public wrong causes injury to person or property, there is nearly always a private action in tort available to the injured party in addition to prosecution available to the state. The public and private actions are independent of each other and are procedurally distinct. In some cases the causes of action may have similar names—battery is a criminal offense as well as a civil cause of action in tort. The crime of rape, in contrast, fits best into the civil cause of action called *battery* (some states have renamed the crime "sexual battery").

Not all torts involve criminal conduct. Because crimes ordinarily require intentional conduct, unintentional infliction of injuries, such as through negligence (e.g., causing an auto accident, medical malpractice) and liability for unsafe products (product liability), is usually not criminal even though the wrongdoer, a **tortfeasor,** may be subject to severe financial liability in tort.

tortfeasor   A person who engages in tortious conduct.

Civil cases can be distinguished from criminal cases by the titles of the cases. *Montagu v. Capulet* and *Hatfield v. McCoy* are civil cases, whereas *Commonwealth v. Ripper, People v. Samson,* and *State v. Miranda* (when defendant appeals to the U.S. Supreme Court, it becomes *Miranda v. Arizona, Ripper v. Massachusetts*) are criminal cases. This distinction is not infallible, however, as states may be parties to civil suits as well.

Tort versus Contract

Private wrongs fall into two categories: tort and contract. Because torts are "private wrongs not arising out of contract," noncontract actions based on wrongful conduct are necessarily torts. The reason for defining tort by what it is *not* can be attributed to the fact that the field of torts consists of a number of causes of action that have little in common, whereas contract actions are predicated on the existence of a valid contract.

The legal significance of this distinction rests on the source of the duty imposed on the defendant. In contract cases, the duties are created by the agreement between the parties and do not exist without it. If a young man offers to mow a neighbor's lawn for ten dollars and the neighbor agrees, the neighbor is obligated by this contract under the law to pay the ten dollars if the man mows the lawn. On the other hand, if the young man simply mows the lawn in the neighbor's absence without any agreement and then demands payment, the neighbor has no obligation to pay; there was no contract. In fact, going on the neighbor's land without consent could technically constitute the tort of trespass.

Rights and duties in tort action, by contrast, are based on obligations imposed by law. For example, our law recognizes an individual's right to a good reputation and a corresponding duty on others not to spread lies that injure an individual's reputation. If such an injury occurs, the injured party may sue in tort under a cause of action for **defamation.** Liability is based on the breach of duties established by law (statutes and cases) rather than on an agreement between the parties found in the terms of a contract.

defamation An injury to reputation and includes *slander* and *libel.*

In a cause of action for breach of contract, the court looks to the contract to determine whether it is valid and enforceable under contract law and then, if valid, to the terms of the contract to determine precisely what obligations were created. If one party failed to fulfill promises made in the contract, liability may be imposed for a resulting injury to the other party. In principle this is simple, but life is complex, so a large body of law has developed to fit this principle to a variety of circumstances (discussed fully in Chapter 11). It should be kept in mind that the law sets the rules for the enforcement of contracts, but the specific duties on which suits are based are to be found in the private agreement of the parties, the contract itself. In a sense, the duty imposed by the law of contracts simply embodies a policy that the law favors the fulfillment of promises made between private parties.

In a cause of action for tort, duties to be enforced must be found in the law. A basic policy of protecting person, property, reputation, or the like is not sufficient. The court needs guidance to determine whether liability should be imposed under the unique circumstances presented by a given case. This is the reason that the common law has been extremely important in the development of tort law. Whenever possible, the court will look to similar cases from past decisions to determine how the duties have been defined. If duties have been established by statute, these may serve as the basis for judicial enforcement in tort. In fact, legislatures often create or redefine tort actions. For example, Congress provided in 42 U.S.C. § 1983 (Civil Rights Act of 1871) for private actions to be brought against state officials who wrongfully deprive individuals of their civil rights.

Often tort actions arise between persons who have relations such that the cause of action may appear to be a contract action. For example, medical malpractice cases arise in a contract relationship—a physician agrees to furnish services in return for payment, a rather typical exchange of promises between parties to a contract. If the physician negligently treats a patient, thereby causing injury, the patient may sue for malpractice in tort based on the duties imposed by law on the physician rather than the duties expressed by the terms of the contract. Although this seems to be a wrong arising out of contract, in fact, the court looks to the law rather than the contract to determine the duties between the parties. There is also a tort called **wrongful interference with contractual relations,** which occurs when a person *not* a party to a contract improperly disrupts the contractual relationship of others, as when a theater owner persuades

wrongful interference with contractual relations When a person *not* a party to a contract improperly disrupts the contractual relationship of others.

a singer to break a contract at another theater. Obviously the tort is predicated on a contract, but in this case the contract is not one between the plaintiff and the defendant.

Elements of Tort

As suits for personal injury developed over the centuries, the courts distinguished types of wrongful conduct. It seemed clear that the intentional infliction of physical injury, for example, was quite different in nature from an injury to reputation, so each required its own definition. Even the *threat* of physical injury—**assault**—was distinguished from the *infliction* of injury—**battery.** The definitions of specific causes of action in tort were framed in terms of elements (crimes are also defined by elements). To succeed in a tort action, the plaintiff must allege sufficient facts in a complaint to satisfy each element of a particular cause of action. If the plaintiff fails to do this, the complaint may be dismissed for failure to state a cause of action (the defendant would make a motion to dismiss "for failure to state a claim upon which relief can be granted"). Of course, the plaintiff must prove these allegations at trial to win the case.

Battery provides a time-tested example of the elements of a tort. It has been defined traditionally as an "unconsented, unprivileged, offensive contact." The definition contains the elements of battery as well as the defenses to battery:

Elements:

1. Intent

2. Bodily contact (extended to clothing, etc.)

3. Offensive in nature

Defenses:

1. Consent to the contact

2. Privilege

Battery is rooted in injury caused by fists or weapons but has been extended generally to offensive bodily contacts, such as sexual touching. It must be intentional and not simply accidental or careless, which might constitute a cause of action for negligence. There must be a contact and not merely a threat of contact (assault). The contact must be offensive. Although a particular form of contact may ordinarily constitute a battery, consent may prevent recovery, as with prizefighters and football players. The contact may be privileged, as when a parent strikes a child as a reasonable disciplinary measure or a policeman subdues a criminal with reasonable force.

Tort Law: An Evolving Field

Preparation of a tort suit begins with the search for an appropriate cause of action and an examination of whether a client's case fits comfortably within the

assault

Putting someone in apprehension of a **battery.** The actor must have the ability to carry out the threatened battery.

battery

An unconsented, unprivileged, offensive contact.

elements of one or more torts. Tort law has experienced and continues to experience an evolution in both its definition as a whole and the definition of specific causes of action. Not only does our notion of appropriate conduct change, but opportunities for injury change as well.

For example, the tort labeled "intentional infliction of mental distress" is a product of the twentieth century, undergoing considerable growth and refinement. Courts of the past were reluctant to compensate for emotional suffering unless accompanied by some physical injury, but modern courts have come to recognize emotional injuries as compensable when caused intentionally by malice or outrageous conduct. Harassing telephone calls, unscrupulous bill collectors, impersonal public and private bureaucracies, and perhaps even the lowering of standards of courtesy on many fronts have all contributed to a recognition that the potential for serious harm to one's emotional well-being is a fact of modern life. The courts have come to impose a legal duty on conduct that custom has always disapproved but not legally condemned. The recognition of **intentional infliction of mental distress** is not designed to compensate for every insult or affront nor to encourage the overly sensitive to sue. Nevertheless, some individuals engage in conduct aimed at causing suffering in ways that the courts feel compelled to condemn. (Example: A man was held liable when he jokingly told a woman that her husband had been in a serious accident and persuaded her to rush down to the hospital.)

The judicial creation of a new tort starts with a dispute before a judge, who will be inclined to recognize right and duty when faced with a compelling set of facts. Tort law has evolved to be highly individualized, based on a recognition of an individual's right to be free from unjustified intrusions on person, personality, personal dignity, and private property. Establishment of a new right of action occurs when an appropriate case demands the redress of a harm that is socially acknowledged and fits within the basic policy of general tort law. In short, the court is unwilling to refuse an injured party a remedy even if the case does not fit precisely into the elements of some traditional cause of action. Whether this will give rise to a cause of action depends on whether other courts agree, and allow the precedent to stand, or whether they criticize it, thus cutting short its life.

As our society changes or as our perception of harm changes, the law comes to recognize new forms of compensable injuries. For example, the law in the twentieth century developed theories of liability for unreasonable intrusions on personal dignity in the form of four varieties of invasion of privacy. In the 1990s, attention was directed to a particularly troublesome phenomenon called "stalking." Some high-profile celebrities were the victims of stalking, and it was soon noted that ordinary citizens were also victims of stalking. The court in *Troncalli v. Jones* was asked to recognize a new tort of stalking. This conduct appears to fall within the tort of invasion of privacy in such a way that this and other courts will address the issues of whether invasion of privacy is sufficient to compensate and protect the victims of stalking and whether stalking is such a serious problem as to deserve a tort of its own.

intentional infliction of mental distress
Almost self-explanatory, it usually requires unreasonable or outrageous conduct and serious mental distress.

Troncalli is complicated by the fact that the Georgia legislature has seen fit to create the new crime of *stalking*. Thus far, we have treated torts as the evolutionary products of judicial decisions. Legislatures, however, may create civil liability through the enactment of statutes. They may also create liability by implication through the passage of criminal statutes. The Supreme Court of Georgia was asked in *Troncalli* to imply a *tort* of stalking by virtue of the *crime* of stalking. Courts are often asked to determine whether such crimes give rise to civil liability. In some cases, a court may find a legislative intent to create liability and other cases may result in the opposite conclusion. The court can always fall back on the argument that the legislature had the power to create civil liability had it so desired. In reading this case, note that the conduct denominated "stalking" was used to establish other causes of action, so that the plaintiff has strong grounds for a remedy even if the stalking argument loses.

TRONCALLI
v.
JONES
Court of Appeals of Georgia
237 Ga.App. 10, 514 S.E.2d 478 (1999)

Regina Jones sued Tom Troncalli. Her complaint set forth one count of stalking; a claim for **intentional infliction of emotional distress;** a claim for **negligent infliction of emotional distress;** a claim for invasion of privacy; and a claim for assault and battery. In addition to the claim for compensatory damages, the complaint sought punitive damages.

The case was tried to a jury; at the conclusion of the evidence, the trial court directed a verdict on the claim for negligent infliction of emotional distress. The jury then returned a general verdict in Jones' favor for $45,000 in compensatory damages; the jury also found that the evidence warranted punitive damages and that Troncalli had acted with specific intent to cause harm. The punitive damages portion of the trial was then held, and the jury awarded $245,891 in punitive damages. The trial court entered judgment, Troncalli appeals, and based on our conclusion in Division 1 that stalking is not a tort, we reverse the judgment.

[The evidence in the case is then discussed. The incidents began when Jones and Troncalli were at a party at a mutual friend's home. Troncalli inappropriately "brushed up" against Jones' breasts on two separate occasions during the night. This act appeared to be intentional and resulted in Jones leaving the party. Troncalli followed her closely despite her reckless driving. Jones eventually spotted police and asked for assistance. Troncalli gave Jones a threatening gesture from his car but was then asked to leave by the police. Jones did not file a report until a week later, a week during which Troncalli harassed her in public and came by her home. Jones "developed shingles, experienced nausea and vomiting, became frightened and depressed, and sought psychological counseling."]

Troncalli testified at trial and claimed that Jones' account of the above incidents was erroneous.

1. In his first enumeration of error, Troncalli claims that the trial court erred in denying his motion for directed verdict on Jones' claim of stalking. Troncalli argues that the court's holding that a tort of stalking was created when the legislature created a criminal statute on

(continued)

(continued)

stalking was erroneous. Jones argues that the court did not err in denying the motion for directed verdict and that the court's charge on stalking simply set forth a duty, which Troncalli breached. Jones claims that because there was a general verdict from the fact that stalking was included as an offense was, at most, harmless error.

The enactment of OCGA § 16-5-90, which defines the crime of stalking, did not automatically create a tort of stalking. It is well settled that "[t]he violation of a penal statute does not automatically give rise to a civil cause of action on the part of one who is injured thereby." . . .

Here, although OCGA § 16-5-90 establishes the public policy of the state, nothing in its provisions creates a private cause of action in tort in favor of the victim. Because there is no cause of action for stalking, the court should have granted Troncalli's motion for directed verdict on this basis.

Jones' argument that there was no harmful error because the jury returned a general verdict lacks merit. In fact, the opposite of this is true: "[S]ince the jury found a general verdict for the plaintiff against [the] defendant, the verdict cannot stand for the reason that this court cannot determine whether the verdict was entered upon a proper basis. [Cits.]" . . .

Similarly, Jones' arguments that the jury was appropriately charged on stalking because the charge outlined Troncalli's duty and because all of the evidence regarding stalking would have been otherwise admissible under other theories are without merit. Stalking was one of Jones' main theories of recovery in the case; it formed a separate count of the complaint. Jones' opening statement listed stalking as the first theory of recovery. In its closing charge, the court gave the jury a lengthy charge regarding stalking, tracking the statutory definition which is set forth in OCGA § 16-5-90. Contrary to Jones' argument, the court did not instruct the jury that stalking simply defined a duty and Jones' argument that stalking was peripheral to her recovery is without merit.

3. Troncalli contends that the trial court erred in denying his motion for directed verdict on Jones' claim of intentional infliction of emotional distress. He argues that his actions did not rise to the level of egregiousness necessary to maintain a claim of this nature. We do not agree.

Judgment reversed.

Case Questions

1. Even though the legislature did not create civil liability for stalking, could the court have created a new tort of stalking? Explain.
2. Might the plaintiff have fared better if she had argued for a separate tort of stalking, independent of the legislative enactment and legislative intent, perhaps citing the crime of stalking as evidence of a serious social problem that the state legislature was attempting to ameliorate? Do you think the plaintiff made this argument as well but the court did not address it? Explain.
3. Do you think there should be a special tort for stalking? Explain.

Case Glossary

intentional infliction of emotional distress and **negligent infliction of emotional distress** Causes of action based on severe emotional distress. While most states recognize the intentional tort, generally requiring outrageous conduct, few recognize the cause of action based on negligence.

Extraneous Factors Influencing Tort Law

The law develops in a social, economic, and political context. As Oliver Wendell Holmes declared in 1881, "The life of the law has not been logic; it has been experience." Lawmaking is not simply a process of refining abstract rules, nor is the process of deciding disputes controlled by the simple expedient of applying abstract rules to concrete events. Tort law has a strong component of logic and common sense. The rights represented by tort law generally reflect what most Americans consider their rights should be (e.g., a person can use force against another person in self-defense). In a sense, tort law more than any other area of law reflects our social values with regard to interpersonal conduct. Nevertheless, there are some special factors that play a large part in tort suits and influence actual outcomes that have little to do with the values expressed in substantive principles.

The Doctrine of *Respondeat Superior* (Vicarious Liability)

respondeat superior
A principle of agency whereby a principal is held responsible for the negligent acts of an agent acting within the scope of the agency; e.g., an employer is liable for the negligence of an employee; also called *vicarious liability*.

The English legal historian Plucknett attributes the birth of this doctrine to Lord Holt, who, in deciding a case in 1691, stated: "Whoever employs another is answerable for him, and undertakes for his care to all that make use of him." Until that time, the doctrine of *respondeat superior*, which places liability on the employer for injuries caused by an employee within the scope of employment, had only been applied to certain public officials when their underlings could not pay damages. Nothing inherent in tort law requires this principle, which is a peculiarity of Anglo-American common law. It contradicts a fundamental principle of tort law, namely, that fault should be the basis for liability. Nonetheless, an employer may be liable without acting wrongfully.

The influence of respondeat superior on modern tort litigation is great. Personal injury cases are costly to litigate, and it is futile to sue a defendant who has limited resources. If, however, a person is injured by someone working on the job for a large corporation, the suit becomes economically feasible. The resources of employees are generally far more limited than those of their employers. As a practical matter, juries tend to be less concerned about the pocketbooks of large businesses than they are about those of workers.

As a result, the availability of compensation may depend more on who may be liable than on the legal merits of the case. When we read in the newspapers of unusually high awards, we can be relatively certain that some "deep pocket" was available to be sued. Respondeat superior creates many deep pockets.

Insurance

insurance The pooling of risk among many insured, typically enabled by a corporation that sells insurance contracts.

The rise of the modern **insurance** industry has abetted tort litigation. The basic principle of insurance is pooling risk. A homeowner who buys fire insurance contributes a small amount to a large pool for protection against the possible but unlikely prospect of a fire. Although the risk of fire is small, the result if it occurs is likely to be financial catastrophe for the uninsured. The insurance company is the pooling agency, collecting payments and maintaining funds from which the unlucky are reimbursed for their losses. The homeowner usually has a homeowner's policy that includes protection against suits from those who may in some way be injured on the homeowner's property. Loss from a fire may be a simple economic loss that can be fairly easily established, but it is quite different when the child next door wanders over and drowns in the swimming pool. The value of that child's life is not easy to fix and will likely produce a protracted negotiation between the insurance company and the bereaved parents (through their attorneys). Insurance companies differ greatly in their willingness to make reasonable settlement offers, so the threat of lawsuit is often necessary; when a settlement cannot be reached, the dispute may be resolved by trial.

The presence of insurance encourages lawsuits for the very reason respondeat superior does—the insurance company has great financial resources. The economic costs of this system are great—attorneys reap large rewards, insurance companies make handsome profits, and injured parties suffer through long delays to receive their (presumably) just compensation.

Given the realities of the economic system and tort law, however, alternative choices are often too risky. For example, physicians commonly pay enormous premiums for malpractice insurance. One might think that a competent, diligent physician need not carry insurance, as the likelihood of suit is minimal. But dedicated, ethical physicians are more concerned with treatment than with liability. Under the law they are held to a high standard of professional care. A simple error of judgment may result in death or serious permanent injury. The potential injuries are so severe that a physician practices without insurance at the peril of financial ruin. The alternative is to practice medicine with the primary purpose of avoiding liability, something neither the medical profession nor the public finds desirable.

Contingency Fees

contingency fee contracts Agreements between an attorney and a client in which the attorney will receive compensation in the form of a percentage of money recovered in a lawsuit; used predominantly in personal injury cases.

The prominence of personal injury lawsuits in the practice of law is encouraged by the custom of **contingency fees.** This is a contract between the lawyer and the client under which the lawyer receives compensation measured by the settlement negotiated with the defendant or the award determined by the court. Rather than charging an hourly fee or a fee fixed in advance, the attorney agrees to represent the client for a percentage of the award. Typically the minimum fee is one third for a settlement, forty percent if the case goes to trial.

Ethically, contingency fees have always been suspect. They not only encourage suits if the potential award is great, but they also give the attorney an interest in the lawsuit, which presents a temptation for the attorney to act on the basis of personal gain rather than in the interests of the client or the law. The contingency fee arrangement is a peculiarly American institution and is not allowed in most countries. The justification for the arrangement most often given is that most injured parties could not afford to pursue a lawsuit if they were forced to pay attorneys as the case proceeds. They would be forced by economic circumstances to settle for much less than their injuries are worth. The individual of limited resources suing an insurance company or a large corporation with sufficient funds to pay attorneys to delay awards indefinitely is necessarily at a great disadvantage. The contingency fee arrangement somewhat equalizes the disparity between the parties. One must question, however, whether this is a natural or artificial product of the tort law.

Contingency fees encourage some sorts of lawsuits and discourage others. If an injury is severe and permanent, especially if it is disabling or disfiguring, compensation may be very great and thus justify the costs of litigation. If the defendant has no financial resources, a lawsuit is unlikely.

Fault

The concept of fault is central to the development of legal theories of tort. Ultimately the resolution of a tort suit involves the question of a transfer of wealth from the defendant to the plaintiff. If someone suffers an injury or a loss, should there be a source of compensation? The law looks to the cause of the injury. If caused by an "act of God," as when someone is struck by lightning, the law cannot allocate compensation, because there is no party at fault.

In contrast, if the cause of the injury can be attributed to human forces, liability may be appropriate. At that point a question of fairness arises. Would it be fair for this person or this organization to surrender some of its resources to the injured party? An affirmative answer to this question is easiest when the injury can be shown to have been caused directly by wrongful conduct of another party to an injured party who is utterly blameless. Unfortunately, causation and blameworthiness are frequently obscure or difficult to prove. What should be the result, for example, when a commercial airline crashes, killing all aboard, but the cause of the crash cannot be determined? Should a widow of one of the passengers be compensated for her loss by the airline? Our sympathies are naturally with the widow, but should the airline compensate her even though she cannot prove fault on the part of the airline? The famous case of *Cox v. Northwest Airlines, Inc.*, 379 F.2d 893 (7th Cir. 1967), resolved this issue through the often-criticized principle of *res ipsa loquitur* ("the thing speaks for itself"). *Res ipsa* is used to infer negligence, specifically a failure of due care, when it would appear that the injury would not have occurred if due care had been exercised. An airplane does not crash without some fault attributable to those in control of it (is this really true?). In this case the principle could be applied without pangs of conscience. The deceased was clearly blameless. The airline was in control of the airplane. In other words, it seems fair that the airline should pay, essentially making the airline the insurer of its passengers; but the fact that fault was established in the absence of proof is troubling to those demanding logic and consistency in the law. Put another way, would it not be better simply to charge airlines (and other common carriers) with the duty to ensure the safety of their passengers rather than apply the questionable principle of *res ipsa loquitur?* Practically speaking, the doctrine of *res ipsa loquitur* is merely a device to get the issue of negligence to the jury.

A different problem of fault was encountered in another famous case, *Summers v. Tice*, 33 Cal. 2d 80, 199 P.2d 1 (1948). Summers was injured in a hunting party when two of his companions fired simultaneously at a quail, hitting Summers in the eye. It was not possible to determine which hunter's shot was responsible for Summers's injury. Logically one was at fault, while the other was not, but the California Supreme Court held both liable because both were negligent in firing in Summers's direction, even though only one could have been the actual *cause* of the injury. "To hold otherwise would be to exonerate both from liability, although each was negligent, and the injury resulted from someone's negligence." The court refused to make Summers suffer the burden of his injuries simply because he could not prove which companion fired the shot that hit his eye.

A similar problem is encountered in the DES (diethylstilbestrol) cases in which an antimiscarriage drug has been alleged to be the cause of cancer in the later life of children born to women who took the drug while pregnant. Assuming the truth of the allegations and assuming that the several drug companies who marketed the drug were legally responsible for the later injuries, who should pay when the medical records, prescriptions, and the mother's memory do not establish which company sold the drug that caused the cancer? One solution proposed to this problem is **enterprise liability** (also known as *market share liability*). Because several companies produced the drug, liability could be pooled among the companies according to their shares of the market for the drug (if one company sold 15 percent of the drug, it would pay 15 percent of the damages). Although enterprise liability is still controversial, it reflects the capacity of tort law to find novel remedies for unusual situations.

enterprise liability
When an injury can be attributed to a number of companies in an industry, *enterprise liability* would apportion the damages according to the market share of each.

Enterprise liability also represents the modern trend in tort law away from the technicalities of finding fault toward emphasizing the search for compensating the innocent victim. The courts and legislatures have been increasingly sensitive to the plight of the consumer, the workforce, the motorist, the homemaker, and the man on the street. Unfortunately, the principles that have arisen do not correct the inequities of the legal system itself. Compensable injuries go uncompensated when the economics of litigation prove an impediment. If there is no "deep pocket," or the injuries are less than the costs of litigation, personal injury attorneys will decline to pursue a case.

The legal profession has the ethical responsibility to provide services to the public in general, not just in cases in which legal fees are readily obtained. The American Bar Association has shown concern for this very problem, but it is up to attorneys to shoulder the responsibility or assist in finding a solution. One promising alternative in this regard is in the growing body of well-trained paralegals. Many of the services provided by attorneys could be provided by paralegals at a much lower cost—not only do paralegals provide their services at a lower fee, they can operate within restricted areas with lower overhead. Full utilization of paralegals by lawyers can significantly reduce costs to clients. Economic necessity together with ethical obligation should result in a growth area for paralegals. This would serve the public and enhance the image of the legal profession. For paralegals this would be a welcome development; helping the nonwealthy may be more personally rewarding than protecting the rich and corporate America.

Should a business enterprise be liable for the intentional torts of a third party on its premises? That is the question in the *Goggin* case. It represents both the search for fault and the plaintiff's search for an affluent defendant.

One of the defenses to negligence is **assumption of risk,** under which the plaintiff voluntarily encounters a known risk (e.g., someone employed to detonate explosives). In *Goggin,* the court not only finds the defendant free of negligence for the harm caused by a third party but also suggests that the plaintiff knew what he was getting into. At the same time, the court acknowledges that the owners of premises open to the public have duties with regard to the safety of patrons. The case raises interesting issues with regard to the assignment of fault.

assumption of risk
May prevent liability for negligence when the plaintiff voluntarily encounters a known risk.

Harold J. GOGGIN
v.
NEW STATE BALLROOM
Supreme Judicial Court of Massachusetts, Suffolk
355 Mass. 718, 247 N.E.2d 350 (1969)

On March 17, 1960, the plaintiff, accompanied by a lady companion, entered the New State Ballroom in Boston at approximately 8:45 P.M. in anticipation of an evening with Terpsichore. Having paid the admission of $2 each and checked clothing, they commenced dancing when the music began. At this time there were approximately 900 people in the hall. The dance floor was waxed and polished and was about 125 feet long with a width of 90 feet. By 9:30 P.M. the crowd had grown to 1,200, and by 10 P.M. it had increased to the point where there were 1,800 to 1,900 people on the dance floor. These dancers were "noisy and boisterous, kicking their feet, bumping into people and doing some real kicking." This kicking occurred in connection with the execution of such dances as the "cha cha and jitterbug," and was accompanied by "bumping." The plaintiff, however, "only danced the waltz and refrained from the cha cha or the jitterbug.". . . While

the plaintiff's partner claimed she saw no attendants, there was testimony from the defendant's manager that two police officers, plus a sergeant, were on duty "along with two employees of the Ballroom who were on the dance floor." This detail was evidently insufficient to aid the plaintiff, for at 10 P.M. "he was dancing the waltz with his partner in a corner as there was one fellow he was trying to keep away from. When it is crowded like that you really can get bumped." He and his partner remained in the corner "but this fellow kept coming and all of a sudden, bang! 'We were pushed right over!' " The plaintiff went down, his head hit the floor, and his partner fell on top of him and ripped her dress in the descent. The plaintiff had been no stranger to the physical activity which took place at the ballroom for he was a regular attendant there on every Saturday evening between March 17, 1959, and March 17, 1960. He also repaired to the ballroom during that period on any holiday nights that fell on a weekday.

On this evidence the defendant moved for a directed verdict on a count in an action of tort brought by the plaintiff wherein he alleged that he was on the defendant's premises by

(continued)

(continued)

invitation, that he had paid an admission, and that he was injured by reason of the defendant's negligence in its failure to conduct its establishment in an orderly manner and in compliance with statutes, ordinances and rules relating to it. The motion was denied, there was a verdict for the plaintiff, and the defendant is here on an exception to that denial.

The law in these circumstances has been often stated. The defendant, which opened its ballroom to the public in furtherance of its business, owed the duty to the plaintiff [**business invitee**], who paid to enter, of reasonable care that no injury occur to the plaintiff through the actions of a third person whether such acts were accidental, negligent or intentional. . . . The defendant, however, was not an insurer of the plaintiff's safety. . . . Its liability in this instance must arise from its knowledge, or the fact that it should have known of or anticipated, in the exercise of reasonable care, the disorderly or rowdy actions of third persons which might lead to injury to the plaintiff. . . . Furthermore, where in a ballroom such as this conditions existing at the time of the accident are open and obvious to

any person of ordinary intelligence, the defendant is under no duty to warn the plaintiff even where a substantial crowd has gathered. . . .

The plaintiff in this case chose on an evening not noted for restraints on exuberance in the city of Boston to go with his lady to a public dance hall where he knew the patrons were lovers of the cha cha and the jitterbug. He knew these dances involved muscular contortions and a degree of abandon not associated with a minuet. A certain amount of innocent bumping in a large crowd would be unavoidable. That the bump which floored the plaintiff may have been deliberate was, in our view, not such a happening that the defendant was bound to anticipate it. It was unusual and not reasonably to be apprehended and affords no basis for treating the defendant as negligent. . . . The vagaries of fashions in the dance and their consequences are better left subject to the judgment of those who engage in them or frequent establishments where they may be found, absent circumstances which may in the light of the principles herein discussed provide a basis for liability. . . .

Exceptions sustained. Judgment for the defendant.

Case Questions

1. To what duty does the court hold the ballroom with regard to the plaintiff invitee?
2. What language in the case suggests assumption of risk?

Case Glossary

business invitee   The most common form of an invitee, businesses, especially retail stores, are often open to the public. By implication, businesses invite members of the public to enter their premises, and they owe a duty of care to those who enter their stores.

Fault and Three Areas of Tort Law

Tort law covers a variety of areas of injury to person and property, but three areas constitute the bulk of tort litigation:

1. Intentional torts

2. Negligence

3. Strict liability (represented primarily by the booming area of products liability)

The most ancient category is intentional torts; negligence flowered in the nineteenth and twentieth centuries; and products liability has come to fruition only in recent decades. It is not possible here to discuss any of these in sufficient detail to suggest a mastery of them, which must be left for later study. They are discussed primarily with regard to the different ways in which they relate to concepts of fault in its historical legal evolution.

Intentional Torts

intentional torts

Torts that require proof of intentional wrongful conduct.

A number of causes of action are lumped together as **intentional torts.** Many of them are quite ancient, such as battery, assault, trespass, false imprisonment, and the like. Some are recent in origin, such as invasion of privacy and intentional infliction of mental distress. Their common bond is the essential element of intent. Intent to do some harm (sometimes the intent to do specific harm) must be alleged and be proven for the plaintiff to prevail. Neither malicious motive nor criminal intent is required for an intentional tort, though **malicious prosecution** specifically requires a showing of malice. Absence of malice may in some cases be a defense against libel.

malicious prosecution

When someone initiates or causes a groundless suit to be brought out of malice. To succeed in this claim, it is essential that the original suit be terminated in favor of the person later suing for *malicious prosecution.*

The requirement of intent demands a proof of fault against the defendant and requires a willful act on the part of the defendant. The law of intentional torts assumes that human beings act from free will and can conform their conduct to societal rules. When they fail to do so, resulting in harm to others, they will be held responsible for their acts to the injured party. If a harmful act was intended, punitive damages are often awarded in addition to compensation. Punitive damages are not ordinarily awarded for nonintentional torts.

The plaintiff must prove intentional conduct, but the defendant has the opportunity to rebut intent. Intent is commonly inferred from the events that gave rise to the injury. In the colorful case of *Katko v. Briney*, 183 N.W.2d 657 (Iowa 1971), an Iowa farmer protected his wife's often-vandalized, unoccupied farm house by wiring a shotgun to a bedroom door to go off when someone opened the door. Katko, a trespasser looking for old bottles, had the misfortune of opening the door and suffered permanent injury to his leg. Briney's attempt to negate intent by stating on the witness stand that he "did not intend to injure anyone" was not believed by the jury, which found that he had acted maliciously and awarded Katko $20,000 in compensatory and $10,000 in punitive damages.

Conversely, when a five-year-old child pulled a lawn chair out from under a woman about to sit in it, the Supreme Court of Washington held that it was insufficient that the child's act was intentional and incurred a risk and remanded the case to the trial judge to determine whether the child realized with a "substantial certainty" that the harmful contact would result (*Garrett v. Dailey*, 46 Wash. 2d 197, 279 P.2d 1091 [1955]). Liability was thus predicated on the knowledge and understanding of a five-year-old. (On remand, the trial court found that the child did in fact have such knowledge.)

In addition to intent, a plaintiff must allege and prove all the other elements of the specific cause of action, as discussed earlier.

Michael POHLE, Appellant-Defendant,
v.
Doris CHEATHAM, Appellee-Plaintiff
Court of Appeals of Indiana
724 N.E.2d 655 (2000)

BAKER, Judge

The facts most favorable to Pohle reveal that on October 13, 1977, Pohle and Cheatham were married. . . . In May 1993, the couple became estranged. However, sometime in late September or early October 1993, during this estrangement, Cheatham and Pohle engaged in sexual relations at Pohle's home. During this visit, in which Cheatham had hopes of reconciliation, she voluntarily posed for Pohle to take Polaroid photographs of her both clothed, in a state of nudity and performing a sex act. At no time during or after these pictures were taken did Cheatham ask what Pohle intended to do with the pictures or attempt to recover them.

Thereafter, on December 29, 1994, the parties' marriage was dissolved. According to a catchall provision in the court-approved **property settlement,** each party was awarded any miscellaneous personal property in their respective possession. Thus, as the pictures remained in Pohle's possession, they were tacitly awarded to him in the dissolution decree. . . . [After the dissolution, Pohle sent a letter to Cheatham threatening to reveal the photos to "friends and family and other people."]

On February 28 or March 1, 1998, Pohle made photocopies of the nude pictures taken years earlier. Each photocopy included several photos of Doris in various sexually explicit poses. . . .

[H]e then posted and scattered them around several locations throughout Jennings County. . . . Moreover, Pohle dispersed several dozen of the photocopies throughout Cheatham's neighborhood and her church. . . . Cheatham, with help from friends and family, then attempted to recover the photos in other locations. In all, approximately sixty photocopies were retrieved from various locations around town. . . . However, Cheatham still received several calls from individuals who encountered pictures that were not recovered.

As a result of the publication of these photographs, Cheatham filed a complaint against Pohle on March 27, 1998, alleging intentional invasion of privacy and intentional infliction of severe emotional distress. In his amended answer, Pohle raised the defense of waiver. On March 31, 1999, Cheatham filed a motion for partial summary judgment, arguing that, as a matter of law, waiver was not a viable affirmative defense in the instant case. Following a hearing, the trial court granted Cheatham's motion for partial summary judgment on June 9, 1999. Pohle now appeals. . . .

Pohle argues that the trial court erred in granting partial summary judgment on his defense of waiver. Specifically, he contends that there exists a genuine issue of material fact regarding whether Cheatham impliedly waived her right to complain about his publication of the photographs. He asserts that waiver is ordinarily a question of fact. Further, Pohle points to the following facts that he alleges give rise to the inference of waiver:

1. [Cheatham] voluntarily posed for nude photographs taken by [Pohle] at his home during a time that the two of them were separated.
2. [Cheatham] voluntarily posed for the photographs without asking [Pohle] what he intended to do with them.
3. [Cheatham] did not take any action to obtain the photographs during the divorce action between she and [Pohle] and allowed them to be awarded to [Pohle] therein.
4. [Cheatham] did not take any action to obtain the photographs when she learned that [Pohle] intended to publish them nor did she take any action to restrain his actions in doing so.

Waiver is an intentional relinquishment of a known right, requiring both knowledge of the existence of the right and intention to relinquish it. . . . Moreover, waiver may be shown either by express or implied consent, and, thus, the right may be lost by a course of conduct which estops its assertion. . . . However, waiver is an affirmative act and mere silence, acquiescence or inactivity does not constitute waiver unless there was a duty to speak or act. . . . Further, any waiver of an individual's right to privacy justifies an invasion only to the extent warranted by the circumstances which brought about the waiver. . . .

[I]t is important to consider the causes of action Cheatham is alleged to have waived. Cheatham's first claim is based on the public disclosure of private facts theory of invasion of privacy. Such a claim for invasion of privacy requires proof of the following essential elements: (1) private information was publicly divulged; (2) to persons who had no legitimate interest in the information; (3) in a manner that was coercive and oppressive; and, (4) such information would be highly offensive and objectionable to a reasonable person of ordinary sensibilities. . . . Cheatham's second claim alleges intentional infliction of emotional distress, which applies when one by extreme or outrageous conduct intentionally or recklessly causes severe emotional distress to another. . . . We note that it is the intent to harm someone emotionally that constitutes the basis for this tort. Id.

It is apparent that Cheatham's causes of action are premised not upon Pohle's taking or possession of the photographs, but upon his distribution of them to the public. Thus, the critical inquiry is whether, as a matter of law, Cheatham has not impliedly waived her right to complain about the public distribution of the photographs.

. . . In the instant appeal, Pohle does not claim, nor do we believe he seriously could claim, that the photographs he distributed of Cheatham were of legitimate public concern.

. . . [T]he undisputed evidence establishes that Cheatham voluntarily submitted to her estranged husband taking sexually explicit pictures of her in the privacy of his home, without inquiring what he planned to do with the pictures. Approximately a year thereafter, she failed to request the pictures during the couple's dissolution. Further, she failed to take any action following an apparent threat by Pohle to publish the pictures.

We cannot agree with Pohle that the trier of fact could reasonably infer from this conduct that Cheatham consented to the publication of the photographs. Rather, it is clear that, in the heat of passion and hopes of reconciliation, she simply consented to being privately photographed by her husband. From such limited consent, it certainly cannot legitimately be inferred that Cheatham intended to waive her right to complain about the public distribution of the photographs. . . . Further, her failure to take action to obtain the photographs during the dissolution or following his apparent threat similarly does not raise an inference that Cheatham intended to consent to their distribution. . . . Therefore, as a matter of law, we find that Cheatham's actions do not amount to waiver, and the trial court properly entered partial summary judgment on Pohle's defense of waiver.

Judgment affirmed.

Case Questions

1. Is the concept of waiver urged here an attempt to argue comparative fault for intentional torts?
2. What problems do you see with using the tort of public disclosure of private facts (invasion of privacy) in husband and wife disputes?
3. What if the husband, instead of taking consented Polaroid shots, had used a hidden video camera, later captured still photos from the video and similarly distributed photocopies of them? Intuitively, this seems far worse than the facts in *Pohle*; how might the outcome be different?

Case Glossary

property settlement (see **property settlement agreement** in glossary)   In divorce (dissolution of marriage) cases, it is common for the parties to divide up the various items of personal property prior to judgment and keep what they have, rather than itemize every last piece of property. This case could have been avoided had the wife demanded the nasty pictures. She might have been understandably reluctant to bring them to anyone's attention.

The *Pohle* case presents one form of the tort of invasion of privacy generally referred to as *public disclosure of private facts,* in this instance, some embarrassing pictures of an ex-wife. (This tort is very different from other forms of invasion of privacy, such as "wrongful appropriation of name or likeness for profit," e.g., using a picture of Michael Jordan to advertise clothing without his consent.)

The issue in this case involves whether an ex-wife waived her right to prevent her ex-husband's distribution of sexually explicit photos of her taken during their marriage. If the central question in a tort case is whether resources should be transferred from the defendant to the plaintiff, as mentioned earlier, and if this determination is based on fairness and fault, the *Pohle* case raises special problems. First, the transfer of wealth will be between ex-husband and ex-wife—not as easy as taking money from Microsoft. Second, while the ex-husband's conduct appears intentionally designed to cause emotional distress to the ex-wife, the pictures were taken with her consent and she did not ask for their return at the time of divorce or later. Is there some fault on her part? Is the defendant trying to sneak in a notion of comparative fault for intentional torts? (We have seen in an earlier chapter the doctrine of comparative negligence.)

Note that the court converts what looks to be a question of fact into a question of law.

Negligence

The Industrial Revolution of the nineteenth century and the automobile of the twentieth both caused a marked increase in serious personal injuries. These injuries were caused by machines and the human beings that control them. Injury was usually accidental rather than intentional, so the traditional notions of intentional fault required elaboration.

A complete *listing* of the names of the causes of action in tort would be dominated by intentional torts, but the cases *brought* for personal injuries would be dominated by the single cause of action called *negligence.* Most people are injured accidentally and not intentionally. In negligence law, liability arises through a different notion of fault than intent. In a sense, negligence is simply culpable carelessness. Poor judgment, momentary inattention, and lack of foresight often result in injury. Negligence law sought and found a measure by which the failure to exercise due care could be categorized as fault and thereby incur liability.

The standard of care is embodied in the *reasonable man* test. Tradition uses the generic male for the standard, but today the test is more properly put as "what a reasonably prudent *person* would have done under the circumstances." Whether someone should be found at fault and held liable is measured by a standard of care based on reasonableness rather than subjective mental state or intent.

Negligence has four elements:

1. Duty (standard of care)

2. Breach of the duty (conduct falling below the standard of care)

3. Causation (the breach must be the cause of the injury)

4. Injury

The breach of the duty establishes fault. Because negligence applies to the myriad injuries incurred daily through oversight and carelessness, it is not possible to cover in the elements the precise circumstances that give rise to liability; they are simply too numerous. The reasonable man standard acknowledges that what may be prudent conduct in one situation may not be prudent in another. The test must be applied on a case-by-case basis, with the standard of care determined by the jury. The "reasonable man" is a hypothetical person of ordinary understanding but prudent in conduct; individuals are not expected to exercise extraordinary care, nor are they excused by the fact that most people are often careless. It would undoubtedly be negligent not to fence in a swimming pool in a neighborhood full of small children, but perhaps not imprudent not to do so on a country estate with no neighboring children; it is up to the jury to decide what is reasonable and prudent.

The standard of care for negligence may vary from the reasonable man standard. Thus, if a statutory standard fits the case, it usually serves for the standard of care. For example, if a motorist runs a stop sign and causes an accident, the breach of the standard of care is satisfied by a statute that requires a full stop at stop signs, so the jury need not question whether a reasonably prudent person stops at stop signs.

For professionals, the standard of care is measured by professional standards in the community in which the professional practices or by a national standard for specialists. It would hardly do for a jury to decide what a reasonably prudent person would do when performing brain surgery. At present, paralegals are not professionals in this legal sense, so negligence on their part ordinarily would result in a suit against the supervising attorney. Should a paralegal who has been certified as a legal assistant by NALA be subject to suit if the paralegal represents himself or herself as a "Certified Paralegal"? At present, many states are questioning whether paralegals should be licensed, which would presumably make them professionals and subject to suit for their negligent mistakes.

While profitable corporations seem much more attractive defendants than the average private citizen, a plaintiff still must establish a basis for liability. Like individuals, corporations are held liable for the injuries they cause, but this liability has its boundaries. As one writer put it, "You can't make a knife that cuts steak but doesn't cut human flesh." In the *Bunn-O-Matic* case, the agent of injury was not a knife but hot coffee, which caused some burns when spilled. The defendant manufactured the coffee maker. Judge Easterbrook weighs the respective duties of both sides in terms of fault. While reading this case, consider whether the plaintiffs hurt themselves in the answers they gave in depositions.

Contributory Negligence/Comparative Negligence   With the rise of negligence suits in the nineteenth century, the requirement of fault (breach of the standard of care) also gave rise to a defense based on fault. It did not seem just to allow recovery if the plaintiff shared some responsibility for causing the injury. A

Angelina and Jack McMAHON, Plaintiffs-Appellants,

v.

BUNN-O-MATIC CORPORATION, James River Paper Company, and Wincup Holdings, L.P., Defendants-Appellees 150 F.3d 651 (7th Cir, 1998)

EASTERBROOK, Circuit Judge.

During a break from a long-distance auto trip, Jack McMahon bought a cup of coffee from the mini mart at a Mobil station. Jack asked Angelina McMahon, his wife, to remove the plastic lid while he drove. Angelina decided to pour some of the coffee into a smaller cup that would be easier for Jack to handle. In the process the coffee flooded her lap; Angelina suffered second and third degree burns that caused her pain for months and produced scars on her left thigh and lower abdomen. Angelina believes that the Styrofoam cup collapsed, either because it was poorly made or because inordinately hot coffee weakened its structure. The McMahons' claims against the producers of the cup and lid have been settled. The third defendant is Bunn-O-Matic Corporation, which manufactured the coffee maker. According to the McMahons, the temperatures at which Bunn's apparatus brews and serves coffee—195°F during the brewing cycle and 179°F as the "holding" temperature of a carafe on its hotplate—are excessive, and its design therefore defective.

The McMahons have two theories of liability under Indiana law (which the parties agree supplies the rule of decision): (i) that Bunn failed to warn consumers about the severity of burns that hot coffee can produce; and (ii) that any coffee served at more than 140°F is unfit for human consumption (and therefore a defective product) because of its power to cause burns more severe than consumers expect, aggravated by its potential to damage the cup and thus increase the probability of spills. After the parties agreed to accept the decision of a magistrate judge . . . the court entered summary judgment for the defendants. . . . The magistrate judge observed that both McMahons conceded during their depositions that "hotness" was one of the elements they value in coffee and that they sought out hot coffee, knew it could burn, and took precautions as a result. . . .

Coffee served at 180°F by a roadside vendor, which doubtless expects that it will cool during the longer interval before consumption, does not seem so abnormal as to require a heads-up warning.

What remains is the argument that Bunn should have provided a detailed warning about the severity of burns that hot liquids can cause, even if 179°F is a standard serving temperature. The McMahons insist that, although they knew that coffee can burn, they thought that the sort of burn involved would be a blister painful for several days (that is, a second degree burn), not a third degree burn of the sort Angelina experienced. . . .

Insistence on more detail can make any warning, however elaborate, seem inadequate. Indiana courts have expressed considerable reluctance to require ever-more detail in warnings. . . . "Extended warnings present several difficulties, first among them that, the more text must be squeezed onto the product, the smaller the type, and the less likely is the consumer to read or remember any of it. Only pithy and bold warnings can be effective. . . . Indiana does not require vendors to give warnings in the detail plaintiffs contemplate. It expects consumers to educate themselves about the hazards of daily life—of matches, knives, and kitchen ranges, of bones in fish, and of hot beverages—by general reading and experience, knowledge they can acquire before they enter a mini mart to buy coffee for a journey.

With warnings out of the way, the remaining theory of liability comes into focus. . . . If the defect in question is a design defect (as opposed to a blunder in the manufacture of a well-designed product), then "the party making the claim must establish that the manufacturer or seller failed to exercise reasonable care under the circumstances in designing the product." In other words, a design-defect claim in Indiana is a negligence claim, subject to the understanding that negligence means failure to take precautions that are less expensive than the net costs of accidents. . . .

Start with the contention that Bunn's coffee maker was negligently designed because, in the words of Professor Diller, "at the temperatures at which this coffee was brewed and maintained the structural integrity of the styrofoam cup into which the coffee was poured would be compromised making it more flexible and likely to give way or collapse when its rigid lid is removed.". . . How does Diller know that hot beverages make Styrofoam cups too flexible? How much more flexible, under what circumstances? How likely to collapse, and how does the failure rate vary with temperature? What is the reasoning (and the data) behind the statement we have quoted? . . . [H]e offers only a bare conclusion. . . . [T]he plaintiffs have no evidence to support this theory of design defect. Naked opinions cannot stave off summary judgment.

At first glance plaintiffs' alternative theory is stronger. Coffee at 180°F is considerably more likely to cause severe burns than is coffee at 135° to 140°F, the maximum at which Diller believes that coffee should be served. . . . Why did the American National Standards Institute set 170°F as the minimum temperature at which coffee should be held ready to serve? Diller does not make any effort to reconcile his "maximum 140°F" position with the ANSI's "minimum 170°F" position. . . . Without some way to compare the benefits of a design change (fewer and less severe burns) against the costs (less pleasure received from drinking coffee), it is impossible to say that designing a coffee maker to hold coffee at 179°F bespeaks negligent inattention to the risks.

It is easy to sympathize with Angelina McMahon, severely injured by a common household beverage—and, for all we can see, without fault on her part. Using the legal system to shift the costs of this injury to someone else may be attractive to the McMahons, but it would have bad consequences for coffee fanciers who like their beverage hot. First-party health and accident insurance deals with injuries of the kind Angelina suffered without the high costs of adjudication, and without potential side effects such as lukewarm coffee. We do not know whether the McMahons carried such insurance (directly or through an employer's health plan), but we are confident that Indiana law does not make Bunn and similar firms insurers through the tort system of the harms, even grievous ones, that are common to the human existence.

AFFIRMED.

Case Questions

1. Why did the court reject plaintiffs' argument that there should have been warnings about the hot coffee?
2. How did the court find fault with plaintiffs' assertions about the proper maximum temperature of coffee?

contributory negligence

A principle by which a recovery will be denied a plaintiff for defendant's negligence if plaintiff is also found to have been at fault.

plaintiff's fault was called **contributory negligence** and constituted a complete defense to a suit for negligence. (It is an affirmative defense that has been replaced by *comparative negligence* in most states.) The courts soon realized that the result of using this doctrine was not always just. In some cases the minor fault of the plaintiff would not allow recovery. Railroad workers, for example, often worked under dangerous conditions in which a moment's inadvertence could result in serious injury or death. It was not sufficient for the widow and children

**workers'
compensation**
A statutory scheme
whereby fixed awards are
made for employment-
related injuries. This
commonly takes the form
of state-regulated
employers' insurance
arrangements.

**comparative
negligence**
A principle whereby
damages are apportioned
between plaintiff and
defendant according to
their relative fault in a
negligence case where
both are found to have
been at fault.

strict liability
A principle, largely
applied to *product
liability*, which creates
liability without proof of
fault, for example, liability
for a "dangerously
defective product";
virtually interchangeable
with *absolute liability*.

to prove that the employer had been responsible for the dangerous conditions; if the employee had not been careful, there could be no recovery.

Legislatures responded to dangers in the workplace with **workers' compensation,** and many courts and legislatures responded with **comparative negligence** for nonworkplace accidents. Under comparative negligence schemes, many of which are statutory, fault is apportioned; that is, if the plaintiff is negligent as well as the defendant, the plaintiff's award is reduced by the plaintiff's percentage of fault. Thus, if the jury, under the judge's instructions, determines that 80 percent of the fault rests with the defendant, while 20 percent is the fault of the plaintiff, the plaintiff is entitled only to 80 percent of the amount of the injuries. If the jury values the plaintiff's injuries at $50,000, the plaintiff would receive $40,000. The percentages are arbitrary approximations, but the jury must estimate them if it finds fault on both parties. Many states will not allow the plaintiff to recover if the jury assigns 50 percent or more of the fault to the plaintiff. Automobile accidents often involve injuries to both drivers, each of whom claims the other was at fault. The final award can differ greatly depending on whether the jurisdiction uses contributory negligence or comparative negligence ("pure" or modified).

Strict Liability/Product Liability

The Age of Technology has confounded the concept of fault in tort. The American consumer acquires a bewildering assortment of machines, appliances, and pharmaceutical drugs, as well as other products that pose unseen dangers. Manufacturers may exercise reasonable precautions to make their products safe and certainly do not intend to injure their customers, so it is difficult to assign fault under theories of negligence or intentional tort. The purchase of products creates a contractual relationship, but ordinary contract remedies do not contemplate compensation for personal injury.

Early in the twentieth century, judges were troubled by innocent victims of defective products who could not prove fault on the part of the producer. As America became a mighty industrial power, courts became less concerned about protecting business from ruinous lawsuits and more concerned about the hapless victims of their products. It did not seem just that a company could reap large profits from sales of its products without compensating those injured by them. A number of cases strained at the concept of fault to protect innocent parties, and in 1963 Justice Traynor of the California Supreme Court wrote the opinion in *Greenman v. Yuba Power Products, Inc.,* 59 Cal. 2d 57, 377 P.2d 897, which announced the birth of product liability. Greenman had purchased a combination power tool for his home workshop that one day inexplicably ejected a piece of wood, striking him in the forehead. Justice Traynor reasoned that traditional requirements of proof of fault were no longer tenable and set the standard for the plaintiff in the case as follows:

> To establish the manufacturer's liability it was sufficient that plaintiff proved
> that he was injured while using the Shopsmith in a way it was intended to be

used as a result of a defect in design and manufacture of which plaintiff was not aware that made the Shopsmith unsafe for its intended use . . .

Perhaps no case in the common law has had a more immediate and far-reaching effect on American law. The *Restatement of Torts* responded two years later with § 402A, which elaborated on the *Greenman* decision. Section 402A was adopted in some form by state after state in rapid succession. In a few short years, numerous cases served to refine the principles of product liability. Never has such a vast body of law so quickly fixed a cause of action so firmly in the law.

implied warranty
A promise imposed by law, for example, an implied warranty of fitness for use or consumption, as distinguished from an *express warranty* stated in a contract.

This was a revolution in tort law waiting to happen. Traynor could appeal to precedent in **implied warranty** theory, which held sellers responsible for the fitness for use of the products they sell. The consumer reasonably relied on the seller to deliver a product fit for use. Implied warranties were in addition to the express warranties given by the seller. The advent of the automobile made implied warranties important because the purchaser was rarely in a position to determine whether the product was properly designed or assembled.

The adoption of the cause of action for product liability was justified on policy grounds, which were stated succinctly by Judge Jacobson in a concurring opinion in *Lechuga, Inc. v. Montgomery*, 12 Ariz. App. 32, 467 P.2d 256:

> It is apparent from a reading of the Restatement, and the leading cases on this subject, that the doctrine of strict liability has evolved to place liability on the party primarily responsible for the injury occurring, that is, the manufacturer of the defective product. This, as Justice Traynor stated in his concurring opinion in *Escola v. Coca Cola Bottling Co. of Fresno*, 24 Cal. 2d 453, 150 P.2d 436 (1944), is based on reasons of public policy: "If public policy demands that a manufacturer of goods be responsible for their quality regardless of negligence there is no reason not to fix that responsibility openly." 150 P.2d, at 441.
>
> These public policy considerations have been variously enumerated as follows:
>
> (1) The manufacturer can anticipate some hazards and guard against their recurrence, which the consumer cannot do. . . .
> (2) The cost of injury may be overwhelming to the person injured while the risk of injury can be insured by the manufacturer and be distributed among the public as a cost of doing business. . . .
> (3) It is in the public interest to discourage the marketing of defective products. . . .
> (4) It is in the public interest to place responsibility for its reaching the market. . . .
> (5) That this responsibility should also be placed upon the retailer and whole-saler of the defective product in order that they may act as the conduit through which liability may flow to reach the manufacturer, where ultimate responsibility lies. . . .
> (6) That because of the complexity of present day manufacturing processes and their secretiveness, the ability to prove negligent conduct by the injured plaintiff is almost impossible. . . .
> (7) That the consumer does not have the ability to investigate for himself the soundness of the product. . . .
> (8) That this consumer's vigilance has been lulled by advertising, marketing devices and trademarks. . . .

Inherent in these policy considerations is not the nature of the transaction by which the consumer obtained possession of the defective product but the character of the defect itself, that is, one occurring in the manufacturing process and the unavailability of an adequate remedy on behalf of the injured plaintiff.

In addition to implied warranty as a ground for product liability, the principle of **absolute liability** for extrahazardous activities furnished precedent. Under this principle, parties engaged in especially dangerous activities, such as the use of explosives, were held liable regardless of fault. The policy grounds were similar. It appeared to the courts unjust that innocent parties could be injured through the direct cause of another's activities and be left without a remedy simply because those engaged in the activities had exercised due care.

Behind liability for dangerously defective products and extrahazardous activities lies a foreseeability issue. Clearly, engaging in activities that present a significant risk to the public makes injury foreseeable in a general sense, even if neither the victim nor the manner of occurrence is precisely foreseeable. And when a manufacturer makes products that are potentially dangerous, the risk of injury has a degree of foreseeability. The law now holds that those who incur risks should bear the cost of the injuries that result. Foreseeability lurks everywhere in tort law. Because of the nature of lawsuits, the foreseeability issue always arises from hindsight—what may seem foreseeable in looking back on the course of events may not have been remotely foreseen at the beginning. The foreseeability issue is both argued and ignored, but further study is beyond the scope of our present discussion.

Damages

A person who loses an arm, a leg, or an eye or is left paraplegic suffers a loss of lifestyle as well. The courts have long considered a reduction in earning potential to be recoverable, but recently attorneys have argued, sometimes successfully, that injured parties should collect for "hedonic" losses, meaning essentially a decrease in enjoyment of life. Imagine an artist made blind by another's wrongful conduct. The artist may lose not only a career and earnings but also much of the meaning and enjoyment of life. The next few years will tell how far courts are willing to go in recognizing such losses as compensable.

The *McDougald* case expresses the nature of **compensatory damages.** Hedonic losses are discussed and their limitations established in the context of a comatose plaintiff.

Punitive (or Exemplary) Damages for Intentional Tort

If compensatory damages aim at returning the plaintiff to the condition enjoyed before the wrongful injury by way of monetary compensation, punitive damages are reserved to punish the outrageous conduct of the defendant. They have

absolute liability
Liability without fault or negligence; often used interchangeably with **strict liability**, though many would contend that there is a difference.

compensatory damages   Awarded to an injured party to make her whole, that is, in tort, to compensate for all injuries, and, in contract, to put the nonbreaching party in the position he would have been in if the contract had been performed; also referred to as *actual damages*.

hedonic damages (losses)   Money awarded in some lawsuits for loss of the ability to enjoy life's pleasures, a recent and controversial basis for damages.

Emma McDOUGALD et al., Respondents,
v.
Sara GARBER et al., Appellants
Court of Appeals of New York
73 N.Y.2d 246, 536 N.E.2d 372,
538 N.Y.S.2d 937 (1989)

This appeal raises fundamental questions about the nature and role of nonpecuniary damages in personal injury litigation. By non-pecuniary damages, we mean those damages awarded to compensate an injured person for the physical and emotional consequences of the injury, such as pain and suffering and the loss of the ability to engage in certain activities. **Pecuniary damages** . . . compensate the victim for the economic consequences of the injury, such as medical expenses, lost earnings and the cost of custodial care.

The specific questions raised here deal with assessment of nonpecuniary damages and are (1) whether some degree of cognitive aware-ness is a prerequisite to recovery for loss of enjoyment of life and (2) whether a jury should be instructed to consider and award damages for loss of enjoyment of life separately from damages for pain and suffering. We answer the first question in the affirmative and the second question in the negative.

* * *

On September 7, 1978, plaintiff Emma McDougald, then 31 years old, underwent a Cae-sarean section and tubal ligation at New York Infirmary. Defendant Garber performed the sur-gery; defendants Armengol and Kulkarni pro-vided anesthesia. During the surgery, Mrs. McDougald suffered oxygen deprivation which resulted in severe brain damage and left her in a permanent comatose condition. This action was brought by Mrs. McDougald and her husband, suing derivatively, alleging that the injuries were caused by the defendants' acts of malpractice.

A jury found all defendants liable and awarded Emma McDougald a total of $9,650,102

in damages, including $1,000,000 for conscious pain and suffering and a separate award of $3,500,000 for loss of the pleasures and pursuits of life. The balance of the damages awarded to her were for pecuniary damages—lost earnings and the cost of custodial and nursing care. Her husband was awarded $1,500,000 on his deriva-tive claim for the loss of his wife's services. On defendants' posttrial motions, the Trial Judge reduced the total award to Emma McDougald to $4,796,728 by striking the entire award for future nursing care ($2,353,374) and by reducing the separate awards for conscious pain and suf-fering and loss of the pleasures and pursuits of life to a single award of $2,000,000. Her hus-band's award was left intact. On cross appeals, the Appellate Division affirmed and later granted defendants leave to appeal to this court.

* * *

We conclude that the court erred, both in instructing the jury that Mrs. McDougald's awareness was irrelevant to their consideration of damages for loss of enjoyment of life and in directing the jury to consider that aspect of damages separately from pain and suffering.

* * *

We begin with the familiar proposition that an award of damages to a person injured by the negligence of another is to compensate the victim, not to punish the wrongdoer. The goal is to restore the injured party, to the extent possible, to the position that would have been occupied had the wrong not occurred. To be sure, placing the burden of compensation on the negligent party also serves as a deterrent, but purely **punitive damages**—that is, those which have no compensatory purpose—are prohibited unless the harmful conduct is inten-tional, malicious, outrageous, or otherwise aggravated beyond mere negligence.

Damages for nonpecuniary losses are, of course, among those that can be awarded as compensation to the victim. This aspect of dam-ages, however, stands on less certain ground

(continued)

(continued)

than does an award for pecuniary damages. An economic loss can be compensated in kind by an economic gain; but recovery for noneconomic losses such as pain and suffering and loss of enjoyment of life rests on "the legal fiction that money damages can compensate for a victim's injury." We accept this fiction, knowing that although money will neither ease the pain nor restore the victim's abilities, this device is as close as the law can come in its effort to right the wrong. We have no hope of evaluating what has been lost, but a monetary award may provide a measure of solace for the condition created.

Our willingness to indulge this fiction comes to an end, however, when it ceases to serve the compensatory goals of tort recovery. When that limit is met, further indulgence can only result in assessing damages that are punitive. The question posed by this case, then, is whether an award of damages for loss of enjoyment of life to a person whose injuries preclude any awareness of the loss serves a compensatory purpose. We conclude that it does not.

Simply put, an award of money damages in such circumstances has no meaning or utility to the injured person. . . .

We recognize that, as the trial court noted, requiring some cognitive awareness as a prerequisite to recovery for loss of enjoyment of life will result in some cases "in the paradoxical situation that the greater the degree of brain injury inflicted by a negligent defendant, the smaller the award the plaintiff can recover in general damages." The force of this argument, however—the temptation to achieve a balance between injury and damages—has nothing to do with meaningful compensation for the victim. Instead, the temptation is rooted in a desire to punish the defendant in proportion to the harm inflicted. However relevant such retributive symmetry may be in the criminal law, it has no place in the law of civil damages, at least in the absence of culpability beyond mere negligence.

Accordingly, we conclude that cognitive awareness is a prerequisite to recovery for loss of enjoyment of life. We do not go so far, however, as to require the fact finder to sort out varying degrees of cognition and determine at what level a particular deprivation can be fully appreciated. With respect to pain and suffering, the trial court charged simply that there must be "some level of awareness" in order for plaintiff to recover. We think that this is an appropriate standard for all aspects of nonpecuniary loss. . . .

Accordingly, the order of the Appellate Division, insofar as appealed from, should be modified, with costs to defendants, by granting a new trial on the issue of nonpecuniary damages of plaintiff Emma McDougald, and as so modified, affirmed.

Case Questions

1. What seems to be the difference in purpose between compensatory damages and punitive damages?
2. What is the inherent weakness in nonpecuniary damages as compensation?
3. What would be required to allow recovery for hedonic losses in New York? Did Emma McDougald meet the test?

Case Glossary

pecuniary damages   Damages that can be measured in terms of cost in money, such as lost wages, medical expenses.

nothing to do with compensation and are a windfall to the plaintiff (after paying 30 or 40 percent of the award to the plaintiff's attorney, the windfall is likely to be erased).

Summary

Tort has traditionally been defined as "a private wrong not arising out of contract." This definition distinguishes between public wrongs, which are classified as crimes, and private wrongs, which are designed to redress wrongful conduct causing injury to a private party. The public prosecutor is responsible for bringing actions in criminal cases; private parties bring actions on their own behalf to redress a wrong. The definition also distinguishes between torts and contract causes of action. In contract, the legal obligations are created by mutual agreement of the parties; the law of contracts simply establishes the requisites for enforcement. In tort law, obligations are imposed by law. Tort law establishes protected private interests relating to person, property, reputation, and so on that are not premised on a contractual relationship, though one may exist (e.g., doctor–patient in medical malpractice).

There are numerous causes of action in tort, each having elements, each of which must be present for the court to accept a lawsuit based on a specific cause of action. However, tort law is a continually evolving field. New causes of action arise with some regularity, and courts exercise flexibility in allowing cases that do not fit into textbook definitions if conduct is clearly wrongful and injury is apparent.

Many factors influence the course of tort law independent of the interest sought to be protected. New law cannot be made by the courts unless disputes are brought, yet the economics of litigation usually influence which suits may be economically rewarding for a plaintiff.

Among the factors facilitating suit is the doctrine of respondeat superior, which holds an employer liable for the wrongful acts of an employee, thus making suits feasible when the wrongdoer/employee has limited funds and the employer has substantial resources. Similarly, the widespread use of insurance presents the opportunity for collecting full compensation for injuries sustained, which might not be possible if the defendant were uninsured and without assets.

In personal injury cases, customary practice includes the use of contingency fee arrangements whereby attorneys receive as their compensation a percentage of the settlement or award at the termination of the case. A great many cases could not be brought if the injured party were required to provide compensation to a lawyer as the case progressed.

Although these factors address practical questions, they affect the development of tort law, as certain sorts of cases are frequently pursued while others remain impractical.

Traditionally, the basis for requiring a defendant to compensate an injured plaintiff was fixing fault on the defendant for a wrongful act. The degree of fault required for a particular tort distinguishes between major categories of tort. The common element of intentional torts is an intentional act, whereas in negligence the standard is not what the defendant intended but the failure to act in a reasonable and prudent manner, the so-called "reasonable man" standard.

The relatively new field of product liability establishes liability without the necessity of proving fault. Manufacturers, in particular, are held liable for distributing dangerously defective products despite a lack of intent to harm or care in production. Although product liability has developed primarily over the last three decades, its roots can be found in much older theories of implied warranty and absolute liability for extrahazardous activities.

An important aspect of tort law is damages, or monetary compensation. Determining the amount of compensation depends on what can be included, but the object is to put the injured party in the position occupied before the wrongdoing occurred, that is, compensation for the difference in the plaintiff's life that the injury imposed. In some cases, punitive damages may be available to punish the wrongdoer. These go beyond actual compensation and require malicious or outrageous conduct on the part of the defendant.

Scenario

Northeastern Printing Corporation of Worcester, Massachusetts, was remodeling its old plant and hired Berkshire-Worcester Electric to rewire part of the plant for a computer laboratory. Berkshire assigned two of its electricians, Fitzgerald and Saltonstall, to complete the work. In the course of rewiring, the electricians drilled holes in the existing countertops, walls, and ceiling. Unbeknownst to them, the countertops contained asbestos fibers. Although the laboratory manager knew of this, he did not warn the workmen of it until they were almost finished and had not used protective gear. It is undisputed that they inhaled some dust containing asbestos fibers although the extent of exposure could not be established. It is also undisputed that the inhalation of asbestos fibers can lead to potentially lethal lung cancer. Expert witnesses testified that the likelihood of Fitzgerald and Saltonstall getting cancer from the asbestos was about one in one hundred and would probably not occur, if at all, for another twenty years (both were thirty-five years old).

Some eighteen months later, Fitzgerald and Saltonstall were examined by Dr. Nathaniel Hawthorne, to whom they had been referred by their attorney. Although Dr. Hawthorne concluded that neither had any asbestos-related disease, they sued Northeastern Printing for mental anguish damages caused by its having negligently exposed them to asbestos fibers.

Dr. Hawthorne testified that the two workmen had been injured by their exposure to asbestos and inhalation of asbestos fibers at the Northeastern Printing lab. He estimated that the chances of their developing a disease as a "high possibility" but not a probability.

Dr. Sigmund Jung, a noted psychiatrist, testified that the men were suffering serious mental distress due to fear of acquiring serious disease from the inhalation of asbestos fibers.

The trial court granted a summary judgment in favor of Northeastern Printing on the ground that Fitzgerald and Saltonstall had not suffered any injury for which they could recover mental anguish damages. (Northeastern Printing argued that plaintiffs' claims for fear of the mere possibility of developing some disease in the future amounted to nothing more than negligent infliction of emotional distress for which they could not recover. Plaintiffs responded that their inhalation of asbestos fibers was a real, physical injury that could eventually lead to disease, and that they were entitled to be compensated for their anxiety over that eventuality.)

The case is now on appeal to the Court of Appeals.

1. Make the argument appealing the summary judgment for plaintiff-appellants, Fitzgerald and Saltonstall.

2. Counter those arguments in behalf of Northeastern Printing.

3. How would you find as the court of appeals? Which argument is most compelling?

CONTRACTS AND COMMERCIAL LAW

Introduction

There are two fundamental, conflicting conceptions of contractual obligations. The earlier, pre-nineteenth century conception embodied equitable principles emphasizing fairness and concepts of property, especially relying on transfer of title. The nineteenth century gave rise to the modern law of contracts, in which the obligations of contracts were cast in the light of the agreement itself, the bargain relationship, and the intent of the parties.

executory contract
A contract that has not yet been fully performed; one that has been fully performed is an *executed* contract.

The title theory of exchange works well for the simultaneous exchange of things of fixed value, as when one pays for groceries at the supermarket. The will theory is more effective for **executory contracts,** that is, contracts relying on promises of future performance. For example, if a food processor contracts with farmers to buy crops for delivery at a fixed price in the future, principles of transfer of property rights at the making of the contract prove very awkward, whereas an examination of the bargain and the intent of the parties usually provides a basis for the enforcement of promises. The will theory is far more suitable for merchants and manufacturers in a commercial society and was gradually adopted by nineteenth-century courts, which viewed the encouragement of commerce and manufacturing as an important instrument of national growth.

A mechanical adherence to the will theory, however, encourages ruthless competition, so many of the adjustments to contract law in the twentieth century were designed to ensure fairness in the market and protection against unfair exploitation. Equitable concepts of fairness are used by the courts to prevent the excesses of the unscrupulous. In addition, legislatures have been active in passing laws, such as recent consumer-oriented legislation, to protect a vulnerable public.

Contract Law in Practice

Most contract obligations are discharged by performance of the parties according to the terms of the agreement. When full performance is not feasible, the parties usually compromise their differences without recourse to law or litigation. Except for the specialist in commercial litigation, lawyer and paralegal alike are most often concerned with making, rather than breaking, contracts. Aiding contract negotiation and drafting contracts constitute most of the work. Precision and clarity of language are the skills most needed for drafting and should be taught as part of a legal writing course (but often are not).

It may appear that we devote an inordinate amount of space in this chapter to contract formation and the conflicting principles that surround it. Although the approach here may seem unduly theoretical for a text for practitioners, the object is to avoid the morass of confusion presented by comprehensive contract texts and the omissions and simplifications of texts on business law.

Definition

Like so many legal concepts, contract is not easily defined. If, as Grant Gilmore has persuasively argued, contract is dead and is being reabsorbed into tort, present definitions may look silly to future generations. Nevertheless, there is a difference between tort and contract in determining obligations from mutual agreements of the parties as opposed to obligations imposed by the law of torts. Even this distinction becomes seriously blurred when a court imposes terms or conditions on parties that they never bargained for and never agreed to.

Tort and contract often overlap. In *Demakos*, a tenant sued a landlord for injuries incurred by other tenants and their visitors. The landlord sought recovery from his insurance company. Although insurance contracts are ordinarily construed in favor of the insured, when the language is clear it is given effect. In contracts, the rights and duties are created by agreement.

The important feature of contract law is not the contract itself, but the contractual relations it creates, and it is the regulation of relationships that is the subject of this chapter. If a court declares a contract void because one of the parties was coerced into agreement, it is saying something not about the nature of contracts but about the nature of contractual relationships. With this caveat in mind, let us look at some definitions of *contract*.

> A contract is a promise or set of promises for the breach of which the law gives a remedy, or the performance of which the law in some way recognizes as a duty.

George DEMAKOS, et al.,
Appellants,

v.

TRAVELERS INSURANCE COMPANY,
Respondent
Supreme Court, Appellate Division,
Second Department
613 N.Y.S.2d 709 (1994)

In an action, inter alia, for a judgment declaring the rights of the parties under a liability insurance policy, the plaintiffs appeal from an order and judgment (one paper) . . . which granted the motion of the defendant insurer for a declaration that it had no duty to defend or indemnify the plaintiffs in an underlying negligence action and to dismiss the plaintiffs' cause of action for damages.

ORDERED that the order and the judgment is affirmed, with costs.

After being sued by a tenant for physical injuries caused by cigarette smoke which allegedly seeped into the tenant's premises from the pool and billiard club in the basement of the building, the insured landlord sought coverage from the insurer under his business liability insurance policies. The insurer disclaimed, based on the pollution exclusion clauses in the policies. Thereafter, the insured brought the instant action. Upon the insurer's motion, the Supreme Court held that the language of the pollution exclusion was clear and unambiguous and that the complaint in the underlying personal injury action fell within the four corners of the exclusion. We agree.

The two identical exclusion clauses in the two policies in effect at the time stated that the insurer was not liable under the policy for any physical or property damage caused by pollutants. The policies also defined the term pollutant to include vapor, smoke, and fumes. The complaint in the underlying personal injury action alleged damages as a result of smoke and noxious fumes and vapors seeping through the basement. The exclusion is unambiguous, and the underlying complaint falls within the exclusion.

Case Questions

1. Why are insurance contracts construed in favor of the insured?
2. To what does the court look to determine what rights and duties are owed?

Restatement (Second) of Contracts § 1 (1981).

"Contract" means the total legal obligation which results from the parties' agreement as affected by this Act and any other applicable rules of law.

Uniform Commercial Code (UCC) § 1–201(11).

The *Restatement* takes the traditional view of contract as an exchange of promises (e.g., "I promise to pay you $10,000 if you promise to give me title to your automobile") that the law recognizes as enforceable. The UCC avoids promissory language and describes a contract as an enforceable agreement. At any rate, it is clear that individuals may make promises or agreements, some of which are legally enforceable and are called contracts.

The *Restatement* definition of contract reflects the will theory mentioned previously, which will henceforth be referred to as the *classical* approach to contracts, reflecting developments in contracts in the nineteenth and early twentieth centuries. It comprises what most legal practitioners need to know about contracts (along with the UCC) in order to draft contracts. Classical contract theory treats the essentials of contract formation in terms of discrete elements necessary to make a valid contract, namely, offer, acceptance, and consideration. It attempts to treat contract law as logical, precise, and self-contained.

Unfortunately, when the promises made at the formation stage are not fulfilled, issues of fairness and morality arise that are not so neatly resolved. A body of law that conflicts with classical theory has evolved to deal with contractual relations. This approach might be called the *moral* or *reliance theory* and is embodied in the somewhat obscure language of § 90 of the first *Restatement*:

> A promise which the promisor should reasonably expect to induce action or forbearance of a definite and substantial character on the part of the promisee and which does induce such action or forbearance is binding if injustice can be avoided only by enforcement of the promise.

In many cases, this principle allows the court to weigh the fairness of enforcement or nonenforcement of contract claims. Although theories of reliance and moral obligation may be of little significance in drafting contracts, they are important once a contract dispute arises. Failure to appreciate that there are two competing theories of contract inevitably leads to confusion. The classical model will be addressed with the issue of contract formation, and the reliance model will be introduced in connection with breach of contract and contract remedies.

Contract Formation: The Classical Model

The requirements of contract formation established in the nineteenth century cast the bargain relationship in idealized form. Parties to contracts were seen as individuals negotiating from equal positions of power, freely arriving at a "meeting of the minds," in which the agreement that constituted the contract was complete and its subject matter and terms were understood by both parties. When such was the case, if one of the parties failed to fulfill contractual promises, it would be necessary only for the court to apply the appropriate remedy for the injured party. Under this scheme, the court inquired into whether the elements of offer, acceptance, and consideration were present; it then interpreted the terms of the contract.

Offer

offer   The first of the three requirements of a traditional contract formation: *offer, acceptance,* and *consideration.*

Contract negotiations typically begin with an **offer;** the party making the offer is the *offeror.* The contract is not complete until an offer has been accepted by an *offeree.* An offer requires:

1. Intent to make an offer on the part of the offeror
2. Definite terms
3. Communication to the offeree

The failure of any of the requisites of an offer may nullify contract formation.

What appears to be an offer may fail because it lacks intent on the part of the offeror. Offers are often distinguished from invitations to negotiate or even solicitations for offers. "No reasonable offer refused," "Would you go as high as $1000?," or "I might sell it for as little as $500" are illusory offers in this category. The circumstances of the offer may also indicate that intent is lacking, as when the offer is made in jest, anger, or intoxication ("I'd sell that money-sucking car for two cents!"). The offeror's post hoc claim that a serious offer was not intended is not sufficient to avoid the contract; the test is whether a reasonable person would conclude from the circumstances that a serious offer had been made.

The offer may be made in terms so indefinite as to render the contract unenforceable; no meeting of the minds was present. Indefiniteness of price, for example, is usually fatal ("just pay me a fair price"). [The UCC takes exception to the indefinite price rule in the sale of goods when certain conditions are met. *See* UCC § 2–305.]

A valid and intended communication must be made to the offeree. The classic example in this category is the offer of a reward. Someone not aware of an offer of a reward who returns a lost dog is not legally entitled to the reward.

Acceptance

An offer does not bind the offeror until it is accepted by the offeree. Prior to **acceptance,** the offeror may revoke the offer, so acceptance subsequent to revocation does not bind the offeror. Acceptance requires:

1. Communication to the offeror
2. Acceptance of the terms of the offer

Because a valid acceptance creates a contract, it is essential that the acceptance be communicated to the offeror. Acceptance has traditionally been classified in two forms:

1. Acceptance by a return promise ("I will pay the $4,000 you are asking for your car")
2. Acceptance by performance required by the offer (acceptance of the offer of a reward for lost property is made by returning the property, not by promising to return the property)

When an offer calls for a return promise, it is called a **bilateral contract.** When the offer calls for acceptance in terms of performance, it is called a **unilateral contract.** Because most contracts are bilateral, it is important for the offeror who insists on performance (rather than a promise to perform) to make this condition quite clear. To "I will pay you $500 to clear my lot by Thursday, October 20" should be added "If you cannot finish by the end of Thursday, do not undertake the job because I will not pay."

The offeror is *master of the offer* and may set specific terms or manner of acceptance. When the offer is silent as to the manner of acceptance, the law has developed a complex set of rules governing the communication of acceptance, to which the UCC has made exceptions with regard to sales of goods.

acceptance
In contract law, the final act in concluding negotiations where an offeree accepts all the terms of the offer.

bilateral contract
A contract accepted by a return promise. It is an exchange of promises, supported by consideration. Compare to **unilateral contract.**

unilateral contract
A contract in which acceptance is accomplished by performance, for example, offer of a reward is acceptance by performing the reward request. Compare to **bilateral contract.**

A valid acceptance requires that the offeree agree to the specific terms of the offer. This is the so-called *mirror image rule*, which has been changed drastically for sales of goods covered by the UCC. If the offeree attempts to change the terms of the offer, the attempted acceptance will be treated as a counter offer rather than an acceptance, and the offeror and offeree change places. If the offeror offers to sell "my first edition of *Moby Dick* for $500," offeree's response of "I'll pay $400" is a counteroffer rather than an acceptance, and the purchaser has become the offeror and the owner the offeree ("I accept your offer of $400" would constitute acceptance and create a contract). Similarly, "I will pay $500 if you furnish a certificate of authenticity" is a counteroffer because it has added a term not present in the original offer.

The meeting-of-the-minds/mirror-image formula is technically simple, but transactions in the real world often defy its application. For example, in something as simple as the first edition sale, when the offeree appears with the personal check for $500, the offeror may insist on cash or a cashier's check. When they agreed on $500, did this mean "cash"? Can the offeror insist on cash? Does the offer to clear land "by" Thursday mean "before" Thursday (midnight Wednesday) or "on" Thursday (before Friday)? An apparent meeting of the minds rarely includes every last detail of performance, and the courts do not require perfection in offer and acceptance; but those who draft contracts must be particularly careful in the precision of their language and use their imaginations to include essential terms and conditions of the contract.

The goal of the attorney may conflict with that of the contracting parties. The attorney aims at protecting a client and providing a contract, the terms of which are sufficiently clear that litigation can be avoided, or if litigation is necessary, so that the court could apply the contract terms as originally intended. The contracting parties, in contrast, are interested in a mutually satisfactory result. Professor Stewart Macaulay has noted that businesspersons are often more concerned about flexibility, cooperation, and continuing good relations than they are about technical problems of contract law. A good legal team should not assume that contracting parties are adversaries—contract relations are ordinarily created because both sides have found a mutual benefit in working together.

If a contract is formed by a "meeting of the minds," what happens when one of the parties later claims the intentions were different? If anyone could avoid a contract simply by asserting a secret intent at the time of making the contract, no contract could be reliable. The courts have developed an "objective" standard for assessing the intent of the parties similar to the reasonable man standard of torts: What would a reasonable person have inferred from the circumstances and conduct of the parties? Such a standard was applied in *Lucy v. Zehmer.*

Consideration

consideration
A requirement in classical contract formation that consists of an exchange of something of value, although this may in some cases be largely symbolic.

Consideration is a somewhat anomalous requirement for contract formation. It is the symbolic proof that the contract was the result of bargaining. In its broadest conception, consideration is represented by the exchange of something of

W.O. LUCY and J.C. Lucy
v.
A.H. ZEHMER and Ida S. Zehmer
Supreme Court of Appeals of Virginia
196 Va. 493, 84 S.E.2d 516 (1954)

This suit was instituted by W.O. Lucy and J.C. Lucy, complainants, against A.H. Zehmer and Ida S. Zehmer, his wife, defendants, to have specific performance of a contract by which it was alleged the Zehmers had sold to W.O. Lucy a tract of land owned by A.H. Zehmer in Dinwiddie county containing 471.6 acres, more or less, known as the Ferguson farm for $50,000. J.C. Lucy, the other complainant, is a brother of W.O. Lucy, to whom W.O. Lucy transferred a half interest in his alleged purchase.

The instrument sought to be enforced was written by A.H. Zehmer on December 20, 1952, in these words: "We hereby agree to sell to W.O. Lucy the Ferguson Farm complete for $50,000, title satisfactory to buyer," and signed by the defendants, A.H. Zehmer and Ida S. Zehmer.

The answer of A.H. Zehmer admitted that at the time mentioned W.O. Lucy offered him $50,000 cash for the farm, but that he, Zehmer, considered that the offer was made in jest; that so thinking, and both he and Lucy having had several drinks, wrote out "the memorandum quoted above and induced his wife to sign it; that he did not deliver the memorandum to Lucy, but that Lucy picked it up, read it, put it in his pocket, attempted to offer Zehmer $5 to bind the bargain, which Zehmer refused to accept, and realizing for the first time that Lucy was serious, Zehmer assured him that he had no intention of selling the farm and that the whole matter was a joke. Lucy left the premises insisting that he had purchased the farm.

* * *

The defendants insist that the evidence was ample to support their contention that the writing sought to be enforced was prepared as a bluff or dare to force Lucy to admit that he did not have $50,000; that the whole matter was a joke; that the writing was not delivered to Lucy and no binding contract was ever made between the parties.

It is an unusual, if not bizarre, defense. When made to the writing admittedly prepared by one of the defendants and signed by both clear evidence is required to sustain it.

In his testimony Zehmer claimed that he "was high as a Georgia pine," and that the transaction "was just a bunch of two doggoned drunks bluffing to see who could talk the biggest and say the most." That claim is inconsistent with his attempt to testify in great detail to what was said and what was done. It is contradicted by other evidence as to the condition of both parties, and rendered of no weight by the testimony of his wife that when Lucy left the restaurant she suggested that Zehmer drive him home. The record is convincing that Zehmer was not intoxicated to the extent of being unable to comprehend the nature and consequences of the instrument he executed, and hence that instrument is not to be invalidated on that ground. It was in fact conceded by defendants' counsel in oral argument that under the evidence Zehmer was not too drunk to make a valid contract.

The evidence is convincing also that Zehmer wrote two agreements, the first one beginning "I hereby agree to sell." Zehmer first said he could not remember about that, then that "I don't think I wrote but one out." Mrs. Zehmer said that what he wrote was "I hereby agree," but that the "I" was changed to "We" after that night. The agreement that was written and signed is in the record and indicates no such change. Neither are the mistakes in spelling that Zehmer sought to point out readily apparent.

The appearance of the contract, the fact that it was under discussion for forty minutes or more before it was signed; Lucy's objection to the first draft because it was written in the singular, and he wanted Mrs. Zehmer to sign it also; the rewriting to meet that objection and the signing by Mrs. Zehmer; the discussion of what was to be included in the sale, the provision for the examination of the title, the completeness of the instrument that was executed, the taking possession of it by Lucy with no request or suggestion by either of the defendants that he give it back, are facts which furnish persuasive evidence that the execution of the contract was a serious business transaction rather than a casual, jesting matter as defendants now contend.

* * *

If it be assumed, contrary to what we think the evidence shows, that Zehmer was jesting about selling his farm to Lucy and that the transaction was intended by him to be a joke, nevertheless the evidence shows that Lucy did not understand it but considered it to be a serious business transaction and the contract to be binding on the Zehmers as well as on himself. The very next day he arranged with his brother to put up half the money and take a half interest in the land. The day after that he employed an attorney to examine the title. The next night, Tuesday, he was back at Zehmer's place and there Zehmer told him for the first time, Lucy said, that he wasn't going to sell and he told Zehmer. "You know you sold that place fair and square." After receiving the report from his attorney that the title was good he wrote to Zehmer that he was ready to close the deal.

Not only did Lucy actually believe, but the evidence shows he was warranted in believing, that the contract represented a serious business transaction and a good faith sale and purchase of the farm.

In the field of contract, as generally elsewhere, "We must look to the outward expression of a person as manifesting his intention rather than to his secret and unexpressed intention. 'The law imputes to a person an intention corresponding to the reasonable meaning of his words and acts.' "

* * *

"The law, therefore, judges of an agreement between two persons exclusively from those expressions of their intentions which are communicated between them.". . . [T]he law imputes to a person an intention corresponding to the reasonable meaning of his words and acts. . . . [I]t is immaterial what may be the real but unexpressed state of his mind.

So a person cannot set up that he was merely jesting when his conduct and words would warrant a reasonable person in believing that he intended a real agreement.

Whether the writing signed by the defendant and now sought to be enforced by the complainants was the result of a serious offer by Lucy and a serious acceptance by the defendants, or was a serious offer by Lucy and an acceptance in secret jest by the defendants, in either event it constituted a binding contract of sale between the parties.

* * *

The complainants are entitled to have specific performance of the contract sued on. . . .

Reversed and remanded.

Case Questions

1. Zehmer had bought the farm eleven years before for $11,000 and had refused an offer seven years prior by Lucy for $20,000. If the contract had been for $10,000, would the court have enforced it? Why, or why not?
2. What if Lucy had known the contract was a joke but proceeded as if it had not been? How might the facts have been different?
3. Could Zehmer have succeeded if he argued that he was drunk at the time claiming intoxication as a defense?

value. Many form contracts include a pro forma recital of consideration, typically one dollar or ten dollars, to satisfy the consideration requirement. Although this is artificial and often illusory (no money actually changes hands), many courts developed the doctrine that the sufficiency of consideration is not to be questioned.

The bargain aspect of consideration is exemplified by § 71 of the *Restatement:* "To constitute consideration, a performance or a return promise must be bargained for." The "something of value" may simply be a return promise. The original purpose of consideration appears to have been the refusal to enforce promises of gifts when the promisee does nothing in return. If Grandmother says to Grandson, "When you reach 25, I'll give you $10,000," and Grandson replies, "I'll be glad to receive it," the appearance is that of acceptance; but when Grandmother's junk bonds become worth twenty cents on the dollar, the court is loath to enforce the agreement, arguing that Grandson neither conferred a benefit on Grandmother nor suffered a "detriment" by forbearing to do something he was entitled to do, so there was no consideration on his part for the contract. In contrast, when Uncle promised Nephew $5,000 on his twenty-fifth birthday if until that time Nephew would refrain from drinking and smoking, the court may find consideration, in that Nephew suffered a legal detriment by forbearing doing something he had a legal right to do. Courts have on occasion found consideration based on "love and affection" to support the promise of a gift when a relative has provided aid and support. It would seem that the courts have attempted to avoid unfairness by invoking the existence of consideration or its absence and have stretched logic to justify their conclusions. Any other explanation suggests a logic and consistency to the concept of consideration that is not corroborated by the cases.

Love and affection have on occasion been construed to be consideration to support enforcement of a contract between persons in close relationships, even though material consideration is lacking. The *Rose* court, however, was unwilling to find consideration on this basis.

Consideration is an artificial legal concept rarely of concern to those engaged in the bargaining relationship. Gilmore traces the rise of the concept to Holmes's *The Common Law,* where it appears mysteriously without authority. The effect of the consideration requirement is to negate many contracts that would be enforceable without it. It is a device that can be used by a court to declare that contract formation was flawed and therefore unenforceable. It is probably of little practical importance to the attorney except as a strategy on behalf of a client trying to avoid enforcement of a contract. Nevertheless, when custom dictates a recital of consideration, it is wise to follow established practice.

Consideration is important in option contracts. Because offers may be revoked prior to acceptance, one way to keep an offer open is to pay for it. A person may purchase an option on land, for example—by paying $1,000 for an option to purchase land for $50,000 before January 1. In this way, the offer to sell the land may not be revoked until the expiration of the option (January 1).

Leah ROSE, Plaintiff-Appellant,

v.

Samuel ELIAS, Defendant-Respondent

Supreme Court, Appellate Division,

First Department

177 A.D.2d 415, 576 N.Y.S.2d 257 (1991)

Order . . . entered May 14, 1990, which granted defendant's motion to dismiss the complaint for failure to state a cause of action, unanimously affirmed, without costs.

Defendant, a married man, promised in writing to purchase an apartment for the plaintiff, his female companion, in return for the "love and affection" that she provided to him during the prior three years. We agree with the [lower] court that the love and affection provided by plaintiff were insufficient consideration for defendant's promise to purchase an apartment for her.

Nor is a cause of action stated by virtue of plaintiff's claim that she forbore job opportunities at defendant's oral request, since defendant's written promise to provide an apartment for plaintiff was unambiguous and complete, and it is apparent that the parties did not view plaintiff's forbearance from accepting job opportunities as consideration for the promise. " 'Nothing is consideration . . . that is not regarded as such by both parties.' "

The defendant asserted that his relationship with the plaintiff was primarily a sexual relationship, and plaintiff did not deny that sexual relations were a part of the relationship. Plaintiff admitted that the proposed purchase of an apartment was intended to facilitate a "comfortable" life together with the defendant. "Agreements tending to dissolve a marriage or to facilitate adultery are closely scrutinized to determine whether the main objective of the agreement is aimed to produce that result." The [lower] court concluded that the words "love and affection" in the circumstances presented suggest adultery, and thus illegal consideration. Since there was found to be no severable legal component of the consideration for defendant's promise, the court correctly ruled in the alternative that the contract was void as against public policy.

We have considered plaintiff's arguments based on theories of estoppel and unjust enrichment, and find them to be without merit.

Case Questions

1. Is there more here than a promise to make a gift?
2. How critical to this decision is the fact that defendant was married?

Because consideration has been paid, a contract has been formed. Of course, if January 1 passes without action, the contract ends, as do the duties of the parties.

Limitations on Contract Formation

Even when offer, acceptance, and consideration are present, the law will not recognize a contract if the bargaining process was flawed by misconduct (fraud, misrepresentation, duress, or undue influence), defect in agreement (mistake), the incapacity of one of the parties (minority or mental incompetence), or illegal purpose. In addition, the law requires that certain contracts must be in writing to be enforceable (Statute of Frauds). Each of these is treated in summary fashion here.

fraud (contract)
A contract induced by intentionally false misrepresentations is voidable for *fraud*.

misrepresentation
May be an innocent false representation and still be voidable by the person to whom the false representation was made.

rescind To annul or cancel a contract, putting the parties back in the position they were in before, as if no contract had been made.

voidable Describes a contract that the innocent party (the other party having contracted wrongfully in certain recognized ways) may avoid by returning to the conditions prior to the agreement.

duress When one party to a contract is threatened with harm to induce agreement.

undue influence
When a contract is induced by relentless pressure, especially from a confidential relationship.

mistake of fact
In contract formation, makes the contract voidable; one or both parties believe some essential fact about the transaction to be other than it really is.

emancipated minor
A person under the age of majority who is totally self-supporting or married; varies by state.

Contract Induced by Misconduct of One of the Parties

Although parties have great latitude in the promises they exchange in a bargaining relationship, the absence of a bargain may be found if one of the parties was deceived as to the bargain or deprived of free will in bargaining.

Fraud and **misrepresentation** are generally distinguished on the basis of intentional false representations (fraud) and innocent false representations (misrepresentation). If a used car dealer sells a 1979 model as a 1980 model, while knowing it to be a 1979 model, it would be fraud; if the dealer believed it to be a 1980 model, it would be misrepresentation. In either case, the innocent party should have the option to accept the contract or to **rescind** it, returning the car and receiving the return of payments made. Such contracts are **voidable**, meaning the innocent party may avoid the contract by returning to the conditions prior to the agreement. This is distinguished from contracts that are *void* (see "Illegality," later in this section).

A contract is also voidable if it can be shown that one of the parties could not exercise free will in the bargaining process (duress). **Duress** occurs when one party is threatened with harm to induce agreement. The threatened harm is ordinarily physical or emotional harm directed against the party, the party's family, or the party's property. Usually economic pressure is not sufficient to constitute duress, nor is the threat to bring lawsuit ("If you don't sell, I'll foreclose").

Undue influence occurs when relentless pressure so weakens a party's will that the bargain is not freely obtained. Undue influence also occurs when the parties have a confidential relationship such as close family relations, attorney-client, physician-patient, or the like.

Mistake

Mutual, or bilateral, **mistake of fact** makes the contract voidable by either party. For example, in one famous case, the violinist Efrem Zimbalist purchased two violins believed by both purchaser and seller to have been made by Guarnerius and Stradivarius. Zimbalist was able to void the contract when the violins proved to be nearly worthless. This example somewhat oversimplifies the complex and confusing area of mistake.

Lack of Capacity to Form a Contract

Lack of capacity may be due to lack of legal competence based on status (minor), lack of mental capacity to form contracts, or temporary incapacitation (intoxication).

In most states, the age of majority is eighteen. Until reaching the age of majority, persons are not legally competent, which includes an incapacity to bind themselves contractually. Exceptions are sometimes made for **emancipated minors.** Contracts with minors may be avoided by the minor, but can be **ratified** upon reaching the age of majority. Contracts for "necessaries," such as food and clothing, are usually enforceable against minors.

ratify   When one
suffering a disability
approves a contract
after the disability has
terminated; for example,
a minor reaches age
of majority and agrees
to a contract made when
a minor.

The invalidity of contracts involving lack of mental capacity is based on the notion that lack of capacity prevents an individual from understanding the bargain. A person may display peculiarities that indicate mental illness yet understand fully the subject matter and obligations entered into by contract, in which case the contract may not be avoided. A person determined to be mentally incompetent by legal authority is not legally competent, and contracts with such persons are in some states void from their inception.

Inability to understand the nature and purpose of contractual obligations may also be established by the intoxication of one of the parties at the time the contract was formed. Intoxication includes all drugs that affect one's mental state and ability to understand the consequences of the bargain. The intoxicated person may later affirm or disaffirm the contract. There is significant variation among jurisdictions as to proof and legal effect of intoxication.

There is a story about Sophocles, the great dramatist of ancient Athens, who had amassed significant wealth from prizes for his plays. When he reached the ripe old age of eighty, his children, then in their fifties, grew tired of waiting for their inheritance and brought Sophocles before the court of Athenian citizens to have him declared senile so that they could manage his wealth. As his only defense, Sophocles read to those assembled a play he had just written. The jury found him to be of sound mind, and his children had to wait another ten years to collect their inheritance. Sophocles would undoubtedly have enjoyed the result in the *Hanks* case.

Illegality

Agreements to do an unlawful act, including tortious as well as criminal acts, or for an unlawful purpose, are deemed void by the courts and will not be enforced. A number of problems, such as what exactly is unlawful and how to handle a contract that is in part unlawful and in part lawful, have had different results in different jurisdictions.

Statute of Frauds

Statute of Frauds
An ancient doctrine that
requires that certain
contracts be in writing
and signed.

An oral contract binds the parties as much as a written one, though a written contract provides more certain evidence of the terms of a contract than personal recollection of what was orally agreed. In 1677 the **Statute of Frauds** was enacted, making certain contracts unenforceable unless written. In 1677 the law of contracts was poorly developed, as were the laws of evidence and proof; the statute was an attempt to prevent fraudulent abuse of legal process. The Statute of Frauds remained largely intact during the creation of American law, often with only minor modifications. Although the statute identified five categories in which a written contract was required, two remain of major importance in the practice of law: (1) contracts for the conveyance of interests in land; (2) contracts not to be performed within one year. The UCC has created its own version of the Statute of Frauds, requiring certain contracts be in writing, the

HANKS
v.
McNEIL COAL CORPORATION et al.
Colorado Supreme Court
114 Colo. 578, 168 P.2d 256 (1946)

Lee A. Hanks, who was a prosperous farmer and businessman in Nebraska, came to Colorado with his family in 1918, at first settling on a farm in Weld county, which included the coal lands involved in this proceeding; then, in 1920 moving to Boulder where he purchased a home, engaged in the retail coal business, and thereafter resided. . . . Shortly after 1922 Lee Hanks discovered that he was afflicted with diabetes, and members of his family noticed a progressive change in his physical and mental condition thereafter. He became irritable and easily upset, very critical of his son's work, and increasingly interested in the emotional type of religion. He began to speculate in oil and other doubtful ventures with money needed for payment of debts and taxes. About 1934 he sent his son what he denominated a secret formula for the manufacture of medicine to cure fistula in horses, which was compounded principally of ground china, brick dust, burnt shoe leather and amber-colored glass. If the infection was in the horse's right shoulder, the mixture was to be poured in the animal's left ear, and if on the left shoulder then in the right ear. In 1937 Mr. Hanks started to advertise this medicine through the press under the name of Crown King Remedy. Thereafter he increasingly devoted his efforts and money to the com-

pounding and attempted sale of this concoction, his business judgment became poor and he finally deteriorated mentally to the point that on May 25, 1940, he was adjudicated insane and his son was appointed conservator of his estate.

[Before being adjudicated insane, in 1937, Hanks sold property to the coal company, which he had learned was hauling coal over his lands. His son, the conservator of his estate brought this suit to avoid the contract.]

. . . The legal test of Hanks' insanity is whether "he was incapable of understanding and appreciating the extent and effect of business transactions in which he engaged."

. . . One may have insane delusions regarding some matters and be insane on some subjects, yet capable of transacting business concerning matters wherein such subjects are not concerned, and such insanity does not make one incompetent to contract unless the subject matter of the contract is so connected with an insane delusion as to render the afflicted party incapable of understanding the nature and effect of the agreement or of acting rationally in the transaction.

. . . Patently Hanks was suffering from insane delusion in 1937 with reference to the efficacy of the horse medicine, but there is no evidence of delusions or hallucinations in connection with this transaction or with his transaction of much of his other business at that time; there is no basis for holding voidable his sale here involved on the ground of his insanity.

Case Questions
1. What difference would it have made if Hanks had been adjudicated insane prior to the sale?
2. Of what significance was the horse medicine?

most notable of which covers the sale of goods for more than $500 and the sale of other forms of personal property valued at more than $5,000.

Today the Statute of Frauds can actually invite fraud, as, for instance, when a person attempts to avoid an obligation by invoking the statute while at the same time benefiting from another's performance. The courts have displayed considerable creativity in getting around the statute when the interests of justice are not served by strict adherence to it.

Compensatory Damages for Breach of Contract

Because contract law is modeled largely on business relations, and contractual relations are created by the parties to the contract, the remedy for breach of contract is quite different from that in tort. Injuries that are not foreseeable or not within the contemplation of the parties are not a usual element of compensatory damages. Physical or emotional injuries are not recoverable except where tort principles have invaded contract territory (e.g., malpractice and products liability).

The overriding policy in compensatory damages for breach of contract is to put the "nonbreaching party in the position he would have been in had the contract been performed." This may include lost profits if they are roughly ascertainable and within the contemplation of the parties. It may mean paying the cost of completion, as with unfinished construction contracts, or cost of replacement, or the difference between contract price and market price. Damages are often rephrased as "giving the nonbreaching party the benefit of his bargain." Several different measures of damages have developed for different categories of contracts, and the Uniform Commercial Code provides its own special rules. The diversity of rules is designed to ensure that the nonbreaching party does not suffer a loss or enjoy a windfall. Although breach represents the fault aspect of contract law, the breaching party is to be protected rather than penalized (punitive damages are rare in contract cases).

This brief summary of damages ignores numerous complicating factors, such as **anticipatory breach, substantial performance,** and cases in which both parties breach, which are normally covered in some detail in contract and business law texts.

Problems with the Classical Model

Classical contract theory, which developed during the period before and after the turn of the century, constructed a logical set of rules based on offer, acceptance, and consideration for the formation of contract and compensatory damages for the resolution of contract disputes. This scheme is satisfactory for a great many contracts, but the diversity of contract relationships creates a variety of situations that defy mechanical solutions:

1. *A person promises to make a gift.* A brother offers his sister the free use of his second home on a permanent basis. She sells her own house and moves her belongings and family. Brother later gets a good offer on the house and reneges on his promise. Under classical consideration principles, the sister has no enforceable contract rights.

anticipatory breach When one party to a contract expresses an intention not to perform; the other party may then treat the contract as *breached*, pursuing an appropriate remedy, rather than wait for performance.

substantial performance When one party has attempted to complete performance in good faith, but a minor variance from the specific terms of the contract has occurred. Under the equitable principle of *substantial performance*, the court may enforce the contract, possibly reducing the payment for performance because of the minor breach.

2. *Charitable pledges.* A church solicits pledges from its parishioners to build a new annex, then enters into a building contract. Was there consideration to support enforcing the pledges?

3. *Confidential professional relationships.* Doctor and patient enter a contract for treatment, but the treatment is negligently performed. Compensatory damages for breach of contract do not compensate for the injuries sustained.

4. *Indefinite oral contracts.* Buyer and seller agree to transfer title to an automobile, but time and place of performance are not mentioned.

5. *Unilateral contracts requiring performance as acceptance when promisee has begun to perform and promisor revokes the offer.* Property owner offers $2,500 to roofer when roof is completed to "owner's satisfaction." Roofer moves trucks and men out to do the work, only to find that owner has hired someone else.

6. *Contracts in which the parties leave the details to be worked out later.*

7. *Performance without a contract.* Contractor blacktops the wrong driveway while owner stands by and watches silently, later disclaiming any liability in the absence of a contract.

8. *Contracts for which compensatory damages create an unfair result.* Seller of house lot refuses to deliver deed as required by contract because a second buyer has offered a higher price. First buyer's costs attributable to the breach of contract are minimal.

9. *Inducements to contract cause a party to incur costs relying on the inducement, but the contract is never completed.* Offer of hardware franchise induces potential franchisee to sell business at loss and work as manager/ trainee to learn business. Franchisor later refuses to enter contract.

10. *Strict adherence to the Statute of Frauds will have grossly unfair results.* Seller and buyer agree orally to transfer land for a fixed price. Buyer clears the land and puts in a foundation for a house, and seller decides not to sell. Under the statute, the contract is unenforceable.

11. *Manufacturer claims no responsibility for person injured by a product because purchaser bought the product from a dealer and had no contractual relation with manufacturer.*

Fault

Historically, judges were naturally reluctant to leave an innocent injured party without a remedy. This presented no problem if the contract was clearly enforceable and one party had breached. If a damages remedy fully compensated the injured party, an easy and just result was available. The breaching party was at fault under contract law, and liability was fixed. In many cases, such as those previously listed, contract principles were unavailing. Judges employed a number of devices to avoid unjust results, some of them old, notably equitable remedies and principles; some of them new; and some of them fictitious.

When fault under common-law contract theory was unworkable, the courts frequently resorted to the developing law of torts. Negligence theory provided a ready remedy for professional malpractice, especially medical malpractice, where compensatory contract damages were inappropriate because the injury was not loss of profits but disability, death, or pain and suffering. The duty of due care was imposed by law rather than by contract, so these cases jumped the fence from contract to tort at an early date without much resistance from the courts. The foreseeability of serious injury from medical malpractice, viewed either from a contract or a tort law perspective, gives strength to the imposition of liability. A high standard of professional care also places the burden on the physician in the doctor-patient relationship, a standard easily implied to the contract.

The shift of products liability from contract to tort was more tortuous (forgive the pun). Although Justice Traynor finally justified the imposition of tort liability for defective products on policy grounds (see Chapter 10), his landmark decision in *Greenman v. Yuba Power Products* rested on a line of cases developed from Judge Cardozo's opinion in *MacPherson v. Buick Motor Co.*, 217 N.Y. 382, 111 N.E. 105 (1916), dispensing with the **privity of contract** requirement and holding the manufacturer as well as the dealer liable. Products liability ultimately rested on the principle of implied warranty, the law imposing duties beyond the express terms of the contract. Although product liability is said to be strict liability without the need to prove fault, the plaintiff must show that the product was "dangerously defective when it left the manufacturer" and that the user was using the product in the manner for which it was designed. In many cases, the plaintiff's burden of proof is not significantly less than showing a manufacturer's negligence.

In other cases, fault in the sense of a legal wrong (e.g., breach of contract, tortious conduct) may be absent, but concepts of commercial morality, such as "good faith," present convenient analogies.

Deceptive Practices

Unscrupulous businesses are very inventive in seducing the innocent consumer into agreements with obscure provisions, penalties, and duties. Most consumers are confronted frequently with contracts that have confusing fine print, often in quite simple transactions where costs appear to be standard and reasonable. While we may not be especially sympathetic to the consumer who signs without reading, neither are we sympathetic to the business that crafts contracts that are indecipherable or misleading, even if they do not contain intentional misrepresentations. Form contracts that do not allow change or negotiation are called **contracts of adhesion** and are viewed skeptically by the courts and interpreted against the party who makes the form and all its terms. Some practices

privity of contract
The relationship between two parties to a contract. Originally, this was a bar to a suit brought by a consumer against a manufacturer when the consumer bought through a dealer and directly from the manufacturer. Modern product liability law does away with this impediment.

contracts of adhesion Contracts in which all the bargaining power (and the contract terms) favor one side, often when the seller uses a pre-printed form contract to unfair advantage.

aimed at deceiving the public have become so common that state legislatures have often passed laws to protect the consumer against unfair business practices that might otherwise stand up in court. The *Hertz* case invokes California statutes specifically designed to protect consumers renting automobiles. Rental car companies are engaged in a highly competitive business in which basic rental rates are advertised in open competition. In order to make a profit, these companies often attempt to exact charges in addition to the advertised rate. The *Hertz* case involves the charges for filling the gas tank after return of the car. An exorbitant rate was charged, which apparently angered one man enough to bring a lawsuit and an appeal.

Peter SCHNALL
v.
The HERTZ Corporation
Court Of Appeal Of California
78 Cal. App. 4th 1144 (2000)

[Appellant's] chief allegation was that, because Hertz's fuel service charge was "excessive and punitive," the rental agreement was unlawful, unfair and fraudulent within the meaning of the unfair competition law (Bus. & Prof. Code, § 17200) (hereafter the UCL) and an unconscionable contract of adhesion that was void as a matter of law. He alleged as well that, apart from the amount of the fuel service charge, provisions of the rental agreement purporting to disclose the charge were incomprehensible and misleading and also constituted an unfair and fraudulent practice under the UCL. Hertz demurred. . . .The trial court sustained the demurrer without leave to amend and entered judgment for Hertz. . . .

. . . In 1995 appellant rented a car from Hertz in New York City for approximately one day. Like all renters, he was provided a car containing a full tank of gas. The standard rental agreement he signed required him to choose at the commencement of the rental whether to purchase fuel from Hertz. . . .

The first option, which was selected by appellant and members of the class he purports to represent and is most directly at issue, is not to purchase fuel from Hertz at the commencement of the rental. If the customer makes this choice and returns the car with a tank as full as when it was delivered, no fuel service charge is imposed. If, however, a renter who selects this option returns the car with less than a full tank, Hertz imposes a charge for fuel and the service of refueling. The amount charged for this service is not disclosed in the rental agreement itself; paragraph 8 simply indicates that the fuel service charge will be based on a "per mile" or "per gallon" rate "specified in the Rental Record." The "Rental Record," which is not described in the rental agreement, is a small single-page computer print-out containing a list of optional services, each designated by abbreviation, together with an indication of which, if any, the renter has "declined."

The complaint alleges that both the per mile and per gallon rates result in a fuel service charge that is "in excess of two and one half times the prevailing average retail price of fuel." . . .

Appellant's first cause of action rests on section 17200 of the Business and Professions Code, the core provision of the UCL. . . . [A]s relevant here, it defines "unfair competition" to include "any unlawful, unfair or fraudulent business act or practice.". . .

Civil Code section 1936 was primarily designed to protect consumers against rental car company overcharges for collision damage waivers. . . . However, subdivision (m)(2) of section 1936—the provision with which we are here primarily concerned—does permit a rental car company to impose additional charges for optional services if the renter knows the charge is avoidable. In material part, subdivision (m)(2) provides as follows: "In addition to the rental rate, taxes and mileage charge, if any, a rental company may charge for an item or service provided in connection with a particular rental transaction *if the renter could have avoided incurring the charge by choosing not to obtain or utilize the optional item or service*". . . .

[Although the contract expressed the avoidability of incurring the refueling charge, it did not give any indication of the cost. Hertz argues that this satisfies the language of the statute and provides it with a "safe harbor." The court agrees that Hertz is protected by this against the simple claim that the charges were exorbitant.]

. . . Fuel service charges imposed under paragraph 8 of Hertz's rental agreement are in our view avoidable within the meaning of subdivision (m)(2) and therefore lawful.

This is not, however, the end of the matter. . . . The second UCL claim we must proceed to examine is that Hertz misleads its customers by deceptively concealing or obscuring the amount of its fuel service charge, and that this conduct is both "unfair" and "fraudulent" under the UCL. . . .

. . . According to the complaint, the practice consists of (1) "purposefully crafting the refueling formulas in the Rental Agreement so that they are incomprehensible to plaintiff and each Class member, especially given the circumstances of the typical four-minute rental transaction"; and (2) "purposefully not including Hertz's actual price per gallon refueling charge in the Rental Agreement, thereby making it even less apparent to the plaintiff and each member of the Class."

The fact that the per gallon rate is not disclosed in the rental agreement but only in the rental record, a small and hard-to-read document consisting for the most part of indecipherable abbreviations, may be indicative of an intent to conceal this important information.

. . . Given the inexplicable use of two different rates to calculate the fuel service charge, and the needlessly complex language in the rental agreement relating to the application of those rates, it would not be surprising if many renters erroneously assumed not only that the per mile rate applies but that it produces a lower fuel service charge, which could be costly mistakes.

The record before us also does not disclose why the per gallon rate—the most useful information to customers who must decide whether to accept the responsibility to refill the tank and, if so, whether to actually do so—is not forthrightly provided. The confusing provisions of the rental agreement and rental record just described, which are very different from the much clearer capitalized language in the agreement describing the conduct that will result in a fuel service charge, appear to violate fundamental rules of honesty and fair dealing. . . .

. . . Since subdivision (m)(2) does not provide Hertz a "safe harbor" against the allegations that it confuses and misleads customers in violation of the "unfair" and "fraud" prongs of the UCL, these allegations sufficiently state a claim under the UCL. . . . For the foregoing reasons, the judgment dismissing the complaint is reversed. Appellant is awarded his costs on appeal.

Case Questions

1. Is the fuel charge unenforceable because it is unreasonable?
2. What would the result have been if the fuel service charge had been 15 percent more than the market price for fuel?

Equitable Remedies

When compensatory damages are inadequate, equitable remedies may be available. Some exist as alternative remedies if certain defects in contract formation can be shown (rescission and reformation). Others ask for something other than money (specific performance and injunctive relief).

Rescission and Reformation

rescission Aims at destroying the contract and its obligations, putting the parties back in their positions prior to the agreement; see **rescind**.

reformation Aims at correcting a contract to reflect the actual intention of the parties.

Rescission aims at destroying the contract and its obligations and putting the parties back in their positions prior to the agreement. Grounds for rescission are defects in formation already mentioned: illegality, undue influence, insanity, and so on. **Reformation** aims at correcting the contract to reflect the actual intent of the parties, usually where mutual mistake exists.

As we have seen in the discussion of equity in Chapter 6, when a court is exercising its equitable jurisdiction, it enjoys considerable discretion to do justice to the parties. Equity is particularly interesting in contract actions because the relationships between contracting parties and their circumstances present every conceivable possibility. Unusual cases call for equitable remedies such as rescission. What should happen when an innocent purchaser buys a haunted house, the unfortunate character of which is known to everyone except the out-of-town purchaser? Just such a situation presented itself in *Stambovsky v. Ackley*. The ancient principle of *caveat emptor*, "let the buyer beware," urges the purchaser to check out his purchase at his peril, but who asks the realtor whether the house on the market is haunted? Nevertheless, one expects the court to be reluctant to acknowledge the "phantasmal" character of property or give any relief. Yet *Stambovsky* resulted in a 3–2 split among the judges on this question (the dissent is omitted). The case presents interesting questions of equity, contract, and property law.

Specific Performance

Specific performance asks the court to order the breaching party to perform rather than compensate, that is, to deliver the goods or the deed to real property. This remedy is available when goods are unique, such as a Stradivarius violin (land is always considered unique, hence the availability of specific performance for enforcing real property sales contracts). This remedy, however, is premised on a valid contract and does not cure formation and consideration problems.

Injunctive Relief

Injunctive relief is sometimes available to order someone not to do something that is prohibited by a contract (e.g., to prevent someone from building a

Jeffrey M. STAMBOVSKY

v.

Helen V. ACKLEY

Supreme Court of New York, Appellate Division, First Department

169 A.D.2d 254; 572 N.Y.S.2d 672; (N.Y. App. Div. 1991)

Plaintiff, to his horror, discovered that the house he had recently contracted to purchase was widely reputed to be possessed by poltergeists, reportedly seen by defendant seller and members of her family on numerous occasions over the last nine years. Plaintiff promptly commenced this action seeking rescission of the contract of sale. Supreme Court reluctantly dismissed the complaint, holding that plaintiff has no remedy at law in this jurisdiction.

The unusual facts of this case, as disclosed by the record, clearly warrant a grant of equitable relief to the buyer who, as a resident of New York City, cannot be expected to have any familiarity with the folklore of the Village of Nyack. Not being a "local," plaintiff could not readily learn that the home he had contracted to purchase is haunted. Whether the source of the spectral apparitions seen by defendant seller are parapsychic or psychogenic, having reported their presence in both a national publication (*Readers' Digest*) and the local press (in 1977 and 1982, respectively), defendant is **estopped** to deny their existence and, as a matter of law, the house is haunted. More to the point, however, no divination is required to conclude that it is defendant's promotional efforts in publicizing her close encounters with these spirits which fostered the home's reputation in the community. . . . The impact of the reputation thus created goes to the very essence of the bargain between the parties, greatly impairing both the value of the property and its potential for resale. . . .

While I agree with Supreme Court that the real estate broker, as agent for the seller, is under no duty to disclose to a potential buyer the phantasmal reputation of the premises and

that, in his pursuit of a legal remedy for fraudulent misrepresentation against the seller, plaintiff hasn't a ghost of a chance, I am nevertheless moved by the spirit of equity to allow the buyer to seek rescission of the contract of sale and recovery of his down payment. . . .

. . . New York adheres to the doctrine of caveat emptor and imposes no duty upon the vendor to disclose any information concerning the premises [with exceptions, especially affirmative misrepresentation].

Caveat emptor is not so all-encompassing a doctrine of common law as to render every act of nondisclosure immune from redress, whether legal or equitable. . . . Where fairness and common sense dictate that an exception should be created, the evolution of the law should not be stifled by rigid application of a legal maxim.

The doctrine of caveat emptor requires that a buyer act prudently to assess the fitness and value of his purchase. . . . It should be apparent, however, that the most meticulous inspection and the search would not reveal the presence of poltergeists at the premises or unearth the property's ghoulish reputation in the community. Therefore, there is no sound policy reason to deny plaintiff relief for failing to discover a state of affairs which the most prudent purchaser would not be expected to even contemplate. . . .

Where a condition which has been created by the seller materially impairs the value of the contract and is peculiarly within the knowledge of the seller or unlikely to be discovered by a prudent purchaser exercising due care with respect to the subject transaction, nondisclosure constitutes a basis for rescission as a matter of equity.

In the case at bar, defendant seller deliberately fostered the public belief that her home was possessed. Having undertaken to inform the public-at-large, to whom she has no legal relationship, about the supernatural occurrences on her property, she may be said to owe

(continued)

(continued)

no less a duty to her contract vendee. . . . Where, as here, the seller not only takes unfair advantage of the buyer's ignorance but has created and perpetuated a condition about which he is unlikely to even inquire, enforcement of the contract (in whole or in part) is offensive to the court's sense of equity. Application of the remedy of rescission, within the bounds of the narrow exception to the doctrine of caveat emptor set forth herein, is entirely appropriate to relieve the unwitting purchaser from the consequences of a most unnatural bargain.

Accordingly, the judgment . . . should be modified, on the law and the facts, and in the exercise of discretion, and the first cause of action seeking rescission of the contract reinstated, without costs.

Case Questions

1. We will encounter estoppel principles shortly under the discussion of *reliance theory*, but it is critical in this case. Does estoppel relieve the court from the embarrassing position of ruling that a house may be haunted?
2. Should caveat emptor require a purchaser to inquire into the supernatural character of a house about to be purchased?

Case Glossary

estopped   In equity, a person may be "estopped"—stopped, prevented—from making assertions contrary to prior assertions on which another has relied to his detriment. See **estoppel.**

carport in a development where deed restrictions require garages and prohibit carports). Such relief also is premised on valid contractual obligations.

Liberal Construction of Consideration

One means of avoiding the arbitrariness of the classical model of contract formation was to construe consideration in the broadest possible terms in order to create a contract. This method was a favorite of Judge Cardozo of the New York Court of Appeals. Cardozo enforced a father's promise to pay an annuity to his daughter following her marriage by finding consideration in her forbearance from breaking off the engagement. *DeCicco v. Schweizer*, 221 N.Y. 431, 117 N.E. 807 (1917). In another case, he found consideration for a pledge to a college endowment campaign in an implied duty of the college to memorialize the donor. *Allegheny College v. National Chatauqua Bank*, 246 N.Y. 369, 159 N.E. 173 (1927). In both of these cases, classical theory should have found a promise to make a gift without consideration on the part of the promisee.

When consideration was designed to deny contracts even when offer and acceptance were present, the liberal construction of consideration undercut its importance. When a powerful moral, as opposed to legal, obligation was present or when a promisee changed position in reliance on a promise, judges at first strained to find consideration.

Moral Obligation and Reliance Theory

Consider the following examples taken from those listed earlier:

1. Contractor makes a contract with Thomas to blacktop Thomas's driveway at 116 Spring Street for $2,000. Contractor mistakenly blacktops Henry's driveway at 114 Spring Street (the two houses are in an urban subdivision where the houses bear a striking similarity to each other). Variations on the facts might be: Henry is away on vacation while the blacktopping occurs and has no knowledge of it until he returns; Henry watches through his window but remains silent, all the while knowing that Thomas was planning to blacktop and that Contractor is mistaken.

2. George, the owner of a small business, opens negotiations with a national hardware chain for a franchise. Franchisor insists that George get experience as manager/trainee in one of the branches and assures George that training plus $25,000 will result in a franchise, although no guarantees are made. George sells his business, moves to another city, and works as trainee. Franchisor increases the cost of the franchise to $35,000. George sells his house to raise the money, but Franchisor decides not to grant the franchise.

Moral Obligation: Quasi-Contract

> **quasi-contract**
> From the theory that a "contract" is created on the basis of moral obligation, called **unjust enrichment,** in which one party receives a benefit to the detriment of another that begs for **restitution;** not an actual contract.

In example 1, there was no contract, but Henry has received a benefit at Contractor's expense. There was no contract, no offer, no acceptance, no consideration on Henry's part; but it would seem unfair for Henry to retain the benefit, particularly if he failed in his moral obligation to inform Contractor of the mistake. In such a situation the court may impose contractual obligations in the name of **quasi-contract,** which is not an actual contract but a "non-contractual obligation that is to be treated procedurally as if it were a contract." *Continental Forest Products, Inc. v. Chandler Supply Co.,* 95 Idaho 739, 518 P.2d 1201 (1974).

> **contract implied in fact**   A contract that can be inferred by the conduct of the parties in the absence of a verbal or express contract.

Quasi-contract is also called *contract implied in law*—distinguished from a **contract implied in fact**—and is based on the concept of **unjust enrichment** and **restitution.** Unjust enrichment is an equitable principle asserting that one receiving a benefit at another's loss owes restitution to the other. Because fairness is the goal of equity, the imposition of contractual obligations depends on the specific circumstances of each case and cannot easily be reduced to mechanical rules. Typically, quasi-contract requires that the recipient of the benefit have the opportunity to decline the benefit and yet fail to do so. In the driveway example, the court might imply such failure if Henry sat idly by and watched the work. It is doubtful that the court would impose the same obligation if Henry had no knowledge of the work (for example, if he was on vacation).

> **unjust enrichment**
> An equitable principle asserting that one receiving a benefit at another's loss owes **restitution** to the other.

> **restitution**   In contract law, usually the amount that puts the plaintiff back in the financial position he or she was in before the contract.

Reliance: Promissory Estoppel

> **promissory estoppel**
> When a person makes a promise to another to induce that other to act to his detriment and that other does so act in reliance on the promise, the court may prevent (estop) the first person from denying or negating the promise; an equitable principle that enforces a promise in the absence of a completed contract.

Example 2 presents a different problem, that of **promissory estoppel.** Although a contract was never complete, George's course of action was determined by assurances made in the course of contract negotiations. George incurred significant costs in reasonably relying on those assurances. The national chain received no benefit at George's expense, so unjust enrichment/quasi-contract is not appropriate, but George has certainly suffered because of the chain's conduct. To impose liability on the chain, the court may resort to another equitable principle called **equitable estoppel,** under which liability is incurred if one by language or conduct leads another to do something he or she would not otherwise have done. This is the basis for the mysterious language of the first *Restatement* § 90:

> A promise which the promisor should reasonably expect to induce action or forbearance of a definite and substantial character on the part of the promisee and which does induce such action or forbearance is binding if injustice can be avoided only by enforcement of the promise.

This section applies to George's plight; it is a concise statement of *reliance theory.* Promises were made on which George relied to his detriment. Although a contract never quite passed the negotiation stage, it would be unjust for George to go without some compensation.

Hoffman is a classic case of promissory estoppel. The plaintiff was induced into a course of conduct by the defendant with the promise of a forthcoming contract that never came. Good faith and reliance on one side were met with vacillation and chicanery on the other. Nevertheless, promissory estoppel is not the same as breach of contract, and the case was ultimately set for new trial on the issue of the amount the plaintiff should receive. Omitted from the case excerpt is the following quotation from Corbin, one of the leading contributors to the *Restatement of Contracts,* the supreme master of reliance theory, showing just how elusive promissory estoppel can be:

> Enforcement of a promise does not necessarily mean Specific Performance. It does not necessarily mean Damages for breach. Moreover the amount allowed as Damages may be determined by the plaintiff's expenditures or change of position in reliance as well as by the value to him of the promised performance. Restitution is also an "enforcing" remedy, although it is often said to be based upon some kind of a rescission. In determining what justice requires, the court must remember all of its powers, derived from equity, **law merchant,** and other sources, as well as the common law. Its decree should be molded accordingly.

Failure of the Classical Model

Out of the chaos of contract law in the nineteenth century, an effort was made by scholars, particularly Langdell and Holmes in this country, to reduce contract law to logical principles in the common law. The effort was doomed from the start because of the nearly infinite variety of promissory situations and bargaining relations. Judges were disinclined to apply mechanical formulas when the results were clearly unjust. The concepts of fairness and good faith in principles of equity provided alternative remedies in some cases, and in other cases

---

equitable estoppel
Being stopped by your own prior acts or statements from claiming a right against another person who has legitimately relied on those acts or statements; also see **estoppel.**

law merchant
The generally accepted customs of merchants, often used to refer to early commercial law developed by the merchants themselves, which later formed the basis for much of commercial common law.

Joseph HOFFMAN
v.
RED OWL STORES, INC.,
a foreign corp., et al., Appellants
Supreme Court of Wisconsin
26 Wis. 2d 683, 133 N.W.2d 267 (1965)

[An agent for Red Owl Stores engaged in continuing negotiations with Hoffman, who operated a bakery but wanted to run a Red Owl supermarket. Negotiations took more than two years, during which Hoffman sold his bakery at the agent's request and bought and worked in a small grocery store. During this period, the price of the franchise was raised from $18,000 to $24,000 to $26,000. When Red Owl insisted that $13,000 put up by Hoffman's father-in-law be considered a gift, Hoffman balked.]

The record here discloses a number of promises and assurances given to Hoffman by Lukowitz in behalf of Red Owl upon which plaintiffs relied and acted upon to their detriment.

Foremost were the promises that for the sum of $18,000 Red Owl would establish Hoffman in a store. After Hoffman had sold his grocery store and paid the $1,000 on the Chilton lot, the $18,000 figure was changed to $24,100. Then in November, 1961, Hoffman was assured that if the $24,100 figure were increased by $2000 the deal would go through. Hoffman was induced to sell his grocery store fixtures and inventory in June, 1961, on the promise that he would be in his new store by fall. In November, plaintiffs sold their bakery building on the urging of defendants and on the assurance that this was the last step necessary to have the deal with Red Owl go through.

We determine that there was ample evidence to sustain the answers of the jury to the questions of the verdict with respect to the promissory representations made by Red Owl, Hoffman's reliance thereon in the exercise of ordinary care, and his fulfillment of the condi-

tions required of him by the terms of the negotiation had with Red Owl.

There remains for consideration the question of law raised by defendants that agreement was never reached on essential factors necessary to establish a contract between Hoffman and Red Owl. Among these were the size, cost, design, and layout of the store building; and the terms of the lease with respect to rent, maintenance, renewal, and purchase options. This poses the question of whether the promise necessary to sustain a cause of action for promissory estoppel must embrace all essential details of a proposed transaction between promisor and promisee so as to be the equivalent of an offer that would result in a binding contract between the parties if the promisee were to accept the same.

Originally the doctrine of promissory estoppel was involved as a substitute for consideration rendering a gratuitous promise enforceable as a contract. In other words, the acts of reliance by the promisee to his detriment provided a substitute for consideration. If promissory estoppel were to be limited to only those situations where the promise giving rise to the cause of action must be so definite with respect to all details that a contract would result were the promise supported by consideration, then the defendants' instant promises to Hoffman would not meet this test. However, [the Restatement of Contracts] does not impose the requirement that the promise giving rise to the cause of action must be so comprehensive in scope as to meet the requirements of an offer that would ripen into a contract if accepted by the promisee. Rather the conditions imposed are:

(1) Was the promise one which the promisor should reasonably expect to induce action or forbearance of a definite and substantial character on the part of the promisee?
(2) Did the promise induce such action or forbearance?
(3) Can injustice be avoided only by enforcement of the promise?

(continued)

(continued)

We deem it would be a mistake to regard an action grounded on promissory estoppel as the equivalent of a breach of contract action. . . .

While the first two of the above listed three requirements of promissory estoppel present issues of fact which ordinarily will be resolved by a jury, the third requirement, that the remedy can only be invoked where necessary to avoid injustice, is one that involves a policy decision by the court. Such a policy decision necessarily embraces an element of discretion.

We conclude that injustice would result here if plaintiffs were not granted some relief because of the failure of defendants to keep their promises which induced plaintiffs to act to their detriment.

* * *

Plaintiffs contend that in a breach of contract action damages may include loss of profits. However, this is not a breach of contract action.

The only relevancy of evidence relating to profits would be with respect to proving the element of goodwill in establishing the fair market value of the grocery inventory and fixtures sold. Therefore, evidence of profits would be admissible to afford a foundation for expert opinion as to fair market value.

Where damages are awarded in promissory estoppel instead of specifically enforcing the promisor's promise, they should be only such as in the opinion of the court are necessary to prevent injustice. Mechanical or rule of thumb approaches to the damage problem should be avoided.

* * *

"The wrong is not primarily in depriving the plaintiff of the promised reward but in causing the plaintiff to change position to his detriment. It would follow that the damages should not exceed the loss caused by the change of position, which would never be more in amount, but might be less, than the promised reward."

* * *

At the time Hoffman bought the equipment and inventory of the small grocery store at Wautoma he did so in order to gain experience in the grocery store business. At that time discussion had already been had with Red Owl representatives that Wautoma might be too small for a Red Owl operation and that a larger city might be more desirable. Thus Hoffman made this purchase more or less as a temporary experiment. Justice does not require that the damages awarded him, because of selling these assets at the behest of defendants, should exceed any actual loss sustained measured by the difference between the sales price and the fair market value.

Since the evidence does not sustain the large award of damages arising from the sale of the Wautoma grocery business, the trial court properly ordered a new trial on this issue.

Case Questions

1. What is the difference in the measure of damages between breach of contract and promissory estoppel?
2. The court cites and rejects the argument that promissory estoppel creates a substitute for consideration. Williston was the foremost proponent of the classical model (offer, acceptance, and consideration) in contract law. *Restatement* § 90 was written by Corbin, the foremost critic of the classical model. How does the court choose one over the other?

alternatives were found in the foundations for quasi-contract and promissory estoppel. The result has been an uneasy coexistence of two contradictory conceptions of contract.

Evidence of the demise of the classical model can be found in the Uniform Commercial Code, which departs from that model at every turn. The UCC emphasizes assisting contract formation rather than restricting it. Consideration is transformed, the mirror image rule is banished, indefinite terms may be implied or determined by the custom of the marketplace, and so on.

For the practitioner, the classical model of offer, acceptance, and consideration must be kept in mind in constructing contracts, but the full range of principles must be appreciated when an agreement fails.

The Field of Commercial Law

Contract law is the starting point for the study of commercial law, as most commercial relationships are contractual in nature. Just as the intricacies of contract law are beyond the scope of this book, so too are the various specialized areas of commercial law, each of which deserves a course by itself in law school curricula. Although they are very important to the paralegal, only a brief introduction to the subject matter of the major subfields of commercial law is presented to acquaint the paralegal with topics covered more fully elsewhere.

The Uniform Commercial Code

The Uniform Commercial Code was designed to establish a set of rules governing commercial transactions, modernizing the concepts of contract and commercial law to suit the marketplace. The UCC encouraged uniformity in state law regarding commercial transactions, and in this it has been largely successful, having been adopted with only minor variations in all states except Louisiana, which has adopted only four of its articles. Separate sections (articles) of the UCC cover the following subjects:

Sales

Commercial paper

Bank deposits and collections

Letters of credit

Bulk transfers

Warehouse receipts, bills of lading, and other documents of title

Investment securities

Secured transactions; sales of accounts, contract rights, and chattel paper

Except for the specialist, the key sections of the UCC concern sales, commercial paper, and secured transactions. Of these, Article 2 (Sales) is extremely important because it clarifies and modifies existing principles of contract law,

negotiable instruments "Commercial paper"; consists of cash substitutes, such as **checks, drafts, promissory notes,** and **certificates of deposit.**

checks Written orders to a bank to pay money to a named person.

draft An order to pay money; a *drawer* orders a *drawee* to pay money to a *payee*. A *check* is a draft on a bank payable on demand.

promissory notes Promises by the maker of the note to pay money to a payee, usually involved in loans and debts.

certificates of deposit Promises by banks to pay money deposited with the bank, ordinarily with interest.

collateral Property pledged to pay a debt; it is a security interest.

mortgage A written instrument creating an interest in land as collateral for the payment of a debt.

mechanic's lien A *lien* arises when property is burdened by an obligation to pay money, as in a mortgage transaction; a *mechanic's lien* arises when someone is not paid for work or improvements to property, ordinarily created by law under state statutes.

corporation A fictional person, a business organization that protects owners and managers from personal liability; it is chartered by a government.

some of which have been noted earlier. The one transactional area *not* covered in detail by the UCC is real property transactions, in which long-standing principles differ widely among the states, defying attempts at unification. The UCC as incorporated in state law should be consulted on any question that comes within its coverage.

Commercial Paper

Commercial paper, or **negotiable instruments** consists of substitutes for cash used to facilitate commercial transactions. **Checks, drafts, promissory notes,** and **certificates of deposit** constitute commercial paper. Commercial paper is thus a signed writing representing an unconditional promise to pay money. It is regulated by Article 3 of the UCC.

Secured Transactions

A secured transaction takes place when the payment of a debt is protected by **collateral.** The most common secured transactions are (1) real property **mortgages,** in which the purchaser or owner of land borrows money, pledging interests in real property to satisfy the debt in case of default; and (2) purchase money installment contracts for personal property, such as an automobile, in which the seller retains rights of repossession in case of default. Article 9 of the UCC covers secured transactions of personal property except for interests arising by operation of law, such as **mechanic's liens.** Secured interests in real property fall outside the UCC, so the law of each state must be consulted for applicable rules.

Obligations to pay money that are unsecured are covered by the state law of debtor and creditor. Discharge of debt through bankruptcy falls within federal jurisdiction under the U.S. Constitution.

Business Organizations

Business organizations consist of variations on three forms: **corporations, partnerships,** and **sole proprietorships.** Attorneys are regularly called upon to advise clients on the choice of business organization that will best suit their needs. Personal liability, tax consequences, and financing are major considerations that affect the choice, but size of the organization, its structure, and its long-range goals are also important considerations. Paralegals frequently draft the documents that create and control business organizations. Once formed, businesses must not only conform to their own rules, but also are subject to numerous requirements of state and federal law with which the commercial lawyer and the paralegal must be familiar.

partnerships
Unincorporated business associations lacking the limited liability of corporations so that suits that cannot be satisfied by partnership property may go after the personal assets of the partners.

sole proprietorships
An unincorporated business owned by one person.

Summary

The law of contracts is concerned with private agreements that the law recognizes as enforceable. Unlike torts, the obligations to be enforced are established by the agreement rather than the law. Under the classical model of contract formation, the requisites of making an enforceable contract consisted of offer, acceptance, and consideration. In its simplest form, consideration is an exchange of promises to perform agreed-upon obligations. The contract is not complete until offeror and offeree agree upon identical terms; an attempted acceptance of an offer that alters a term of the contract is considered a counteroffer rather than acceptance.

Even when offer, acceptance, and consideration are present, contract formation is corrupted by misconduct of one of the parties, mistake, lack of contractual capacity, or illegality. Certain kinds of contracts are required to be in writing by the Statute of Frauds and the Uniform Commercial Code, the latter making significant changes in the model of offer, acceptance, and consideration.

When a contract is not fulfilled, compensatory damages are available to put the nonbreaching party in the position he or she would have been in if the contract had been performed. Punitive damages and recovery for emotional damages are not ordinarily available in contract, but the lines between contract and tort have become increasingly blurred, as witnessed by medical malpractice and products liability.

Strict adherence to the classical model provides little flexibility in the nearly infinite variety of contractual situations, so the courts have devised a number of ways around what appear to be unjust results. The classical model based on the common law must compete with traditional concepts of fairness emanating from equity. A number of equitable remedies are available that depart from monetary compensation. In addition, equitable principles have given rise to enforcement of moral obligations in the form of quasi-contract, whereby the law imposes a contract to avoid unjust enrichment, and promissory estoppel, whereby a party suffers a detriment in relying on inducements made by another when a contract is not enforceable under common-law principles. Although common-law contract principles and theories of moral obligation and reliance in equity exist side by side, they are intrinsically contradictory, resulting in inconsistency in contract law.

The field of commercial law covers a number of subfields such as commercial paper, secured transactions, and business organization. Much of the law in this area is statutory, including the Uniform Commercial Code, which has been adopted by most states and which provides uniformity in interstate commercial transactions.

Scenario

In general, parties to a contract are free to set whatever terms and conditions they please if they are legally competent and the contract does not have an illegal purpose. The following contract is unusual and untested in the courts, to the best of this author's knowledge. The author came across a contract on which this is modeled on the World Wide Web and soon discovered there were several other similar contracts. There is a private world of "bondage enthusiasts," for want of a better word, who take such contracts quite seriously.

Master and Slave Contract

I hereby offer myself in slavery to my Master in consideration of his love and affection. I make these promises voluntarily out of a desire to serve my Master whom I love and adore. This contract shall begin _____ and end _____.

Terms and Conditions

The slave agrees to obey her Master in every way. Her body is available for her Master at all times and she agrees that he may determine whether others may use her body and for what purpose. The slave accepts that her Master may hurt her to gain pleasure for himself. The slave may on appropriate circumstances utter the *safeword*, a word agreed upon entering this contract, that temporarily suspends the obligations of this contract.

The slave will address the Master as "Master" or "Sir" and will always show him deference and respect. On days when the Master works, the slave will greet him at his return wearing wrist restraints, a neck collar with a leash, or such garments as the Master shall desire. She must ask the Master for permission to leave the room, to eat, and to use the toilet. Failure in any of these will result in a punishment of the Master's choosing.

None of the foregoing terms and conditions shall interfere with the slave's career. She is expected to work hard and dress and act as expected in her career.

I consign my body and soul to my Master according to the terms set herein.
(*signature*) _____ Slave _____ date

I accept my slave's promise of obedient service and take responsibility for her care and discipline to see that she serves my will.
(*signature*) _____ Master _____ date

As an attorney, you are visited by the "slave" who signed this contract. She acknowledges that she was strongly attracted to sexual bondage and sado-masochism, but her "master," a man of independent wealth, beat her so severely over several months that she has lost the use of her left hand and has several permanent scars on her body. She wants to sue in tort for her injuries. What part does this contract play in such a suit? On what grounds can the contract be attacked? How can the Master use the contract as a defense to suit for battery?

THE LAW
OF PROPERTY

CHAPTER OUTLINE

Introduction

The previous chapters have probably given the impression that disputes and litigation form the core of the law, but this is a false impression of the practice of law. Particularly in the area of property, litigation is rare because good "lawyerly" work prevents the need for litigation. A properly drafted and executed will should avoid all but unreasonable challenges. A carefully executed real estate transaction transfers title without loose ends and settles all important future questions about ownership.

Property law is extremely important for paralegals because it involves a great deal of work that does not require an attorney except as legal advisor and supervisor. Within the area of property law are a number of important subfields, such as real estate transactions, landlord and tenant law, estates and trusts, estate planning, planning and zoning, environmental law, and commercial leases. Other areas present specialized property law aspects, such as community property, equitable distribution, and marital estates in family law, and leases and real property transactions in contract law. Taxation is an important consideration in legal advising on all aspects of property law. There are specific causes of action in tort to protect property interests: trespass, **nuisance, ejectment.** In recent years government regulation of property by planning, zoning, and environmental law has placed severe restrictions on land use and created a need for legal specialization in these areas. Bankruptcy, **foreclosure,** mortgages, and mechanic's liens concern rights of third parties in property. In short, all of private law that is not concerned with wrongful misconduct (and much that is)

nuisance A private *nuisance* is basically a continuing trespass, as when one discharges polluting effluents that seep into a neighbor's pond.

ejectment A common law cause of action designed to return rightful possession of real property, commonly called *eviction* in modern landlord and tenant law.

foreclosure The process whereby real property is sold to satisfy a mortgage under default.

revolves around property law. Perhaps in no other field of law is a more comprehensive knowledge of law required for legal advice, even on what may appear to be a relatively simple problem or transaction, as in the area of real property law.

Property Is an Abstraction

Natural property does not exist. From a legal point of view, a mountain is not property, nor a lake, nor a book. Until we assign legal rights in a thing, it is not property. When a person building a new home says, "I am going out to the property," we understand a building site, a piece of land, in its natural or altered state, but we also understand that the statement asserts rights of ownership over something that has been defined on a map with boundaries, the title to which has been transferred from one hand to another and recorded in the records of the county in which it is situated. But the most important, albeit often unconscious, assertion in this use of the word *property* is that the owner has rights that the law will defend. The definition, determination, and allocation of these rights are the subject matter of property law.

The abstract nature of property may be illustrated by a few examples:

1. A retailer builds up a profitable business over many years and then decides to sell it and retire. Not only may the retailer sell the premises and the inventory of the store, but a major part of the sales price may be for "goodwill," which is valuable property.

2. A professional basketball player may be paid a very large sum of money just to have his name associated with a line of sneakers. He has property rights in his name.

3. A person buys a fifth-story **condominium** on the beach before it is built. Until constructed, ownership is of a piece of air.

4. Someone pays for a **franchise** to operate a fast-food restaurant.

5. Amazon.com invents a software program to keep on-line buyer information to enable one-click purchases from repeat buyers. Amazon patents the process and successfully stops Barnes & Noble from using a virtually identical program for its on-line shoppers.

6. A state university professor receives **tenure,** which grants a right to permanent employment at the university.

7. Someone registers the Internet domain name http://www.beautiful.com with Network Solutions and is later offered and accepts one million dollars for the domain name.

8. A physician challenges antiabortion statutes on the grounds that the right to practice medicine has been unconstitutionally restricted.

All these examples express valuable property rights of which the law takes cognizance. Note that the government not only restricts property rights (exam-

condominium A form of ownership in real property where owners typically share ownership in common areas, such as the land, sidewalks, swimming pool, but have individual rights in a building, as if each owner owned an apartment or townhouse.

franchise A collaborative relationship in which the franchisee pays a franchisor for the use of the franchisor's trade name and products, like McDonald's restaurants.

tenure In higher education, job security granted to faculty members, usually after a period of several years and based on an extensive approval process. Tenured faculty cannot be fired without cause.

ple 8), but also creates them (examples 5 and 6). In fact, the government through its laws can create or destroy property rights, subject only to due process of law and just compensation for property taken for a public purpose.

The law may recognize something as property for one purpose but not for another. In New York, for example, a professional license may be "marital property," the value of which can be divided in a divorce, but it is not property for the purposes of sale or gift. In *Community Redevelopment Agency v. Abrams*, 15 Cal. 3d 813, 543 P.2d 905, 126 Cal. Rptr. 423 (1975), the California Supreme Court held that goodwill in a pharmacy that was taken in order to redevelop an urban center was not property, even though it would be property for the purposes of a private sale of the pharmacy. In relation to this last example, Professor Berger asked the unanswerable question, "Did the pharmacist lose because he had no property or did he have no property because he lost?" Goodwill is an abstract concept, but goodwill as property raises it to an even higher level of abstraction. Property itself is an abstraction of the rights that the law recognizes.

Real Property's "Bundle of Rights" Model

In an effort to simplify the abstraction of property, legal scholars refer to a *bundle of rights* that a person may enjoy. This model is used to explain the complex laws of real property ownership. Real property consists of land and its improvements (buildings, fences, wells, etc.—those valuable changes that humans inflict on their land). Other things that may be owned, such as money, goods, stocks and bonds, and the like, are called *personal property* and have a much smaller bundle of rights.

The most important property rights are rights of possession, use, and transfer. Each of these includes other rights. The *right of possession* allows one not only to be present on the land but also to exclude others. The causes of action for trespass, ejectment, and nuisance are based on this right. *Use rights* include the right to improve the land, to exploit it for agriculture, mining, cut timber, and so on. The *right of transfer or conveyance* includes the right to sell, lease, or give away real property. Real property is also transferred at death by will or intestate succession; these are important rights of ownership.

The nature and duration of these rights are restricted by a number of features of property law and property rights. Consider a married couple that "owns" a home. If they acquired the home after they were married, it is likely that they have a form of co-ownership called a **tenancy by the entirety,** whereby the surviving spouse would own the entire property in the event of the other's death. Even if title to the home is held in only one name, the other may have a marital interest based on **dower** or **curtesy** or on community property rights in some states. If there is a **mortgage** on the home, someone else has a right to sell the property in foreclosure if they default on the payments, and their capacity to sell the property may be severely restricted by the terms of their mortgage.

What they can do with their land may be subject to many limitations— **restrictive covenants**—placed in their deed if the home was part of a housing

tenancy by the entirety A form of co-ownership with a *right of survivorship* that can only be held by husband and wife.

dower and **curtesy** Formerly, interests in property held by wife (dower) and husband (curtesy), the primary purpose of which was to guarantee real property interests for a surviving spouse. The husband was favored, and these interests have been equalized or combined in recent times so as not to discriminate.

mortgage A written instrument creating an interest in land as collateral for the payment of a debt.

restrictive covenants In real property, take many forms including minimum square footage for a house, lawn maintenance, and signage. Racially restrictive covenants and other discriminatory practices have long been held unconstitutional.

easement   A right of use in another's property as, for example, when someone has a right-of-way to cross another's land.

development. The use of their land is limited by local, state, and federal law — they may not be able to cut down a tree or have a garage sale without a permit. If their house is on a city street, the city has an **easement** along the street that gives the city a number of rights and the owners little but duties. The electric company has an easement for lines across the property, as does the city water department. There could be other private easements allowing other persons a right-of-way across their land. They might not own the mineral rights below the surface of their land. The city, county, state, or federal governments could take away their property to build a highway or for other public use, only providing them with just compensation. Despite these restrictions, they are taxed on the value of the entire property, which could be sold for nonpayment of the taxes.

lease   An agreement by an owner of property, the *lessor*, with a renter, a *tenant* or *lessee*, whereby the lessee pays for the right of possession and use but does not acquire title.

The duration of property rights may also be limited. If possession is held by a **lease,** the right of possession is subject to limitations of time as well as any other conditions the lessor includes in the lease agreement. A title may be limited in duration, such as for life (life estate) or until the fulfillment of a condition. When title has a limited duration, someone other than the present possessor has a future interest in the property, so that the present possessor has duties and limitations on use for the benefit of the future interest.

The bundle of rights may be viewed as the totality of rights and restrictions on rights held by a person with regard to real property. In view of the complexities of property rights, the term *ownership* has limited usefulness in the field of real property. The law deals with rights, and the extent of a person's ownership depends on how much of the bundle a person has.

The Deed

deed   A document that describes a piece of real property and its transfer of title to a new owner.

grantor   A party transferring an interest in real property to another, the **grantee.**

The conservatism and formality of real property law can be shown by the *Moseley* case, which follows. As we shall see shortly, a will must satisfy rigid formalities to be valid. **Deeds** are the documents that express the intention to transfer real property interests from one owner, the **grantor,** to another, the **grantee.** Generally, a deed has the following requirements:

- The deed must be in writing.
- The grantor must be competent.
- The grantee must be identified.
- There must be an adequate description of the property.
- Consideration — a mere recital of consideration is usually sufficient.
- The grantor must sign.
- Witnesses are commonly required.
- The deed must be delivered to the grantee.

Different states have their own variations that could trap the unwary. The *Moseley* case is concerned with the very last requirement, delivery. *Moseley* demonstrates a major difference between the law or real property and other areas of law. We have seen that the court in tort and contract disputes will often search for novel ways to do justice to the parties. In real property disputes, the court, to the contrary, will often elevate formality above intent and even fairness. The court has two considerations that are special to property law. First, property transactions are formal events that are often part of an official record. Second, the grantor is often—and the testator is always—deceased and therefore not available to testify. In the *Moseley* case, the grantor of a deed was deceased. The testimony certainly indicates he wanted a married woman of whom he was enamored to get his home upon his death (or maybe before) in lieu of his stepchildren, who were named in the will. He executed a deed to this effect but did not deliver it, an essential part of the transfer. He was a lawyer and should have known better, as his own attorney advised.

Ralph S. MOSELEY, Special Administrator of the Estate of Otto W. Miller, et al., Appellees

v.

Mary S. ZIEG et al., Appellants
Supreme Court of Nebraska
180 Neb. 810; 146 N.W.2d 72 (1966)

BROWER, J.

The appellees, Ralph S. Moseley as special administrator of the estate of Otto W. Miller, deceased, and Seth E. Cole, Sr., Robert A. Cole, Sr., Mamie Whitmarsh, and Margaret A. Hostreiter, the devisees and legatees under the will of said deceased, as plaintiffs, brought this action in the district court for Lancaster County against the defendants and appellants Mary S. Zieg and Henry G. Zieg, her husband, to cancel and declare void a deed conveying a lot and residence. . . . A trial to the court resulted in a judgment finding that the grantor never delivered the deed in his lifetime to anyone, but retained the same in his own personal possession, and granting the plaintiffs the relief prayed for.

[The pertinent facts and testimony in this case may be summarized as follows:

Otto W. Miller was the grantor of the deed in question and Mary S. Zieg the grantee. He died on March 18, 1964, and left a will executed on May 4, 1960, which named four children (named

above as Appellees) of a wife who predeceased him. These were children of a prior marriage of the wife. Miller lived in the house named in the deed and rented appartments in the house until his death. On November 9, 1961, Miller had his attorney, Ralph S. Moseley, prepare the deed in question, conveying the premises mentioned to the defendant Mrs. Zieg. The deed was witnessed by Moseley and was acknowledged by Miller before Ollie R. McMeen, a lady and notary public in Moseley's office. Harold Foster, a student at the University of Nebraska and a tenant of the deceased Miller, testified with respect to conversations had alone with the latter on an evening near the middle of February 1964. The witness stated Miller said he was in love with Mrs. Zieg and was going to see she got the property after he died. Miller said he had made a new will within the past year that would give her the property and that she had been given a deed to the property. Mrs. Lillith Gluesing, the occupant of Miller's upstairs apartment, testified by deposition. Miller had told her he would marry Mrs. Zieg if she were single and Mrs. Zieg had stated to her that if single she would marry Miller. In July or August 1963, he said, "'This house belongs to Mary. I have taken care of that,' something about all the paper work has been done. 'I have been to see my lawyer, all the paper work is signed and it has been delivered.'" William H. Owen, a

(continued)

(continued)

son of Mrs. Zieg, testified that Miller stated he had been to see his lawyer and that he had taken the deed to his house over to "my mother's house" the day before, after he had come home. He stated John Steinacher "'knows all about this.'" "'John will take your mother and have the deed recorded on my death.'" "'Be sure that they do it immediately; don't wait one day.'" Ralph S. Moseley, the attorney, testified for plaintiffs. He stated Miller came to his office and requested him to prepare the deed on November 9, 1961. It was prepared, signed, and witnessed, and acknowledged by Miller there at that time. The witness told Miller that he would have to give it to Mrs. Zieg to make good delivery, but he knew Miller was an attorney. Miller stated the deed would not be effective until after his death. He testified that after Miller's death, Mrs. Zieg contacted him about the deed and she and Steinacher went with him to the safe deposit box in the basement of the National Bank of Commerce where Mrs. Zieg signed for admission to the box. She had a key that would permit her to open it. He testified that in the box was the deed in question which was in an old envelope on which was written "'To be filed at my death.'" The deed was given by him to Mrs. Zieg at that time and he advised her to put revenue stamps thereon and to record it, and told the defendant the place was then hers.

John J. Steinacher, a witness for the defendants and a neighbor of Miller, testified that Miller had told him in August 1963 that "Mary gets the house when he is gone." Miller instructed Steinacher to take Mary to his safety deposit box in the event of Miller's death and get the deed and record it. Steinacher's subsequent testimony was inconsistent, first indicating that he took Mary, who had a key to the box, to the bank from which she emerged with a deed she did not appear to have when entering. He then went with Mary to Moseley's office, then back to the bank but testified that Mary had the deed all along. A vice president

of the bank testified to some important dates of record. He identified a rental contract for the safe deposit box between the bank and O. W. Miller and Mary Owen Zieg with a record of entries attached, which is in evidence. The contract is dated March 2, 1961. The record of entries shows Miller signed the entry sheet only on November 9, 1961, and November 12, 1963, and that Mary Owen Zieg signed it on March 18, 1964, at both 10 a.m., and 10:43 a.m., and on March 20, 1964, and several times thereafter, i.e., all after the death of Miller.]

This court, in the case of *Lewis v. Marker*, 145 Neb. 763, 18 N.W.2d 210, laid down the following rules in its syllabi which we deem applicable to the case before us: "It is essential to the validity of a deed that there be a delivery and the burden of proof rests upon the party asserting delivery to establish it by a preponderance of the evidence.

"To constitute a valid delivery of a deed there must be an intent on the part of the grantor that the deed shall operate as a muniment of title to take effect presently.

"Where an unrecorded deed is found, after grantor's decease, in a safety deposit box to which the grantee had a right of access as a joint lessee thereof with such grantor, this of itself will not sustain a finding that the deed was delivered when the grantor retained control of the property, collected the rents, made repairs and paid taxes thereon as he did before the date of the purported delivery." See, also, *Owens v. Reed*, 141 Neb. 796, 4 N.W.2d 914, cited in *Lewis v. Marker, supra*.

In the present case we think the defendants have failed to show that the deed was in the possession of the defendant Mary S. Zieg during her lifetime. Although the testimony of attorney Moseley and the witness Steinacher is not in complete harmony, it plainly appears that the latter took Mrs. Zieg to the bank that she procure the deed from the safe deposit box. Parts of Steinacher's testimony clearly indicates she got it there. They went together to the safe deposit box of Miller after his death pursuant to the instruction given by Miller in his lifetime. It stretches credulity to believe that if Mrs. Zieg carried the deed with her before arriving at the bank she would not have told the person she accompanied that she already had it and exhibited it to him. It is of some significance also that William H. Owen on being informed by Miller that he had taken the deed to his mother the day before did not thereafter observe it in her possession. Steinacher's testimony, from which defendants claim it might be inferred she had it at all times, is inconsistent and unsatisfactory. We think it must be conceded the deed was procured from the joint

safe deposit box. If so, it was placed there by Miller in his lifetime because he was the only person who had access to it before his death. The presumption of delivery of a deed found in the possession of a grantee in the grantor's lifetime does not obtain in the present case. The burden here was on the defendants to prove delivery.

We conclude the defendants have not sustained the burden of proof to show the delivery of the deed in question.

The judgment of the trial court was without error and should be and is affirmed.

Affirmed.

Case Questions

1. Which facts were most devastating to Mrs. Zieg's case?
2. Why is delivery of the deed so important?

Estates in Land

In a highly commercial society such as ours, real estate is often perceived as a commodity to be bought and sold for investment or speculation. But it is not a commodity like pencils, where monetary payment and delivery of the goods pass title from one hand to the next without either side considering problems of title. Even the simplest real estate sale involves lawyers, title companies, tax stamps, recording at the court house, realtors, closing agents, mortgage companies, and so forth. The need for all of these has a lot to do with the ancient law of estates.

The law of tort and contract is a model of common sense compared to property law. Law based on private wrong must adapt to changing values and daily life, whether personal or commercial. Property law, in contrast, reflects the accumulation of technical principles establishing ownership rights. Land law is conservative; many basic principles have changed little over the centuries.

The conservatism of land law is partly due to concern on the part of those who have property that their rights remain secure; and because, over the centuries, those with wealth in property have either made the law or had extraordinary influence over those who make the law, tinkering with the rules of property rights has been disfavored. Another reason for the conservatism can be attributed to the very law that has given us the bundle-of-rights principles. Title to land, as we have seen, is a complex matter. Intrusions into ownership rights may take place at any time—a second mortgage, a tax lien, a lease or marriage or divorce can occur during the course of possession and will affect how various rights are distributed and limited. When someone sells real estate, the buyer will want to know the status of all rights pertaining to the property in question. The current status of a piece of real property depends upon its history. A search of the history—**chain of title**—of the property may even reveal that the seller's claims of ownership are much in doubt, or that someone else claims to be the owner, or that there are restrictions that make the property unsuitable for the purchaser's intended use.

To many, our land law is simply a cumbersome relic of the past, but it is self-perpetuating—its technical complexity makes it difficult to change. What may appear to be a minor change may turn out to require adjustments through the entire system, and anything that potentially casts doubt on ownership is unfavorably viewed by property owners, lawyers, and those who make the law. Modernization of land law would be a monumental task and an agonizing ordeal that few seem ready to undertake.

The result of this conservatism is land law based on an ancient system that bears little relation to present realities. At the core of land law are the common law estates, which were developed in the first centuries following the Norman Conquest in 1066. These came into being during England's feudal period when a person's status in society depended almost entirely on rights in land. Society and government were built on a military model with the king at its apex. Technically all land was held by the king, but it was divided among his subjects, who thereby owed the king certain fees and military service. Thus, a certain baron might control a certain area of land and the peasants working the land and be required to furnish his overlord with fees and a specified number of knights and soldiers in time of conflict. The overlord, in turn, was similarly responsible to his overlord, and so forth up to the king. At the base of the pyramid were the peasants who worked the land, providing a portion of their crops and personal service to the landlord, who was their protector. Although no one owned the land in the modern sense of the word, the status attached to the land passed from father to eldest son—**primogeniture**—as long as the son was acceptable to the lord and swore fealty to him. A baron's (or count's) land was inherited by his son (land could not be passed by will until the Statute of Wills in 1540), who then became the baron.

Although the system of primogeniture and certain other features of aristocratic land ownership were not adopted in the United States, the system of common law estates continues to this day. The estates were divided between freehold and nonfreehold estates; freeholders were free men, and nonfreeholders were called "villeins." Except for the last term, which has come to mean something quite different, the terms have been preserved intact. It is more common to call a nonfreehold a leasehold estate with a lease, a lessor, and a lessee.

Fee Simple Absolute

The inheritable freehold estates were called fees; the most important one, then and today, was the **fee simple absolute**. This estate represents the maximum bundle of rights with the fewest strings attached. Among its important features

chain of title The history of the transfer of title to real property. It is comprised of a series of grantors to grantees showing who is the present holder of title.

primogeniture A system under the common law whereby title to land passed to the eldest son (primo- first-, geni-born).

fee simple absolute An estate in land having the maximum rights, that is, without future interests.

are that it is *alienable* (it can be sold or given away), **inheritable,** and **devisable** (it can be passed by will). A fee simple absolute is unconditional and has potentially infinite duration. Standard real estate sales contracts call for a fee simple absolute, and that is what purchasers want and expect, whether or not they are familiar with its name. Such an estate still represents what it did several hundred years ago: the complete bundle of rights to possession, use, and transferability.

Life Estate

Contrast fee simple absolute with **life estate,** which is a freehold estate that is not inheritable. A life estate is created to last for a person's lifetime. It cannot be inherited or passed by will because it ends immediately upon the death of the owner life tenant. Otherwise, it has the attributes of a fee simple absolute. It can be leased, given away; of course, the life tenant cannot transfer more than he the purchaser gets an estate that lasts only as long as the original life tenant. A life estate always creates a future interest; someone must have title after tenant dies, which imposes a duty on the life tenant to preserve the estate able for "waste." For example, a father conveys real property "to my son for life, and then to my grandson George." If no other limiting language ed, when Michael dies, George will hold the property in fee simple absolute (while Michael is alive, George's future interest is called a **remainder**).

Saltzman v. Ahern presents the problem of an owner of property, here the grantor, delivering two deeds to the property to two different grantees. The first grantee, Ahern, brought a suit to quiet title, an appropriate action requesting the court to determine who has title. The Saltzmans challenged Ahern's deed, claiming it did not pass title but was an attempt to pass title at the grantor's death, the grantor having reserved a life estate in the property in the deed. In other words, the Saltzmans argued that the deed should be treated as if it were a will. As a will can be revoked at any time prior to death, the subsequent deed to the Saltzmans served as a revocation. Revocation may in fact have been the grantor's intention; but if it was, he certainly chose the wrong means for accomplishing his purpose and compounded the problem by the subsequent grant to the Saltzmans.

The Saltzmans' argument at first sight seems to strain logic, but the history of property law shows a concern for technicality that lends some support to their challenge. They make much of the fact that the terms "warranty" and "in fee simple" were deleted from the standard printed form. At common law, the words "and his [her, their] heirs" were required for conveying a fee simple absolute because the phrase meant the conveyance of a heritable estate; without the inclusion of this phrase, only a life estate was conveyed. In Florida, as in most states, this technicality has been dispensed with, and a fee simple absolute is presumed when other qualifying language is absent. The grantor's deletion of the phrase "in fee simple" might suggest that some other estate was intended, but the grantor did not delete "and their heirs and assigns." The deletion of words of warranty might suggest that the grantor intended something other than a **warranty deed,** which warrants title and promises to defend it, but there is nothing in the deed to suggest that it is anything but a warranty deed.

warranty deed   A *deed* that includes promises or warranties, especially the promise to defend the title.

...that ...ows a *life estate.*

Herman SALTZMAN and Irene P. Saltzman, his wife, et al., Appellants,
v.
Lacey N. AHERN, Appellee
District Court of Appeal of Florida, First District
306 So. 2d 537 (1975)

Both appellants and appellee claim title to a parcel of real estate, each claiming under separate conveyances from a common grantor, one James M. Dudley. Appellee filed a complaint to **quiet title** and appellants counterclaimed. The trial judge granted a motion for summary judgment, quieting title in appellee and appellants appealed.

* * *

The questioned deed was executed by Dudley on August 24, 1953. A standard printed form was utilized, but the grantor deleted the word "warranty" and the "warranting clause" as well as the words "in fee simple," causing the deed to read (in material part) as follows:

"WITNESSETH, that the said grantor, in consideration of Ten ($10.00) dollars and other valuable consideration, the receipt whereof is hereby acknowledged, does give, grant, bargain, sell, alien, remise, release, enfeoff, convey and confirm unto the said grantees and their heirs and assigns the lands situate in Duval County, State of Florida, . . .

"BUT RESERVING, HOWEVER, unto the said grantor a life estate in said above described lands for the period of his natural life.

"TO HAVE AND TO HOLD the same together with the hereditaments and appurtenances, unto the said grantees, and their heirs and assigns forever, subject, however, to the estate for the life of the said grantor therein."

. . . Appellants' sole contention is that the grantor, by making the changes in the deed form above mentioned, and by subsequently conveying the identical property to appellants' predecessors in title thereby evinced an intention that the subject deed not take effect during his lifetime but be considered instead as an attempted testamentary disposition.

In order to resolve the issue, there being no question as to execution, consideration or delivery, we must examine the deed itself. When the language of a deed is clear and certain in meaning and the grantor's intention is reflected by the language employed, there is no room for judicial construction of the language nor interpretation of the words used. . . . The recitation of consideration in an instrument raises a presumption thereof and when a person executes and delivers a deed for consideration there is raised a presumption that the words employed in the deed were intended to be effective in accordance with their ordinary meaning. If a deed is, by virtue of execution, delivery, consideration and language employed, impervious to attack by the grantor executing same, then it may not be successfully collaterally attacked by another.

* * *

The judgment appealed is accordingly Affirmed.

Case Questions

1. In its opinion, the court does not delve into the circumstances of the making of the deed. What is more important here, the grantor's intent or the interpretation of his intent from the language of the deed?
2. Does the treatment here conform to contract law with regard to consideration? Explain.
3. What is the status of the Saltzmans' deed?
4. Why did the grantor deed the property twice? Is that relevant? Explain.

Case Glossary

quiet title   When the examination of title to real property reveals a questionable claim or interest casting a cloud on the title, a suit to quiet title is commonly brought to obtain a judicial order declaring that claim or interest to have no effect on the title.

Nonfreehold Estates

nonfreehold estate
An interest in real property that does not include holding of title. This is primarily the right of possession and occupancy as in a lease agreement. This is also called a **leasehold estate**.

Nonfreehold estates are also called **leasehold estates** and are most commonly represented by formal leases, commercial or residential, which spell out rights, duties, commencement, and termination as well as rental terms. Because these are contractual in nature and do not pass title, problems are resolved under contract law and state landlord and tenant law. Oral and informal arrangements present special problems that are usually handled in small claims court, as most rentals involving substantial amounts of money are evidenced by written contracts that are the products of professional legal advice.

Co-Ownership

right of survivorship
An incident to certain forms of co-ownership whereby a co-owner, if there are but two co-owners, will own the entire interest upon the death of the other co-owner.

joint tenancy   A form of co-ownership that includes a right of survivorship.

tenancy in common
A form of co-ownership that does not have a *right of survivorship* and that permits unequal shares.

Title may be held by more than one owner. Mention has been made of tenancy by the entirety, which is a species of co-ownership that can be held only by husband and wife. It includes a **right of survivorship**, as does **joint tenancy**, which can be held by two or more people as equal owners with equal rights of use and possession. Under the right of survivorship, if one co-owner dies, the share of the deceased is owned equally by the survivors. Sale or gift prior to death defeats the right of survivorship, but an attempted gift by will fails because death terminates all property interests in a joint tenancy or tenancy by the entirety. A remaining form of co-ownership is **tenancy in common,** which does not have a right of survivorship and which permits unequal shares among the co-owners.

An important example of co-ownership today is the condominium, in which owners of individual housing units are also tenants in common with regard to common areas—stairs, walkways, parking lots, and so on—and are equally obligated for their maintenance. Time-share arrangements are a relatively new phenomenon commonly associated with a condominium-like land use. Under time-share, owners are tenants in common but restricted in their use to certain time periods during the year. States in which condominiums and time-share are common have adopted comprehensive statutes governing them.

Implications

Clearly the holder of a life estate is missing some of the rights enjoyed by the owner in fee simple absolute. There are other less frequently used freehold estates that are not described here, but keep in mind that in a sale of land, the purchaser ordinarily expects a fee simple absolute, and it is the responsibility of the person examining the land's past to determine whether the asserted owner does in fact have a clear title with the full bundle of rights.

The purchaser must be informed of any encumbrances. Attorneys are called upon to search titles, that is, to examine the records to establish the present owner and the extent of ownership. If there are any of the numerous intrusions on ownership mentioned previously, the purchaser should know of these and their legal ramifications—for instance, the significance of a utility easement that allows the electric company to cross the land to serve other properties. Inconsistencies and questions should be resolved: Has an old mortgage been satisfied even though satisfaction of mortgage has not been recorded? What was the effect of the divorce of a prior owner? An attorney may be retained not only to help conduct the transaction but also to provide a title opinion describing the current status of the title. Title insurance companies, which maintain extensive records on land within the territory they cover, offer additional protection to the prudent buyer.

Title searches, title opinions, and title insurance are made necessary by the system of estates that has been inherited over the centuries. Land sales call for a methodical approach that typically follows an orderly checklist to prepare for a smooth closing at which the purchase price is exchanged for delivery of a deed to the property. Much of the work in real property transactions can and should, for reasons of cost, be done by paralegals. In fact, a person who specializes in such transactions, or even one who specializes in residential or commercial sales or leases, is preferable to a general practitioner. Experience develops an awareness of the myriad problems that may arise.

Liability of Landowners

Landowners have duties toward others present on their land. The common law distinguished three major categories of people who entered another's land: invitee, licensee, and trespasser. In this order, the landowner (or occupier of land) owed a diminishing duty. To the trespasser was owed almost no duty at all, except perhaps a duty not to set hidden traps; a trespasser is on the land wrongfully, without consent or invitation, express or implied. The invitee is usually someone who enters premises on business involving the landowner, by invitation express or implied; this is most usually a business visitor. The invitee is owed a duty of protection against dangers known, or reasonably should have been known, to the landowner. The licensee is a person privileged to enter the land by permission or consent, express or implied, but whose purpose is the licensee's, not any interest of the landowner. The licensee is owed a lesser standard of care than the invitee. The difference today between a licensee and an invitee is blurred or nonexistent. The courts are more likely to look at reasonable duty of care in either case. Trespassers are a different story, however.

State and federal governments are landowners as well. What duties do they owe those who enter their lands? In the *Gould* case, two plaintiffs sued the United States for injuries received on property owned by the United States located in Missouri. Note that the court looks to Missouri law to determine liability.

C. Russell GOULD, Appellant,

v.

UNITED STATES of America, Appellee
William R. ZANETELLO, Appellant,

v.

UNITED STATES of America, Appellee
United States Court of Appeals
160 F.3d 1194 (8th Cir. 1998)

William Zanetello and Russell Gould, strangers to each other at the time, were injured on different days while sledding down the back of a dam built, operated, and owned by the Army Corps of Engineers (the Corps) at Longview Lake in Jackson County, Missouri. Each of them was seriously hurt when his sled crashed after having been propelled into the air upon contact with a sloped terrace that was three or four feet high. Each sued the United States under the **Federal Tort Claims Act.** . . .

Both lawsuits asserted a theory of "premises liability," that is, they claimed that the plaintiff was injured by an unreasonably dangerous condition that existed on property of the United States. After a bench trial, the court entered judgment for the United States based on its findings that both Mr. Zanetello and Mr. Gould actually knew, or in any event could reasonably have been expected to discover, the risk of becoming airborne. . . .

I.

Mr. Zanetello and Mr. Gould contend that the unreasonably dangerous condition relevant in this case was the presence of the terrace and that the relevant risk was that a person's sled could be propelled four to six feet high after crossing the terrace. That risk is relevant, of course, only if it is what actually caused the plaintiffs' injuries.

With respect to Mr. Zanetello, however, there was no evidence that he in fact reached such a height. . . . The evidence was simply insufficient to support a conclusion that Mr. Zanetello was injured after being propelled four to six feet in the air. We therefore affirm the trial court's judgment for the United States with respect to Mr. Zanetello.

With respect to Mr. Gould, David Gross testified that Mr. Gould achieved a height of four to six feet. Adam Gross testified that . . . Mr. Gould "flew close to eight feet, somewhere around there, five to ten feet." . . . The trial court's decision relied substantially on Mr. Gross's testimony for the crucial facts that the terrace was visible on the day of the accident, that Mr. Gross made a sled run and went airborne prior to Mr. Gould's run, and that Mr. Gould's sled "lost contact with the ground and flew a number of feet through the air." It thus appears to us that the trial court credited Mr. Gross's testimony concerning the height Mr. Gould's sled reached, and we therefore turn to a consideration of the Missouri law applicable to this kind of case.

II.

Missouri law imposes liability on a landowner when a licensee is injured on the owner's land only if the owner had actual knowledge of a condition presenting an unreasonable risk, and had a reason to believe that a licensee would not discover the condition or realize the risk.

The Missouri courts have held that landowners have no reason to believe that open and obvious conditions or risks will not be discovered, and that landowners do have a reason to believe that conditions or risks will not be discovered if they are not open and obvious. . . . "[T]he fact that the condition is obvious," so that a licensee could reasonably be expected to know of or discover it, "is usually sufficient to apprise [a licensee], as fully as the possessor, of the full extent of the risk involved in it." [Citation omitted]

A frequently cited Missouri case, moreover, states that a dangerous condition is open and obvious as a matter of law only if the injured party "should reasonably be expected to discover it and realize the danger." . . . "'[K]nowledge' of the risk involved in a particular condition implies not only that the condition is recognized as dangerous but also that the chance of harm and the gravity of the threatened harm are appreciated." . . .

We do not believe that an appreciation of the risk involved in this case necessarily

(continued)

(continued)

followed from the obviousness of the physical condition. The question here is not simply whether Mr. Gould knew of or could reasonably have been expected to discover the terrace itself, or even the possibility of becoming airborne upon contact with it, but whether he knew of or could reasonably have been expected to discover the risk of flying four to six feet into the air—a risk significantly different from the risk of merely becoming airborne.

Before Mr. Gould's own sled run, the trial court found, Mr. Gould had seen David Gross achieve a height of "a couple of feet." There was no evidence, however, that Mr. Gould saw anyone reach a height above four feet. . . . It seems clear to us that the risk associated with achieving a height of four feet or more on a speeding sled is of a different order of magnitude from the risk associated with achieving a height of a "couple of feet." . . . The evidence is that Mr. Gould did not know of, and, we hold, could not reasonably have been expected to discover, the risk of being propelled more than four feet high. Because this risk was not open and obvious, the Corps had a reason to believe that Mr. Gould would not discover it.

The trial court found that the Corps did not know of the risk that a sled could be propelled up to six feet high. The only evidence at trial in this respect, however, was from the park ranger responsible for the dam. He stated unequivocally that he had seen sledders fly up to six feet in the air after hitting the terrace. We therefore hold that the trial court's finding with respect to the knowledge of the risk by the Corps was clearly erroneous.

Since the Corps did in fact know of the risk that injured Mr. Gould, since Mr. Gould did not know of that risk and could not reasonably have been expected to discover it, and since the Corps had a reason to believe that Mr. Gould would not discover it, the Corps failed in its duty to take reasonable steps to protect Mr. Gould from that risk. It is therefore liable for the injuries that the risk caused Mr. Gould. Since we have no findings by the trial court, however, on the question of whether, or to what extent, the risk that Mr. Gould faced caused his injuries, we remand the case to the trial court for further proceedings on that issue. If the evidence presented to the court does not prove by a preponderance of the evidence that Mr. Gould suffered injuries attributable to the risk of being propelled four to six feet in the air, then the Corps is entitled to judgment. *In other words, Mr. Gould can recover only for such injuries as would not have occurred but for the risk that he did not appreciate. If the injuries were caused by a risk that he did appreciate, namely, the risk of being propelled a "couple of feet" into the air, then he can recover nothing* [emphasis added]. Mr. Gould, as plaintiff, of course bears the burden of proof on the issue of damages.

III.

For the reasons stated, we affirm the judgment of the trial court with respect to Mr. Zanetello. With respect to Mr. Gould, we vacate the judgment and remand to the trial court for further proceedings not inconsistent with this opinion.

Case Questions

1. Why did Zanetello lose and Gould win?
2. What did Gould win?
3. What must the trial court now do?

Case Glossary

Federal Tort Claims Act   Under the doctrine of *sovereign immunity*, state and federal governments were immune from tort suits, unless the government consented to the suit. In 1947, Congress remedied this situation by passing the Federal Tort Claims Act, which made the federal government liable, with certain exceptions, as if it were a private party. (See Chapter 14, "Liability of Government and Its Officers.")

Title

title Formal ownership of property; has many nuances of meaning.

The word **title** has been used frequently thus far; its definition cannot be postponed. It is an important concept but one that is often misunderstood. The definition of title is curiously absent from or cursorily treated in law texts covering real property. The concept of title is abstract to the point of mystery.

In its beginnings it was embodied in the concept of *seisin*, which originally meant possession but gradually came to signify possession under the right to claim a freehold estate. Seisin originally referred to what seems today to have been a rather mystical relationship between an owner and his land; seisin was passed from one man to another by a ritual called *livery of seisin*, symbolized by handing over a twig or a clump of dirt from the land. When seisin passed, so did the right of possession.

The concept of title is similar. Its definition takes three forms:

1. The right to ownership and possession of land
2. The means whereby an owner of land has just possession
3. The evidence of ownership of land.

Title is not a document, such as a deed, though the term is often loosely used in such a reference. A deed is simply one of many bits of evidence of title. In a sense, title is held by the one who holds the greatest number of the bundle of rights that constitute a freehold estate; a lessee does not have title despite having the right of possession.

adverse possession A means of acquiring title by occupying and using land for a certain length of time even though the occupier does not have title. The period at common law was twenty years, shorter in most states by statute.

The three definitions of title treat different aspects of title. As evidence of title, there are numerous documents that, combined in a somewhat mystical union, tell us who has title. Documents alone may not be sufficient. One in wrongful possession for a sufficient period of time may acquire title—**adverse possession.** Treating title as a means of claiming possession refers to the need on occasion for one holding title to prove title against other claimants for title or possession. Finally, the right of ownership represented by the concept of title is its most common meaning, especially when ownership is not in question. "Right of ownership" must remain abstract, because the law is normally concerned with acknowledging and enforcing specific rights.

If the concept of title is still obscure, it is because it is relative and abstract. It is used in preference to ownership because it signifies the application of all the rules that identify ownership. Perhaps it is best explained by the barb, "I don't own the house, the bank owns it." This is an obvious reference to the lender on a mortgage, who usually puts up a far greater portion of the purchase price than the actual purchaser. In most states, however, the bank merely holds a lien on the property and no part of the title. Nevertheless, the title to the land in question is encumbered by the mortgage, and no prudent purchaser would buy the land without resolving the mortgage question. (A mortgage may not prevent a sale of land, but because the mortgage is secured by the land, a failure to pay the mortgage could result in foreclosure no matter who has title.)

Personal Property

Title to personal property does not usually raise the complex problems associated with chain of title to real property. Because tangible personal property is commonly exchanged by sale or gift, mere possession is significant evidence of exchange of title. Most problems arise with **bailments** and lost, stolen, or abandoned property, which is usually covered by well-established legal rules. The Uniform Commercial Code gives specific guidance on sale of goods and intangible personal property in the form of negotiable instruments.

bailment When the owner of personal property delivers possession without intent to pass title, as when one leaves an automobile with an auto mechanic.

What happens to an engagement ring when the marriage does not take place? Devising fair principles is not as easy as it may seem. The problem is complicated by the intersection of several fields of law:

1. *Contract law.* Is an engagement a contract? If the contract is breached, is restitution in the form of return of the engagement ring an appropriate remedy?

2. *Tort law.* There was at one time an action at common law called "breach of promise to marry" with a consequent suit for damages. Many states have abolished this cause of action. Could the engagement ring be an element of damages? Does abolishing the cause of action put the ring beyond reach?

3. *Family law.* Should the marriage (and engagement) contract be treated like any other contract, or should the state's interest in the sanctity of the family treat this contract specially, including the right to the engagement ring? If the state's public policy is not to force incompatible couples to marry, how should the court decide on the ring?

4. *Property law.* Is the engagement ring a gift? Consideration for a contract? A pledge? Has title passed?

The basic principles that developed concerning return of the ring were as follows: (1) If the donee breaks off the engagement without fault on the part of the donor, the donor is entitled to its return. (2) If the donor breaks off the engagement, the donee keeps the ring. (3) An engagement broken by mutual consent obliges the return of the ring.

In the state of New York, these common law rules applied until 1935, when the legislature abolished actions for breach of promise to marry, which was interpreted by the courts to bar an action for recovery of engagement rings. In 1965, the legislature enacted law to allow recovery of engagement rings when "justice so requires." This moral tone is echoed in the *Cohen* case, in which the fiance was killed in an auto accident shortly before the wedding and the personal representative of his estate attempted to recover the ring.

A somewhat similar case had occurred in Massachusetts a few years before with different results. In *DeCicco v. Barker*, 339 Mass. 457, 159 N.E.2d 534 (1959), a married man gave several rings to a woman, at least one of which, a six-carat diamond ring, was apparently an engagement ring. His wife was in the hospital at the time, and the engagement was conditioned on her death, which occurred two months later. Subsequent to the wife's death, the fiancee bought him an engagement ring but several months later broke the engagement.

She relied on the Massachusetts legislative abolishment of the cause of action for breach of promise to marry, but the court gave him the six-carat ring, stating:

> . . . It is a proceeding not to recover damages, either directly or indirectly for breach of the contract to marry but to obtain on established equitable principles restitution of property held on a condition which the defendant was unwilling to fulfil. It seeks to prevent unjust enrichment.

COHEN
v.
BAYSIDE FEDERAL SAVINGS AND LOAN ASSOCIATION
Supreme Court of New York
62 Misc. 2d 738, 309 N.Y.S.2d 980 (1970)

Some courts have propounded a pledge theory. Other courts state that principles of unjust enrichment govern and the most popular rationale is that the ring is given as a gift on condition subsequent. It is not always clear, however, whether it is the actual marriage of the parties or the donee's not performing any act that would prevent the marriage that is the actual condition of the "transaction."

Thus a confusing body of law has grown up around the engagement ring and, after careful consideration of these principles, this court has decided that Carol should keep the ring because that result is equitable and because "justice so requires". . . .

I cannot believe that the age-old ritual of giving an engagement ring to bind the mutual premarital vows can be or is intended to be treated as an exchange of consideration as practiced in the everyday market place. Can it be seriously urged that the giving of this ring by the decedent "groom" to his loved one and bride-to-be can be treated as the ordinary commercial or business transaction requiring the ultimate in consideration and payment? I think

not. To treat this special and usually once in a lifetime occasion, one as requiring quid pro quo, is a mistake and unrealistic.

[Carol Cohen's ring was worth only one thousand dollars. In *Lowe v. Quinn* the ring was valued at $60,000, which explains why she wanted to keep it and he went to the highest state court to get it back. Although she broke off the engagement, he was in a special dilemma—he was still married.]

Edwin S. LOWE, Appellant
v.
Jayne D. QUINN, Respondent
Court of Appeals of New York
27 N.Y.2d 397, 267 N.E.2d 251 (1971)

An engagement ring "is in the nature of a pledge for the contract of marriage" and, under the common law, it was settled—at least in a case where no impediment existed to a marriage— that, if the recipient broke the "engagement," she was required, upon demand, to return the ring on the theory that it constituted a conditional gift. However, a different result is compelled where, as here, one of the parties is married. An agreement to marry under such circumstances is void as against public policy, and it is not saved or rendered valid by the fact that the married individual contemplated divorce

(continued)

(continued)

and that the agreement was conditioned on procurement of the divorce. Based on such reasoning, the few courts which have had occasion to consider the question have held that a plaintiff may not recover the engagement ring or any other property he may have given the woman. . . .

[The court goes on to argue that the legislative reenactment of the right to recover an engagement ring did not apply to a situation in which either of the parties is married at the time of the gift of the ring.]

Case Questions

1. Is *Cohen* decided on the basis of contract, tort, family, or property law, as suggested in the comments prior to the cases?
2. Is *Lowe* decided on the basis of contract, tort, family, or property law, as suggested in the comments prior to the cases?

Estate Planning

An important area of law practice is estate planning, which deals with the orderly distribution of assets at death. If no provision is made in advance, the property of a deceased person, called the *estate* or *decedent's estate*, passes by intestate succession as ordered by state law. Most persons would distribute their property somewhat differently than will the state and should so provide in advance by will and/or trust. The estate planner not only assists in preparing the documents of distribution but also advises clients on tax and other legal consequences of different distributions. Advice is not merely legal and financial but can be very personal as well.

Wills

The primary purpose of wills is distribution of the financial assets of the deceased according to directions provided prior to death in the will itself. Many persons wish to control the use of their property long after death or want to specify in great detail how everything they own will pass to intended beneficiaries. All this can be accomplished through a will. However, unnecessary complexity not only makes administration of the estate cumbersome but also tends to anger and frustrate beneficiaries and encourage suits to contest the validity of the will. When specific problems, such as a spendthrift child or spouse, warrant limitations on the distribution or use of property, a trust is often the more appropriate solution.

Will drafting is often left to paralegals, who can use the language and form of past models to express the intent of the testator, to be reviewed by the responsible attorney prior to signing by the testator and witnesses. Today, drafting wills can be greatly facilitated by computers programmed with standard clauses and paragraphs that reflect the requirements of state law. In some instances, an attorney or paralegal may simply follow a checklist of questions, the answers to which are entered into a computer, which then prints a will. If the computer program is comprehensive, the possibility of human error is minimized.

Each state requires specific formalities for the signing and attesting of wills that must be strictly adhered to in order to create a valid will. The legal advisor's goal should be to give force to the intent of the testator in a form that will discourage and overcome legal challenge. The process of settling an estate through the court is called *probate*, and the court responsible is commonly called *probate* or *surrogacy* court.

Working with clients who wish to have wills drafted calls for delicacy, tact, common sense, and a basic understanding of human nature. Contemplation of death is unpleasant at best, and letting go of the acquisitions of a lifetime is not easy.

A special note is warranted here. Making a will for a client usually results in the attorney and staff acquiring a detailed knowledge of the client's finances and personal relationships. All of this information is strictly confidential, and all members of the legal staff must scrupulously avoid revealing any knowledge thus acquired.

Trusts

A *trust* is a device dating back to the fourteenth century, when it was used to avoid certain features of the ownership of common law freehold estates. It was enforced in the courts of equity and is still governed by equity today. A trust involves a transfer of title of real or personal property to a trustee who is charged with a duty to hold the property for the benefit of another, a beneficiary (*cestui que* trust). The trust instrument provides instructions for the trustee to follow in distributing property to the beneficiary.

living trust or inter vivos trust An ordinary trust as opposed to a trust established by a will at death (inter vivos— "between living persons").

By setting up a **living (inter vivos) trust,** a person can put property into the trust that will go to named parties immediately or when the donor dies. In this way the trust can be used as a will substitute and has the advantage of making possible detailed instructions on the distribution of property at the same time that it avoids probate of the property. When a trust is used as a will substitute, the donor can make himself or herself trustee and beneficiary for his or her lifetime and thereby both control and benefit from the property. Trusts can also be used to transfer property without regard to death, as with a trust fund to send one's children to college; the donor may relinquish any control (*irrevocable trust*).

The advantage of a trust over a will is that it names a trustee to carry out the wishes of the donor. Without such an arrangement, future decisions would be based on interpretations of the intent of the testator, which might prove inappropriate as times and situations change. The donor may provide for flexibility that would not be possible in an outright distribution. Also, the trustee has a fiduciary duty toward the beneficiary that can make the trustee more accountable than someone who misuses distributed property. For someone with minor children or others who cannot properly take care of their affairs, a trust can be established that provides temporarily for financial needs while preserving assets for later distribution. In short, the trust can be tailored to very special problems that would be very awkward to handle in a will.

A good deal of the work involving trusts can be efficiently done by paralegals.

Government Regulation of Real Property

Ownership of real property today is subject to many intrusions by government. Most of these take the form of restrictions on use. In addition, governments may take property under the power of eminent domain, and the federal government has authority over navigable waters. Former rights over airspace above an owner's property have been restricted primarily because of the advent of the airplane.

Eminent Domain

eminent domain The power of the government to take private property for a public use, for which just compensation is required by the Constitution.

The Fifth Amendment to the U.S. Constitution, the repository of basic rights in criminal law, ends with the clause, "nor shall private property be taken for a public use, without just compensation." This, along with similar language in state constitutions, is the basis for the power our governments exercise called **eminent domain.** This power is used to take property for highways, parks, urban redevelopment, and protection of the environment. "Public use" has been broadly defined to cover laws allowing private railroads to acquire property for their routes, electric utilities to obtain rights-of-way, and so forth.

Compensation for the taking of property is often subject to dispute, but state and federal governments have procedures designed to determine fair market value and to give the opportunity to challenge assessments. The major issue in litigation has been interpretation of the word "taking." When government takes title to an entire piece of property, the problem may be simple—pay fair market value. If, however, the state builds a new highway, reducing traffic on an old highway and thereby making a filling station unprofitable, there is no "taking"—it is considered *damnum absque injuria*, a harm without a legal injury, and not compensable. Thus, some effects of government action constitute taking and some do not. The issue arose early in this century with planning and zoning.

Planning and Zoning

The most direct intrusions into a private property owner's rights have come from governmental attempts to regulate land use. For both residential and commercial owners, planning and zoning have resulted in severe restrictions on property owners' rights. The classic example of planning that is still to be found everywhere is the comprehensive zoning ordinance. Starting in the 1920s, cities and counties throughout the country adopted the practice of mapping land use zones, which restrict areas to categories of use such as residential, professional, commercial, and industrial. Generally these zones reflect contemporary uses but restrict future development. The object of zones is to diminish the effects of urban blight, save agricultural and green areas, and prevent the intrusion of incompatible uses in adjacent areas. Because zoning clearly represents the government depriving property owners of use rights they would otherwise enjoy, it was challenged as a taking under eminent domain for which no compensation was provided.

The U.S. Supreme Court in *Euclid v. Ambler*, 272 U.S. 365, 47 S. Ct. 114, 71 L. Ed. 303 (1926) upheld comprehensive zoning in the village of Euclid, Ohio, under the state's power to regulate health, safety, and welfare, but found a taking in *Nectow v. City of Cambridge*, 277 U.S. 183, 48 S. Ct. 447, 72 L. Ed. 842 (1928), where zoning effectively deprived the owner of any economically feasible use of his property (property zoned residential, though adjacent properties were occupied by industrial enterprises). The judgment relied on the Fourteenth Amendment's prohibition of deprivation of property without due process of law. Subsequent constitutional history has affirmed the resulting balancing test between the rights of communities to control land use and the rights of individual property owners to make reasonable use of their land.

Today planning has taken on additional tasks. Zoning maps are only a temporary solution to the problems that intensive growth has created in many areas. Comprehensive, long-range planning prevails in populous states, along with environmental concerns. Residential and commercial development is frequently carried out on a grand scale, and federal and state laws have been enacted to require exhaustive studies of the impact of such development on the environment and the capacity of local resources to support new building. Government has taken a serious role in controlling and directing growth. Major projects, airports, shopping malls, large residential developments, and the like are subject to intense scrutiny to assure compliance with the law, and it is unlikely that legal requirements will decrease in the future.

Lawyers find much work in this area in advising, negotiating, and facilitating cooperation between developers and local governmental bodies. Paralegals can be invaluable in the process.

Summary

Property is an abstract concept, not a natural or physical object or feature. It is best explained in terms of legal rights, such as rights to possess, exclude, and transfer. Rights can also be limited in time, such as a lease or a life estate, and in the nature of use and transferability. Rights may be restricted by a deed, by zoning ordinances, and by rights of others, such as utility easements and rights of way.

Property is divided into real and personal property. Real property, which consists of land and its improvements, is based on common law estates, which have endured for many centuries because of the basic conservatism of real property law. Under this system a person owns rights in land (the bundle-of-rights concept) rather than owning the land itself. When a person owns the maximum bundle of rights, the estate is called a fee simple absolute and corresponds to what we casually refer to as ownership. Lesser estates may be held, of which the most common is the life estate, which allows the life tenant to exercise rights over the property while alive. Upon death, the rights automatically transfer to a person who until that time held only a future interest.

Leasehold (or nonfreehold) estates involve the temporary transfer of the right of possession and are regulated by landlord and tenant laws of each state.

Title is an important concept in property law. It is not a document like a deed, but an abstraction based on the history of the ownership of property that describes the extent of rights and limitations on rights; it can be determined by examining the records of transactions dealing with a particular piece of land. Title to personal property is generally much simpler, especially when physical property is directly exchanged for cash or a cash equivalent—title passes instantaneously.

An important aspect of the practice of property law involves estate planning, preparing for the distribution of a person's estate (the totality of one's property, real and personal). The most common devices used in estate planning are wills and trusts. A will provides for the distribution of property at death. A trust may distribute property at death or during one's lifetime; it establishes a trustee who distributes property to a beneficiary according to instructions in the trust instrument.

Today property is extensively regulated by government. Particularly affecting real property are restrictions on land use covered by local government planning and zoning, but state and federal governments have become more and more active in limiting land use, especially in the area of environmental law.

Scenario

Eileen Slipslope was staying at the Holiday Six Hotel in Williwonky, Maryland, when she was injured walking from the parking lot to the hotel. Mrs. Slipslope slipped on some ice and fell forward onto the sloping pavement.

The court is considering Holiday Six's motion for summary judgment and Slipslope response, which present contrasting legal bases for Slipslope's claim. The Holiday Six argues that it has no liability to Slipslope under the Maryland "ridges and hills" doctrine regarding liability for snow and ice accumulation. In her response, Slipslope argues that she does not rely on the "ridges and hills" doctrine but, instead, alleges a design defect in the parking lot.

The "ridges and hills" doctrine is a long-standing and well entrenched legal principle that protects an owner or occupier of land from liability for generally slippery conditions resulting from ice and snow where the owner has not permitted the ice and snow to unreasonably accumulate in ridges or elevations. In order to show liability under such circumstances, the plaintiff must demonstrate: (1) that snow and ice had accumulated on the sidewalk in ridges or elevations of such size and character as to unreasonably obstruct travel and constitute a danger to pedestrians traveling thereon; (2) that the property owner had notice, either actual or constructive, of the existence of such condition; and (3) that it was the dangerous accumulation of snow and ice that caused the injury.

The doctrine's application has been extended to cases where a business invitee falls on snow or ice covering a parking lot, and the parties stipulate that Slipslope was a business invitee of the Holiday Six, and that the parking lot in question belonged to the Holiday Six.

Assume the following facts: The evidence shows that snow stopped falling only about ten hours before the accident, and that temperatures had not risen to the point where the snow might have melted away. Thus, there is no disputed issue of material fact over whether "generally slippery conditions" existed in the Holiday Six's parking lot on that March 8 evening. Similarly, there is no dispute that the ice that allegedly caused Mrs. Slipslope's fall had not accumulated in a "hill" or "ridge" but instead was evidently barely perceptible.

Thus, if it applies, the "ridges and hills" doctrine prevents Slipslope from holding the Holiday Six liable for the existence of the patch of ice on the parking lot.

Slipslope argues that she does not rely on the "ridges and hills" doctrine. Instead, she contends that there was a design defect in the parking lot, which "at a minimum, was a concurrent cause of the accident coupled with the inclement weather." In particular, she alleges that the portion of the parking lot on which she fell is "too steep a slope for any pedestrian to traverse, and creates a danger in all inclement weather."

Slipslope offered the testimony of an expert witness who testified that the area in question "could have easily been more gradually graded as was done at the other parking lanes." He also performed an analysis of the forces operating on a one-hundred-fifty-pound adult attempting to walk down a snow- or ice-covered surface sloped as the one at issue, and concluded that there would always exist a downhill force causing the pedestrian to lose balance.

Assignment   Sitting as the judge in this case, write an opinion discussing the issues on each side and explain why you think one side should win rather than the other. In your discussion consider the following persuasive authority:

The Restatement (Second) of Torts §343 reads:

A possessor of land is subject to liability for physical harm caused to his invitees by a condition on the land if, but only if, he

(a) knows or by the exercise of reasonable care would discover the condition, and should realize that it involves an unreasonable risk of harm to such invitees, and

(b) should expect that they will not discover or realize the danger, or will fail to protect themselves against it, and

(c) fails to exercise reasonable care to protect them against the danger.

FAMILY LAW

CHAPTER OUTLINE

Historical Roots of Family Law

Probably no area of law has changed more in American history than family law. Family and family life have changed radically, and the law has changed along with them. Regulation of the family by legislatures and courts has followed a tortuous course. The degree to which the state should intrude into family relationships has always been controversial. For example, public policy supports the protection of children from abuse and neglect, but traditional values also protect parental authority against interference by the government.

Regulation of the family involves limiting choices by law in an area of human life where choices are jealously guarded. Should individuals be free to marry, **divorce,** and bear children at their whim? In our society, some would place severe restrictions on each of these; others would insist that each is purely a matter of individual choice and not a concern of government.

divorce The severance of the bonds of matrimony; also referred to as *dissolution of marriage*.

Whereas other areas of law, such as the law of property, may be seen as a logical evolution from ancient English roots, family law is largely an American creation, consciously departing from English legal traditions. For example, Connecticut allowed absolute divorce long before England did. Divorce is really an American legal institution.

The archetypal family consists of a father, a mother, and children. Although there are contemporary pressures to define *family* in much broader terms, the legal foundations of family law are premised on legitimizing a sexual relation between husband and wife that encourages childbearing and child rearing. American courts have, throughout their history, regarded themselves as the protectors of the family, often invoking rules on purely moral grounds.

marriage The legal joining together of husband and wife, having among its important effects the legitimatization of their offspring; also, the Christian sacrament that joins husband and wife.

canon law Church, or ecclesiastical, law traditionally associated with the Roman Catholic Church, which in English law was continued by the Church of England. Separation of church and state in the United States created gaps in the law, most notably in the area of domestic relations (family law).

child custody The rights and duties of those legally entrusted with the care and control of a child, usually the parents.

child support An obligation of parents; the payments due from one parent to another for the care of children following divorce.

alimony Payments for personal maintenance from one ex-spouse to the other following divorce.

community property A regime in which the earnings of husband and wife during marriage are owned equally by both; eight states borrowing from French (Louisiana) or Spanish (Texas west to California) law incorporated the concept of community property into marital law.

The moral basis of family law was formalized when the Church assumed responsibility for regulating domestic relations in the late Middle Ages. At that time, **marriage** became a sacrament, subjecting the marital relationship to regulation by the Church. Our family law originated in the **canon law,** the law of the ecclesiastical courts. Because America did not employ ecclesiastical courts or canon law, the area of domestic relations was subsumed under the courts of equity, except in colonies like Connecticut and Massachusetts that refused to adopt courts of equity. At the founding of the American republic, the division between courts of equity and common law courts was still very strong. There was no common law tradition of family law except for property rights, and the common law was most appropriately charged with formal legal matters such as the remedies for injury to person or property, for crimes, and for breach of contract.

Despite the American rejection of ecclesiastical law, the marriage contract retains some elements of its former sacred character. In former times, the betrothal was the critical event in marriage, as marriage partners were chosen by the parents of the bride and groom as part of a family alliance that benefited the respective families as well as the couple. In recent times, the wedding has become the significant event, as people have become free to choose their own partners. Both church and state have retreated from their former authority, leaving individuals free to form and dissolve the marital union.

Law and Marriage

The legal requirements for marriage are minimal. The bride and groom must meet minimum age requirements; for the moment, they must ordinarily be of different sexes; they must have legal capacity to contract marriage; they must not be married to someone else; and they must not be closely related by blood. In short, it is easy to get married. Lawyers are rarely consulted.

Divorce, in contrast, is far more complicated. The principal subjects of family law are in one way or another concerned with divorce and its aftermath: **child custody, child support,** spousal support (**alimony**), **community property,** and **equitable distribution.**

Marriage as Contract

The marriage itself is traditionally viewed as a contractual arrangement, because the parties voluntarily assume the relationship of husband and wife, but the most important duties are those imposed by law rather than the agreement of the parties. For example, husband and wife are obligated to provide mutual support for each other and support and nurture for their children. Individuals may avoid these duties by agreement only under special circumstances allowed by the law.

Although marriage has long been characterized as a contract, it has not been an ordinary contract in the eyes of the law, that is, one that could be freely made, altered, and broken. The sacred aspect of the family and procreation

equitable distribution
Designed to equalize the marital shares of husband and wife for purposes of divorce; many states that are not *community property* states have principles of equitable distribution.

argued for a sacred contract. In recent decades, however, the state, which in America had assumed responsibility for domestic regulation, moved toward making the marriage contract much more like other contracts, in which the contracting parties controlled the relationship. Many of the features of family law can be explained by the tension between the special regard with which we view marriage and the family and the objective contractual rights and duties that the law imposes on family relationships.

> It is also to be observed that, although marriage is often termed by text writers and in court decisions as a civil contract—generally to indicate that it might be founded upon the agreement of the parties, and does not require any religious ceremony for its solemnization—it is something more than a mere contract. The consent of the parties is of course essential to its existence; but when the contract to marry is executed by the marriage, a relation between the parties is created which they cannot change. Other contracts may be modified, restricted, or enlarged, or entirely released upon consent of the parties. Not so with marriage. Once the relation is formed, the law steps in and holds the parties to various obligations and liabilities. It is an institution, in the maintenance and purity of which the public is deeply interested, for it is the foundation of the family and of society, without which there would be neither civilization nor progress.

Maynard v. Hill, 125 U.S. 190, 210 (1888).

Marriage as a Partnership

From an economic standpoint, the marriage contract establishes an ongoing, cooperative unit like a business partnership. In some instances, the reciprocal nature of the business is clear, as when the wife works as a secretary to support her husband while he gets through law school, with the understanding that, once the husband's practice is prospering, the wife will quit working and bear and raise the couple's children. Success of the partnership depends upon each spouse meeting the terms of the contract. Other marriage partners may be business partners in an objective sense, that is, they may jointly manage their own commercial enterprise. Often the division of profits does not take place in the way unmarried partners would ordinarily conduct a business, but in every other respect the differences may be insignificant. Perhaps the majority of marriages do not have the usual characteristics of a business venture, but nearly all marriages involve important cost and savings sharing for mutual benefit, similar to a business enterprise.

Divorce may be treated like the dissolution of a business partnership. To the extent that property assets have been acquired by the joint efforts of the spouses, this model may, when used with caution, effect a fair distribution of the marital property.

domestic relations
The field of law governing the rights and duties of family relations, particularly divorce; usually synonymous with *family law.*

Children

Family law, often called **domestic relations,** might more properly be titled the *law of intimate relations,* especially in this period in our society when couples exercise considerable freedom in the partners they choose and the lifestyles those partnerships express. Even though we have moved away from the traditional marriage-and-children model of adult relationships, the idealized model of the family continues to be a heterosexual union having as its major motivation the creation and nurture of children. Children add a dimension to family law that distinguishes it from other areas of law: Family law commonly deals with the welfare of human beings who have not reached the age of legal competence (majority), who are vulnerable to abuse or exploitation, and who must be protected by society through its legal institutions when the family, the primary social institution, fails. Problems in other areas of law are often neatly handled by the transfer of wealth from one pocket to another; family law involves issues that are not readily measured in dollars and cents.

Family Law and the Adversarial Process

American legal procedure has developed around an adversarial process in which disputing parties arm themselves with legal representatives and ultimately try their cases before an impartial judge if the lawyers and the parties cannot reach an agreement. The sides are viewed as hostile, and the lawyers are duty-bound to fight for the interests of their clients. This model quite naturally tends to focus and intensify the dispute, one of the reasons the states attempted to soften the process by adopting **no-fault divorce** statutes. Divorcing couples with minor children pose a serious problem for the legal system. We assume that parents will care for the interests of their children, but divorcing parents often aggravate the damage the divorce causes to children by drawing them into a continuing dispute.

no-fault divorce
Contemporary divorce that does away with the need to prove fault, that is, state grounds, against the other spouse.

Annulment

annulment   Ends the relation of husband and wife by invalidating the marriage contract, as if they were never married.

An examination of **annulment** is valuable because it reveals the requirements for a valid marriage. An action for annulment challenges the validity of the original marriage contract. Annulment is uncommon today largely because the adoption of no-fault divorce statutes has made divorce easier than annulment. Nevertheless, for religious or other reasons, some individuals may prefer to seek annulment.

The most important aspect of the difference between annulment and divorce relates to the grounds for ending the marriage. Annulment is based on a defect in existence when the marriage was contracted. Divorce is based on grounds arising during the marriage itself. For instance, it is often possible to obtain an annulment if one of the parties to the marriage was impotent or sterile at the time of the marriage (usually assuming this fact was unknown to the other party); impotence or sterility developing after the marriage contract would not ordinarily be grounds for annulment—the complaining party would be forced to resort to divorce to get out of the marriage.

Divorce terminates the marriage from the time of the final decree, but annulment operates retroactively to invalidate the marriage from its beginning.

This is so because the cause of action for annulment asserts some impediment to the formation of the marriage contract itself—if the contract was invalid, no marriage resulted. One of the important consequences of annulment is the general unavailability of alimony, which most American courts award only upon dissolution of a valid marriage.

Void or Voidable?

Under traditional contract theory, some contracts are deemed void and some are merely voidable. A *void contract* is one that was never valid; a *voidable contract* is valid until a court declares it invalid. Through the passage of time and removal of the impediment to validity, a voidable contract may become enforceable. Marriage contracts are similarly subject to the void–voidable distinction. Because of the special nature of the marriage contract, the grounds for invalidity are somewhat different from other contracts.

Marriages generally considered void include:

bigamous Referring to the marriage of a person who is already married to another person. Bigamy is a crime, and a bigamous marriage is void.

1. **Bigamous** marriage, when one of the parties is already married
2. **Incestuous** marriage, within a prohibited relationship for marriage (e.g., brother-sister)
3. **Mental incompetence,** when one of the parties lacks mental capacity to contract marriage
4. **Nonage,** when at least one of the parties is below the minimum age to marry.

incestuous Referring to the marriage of two persons who stand in a family relationship in which the law prohibits marriage. *Incest* refers to the sexual relations of persons in such a relationship, for example, father-daughter, brother-sister.

nonage The condition of being a minor, not having reached the age of majority.

Marriages may be merely voidable on the ground of *formalities,* that is, failure to meet the formal requirements for a licensed marriage; and *fraud.* Fraud, which accounts for the largest number of attacks on marriages through annulment proceedings, includes three categories:

1. *Fraud with regard to essentials of marriage.* Many courts have adopted the rule that fraud as to the essentials of marriage must be of an extreme nature. This is often referred to as the *Massachusetts rule,* derived from *Reynolds v. Reynolds,* 85 Mass. (3 Allen) 605 (1862), in which an annulment was granted to a husband whose wife had represented herself as chaste even though she was already pregnant by another man. An annulment was granted to the husband.

2. *Fraud with regard to inability or unwillingness to have children.* Perhaps the oldest ground for annulment known to our law has to do with sex and procreation. When one spouse misrepresents his or her ability to have children, the law traditionally permits annulment.

3. *Fraud on the court or legal process.* Certain cases of collusion between parties involve fraud on the legal system rather than fraud on the other party. This occurs with sham marriages, wherein some purpose other than marriage, cohabitation, and procreation is intended, such as marrying to qualify for a visa or legitimizing a child. When there was no intent to consum-

mate the marriage and the marriage was not in fact consummated, annulment may be available.

Consequences of Annulment

Historically, annulment treated the marriage as if it had never occurred, but the harshness of this rule has been softened in recent times. In particular, annulment should not bastardize the offspring of an annulled marriage. The Uniform Marriage and Divorce Act (UMDA) § 207(c) states: "Children born of a prohibited marriage are legitimate." (The UMDA was drafted by the National Conference of Commissioners on Uniform State Laws to propose legislation for the states that would cover the principal subject of marriage and divorce. Several states have adopted the Act, and many judicial opinions cite it as supporting authority.)

Alimony is another matter. Under the common law, it was the duty of the husband to provide for the wife and this extended to legal separations (i.e., divorce from bed and board), as well as absolute divorce. This duty, however, depended upon a valid marital contract and was therefore inconsistent with annulment. A number of states have passed legislation allowing alimony following annulment under restricted circumstances, as when the receiving spouse is an innocent party.

Antenuptial (Premarital) Agreements

Dower and **curtesy** under the common law, and their modern representatives such as **elective share,** provide that a surviving spouse is entitled to a large share of the decedent's estate despite testamentary provisions (the laws of intestacy apply when no valid will exists). Community property or equitable distribution favor a fifty-fifty split in case of divorce. In most states, the only way to decrease this share upon death or divorce is through an agreement signed before the marriage: an **antenuptial** or **premarital agreement.** Until the twentieth century, such agreements were judicially disapproved as violating public policy, which disfavored any agreement tending to promote divorce. By the end of the twentieth century, this policy had reversed, and now most states enforce antenuptial contracts, especially when financial disclosure precedes the contract and coercive conduct is absent.

Antenuptial agreements are private contracts setting the terms of the marital contract in advance. Both their popularity and their use have increased in recent years. In the practice of law, the important features of antenuptial agreements are concerned with the distribution of property at death or divorce. Jurisdictions that approve antenuptial agreements have tended to treat them in most respects like other contracts. Their validity may be challenged on traditional contract grounds, such as voluntariness, fraud, and conscionability. Some jurisdictions, however, have been reluctant to treat antenuptial agreements like

dower and **curtesy**
Formerly, interests in property held by wife (dower) and husband (curtesy), the primary purpose of which was to guarantee real property interests for a surviving spouse. The husband was favored, and these interests have been equalized or combined in recent times so as not to discriminate.

elective share   The phrase representing what was formerly *dower* and *curtesy* in the common law, the share of a surviving spouse in the deceased spouse's property that the surviving spouse may elect to take instead of the property that a will would distribute.

antenuptial or **premarital agreement**
A contract agreed to by persons before their marriage, primarily concerned with the distribution of personal and marital assets in the event of divorce or death.

other contracts, expressing traditional public policy concerns for the stability of the family and protection of its members.

Certain situations are ready-made for antenuptial agreements, as when someone remarries and wants to ensure that a major portion of his or her assets will be preserved for children of a prior marriage. Spouses, most commonly women, who sacrifice to put their spouses through a long and expensive education, may want to protect themselves in case of divorce so that they recoup their investments.

Postmarital Contracts

postnuptial agreement
An agreement between spouses, usually distributing family property in the event of death or divorce.

separation agreement or **property settlement agreement** A contract between husband and wife after they have already married to distribute property in case of death or divorce. The agreement is usually executed in preparation for divorce, but it is used occasionally between couples who merely wish to live separately.

Postmarital contracts may be labeled **postnuptial agreements, separation agreements,** or **property settlement agreements.** Postnuptial agreements executed while the marriage is still harmonious are subject to the same public policy challenge as antenuptial agreements, and they lack the consideration essential to a valid contract. Separation agreements and property settlements executed in contemplation of an impending divorce are generally exempt from these attacks. The modern trend in most states increasingly favors recognition of the validity of postmarital agreements.

A major issue regarding agreements submitted to the courts in divorce proceedings concerns whether the agreement is merged into the final decree, so that it loses its separate existence as a contract. On the answer to this question rests the availability of a suit or petition for modification to change or extend the terms of the agreement at a later date. The means of enforcement also depend on whether the agreement is said to be merged in the decree. If merged, contempt of court is available to enforce compliance, on the ground that noncompliance defies the order of the court. Without merger, traditional contract actions may be necessary to remedy noncompliance. If the agreement is merged so that its terms are ordered by the court, those orders may be modified like other orders (custody and support) emanating from the court. If the agreement is not merged, the contract may only be modified by mutual agreement of the parties. The common exception to this concerns children, whose interests most courts will not allow to be bargained away.

Divorce: Property Settlements

The principal legal issues at divorce are the division of property and rights and duties with regard to children. These issues should be explicitly resolved in the property settlement or marital settlement agreement. Although the judge in a divorce case is ultimately responsible for recognizing the agreement or setting its provisions, most judges will avoid making difficult choices if at all possible. Because the judge in a divorce case is vested with great discretion, lawyers are extremely reluctant to take chances on the vagaries of judicial choice and advise their clients against such a course. This means that the lawyers will hammer out a property settlement, often through extended negotiations, with obstinate spouses. The negotiations are limited by principles enunciated by state legislatures and the courts.

The distribution of assets at divorce is treated differently in different states, but the underlying goal is fairness to both parties. In the past, a major theme of distribution was the effort to protect dependent spouses. More recently, this has been restated in terms of valuing homemaking in the distribution of marital assets. Now that wives have taken their place in the workforce, the valuation of respective contributions has an added feature. The questions that arise in this context concern classification and valuation. Fairness requires that the courts be open to a variety of economic claims that were rare a few decades ago. For example, is a spouse entitled to share in the value of a professional license acquired by the other spouse during the marriage? Are future pension benefits classified as property, or marital property, or something else? What if one of the spouses dissipates marital assets (say, through gambling or extravagance)? Does this entitle the other spouse to a larger share of what is left? The answer to these questions is yes, in *some* states. Regardless of the nature of the property that is subject to distribution, its valuation is a major problem when market value is less than obvious.

In community property states (Arizona, California, Idaho, Louisiana, New Mexico, Nevada, Texas, and Washington), property acquired during the marriage is owned equally, so disputes in divorce concern whether property is community or *separate property*. The latter consists of property owned prior to the marriage or acquired during the marriage by gift, will, or inheritance. Separate property can be transmuted into community property by transfer or gift or by commingling funds so as to render them untraceable as separate property.

Community property embodies a partnership model that has been borrowed in so-called common law states with the label *equitable distribution*. This scheme is designed to treat the partners fairly, especially considering domestic contributions equal to financial contributions. Although equitable distribution generally takes a broad, inclusive view of marital property, the distinction between marital and separate property is similar to community property. It would be a mistake, however, to conclude that divorces in any of the states involved will result in either a fifty-fifty split in property or a division regarded as fair by both sides.

Under basic community property theory, property acquired during marriage is owned equally by husband and wife because they are a community. What exactly may be included varies somewhat from state to state. In the *Lynch* case, the court argues that the rules may be drastically opposed in different states.

LYNCH
v.
LYNCH
Court of Appeals of Arizona
164 Ariz. 127, 791 P.2d 653 (1990)

A man who won the lottery before the pending dissolution of his marriage seeks to reverse the trial court's grant of half his winnings to his wife. We hold that the winnings were community property and affirm. . . .

Michael Lynch (husband) and Bonnie Lynch (wife) were married in 1968. Their only child was born in 1971. The couple separated in 1985, and within a year husband began living with a woman named Donna Williams. Wife filed for dissolution shortly after.

Wife's petition was uncontested, and at a default hearing on February 10, 1987, wife testified that the marriage was irretrievably broken. A decree of dissolution is ordinarily entered at the conclusion of a default hearing. However, on February 10, the trial court took the matter under advisement and, on February 19, vacated the hearing because husband had received untimely notice. . . .

On February 21, husband and Donna Williams won a $2.2 million jackpot in the Arizona State Lottery. Each owned half a share of the winning ticket. Wife then filed an amended petition in the unconcluded dissolution seeking half of husband's share. This time husband answered, the case went on to trial, and in the ultimate decree of dissolution the trial court awarded wife half of husband's lottery share.

Husband has appealed the trial court's ruling on three grounds. . . . By each argument, he attempts to establish that the parties acquired no community property after February 10, 1987, when the invalid default hearing was held. First, he argues that a marital community lasts only as long as the parties' will to union and that these parties' will to union had ended by the time of wife's testimony on Feb-

ruary 10 that the marriage was irretrievably broken. Second, he argues that, by this testimony, wife waived her community interest in his future acquisitions. Last, he contends that, because wife's lawyers gave untimely notice of the February 10 hearing, wife is estopped from denying that the marital community ended on that date.

Community Duration

When an Arizona spouse acquires an asset before marital dissolution, Arizona law treats the asset as community property unless it falls within one of several statutory exceptions. . . . A marriage endures in Arizona—and thus the acquisition of community property continues—"until the final dissolution is ordered by the court."

In some jurisdictions, acquisition of community property ceases when spouses begin to live separate and apart. In Arizona, however, demarcation by decree "avoids the factual issue of when the couple began living apart, and provides appropriate treatment for the on-again off-again manner in which some couples try to resolve their differences and patch up their marriages."

An Arizona couple that wishes to end the acquisition of community property before (or without) dissolution has a statutory means to do so. [State statute] provides for entry of a decree of legal separation that terminates "community property rights and liabilities. . . . as to all property, income and liabilities received or incurred after [its] entry." In the absence of a decree of legal separation, however, acquisition of community property continues in Arizona until the decree of dissolution is filed.

[The court then rejected husband's argument based on the will-to-union doctrine, a Spanish rule which holds that property acquired after the union of the wills has ceased would not be community property. On the facts, the court found some basis to doubt that the will to union had really ceased.]

Waiver

Husband makes the related argument that wife waived any interest in his further acquisitions on February 10 when she testified that the marriage was irretrievably broken, expecting a decree of dissolution to issue on that date. We disagree. Waiver is the intentional relinquishment of a known right. Wife surely waived her interest in husband's acquisitions beyond the dissolution of their marriage, but her waiver went no further. She did not relinquish what might accrue to the marital community if the marriage lasted beyond its anticipated end. . . .

Conclusion

This case displays the hand of chance. Fortune favored husband with a jackpot, but, because his marriage had not ended, fortune dealt his wife a share. Though the lottery was a windfall, spouses marry for better or for worse and share no less in windfalls than in labor's wages. Husband claims that his marriage ended equitably, though not formally, before the winning ticket was acquired. We have given our reasons for rejecting his arguments. The judgment of the trial court is affirmed.

Case Questions

1. Why wasn't a default entered on February 10, 1987? What would its effect have been if it had been entered? Do you think Bonnie Lynch could have challenged a default if entered?
2. Bonnie Lynch's attorney made a mistake in the hearing notice procedure. Was she mad at him? Explain.

---

spousal support
Payments made to an ex-spouse following divorce that are designed as support rather than a division of the marital property. Traditionally this was called *alimony*, and in many jurisdictions the term *maintenance* is used.

rehabilitative alimony
Ordinarily a form of periodic payment, temporary in duration, designed to provide for an ex-spouse until he or she can become self-supporting.

lump-sum alimony
Alimony that is established as one lump-sum amount, usually in the form of one payment but occasionally in installments.

Alimony

The traditional term for **spousal support** was **alimony.** In many jurisdictions it is called **maintenance,** and all three terms may be used interchangeably in many states. For some, alimony has a negative connotation because it is associated with an earlier time when a husband had a lifelong duty to support his dependent wife, whether married or divorced. Because of equal rights guaranteed by the Constitution, alimony today requires that a husband may receive alimony if a wife can. In recent times, courts and legislatures have come to disfavor both permanent alimony and alimony in general. Most awards of alimony today come in the form of periodic payments lasting a few months or years, classified as **rehabilitative alimony** and designed to return a homemaker to the job market (i.e., to help a dependent spouse get through the post-divorce period of adjustment to self-sufficiency). **Lump-sum alimony** is occasionally awarded, often to provide compensation for contributions by one spouse, such as one spouse who worked to put the other through a professional education.

Alimony is part of a more comprehensive plan dividing the resources and obligations of the spouses. The distribution of assets and child support are the other two important economic ingredients of this plan.

Alimony is characterized by a high degree of discretion on the part of the judiciary, although most states have provided more or less detailed guidelines for judges to weigh when awarding alimony. Alimony is principally based on the need of the recipient and the other spouse's ability to pay. Need is a relative concept, depending to a large degree on the standard of living enjoyed during the marriage. Alimony is usually terminated by the death of either party or by remarriage of the recipient. Depending on the jurisdiction, this may be waived in the property settlement agreement.

A post-divorce procedure in the form of a petition for **modification** is available to increase or decrease alimony or to extend or shorten the period during which payments are made. The key element in a successful suit for modification is proof of *changed circumstances* justifying modification. For the recipient of alimony to obtain an upward modification, it must be shown also that the payor has the ability to pay the increased amount.

The *Brown* case traces the history of alimony in Florida over more than a century. Although the dates may differ from state to state, the path from a preference for permanent periodic monthly payments for a divorced wife to the general disfavor in which alimony is held today is echoed in state after state. In most instances, changes in the law of alimony directly reflect the changing status of women in our society.

modification   When applied to divorce, a court-approved change in the amount or terms of alimony, child support, or child custody.

BROWN
v.
BROWN
First District Court of Appeal of Florida
300 So. 2d 719 (Fla. Dist. Ct. App. 1974)

For at least forty years prior to the recent enactments repealing divorce and instituting dissolution of marriage (commonly referred to as no fault), the courts awarded a divorced wife periodic alimony almost as a matter of constitutional right. In *Phelan v. Phelan,* 12 Fla. 449 (1868) the Supreme Court [said:] "Permanent alimony is not a sum of money or a specific proportion of the husband's estate given absolutely to the wife. It is a continuous allotment of sums payable at regular periods for her support from year to year."

This definition of permanent alimony was reaffirmed in. . . . 1948 [in a case holding that a wife was entitled to periodic alimony based upon her needs and her husband's ability to pay. The court refused to apply retroactively a newly enacted statute permitting the award of lump-sum alimony.]

The next development in the law of alimony was the appearance of the doctrine of special equity. As early as 1919, the Supreme Court . . . , after noticing that the wife, mother of six children, had contributed generously in funds and

by her personal exertion and industry through a long period of time to the acquisition and development of [the] home and other property and the establishment of [a] fortune, held that the wife possessed a special equity in the property which she aided in acquiring and possessing.

In 1932, the Supreme Court utilized the doctrine of special equity to relieve a wife from the harshness of the statutory prohibition of awarding alimony to an adulteress.

* * *

[The court was again confronted with the question of lump-sum alimony in 1968. [T]he original final judgment for payment of periodic alimony by the husband to the wife was amended to provide lump-sum alimony payable in monthly installments.]

In 1955, Justice Roberts, speaking for our Supreme Court, announced:

Times have now changed. The broad, practically unlimited opportunities for women in the business world of today are a matter of common knowledge. Thus, in an era where the opportunities for self-support by the wife are so abundant, the fact that the marriage has been brought to an end because of the fault of the husband does not necessarily entitle the wife to be forever supported by a former husband who has little, if any, more economic advantages than she has.

This pronouncement marks the entry in the jurisprudence of this state of the concept of rehabilitative alimony. Rehabilitative means the restoration of property that has been lost. The concept of rehabilitative alimony appeared in the statutory scheme of this state in 1971 when the legislature made a major change. . . . The salient provisions are:

> . . . [T]he court may grant alimony to either party, which alimony may be rehabilitative or permanent in nature. In any award of alimony, the court may order periodic payment or payments in lump sum or both. . . .
>
> In determining a proper award of alimony, the court may consider any factor necessary to do equity and justice between the parties.

In 1966, [another Florida district court] clearly stated the rule that prevailed as to awarding alimony prior to the dissolution of marriage act in 1971 as: "The accepted principles are that a divorced wife is entitled to alimony which will permit her to live in a manner commensurate with that provided by her husband during coverture, if he has the ability to pay."

Post 1971 alimony

[In 1972], the trial court found (as is probably true in more than 90 percent of marriage failures) that although neither party was without fault, "the preponderance of the equities lies with appellant husband and he is entitled to a divorce from appellee wife on the ground of habitual intemperance and indulgence in alcoholic beverages." [The court reversed an award of $100 per month permanent alimony with the following statement:]

> They now occupy a position of equal partners in the family relationship resulting from marriage, and more often than not contribute a full measure to the economic well-being of the family unit. Whether the marriage continues to exist or is severed through the device of

judicial decree, the woman continues to be as fully equipped as the man to earn a living and provide for her essential needs. The fortuitous circumstance created by recitation of the marriage vows neither diminishes her capacity for self-support nor does it give her a vested right in her husband's earnings for the remainder of her life. . . .

"The new concept of the marriage relation implicit in the so-called no fault divorce law enacted by the legislature in 1971 places both parties to the marriage on a basis of complete equality as partners sharing equal rights and obligations in the marriage relationship and sharing equal burdens in the event of dissolution."

. . . Either spouse may contribute either by working in the market place or by working as a homemaker. The fact that in one marital venture a spouse is gainfully employed in the market place and pays a housekeeper to rear the children and keep house is not distinguishable from the spouse who devotes his or her full time to the profession of homemaker. The primary factual circumstance is each spouse's contribution to the marital partnership. In the case sub judice, the wife has been short changed. The wife has not been adequately compensated for the contribution that she made as a full time mother and homemaker to the equal partnership marriage. We hold that the trial court abused its discretion in awarding the wife a pittance of the material assets accumulated in the husband's name during 21 years.

McCORD, Judge (specially concurring):

[Rehabilitative alimony is defined as] financially supporting an ill spouse until his or her health is restored, or financially supporting a spouse until he or she can be trained for employment, or, in some circumstances, until the spouse has a reasonable time to recover from the trauma of the dissolution.

Case Questions

1. Why does Judge McCord's definition of rehabilitative alimony fit the commonly accepted meaning of the phrase better than the definition given in the main opinion?
2. How does the evolution of alimony reflect the changing status of American women?

Child Support

After divorce, one parent usually becomes the primary caregiver of the children. When one parent is responsible for the physical custody of the children more than the other, the primary caregiver is entitled to contribution for providing more than his or her share of support. Today both parents are obligated to support their children, and that obligation is measured in terms of their respective ability to pay and the needs of the children. Legal issues with regard to child support range from the basic questions of how much support should be paid and how to collect arrearages to questions of who should pay and what should be covered. Legislation in this area has focused on establishing precise guidelines for payment and the means to enforce them.

Parental Duty to Support

As the duty of support was first legally recognized, it applied only to the father. In the twentieth century, the duty of support was extended to mothers as *secondarily* liable for support. This concept was destined to fail as focus on the equal protection clause of the Fourteenth Amendment was applied with greater force to legal distinctions based on gender. Eventually, the law required equal duty of support from mother and father.

Unmarried fathers are also obligated to support their offspring. Adoptive parents are legally bound to support their adoptive children—adoption severs the legal bond between a child and its natural parents and treats the child as having the same legal relationship to its adoptive parents as a natural child would have. There is even a trend toward recognizing stepparents' legal obligations to support their stepchildren.

Need and Ability to Pay

Like alimony, child support is based on (children's) *need* for support and (parents') *ability to pay*. Even when the mother is the primary custodian of the children, her resources may be considered in the amount ordered to be paid by the father, as she is obligated to support her children, too. Similarly, when the father has custody of the children, the mother may be ordered to pay child support to the father. Unlike alimony, the resources of the beneficiary have only a limited impact on the award. A child's resources (e.g., a trust set up by grandparents) do not ordinarily reduce the parental obligation for furnishing necessaries.

Need is a relative concept. The courts do not limit parental contributions to necessaries after divorce. In this instance, the child of divorce may be entitled to more (and usually receives less) than the child of an intact family, who has only a right to necessaries. The rationale is that a child should not be required to drastically reduce an accustomed lifestyle simply because one of the parents has moved to other quarters.

Setting and Enforcing Child Support

During the 1980s and 1990s, both states and the federal government made a major effort at reducing welfare costs by collecting child support arrearages. A federal law made crossing state lines to avoid paying child support a federal crime. The motivation for government action was not a simple and direct response to the woeful record of support payments, although statistics in that regard demanded attention and action. The governments aimed to reduce the governments' share in welfare payments to single-parent families. In many instances, public assistance provided support when parents (fathers in particular) failed to meet their legal support obligations. New laws provide means for collecting arrears that can then be credited to welfare amounts that had been paid.

These efforts were begun primarily through the Office of Child Support Enforcement (OCSE) of the U.S. Department of Health and Human Services, beginning in 1974, and are presently collecting several billion dollars yearly. The federal government furnishes funds for state enforcement programs at the same time that it imposes requirements on the states that receive the funds. Amendments to the law (the Federal Enforcement Initiative of 1974) in 1984 and 1988 have added more requirements and made more drastic the means of enforcement. AFDC applicants assign their uncollected support rights to the state and must assist efforts to collect. Both the states and the federal government maintain records to assist in locating parents in arrears.

Under the requirements imposed on the state, new laws must require employee withholding of child support from paychecks of those in arrears. Arrears in excess of $1,000 must be deducted from state and federal income tax refunds. Under the 1988 amendments, orders for support or orders modifying support cause support payments to be automatically deducted from paychecks whether the payor is in arrears or not. The 1988 amendments also provided new standards for paternity and federal funds for paternity testing, in an obvious effort to make unwed fathers financially responsible for their offspring.

Child Support Guidelines

One of the most far-reaching requirements of the 1984 amendments provided: "Each state, as a condition for having its State plan approved under this part, must establish guidelines for child support award amounts within the state. The guidelines may be established by law or by judicial or administrative action." Although need and ability to pay are the foundation for determining the amount of child support the noncustodial parent must pay, a powerful movement toward establishing statutory (sometimes judicial) guidelines has resulted in numerous schemes, from criteria to formulas to lengthy tables, by which to calculate child support.

Interstate Enforcement—URESA

The Uniform Reciprocal Enforcement of Support Act (URESA) and its latest revised version (RURESA), was produced by the National Conference of Commissioners on Uniform State Laws. URESA was formulated because of the national problem with interstate enforcement of child support orders. URESA provides a means of enforcement when defaulted payments have not been reduced to judgment, as well as provisions for when the defaulting obligor has been ordered in contempt of court. It is a means by which the recipient of child support payments may bring an action in his or her own state that will be tried in the state of the debtor. This solves the problem of lack of personal jurisdiction over the debtor by the state of the creditor and saves the creditor the expense of traveling to the debtor's state.

A complaint is filed in the appropriate court in the creditor's state. The complaint is forwarded to the court having jurisdiction over the debtor-defendant and the case is tried there, with a local official representing the creditor.

Once the case is decided, the state ordering compliance receives the payments and forwards them to the court of the creditor. Failure to pay subjects the debtor to the usual sanctions (contempt, garnishment, etc.) available in the state with personal jurisdiction over the defendant.

Unwed fathers may also be subject to URESA. If paternity has already been adjudicated, they may be treated the same as divorced fathers. URESA also provides for the responding state to adjudicate paternity.

Child Custody

Battles over custody of children may be the most intense of all legal encounters. The introduction of no-fault divorce did not seriously change the volatile nature of custody cases, which pose special problems. Those most deeply affected—namely, minor children—are not parties to the lawsuit. In custody battles, children often become pawns in a political struggle between men and women. Complicating this situation is the fact that the court departs from its usual role of resolving a dispute over *past* events and must predict the best course of action for the *future* welfare of the children.

Historical Overview

The English common law carried on the Western European tradition of Roman law, which gave the father absolute control over his children. Because the father-husband enjoyed and exercised legal rights in behalf of the family, his duty of support was balanced by custodial rights. In America, where divorce was early recognized, issues of custody and support became problems for ordinary people. As the revolutionary family was cast in the companionate mold, with the wife responsible for home and children, the father's right to custody was disputed and lost, particularly for children of tender years.

It was not until the twentieth century that this custodial double standard was challenged. The movement for equality of women caused two ideological changes in the legal view of custody. First, if the sexes are equal and should have equal rights, as embodied in the equal protection clause of the Fourteenth Amendment, the tender years doctrine could no longer stand. Second, as the country grew more prosperous and new opportunities for employment of women became available, judicial opinions began to argue that women were no longer unable to join men in the workplace. The custodian of the children then became a matter of choice, giving rise to the ultimate standard, the best interests of the child.

The most recent turn in this story has been a shift from parental rights toward parental responsibilities. The best interests of the child standard emphasizes rights of the child rather than those of the parents. This change of focus has encouraged extensive study of children of divorce, single-parent families, and adopted and foster children, all of which we now have in large supply. Psychological and sociological studies have influenced both statute and court decisions. Child custody is but one part of a larger picture in which many of our youth appear to be at risk.

joint custody The continued sharing of rights and duties with regard to children following divorce.

sole custody The award of *child custody* exclusively to one parent upon divorce; the other parent usually enjoys visitation rights.

Many states have attempted to reduce the injury that divorce does to children by adopting **joint custody** as the preferred form of parental responsibility. Formerly, **sole custody** was granted to one parent, who made all decisions for the children, while the other parent was granted visitation rights. Under the joint custody scheme, both parents share in the decision making over the vital concerns of the children, and both have frequent contact with the children. There is a fundamental weakness in the premise of joint custody: We are asking two individuals who were unable to cooperative effectively while married to cooperate after the destructive ordeal of divorce. Fortunately, most parents continue to love their children long after they have lost their love for each other, and may be able to cooperate for the sake of the children. That, at least, is the hope that joint custody offers.

Best Interests of the Child

Case after case insists that the polestar of custody decisions is the best interests of the child. This is a significant departure from the older common law paternal rights approach, but the common law rule really acted as a presumption in favor of the father and existed in an era when divorce was rare. Today, despite the best-interests standard, custody decisions are made in the context of presumptions, preferences, and legislative and judicial guidelines. For example, the tender years doctrine, popular during the latter part of the nineteenth century and most of the twentieth, expressed a presumption or preference, depending on the state, that young children should be in the custody of their mother. Even in jurisdictions that have clearly abolished the tender years doctrine by judicial decision, the mother of small children asserts an unspoken claim that judges are likely to heed. After all, the suckling infant will not be forcibly weaned in the name of parental equality. Other policies underlying custody decisions include the wishes of the child; avoidance of splitting siblings; minimizing dislocation of children from school, community, and extended family; and protecting parents' rights against third parties.

Formerly, the adultery of the mother could cause her to lose custody; a strict moral code was in force, including a double standard censuring extramarital conduct on the part of the wife and mother. Not only was a woman at fault with regard to the divorce itself, but the moral code presumed that her conduct would have a bad impact on the children. This sometimes overcame the preference in favor of awarding custody to the mother. More recently, however, sexual misconduct has generally been abandoned as grounds to deny custody, unless the father can demonstrate that the mother's sexual behavior has a detrimental impact on the children. The issue continues to be cloudy, however, because judges have very different perceptions of improper sexual conduct and different beliefs about the impact of parental sexuality on children.

Modification

Custody awards may be modifiable, like alimony and child support, but modification is more difficult to obtain than alimony and child support because of judges' reluctance to switch custody and remove a child from a stable environment. Many states have adopted provisions prohibiting modification of custody for two years following a custody order, absent a showing of danger to the child posed by its environment. The most common form of modification attack addresses the sexual misconduct of a custodial mother—the moral leper approach used to gain custody at divorce. When the single mother begins to court, the ex-husband may use this to seek custody (and sometimes as a device to negotiate reductions in support payments). Formerly, courts concluded without proof that extramarital sexual encounters by the mother automatically created an immoral environment for children. Sensitivity in the courts to the impropriety of a sexual double standard, along with a focus on the welfare of the child rather than the rights of the parents, has reversed this custom. Today, a mother's sexuality does not justify modification of custody without a clear showing that the mother's conduct has an injurious effect on the children.

The Natural Father

When children are born to unmarried parents, a special set of problems arises. On the one hand, there is no body of law from which to fashion rights of the unofficial family. On the other hand, the recognition of Fourteenth Amendment equal protection rights has generated a continuing inquiry into discrimination against the relationships within a nonmarital family. As a general rule, nonmarital relationships should not invoke different treatment. The unwed father should have the same rights as the man married to a child's mother. Although it may pose a moral issue for some, the nonmarital family does not pose a legal quandary when it is an intact family or when an intact family splits up. In many cases, however, the illegitimate child is the product of a relatively brief relationship, sometimes terminating before the child's birth. This may constitute abandonment of a relationship that was never established except biologically.

Uniform Child Custody Jurisdiction Act

The outcome of custody disputes can be radically different in different states. In the past, a parent could grab the kids, run to another state, and thwart the other parent's custodial rights not only by hiding but also by making recovery of the children dependent on a cumbersome process in which state jurisdiction became a legal issue of considerable complexity. The Uniform Child Custody Jurisdiction Act (UCCJA) was proposed to ameliorate this situation, discourage child snatching, and provide a uniform basis for jurisdiction that could be applied reciprocally by the states.

The UCCJA resolves three problems that arose in the past. First, jurisdiction was commonly premised on the physical whereabouts of the child, which encouraged child snatching and interstate flight as well as forum-shopping. Second, parents often attempted to undo custody orders by seeking modification in another state. Although full faith and credit applied to the original order, this did not prevent another state from assuming jurisdiction for the sake of modification. Third, the UCCJA promotes swift enforcement of the custody orders of other states.

Adoption

adoption   In family law, the legal establishment of parent-child bonds between persons who did not formerly have them; commonly, this entails the severance of those bonds with a former parent.

Adoption creates bonds of parent and child between persons who did not previously have this relationship. Ordinarily this involves the severance of legal bonds between a child and its natural parent or parents and the substitution of a new parent or parents, with all the legal consequences of the parent-child relationship.

Adoption was not recognized in England until 1926. The American law of adoption traces its roots to Massachusetts statutes in 1851. Until recently, adoption was primarily concerned with finding children for childless couples; providing parents for children was an incidental benefit. As the focus of public policy turned away from parental rights toward the interests of children, some reorientation in adoption has taken place. An early issue in the law of adoption was the degree to which judicial intervention was appropriate. Today governmental administrative agencies concern themselves with the adoption process and legislatures have enacted increasing numbers of laws to regulate the adoption process.

Government has entered the adoption process in favor of children with special needs, creating subsidies for parents to adopt children when their resources would otherwise be insufficient. The National Conference of Commissioners on Uniform State Laws published the Uniform Adoption Act in 1953 and revised in

1969, and the Department of Health, Education, and Welfare proposed a model act for the states called "An Act for the Adoption of Children."

The Parties

Other than the status of adulthood, the states place few statutory requirements on the prospective adopting parent. Administrative or judicial approval, however, is another matter. The law has been reluctant to grant anyone a *right* to adopt, but clear preferences may be found in the law and in the decisions approving and disapproving particular adoptions. An examination of some of the most common situations clarifies the adoption picture:

1. *Blood relatives.* By custom, orphans became the wards of their close relatives. For divorced parents with minimal resources or for working single mothers, parental duties may be overwhelming, and children are often placed in the care of grandparents or aunts and uncles. Although these may be purely temporary placements, with legal custody remaining with the parent or parents, the desire to adopt may arise for many reasons. With orphans, de facto adoption may be followed by legal adoption. The court or agency looks for the same factors applicable to custody disputes—wholesome environment, continuity of care (same home, school, neighborhood, etc.), keeping siblings together.

2. *Foster parents.* Children who have been placed in the care of strangers may remain with them via adoption even though the foster care administered through the state was traditionally conditioned on the **foster parents** not attempting adoption.

3. *Stepparents.* One of the most common relationships involved in adoption is **stepparent-stepchild.** A typical scenario: A stepfather is actively involved in raising his wife's children by a former marriage, with the natural father mostly or completely absent and perhaps totally neglecting support obligations. The greatest stumbling block to such an adoption is denial of consent by the natural parent. Although this may be overcome by a court finding that abandonment or neglect has severed the bonds between parent and child, the law so strongly favors continuance of the biological bond as a legal bond that lack of consent in many instances is fatal to the adoption process. Adoption severs the natural parents' rights with regard to the child, something the court is extremely reluctant to do.

4. *Childless strangers.* Couples unable to bear children are most likely to go to adoption agencies or lawyers to seek children to adopt. Adoption agencies are usually extensively regulated and subject to statutory restriction. Potential adoptive parents are in theory carefully scrutinized both for the environment they can provide and their capacity to be good parents. The process may be lengthy and cumbersome, so many couples employ attorneys to facilitate the process.

foster parents
Caretakers of children who are not their parents, stepparents, nor adoptive parents, whom the law has recognized as parental caretakers, commonly when children are taken away from their parents for cause.

stepparent A person in a relationship with a child by virtue of marriage to the child's legal parent; the child in that relationship is a **stepchild.**

illegitimate Referring to a child born to an unwed mother. In most states, the acknowledgment of paternity by a natural father may legitimate the child despite being born out of wedlock.

5. *Unwed (nonmarital) fathers*. Until recent years, fathers of **illegitimate** offspring had no rights or legal relationship with their children. With the advent of financial responsibility through paternity suits, the fathers could expect to have rights as well. Visitation rights were forthcoming and custody was possible when the mother died or her custody was detrimental to the child. Still, because the father had not married the mother and usually had not otherwise acknowledged paternity, his rights inevitably threatened the maternal bond. Courts and legislatures have created a balancing act between recognition of the special place of the mother without depriving the father of rights.

Surrogacy

surrogacy contract A contract by which the natural father takes custody of a child and the mother relinquishes custody in favor of adoption by the father's wife.

Because of the *Baby M* case in 1988, much public attention was directed at so-called **surrogacy contracts.** In surrogacy contracts, the natural father takes custody of the child while the mother relinquishes custody in favor of adoption by the natural father's wife. Conception is ordinarily achieved by artificial insemination with the contracting father's sperm or by implanting a fertilized ovum in the surrogate mother. In the former case, the childbearer is the genetic mother, but not in the latter case. Although in theory surrogacy contracts are simple, their subject matter is unique. From one point of view, they seem to be agreements to sell babies and thus clearly illegal. In contrast, because the natural fathers are assuming custody, they cannot be said to be buying something to which they have no right. These contracts have also been considered offensive because they imply that womens' bodies may be rented for a period of time, suggesting exploitation of the poor by the rich. Additionally, surrogacy involves the psychobiology of rending an infant from its natural mother, whose feelings and state of mind have undoubtedly changed considerably from the time of contracting. For all these (and perhaps other) reasons, the *Baby M* case, in which a surrogate mother changed her mind after the birth of the child, prompted a diversity of intense emotional and intellectual responses, and state legislatures hurriedly passed legislation to regulate surrogacy contracts.

Summary

Family law has undergone continuous revision since the founding of American law, changing to keep up with American society. The principal subject of family law is divorce, although annulment remains an alternative. Divorce inevitably raises the issues of distribution of marital property, spousal and child support, and child custody. Although these are the most litigated issues of family law, in most instances their resolution occurs outside of court during lawyers' negotiations. This is due in part to the uncertainty created by the vast discretion judges exercise when forced to decide domestic relations issues.

Adoption and premarital, or antenuptial, agreements pose additional areas of legal concern in family law.

Scenario

Henry A. Fuller (Henry) was born to Audrey Fuller (Fuller) in 1951. Paternity was never established. Fuller decided to give up her son for adoption. In 1947, the Columbia County Juvenile Court entered a parental termination order stating Fuller was "permanently deprived of any and all maternal rights and interests in and to the said Baby Boy Fuller." The order also placed Henry into the permanent custody of the Catholic Charities of the Diocese, authorizing that organization to consent to his adoption. Henry was never adopted. The parent-child relationship between Henry and Fuller was never reestablished.

Henry died intestate in 1996. He was not married and had no children. Two biological relatives survived Henry—his biological mother and his half-brother, William Gilbert, who was born to Fuller after she terminated her parental rights to Henry.

In 1998, the personal administrator of Henry's estate filed a petition for determination of heirship. She asked the court to find that Fuller and Gilbert were not entitled to inherit from Henry because by court order all maternal rights had been terminated. She argued that Henry's estate should escheat to the State because he died intestate without any legal heirs.

Fuller and Gilbert filed a response and objection to the petition. The superior court commissioner agreed with Renfrew and ruled the estate escheats to the State because Henry was without legal heirs. The commissioner found that the 1947 order terminating Fuller's maternal rights to Henry also extinguished her right to inherit intestate, and that Gilbert could not inherit from Henry because there was no longer a common ancestor between them.

Fuller died soon after the commissioner ruled. Gilbert was appointed personal representative of her estate. After her death, Gilbert continued to assert a claim to Henry's estate, filing a motion in superior court to revise the ruling of the commissioner. The superior court upheld the commissioner's order.

The statute in effect at the time of the court-ordered surrender of Henry provided that when a parent surrendered a child to a charitable organization, "the rights of its natural parents or of the guardian of its person (if any) shall cease and such corporation shall become entitled to the custody of such a child."

The statute regarding intestate succession reads as follows:

(1) Shares of others than surviving spouse. The shares of the net estate not distributable to the surviving spouse, or the entire net estate if there is no surviving spouse, shall descend and be distributed as follows:
    (a) To the issue of the intestate. . . .
    (b) If the intestate not be survived by issue, then to the parent or parents who survive the intestate.
    (c) If the intestate not be survived by issue or by either parent, then to those issue of the parent or parents who survive the intestate[.]

If no person qualified to inherit under the intestate law, the property belongs to the State.

Query   There are two ways that Gilbert might acquire Henry's estate. Make an argument that will favor Gilbert using two alternative ways that could happen. Argue the intent of the legislature. Argue policy—why the law would favor an interpretation that would give Gilbert the estate rather than the State. Argue justice—why the facts of the case are special and the equities are in Gilbert's favor. How can you define "apparent" in such a way that Gilbert can prevail?

14

ADMINISTRATIVE LAW AND PROCEDURE

CHAPTER OUTLINE

Introduction

administrative law
The body of law that controls the way in which administrative agencies operate covered by state and federal Administrative Procedure Acts; also deals with regulations issued by administrative agencies.

Administrative law refers to the law that governs administrative action by government. It regulates the relationship between the citizen and the government. Although it is poorly understood by laypersons and many practitioners, it has a greater impact on the daily lives of Americans than any other area of law. Most people have few, if any, brushes with criminal law; few are often involved in personal injury law; contract and property law are matters of occasional concern for the nonbusinessperson. But the rules and regulations of government agencies are encountered throughout a lifetime. The water we drink, the air we breathe, the places we work, the schools we attend, the social security system, and a host of other facets of our lives are subject to regulations by agencies governed by administrative law.

The Field of Administrative Law

Administrative law was born in the twentieth century. In theory, it can be traced back through the centuries, but the field as it is defined today emanates principally from the U.S. Constitution as it has come to be interpreted in recent decades. The federal Administrative Procedure Act, first enacted in 1946, may have been the most important event in administrative law, although its provisions drew heavily on prior case law. Because administrative law is relatively

bureaucracy That
part of the government
composed of agencies
staffed by civil servants;
forms the major part of
the administrative
branch.

young, it is still dynamic and changing. Our **bureaucracy** has expanded and
blossomed, particularly in the years since Roosevelt's New Deal. The greatest
expansion has come in social services agencies, such as social security, the Veterans Administration, Medicare, and the social welfare agencies. The new agencies and the expanding scope of government activities have presented numerous problems that have encouraged the growth of administrative law and the
litigation that often shapes it. Charting new ground for law has left a confusing
array of cases and rules that makes administrative law a great challenge.

Substantive Law

The academic study of administrative law is generally confined to procedural
law because of the impossibility of learning the substantive law. Each agency
has its own set of substantive rules and regulations, sometimes a product of the
legislature and sometimes the legislative product of the agency itself. The regulations of the Social Security Administration bear little resemblance to those
of the Securities and Exchange Commission or the Environmental Protection
Agency, and their regulations are collected in the *Code of Federal Regulations*,
which is a huge compendium that no one has ever mastered. It would be a
major undertaking simply to gain a relatively complete understanding of the
rules and regulations of the Social Security Administration.

Procedural Law

Administrative procedural law encompasses most of what is usually meant when
the term *administrative law* is used. There are certain principles governing
administrative action regardless of the agency concerned. Administrative agencies pose a special problem for the law because most agencies engage in all
three governmental functions. Although they belong to the executive branch of
government, most agencies engage in rulemaking, which is the administrative
agency equivalent of legislation; and most large agencies (and many small agencies) have an adjudicatory function as well.

Administrative procedure is particularly concerned with the legislative
(rulemaking) and adjudicatory functions of agencies. Because these involve
state or federal action, they are constrained by the due process clauses of the
Fifth and Fourteenth Amendments requiring fundamental fairness in substance
and procedure. What makes administrative procedural law different from the
procedural principles that apply in suits between private parties derives from the
nature of the parties involved.

Every administrative law case potentially involves weighing the important
interests of the individual against the interests of society as represented by government. A prime example is sovereign immunity from suit. In the nineteenth
century, the courts and some state legislatures concluded that it made no sense
for a private citizen to sue the government. At that time, of course, government
was small, offered few services, and intruded very little into private affairs. A

democratic government was perceived as benevolent, as representing the people, so it was illogical for the people to sue themselves. By the 1960s and 1970s, it had become apparent that a democratic government could indeed be intrusive and abusive, and that sovereign immunity was often viewed as a license for government to run roughshod over private interests.

Administrative Law in Practice

The study of administrative law is a worthwhile endeavor for the paralegal student for a number of reasons. Only by studying administrative law can a person gain a deep understanding of the basic process of upholding the rights of the citizen against the intrusions of government. It is also a rewarding education into constitutional law. But the study of administrative law can also be very practical. Litigation against the government increases as the scope of government activities increases, and there seems to be no end to this increase. Administrative law cases frequently involve lengthy litigation with copious amounts of research that should be done by paralegals for reasons of cost efficiency. In addition, many agencies, such as the Social Security Administration and other social service agencies, permit claimants to be represented by anyone of their choosing. The California Bar Association in 1989 issued an opinion allowing paralegals employed by law firms to represent the firm's clients in administrative hearings. This affords paralegals an opportunity to do trial work. Many legal aid offices employ paralegals to represent indigents at administrative hearings. Administrative law thus presents a promising area for employment of paralegals. Although many (perhaps most) paralegals will never handle administrative law work, many others will be administrative law specialists.

Independent Regulatory Agencies

Administrative law questions ultimately concern the power of government to regulate and the right of private parties to challenge regulation. Most of the major principles of the law of administrative procedure grew out of challenges to government regulation of business against government agencies established for the purpose of regulating business.

independent regulatory agencies
Those agencies of the government that exercise relative autonomy because their heads cannot be removed at the whim of the chief executive, for example, the president, as distinguished from *departments*, which are under the direct control of *secretaries*, who serve at the pleasure of the president.

The discussion of administrative law in this chapter uses federal administrative procedure as its model. Most states have adopted comprehensive administrative procedure statutes, modeled on the federal act with modifications. Nevertheless, administrative law at the federal level has tended to lead the way—the federal Administrative Procedure Act (APA) predates state acts by two to four decades. Congress and the federal courts naturally became involved at an earlier stage because of the creation of **independent regulatory agencies** with national authority and great power.

Independent regulatory agencies were originally created to control the devastating effects of cutthroat competition in certain industries. The first great agency to be created was the Interstate Commerce Commission, created in

1887. Since that time Congress has periodically created new agencies; there now exist a dozen major independent regulatory agencies and more than fifty smaller ones. Regulating an industry is essentially anticompetitive and counter to a pure market model of free enterprise. Americans, especially politicians, often speak of free enterprise as if it has always characterized—and continues to characterize—the American economy. Even a cursory review of world history shows that free enterprise unregulated by government probably never existed, though the United States may have come closest to the model at one time or another. In a legal sense, we have been more committed to a *fair* market than a *free* market. It is the nature of government to allocate and distribute power and wealth, which makes it inevitable that business will be taxed and regulated.

The Interstate Commerce Commission (ICC) is a good illustration of the rationale of regulation. The ICC was formed to serve the railroad industry and the public. Vicious competition combined with monopolistic practices often undermined individual companies on the one hand and allowed excessive rates on the other. The industry was unstable at a time when the railroads were a major vehicle for economic growth of the country. Railroads are different from some other businesses in that they must operate on fixed routes—the investment in land and track must result in a level of use that will repay the investment. If 100 railroads build tracks from Chicago to St. Louis, none of them will make money until most have abandoned the route. The ICC was charged with regulating routes and rates in such a way that the railroads could make a reasonable profit charging rates that business and the public could afford so that everyone would benefit. Regulatory schemes are not perfect—sometimes they benefit the country and sometimes they are a burden—but the fact remains that some business activities are so central to the national economy that the government is unlikely to relinquish control.

Some activities must be controlled because they are by nature monopolistic. Public utilities are the prime example. The furnishing of water, sewer, gas, and electricity is an activity that can only be accomplished efficiently by one company serving a community, locality, or region. In fact, these activities are often performed by government. Where they are not, public service commissions monitor their activities and particularly their rates. Because these activities provide absolutely essential services to the community, government does not allow the utilities a free rein.

Independent agencies may be distinguished on the federal level by the following rule of thumb: an independent agency is one whose head cannot be removed by the president without cause. By contrast, cabinet chiefs (the secretaries of state, labor, defense, etc.) occupy their positions at the pleasure of the president. Although the president must obtain Congress's approval for appointment, he can remove a cabinet secretary at any time. The president may remove the chiefs or commissioners of the independent regulatory agencies only upon showing just cause for their removal.

Since the Roosevelt New Deal era, Congress has moved away from creating new industry-regulating agencies toward the establishment of social service agencies such as the Social Security Administration; the Occupational Safety and Health Review Commission, established by the Occupational Safety and Health Act (OSHA); and the Consumer Product Safety Commission (CPSC).

The importance of independent regulatory agencies for administrative law is twofold. First, the creation of these agencies brought into question the authority of Congress to delegate its legislative powers granted by the Constitution. Second, authority was delegated to administrative agencies with a degree of independence from the executive branch of government of which they were a part. Because the agencies often regulated national industries and administrative activities, the regulations they promulgated, the enforcement procedures they used, and their activities were frequently challenged by business interests that could afford to pursue their remedies all the way to the U.S. Supreme Court. As the initial legal issues were basic constitutional questions, many of the fundamental principles of administrative procedure were formulated in the context of the regulation of business.

Thus, many of the landmark cases in administrative law seem remote from daily life. For example, *United States v. Morgan*, 313 U.S. 409 (1941), involved the fixing of rates for buying and selling livestock at the Kansas City Stock Yards, but it went to the U.S. Supreme Court four times and ultimately set standards for the extent to which litigants could inquire into the decision making of high-level policymakers. *Abbott Laboratories v. Gardner*, 387 U.S. 136 (1967), concerned Food and Drug Administration regulation of drug labeling but set forth the fundamental interpretation of judicial review under the APA, namely, that agency action is presumptively reviewable by the courts.

Research and argument in administrative procedural law differ from other areas of law because the cases deal with a myriad of agencies. Whereas in most private law cases, especially substantive questions of law, the researcher looks for cases with a similar fact pattern (argument in a slip-and-fall case will usually revolve around prior slip-and-fall decisions), administrative procedure arguments are constructed from a line of precedent-setting cases that bear no fact resemblance other than the procedural issue raised.

Delegation of Legislative Authority

In the nineteenth century, the courts frequently repeated the doctrine that Congress could not delegate its legislative authority, on the ground that the Constitution restricted this authority to Congress. In actual fact, Congress from the very beginning delegated its authority to administrative agencies, but the courts did not strike down such delegation until 1935, when a broad delegation of authority under the National Industrial Recovery Act was held by the U.S. Supreme Court to be unconstitutional in two cases. Since that time, the nondelegation doctrine has been all but dead, though it was partially resurrected in *Immigration and Naturalization Service v. Chadha*, 462 U.S. 919 (1983). The principle is still occasionally raised in administrative law cases with state agencies.

Judicial Review of Agency Action

Critical topics in the field of administrative law are judicial review and the scope of judicial review. These issues address basic questions concerning whether a dispute over agency action is a matter for the courts, who may bring such an action, and what exactly the courts should consider. These problems are constitutional ones. Because the U.S. Constitution establishes the doctrine of separation of powers, it was thought in the nineteenth century that the courts had no authority to question actions by the executive branch of government. An opposing constitutional premise, however, is that the executive branch may not violate the Constitution; and because the federal courts are responsible for interpreting the Constitution, logically the courts should be the forum for preventing the executive branch from exceeding its constitutional authority.

The demise of the doctrine of nonreviewability was signaled by *American School of Magnetic Healing v. McAnnulty*, 187 U.S. 94 (1902), in which the postmaster general prohibited the school from using the mail. It was clear that the postmaster general did not have such authority, and the court was faced with either dismissing the case for nonreviewability, thereby allowing the postmaster general unbridled authority, or reviewing the case and limiting the postmaster general to his legal authority. There really was no choice; our democratic legal principles could not allow a public official to act unlawfully. The postmaster general lost, and judicial review assumed respectability. Thereafter, the doctrine of judicial review was formulated in a series of cases that culminated in the enactment of Chapter 7 of the APA, which states in relevant part:

§ 701.   *Application; definitions*

(a) *This chapter applies, according to the provisions thereof, except to the extent that—*
   (1) statutes preclude judicial review; or
   (2) agency action is committed to agency discretion by law.

---

§ 704.   *Actions reviewable*

Agency action made reviewable by statute and final agency action for which there is no other adequate remedy in a court are subject to judicial review.

What exactly these two sections mean in combination has been the subject of much commentary and will undoubtedly continue to require clarification. What is clear, in theory if not always in fact, is that § 701(a)(1) means that Congress may specifically exempt some agency action from court review by statute, but when review is specifically authorized by statute, review is available. If Congress states that action cannot be reviewed, it cannot be reviewed; if Congress states action can be reviewed, it can be reviewed. This is simple enough except that Congress is usually silent with regard to review. In that case, § 704 would seem to indicate that review is available, except where "agency action is committed to agency discretion by law," a proviso that is less than crystal clear. *Abbott Laboratories v. Gardner*, 387 U.S. 136 (1967), resolved the issue by ignoring the lack of clarity in the language of the APA and stating that the APA expresses a "presumption of reviewability." The courts and Congress seem content with that principle and have left the debate over the nuances of the APA to legal scholars.

Review of Discretionary Acts of Officials

The actions of public officials often fall within areas of discretion recognized by the law. The very term *discretion* implies unreviewability, and § 701(a)(2) "agency action is committed to agency discretion by law" suggests that discretionary action may not be reviewed. Nevertheless, "committed . . . by law" invites various interpretations. Certainly Congress may use statutory language specifically using the term *discretion* or *discretionary* to leave no doubt of its delegation of authority. If the court concludes such a delegation is proper, it is unlikely to challenge an exercise of discretion. In many instances, the statutory language suggests a delegation of discretion that a court might conclude was not fully committed by law. In addition, the precise scope of discretion may be unclear and an official might act within the scope of her duties without acting within the area of committed discretion. At the highest levels of government, official decisions are commonly policy decisions, not only discretionary but protected by principles of separation of powers. At lower levels of action, decision making enjoys less respect, and when decisions affect rights, assuming a quasi-judicial flavor, the separation of powers protection is less persuasive.

When the exercise of discretion is challenged, the standard of review is different from the standards of review applied to lower courts of law but follows equity instead. Recall from our discussion of equity in Chapter 6 that courts of equity have always enjoyed considerable discretion. Discretionary acts of public officials are judged by the same standard: abuse of discretion. Logically, while the people, the government, and the law may give an official discretion, that discretion must not be abused. Another way of putting this: Courts, in our system of separate powers, are reluctant to question the acts of other branches of government of the acts of officials of those other branches; no one has absolute power and every official must act within reasonable bounds. We must have some basis to hold officials accountable for clearly unreasonable actions.

The litigation surrounding the presidential election of 2000 offers an illustration of the application of abuse of discretion at the state level. Katherine Harris, the Florida secretary of state, was invested by the Florida legislature with the authority to certify the electors for the State of Florida along with the responsibility to supervise voting standards and procedures. Although she had great discretion, that discretion was limited. Judge Lewis of the Circuit Court for Leon County recognized this discretion but commanded her to exercise discretion within the limits appropriate to her task.

In *McDermott v. Harris* [*McDermott* I], Judge Lewis describes in precise terms the nature of official discretion and its limitation in the election controversy.

[McDermott I]

McDERMOTT

v.

HARRIS

Florida Circuit Court, Leon County
No. 00-2700 (Fla. 2d Cir. Ct. Nov. 14, 2000)

The heart of the issue raised by the Motion [for Declaratory Judgment] is this: Section 102.166, Florida Statutes, contemplates that upon request a county canvassing board may authorize a manual recount of votes cast in an election. Both Volusia and Palm Beach Counties have so authorized, and are in the process of conducting, a manual recount. The Boards are concerned that the manual recounts may not be completed by 5:00 p.m. today, November 14, 2000, which is the deadline imposed upon them by Section 102.112, Florida Statutes, to certify and report the election returns to the Secretary of State. This Section provides that if the returns are not received by the deadline, such returns *may* be ignored by the Secretary in her certification of results statewide.

The Plaintiffs insist that the Secretary of State *must* consider the certified results from Volusia and Palm Beach Counties, even if they are filed late, if they are still engaged in the manual recount of the votes. The Secretary of State insists that, absent an Act of God such as a hurricane, any returns not received by the statutory deadline *will not* be counted in the statewide tabulations and certification of the election results. For the reasons set forth below, I find that the County Canvassing Boards must certify and file what election returns they have by the statutory deadline of 5:00 P.M. of November 14, 2000, with due notification to the Secretary of State of any pending manual recount, and may thereafter file supplemental or corrective returns. The Secretary of State may ignore such late filed returns, but may not do so arbitrarily, rather, only by the proper exercise of discretion after consideration of all appropriate facts and circumstances. . . .

It is unlikely that the Legislature would give the right to protest returns, but make it meaningless because it could not be acted upon in time. . . .

To determine ahead of time that such returns *will* be ignored, however, unless caused by some Act of God, is not the exercise of discretion. It is the abdication of that discretion. . . .

I can lawfully direct the Secretary to properly exercise her discretion in making a decision on the returns, but I cannot enjoin the Secretary to make a particular decision, nor can I rewrite the Statute that, by its plain meaning, mandates the filing of returns by the Canvassing Boards by 5:00 P.M. on November 14, 2000. . . .

Accordingly, it is

ORDERED AND ADJUDGED that the Secretary of State is directed to withhold determination as to whether or not to ignore late filed returns, if any, from Plaintiff Canvassing Boards, until due consideration of all relevant facts and circumstances consistent with the sound exercise of discretion. In all other respects, the Motion for Temporary Injunction is denied.

In response to Judge Lewis's warnings, Secretary Harris instructed the county canvassing boards to furnish reasons for submitting amended vote counts based on manual counts. Furnished with their reasons, Harris rejected the changes in vote on the ground that none of the reasons were justified by the statutes, which she interpreted to include Acts of God, machine malfunction, and fraud, none of which had been given as reasons.

Secretary Harris's conclusions were challenged as the case returned to Judge Lewis, who gave a brief order [*McDermott* II].

[McDermott II]

McDERMOTT
v.
HARRIS
Florida Circuit Court, Leon County
No. 00-2700 (Fla. 2d Cir. Ct. Nov. 17, 2000)

ORDER DENYING EMERGENCY MOTION TO COMPEL COMPLIANCE WITH AND FOR ENFORCEMENT OF INJUNCTION

The limited issue before me on this Motion is whether the Secretary of State has violated my Order of November 14, 2000. The Plaintiffs assert that she has acted arbitrarily in deciding to ignore amended returns from counties conducting manual recounts. I disagree.

As noted in my previous Order, Florida law grants to the Secretary, as the Chief Elections Officer, broad discretionary authority to accept or reject late filed returns. The purpose and intent of my Order was to insure that she in fact properly exercised her discretion, rather than automatically reject returns that came in after the statutory deadline.

On the limited evidence presented, it appears that the Secretary has exercised her reasoned judgment to determine what relevant factors and criteria should be considered, applied them to the facts and circumstances pertinent to the individual counties involved, and made her decision. My Order requires nothing more.

Accordingly, it is

ORDERED AND ADJUDGED that the Motion is hereby denied.

DONE AND ORDERED in Chambers at Tallahassee, Leon County, Florida, this 17th day of November, 2000.

Terry P. Lewis, Circuit Judge

Case Questions

1. Are these two cases consistent?
2. Was the judge motivated by political considerations? Explain your answer.

Scope of Review

The courts will review agency pending if a case is brought forth ?

The reluctance of the early courts to review administrative action was due in part to a desire to avoid retrying the facts. When an agency had made a determination of rights, especially if a hearing had been provided, the courts saw no need to conduct another hearing. When facts were found by the agency, the courts did not want to engage in a new round of factfinding. In addition, the agency was presumably better at finding facts because it employed experts in the field for which it was established. It was reasoned, for example, that the ICC was better able to understand the intricacies of the railroad business than were ordinary judges and juries, so the courts were reluctant to interfere with policy-making by the agencies entrusted with that function.

The resolution of this problem came about through the gradual transformation of judicial review into an appellate procedure, with the agencies serving in the place of trial courts (conducting the hearings, finding fact, and applying rules) and the court of appeals reviewing agency determinations much like an appellate court reviews an appeal from a trial court. Today, nearly all judicial review in both state and federal courts takes place at the appellate level.

In this way, the courts have limited the scope of judicial review to the legal questions with which appellate judges are competent and comfortable. Issues of jurisdiction, the interpretation of statutes, and due process raise questions that the courts treat on a daily basis. When factfinding is questioned, the courts borrow the substantial evidence test used for appellate review of jury factfinding. By limiting the scope of review, the courts remove themselves from making policy decisions and assume responsibility for monitoring the fairness of procedure.

A celebrated example of this was *Environmental Defense Fund, Inc. v. Ruckelshaus*, 439 F.2d 584 (D.C. Cir. 1971), in which the Secretary of Agriculture was sued by an environmental group in an effort to ban the pesticide DDT. Judge Bazelon separated the questions of fact from the questions of law. He declined to examine the conclusion of the secretary that DDT did not present an "imminent hazard," which would warrant summary suspension—this was a fact question left to the determination of the agency. However, the issue raised by EDF concerning whether the standard of proof used by the secretary conflicted with legislative intent in the applicable statute was a legal question appropriate for judicial determination. In this way, the court avoided making policy as to whether DDT should be banned and restricted the scope of review to whether the agency acted properly within the statute.

Rulemaking

The major innovation made by the APA was § 553, "Rule Making." With acceptance of Congress's authority to delegate its legislative powers, a standard was needed to ensure that those powers were exercised with procedural fairness. **Rulemaking** is simply the name applied to the agency's legislative function. In some cases, Congress specifically charges an agency with rulemaking authority; sometimes Congress is silent, but rulemaking authority is implied from the agency's statutory mission; and occasionally Congress denies an agency rulemaking authority (the Federal Trade Commission, for example, is an investigatory rather than a regulatory agency).

rulemaking Generic meaning of making rules; but, also, a specific meaning referring to the legislative function of administrative agencies, as distinguished from their usual administrative function.

When an agency engages in rulemaking, it must follow the procedure of the APA, or the rule is invalid and unenforceable. The steps required by the APA are simple:

§ 553. *Rule Making*

(b) *General notice of proposed rule making shall be published in the Federal Register, unless persons subject thereto are named and either personally served or otherwise have actual notice thereof in accordance with law. The notice shall include—*
   (1) *A statement of the time, place, and nature of public rule making proceedings;*
   (2) *reference to the legal authority under which the rule is proposed; and*
   (3) *either the terms or substance of the proposed rule or a description of the subjects and issues involved.*

* * *

(c) *After notice required by this section, the agency shall give interested persons an opportunity to participate in the rule making through submission of written data, views, or arguments with or without opportunity for oral presentation. After consideration of the relevant matter presented, the agency shall incorporate in the rules adopted a concise general statement of their basis and purpose. . . .*

(d) *The required publication or service of a substantive rule shall be made not less than 30 days before its effective date [with exceptions].*

Although § 553 presents some burden to the agencies, the steps are not cumbersome. Basically it requires public notice of proposed rules and an opportunity for public input. Legally there is nothing to prevent an agency from making rules despite major opposition as long as it follows the procedure. The innovation of § 553 is in requiring that the process be public and provide for public participation. The weaknesses and unpopularity of a proposed rule may thus be brought into the open. An agency cannot long defy the public interest without a response from Congress and the president, who ultimately control the power that the agency exercises.

Section 553 has some significant exceptions. Internal housekeeping rules, those concerning personnel and internal management, are not covered by it. So-called "interpretative rules" need not go through the § 553 procedure. In a loose sense, interpretative rules are those that carry out the meaning of a statute, interpreting it rather than adding to it. The distinction between interpretative and legislative or substantive rules is far from clear—a technical question that several cases have confused rather than clarified. The question seems purely academic until an agency attempts to make an interpretative rule without going through § 553 procedure, only to find a complaining party asserting that the rule is substantive and therefore invalid for lack of proper procedure. If the court agrees with the complaining party and concludes that the rule is substantive (legislative), the failure to follow § 553 procedure makes the rule invalid.

When Congress specifically authorizes an agency to make rules under § 553, those rules are said to have the "binding force of law," meaning that the courts will accord them the same respect as if the rules had been passed by Congress. Interpretative rules do not enjoy this stature, though as a practical matter they ordinarily are enforced by the courts.

The Right to Be Heard

Section 553 leaves to the agency the discretion to allow oral presentation and argument and its scope, but some rules call for more than the mere opportunity for written submission of argument. Some questions are better left to an adjudicatory process by the agency.

An issue that often arises in suits against governmental bodies is whether the plaintiffs have *standing,* that is, do they have the right to sue, or, as it is described in *Norris,* do they have a "legally cognizable interest"?

As discussed in earlier chapters, legislation and adjudication are different processes appropriate to different situations. In the administrative field, two

cases arising in Colorado have been used repeatedly as examples of this distinction. In *Bi-Metallic Investment Co. v. State Board of Equalization*, 239 U.S. 441 (1915), the state had increased the valuation of all real estate in Denver by 40 percent. The court denied a suit for an injunction by the company, holding that no hearing was necessary. The court distinguished the earlier case of *Londoner v. Denver*, 210 U.S. 373 (1908), in which it had required a hearing ("by argument however brief, and, if need be, by proof, however informal") on the assessment of the plaintiff's land for the cost of paving a street. The distinction was made on the difference between policy that treated the entire community equally (*Bi-Metallic*) and a decision in which a few persons were affected individually (*Londoner*). In other words, the decision to set valuations in general is a legislative question, whereas assessing costs individually and differentially is an adjudicative question, as the individual may have special reasons why the assessment is unfair. Highly particularized disputes of this sort call for a hearing.

Donald L. NORRIS, et al., Petitioners/Plaintiffs,

v.

Town of WHEATLAND, et al., Respondents/Defendant
Supreme Court, Monroe County, N.Y.
613 N.Y.S.2d 817 (1994)

After eighteen months of divisive debate about the future of their police department, the Town of Wheatland voters elected two board members and a supervisor who stood for its abolition. Upon taking office in January 1994, the Town Board, by a three to two vote, immediately approved the Wheatland Police Department for only three months. On March 3, 1994 the Town Board proposed, and on March 30, 1994 passed, Local Law No. 1 abolishing the Wheatland Police Department as of June 1, 1994.

This action was brought . . . seeking to set aside and annul the decision of the Wheatland Town Board pursuant to Local Law No. 1. The Petitioners, which include the Wheatland Police Chief and 41 residents of the town, allege the Town Board acted improperly by: 1) not procedurally complying with the appropriate provisions of the State Environment

Quality Review Act (SEQRA) and by failing to consider the "socioeconomic effect" of the Local Law; 2) acting arbitrarily and capriciously; 3) failing to comply with the requirements of the Municipal Home Rule Law; 4) not referring the Local Law to a referendum; and 5) one of the Board Members voting in favor of the Local Law No. 1 not being a resident of the Town of Wheatland at the time of the vote.

In rejoinder, the respondents deny the allegations of the petition and questioned whether the petitioners have standing to bring the action.

STANDING

. . . "It is established law that to be entitled to seek judicial review of an administrative determination, the petitioning party must have a legally cognizable interest that is or will be affected by the determination. A showing of special damage or actual injury is not necessary to establish a party's standing."

Unlike a zoning matter, the abolition of a town police department is all-pervasive. To require a showing of special damage or actual injury to one resident vis-à-vis another is unlikely and counteracts the intent of SEQRA,

(continued)

(continued)

which is "to assure that those charged with decision-making responsibility are aware of their obligations to protect the environment for the use and enjoyment of this and all future generations." Furthermore, to deny standing in this matter would be to insulate governmental action from scrutiny. In a matter affecting a town-wide service, either all residents have standing, or none do. In this matter, any resident of the Town of Wheatland has standing.

* * *

[In a lengthy discussion of whether the Board had properly complied with the procedural requirements related to abolishing the police force, the court concluded that it had.]

SEQRA COMPLIANCE-SUBSTANTIVE

It must now be reviewed whether the Town Board, as lead agency, by issuing a Negative Decision, ". . . determine(d) either that there will be no environmental effect or that the identified environmental effects will not be significant," and did the Town Board ". . . take a hard look at all relevant impacts . . . in making this decision and document its reasons in writing."

Those supporting the retention of the Police Department provided the Town Board with reports, letters and testimony which raised questions as to the environmental, economic and social effects on the community. In addition, there existed a thorough and comprehensive task force report supporting the retention.

In response, the Town Board undertook the following steps: 1. The Town solicited comments from all the Town Supervisors in Monroe County who relied on the Monroe County Sheriff's Department for their police services. The request for information specifically related questions concerning response time, community involvement, professionalism and effectiveness. 2. The Town contacted the Monroe County Sheriff's Office and requested information concerning its ability to provide police services to the Town of Wheatland. Sheriff

Andrew Meloni, in part, stated: "I am confident that the Monroe County Office of Sheriff has all the necessary resources to provide professional, effective and efficient services to the Town of Wheatland." 3. The Supervisor conducted a review of crime statistics, the capacity of Monroe County Sheriff's Office, the degree of activities of various districts of the Monroe County Sheriff's Office and the ability of the Monroe County Sheriff's Office to handle the Town of Wheatland. The Town of Wheatland invited the public to comment on issues including environmental significance of the proposed action and heard all parties wishing to address the issue and received and filed all documents concerning this subject. The Town Board also held a public informational meeting on March 1, 1994 at which the public addressed questions to Undersheriff O'Flynn.

The Court's role in reviewing SEQRA determinations is to, first, review the agency procedures to determine whether they were lawful. As set forth above, the only procedural defect, an inadvertent reference to a hearing, has been satisfactorily resolved. Second, courts may review the record to determine whether the agency identified the relevant areas of environmental concern, took a "hard look" at them, and made a "reasoned elaboration" of the basis for its determination. When doing so the Courts are to remember that an agency's substantive obligations under SEQRA must be viewed in light of a rule of reason. Although agencies have considerable latitude in evaluating environmental effects and choosing among alternatives, "[n]othing in the law requires an agency to reach a particular result on an issue, or permits the courts to second-guess the agency's choice, which can be annulled only if arbitrary, capricious or unsupported by substantial evidence."

[T]he court finds that the Wheatland Town Board identified the relevant areas of environmental concern, took a hard look at them and made a "reasoned elaboration" for the basis of its determination.

* * *

ARBITRARY AND CAPRICIOUS

Considering its extensive experience with and regard for local police, this Court does not necessarily agree with the Board's abolition of the Police Department. However, it cannot be said that the Board's actions, as set forth in the legislative findings, are unsupportable or were arbitrary or capricious. Ultimately, in the representative democracy of Wheatland, New York, the wisdom of the abolition of the police department by the Town Board can be reviewed by the voters on November 7, 1995.

Case Questions

1. Can a town through its elected representatives abolish the police force? Explain.
2. On what basis do the plaintiffs have standing?
3. Why is the statute (SEQRA) at issue here?

What Kind of a Hearing?

The right to a hearing in administrative law does not necessarily mean an on-the-record, trial-type, or evidentiary hearing. Such events present a significant burden to an agency, which may devote significant resources and time when the full complement of rights and procedures must be respected. The extent of a person's rights in a hearing run the gamut from extremely informal meetings to hearings that are virtually indistinguishable from trials. The extremes are represented by *Goss v. Lopez*, 419 U.S. 565 (1975), and *Goldberg v. Kelly*, 397 U.S. 254 (1970). *Goss* involved ten-day suspensions of high school students. The U.S. Supreme Court held that they were entitled to a hearing, but the rights of the students were limited to (1) notice of the charges against them; (2) explanation of the evidence against them; and (3) the opportunity to present their side of the facts. By contrast, *Goldberg* concerned the right of a welfare recipient to a hearing prior to termination of benefits. The court held that she was entitled to a hearing before termination, including the following rights in connection with the hearing:

1. Notice with reasons for the termination
2. Confrontation of witnesses against her
3. Oral argument
4. Cross-examination of adverse witnesses
5. Disclosure of evidence for the other side
6. Representation by an attorney
7. Determination on the record
8. Statement of reasons relied on for decision
9. Impartial decision maker

Practically speaking, this is a catalog of the rights ordinarily enjoyed in a civil trial.

Administrative Hearings

Most agencies provide procedural steps within the agency for processing grievances and complaints. Judicial review is premised on "final agency action," which requires some authoritative determination of rights; the APA allows agencies to require that a claimant exhaust some or all of these steps prior to seeking judicial review. Prior to the APA, claimants were required to exhaust all administrative remedies before judicial review, and many states still require this.

Agencies are hierarchical bureaucracies and typically provide aggrieved parties the opportunity to pursue review of determinations from lower levels all the way to the top of the bureaucratic pyramid. Someone once counted thirty-three steps in the social security system that would have to be completed to fully exhaust the administrative remedies available. It is unrealistic to think that the reviewing court would reverse a consistent determination through all these steps except on the ground that the procedure itself was constitutionally defective.

Hearings at the highest level are held by hearing officers called *administrative law judges*, who are employed by the government to hold recorded hearings, make findings of fact, and recommend action to the highest level of the agency. In most instances, the agency will follow the recommendations of the administrative law judge.

Liability of Government and Its Officers

Recent decades have seen a major change in liability for agency action. When sovereign immunity was in its heyday, the only remedy for a person injured by official action was a suit against the public employee who caused the injury. Even there, the courts developed a doctrine of official immunity for injuries caused by "discretionary" acts within the scope of the employee's duties. Policy makers and planners were thus immunized for most of their acts.

The death knell of sovereign immunity for tort suits came with enactment of the Federal Tort Claims Act (FTCA) in 1947. The FTCA continued the judicial doctrine of discretionary immunity, and exempted a number of intentional torts, but held the federal government "liable, respecting the provisions of this title relating to tort claims, in the same manner and to the same extent as a private individual under like circumstances." This formally enacted a judicial doctrine that had developed to disallow governmental immunity when the activities were the same as those performed by private enterprise, the so-called "governmental–proprietary function test." The states gradually followed suit, though they did so with a variety of statutes, many of which retained varying degrees of immunity.

With the availability of suits against the government, the courts became more protective of government officers. Not only was the discretionary immunity expanded, but also a form of *qualified immunity* was invented that immunized from suit officers acting in good faith and under a reasonable belief that their actions were proper. This was a logical result of the dilemma in which public officers, especially police, found themselves when acting pursuant to statutory authority, only to have a court hold the statute unconstitutional. For example, a police officer makes an arrest under a state statute, but the statute is found by the court to be unconstitutional, so the arrest was illegal and the officer subject to suit for false arrest and false imprisonment. If the standards of the doctrine are met, the officer enjoys qualified (as distinguished from absolute) immunity.

42 U.S.C. § 1983

To protect former slaves from abuse at the hands of white authorities following the Civil War, Congress passed the Civil Rights Act of 1871, from which 42 U.S.C. § 1983 reads:

> Every person who, under color of any statute, ordinance, regulation, custom, or usage, of any State or Territory, subjects, or causes to be subjected, any citizen of the United States or other person within the jurisdiction thereof to the deprivation of any rights, privileges, or immunities secured by the Constitution and laws, shall be liable to the party injured in an action at law, suit in equity, or other proper proceeding for redress.

The broad provisions of this act were rarely used until 1961, when a suit brought against Chicago police officers and the City of Chicago was successful (*Monroe v. Pape*, 365 U.S. 167). *Monroe* held, however, that the city was not a "person" under the act and could not be sued; but in 1978 the U.S. Supreme Court overruled *Monroe* and allowed a suit against the City of New York in *Monell v. Department of Social Services*, 436 U.S. 658. Since *Monell*, § 1983 suits have proliferated and are a constant concern of local governments, especially for the conduct of their police; a § 1983 suit was even brought against the governor of Ohio over the National Guard shootings of Kent State University students during antiwar demonstrations in 1970. (The U.S. Supreme Court held that the governor had qualified immunity.) The broad scope of the language of § 1983 and its expanding application have made it a frequent basis for litigation.

Although the scope of 42 U.S.C. § 1983 has been greatly expanded with regard to suing state and local governments, suits against government officials have confronted an increasing recognition of absolute and qualified immunities. The courts have been steadfast in upholding absolute immunity of judges acting in their judicial capacity. *Stump v. Sparkman* expresses the most extreme application of judicial immunity. The mother of a "somewhat retarded" daughter petitioned Judge Stump of an Indiana Circuit Court for an order permitting the daughter to be sterilized. Judge Stump met with the mother in chambers and wrote and signed the order. The sterilization procedure was performed, the daughter being told that her appendix was being removed. When the daughter married two years later, she soon discovered what had happened. She sued Judge Stump under § 1983. The U.S. District Court held the judge enjoyed immunity from suit, but the Court of Appeals reversed and the case reached the U.S. Supreme Court on certiorari.

STUMP
v.
SPARKMAN
U.S. Supreme Court
435 U.S. 349 (1978)

The governing principle of law is well established and is not questioned by the parties. As early as 1872, the Court recognized that it was "a general principle of the highest importance to the proper administration of justice that a judicial officer, in exercising the authority vested in him, [should] be free to act upon his own convictions, without apprehension of personal consequences to himself." For that reason the Court held that "judges of courts of superior or general jurisdiction are not liable to civil actions for their judicial acts, even when such acts are in excess of their jurisdiction, and are alleged to have been done maliciously or corruptly." Later we held that this doctrine of judicial immunity was applicable in suits under § 1 of the Civil Rights Act of 1871, 42 U.S.C.A. § 1983, for the legislative record gave no indication that Congress intended to abolish this long-established principle.

* * *

Perhaps realizing the broad scope of Judge Stump's jurisdiction, the Court of Appeals stated that, even if the action taken by him was not foreclosed under the Indiana statutory scheme, it would still be "an illegitimate exercise of his common law power because of his failure to comply with elementary principles of procedural due process." This misconceives the doctrine of judicial immunity. A judge is absolutely immune from liability for his judicial acts even if his exercise of authority is flawed by the commission of grave procedural errors. . . .

Disagreement with the action taken by the judge, however, does not justify depriving that judge of his immunity. Despite the unfairness to litigants that sometimes results, the doctrine of judicial immunity is thought to be in the best interests of "the proper administration of justice . . . for it allows] a judicial officer, in exercising the authority vested in him [to] be free to act upon his own convictions, without apprehension of personal consequences to him-self." The fact that the issue before the judge is a controversial one is all the more reason that he should be able to act without fear of suit. . . .

Mr. Justice STEWART, with whom Mr. Justice MARSHALL and Mr. Justice POWELL join, dissenting.

It is established federal law that judges of general jurisdiction are absolutely immune from monetary liability "for judicial acts, even when such acts are in excess of their jurisdiction, and are alleged to have been done maliciously or corruptly." It is also established that this immunity is in no way diminished in a proceeding under 42 U.S.C.A. § 1983. But the scope of judicial immunity is limited to liability for "judicial acts," and I think that what Judge Stump did on July 9, 1971, was beyond the pale of anything that could sensibly be called a judicial act.

* * *

When the Court says that what Judge Stump did was an act "normally performed by a judge," it is not clear to me whether the Court means that a judge "normally" is asked to approve a mother's decision to have her child given surgical treatment generally, or that a judge "normally" is asked to approve a mother's wish to have her daughter sterilized. But whichever way the Court's statement is to be taken, it is factually inaccurate. In Indiana, as elsewhere in our country, a parent is authorized to arrange for and consent to medical and surgical treatment of his minor child. And when a parent decides to call a physician to care for his sick child or arranges to have a surgeon remove his child's tonsils, he does not, "normally" or otherwise, need to seek the approval of a judge. On the other hand, Indiana did in 1971 have statutory procedures for the sterilization of certain people who were *institutionalized.* But these statutes provided for *administrative proceedings* before a board established by the superintendent of each public hospital. Only if after notice and an evidentiary hearing, an order of sterilization was entered in these proceedings could there be review in a circuit court.

* * *

Mr. Justice POWELL, dissenting.

While I join the opinion of Mr. Justice STEW-ART, I wish to emphasize what I take to be the central feature of this case—petitioner's preclusion of any possibility for the vindication of respondent's rights elsewhere in the judicial system.

* * *

But where a judicial officer acts in a manner that precludes all resort to appellate or other judicial remedies that otherwise would be available, the underlying assumption of the *Bradley* doctrine is inoperative. . . . The complete absence of normal judicial process foreclosed resort to any of the "numerous remedies" that "the law has provided for private parties."

Case Questions

1. Was Judge Stump's order a judicial act? Explain.
2. Judicial immunity was again tested in the U.S. Supreme Court in 1988 in *Forrester v. White*, 108 S. Ct. 538, in which a female probation officer was fired by Judge White, who was responsible for hiring and firing probation officers. Ms. Forrester sued under § 1983 on the grounds that she had been discriminated against because of her sex. Writing the opinion of the Court, Justice O'Connor applied the "judicial function" test that asserts absolute immunity for a judge's actions while exercising a judicial function. Justice O'Connor concluded that Judge White's authority over personnel was an administrative function separate from his judicial function, rendering him amenable to suit for improper actions in his administrative function, and the suit was allowed to proceed. Can you reconcile *Forrester* with *Stump*?

Summary

Administrative law covers the rules relating to legal action taken against the administrative agencies of the government. Although each agency has its own substantive rules and regulations, procedural law has evolved, and is still evolving, first from the Constitution and more recently from the enactment of federal and state administrative procedure legislation.

The last hundred years have witnessed reversals in the major areas of administrative law. In the nineteenth century, sovereign immunity was doctrine throughout the United States—officers could be sued but not the government. It was presumed that Congress could not delegate its legislative authority to other government agencies. There was a presumption of nonreviewability of administrative action by the courts. All of these doctrines met their demise in the twentieth century. Rather than challenging legislative delegation, the courts have concentrated on the question of whether the agencies adhere to legislative intent. Rather than refusing to review, the courts have limited the scope of review along lines similar to appellate review. With the erosion of sovereign immunity, the courts have expanded the liability of government and narrowed the liability of public officers.

The enactment of the Administrative Procedure Act in 1946 put administrative law on a firm footing. The major innovation of the APA was its provisions for rulemaking, requiring public notice and the opportunity for public input prior to the promulgation of agency rules.

Administrative law was forced to change as government changed from performing relatively few services into an immense bureaucracy regulating every aspect of our daily lives. Administrative law changed to hold government more accountable to the public.

Scenario

Morgan Pierpont, a small-time investor in common stocks, about a million dollars in the market at the height of his powers, has lost two-thirds of his wealth on a recent crash in the stock market. The catalyst for the crash seems to have been the decision of the Federal Reserve Board (the Fed) to raise the interest rate at which the Fed lends funds to member banks a full point at a surprise meeting of the Fed called by Alan Redspan, its chairman and dominant leader and policymaker. The Fed interest rate, especially when raised or cut, for a long time has been considered the single most important means by which the stock market can be sent up or down, especially when the change is unanticipated by investors and especially when the change is a half point or more. While the effect of interest rate changes on the economy as a whole tends to take six months or a year, the effect on the stock market can be instantaneous. Redspan and the Fed have consistently expressed their overriding concern for inflation, which they fight aggressively with rate hikes, although they tend to gradually lower interest rates when inflationary pressures are minimal and the specter of recession looms on the horizon. The reason for the sudden raise in the Fed rate, as expressed publicly by Redspan, was the announcement three days before of an unexpected rise of 5 percent of the consumer price index (CPI), an indicator of inflation, which reached a level much higher than anticipated and well beyond the level Redspan finds acceptable. A month later, when all the data were in, the CPI was adjusted downward for March to 3.5 percent, but by then the damage had been done. The market had gone into a steady downward spiral and consumer confidence was at a ten-year low.

Pierpont and other investors are both impoverished and furious. He brings a lawsuit against the president of the United States demanding that the president fire the chairman of the Federal Reserve Board. Pierpont bases his standing on the economic losses he sustained because of government action and as a taxpayer. The Federal District Court dismisses for lack of standing. Pierpont appeals to the Circuit Court of Appeals, which acknowledges that economic losses due to government action have traditionally established standing. Because the lower court made no findings of fact with regard to the nexus between the action of the government and actual damages to the plaintiff/appellant, the Circuit Court of Appeals proceeds beyond the standing question to dismiss the case on other grounds.

Discuss the many policy grounds that might support the dismissal of Pierpont's lawsuit. Section 701 of the Administrative Procedure Act regarding judicial review of agency action may be a useful starting point, but many common-sense arguments apply here as well. Common sense, however, only makes a good legal argument with an understanding of the law and the legal system as well as a basic understanding of constitutional principles, which extends to administrative law. Pierpont really has nothing going for him, but your job is to frame his weaknesses in lawyerly arguments.

LAW IN THE AGE OF COMPUTERS

Introduction

Since the last edition of this book, changes in computer use have advanced at an unbelievable pace. The last decade of the twentieth century witnessed an incredible proliferation of software and systems used in business offices throughout the country; and law offices, which were latecomers to computerization, have become highly automated in virtually every aspect of their activities. The World Wide Web introduced graphical enhancement to the Internet that made computers user-friendly, which meant that lawyers, accustomed to words and not machines, quickly learned how useful computers could be. Thus, two avenues opened for law offices. One entailed a revolution in legal research, moving from a nearly exclusive use of the print sources in the extensive law libraries necessary for lawyers to conduct their research to on-line research, which means that lawyers and their staff hardly need to leave their desks to find what they are looking for. The second major change was the automation of the law office itself, with computerized billing, litigation assistance, downloadable forms, and numerous other changes that allowed formerly onerous tasks to be accomplished speedily.

Both of these areas are complex and changing. Both deserve books and courses of their own. "Legal research," the course, now must address both print and electronic versions. Meanwhile, "law office management" is no longer simply a subdivision of business administration but is principally concerned with the efficient use of technology particularized to the legal field and the law office. These two fields are beyond the scope of this book, and we can no longer simply predict the changes for the future, as we did in previous editions. Rather, we must give an overview of the changes that are no longer coming—they have arrived. Of course, the pace of techonology has not abated and what we state here may soon become obsolete. We will concentrate on computer-assisted legal research (CALR) since the law office technology other than basic research varies from one law office to another and is best learned on the job or in an up-to-date book or course on the subject.

Computer-Assisted Legal Research

Unlike other chapters, this one introduces the reader to some activities that can be immediately put to good use. Some wonderful legal websites are free and open to the public wherein cases, statutes, and legal articles may be found easily. For the inquisitive, it is almost dangerous—so much information and so little time. Sites for lawyer jokes, wild cases, and a wealth of intriguing legal stories are available to distract the curious; but, first, let us acquire some background in the area.

Some websites are free or very close to free. Others require subscriptions or fees. Most of the practice-oriented sites are not free, and some are even rather price-prohibitive except for the large law firm. Some specialized law firms have created websites with useful information that is truly amazing; the outstanding examples can be found in **intellectual property** fields. Intellectual property as related to cyberspace is perhaps the fastest growing specialization within the legal field, and many of the prominent law firms practicing in this area have consolidated their positions by creating great and informative websites. A number of universities have created websites with links to most important legal materials. Some law reviews make some or all of their articles available electronically, although at the time of this writing the problem of diminishing subscriptions has created something of a crisis for university-based scholarly writing, which in the past depended on subscriptions to underwrite some of the cost of publication.

intellectual property
Ideas in the form of writings, works of art, commercial symbols, and inventions that are protected by government license, usually by registration, in the form of copyright, patent, and trademark. The law of trade secrets is also part of intellectual property law.

Westlaw® and Lexis-Nexis®

The field of legal databases has been dominated by two sources that are commercial and not freely available to the public. Building on a project begun by the Ohio State Bar Association, Mead Corporation in 1973 offered subscribers a legal database including federal cases and statutes along with selected state databases, adding materials continually to expand its coverage. In 1980, Mead added Nexis, which included nonlegal news and business information. In 1994, Mead sold rights to Lexis-Nexis to the publishing conglomerate Reed Elsevier, Inc.

Meanwhile, starting in 1973, West Publishing Co. (now West Group, Inc.) weighed into the electronic field. As the predominant publisher of legal mate-

Westlaw®   A legal database maintained by West Group, Inc., widely used by the legal profession.

Lexis®   A legal database maintained by Reed Elsevier, Inc., widely used by the legal profession.

rials, including all of the regional reporters, the source of all the cases excerpted in this book, West was anxious to preserve its dominance and realized that the future would include electronic databases for the cases they had long put in print form. West launched **Westlaw** in 1975, although it took awhile to compete fully with **Lexis**. Both of these services have since added immense amounts of legal materials and are the primary sources of the most recent cases and statutes to the extent that search results of new cases often can only site to Westlaw or Lexis because they have not been assigned a volume or page number in the reporters.

Consensus is lacking as to whether Westlaw or Lexis is a better service, depending in part on particular use desired. Most large law firms subscribe to both. Law schools commonly pay subscription rates that allow access of all their students to both services, often providing temporary passwords to each student. Business and industry frequently use these two services, which, with full subscription, provide access to many nonlegal sources such as newspapers, news magazines, and scholarly journals, in addition to financial data and public records.

Legal research by computer is different in nature from research using print materials. The computer is magnificent in the speed with which it can search for character strings, that is, it can look in all the cases in the United States for the character string "Microsoft" in a matter of minutes and return the cites for those cases. The computer cannot think, however, or at least not very well—not yet. Some law schools prohibit the use of Lexis and Westlaw for beginning law students to force them to learn the print media first. It might be worthwhile to speculate on why they follow such a policy. Although the legal databases are used for word searches, they are organized according to principles formulated in the printed materials. Cases, of course, are reported chronologically because they are issued chronologically and because the most recent cases have the greatest precedential value. Another very good reason is that, if they were organized topically, the series would require republication on a regular basis. The legal encyclopedias, for example, *Corpus Juris Secundum* and *American Jurisprudence*, are organized by topics, requiring pocket parts in the back of each volume into which are inserted periodic supplements until the supplements grow to a size requiring republication of the volume.

Let us compare the research process using printed materials as compared to electronic resources. When an attorney is presented with a legal issue in a case that is unfamiliar, novel, or within an area over which the attorney has limited mastery, the law library may be consulted to research that issue. The attorney may consult the statutes, which are organized by topic, albeit many states seem to preserve somewhat archaic headings and numerical sequences. If the issue has a statutory component, it is always wise to consult cases interpreting the feature of the statute relevant to the case at hand. If there is no statutory component, the cases must be consulted. How are these found? To a certain extent, finding the materials is a bit of an art, but legal encyclopedias, digests, practice books, treatises, and article indexes provide clues to the materials. If the issue and topic are unfamiliar or the attorney's memory is a bit rusty, the natural place to start research is at the lowest level of competence. Thus, if the issue is the liability of the ninth car in a ten-car collision, the attorney thinks of causation and joint liability, remembering the magic phrases "proximate cause" and "joint and several liability of tortfeasors." Finding these topics, the researcher will work down until appropriate topics and annotations to cases are found. In the process, the researcher is rewarded with memory refreshment and the acquisition of a broad knowledge of the specific topic investigated. Analogous cases having nothing to do with vehicular collisions may be discovered that might prove to have useful arguments. If national sources are researched, cases from other states will be discovered. An educational process occurs that follows the lines of the lawyer's law school training that has been reinforced in subsequent legal training. In this way, the attorney not only finds materials relevant to the issue but builds on that ever-expanding body of knowledge that he or she possesses.

Compare this to electronic research. The researcher sits before the computer, pulls up Westlaw, narrows the database to Virginia where the collision occurred, and puts in search words likely to pinpoint the issue. Of course, the magic phrases could be inputted, but "proximate cause" will likely bring up two thousand cases, entirely unmanageable. More likely, the researcher will choose words relating to the fact pattern since that is ultimately very important since the closer a case is to the fact pattern, the more persuasive the precedent; the ideal case would be a multiple-vehicle accident involving the liability of the next-to-last vehicle. A number of words come to mind: vehicle, automobile, car, multiple, proximate cause, joint, liability. Perhaps additional words would be pertinent to the search such as "snow," "visibility," "night," "act of God." Except for the words of legal significance—"proximate cause," "joint," "liability"—these words are not to be expected in the broader print resources except when getting down to case annotations and references. They are immediately available in a word search, however. On the computer, the most analogous case may be found in a fraction of the time it takes with print materials. Finding such a case, the researcher may then expand the search to cited cases and search forward in time to new cases citing this and other cases (this can be done in print searches through the indexing tool called *Shepard's Citations*, known as "shepardizing" a case).

Ultimately, a good and thorough researcher may find the same cases and statutes through either medium. A problem may occur, however, where one researcher fails to find relevant materials that would have been found through a different medium of research. This raises problems of competence and malpractice that should encourage the researcher—particularly the print researcher, if there are any left—to double check through the electronic databases. This problem can be solved by good habits. The point we want to make here, however, is that researching the printed materials involves a continuing education building on a body of knowledge acquired through traditional methods of learning [by the fourth edition of this book, perhaps law students will no longer buy books and engage only in electronic study]. Researching Westlaw and Lexis, on the other hand, requires skills of a different nature—clever word searching that, while premised on a body of knowledge acquired initially by study, is efficiently restricted to the case at hand and focuses on facts rather than law.

Not everyone would agree with this analysis. We are moving toward exclusive use of electronic media; by the time this book is printed, many courts may use an electronic standard, that is, a thorough database search might meet an acceptable professional standard. Many courts are now accepting electronic documents; printed briefs, memoranda of law, and other documents may soon be all electronic, with an original electronic document filed with the clerk of court. At present, a printed document may be necessary to check against electronic alterations, but "watermarking" and other means of dating original electronic documents will soon solve that problem.

CD-ROM Programs and More

One impediment to computer use formerly was storage capacity, particularly for movable storage, originally contained on large "floppy disks" and for some time now on smaller diskettes (3.5") that hold 1.44 megabytes of data. Now Zip disks and other forms of storage are common, but the major breakthrough came with the addition of CD-ROM drives to computers. When preparing the second edition of this book in late 1995, we considered producing an accompanying CD but decided against that because most of the students using the book would not have CD-ROM drives on their computers. Five years later, the CD-ROM drive was an indispensable part of all personal computers except for those opting for the bigger and better DVD drives. Having capacity for about 750 megabytes of storage capacity, the CD provides enough space for complex software programs or an encyclopedia. The disks cost less than a dollar and are easily dispensable—witness the quarterly mailing of America Online advertising diskettes received unsolicited in the mail.

While CD-ROMs can be used to store large amounts of data, such as the complete state statutes on a single CD or a law firm's documents in large litigation projects, one of the most useful tools is the inclusion of legal forms on CDs, which has even resulted in do-it-yourself legal products for the public. One of the perennial aspects of the practice of law is filling in forms. Sometimes these forms resemble the sort of forms ubiquitous in modern life, like the IRS income tax form, which can now be downloaded directly from the government website. But law firms have for a long time expanded the meaning of "form" beyond that of a series of labeled boxes to be filled in by the user. Most legal documents, for example, a warranty deed or a simple will, contain "boilerplate" language, which is repeated verbatim over and over again. Computers can store forms that contain such language to be entered into a document in a variety of ways. There are CDs for writing wills, and there are CDs for law firms to write wills. Some states have established standard will forms to be used by attorneys with a series of questions to ask a client in such a way that a will may be printed and witnessed in the law office in a single visit, an efficient and cost-effective service that turns what was once a marginally profitable legal service into a simple transaction that is inexpensive for a client while still profitable for the firm. (Complex wills and large estates are another matter, of course.)

Law firms use other forms extensively that might not be considered forms in the usual sense. The use of formbooks has a long tradition. An attorney engaged in a product liability practice, for example, might reach for a number of books that provide forms for complaints, defenses, requests for documents, interrogatories, and a myriad of other forms common to such a practice, with many variations likely to occur. In former times, secretaries spent long hours copying such forms with the insertions and deletions noted by the attorney. Today, the language is programmed into a CD-ROM or the law firm's permanent storage. More than likely, much of the firm's storage began as a CD that was downloaded. As broadband delivery of data becomes common, even CDs and DVDs may be dispensed with for such forms, and services will update forms, statutes, and cases automatically, especially when and if the security problems are resolved.

All of these forms do not relieve the attorneys of the need to read, write, and understand legal and ordinary language. Once we get away from simple property documents, debt collection, and other forms of legal practice that use a lot of boilerplate, the need for effective writing and persuasion remains. Writing an appellate brief requires considerable knowledge, intelligence, and writing skill. Nevertheless, briefs follow rigid formats (statement of facts, statement of issues, summary, list of cases, etc.) that should now be programmed into a computer, facilitating the writing of a brief. Software programs have been developed that check citations for correct form and detect mistakes, freeing the attorney's time for thinking and writing.

On-Line Services

It is now possible to write a will by going on-line to a law firm and providing answers to basic questions, a sophisticated checklist, and receive a completed will in the mail or by fax with instructions concerning the proper witnessing and signatures. The law firm will maintain the will in its database, much as an attorney customarily keeps a copy of a will on file, ignoring for the moment the significant difference between a signed copy and an electronic version. The purchaser of such a will should receive periodic reminders to review and change the will just as estate attorneys send notices to clients of the same nature. A logical approach is to send the customer/testator a checklist full of questions about change in position (any new children? a divorce? death? acquisitions? new business?) that would trigger the need for a new will.

We can expect a proliferation of self-help legal services both from proprietary organizations and from the government, the latter recognizing that a tremendous savings in time and personnel may be gained by providing information and forms on-line. In the state of Florida, for example, it is possible to check on lost funds, stock certificates, and other property where the owner's whereabouts have been lost and the property turned over to the state. Once discovered, the owner files appropriate forms with the state and, if all the requirements are fulfilled, will receive the lost funds by check in the mail. This can be accomplished with property of a deceased as well, although the process is more complicated; and probate and tax consequences may require the help of an attorney.

Computer Dangers

Discussion of the wonders of the computer must include some reference to its dangers. Obviously the do-it-yourselfer risks the danger of taking legal action without competent legal advice. Writing a simple will is different than knowing that a simple will is appropriate to the situation. Attorneys, too, may become overreliant on computer forms and language; the press of business may cause an attorney to cut corners. Computers seem so efficient that we may begin to believe that a computer program has foreseen every possibility and resolved all the problems. The knowledge, experience, and skills of attorneys will continue to be valuable to the public despite computerization.

Computers present their own legal problems. Most of us have quite a bit of experience with computers, but few of us understand how they work, and fewer still appreciate the security risks they present. Unfortunately, some of those few are unscrupulous and prey upon the public through computers. A recent example may suffice to indicate the many ways these problems may arise. A small retail business recently received a long-distance telephone bill from a provider that the owner had never heard of before. She inquired of the service what authority they had to charge her; she had not subscribed to the service, and she was certain that none of her five employees had either. It was difficult to imagine any scenario in which one of her employees would switch the long-distance provider. The provider claimed it recorded all transactions of that nature. She asked for the recording but never received it. She contacted her local service, Bell South, which told her it had switched her at the insistance of the long-distance provider and added that fraudulent switches of that sort were not uncommon. In the meantime, she received a letter from a collection agency in behalf of the provider. Her attorney advised her to report this incident to the state attorney.

In summary, computers provide wonderful services and cost-effectiveness in many areas while incurring often unforeseen risks. The most frustrating aspect of writing this section of the book is that it may be obsolete a few months after it is written. It is no longer possible to practice law and even be semi-literate with computers. Following are a few useful links to the World Wide Web that provide useful legal information.

Commercial Databases

http://www.westlaw.com
Westlaw is one of the two primary legal sources used by law firms and is commonly available to law students through their law schools.

http://www.lexis-nexis.com
Lexis is one of the two primary legal sources used by law firms and is commonly available to law students through their law schools.

http://web.lexis-nexis.com/universe
Lexis-Nexis Universe may be available through a student's college or university website or library.

http://www.versuslaw.com
VersusLaw provides a case search at a subscription rate of $6.95 per month.

Public Access Databases

Cornell Law School is one of the richest sources of legal information, with thorough and intelligent access to federal materials. Many state materials are available, but cases may be limited to fairly recent decisions.

http://www.law.cornell.edu
Cornell Legal Institute (LII) homepage

http://www4.law.cornell.edu/uscode
Page for access to United States Code

http://www.law.cornell.edu/ethics
Legal Ethics Library

http://www.law.cornell.edu/citation
LII's Introduction to Legal Citation, based on the "Bluebook" by Peter W. Martin

http://www.findlaw.com
Findlaw is a portal for legal information, an outstanding site that is well worth investigating thoroughly. Findlaw was bought by West Group on January 26, 2001. West Group also publishes the book you are now reading. [We hope West Group will continue to keep Findlaw free to the public but get real money for our book.]

http://www.washburnlaw.edu
Washburn University School of Law provides resources and links to legal materials.

http://www.lawresearch.com
A commercial research and resource page with many links

http://www.lectlaw.com/ref.html
The 'Lectric Law Library Reference Room has links to many useful topical articles and a law dictionary that has extensive information and even case citations.

Scenario

Your sister tells you she has 200 songs that she downloaded in 2000 from the Napster (http://www.napster.com) website. They are on her harddrive, but she wants to burn them all to CDs or DVDs. She wants to have the pertinent information as to whether she has or is about to break the law and what consequences are likely to follow. She knows you are familiar with the legal materials on the Web. See what material you can find and what is the latest situation with regard to the status of materials downloaded in the year 2000 as well as putting these on CD or DVD next month. If you were licensed to give her legal advice, what would you advise her?

APPENDIX A

How to Read a Case

Introduction

Reported judicial decisions have a style and format all their own. This discussion is designed to acquaint readers with the form and the nature of judicial decisions. Although judges have considerable freedom in how they write opinions, some uniformity of pattern comes from the similarity of purpose for decisions, especially decisions of appellate courts, which frequently serve as authority for later cases.

Similarity is also a product of custom. The influence of West Group, Inc., which publishes the regional reporter series and the federal reporters, as well as the Westlaw® database, has been great. Some of this material repeats discussions in the first chapters of the book, but this appendix is designed to be read at almost any point during the book—the sooner, the better, as judicial decisions are interspersed throughout the text.

Which Court?

Knowing which court issued the opinion is extremely important. As a general rule, the higher the court, the more compelling its authority. The binding force of precedent depends on the relationship between the court which issues it and the court applying it. A decision of the Iowa Supreme Court has no precedential power over courts in Tennessee because each state has its own laws and legal system. Iowa courts may not dictate to Tennessee what Tennessee law is or should be. However, decisions of the Supreme Court of Tennessee, the highest court of that state, are binding precedent on other state courts in Tennessee; lower courts must follow the law as stated by a higher court in their jurisdiction.

Federal and State Courts

The United States has two parallel legal structures. Each state has its own set of laws and courts. In addition, the federal government has a separate legal authority through courts located in every state. Federal courts are not superior to state courts but parallel to them, having authority over different types of cases. For example, the U.S. Constitution restricts authority over patents and copyrights to the federal government. Thus, a patent case will be heard in federal court but not in a state court. In contrast, there are both federal and state civil rights laws, so a particular case might be filed in one or the other. When federal and state courts have concurrent jurisdiction of this sort, exercise of authority is governed by custom or law; but when state and federal law overlap and conflict, state law must yield to federal law.

Trial and Appellate Courts

State and federal courts are divided into trial and appellate courts. Most cases originate in trial courts, where evidence is presented, witnesses are questioned, and a judgment determining the rights of the parties is entered. If one of the parties to the case is dissatisfied with the result, the case may be appealed; an appellate court is petitioned to review the proceedings of the lower, or trial, court to determine if errors were made that would justify changing the outcome of the case.

The federal system provides a model followed in general terms by a majority of state systems. The U.S. District Court is the primary federal trial court. The next higher federal court is the United States Court of Appeals. It is called an intermediate appellate court because it is subordinate to the highest court, the U.S. Supreme Court.

Most states name their highest court Supreme Court; New York, a notable exception, calls its highest court the Court of Appeals and uses the designation Supreme Court for lower courts. Some states do not have intermediate appellate courts. There is also considerable variety in state trial courts and the names applied to them.

The careful researcher always takes note of the court issuing a decision because the higher the court, the greater the force of its decision. The decision of a court is binding on lower courts within its jurisdiction, meaning that the rules it lays down must be followed by lower courts faced with the same issue.

For Whom Are Judicial Opinions Written?

In evaluating any written material, the reader should assess the audience the writer is addressing and the writer's goals. Judges write decisions for two reasons. The first is to inform the parties to the dispute who won and who lost, giving the rules and reasoning the judge applied to the facts. The second is to inform the legal profession, attorneys and judges, of the rules applied to a given set of facts and the reasons for the decision.

Attorneys and Judges Read Judicial Opinions

Very few laypersons ever enter a law library to find and read cases. The people found in the county law library are usually lawyers, paralegals, and judges. Cases are rarely intended to be entertaining, and judges are not motivated to make their cases "reader-friendly." Their tasks are quite specific. Because any case may serve as precedent, or at least form a basis for subsequent legal arguments, judges are especially concerned with conveying a precise meaning by carefully framing the rules and providing the reasoning behind them. The higher the court, the greater this concern will be. Imagine writing an opinion for a highly skilled, highly intelligent readership that critically analyzes every word and phrase, an opinion that may well affect important rights of citizens in the future.

Judicial writing is different from most other kinds of writing in that its goal is neither simply to pass on information nor to persuade the reader of the author's point of view. The judge is stating the law and making a final judgment but must do so with caution so that the statements are not misinterpreted or misused. An appreciation of the judge's dilemma is essential to critical evaluation of cases.

The Effect of Setting Precedent

The cost of litigation is great, and appeal of a decision incurs significant additional cost. It makes sense to appeal if the losing party reasonably concludes that the lower court was incorrect in its application of the law. It would be quite foolish to spend large sums of money to go to the higher court if the chances of winning were slim and the stakes were small. This means that the cases we read from appellate courts, and especially from the highest courts, generally involve questions with strong arguments on both sides. The judges of these courts are faced with difficult decisions and must respect the reasonable arguments of both sides in deciding which side will prevail.

Clarity versus Confusion

Judicial writing is often difficult and obscure, but such criticism of judicial writing often neglects to recognize that not only are the issues difficult to present with clarity, but also that often the importance of narrowing the application of the decision encourages tortuous reasoning. For example, when faced with a landmark case of reverse discrimination (a white applicant for medical school was denied admission, while less-qualified minority students were admitted), the U.S. Supreme Court was expected to lay down a rule concerning the constitutionality of such admissions programs. Those expectations were disappointed. The justices wrote divergent opinions that made it very difficult to discover exactly what the rule was. At the time the issue was quite controversial, and the decision potentially could have affected efforts by the administration and Congress to help the position of disadvantaged minorities. Any precedent of the Court would have far-reaching consequences. Although the plaintiff won and subsequently entered medical school, there was some confusion as to why he won. The effect of the decision was to stifle future efforts to pursue reverse discrimination cases. Each justice of the Court viewed the problem in a different light, and the result was a resolution of the dispute without a clear picture of the rule to be applied in such cases.

Thus, the reader of cases should be aware that the complex reasoning of a judge's writing is not always due to the complexity of the issues but may also be caused by the judge's desire to narrow the effect of the precedent.

Most appellate decisions are the product of three or more judges. A unanimous or majority opinion is not the reasoning of a single person. The author of an opinion must take into consideration the views of the judges who join in the opinion. In some cases, especially with the nine justices of the U.S. Supreme Court, achieving a majority involves negotiation—one justice may vote with the majority only if a key point in his or her reasoning is included or only if the rule is narrowed to cover a limited number of situations. The author of the opinion may thus be stating someone else's reasoning or opinion, or may be stating the argument to appease a justice who is reluctant to join in the opinion. The politics of decision making may make it quite difficult to write a cohesive opinion that makes everyone happy.

Doing Justice to the Parties

It is a mistake to assume that judges are dispassionate, totally rational, and objective interpreters of the law. The notion that judges reason directly from the facts to the law in a rather mechanical fashion neglects the obvious fact that judges are human beings doing their best to dispense justice. We must suspect that in any given case, the judge or judges form an opinion as to which side should win and then select rules and arguments to support that side. (If justice clearly favors one side, it is usually not difficult to frame a convincing legal argument for that side to win.)

Sometimes a strict application of the law causes a very undesirable result. The Kentucky Court of Appeals was faced with such circumstances in *Strunk v. Strunk*, 445 S.W.2d 145, in which a man was dying of a kidney problem and his brother was the only appropriate donor for a life-saving kidney transplant. The problem was that the brother with the healthy kidneys was severely mentally retarded and therefore legally incompetent to consent to the operation. The issue facing the court was whether the mother of the two brothers could consent to the operation, acting as the guardian of the retarded brother. Kentucky precedents (cited by the dissenting judges, but ignored by the majority) seemed to show clearly that a guardian's authority did not extend to making such a decision. Faced with a heartrending life-or-death decision, four of seven judges deciding the case ignored prior precedents. Three of the judges disagreed, and one wrote a vigorous dissenting opinion. The reasoning of the majority opinion was weak, but it is difficult to fault the judges under the circumstances.

The Format for a Reported Decision

The cases found in the reporters generally follow a uniform format with which researchers must become familiar. The first part of the case has no official authority. Authoritative statements begin with the actual text of the opinion.

All of the comments and the example that follows represent the print version of the cases, following a format developed by West Publishing Company many years ago and cross-indexed to its many publications. Naturally, the appearance is different from the electronic versions found on Westlaw®, but the elements will be familiar to anyone conversant with the print version. The **headnotes** with accompanying key numbers are a West invention and therefore copyrighted and not found on other electronic versions unless West has given its permission. The decision itself is a public document and falls within the public domain exception to copyright. This sometimes presents a problem since the **syllabus** section of the case may have been written by a court official or by the private reporter, for example, West. Whether it falls under copyright or not must be determined by examination. While this may not be significant to the reader, copyright issues are important to the author of this book and others who publish from the cases.

Other electronic versions may have a different style, but the case itself should be identical. The great advantage of electronic versions is the inclusion of links to cited materials and related authorities; in other words, speed and convenience of research far surpass the print materials. Although many law firms are converting to electronic law libraries, virtually every lawyer working today started with the books and many prefer to read from the printed page, whether it is a book or the "hard copy" of a digital version. The effect of the electronic law library on the format and style of legal writing has yet to be determined. For the time being, it is best to become familiar with the format of the printed version.

headnotes Statements of the major points of law discussed in a case; these are found in the law reports published by West Group, Inc., formerly West Publishing Company.

syllabus A summary of a case often included with a report decision and preceding the official text of the opinion.

Format Preceding the Opinion

West Group, Inc. publishes the reporter series for which it has established a uniform format. The first page of *United States v. National Lead Co.*, 438 F.2d 935 (8th Cir. 1971) illustrates all the elements (Figure A-1).

The Citation

The heading of the page indicates the citation: "**UNITED STATES v. NATIONAL LEAD COMPANY**" and "Cite as 438 F.2d 935 (1971)." This is the name of the case and where it can be found, namely, on page 935 in Volume 438 of the Federal Reporter, Second Series. Note that this differs from the official citation, *United States v. National Lead Co.*, 438 F.2d 935 (8th Cir. 1971), that would be used in legal texts and opinions. The official citation indicates that the case was decided by the U.S. Court of Appeals for the Eighth Circuit.

FIGURE A-1

UNITED STATES v. NATIONAL LEAD COMPANY
Cite as 438 F.2d 935 (1971)

UNITED STATES of America,
Plaintiff-Appellant,
v.
NATIONAL LEAD COMPANY,
a Corporation, and Chemical
Workers' Basic Union Local 1744,
AFL-CIO, Defendants-Appellees.
No. 20427.
United States Court of Appeals,
Eighth Circuit. Feb. 26, 1971.

Action by government against company and union for alleged violations of Civil Rights Act of 1964. The United States District Court for the Eastern District of Missouri, Roy W. Harper, Senior District Judge, 315 F.Supp. 912, denied government's motion for preliminary injunction, and government appealed. The Court of Appeals, Bright, Circuit Judge, held that although, under facts, some vestiges of employer's past discrimination seemed preserved in employer's transfer and promotion procedures, in view of fact that actual impact of this discrimination upon black employees possessing seniority dating back prior to end of discrimination was unclear, and in view of fact that an appropriate solution was not readily apparent from partial development of facts, denial of relief by way of a preliminary injunction was not error.

Affirmed and remanded.

1. Civil Rights   3

Employment policies which appear racially neutral but build upon bias that existed prior to enactment of 1964 Civil Rights Act to produce present discrimination are actionable. Civil Rights Act of 1964, § 701 et seq., 42 U.S.C.A. § 2000e et seq.

2. Civil Rights   3

Policy of 1964 Civil Rights Act is not fulfilled by a showing that black employees may enjoy substantially equal pay with others in similar capacities; the test is whether all employees possess an equal opportunity to fully enjoy all employment rights. Civil Rights Act of 1964, §§ 703(h), 706(g), 42 U.S.C.A. §§ 2000e–2(h), 2000e–5(g).

3. Injunction   137(4)

Although, under facts, some vestiges of employer's past discrimination seemed preserved in employer's transfer and promotion procedures, in view of fact that actual impact of this discrimination upon black employees possessing seniority dating back prior to end of discrimination was unclear, and in view of fact that an appropriate solution was not readily apparent from partial development of facts, denial of relief by way of a preliminary injunction was not error. Civil Rights Act of 1964, §§ 701 et seq., 707(a) 42 U.S.C.A. §§ 2000e et seq., 2000e–6(a).

4. Injunction   147

In view of evidence disclosing that in recent years blacks had filled three of six vacancies for guard positions and that employer planned no immediate expansion of present guard force or filling of any existing vacancies, no need for preliminary injunction was shown with respect to guard force. Civil Rights Act of 1964, §§ 701 et seq., 707(a), 42 U.S.C.A. §§ 2000e et seq., 2000e–6(a).

Jerris Leonard, Asst. Atty. Gen., Daniel Bartlett, Jr., U. S. Atty., David L. Rose, Stuart P. Herman, Attys., Dept of Justice, Washington, D.C., for plaintiff-appellant.

Edward Weakley, Howard Elliott, Boyle, Priest, Elliot & Weakley, St. Louis, Mo., for National Lead Co.

Harry Moline, Jr., Thomas, Busse, Cullen, Clooney, Weil & King, St. Louis, Mo., for Chemical Workers' Basic Union, Local 1744, AFL-CIO.

Before GIBSON and BRIGHT, Circuit Judges, and McMANUS, Chief District Judge.

BRIGHT, Circuit Judge.

The United States by its Attorney General brings this action seeking . . .

FIGURE A-2

> UNITED STATES of America,
> Plaintiff-Appellant,
> v.
> NATIONAL LEAD COMPANY,
> a Corporation, and Chemical Workers'
> Basic Union Local 1744, AFL-CIO,
> Defendants-Appellees.
> No. 20427.
> United States Court of Appeals,
> Eighth Circuit.
> Feb. 26, 1971.

The Caption

Figure A-2 shows the caption of the case, which names the parties. Note that the citation names only one party for each side, whereas the caption includes a co-defendant, a union local of the AFL-CIO. The caption also indicates the status of the parties with regard to the suit as "Plaintiff-Appellant" and "Defendants-Appellees." We can surmise from this that the United States brought the original suit as plaintiff and then also the appeal, apparently having lost the original suit.

Commonly, the caption simply states "appellant" and "appellee," and the reader must discover from the text who brought the suit originally. It is important to note who is appellant and who is appellee because many opinions refer to the parties by those terms. In *National Lead*, Judge Bright refers to "the government" and "National Lead," which makes reading much less confusing.

Below the parties we find "No. 20427," the docket number, which is a number assigned to the case upon initial filing with the clerk of the court and by which it is identified prior to assigning it a volume and page number in the reporter series. This number is important when attempting to research the case prior to its official publication. Below the docket number is the name of the court issuing the decision and the date of the decision.

The Syllabus

Following the caption is a brief summary of the case called the syllabus (Figure A-3). Although this is sometimes written by the court or a reporter appointed by the court, it is a narrow condensation of the court's ruling and cannot be relied upon as the precise holding of the court. The syllabus can be useful in obtaining a quick idea of what the case concerns—a summary of the issue and the holding of the court. Frequently, legal researchers follow leads to cases that upon reading prove to be unrelated to the issue being researched. Reading the syllabus may make reading the entire opinion unnecessary. However, if the syllabus suggests that the case may be important, a careful reading of the entire text of the opinion is usually necessary.

FIGURE A-3

Action by government against company and union for alleged violations of Civil Rights Act of 1964. The United States District Court for the Eastern District of Missouri, Roy W. Harper, Senior District Judge, 315 F.Supp. 912, denied government's motion for preliminary injunction, and government appealed. The Court of Appeals, Bright, Circuit Judge, held that although, under facts, some vestiges of employer's past discrimination seemed preserved in employer's transfer and promotion procedures, in view of fact that actual impact of this discrimination upon black employees possessing seniority dating back prior to end of discrimination was unclear, and in view of fact that an appropriate solution was not readily apparent from partial development of facts, denial of relief by way of a preliminary injunction was not error.

Affirmed and remanded.

FIGURE A-4

3. Injunction   137(4)

Although, under facts, some of vestiges of employer's past discrimination seemed preserved in employer's transfer and promotion procedures, in view of fact that actual impact of this discrimination upon black employees possessing seniority dating back prior to end of discrimination was unclear, and in view of fact that an appropriate solution was not readily apparent from partial development of facts, denial of relief by way of a preliminary injunction was not error. Civil Rights Act of 1964, §§ 701 et seq., 707(a) 42 U.S.C.A. §§ 2000e et seq., 2000e–6(a).

4. Injunction   147

In view of evidence disclosing that in recent years blacks had filled three of six vacancies for guard positions and that employer planned no immediate expansion of present guard force or filling of any existing vacancies, no need for preliminary injunction was shown with respect to guard force. Civil Rights Act of 1964, §§ 701 et seq., 707(a), 42 U.S.C.A. §§ 2000e et seq., 2000e–6(a).

Headnotes

Figure A-4 illustrates the headnotes, which are statements of the major points of law discussed in the case. With limited editing, the headnotes tend to be nearly verbatim statements lifted from the opinion. The headnotes are listed in numerical order, starting at the beginning of the opinion, so that the reader may look quickly for the context of a point expressed by a headnote. For example, the part of the text that deals with a particular point made in the headnote will have the number of the headnote in brackets, for example, [4], at the beginning of the paragraph or section in which it is discussed. This is very helpful when researching lengthy cases in which only one issue is of concern to the researcher.

To the right of the headnote number is a generic heading, such as "Civil Rights," and a *key* number. Because this reporter is published by West Law, Inc.,

FIGURE A-5

Jerris Leonard, Asst. Atty. Gen., Daniel Bartlett, Jr., U. S. Atty., David L. Rose, Stuart P. Herman, Attys., Dept of Justice, Washington, D.C., for plaintiff-appellant.

Edward Weakley, Howard Elliott, Boyle, Priest, Elliot & Weakley, St. Louis, Mo., for National Lead Co.

Harry Moline, Jr., Thomas, Busse, Cullen, Clooney, Weil & King, St. Louis, Mo., for Chemical Workers' Basic Union, Local 1744, AFL-CIO.

Before GIBSON and BRIGHT, Circuit Judges, and McMANUS, Chief District Judge.

FIGURE A-6

BRIGHT, Circuit Judge.
The United States by its Attorney
General brings this action seeking . . .

it uses an indexing title and number that can be used throughout the many West indexes, reporters, and encyclopedias.

Although syllabi and headnotes are useful, they are not authoritative.

Attorneys for the Parties

Figure A-5 shows the *attorneys for the parties* as well as the judges sitting on the case. These are listed just above the beginning of the opinion, shown in Figure A-6.

Format of the Opinion

Following the names of the attorneys and a list of the judges sitting on the case, the formal opinion (that is, the official discussion of the case) begins with the name of the judge writing the opinion, for example, "Bright, Circuit Judge," in *National Lead*. The author of the opinion has considerable freedom in presentation. Some opinions are written mechanically; a few are almost poetic. The peculiarities of any particular case may dictate a special logical order of their own. Nevertheless, the majority of opinions follow a standard format. When this format is followed, reading and understanding are simplified, but no judge is required to make an opinion easy reading. The following format is the one most frequently used.

Procedure

Most opinions begin with some reference to the outcome of the trial in the lower court and the basis for appeal. In a criminal case, for example, the opinion may state that the defendant was found guilty of aggravated assault and is appealing the judge's ruling to admit certain evidence over the defendant's objections that the evidence was prejudicial to the defendant's case. Often the remarks about procedure are brief and confusing, especially if the reader is not familiar with procedural rules. If the procedure is important to the opinion, a more elaborate discussion is usually found in the body of the opinion. Many things in the opinion become clear only upon further reading, and many opinions must be read at least twice for a full understanding. An opinion is like a jigsaw puzzle—the reader must put the parts together to see the full picture.

The Facts

Most of the text of an opinion in appellate decisions is concerned with a discussion of the law, but because a case revolves around a dispute concerning events that occurred between the parties, no opinion is complete without some discussion of the events that led to the trial. Trials generally explore these events in great detail and judge or jury settle the facts, so appellate opinions usually narrow the fact statement to the most relevant facts. In an interesting case, the reader is often left wanting to know more about what happened, but the judge is not writing a story. The important element in the opinion is the application of law.

The Issue

Following a summary of relevant facts, many writers describe the questions of law that must be decided. Rarely, this is made quite clear: "The only issue presented to the court is. . . ." Unfortunately, few writers pinpoint the issue in this fashion, so the reader must search the text for the issue. At this point it is appropriate to introduce a favorite term used by attorneys: *caveat*. This means "warning" or, literally, "Let him beware."

Caveat: The issue is the most important element in an opinion. If the issue is not understood, the significance of the rule laid down by the court can easily be misunderstood. This point cannot be emphasized too strongly. Law students study cases for three years with one primary goal: "Identify the issues." Anyone can fill out forms, but a competently trained person can go right to the heart of a case and recognize its strengths and weaknesses.

The Discussion

The main body of the text of an opinion, often 90 percent of it, discusses the meaning of the issue(s) and offers a line of reasoning that leads to a disposition of the case and explains why a certain rule or rules must apply to the dispute. This part of the opinion is the most difficult to follow. The writer has a goal, but the goal is often not clear to the reader until the end. For this reason, it is usually helpful to look at the final paragraph in the case to see whether the appellate court affirmed (agreed with the lower court) or reversed (disagreed with the lower court). Many judges seem to like to hold the reader in suspense, but the reader need not play this game. By finding out the outcome of the decision, the reader can see how the writer of an opinion is building the conclusion. By recognizing the issue and knowing the rule applied, the reader can see the structure of the argument. The discussion section is the writer's justification of the holding.

The Holding

holding The core of a judge's decision in a case; that part of the written opinion that applies the law to the facts of the case; it expresses the **rule of the case** as distinguished from *dicta*.

rule of the case That part of a written judicial opinion that decides the case; it is what the case stands for as far as applying a rule to the facts of the case.

The **holding** states the **rule of the case,** that is, the rule the court applies to conclude whether the lower court was correct. The rule is *the law*, meaning that it determines the rights of the parties unless reversed by a higher court. It binds lower courts faced with a similar dispute in future cases. It is best to think of the holding as an answer to the issue.

Let us give a real-life example. A woman is suing for wrongful death. Her husband was killed in an auto accident, and she is attempting to collect damages based on the income her husband would have received had he lived, in which income she would have shared. Since the death, however, she has married an affluent man, and her lifestyle has not diminished. The issue is whether the jury can be informed of her remarriage. The court holds that the fact of her remarriage may not be kept from the jury. The court also holds that evidence of her new husband's earnings may *not* be presented to the jury. In this instance, the holding goes a bit beyond the issue and clarifies it. (This particular issue has been answered quite differently in different states.) The reasoning for the holding is as follows: There is no justification for deliberately deceiving the jury about the woman's marital status. However, her current husband's earnings are irrelevant to the damage she suffered in losing her former husband. Fairness on this issue is difficult.

Evaluating Cases

Once the purpose, style, and structure of appellate decisions are grasped, mastering the content is a matter of concentration and experience. Researching cases generally has one or more of the following three goals:

1. Finding statements of the law
2. Assessing the law in relation to the client's case
3. Building an argument

Finding the Law

Research of cases is done for a number of reasons. The principles that apply to a dispute may be unknown, unfamiliar, or forgotten. With experience, legal professionals come to develop a knack for guessing how a dispute will be decided and can even predict what rules will be applied. Once the issues of a case are recognized, a reasonable prediction of a fair outcome can be made. This is, however, merely tentative; the researchers must check their knowledge and memory against definitive statements of the law. In some instances a statute clearly defines the rights and duties that pertain to the case at hand; in others the elaboration of the law in the cases leaves little room for doubt. Frequently, however, the issue in a client's case is complex or unique, and no case can be found that is directly "on point." Ideally, research will result in finding a case that contains a fact situation so similar to that of the client that an assumption can be made that the same rule will apply. A case with a factual background identical to that of the client is said to be *on point*, as illustrated in the following example.

Suppose Laura Lee, while waiting for a bus, was hit and injured by an automobile. The driver had lost control because of a defective steering mechanism. Laura was seriously injured, and the driver has minimal insurance (and may not have been at fault). The issue is whether the manufacturer of the automobile is liable. The owner could sue the automobile manufacturer, but can a bystander sue as well? A search reveals several cases involving bystanders who were injured by defective brakes and were able to sue the manufacturer for product liability. Although the facts are not identical, these cases are on point, because the issue is not what kind of defect caused the accident but whether a bystander can sue.

Distinguishing Cases

In some instances, the facts of a dispute are used to *distinguish* it from similar cases. For example, in researching Laura Lee's case, a case is encountered in which a bystander was injured by an automobile with a defective steering mechanism. In that case, the bystander did not collect damages from the manufacturer. The case was distinguishable because the driver was intoxicated. The driver's negligence was not merely passive, such as procrastinating in obtaining repairs, but was actively caused by his intoxication. The intoxication was the true cause of the injury, so it would have been unfair to place liability on the manufacturer. (The manufacturer would probably be sued anyway simply because it has the resources to compensate for the injury.)

Only experience and knowledge of the law will develop the keen sense it takes to separate cases that are on point from those that are distinguishable. It is often the advocate's job to persuade on the basis of threading a way through a host of seemingly conflicting cases.

Summary

Judicial opinions are unique as a literary form in that their statements of law as defined by the court become precedent for future legal arguments and decisions. Judges must not only do justice to the parties but also remain aware that their decisions determine rights of other parties in the future. Complex issues often result in opinions that are difficult to follow. Controversial issues may cause judges to be evasive in their conclusions.

A standard publishing format is followed in reported judicial decisions. In addition, custom has dictated a format for the text of the opinion itself. Judges are under no requirement to follow this format, and it is up to the reader to ferret out the issues and follow the reasoning.

APPENDIX B

The Constitution
of the United States of America

PREAMBLE

We the People of the United States, in Order to form a more perfect Union, establish Justice, insure domestic Tranquility, provide for the common defence, promote the general Welfare, and secure the Blessings of Liberty to ourselves and our Posterity, do ordain and establish this Constitution for the United States of America.

ARTICLE I

Section 1 All legislative Powers herein granted shall be vested in a Congress of the United States, which shall consist of a Senate and House of Representatives.

Section 2 (1) The House of Representatives shall be composed of Members chosen every second Year by the People of the several States, and the Electors in each State shall have the Qualifications requisite for Electors of the most numerous Branch of the State Legislature.

(2) No Person shall be a Representative who shall not have attained to the age of twenty-five Years, and been seven Years a Citizen of the United States, and who shall not, when elected, be an Inhabitant of that State in which he shall be chosen.

(3) Representatives and direct Taxes shall be apportioned among the several States which may be included within this Union, according to their respective Numbers, which shall be determined by adding to the whole Number of free Persons, including those bound to Service for a Term of Years, and excluding Indians not taxed, three fifths of all other Persons. The actual Enumeration shall be made within three Years after the first Meeting of the Congress of the United States, and within every subsequent Term of ten Years, in such Manner as they shall by Law direct. The Number of Representatives shall not exceed one for every thirty Thousand, but each State shall have at Least one Representative; and until such enumeration shall be made, the State of New Hampshire shall be entitled to chuse three, Massachusetts eight, Rhode Island and Providence Plantations one, Connecticut five, New York six, New Jersey four, Pennsylvania eight, Delaware one, Maryland six, Virginia ten, North Carolina five, South Carolina five, and Georgia three.

(4) When vacancies happen in the Representation from any State, the Executive Authority thereof shall issue Writs of Election to fill such Vacancies.

(5) The House of Representatives shall chuse their Speaker and other Officers; and shall have the sole Power of Impeachment.

Section 3 (1) The Senate of the United States shall be composed of two Senators from each State, chosen by the Legislature thereof, for six Years; and each Senator shall have one Vote.

(2) Immediately after they shall be assembled in Consequence of the first Election, they shall be divided as equally as may be into three Classes. The Seats of the Senators of the first Class shall be vacated at the Expiration of the second Year, of the second Class at the

Expiration of the fourth Year, and of the third Class at the Expiration of the sixth Year, so that one third may be chosen every second Year; and if Vacancies happen by Resignation, or otherwise, during the Recess of the Legislature of any State, the Executive thereof may make temporary Appointments until the next Meeting of the Legislature, which shall then fill such Vacancies.

(3) No Person shall be a Senator who shall not have attained to the Age of thirty Years, and been nine Years a Citizen of the United States, and who shall not, when elected, be an Inhabitant of that State for which he shall be chosen.

(4) The Vice President of the United States shall be President of the Senate, but shall have no Vote, unless they be equally divided.

(5) The Senate shall chuse their other Officers, and also a President pro tempore, in the Absence of the Vice President, or when he shall exercise the Office of the President of the United States.

(6) The Senate shall have the sole Power to try all Impeachments. When sitting for that Purpose, they shall be on Oath or Affirmation. When the President of the United States is tried, the Chief Justice shall preside: And no Person shall be convicted without the Concurrence of two thirds of the Members present.

(7) Judgment in Cases of Impeachment shall not extend further than to removal from Office, and disqualification to hold and enjoy any Office of honor, Trust or Profit under the United States: but the Party convicted shall nevertheless be liable and subject to Indictment, Trial, Judgment and Punishment, according to Law.

Section 4 (1) The Times, Places and Manner of holding Elections for Senators and Representatives, shall be prescribed in each State by the Legislature thereof; but the Congress may at any time by Law make or alter such Regulations, except as to the Places of chusing Senators.

(2) The Congress shall assemble at least once in every Year, and such Meeting shall be on the first Monday in December, unless they shall by Law appoint a different Day.

Section 5 (1) Each House shall be the Judge of the Elections, Returns and Qualifications of its own Members, and a Majority of each shall constitute a Quorum to do Business; but a smaller Number may adjourn from day to day, and may be authorized to compel the Attendance of absent Members, in such Manner, and under such Penalties as each House may provide.

(2) Each House may determine the Rules of its Proceedings, punish its Members for disorderly Behaviour, and, with the Concurrence of two thirds, expel a Member.

(3) Each House shall keep a Journal of its Proceedings, and from time to time publish the same, excepting such Parts as may in their Judgment require Secrecy; and the Yeas and Nays of the Members of either House on any question shall, at the Desire of one fifth of those Present, be entered on the Journal.

(4) Neither House, during the Session of Congress, shall, without the Consent of the other, adjourn for more than three days, nor to any other Place than that in which the two Houses shall be sitting.

Section 6 (1) The Senators and Representatives shall receive a Compensation for their Services, to be ascertained by Law, and paid out of the Treasury of the United States. They shall in all Cases, except Treason, Felony and Breach of the Peace, be privileged from Arrest during their Attendance at the Session of their respective Houses, and in going to and returning from the same; and for any Speech or Debate in either House, they shall not be questioned in any other Place.

(2) No Senator or Representative shall, during the Time for which he was elected, be appointed to any civil Office under the Authority of the United States, which shall have been created, or the Emoluments whereof shall have been encreased during such time; and no Person holding any Office under the United States, shall be a Member of either House during his Continuance in Office.

Section 7 (1) All Bills for raising Revenue shall originate in the House of Representatives; but the Senate may propose or concur with Amendments as on other Bills.

(2) Every Bill which shall have passed the House of Representatives and the Senate, shall, before it become a Law, be presented to the President of the United States; If he approve he shall sign it, but if not he shall return it, with his Objections to that House in which it shall have originated, who shall enter the Objections at large on their Journal, and proceed to reconsider it. If after such Reconsideration two thirds of that House shall agree to pass the Bill, it shall be sent, together with the Objections, to the other House, by which it shall likewise be reconsidered, and if approved by two thirds of that House, it shall become a law. But in all such Cases the Votes of both Houses shall be determined by Yeas and Nays, and the Names

of the Persons voting for and against the Bill shall be entered on the Journal of each House respectively. If any Bill shall not be returned by the President within ten Days (Sunday excepted) after it shall have been presented to him, the Same shall be a Law, in like Manner as if he had signed it, unless the Congress by their Adjournment prevent its Return, in which Case it shall not be a Law.

(3) Every Order, Resolution, or Vote to which the Concurrence of the Senate and House of Representatives may be necessary (except on a question of Adjournment) shall be presented to the President of the United States; and before the Same shall take Effect, shall be approved by him, or being disapproved by him, shall be repassed by two thirds of the Senate and House of Representatives, according to the Rules and Limitations prescribed in the Case of a Bill.

Section 8   (1) The Congress shall have Power To lay and collect Taxes, Duties, Imposts and Excises, to pay the Debts and provide for the common Defence and general Welfare of the United States; but all Duties, Imposts and Excises shall be uniform throughout the United States;

(2) To borrow Money on the credit of the United States;

(3) To regulate Commerce with foreign Nations, and among the several States, and with the Indian Tribes;

(4) To establish an uniform Rule of Naturalization, and uniform Laws on the subject of Bankruptcies throughout the United States;

(5) To coin Money, regulate the Value thereof, and of foreign Coin, and to fix the Standard of Weights and Measures;

(6) To provide for the Punishment of counterfeiting the Securities and current Coin of the United States;

(7) To establish Post Offices and post Roads;

(8) To promote the Progress of Science and useful Arts, by securing for limited Times to Authors and Inventors the exclusive Right to their respective Writings and Discoveries;

(9) To constitute Tribunals inferior to the Supreme Court;

(10) To define and punish Piracies and Felonies committed on the high Seas, and Offenses against the Law of Nations;

(11) To declare War, grant Letters of Marque and Reprisal, and make Rules concerning Captures on Land and Water;

(12) To raise and support Armies, but no Appropriation of Money to that Use shall be for a longer Term than two Years;

(13) To provide and maintain a Navy;

(14) To make Rules for the Government and Regulation of the land and naval Forces;

(15) To provide for calling forth the Militia to execute the Laws of the Union, suppress Insurrections and repel Invasions;

(16) To provide for organizing, arming, and disciplining, the Militia, and for governing such Part of them as may be employed in the Service of the United States, reserving to the States respectively, the Appointment of the Officers, and the Authority of training the Militia according to the discipline prescribed by Congress;

(17) To exercise exclusive Legislation in all Cases whatsoever, over such District (not exceeding ten Miles square) as may, by Cession of particular States, and the Acceptance of Congress, become the Seat of the Government of the United States, and to exercise like Authority over all Places purchased by the Consent of the Legislature of the State in which the Same shall be, for the Erection of Forts, Magazines, Arsenals, dock-Yards, and other needful Buildings;—And

(18) To make all Laws which shall be necessary and proper for carrying into Execution the foregoing Powers, and all other Powers vested by this Constitution in the Government of the United States, or in any Department or Officer thereof.

Section 9   (1) The Migration or Importation of such Persons as any of the States now existing shall think proper to admit, shall not be prohibited by the Congress prior to the Year one thousand eight hundred and eight, but a Tax or Duty may be imposed on such Importation, not exceeding ten dollars for each Person.

(2) The Privilege of the Writ of Habeas Corpus shall not be suspended unless when in Cases of Rebellion or Invasion the public Safety may require it.

(3) No Bill of Attainder or ex post facto Law shall be passed.

(4) No Capitation, or other direct, Tax shall be laid, unless in Proportion to the Census or Enumeration herein before directed to be taken.

(5) No Tax or Duty shall be laid on Articles exported from any State.

(6) No Preference shall be given by any Regulation of Commerce or Revenue to the Ports of one State over those of another; nor shall Vessels bound to, or

from, one State, be obliged to enter, clear or pay Duties in another.

(7) No Money shall be drawn from the Treasury, but in Consequence of Appropriations made by Law; and a regular Statement and Account of the Receipts and Expenditures of all public Money shall be published from time to time.

(8) No Title of Nobility shall be granted by the United States: And no Person holding any Office of Profit or Trust under them, shall, without the Consent of the Congress, accept of any present, Emolument, Office, or Title, of any kind whatever, from any King, Prince or foreign State.

Section 10 (1) No State shall enter into any Treaty, Alliance, or Confederation; grant Letters of Marque and Reprisal; coin Money; emit Bills of Credit; make any Thing but gold and silver Coin a Tender in Payment of Debts; pass any Bill of Attainder, ex post facto Law, or Law impairing the Obligation of Contracts, or grant any Title of Nobility.

(2) No State shall, without the Consent of Congress, lay any Imposts or Duties on Imports or Exports, except what may be absolutely necessary for executing its inspection Laws: and the net Produce of all Duties and Imposts, laid by any State on Imports or Exports, shall be for the Use of the Treasury of the United States; and all such Laws shall be subject to the Revision and Controul of the Congress.

(3) No State shall, without the Consent of Congress, lay any Duty of Tonnage, keep Troops, or Ships of War in time of Peace, enter into any Agreement or Compact with another State, or with a foreign Power, or engage in War, unless actually invaded, or in such imminent Danger as will not admit of Delay.

ARTICLE II

Section 1 (1) The executive Power shall be vested in a President of the United States of America. He shall hold his Office during the Term of four Years, and, together with the Vice President, chosen for the same Term, be elected, as follows:

(2) Each State shall appoint, in such Manner as the Legislature thereof may direct, a Number of Electors, equal to the whole Number of Senators and Representatives to which the State may be entitled in the Congress: but no Senator or Representative, or Person holding an Office of Trust or Profit under the United States, shall be appointed an Elector.

The Electors shall meet in their respective States, and vote by Ballot for two Persons, of whom one at least shall not be an Inhabitant of the same State with themselves. And they shall make a List of all the Persons voted for, and of the Number of Votes for each; which List they shall sign and certify, and transmit sealed to the Seat of the Government of the United States, directed to the President of the Senate. The President of the Senate shall, in the presence of the Senate and House of Representatives, open all the Certificates, and the Votes shall then be counted. The Person having the greatest Number of Votes shall be the President, if such Number be a Majority of the whole Number of Electors appointed; and if there be more than one who have such Majority, and have an equal Number of Votes, then the House of Representatives shall immediately chuse by Ballot one of them for President; and if no Person have a Majority, then from the five highest on the List the said House shall in like Manner chuse the President. But in chusing the President, the Votes shall be taken by States, the Representation from each State having one Vote; a quorum for this Purpose shall consist of a Member or Members from two thirds of the States, and a Majority of all the States shall be necessary to a Choice. In every Case, after the Choice of the President, the Person having the greatest Number of Votes of the Electors shall be the Vice President. But if there should remain two or more who have equal Votes, the Senate shall chuse from them by Ballot the Vice President.

(3) The Congress may determine the Time of choosing the Electors, and the Day on which they shall give their Votes; which Day shall be the same throughout the United States.

(4) No Person except a natural born Citizen, or a Citizen of the United States, at the time of the Adoption of this Constitution, shall be eligible to the Office of President; neither shall any Person be eligible to that Office who shall not have attained to the Age of thirty five Years, and been fourteen Years a Resident within the United States.

(5) In Case of the Removal of the President from Office, or of his Death, Resignation, or Inability to discharge the Powers and Duties of the said Office, the Same shall devolve on the Vice President, and the Congress may by Law provide for the Case of Removal, Death, Resignation or Inability, both of the President and Vice President, declaring what Officer shall then act as President, and such Officer shall act accordingly, until the Disability be removed, or a President shall be elected.

(6) The President shall, at stated Times, receive for his Services, a Compensation, which shall neither be increased nor diminished during the Period for which he shall have been elected, and he shall not receive within that Period any other Emolument from the United States, or any of them.

(7) Before he enter on the Execution of his Office, he shall take the following Oath or Affirmation:—"I do solemnly swear (or affirm) that I will faithfully execute the Office of President of the United States, and will to the best of my Ability, preserve, protect and defend the Constitution of the United States."

Section 2   (1) The President shall be Commander in Chief of the Army and Navy of the United States, and of the Militia of the several States, when called into the actual Service of the United States; he may require the Opinion, in writing, of the principal Officer in each of the executive Departments, upon any Subject relating to the Duties of their respective Offices, and he shall have Power to grant Reprieves and Pardons for Offenses against the United States, except in Cases of Impeachment.

(2) He shall have Power, by and with the Advice and Consent of the Senate, to make Treaties, provided two thirds of the Senators present concur; and he shall nominate, and by and with the Advice and Consent of the Senate, shall appoint Ambassadors, other public Ministers and Consuls, Judges of the supreme Court, and all other Officers of the United States, whose Appointments are not herein otherwise provided for, and which shall be established by Law: but the Congress may by Law vest the Appointment of such inferior Officers, as they think proper, in the President alone, in the Courts of Law, or in the Heads of Departments.

(3) The President shall have Power to fill up all Vacancies that may happen during the Recess of the Senate, by granting Commissions which shall expire at the End of their next Session.

Section 3   He shall from time to time give to the Congress Information of the State of the Union, and recommend to their Consideration such Measures as he shall judge necessary and expedient; he may, on extraordinary Occasions, convene both Houses, or either of them, and in Case of Disagreement between them, with Respect to the Time of Adjournment, he may adjourn them to such Time as he shall think proper; he shall receive Ambassadors and other public Ministers; he shall take Care that the Laws be faithfully executed, and shall Commission all the Officers of the United States.

Section 4   The President, Vice President and all Civil Officers of the United States, shall be removed from Office on Impeachment for, and Conviction of, Treason, Bribery, or other high Crimes and Misdemeanors.

ARTICLE III

Section 1   The judicial Power of the United States, shall be vested in one supreme Court, and in such inferior Courts as the Congress may from time to time ordain and establish. The Judges, both of the supreme and inferior Courts, shall hold their Offices during good Behaviour, and shall, at stated Times, receive for their Services, a Compensation, which shall not be diminished during their Continuance in Office.

Section 2   (1) The judicial Power shall extend to all Cases, in Law and Equity, arising under this Constitution, the Laws of the United States, and Treaties made, or which shall be made, under their Authority;—to all Cases affecting Ambassadors, other public Ministers and Consuls;—to all Cases of admiralty and maritime Jurisdiction;—to Controversies to which the United States shall be a party;—to Controversies between two or more States;—between a State and Citizens of another State;—between Citizens of different States;—between Citizens of the same State claiming Lands under Grants of different States, and between a State, or the Citizens thereof, and foreign States, Citizens or Subjects.

(2) In all Cases affecting Ambassadors, other public Ministers and Consuls, and those in which a State shall be Party, the supreme Court shall have original Jurisdiction. In all the other Cases before mentioned, the supreme Court shall have appellate Jurisdiction, both as to Law and Fact, with such Exceptions, and under such Regulations as the Congress shall make.

(3) The Trial of all Crimes, except in Cases of Impeachment, shall be by Jury; and such Trial shall be held in the State where the said Crimes shall have been committed; but when not committed within any State, the Trial shall be at such Place or Places as the Congress may by Law have directed.

Section 3   (1) Treason against the United States, shall consist only in levying War against them, or in adhering to their Enemies, giving them Aid and Comfort. No Person shall be convicted of Treason unless on the Testimony of two Witnesses to the same overt Act, or on Confession in open Court.

(2) The Congress shall have Power to declare the Punishment of Treason, but no Attainder of Treason shall work Corruption of Blood, or Forfeiture except during the Life of the Person attainted.

ARTICLE IV

Section 1   Full Faith and Credit shall be given in each State to the public Acts, Records, and judicial Proceedings of every other State. And the Congress may by general Laws prescribe the Manner in which such Acts, Records and Proceedings shall be proved, and the Effect thereof.

Section 2   (1) The Citizens of each State shall be entitled to all privileges and Immunities of Citizens in the several States.

(2) A Person charged in any State with Treason, Felony, or other Crime, who shall flee from Justice, and be found in another State, shall on Demand of the executive Authority of the State from which he fled, be delivered up, to be removed to the State having Jurisdiction of the Crime.

(3) No Person held to Service of Labour in one State, under the Laws thereof, escaping into another, shall, in Consequence of any Law or Regulation therein, be discharged from such Service or Labour, but shall be delivered up on Claim of the Party to whom such Service or Labour may be due.

Section 3   (1) New States may be admitted by the Congress into this Union; but no new State shall be formed or erected within the Jurisdiction of any other State; nor any State be formed by the Junction of two or more States, or Parts of States, without the Consent of the Legislatures of the States concerned as well as of the Congress.

(2) The Congress shall have power to dispose of and make all needful Rules and Regulations respecting the Territory or other Property belonging to the United States; and nothing in this Constitution shall be so construed as to Prejudice any Claims of the United States, or of any particular State.

Section 4   The United States shall guarantee to every State in this Union a Republican Form of Government, and shall protect each of them against Invasion; and on Application of the Legislature, or of the Executive (when the Legislature cannot be convened) against domestic Violence.

ARTICLE V

The Congress, whenever two thirds of both Houses shall deem it necessary, shall propose Amendments to this Constitution, or, on the Application of the Legislatures of two thirds of the several States, shall call a Convention for proposing Amendments, which, in either Case, shall be valid to all Intents and Purposes, as Part of this Constitution, when ratified by the Legislatures of three fourths of the several States, or by Conventions in three fourths thereof, as the one or the other Mode of Ratification may be proposed by the Congress; Provided that no Amendment which may be made prior to the Year One thousand eight hundred and eight shall in any Manner affect the first and fourth Clauses in the Ninth Section of the first Article; and that no State, without its Consent, shall be deprived of its equal Suffrage in the Senate.

ARTICLE VI

(1) All Debts contracted and Engagements entered into, before the Adoption of this Constitution, shall be as valid against the United States under this Constitution, as under the Confederation.

(2) This Constitution, and the Laws of the United States which shall be made in Pursuance thereof; and all Treaties made, or which shall be made, under the Authority of the United States, shall be the supreme Law of the Land; and the Judges in every State shall be bound thereby, any Thing in the Constitution or Laws of any State to the Contrary notwithstanding.

(3) The Senators and Representatives before mentioned, and the Members of the several State Legislatures, and all executive and judicial Officers, both of the United States and of the several States, shall be bound by Oath or Affirmation, to support this Constitution; but no religious Test shall ever be required as a Qualification to any Office or public Trust under the United States.

ARTICLE VII

The Ratification of the Conventions of nine States, shall be sufficient for the Establishment of this Constitution between the States so ratifying the Same.

ARTICLES IN ADDITION TO, AND AMENDMENT OF, THE CONSTITUTION OF THE UNITED STATES OF AMERICA, PROPOSED BY CONGRESS, AND RATIFIED BY THE SEVERAL STATES, PURSUANT TO THE FIFTH ARTICLE OF THE ORIGINAL CONSTITUTION

AMENDMENT I (1791)

Congress shall make no law respecting an establishment of religion, or prohibiting the free exercise thereof; or abridging the freedom of speech, or of the press; or the right of the people peaceably to assemble, and to petition the Government for a redress of grievances.

AMENDMENT II (1791)

A well regulated Militia, being necessary to the security of a free state, the right of the people to keep and bear Arms, shall not be infringed.

AMENDMENT III (1791)

No Soldier shall, in time of peace be quartered in any house, without the consent of the Owner, nor in time of war, but in a manner to be prescribed by law.

AMENDMENT IV (1791)

The right of the people to be secure in their persons, houses, papers, and effects, against unreasonable searches and seizures, shall not be violated, and no Warrants shall issue, but upon probable cause, supported by Oath or affirmation, and particularly describing the place to be searched, and the persons or things to be seized.

AMENDMENT V (1791)

No person shall be held to answer for a capital, or otherwise infamous crime, unless on a presentment or indictment of a Grand Jury, except in cases arising in the land or naval forces, or in the Militia, when in actual service in time of War or public danger; nor shall any person be subject for the same offence to be twice put in jeopardy of life or limb; nor shall be compelled in any criminal case to be a witness against himself, nor be deprived of life, liberty, or property, without due process of law; nor shall private property be taken for public use, without just compensation.

AMENDMENT VI (1791)

In all criminal prosecutions, the accused shall enjoy the right to a speedy and public trial, by an impartial jury of the State and district wherein the crime shall have been committed, which district shall have been previously ascertained by law, and to be informed of the nature and cause of the accusation; to be confronted with the witnesses against him; to have compulsory process for obtaining witnesses in his favor, and to have the Assistance of Counsel for his defence.

AMENDMENT VII (1791)

In Suits at common law, where the value in controversy shall exceed twenty dollars, the right of trial by jury shall be preserved, and no fact tried by a jury, shall be otherwise re-examined in any Court of the United States, than according to the rules of the common law.

AMENDMENT VIII (1791)

Excessive bail shall not be required, nor excessive fines imposed, nor cruel and unusual punishments inflicted.

AMENDMENT IX (1791)

The enumeration in the Constitution, of certain rights, shall not be construed to deny or disparage others retained by the people.

AMENDMENT X (1791)

The powers not delegated to the United States by the Constitution, nor prohibited by it to the States, are reserved to the States respectively, or to the people.

AMENDMENT XI (1798)

The Judicial power of the United States shall not be construed to extend to any suit in law or equity, commenced or prosecuted against one of the United States by Citizens of another State, or by Citizens or Subjects of any Foreign State.

AMENDMENT XII (1804)

The Electors shall meet in their respective states and vote by ballot for President and Vice-President, one of whom, at least, shall not be an inhabitant of the same state with themselves; they shall name in their ballots the person voted for as President, and in distinct ballots the person voted for as Vice-President, and they shall make distinct lists of all persons voted for as President, and of all persons voted for as Vice-President, and of the number of votes for each, which lists they shall sign and certify, and transmit sealed to the seat of the government of the United States, directed to the President of the Senate;—The President of the Senate shall, in the presence of the Senate and House of Representatives, open all the certificates and the votes shall then be counted;—The person having the greatest number of votes for President, shall be the President, if such number be a majority of the whole number of Electors appointed; and if no person have such majority, then from the persons having the highest numbers not exceeding three on the list of those voted for as President, the House of Representatives shall choose immediately, by ballot, the President. But in choosing the President, the votes shall be taken by states, the representation from each state having one vote; a quorum for this purpose shall consist of a member or members from two-thirds of the states, and a majority of all the states shall be necessary to a choice. And if the House of Representatives shall not choose a President whenever the right of choice shall devolve upon them, before the fourth day of March next following, then the Vice-President shall act as President, as in the case of the death or other constitutional disability of the President—The person having the greatest number of votes as Vice-President, shall be the Vice-President, if such number be a majority of the whole number of Electors appointed, and if no person have a majority, then from the two highest numbers on the list, the Senate shall choose the Vice-President; A quorum for the purpose shall consist of two-thirds of the whole number of Senators, and a majority of the whole number shall be necessary to a choice. But no person constitutionally ineligible to the office of President shall be eligible to that of Vice-President of the United States.

AMENDMENT XIII (1865)

Section 1   Neither slavery nor involuntary servitude, except as a punishment for crime whereof the party shall have been duly convicted, shall exist within the United States, or any place subject to their jurisdiction.

Section 2   Congress shall have power to enforce this article by appropriate legislation.

AMENDMENT XIV (1868)

Section 1   All persons born or naturalized in the United States and subject to the jurisdiction thereof, are citizens of the United States and of the State wherein they reside. No State shall make or enforce any law which shall abridge the privileges or immunities of citizens of the United States; nor shall any State deprive any person of life, liberty, or property, without due process of law; nor deny to any person within its jurisdiction the equal protection of the laws.

Section 2   Representatives shall be apportioned among the several States according to their respective numbers, counting the whole number of persons in each State, excluding Indians not taxed. But when the right to vote at any election for the choice of electors for President and Vice-President of the United States, Representatives in Congress, the Executive and Judicial officers of a State, or the members of the Legislature thereof, is denied to any of the male inhabitants of such State, being twenty-one years of age, and citizens of the United States, or in any way abridged, except for participation in rebellion, or other crime, the basis of representation therein shall be reduced in the proportion which the number of such male citizens shall bear to the whole number of male citizens twenty-one years of age in such State.

Section 3 No person shall be a Senator or Representative in Congress, or elector of President and Vice President, or hold any office, civil or military, under the United States, or under any State, who, having previously taken an oath, as a member of Congress, or as an officer of the United States, or as a member of any State legislature, or as an executive or judicial officer of any State, to support the Constitution of the United States, shall have engaged in insurrection or rebellion against the same, or given aid or comfort to the enemies thereof. But Congress may by a vote of two-thirds of each House, remove such disability.

Section 4 The validity of the public debt of the United States, authorized by law, including debts incurred for payment of pensions and bounties for services in suppressing insurrection or rebellion, shall not be questioned. But neither the United States nor any State shall assume or pay any debt or obligation incurred in aid of insurrection or rebellion against the United States, or any claim for the loss or emancipation of any slave; but all such debts, obligations and claims shall be held illegal and void.

Section 5 The Congress shall have power to enforce, by appropriate legislation, the provisions of this article.

AMENDMENT XV (1870)

Section 1 The right of citizens of the United States to vote shall not be denied or abridged by the United States or by any State on account of race, color, or previous condition of servitude.

Section 2 The Congress shall have power to enforce this article by appropriate legislation.

AMENDMENT XVI (1913)

The Congress shall have power to lay and collect taxes on incomes, from whatever source derived, without apportionment among the several States, and without regard to any census or enumeration.

AMENDMENT XVII (1913)

The Senate of the United States shall be composed of two Senators from each State, elected by the people

thereof, for six years; and each Senator shall have one vote. The electors in each State shall have the qualifications requisite for electors of the most numerous branch of the State legislatures.

When vacancies happen in the representation of any State in the Senate, the executive authority of such State shall issue writs of election to fill such vacancies: *Provided,* That the legislature of any State may empower the executive thereof to make temporary appointments until the people fill the vacancies by election as the legislature may direct.

This amendment shall not be so construed as to affect the election or term of any Senator chosen before it becomes valid as part of the Constitution.

AMENDMENT XVIII (1919)

Section 1 After one year from the ratification of this article the manufacture, sale, or transportation of intoxicating liquors within, the importation thereof into, or the exportation thereof from the United States and all territory subject to the jurisdiction thereof for beverage purposes is hereby prohibited.

Section 2 The Congress and the several States shall have concurrent power to enforce this article by appropriate legislation.

Section 3 This article shall be inoperative unless it shall have been ratified as an amendment to the Constitution by the legislatures of the several States, as provided in the Constitution, within seven years from the date of the submission hereof to the States by the Congress.

AMENDMENT XIX (1920)

The right of citizens of the United States to vote shall not be denied or abridged by the United States or by any State on account of sex.

Congress shall have power to enforce this article by appropriate legislation.

AMENDMENT XX (1933)

Section 1 The terms of the President and Vice President shall end at noon on the 20th day of January, and the terms of Senators and Representatives at noon on the 3d day of January, of the years in which such terms would have ended if this article had not been ratified; and the terms of their successors shall then begin.

Section 2 The Congress shall assemble at least once in every year, and such meeting shall begin at noon on the 3d day of January, unless they shall by law appoint a different day.

Section 3 If, at the time fixed for the beginning of the term of the President, the President elect shall have died, the Vice President elect shall become President. If a President shall not have been chosen before the time fixed for the beginning of his term, or if the President elect shall have failed to qualify, then the Vice President elect shall act as President until a President shall have qualified; and the Congress may by law provide for the case wherein neither a President elect nor a Vice President elect shall have qualified, declaring who shall then act as President, or the manner in which one who is to act shall be selected, and such person shall act accordingly until a President or Vice President shall have qualified.

Section 4 The Congress may by law provide for the case of the death of any of the persons from whom the House of Representatives may choose a President whenever the right of choice shall have devolved upon them, and for the case of the death of any of the persons from whom the Senate may choose a Vice President whenever the right of choice shall have devolved upon them.

Section 5 Sections 1 and 2 shall take effect on the 15th day of October following the ratification of this article.

Section 6 This article shall be inoperative unless it shall have been ratified as an amendment to the Constitution by the legislatures of three-fourths of the several States within seven years from the date of its submission.

AMENDMENT XXI (1933)

Section 1 The eighteenth article of amendment to the Constitution of the United States is hereby repealed.

Section 2 The transportation or importation into any State, Territory or possession of the United States for delivery or use therein of intoxicating liquors, in violation of the laws thereof, is hereby prohibited.

Section 3 This article shall be inoperative unless it shall have been ratified as an amendment to the Constitution by conventions in the several States, as provided in the Constitution, within seven years from the

date of the submission hereof to the States by the Congress.

AMENDMENT XXII (1951)

Section 1 No person shall be elected to the office of the President more than twice, and no person who has held the office of President, or acted as President, for more than two years of a term to which some other person was elected President shall be elected to the office of the President more than once. But this Article shall not apply to any person holding the office of President when this Article was proposed by the Congress, and shall not prevent any person who may be holding the office of President, or acting as President, during the term within which this Article becomes operative from holding the office of President or acting as President during the remainder of such term.

Section 2 This Article shall be inoperative unless it shall have been ratified as an amendment to the Constitution by the legislatures of three-fourths of the several States within seven years from the date of its submission to the States by the Congress.

AMENDMENT XXIII (1961)

Section 1 The District constituting the seat of Government of the United States shall appoint in such manner as the Congress may direct:

A number of electors of President and Vice President equal to the whole number of Senators and Representatives in Congress to which the District would be entitled if it were a State, but in no event more than the least populous State; they shall be in addition to those appointed by the States, but they shall be considered, for the purposes of the election of President and Vice President, to be electors appointed by a State; and they shall meet in the District and perform such duties as provided by the twelfth article of amendment.

Section 2 The Congress shall have power to enforce this article by appropriate legislation.

AMENDMENT XXIV (1964)

Section 1 The right of citizens of the United States to vote in any primary or other election for President or Vice President, for electors for President or Vice

President, or for Senator or Representative in Congress, shall not be denied or abridged by the United States or any State by reason of failure to pay any poll tax or other tax.

Section 2 The Congress shall have power to enforce this article by appropriate legislation.

AMENDMENT XXV (1967)

Section 1 In case of the removal of the President from office or of his death or resignation, the Vice President shall become President.

Section 2 Whenever there is a vacancy in the office of the Vice President, the President shall nominate a Vice President who shall take office upon confirmation by a majority vote of both Houses of Congress.

Section 3 Whenever the President transmits to the President pro tempore of the Senate and the Speaker of the House of Representatives his written declaration that he is unable to discharge the powers and duties of his office, and until he transmits to them a written declaration to the contrary, such powers and duties shall be discharged by the Vice President as Acting President.

Section 4 Whenever the Vice President and a majority of either the principal officers of the executive departments or of such other body as Congress may by law provide, transmit to the President pro tempore of the Senate and the Speaker of the House of Representatives their written declaration that the President is unable to discharge the powers and duties of his office, the Vice President shall immediately assume the powers and duties of the office as Acting President.

Thereafter, when the President transmits to the President pro tempore of the Senate and the Speaker of the House of Representatives his written declaration that no inability exists, he shall resume the powers and duties of his office unless the Vice President and a majority of either the principal officers of the executive department or of such other body as Congress may by law provide, transmit within four days to the President pro tempore of the Senate and the Speaker of the House of Representatives their written declaration that the President is unable to discharge the powers and duties of his office. Thereupon Congress shall decide the issue, assembling within forty-eight hours for that purpose if not in session. If the Congress, within twenty-one days after receipt of the latter written declaration, or, if Congress is not in session, within twenty-one days after Congress is required to assemble, determines by two-thirds vote of both Houses that the President is unable to discharge the powers and duties of his office, the Vice President shall continue to discharge the same as Acting President; otherwise, the President shall resume the powers and duties of his office.

AMENDMENT XXVI (1971)

Section 1 The right of citizens of the United States, who are eighteen years of age or older, to vote shall not be denied or abridged by the United States or by any State on account of age.

Section 2 The Congress shall have power to enforce this article by appropriate legislation.

AMENDMENT XXVII (1992)

No law varying the compensation for the services of the senators and representatives shall take effect, until an election of representatives shall have intervened.

GLOSSARY

ABA The American Bar Association, a voluntary association for lawyers.

absolute liability Liability without fault or negligence; often used interchangeably with *strict liability*, though many would contend that there is a difference.

abuse of discretion A standard of review of official or judicial acts that are committed to discretion, as when the certification of electors is committed to the discretion of the Florida Secretary of State. Courts show deference to discretionary acts and decisions unless they constitute an unreasonable exercise of discretion.

acceptance In contract law, the final act in concluding negotiations where an offeree accepts all the terms of the offer.

actus reus Criminal act; conduct that the law prohibits or absence of conduct that the law requires.

adjudication The formal act of deciding disputes by a court or tribunal.

administrative law The body of law that controls the way in which administrative agencies operate covered by state and federal Administrative Procedure Acts; also deals with regulations issued by administrative agencies.

administrator A person appointed by a court to manage the distribution of the estate of a deceased person.

admiralty That branch of law pertaining to maritime commerce and navigation.

adoption In family law, the legal establishment of parent-child bonds between persons who did not

formerly have them; commonly, this entails the severance of those bonds with a former parent.

adversarial system The U.S. legal system in which litigants, typically represented by attorneys, argue their respective sides in a dispute before an impartial judge and jury; often contrasted with an inquisitorial system in which an accused is questioned by officials without rights of defense in a relentless search for the truth.

adverse possession A means of acquiring title by occupying and using land for a certain length of time even though the occupier does not have title. The period at common law was twenty years, shorter in most states by statute.

affidavit A statement in writing sworn to before a person authorized to administer an oath.

affirmative defense A claim made by the defendant that, if it prevails, will negate the plaintiff's case.

alienation of affection Taking away the love, companionship, or help of another person's husband or wife; still recognized in a few states.

alimony Payments for personal maintenance from one ex-spouse to the other following divorce. It is most commonly periodic, for example, monthly, but may also be in the form of a lump-sum payment.

amicus curiae Latin for a "friend of the court." A person who is interested in the outcome of the case, but who is not a party, whom the court permits to file a brief for the purpose of providing the court with a position or a point of view that it might not otherwise have.

annulment   Ends the relation of husband and wife by invalidating the marriage contract, as if they were never married.

answer   A pleading that responds to the complaint, admitting and denying specific allegations and presenting defenses.

antenuptial or **premarital agreement**   A contract agreed to by persons before their marriage, primarily concerned with the distribution of personal and marital assets in the event of divorce or death.

anticipatory breach   When one party to a contract expresses an intention not to perform; the other party may then treat the contract as *breached*, pursuing an appropriate remedy, rather than wait for performance.

appeal   The process by which a higher court is requested by a party to a lawsuit to review the decision of a lower court. Such reconsideration is normally confined to a review of the record from the lower court, with neither new testimony taken nor new issues raised.

appellant   The party bringing an appeal against the other party, the *appellee*.

appellate   Pertaining to the taking of an "appeal"; the adjectival form of "appeal."

appellate brief   A formal statement submitted to the appellate court. When a case is appealed, the appellant submits a written statement to the appellate court raising legal issues to be decided. The appellee then has a period within which the appellee's brief must be filed, challenging the appellant's arguments on the issues.

appellate courts   As distinguished from *trial courts*, appellate courts function primarily to correct errors of the lower, trial courts and do not ordinarily serve as factfinders. The two common forms of appellate courts are intermediate appellate courts, usually called courts of appeal(s), and the highest courts, usually called supreme courts.

arraignment   Brings the defendant before the court to make a plea.

arrest   Usually refers to detaining someone to answer for a crime.

assault   Putting someone in apprehension of a *battery*. The actor must have the ability to carry out the threatened battery.

associate   The title usually given to a full-time member of a law firm who has not yet been elevated to *partner*; the associate is salaried, whereas the partners share in the profits of the firm.

assumption of risk   May prevent liability for negligence when the plaintiff voluntarily encounters a known risk.

attachment   Formally seizing property in order to bring it under the control of the court; this is usually done by getting a court order to have a law enforcement officer take control of the property.

attempt to commit a crime   An act that goes beyond mere preparation to commit a crime but that is not completed.

attorney-client privilege   Confidential statements made by a client to an attorney may not be disclosed to others by the attorney without the client's permission.

bailiff   An officer of the court charged with keeping order in the courtroom, having custody over prisoners and the jury.

bailment   When the owner of personal property delivers possession without intent to pass title, as when one leaves an automobile with an auto mechanic.

bankruptcy   Generally, the situation in which a person, business, or government cannot or will not pay its debts, so its property is entrusted to a "trustee in bankruptcy" who distributes the property to creditors.

bar   The term used to refer collectively to licensed members of the legal profession, attorneys as a group, that is, "the bar."

bar examination   A written test required of applicants for license to practice law.

barrister   An English lawyer who specializes in trial work.

battery   An unconsented, unprivileged, offensive contact.

bench Drawn from the term referring to the seat occupied by judges in court, "the bench" refers to all judges collectively.

bench trial A trial before a judge without a jury; a nonjury trial.

bequest A gift in a will. Traditionally this referred to personal property, but today it is often used for testamentary gifts of real property (real estate) as well.

bicameral Referring to a legislature with two bodies, such as a House of Representatives and a Senate; only Nebraska has a single, or *unicameral*, legislature.

bigamous Referring to the marriage of a person who is already married to another person. Bigamy is a crime, and a bigamous marriage is void.

bilateral contract A contract accepted by a return promise. It is an exchange of promises, supported by consideration. Compare to **unilateral contract**.

black letter law Lawyers' slang for the basic, well-established rules of law.

breach of contract When a party fails to render the performance required by a contract; also the name of the *cause of action* that results if the nonbreaching party sues for compensation.

breach of promise to marry A cause of action based on breaking off an engagement to marry; today a thoroughly disfavored heart balm remedy.

breached Commonly means breaking a law or obligation. In contract law, a breaching party is one who fails to perform part or all of his obligations under the contract.

brief A written statement submitted to a court; also see **appellate brief.**

burden of proof The duty of proving a fact that is in dispute. In a trial, the plaintiff has the burden of proving through the presentation of evidence the allegations on which the case is brought. If the plaintiff fails to present sufficient evidence to prevail if that evidence were believed, the burden of proof has not been met and the case should be dismissed in defendant's favor.

bureaucracy That part of the government composed of agencies staffed by civil servants; forms the major part of the administrative branch.

business invitee The most common form of an invitee, businesses, especially retail stores, are often open to the public; they impliedely invite members of the public to enter their premises, and they owe a duty of care to those who enter their stores.

canon law Church, or ecclesiastical, law traditionally associated with the Roman Catholic Church, which in English law was continued by the Church of England. Separation of church and state in the United States created gaps in the law, most notably in the area of domestic relations (family law).

Canons of Ethics A set of basic principles established by the ABA to govern professional conduct; formerly adopted by most states.

caption The heading of a court paper, usually including the names of the parties, the court, and the case number.

case and controversy Terms used in Article III, Section 2, of the U.S. Constitution regarding the judicial power; the terms have been interpreted to mean that the courts have authority over real disputes between real parties, as opposed to hypothetical disputes or nonadversarial parties. The courts do not answer questions about the law but decide actual disputes.

case law That body of the law that is expressed in judicial opinions. *Case law* is often used interchangeably with "common law" (precedents), but case law may refer to statutory interpretation as well.

case method Since its introduction by Dean Langdell at Harvard Law School, the method of reading judicial opinions (cases) and analyzing them under the law professor's questioning has been the standard approach to law school instruction in America.

case of first impression A case that presents a fact situation the court has never decided before.

case-in-chief The main evidence offered by one side in a lawsuit. This does not include evidence offered to oppose the other side's case.

cause of action   In order to bring a lawsuit, one must state a *cause of action*. The court must recognize the action (suit) as one of the many kinds that a court can decide. In a sense, a cause of action is a label for a type of lawsuit. For example, slander, breach of contract, invasion of privacy, and trespass are causes of action.

certificates of deposit   Promises by banks to pay money deposited with the bank, ordinarily with interest.

certiorari   To be informed of, to be made certain in regard to. Also see **writ of certiorari.**

chain of title   The history of the transfer of title to real property. It is comprised of a series of grantors to grantees showing who is the present holder of title.

challenge for cause   In qualifying jurors during *voir dire*, either party may challenge the seating of a juror for bias or other disqualification. Challenges for cause are unlimited.

chambers   The private office of a judge where matters not required to be heard in open court can be discussed and appropriate orders issued.

chancellor   A judge of a court of chancery or court of equity; also called a *master in equity*.

chancery   Equity, equitable jurisdiction, a court of equity; a court that administers justice and decides controversies in accordance with the rules, principles, and precedents of equity and that follows the forms and procedures of chancery; as distinguished from a court having the jurisdiction, rules, principles, and practice of the common law.

charges to the jury   Jury instruction, given to the jury prior to their deliberations.

checks   Written orders to a bank to pay money to a named person.

child custody   The rights and duties of those legally entrusted with the care and control of a child, usually the parents.

child support   An obligation of parents; the payments due from one parent to another for the care of children following divorce.

civil procedure   Addresses the complex rules governing the steps appropriate to noncriminal cases from filing a complaint through trial.

class action suits   A modern form of suit in which a group of persons is represented by some members of the class in pursuing a lawsuit. It was designed to enable a class with numerous members to bring a suit in the name of all.

clean hands doctrine   An *equitable maxim* according to which the court of equity will refuse to provide a remedy to a petitioner who has acted in bad faith (with "unclean hands").

clearly erroneous   This phrase refers to the test or standard that is used at the appellate level to determine whether factfinding at a lower level (e.g., the trial court) constitutes reversible error. It represents the deferential attitude of appellate courts to lower court factfinding. It is commonly expressed as, "We cannot say that the factfinding below was *clearly erroneous.*"

clinical programs   Programs found in most law schools in which students provide legal services to the public under the supervision of law professors and sanctioned by the courts and the bar; some schools require enrollment, but in most law schools "clinic" is a voluntary course for credit.

code   The word used to refer to statutes or legislation, as in "criminal code," or to the entire body of statutes such as the United States Code (USC). Some states refer to their code as statutes, as in Florida Statutes. Others refer to them as a code, as in the Code of Georgia.

codicil   A supplement to a will that modifies or adds to the will without revoking it.

codification   The term *codify* may refer to the simple process of turning a custom or common law rule into legislation, but usually it refers to making *codes*.

cohabitation   Living together in a marital-like relationship. Sometimes simply refers to a sexual relationship.

collateral   Property pledged to pay a debt; it is a security interest.

collateral estoppel   Bars the relitigation of issues that have been previously adjudicated.

common law   In the first century after the Norman Conquest, the Normans established a legal regime for the entire kingdom of England, with laws common to all inhabitants of the realm. Under the system, three common law courts were established (Kings bench, common pleas, exchequer). The decisions of these courts and especially the decisions of the appeals of these courts became binding precedents on lower courts under a doctrine called *stare decisis*.

community property   A regime in which the earnings of husband and wife during marriage are owned equally by both; eight states borrowing from French (Louisiana) or Spanish (Texas west to California) law incorporated the concept of community property into marital law.

comparative negligence   A principle whereby damages are apportioned between plaintiff and defendant according to their relative fault in a negligence case where both are found to have been at fault.

compensatory damages   Awarded to an injured party to make her whole, that is, in tort, to compensate for all injuries, and, in contract, to put the nonbreaching party in the position he would have been in if the contract had been performed; also referred to as *exemplary damages*.

complainant   The plaintiff in a lawsuit.

complaint   The initial pleading in a civil action in which the plaintiff alleges a cause of action and asks that the wrong done to the plaintiff be remedied by the court.

concur   To join with.

concurring opinion   An opinion issued by one or more judges that agrees with the result reached by the majority opinion rendered by the court but reaches that result for different reasons.

condominium   A form of ownership in real property where owners typically share ownership in common areas, such as the land, sidewalks, swimming pool, but have individual rights in a building, as if each owner owned an apartment or townhouse.

conflict of laws   Also called *choice of law*, concerns the problem that arises when there is a question about which state law should apply in a particular case.

consideration   A requirement in classical contract formation that consists of an exchange of something of value, although this may in some cases be largely symbolic.

conspiracy   A crime involving two or more persons who agree to commit a crime or agree to plan a crime.

constitution   The basic charter of government. In the American tradition, a constitution describes the allocation of power among the primary branches of government (legislative, executive, judicial) as well as starting fundamental rights of the citizen. NB: The United States Constitution is unusual in recognizing independent state and federal governments.

contingency fee contracts   Agreements between an attorney and a client in which the attorney will receive compensation in the form of a percentage of money recovered in a lawsuit; used predominantly in personal injury cases.

contract   An agreement that creates a legal relationship between two or more parties; while the parties create the rights and duties, the law establishes the requirements for the validity of a contract.

contract implied in fact   A contract that can be inferred by the conduct of the parties in the absence of a verbal or express contract.

contracts of adhesion   Contracts in which all the bargaining power (and the contract terms) favor one side, often when the seller uses a pre-printed form contract to unfair advantage.

contributory negligence   A principle by which a recovery will be denied a plaintiff for defendant's negligence if plaintiff is also found to have been at fault. It is an affirmative defense that has been replaced by *comparative negligence* in most states.

copyright   A right in literary property giving an author exclusive rights over her works for a limited period of time.

corporation A fictional person, a business organization that protects owners and managers from personal liability; it is chartered by a government.

corpus juris Literally, the "body of the law"; the name later given to a compilation of Roman civil law ordered by the Emperor Justinian in the sixth century. It was studied and revised in the late Renaissance in Europe, except for England, which clung stubbornly to the common law. A major American encyclopedia of the common law, *Corpus Juris Secundum* ("the second body of the laws"), borrowed the name without borrowing from the code.

counterclaim A cause of action brought by a defendant against the plaintiff in a single case; for example, in an auto collision, both drivers often sue each other—one files a complaint and the other counterclaims.

court of appeals An intermediate appellate court in a three-tiered system with trial courts at the bottom and a supreme court at the top. The names may vary with the jurisdiction, but both Florida and the United States refer to these intermediate courts as courts of appeals.

court reporter A person who makes verbatim recordings of court proceedings and other sworn statements, such as depositions, which can be reduced to printed transcripts.

crime An act that violates the criminal law. If this seems redundant, compare *Orans*: "Any violation of the government's penal laws. An illegal act."

criminal conversation Causing a married man or woman to commit adultery. Despite its name, this is a tort, not a crime, and it is generally abolished in most states as a cause of action.

criminal law The list of crimes promulgated by the state, including the mental states required for particular crimes, for example, specific intent, premeditation.

criminal procedure Ordinarily taught as a separate course from civil procedure since its rules differ in important respects, such as search and seizure evidence and the privilege against self-incrimination.

cross-examination The questioning of an opposing witness during a trial or hearing.

curtesy and **dower** Formerly, interests in property held by wife (dower) and husband (curtesy), the primary purpose of which was to guarantee real property interests for a surviving spouse. The husband was favored, and these interests have been equalized or combined, for example, Florida's *elective share*, in recent times so as not to discriminate.

damages Legal remedies, which seek compensation in the form of money. Although damages normally aim at compensating an injured party for losses (compensatory or actual damages), under limited circumstances, money may be awarded beyond compensation to punish the wrongdoer (*punitive damages*).

de novo Over again, from the beginning. Trial de novo is a new trial in an appellate court in which the whole case is gone into as if no trial whatever had taken place.

decision The conclusion of a court after hearing and settling a case by judicial procedure.

declaratory judgment A judgment that specifies the rights of the parties but orders no relief. It is a binding judgment and the appropriate remedy for the determination of an actionable dispute when the plaintiff's legal rights are in doubt.

deed A document that describes a piece of real property and its transfer of title to a new owner.

defamation An injury to reputation and includes *slander* and *libel*.

default judgment May be entered against a party failing to file a required document in a lawsuit, particularly failing to file an answer.

defendant The person against whom an action is brought.

deference Courteous submission or yielding to the opinion or judgment of another, also courteous respect.

demurrer A motion to dismiss a case, alleging that the complaint is insufficient to state a legal cause of action.

deposition Oral examination of a witness transcribed by a court reporter. Ordinarily, attorneys for both sides are present, one having requested the deposition. A deposition is part of the pretrial procedure called *discovery*, and is usually conducted without any participation by the judge.

deterrence   Theory in criminal law that holds that the purpose of the sanctions imposed by the law is to deter, rather than simply punish, criminal conduct.

devisable   The character of an estate in land that is capable of being passed by will upon death. Personal property is usually devisable.

dictum, dicta, obiter dictum   *Dictum* is a Latin word meaning "said" or "stated." *Obiter* means "by the way" or "incidentally." *Obiter dictum*, then, means something stated incidentally and not necessary to the discussion, usually shortened to *dictum* or its plural *dicta*. In law, it refers to a part of a judicial decision that goes beyond the scope of the issues and is considered mere opinion and not binding precedent.

direct examination   The first questioning of a witness in a trial by the side that called the witness.

directed verdict   The judge may order a verdict against the plaintiffs when they have failed to meet their burden of proof. Formerly, the judge ordered the jury to enter a verdict against the plaintiff. Today, the judge grants a motion for a directed verdict and enters a judgment.

disbarment   The most severe professional disciplinary sanction, canceling an attorney's license to practice law.

discovery   A pretrial procedure in which parties to a lawsuit ask for and receive information such as testimony, records, or other evidence from each other.

dissent   The point of view expressed by a judge who disagrees with the position taken by the majority of judges in a case.

dissenting opinion   A written opinion filed by a judge of an appellate court who disagrees with the decision of the majority of judges in a case and giving the reasons for the differing view.

diversity of citizenship   The subject matter jurisdiction of federal courts to hear cases between citizens of different states.

divorce   The severance of the bonds of matrimony; also referred to as *dissolution of marriage*.

docket   The court calendar of proceedings.

domestic relations   The field of law governing the rights and duties of family relations, particularly divorce; usually synonymous with *family law*.

double jeopardy   Prevents a person from being tried twice for the same crime.

dower   Property interests acquired in a husband's estate upon marriage. In old common law, a wife was entitled to one-third of her husband's real property upon his death. Today, husband and wife have equal rights as surviving spouses, but these vary from state to state.

dower and **curtesy**   See **curtesy and dower.**

draft   An order to pay money; a *drawer* orders a *drawee* to pay money to a *payee*. A *check* is a draft on a bank payable on demand.

due process of law   A guarantee of the Fifth Amendment and the Fourteenth Amendment to the U.S. Constitution. It provides that law administered through courts of justice is equally applied to all under established rules that do not violate fundamental principles of fairness. The process that is due before government may deprive a person of life, liberty, or property.

duress   When one party to a contract is threatened with harm to induce agreement.

easement   A right of use in another's property as, for example, when someone has a right-of-way to cross another's land.

ejectment   A common law cause of action designed to return rightful possession of real property, commonly called *eviction* in modern landlord and tenant law.

elective share   The phrase representing what was formerly *dower* and *curtesy* in the common law, the share of a surviving spouse in the deceased spouse's property that the surviving spouse may elect to take instead of the property that a will would distribute.

electoral college   The body of electors of a state who are empowered by the Constitution and chosen to elect the president and vice president of the United States.

elements The specific parts of a cause of action that must be alleged and proved to make out that cause of action.

emancipated minor A person under the age of majority who is totally self-supporting or married; varies by state.

eminent domain The power of the government to take private property for a public use, for which just compensation is required by the Constitution.

enjoin To prohibit (or require) a person from certain acts; an order typically emanating from an *injunction.*

enterprise liability When an injury can be attributed to a number of companies in an industry, *enterprise liability* would apportion the damages according to the market share of each.

equal protection of the laws A Constitutional guaranty that specifies that every state must give equal treatment to every person who is similarly situated or to persons who are members of the same class; this protection is a requirement of the Fourteenth Amendment enacted originally to protect former slaves.

equitable distribution Designed to equalize the marital shares of husband and wife for purposes of divorce; many states that are not *community property* states have principles of equitable distribution.

equitable estoppel Being stopped by your own prior acts or statements from claiming a right against another person who has legitimately relied on those acts or statements; also see **estoppel.**

equitable maxim A general rule or principle guiding decision making in courts of equity, often serving the function that *precedent* would serve in a common law court.

equitable remedy A special remedy, such as an injunction, or specific performance, not available at common law.

equity A system for ensuring justice in circumstances where the remedies customarily available under conventional law are not adequate to ensure a fair result. Also see **chancery.**

error A mistake of the court during the trial of a lawsuit that forms a basis for filing an appeal requesting an appellate court to review the proceedings.

estate *Estate* has several legal meanings, but when used in reference to a decedent it means the property rights to be distributed following death.

estate planning The process of planning for the management of a person's property in preparation for retirement and death.

estoppel A principle used by the courts to prevent someone from making an assertion inconsistent with prior words or conduct that led another to act to his or her detriment if the assertion were allowed (as *evidence*).

ethics Concerns right or proper conduct and often refers to the fairness and honesty of a person's character. In philosophy, it covers the area of inquiry into right conduct.

evidence The information presented at trial; the *rules of evidence* are part of the procedural law.

evidentiary facts The specific facts presented at trial, as distinguished from the more general *ultimate facts.*

evidentiary hearing A proceeding in which evidence is introduced and witnesses are examined so that findings of fact can be made and a determination rendered, for example, a trial.

ex post facto law A penal law that operates retroactively.

executory contract A contract that has not yet been fully performed; one that has been fully performed is an *executed* contract.

expert witness When qualified as an expert, a witness may offer opinion testimony, which would be objectionable in a "lay" witness.

fact Generally, an event, an act, or information about an event or an act, as distinguished from *law,* that is, the legal consequences of an event or act.

factfinding The process of a jury, or a judge in a nonjury proceeding, to reach a conclusion with respect to disputed facts in a legal action, reasoned or inferred from the evidence.

federal question Federal courts have subject matter jurisdiction over cases arising under the Constitution, laws, and treaties of the United States; these raise "federal questions."

Federal Tort Claims Act Under the doctrine of *soverign immunity*, state and federal governments were immune from tort suits, unless the government consented to the suit. In 1947, Congress remedied this situation by passing the Federal Tort Claims Act, which made the federal government liable, with certain exceptions, as if it were a private party. (See Chapter 14, "Liability of Government and Its Officers.")

fee simple absolute An estate in land having the maximum rights, that is, without future interests.

felony A serious crime, commonly defined by a penalty of a year or more in prison.

felony-murder rule Provides for conviction of murder where someone is killed during the commission of a felony; premeditation need not be proven.

Florida Statutes Laws enacted by the Florida legislature.

forcible rape Distinguished from *statutory rape,* or its modern equivalents; requires force or threat of force and lack of consent. In statutory rape, consent is irrelevant because of the age or mental condition or status of the victim.

foreclosure The process whereby real property is sold to satisfy a mortgage under default.

forum non conveniens If two or more courts both have proper *venue* for a case, a judge may rule that a lawsuit must be brought in the other court for either the convenience of or fairness to the parties.

foster parents Caretakers of children who are not their parents, stepparents, nor adoptive parents, whom the law has recognized as parental caretakers, commonly when children are taken away from their parents for cause.

Founding Fathers The members of the American Constitutional Convention of 1787 who adopted the Constitution of the United States.

franchise A collaborative relationship in which the franchisee pays a franchisor for the use of the franchisor's trade name and products, like McDonald's restaurants.

fraud (contract) A contract induced by intentionally false misrepresentations is voidable for *fraud.*

full faith and credit The Constitution requires that each state respect the legal pronouncements of sister states: "Full faith and credit shall be given in each State to the public acts, records, and judicial proceedings of every other State" (Article IV).

garnishment An action by which one who is owed a debt may collect payments through a third party, often an employer.

general intent For criminal law, *general intent* requires merely that the actor intended a harmful act, not necessarily the specific result. Also see **specific intent.**

general retainer The first payment made in hiring an attorney. A general retainer occurs when a client furnishes a sum of money to an attorney to ensure that the attorney will represent the client in whatever legal matters may arise.

general subject matter jurisdiction A court's authority to hear and decide a broad range of cases.

grand jury A body of citizens who receive complaints and accusations of crime and decide whether an *indictment* should issue.

grant A word used in conveying real property; that which is conveyed, conferred, or given.

grantor A party transferring an interest in real property to another, the **grantee.**

gratuitous bailment A *bailment* for which no compensation is made.

gross negligence Negligence reflecting a reckless disregard for the rights of others, in contrast to *ordinary negligence*, which is commonly characterized by simple carelessness or inattention.

guilt beyond a reasonable doubt The standard of proof the prosecution must meet in a criminal case.

habeas corpus An ancient remedy used to challenge the lawfulness of a detention by a government.

harmful error   Mistakes made at trial that are sufficiently serious to prejudice the result against one of the parties; in other words, it is sufficiently serious that, if it had not occurred, the case might have reached a different result. Also called *reversible* or *prejudicial* error.

headnotes   Statements of the major points of law discussed in a case; these are found in the law reports published by West Group, Inc., formerly West Publishing Company.

hearing   The presentation of evidence and argument before a tribunal. Under *procedural due process*, the hearing, usually the trial, must be fair and evenhanded. Most of the elements of a fair hearing have been established by custom and precedent.

hearsay rule   Excludes from testimony out-of-court statements made by a person not present in court; a complex rule with many exceptions.

heart balm suits   Now largely discredited lawsuits for emotional injuries such as *seduction, breach of promise to marry, criminal conversation,* and *alienation of affections.*

hedonic damages (losses)   Money awarded in some lawsuits for loss of the ability to enjoy life's pleasures, a recent and controversial basis for damages.

heirs   The persons who take the property of a deceased when no valid will is present. Heirs are determined by intestate succession according to state law. A living person does not have heirs.

holding   The core of a judge's decision in a case; that part of the written opinion that applies the law to the facts of the case; it expresses the *rule of the case* as distinguished from *dicta.*

house counsel   Full-time attorneys employed by many corporations and other businesses as part of the administrative staff; distinguish from "outside counsel."

illegitimate   Referring to a child born to an unwed mother. In most states, the acknowledgment of paternity by a natural father may legitimate the child despite being born out of wedlock.

implied warranty   A promise imposed by law, for example, an implied warranty of fitness for use or consumption, as distinguished from an *express warranty* stated in a contract.

in personam   See **personal jurisdiction.**

in rem jurisdiction   Describes a lawsuit brought to enforce rights in a thing against the whole world as opposed to one brought to enforce rights against another person; see **personal jurisdiction.**

incestuous   Referring to the marriage of two persons who stand in a family relationship in which the law prohibits marriage. *Incest* refers to the sexual relations of persons in such a relationship, for example, father-daughter, brother-sister.

independent regulatory agencies   Those agencies of the government that exercise relative autonomy because their heads cannot be removed at the whim of the chief executive, for example, the president, as distinguished from *departments*, which are under the direct control of *secretaries*, who serve at the pleasure of the president.

indictment   A written accusation by a *grand jury* charging the accused with a crime. Also called a "true bill." When the grand jury does not indict, it is called a "no bill."

infamous crime   A major crime, for which a heavy penalty may be awarded. Used in the Constitution but now out of date and would probably mean *felony* today.

information   A written accusation made by a public prosecutor.

inheritable   The character of an estate in land that may pass to heirs upon death (with no will). Personal property is usually inheritable. *Inheritable* has the same meaning as *heritable.*

initial or **first appearance**   A person arrested for a crime must be brought before a magistrate promptly after arrest to be informed of the charges and the legal rights of the accused.

injunction   A court order that commands or prohibits some act or course of conduct; it is preventive in nature and designed to protect a plaintiff from irreparable injury to his or her property or property rights by prohibiting or commanding the doing of certain acts; a form of equitable relief.

Inns of Court   For centuries, English lawyers were trained in the Inns of Court, where students learned the law in association with legal scholars, lawyers, and judges.

insurance   The pooling of risk among many insured, typically enabled by a corporation that sells insurance contracts.

integrated bar   A state bar association in which membership is required in order to practice law.

intellectual property   Ideas in the form of writings, works of art, commercial symbols, and inventions that are protected by government license, usually by registration, in the form of copyright, patent, and trademark. The law of trade secrets is also part of intellectual property law.

intentional infliction of mental distress   Almost self-explanatory, it usually requires unreasonable or outrageous conduct and serious mental distress. *Intentional infliction of emotional distress* and *negligent infliction of emotional distress* are causes of action based on severe emotional distress; while most states recognize the intentional tort, generally requiring outrageous conduct, few recognize the cause of action based on negligence.

intentional torts   *Torts* that require proof of intentional wrongful conduct.

intermediate appellate court   See **court of appeals**.

interrogatories   A *discovery* device, pretrial written questions sent from one party to the other party.

intestate   A person who dies without a will. Also used as an adjective to refer to the state of dying without a will.

invasion of privacy   Actually is composed of four different forms of misconduct that harm a person's reasonable expectations of privacy, including the wrongful use of another's name, likeness, or private history, as well as unreasonable intrusion into another's private life and affairs.

issue   A material point or question arising out of the pleadings in a case, which is disputed by the parties, and which they wish the court to decide. Appellate courts are ordinarily concerned with addressing those legal issues presented to them for determination.

J.D.   The basic law degree; it stands for "juris doctor" and is equivalent to the more traditional **LL.B.**

Jim Crow laws   Enacted by Southern states following the Civil War and Reconstruction to enforce segregation of African Americans primarily in lodging and transportation. In retrospect, these laws are viewed as an outrageous denial of civil rights under color of law.

joinder   The bringing in of a new person who joins together with the plaintiff as a plaintiff or the defendant as a defendant.

joint custody   The continued sharing of rights and duties with regard to children following divorce.

joint tenancy   A form of co-ownership that includes a right of survivorship.

judges   Public officers who conduct or preside over courts of justice. The words *judge*, *court*, and *justice* are often used interchangeably and, in context, have the same meaning.

judgment   The official decision of a court about the rights and claims of each side in a lawsuit; usually a final decision after trial based on findings of fact and making conclusions of law.

judgment notwithstanding the verdict, motion for   This is a motion made at the end of a trial asking the judge to enter a judgment contrary to the jury's verdict on the grounds that the verdict is against the manifest weight of the evidence. Also called a *motion for judgement n.o.v.*

judgment n.o.v., motion for   The abbreviation n.o.v. is *non obstante veredicto*, Latin for "notwithstanding the verdict." This is a motion made at the end of a trial asking the judge to enter a judgment contrary to the jury's verdict on the grounds that the verdict is against the manifest weight of the evidence. Also called a *motion for judgment notwithstanding the verdict*.

judicial notice   The act of a judge in recognizing the existence or truth of certain facts without bothering to make one side in a lawsuit prove them.

judicial opinion   An opinion issued by a court. The statement by a judge or court of the decision reached in regard to a case tried or argued before it, explaining the law as applied to the case, and detailing the reasons upon which the judgment is based.

judicial restraint   An accepted, customary policy of courts to restrict themselves to consideration of the questions presented to them and to restrain from legislating or interfering unduly with the executive or legislative branches. The principle also refers to the customary restraint federal courts exercise to leave questions of state law to state courts.

judicial review   Review by an appellate court of a determination by a lower court; also, the power of the federal courts to declare acts contrary to the Constitution null and void.

jurisdiction   The authority, capacity, power, or right of a court to render a binding decision in a case; jurisdiction has several aspects such as jurisdiction over the subject of a case (subject matter jurisdiction), jurisdiction over the parties (personal jurisdiction), and the territorial or sovereignty feature of jurisdiction, for example, state jurisdiction, federal jurisdiction.

jurisprudence   Commonly defined as the science of philosophy of law; it is generally concerned with the nature of law and legal systems.

jury   The right to a *jury* in the Constitution refers to a petit jury, which is the trier of fact in a criminal case. Also see **grand jury.**

justice   The title given to the judges of the Supreme Court of the United States and to the judges of the appellate courts of many of the states.

laches   An equitable principle, roughly equivalent to a statute of limitations at common law; it prevents a party from bringing a petition (suit) where there has been an unreasonable delay in doing so.

law clerks   Law school students who work summers or part time for private attorneys; also, top law students who obtain clerkships with judges after graduating from law school, an honor that increases with the level and prestige of the court.

law merchant   The generally accepted customs of merchants, often used to refer to early commercial law developed by the merchants themselves, which later formed the basis for much of commercial common law.

law review   Most accredited law schools publish a "law review" on a quarterly basis with scholarly articles and comments on legal issues. Law reviews are edited by outstanding students and give students special prestige, especially when they are seeking employment. Because of Harvard Law School's traditional prestige, the *Harvard Law Review* has a nearly mythical status as a fount of legal scholarship.

lawyer   A person learned in the law; an attorney or counsel; a person licensed to practice law. Any person who, for fee or reward, prosecutes or defends causes in courts of record or other judicial tribunals of the United States.

lease   An agreement by an owner of property, the *lessor,* with a renter, a *tenant* or *lessee,* whereby the lessee pays for the right of possession and use but does not acquire title.

legal assistant   Refers generally to a worker in a law office who performs legal tasks under attorney supervision but who is not licensed to practice law. Some states allow legal assistants to provide limited legal services without supervision. "Legal assistant" as a title and a job is usually interchangeable with *paralegal.*

legal authority   The power of the law to require obedience. A decision made by a court that must be taken into account in subsequent cases presenting similar facts and involving the same legal problem.

legal ethics   Synonymous with "professional responsibility"; the legal profession promulgates specific rules to cover important areas of professional misconduct and disciplines transgressors.

legal reasoning   A specialized, formal reasoning, based on argument and legal authority and characterized by syllogistic reasoning, q.v.

legal remedy   A remedy under the common law, as distinguished from an *equitable remedy.*

legal technicians   Persons who provide legal services for compensation without attorney supervision.

legislation   The act of giving or enacting laws; preparation and enactment of laws; lawmaking, ordinarily the prerogative of legislatures or legislative bodies.

legislative history   Recorded events that provide a basis for determining the legislative intent underlying a statute enacted by a legislature; the sources for legislative history include legislative committee hearings and debates on the floor of the legislature.

legislative intent   That which the legislature wanted or intended to achieve when it enacted a statute; the determination of which is the goal of the court when the language of a statute is in doubt.

legislature   The branch of government that enacts statutory law. In Florida and the federal governments, it consists of two houses; a Senate and a House of Representatives made up of members representing districts and elected by the voters of those districts. The national legislature collectively is called Congress.

lex loci delicti (Latin)   "The law of the place of the wrong." In a *conflict of laws* question in a tort action, this ancient rule held that the court would apply the law of that place (state) where the last act necessary to complete the tort occurred or the last act necessary to make the actor liable occurred.

Lexis®   A legal database maintained by Reed Elsevier, Inc., widely used by the legal profession.

life estate   An estate, especially in land, that lasts until someone dies (the *life tenant*).

limited subject matter jurisdiction   A court's restricted authority to decide only certain kinds of cases; for example, a probate court only hears cases concerning decedents' estates.

litigation   A dispute brought to court; derived from the Latin *lis*, which means lawsuit; also refers to the subject of lawsuits, for example, "Litigation increased last year nationwide."

living trust or **inter vivos trust**   An ordinary trust as opposed to a trust established by a will at death (inter vivos—"between living persons").

LL.B.   The basic law degree, a "bachelor of laws," replaced in most law schools today by J.D. (juris doctor).

long-arm statutes   Statutes that provide a state with jurisdiction over persons or entities ordinarily beyond its territory and usual jurisdiction.

LSAT   "Law School Admissions Test," a written, largely multiple-choice test required at most law schools for admission.

lump-sum alimony   *Alimony* that is established as one lump-sum amount, usually in the form of one payment but occasionally in installments.

mala in se (Latin)   "Wrong in and of itself"; crimes that are morally wrong.

mala prohibita (Latin)   "Prohibited wrongs." Crimes that are not inherently evil, usually regulatory crimes.

malicious prosecution   When someone initiates or causes a groundless suit to be brought out of malice. To succeed in this claim, it is essential that the original suit be terminated in favor of the person later suing for *malicious prosecution.*

malpractice   Professional negligence; those who are licensed professionals are held to a higher standard of care for their services than is required in ordinary negligence.

marital settlement agreement   A contract drawn up for a divorcing couple to distribute marital property and set the terms for child custody, child support payments, and alimony.

marriage   The legal joining together of husband and wife, having among its important effects the legitimatization of their offspring; also, the Christian sacrament that joins husband and wife.

master in equity   *Chancellor*, a judge sitting in *equity.*

mechanic's lien   A *lien* arises when property is burdened by an obligation to pay money, as in a mortgage transaction; a *mechanic's lien* arises when someone is not paid for work or improvements to property, ordinarily created by law under state statutes.

mediation   A form of conflict resolution often used in conjunction with litigation or as an alternative to it. Mediation deals with adversarial parties, as in divorce mediation, but is not an adversarial process. The mediator's task is to facilitate agreement and resolution, bringing the parties together without taking sides.

medical malpractice   A form of professional misconduct restricted to negligence in the medical field; an important field of legal specialization.

memorandum decision   A court's decision that gives the ruling (what it decides and orders done), but no opinion (reasons for the decision). A *memorandum opinion* is the same as a *per curiam opinion*, which is an opinion without a named author, usually a brief and unanimous decision.

mens rea   Literally, "criminal mind"; criminal intent.

misrepresentation   May be an innocent false representation and still be voidable by the person to whom the false representation was made.

mistake of fact   In contract formation, makes the contract voidable; one or both parties believe some essential fact about the transaction to be other than it really is.

mistrial   A trial that the judge ends and declares will have no legal effect because of a major defect in procedure or because of the death of a juror, a deadlocked jury, or other major problem.

modification   When applied to divorce, a court-approved change in the amount or terms of alimony, child support, or child custody.

mortgage   A written instrument creating an interest in land as collateral for the payment of a debt.

motion   Generally, a formal request by a party for a ruling by the court in favor of that party. There are many types of motions; dismissal motions are discussed in Chapter 7.

movant   The party making a motion.

Multistate Bar Examination   A standardized national test of general legal subjects, such as property, contracts, and constitutional law.

murder   The wrongful killing of another human being with malice aforethought (premeditation).

negligence   A cause of action based on a failure to meet a reasonable standard of conduct that results in an injury.

negotiable instruments   "Commercial paper"; consists of cash substitutes, such as *checks, drafts, promissory notes,* and *certificates of deposit.*

no-fault divorce   Contemporary divorce that does away with the need to prove fault, that is, state grounds, against the other spouse.

nolo contendere (Latin)   "I do not want to contest." Accepts responsibility without an admission of guilt.

nonage   The condition of being a minor, not having reached the age of majority.

nonfreehold estate   An interest in real property that does not include holding of title. This is primarily the right of possession and occupancy as in a lease agreement. This is also called a *leasehold estate.*

nonmoving party   The party against whom a motion is made.

not guilty by reason of insanity   A plea in a criminal case that admits commission of the acts charged but denies intent on the basis of defendant's insanity.

notice   In law, represents the time requirement of notification of the opposing party. Under *procedural due process,* the fairness of legal procedure requires that a party must have sufficient notice to prepare a response to legal action.

nuisance   A private *nuisance* is basically a continuing trespass, as when one discharges polluting effluents that seep into a neighbor's pond.

obiter dictum   *Dictum* is a Latin word meaning "said" or "stated." *Obiter* means "by the way" or "incidentally." *Obiter dictum,* then, means something stated incidentally and not necessary to the discussion, usually shortened to *dictum* or the plural *dicta.*

offer   The first of the three requirements of a traditional contract formation: *offer, acceptance,* and *consideration.*

opening statements   The introductory statements made at the start of a trial by lawyers for each side.

The lawyers typically explain the version of the facts best supporting their side of the case, how these facts will be proved, and how they think the law applies to the case.

ordinance Legislation at the local level, typically, city councils, county commissions.

original service The first presentation of legal documents to the defendant, after which service is usually made to the defendant's attorney.

output contract A contract that binds the buyer to buy and the seller to sell all the product produced by the seller.

paralegal Refers generally to a worker in a law office who performs legal tasks under attorney supervision but who is not licensed to practice law. Some states allow paralegals to provide limited legal services without supervision. "Paralegal" as a title and a job is usually interchangeable with *legal assistant.*

partnerships Unincorporated business associations lacking the limited liability of corporations so that suits that cannot be satisfied by partnership property may go after the personal assets of the partners.

party In a lawsuit, the plaintiff or defendant, whether composed of one or more individuals, and all others who may be affected by the suit, indirectly or consequentially.

patent An exclusive right granted by the government to use one's invention.

pecuniary damages Damages that can be measured in terms of cost in money, such as lost wages or medical expenses.

per curiam (Latin) "By the court." *Per curiam opinions* are anonymous opinions, departing from the custom of naming the author of the majority opinion. These are often used in unanimous opinions lacking extensive argumentation.

per curiam opinion An opinion without a named author, usually a brief and unanimous decision.

peremptory challenge Each side in a trial is allowed a specific number of exclusions of individual jurors without the necessity of giving reasons for the exclusions.

perjury Committed by knowingly making a false statement under oath in a judicial proceeding; the false statement must concern a material issue or fact in the proceeding.

personal jurisdiction The power a court has over the person of a defendant to subject that person to decisions and rulings made in a case; also called *in personam.*

personal service The presentation of the summons and complaint upon the defendant personally.

persuasive authority Authority that carries great weight even though not qualifying as precedent, for example, decisions of other state courts.

petition Sometimes also known as a *complaint* or *pleading*, it alleges a cause of action. It is a formal, written request, addressed to a person or body in a position of authority.

petitioner One who presents a *petition.* One who opposes the prayer of the petition is called the *respondent.*

physical evidence Physical objects introduced as evidence, such as a gun, a lock, drugs, and so on.

plain meaning rule A rule of statutory construction that states that if the language of a statute is unambiguous, the terms of the statute should be construed according to their ordinary meaning.

plaintiff A person who brings a lawsuit, a party who complains and is named on the record. Also known as a *petitioner.*

plea bargaining One accused of a crime can "bargain" through her attorney with the prosecutor; the bargain usually involves an agreement by the accused to plead guilty in return for favorable treatment, such as a lenient sentence, reduction to a lesser charge, or probation in lieu of incarceration.

pleadings Written formal documents framing the issues of a lawsuit, consisting primarily of what is alleged on the one side, for example, the plaintiff's *complaint*, or denied on the other, for example, the defendant's *answer.*

postnuptial agreement An agreement between spouses, usually distributing family property in the event of death or divorce.

political branches Executive and legislative branches of government. See **Separation of Powers.**

prayer for relief Also known as *demand for relief,* it is that portion of a complaint or claim for relief that specifies the type of relief to which the plaintiffs feel they are entitled and they are requesting. See **wherefore clause.**

precedent Prior decisions of the same court, or a higher court, which a judge must follow in deciding a subsequent case presenting similar facts and the same legal problem. Precedent consists of the rule applied in a case and encompasses the reasoning that requires it. In a given decision, the precedent may be distinguished from *dictum,* which includes extraneous or conjectural statements not necessary to the decision and which are not binding on future decisions.

preemption The principle or doctrine that federal statutes that overlap or are in conflict with state statutes will take preference and prevail, even to the point of invalidating state statutes entirely.

prejudicial error Mistakes made at trial that are sufficiently serious to prejudice the result against one of the parties; in other words, it is sufficiently serious that, if it had not occurred, the case might have reached a different result. Also called **reversible** or **harmful** error.

preliminary hearing A criminal defendant is ordinarily afforded an opportunity to challenge the case before the judge in a hearing that determines the sufficiency of the charges without a determination of guilt.

premarital or **antenuptial agreement** A contract agreed to by persons before their marriage, primarily concerned with the distribution of personal and marital assets in the event of divorce or death.

preponderance of the evidence The standard of proof required in most civil actions. The party whose evidence, when fairly considered, is more convincing as to its truth has the *preponderance of evidence* on its side.

pretrial conference or **hearing** A meeting of attorneys in a case with the judge to discuss the issues in the case and plan for the trial.

pretrial diversion Postpones and usually obviates the need for trial if the accused meets certain conditions, typically the performance of community service.

prima facie case A case that will win unless the other side comes forward with evidence to disprove it.

primogeniture A system under the common law whereby title to land passed to the eldest son (primo: first; geni: born).

prior restraint An action by the government to impose limits on the exercise of free speech, especially publication, prior to its exercise, as distinguished from punishing a person after publication.

privilege against self-incrimination A person accused of a crime cannot be required to testify against himself.

privity of contract The relationship between two parties to a contract. Originally, this was a bar to a suit brought by a consumer against a manufacturer when the consumer bought through a dealer and directly from the manufacturer. Modern product liability law does away with this impediment.

pro bono (publico) (Latin) "For the (public) good." Traditionally, members of the bar were under a moral obligation to render free services to the public, typically to provide services to people who could not afford to pay. States now make this a requirement of membership in the bar, typically with specific minimum contributions of time.

pro se (Latin) "For oneself," "in one's own behalf." American law recognizes not only the right to be represented by an attorney but also the right to represent oneself in court.

probate The process of handling the will and the estate of a deceased person.

probation An alternative to incarceration that sets a period of time during which the probationer must adhere to conditions set by the court and be supervised by a probation officer. Violation of the conditions may result in incarceration.

procedural due process That due process that is concerned with the fairness of *notice* and *hearing* provided by government in the adjudication of rights and duties.

procedural law   That part of law that deals with the method of enforcing rights.

process   In criminal law, the document commanding a party to do or not to do something; see **service of process.**

production of documents   Requests used in *discovery* to obtain documents from the other side of a case that are pertinent to issues in the case.

product liability   A branch of tort law that assigns liability to a manufacturer when injury occurs due to a "dangerously defective product." It dispenses with traditional requirements of proving fault, as in *intentional torts* and *negligence.*

promissory estoppel   When a person makes a promise to another to induce that other to act to his detriment and that other does so act in reliance on the promise, the court may prevent (estop) the first person from denying or negating the promise; an equitable principle that enforces a promise in the absence of a completed contract.

promissory notes   Promises by the maker of the note to pay money to a payee, usually involved in loans and debts.

property settlement agreement   A contract between husband and wife after they have already married to distribute property in case of death or divorce. The agreement is usually executed in preparation for divorce, but it is used occasionally between couples who merely wish to live separately.

prosecutor   The attorney charged with prosecuting criminal cases on behalf of a state or the United States; a public employee commonly titled state attorney, district attorney, or United States attorney.

public defender's office   A government agency that provides criminal defense services to indigents.

publication   1. In *defamation* (libel or slander), a public communication of a defamatory utterance. This may be constituted by an oral statement (slander) made in front of a single third party. 2. In reference to *service of process*, a means of service by

publishing notice in the legal section of a newspaper periodically as prescribed by statute.

punishment, or retribution   Has as the primary goal of criminal law punishing a person for criminal conduct. The other theories of the treatment of criminals are *deterrence* of crime (defined elsewhere); *incapacitation*, that is, removing the criminal from society through incarceration; and *rehabilitation*, helping the criminal toward a productive role in society.

punitive damages   Sometimes awarded beyond mere compensation (see **compensatory damages**) to punish a defendant for outrageous conduct in tort.

quasi in rem   Actions that are really directed against a person, but are formally directed only against property.

quasi-contract   From the theory that a "contract" is created on the basis of moral obligation, called *unjust enrichment*, in which one party receives a benefit to the detriment of another that begs for *restitution*; not an actual contract.

question of fact   A question to be decided by the jury in a trial by jury or by the judge in a *bench trial*. Fact questions are evidentiary questions—questions of who, when, where, and what. See **question of law.**

question of law   A question to be decided by the judge (*quieting title*), that is, a question as to the appropriate law to be applied in a case, or the law's correct interpretation; distinguished from *question of fact*.

quiet title   When the examination of title to real property reveals a questionable claim or interest casting a cloud on the title, a suit to quiet title is commonly brought to obtain a judicial order declaring that claim or interest to have no effect on the title.

quo warranto   Writs of quo warranto are extraordinary writs used to secure judicial determinations of whether public officers are legally exercising their power, for example, whether the law has granted their office the powers they are exercising.

rape   At common law, this was forcible sexual intercourse by a man on a woman against her will. Add to this modern *statutory rape*, which makes consent irrelevant because of the status or mental state of the victim. Modern law recognizes a variety of sexual assaults.

ratify When one suffering a disability approves a contract after the disability has terminated; for example, a minor reaches age of majority and agrees to a contract made when a minor.

real estate closing Real estate transactions are completed by a closing, at which numerous documents are signed and exchanged, payment is made, and property deeds are transferred.

record All the evidence presented at trial, whether or not recorded.

recross The questioning of a witness by the party that did not call the witness following *redirect.*

recuse, recusal To disqualify oneself from sitting as a judge in a case, either on the motion of a party or on the judge's own motion, usually because of bias or some interest in the outcome of the litigation.

redirect When the party calling a witness asks questions of the witness following *cross-examination.*

reformation Aims at correcting a contract to reflect the actual intention of the parties.

rehabilitative alimony Ordinarily a form of periodic payment, temporary in duration, designed to provide for an ex-spouse until he or she can become self-supporting.

remainder A future interest in land that follows a *life estate.*

remand Sending the case back to the same court out of which it came, for the purpose of having some action on it there. For example, the return of a case by an appellate court to the trial court for further proceedings, for a new trial, or for entry of judgment in accordance with an order of the appellate court.

remedy The means by which a right is enforced or the violation of a right is prevented, corrected, or compensated.

replevin A common law cause of action to recover personal property wrongfully possessed by another person.

reply A pleading made by a plaintiff when a defendant makes a counterclaim or affirmative defenses that require a response.

requests for admissions One side in a lawsuit giving a list of facts to the other and requesting that they be admitted or denied; those admitted need not be proved at trial.

res Thing. In Latin, nouns have different forms for subjective and ojective positions in the sentence. Thus, res is the same noun as rem in "in rem," except that the latter takes a different ending because it follows the preposition. Note that "in personam" also adds an "m" to "persona" because it follows the preposition.

res judicata Latin for "the thing has been judged." This is an affirmative defense that prevents a civil case from being brought a second time.

rescind To annul or cancel a contract, putting the parties back in the position they were in before, as if no contract had been made.

rescission Aims at destroying the contract and its obligations, putting the parties back in their positions prior to the agreement; see **rescind.**

respondeat superior A principle of agency whereby a principal is held responsible for the negligent acts of an agent acting within the scope of the agency; e.g., an employer is liable for the negligence of an employee; also called *vicarious liability.*

respondent The party who is successful in a lower court and is taken to a higher court for an appeal by the petitioner, the party who lost in the lower court; a party against whom a legal action is brought; equivalent to a defendant and sometimes referred to as such even when the action is brought by petition.

restatements of the law The compilation of general interpretations of major fields of common law, sponsored and published by the American Law Institute, founded in 1923; for example, the *Restatement of Torts.*

restitution In contract law, usually the amount that puts the plaintiff back in the financial position he or she was in before the contract.

restrictive covenants In real property, take many forms including minimum square footage for a house, lawn maintenance, and signage. Racially restrictive covenants and other discriminatory practices have long been held unconstitutional.

reversal   The act of an appellate court in turning around; a term used in appellate court opinions to indicate that the court has set aside the judgment of the trial court.

reversible error   Mistakes made at trial that are sufficiently serious to prejudice the result against one of the parties; in other words, it is sufficiently serious that, if it had not occurred, the case might have reached a different result. Also called *prejudicial* or *harmful* error.

right of survivorship   An incident to certain forms of co-ownership whereby a co-owner, if there are but two co-owners, will own the entire interest upon the death of the other co-owner.

rule of the case   That part of a written judicial opinion that decides the case; it is what the case stands for as far as applying a rule to the facts of the case.

rulemaking   Generic meaning of making rules; but, also, has a specific meaning referring to the legislative function of administrative agencies, as distinguished from their usual administrative function.

rules of construction   A tradition of customs for statutory interpretation; **construe** is the verb from which the noun *construction* is derived and is very close in meaning to *interpret*.

rules of court   The rules for regulating the practice of the different courts, which the judges are empowered to frame and put in force as occasion may require. These may be quite detailed, as in requiring a specific typeface and point size for appellate briefs.

secondary authority   Authoritative statements of law other than statutes and cases, such as law review articles, treatises, and the restatements.

seduction   Inducing (usually by deception or promise to marry) a person (usually a chaste, unmarried woman) to have sex; among the heart balm remedies now generally abolished.

sentencing guidelines   Many states have adopted guidelines that establish specific sentences for specific crimes. Some states have also adopted minimum sentences for certain crimes.

separation agreement or **property settlement agreement**   A contract between husband and wife after they have already married to distribute property in case of death or divorce. The agreement is usually executed in preparation for divorce, but it is used occasionally between couples who merely wish to live separately.

separation of powers   A fundamental principle of the Constitution that gives exclusive power to the legislative branch to make the law, exclusive power to the executive branch to administer it, and exclusive power to the judicial branch to interpret it. The authors of the Constitution believed that the separation of powers would make abuse of power less likely.

service of process   Delivery of a summons, writ, complaint, or other process to the opposite party or other person entitled to receive it, in such manner as the law prescribes; it is an essential component of procedural due process, the other being a (fair) hearing.

set aside   To vacate, annul, void, or reverse a judgment or order of a court.

show cause   A court may issue a rule to show cause when it wants a hearing on the question of why it should not take certain action. A party shows cause by providing a compelling reason to prevent the action.

significant relationship test   The modern rule followed in a *conflict of laws* setting; it is used in both tort and contract contexts and makes the court apply the law of the state that had the most "significant relationship" to the cause of action.

slander   An injury to reputation ordinarily caused by the communication of lies to third parties. It is the spoken form of defamation, *libel* being written defamation.

sole custody   The award of *child custody* exclusively to one parent upon divorce; the other parent usually enjoys visitation rights.

sole proprietorship   An unincorporated business owned by one person.

solicitation   In legal ethics, using improper means to drum up business. For example, the practice of "ambulance chasing," such as approaching hospital patients to solicit business, is unethical.

solicitor   A lawyer in England who handles all legal matters except trial work.

sovereign The independent, highest, and final authority. Sovereign power is the power to make and enforce laws to which everyone must conform. In the United States, the federal government and state governments both have sovereignty within the areas of their authority.

special appearance A defendant may make a special appearance for the purpose of challenging personal jurisdiction without the fact of the appearance conferring personal jurisdiction as it would otherwise do.

specific intent In criminal law, *specific intent* requires that the actor intended the precise result of a harmful act. Also see **general intent.**

specific performance An equitable remedy that asks the court to order a party to a contract to perform the terms of the contract.

spousal support Payments made to an ex-spouse following divorce that are designed as support rather than a division of the marital property. Traditionally this was called *alimony*, and in many jurisdictions the term *maintenance* is used.

standing "Standing to sue" is a person's right to bring a lawsuit because he or she is directly affected by the issues presented, having a stake in the outcome of the suit.

stare decisis The doctrine that judicial decisions stand as precedents for cases arising in the future. It is a fundamental policy of our law that, except in unusual circumstances, a court's determination on a point of law will be followed by courts of the same or lower rank in later cases presenting the same legal issue. It means to stand by a decision. The conventional translation is "Let the decision stand," probably not very helpful.

statute A law enacted by the legislative branch of government declaring, commanding, or prohibiting something.

Statute of Frauds An ancient doctrine that requires that certain contracts be in writing and signed.

statute of limitations A federal or state law that specifies time limits within which suits must be filed for civil and criminal actions: they vary from state to state and from action to action.

stay An order of a court to postpone an action.

stepparent A person in a relationship with a child by virtue of marriage to the child's legal parent; the child in that relationship is a *stepchild.*

stipulate To arrange or settle definitely so that proof is not required. "We will stipulate that the ballots in question are all undervotes."

strict construction Narrowly interpreted by a very literal reading of the statutes; criminal statutes, in particular, are *strictly construed.*

strict criminal liability A few crimes may be proven without proving intent; see **strict liability.**

strict liability A principle, largely applied to *product liability*, which creates liability without proof of fault, for example, liability for a "dangerously defective product"; virtually interchangeable with *absolute liability.*

subject matter jurisdiction The jurisdiction of a court to hear and determine the type of case before it. For example, in Florida, election contests are heard in the circuit court but not in county court. The reference to Leon County in "the Circuit Court for Leon County" refers to the location of the court—it is a circuit court, not a county court.

subpoena A court's order to a person that he or she appear in court to testify in a case.

substantial evidence The test or standard that is used at the appellate level to determine whether factfinding at a lower level (e.g., the trial court) constitutes reversible error. The test is whether there is substantial evidence to support the factfinding. If so, the factfinding will be accepted by the appellate court.

substantial performance When one party has attempted to complete performance in good faith, but a minor variance from the specific terms of the contract has occurred. Under the equitable principle of *substantial performance*, the court may enforce the contract, possibly reducing the payment for performance because of the minor breach.

substantive An essential part or relating to what is essential. Usually contrasted with *formal*, which in law is usually called *procedural.*

substantive due process of law A theory of due process that emphasizes judging the content of a law by a subjective standard of fundamental fairness; the government may not act arbitrarily or capriciously in making, interpreting, or enforcing the law.

substantive law   That part of law that creates, defines, and regulates rights; compare to **procedural law,** which deals with the method of enforcing rights.

substituted service   Service of process to someone other than the defendant, such as a relative living at the defendant's abode; requirements usually defined by statute.

substitution of judgment   The standard of review by an appellate court over conclusions of law by a trial court. The appellate court is free to substitute its judgment for that of the trial court.

summary judgment, motion for   A dismissal motion that is a pretrial motion and also a trial motion in a *bench trial.*

summation or **closing argument**   Each lawyer's presentation of a review of the evidence at the close of trial.

supersedeas   An order staying the execution of judgment by a trial court. Suspension of the trial court's power, as where an appeal halts the court's power to execute judgment.

supremacy clause   Article VI of the U.S. Constitution, which provides: "This Constitution and the laws of the United States which shall be made in pursuance thereof; and all treaties made, or which shall be made, under the authority of the United States, shall be supreme law of the land, and the Judges in every State shall be bound thereby, any thing in the Constitution or laws of any State to the contrary notwithstanding."

surrogacy contract   A contract by which the natural father takes custody of a child and the mother relinquishes custody in favor of adoption by the father's wife.

syllabus   A summary of a case often included with a reported decision and preceding the official text of the opinion.

syllogism   See syllogistic reasoning.

syllogistic reasoning   A *syllogism* has two premises and a conclusion. All men are mortal; Socrates is a man; therefore, (conclusion) Socrates is a mortal. Syllogistic reasoning in the law refers to the application of a rule (a conviction for murder requires

premeditation) to fact (the defendant's conduct demonstrated that his act was premeditated) to draw a conclusion (the defendant had the requisite intent for a conviction for murder). It is rarely this simple, but the model has heuristic value.

tenancy by the entirety   A form of co-ownership with a *right of survivorship* that can only be held by husband and wife.

tenancy in common   A form of co-ownership that does not have a *right of survivorship* and that permits unequal shares.

tenure   In higher education, job security granted to faculty members, usually after a period of several years and based on an extensive approval process. Tenured faculty cannot be fired without cause.

testimony   Consists of statements made by witnesses in the course of trial.

title   Formal ownership of property; has many nuances of meaning.

tort   A major area of substantive law including causes of action to redress injuries that arise out of noncontractual events. Tort includes three major divisions: *intentional torts, negligence,* and *strict liability.*

tortfeasor   A person who engages in tortious conduct.

trademark   A distinctive mark in symbols or words used to distinguish products of manufacturers or merchants.

transcript   A written verbatim version of an oral statement. In law, transcripts are used most frequently in reference to depositions and trials.

treatises   In the legal context, scholarly books about the law, usually covering one of the basic fields of law, such as torts or contracts, or a significant subfield of the law, such as worker's compensation. The persuasiveness of a treatise rests largely on the prestige of the author.

trespass   Originally covered a wide variety of wrongs, one species of which, *trespass quare clausum fregit,* constituted "trespass to land," which is a wrongful intrusion on the land of another.

trial   A judicial examination, in accordance with the law, of a criminal or civil action. It is an "on-the-record hearing," which means the determination is to be made on the basis of what is presented in court. It is a trial of fact with judgment entered on the law.

trier of fact   Also called *factfinder*, the entity that determines fact in a trial. In a jury trial, the jury is entrusted with factfinding; in a bench trial, the judge necessarily must find the facts as well as make conclusions of law.

trust   A device whereby title to property is transferred to one person, the trustee, for the benefit of another, the beneficiary.

trust account   In the practice of law, a special bank account in which fess paid by clients are kept until an attorney may properly claim the funds for fees or expenses.

ultimate facts   The general statements of fact that support a cause of action, for example, the allegations of fact in the complaint. Compare to **evidentiary facts.**

undue influence   Excessive pressure placed on a person by another person, usually in a position of influence, such that the will of other overcomes the will of the first person. Used primarily to challenge the voluntariness of a person making a contract.

Uniform Commercial Code   Commonly referred to simply as the UCC, a set of comprehensive statutes governing most commercial transactions and has been adopted in every state except Louisiana.

unilateral contract   A contract in which acceptance is accomplished by performance, for example, offer of a reward is acceptance by performing the reward request. Compare to **bilateral contract.**

uninsured motorist coverage   Supplemental coverage in auto insurance that covers the insured in the event that there is a collision with an uninsured motorist to cover the liability of the latter.

United States Code (USC)   The official codified version of federal statutes; divided into fifty titles, each dealing with a particular topic, for example, Title 3, The President, hence 3 USC § 5 is about certifying electors to the Electoral College.

unjust enrichment   An equitable principle asserting that one receiving a benefit at another's loss owes *restitution* to the other.

venue   The *place* where jurisdiction is exercised—many courts may have jurisdiction over a case, but it is filed in only one place. See **forum non conveniens.**

verdict   The factfinding by a jury; for example, in a civil case, the jury might find the defendant liable in a dollar amount; in a criminal case, the verdict is usually *guilty* or *not guilty* of each criminal charge.

void for vagueness   A constitutional principle of substantive due process that is used to invalidate legislation that fails to give a person of ordinary intelligence fair notice that his contemplated conduct is forbidden by the statute.

voidable   Describes a contract that the innocent party (the other party having contracted wrongfully in certain recognized ways) may avoid by returning to the conditions prior to the agreement.

voir dire   The examination of potential jurors to qualify them for the trial.

voluntary   When used in reference to criminal law, *voluntary* means an act of free will, though this is different from its use in contract law, where coercion may negate voluntariness. In criminal law, acts are not voluntary when occurring during sleep, unconsciousness, or hypnosis or by reflex or convulsions.

warrant   Written permission given by a judge to arrest a person or conduct a search or make a seizure.

warranty deed   A *deed* that includes promises or warranties, especially the promise to defend the title.

Westlaw®   A legal database maintained by West Group, Inc., widely used by the legal profession.

wherefore clause   Meaning "for this reason," this refers to the *prayer for relief*, the final clause in a complaint asking the court for some sort of remedy: "Wherefore, the plaintiff prays that. . . ."

will   A document through which a person directs how his or her property will be distributed at death;

each state has formal requirements for the execution of a valid will.

workers' compensation   A statutory scheme whereby fixed awards are made for employment-related injuries. This commonly takes the form of state-regulated employers' insurance arrangements.

writ   A written order directing that a specific act be performed; in ancient times, it was roughly the equivalent of a complaint, or a complaint on which was based an order of the court (not easily defined without a study of legal history).

writ of certiorari   A writ issued by a higher court to a lower court requiring the certification of the record in a particular case so that the higher court can review the record and correct any actions taken in the case that were not in accordance with the law. Also see **certiorari**.

writ of habeas corpus   Brought by petition to challenge the lawfulness of a detention.

writ of mandamus   An order requiring a public officer to perform a duty.

writ of prohibition   An order by a higher court directing a lower court not to do something.

wrongful interference with contractual relations   When a person *not* a party to a contract improperly disrupts the contractual relationship of others.

zoning variance   It is customary in the United States for local governments to create *zones* within city and county boundaries with restrictions primarily on the form of use, for example, agricultural, residential. Permission by local government to depart from the restrictions is called a *variance*.

INDEX

NOTE: Page numbers in **boldface** refer to definitions in margins, in text, or in Case Glossaries.